BIRDS IN SANSKRIT LITERATURE

BIRDS
IN
SANSKRIT LITERATURE
With 107 Bird Illustrations

K. N. Dave

MOTILAL BANARSIDASS PUBLISHERS
PRIVATE LIMITED • DELHI

First Edition: 1985
Revised Edition: Delhi, 2005

ISBN: 81-208-1842-3

MOTILAL BANARSIDASS
41 U.A. Bungalow Road, Jawahar Nagar, Delhi 110 007
8 Mahalaxmi Chamber, 22 Bhulabhai Desai Road, Mumbai 400 026
236, 9th Main III Block, Jayanagar, Bangalore 560 011
120 Royapettah High Road, Mylapore, Chennai 600 004
Sanas Plaza, 1302 Baji Rao Road, Pune 411 002
8 Camac Street, Kolkata 700 017
Ashok Rajpath, Patna 800 004
Chowk, Varanasi 221 001

Printed in India
BY JAINENDRA PRAKASH JAIN AT SHRI JAINENDRA PRESS,
A-45 NARAINA, PHASE-I, NEW DELHI 110 028
AND PUBLISHED BY NARENDRA PRAKASH JAIN FOR
MOTILAL BANARSIDASS PUBLISHERS PRIVATE LIMITED,
BUNGALOW ROAD, DELHI 110 007

CONTENTS

INTRODUCTION

I

I have been interested in birds from my younger days and have kept talking Parrots, the smaller Skylarks, Mynas, Lal Munias, Racket-tailed Drongo, and Love-birds. This led my friend, Kamta Prasad Sagreiya, I.F.S., to ask me to prepare a list of Hindi names for the birds exhibited in the Museum at Nagpur. In the course of that work I had often to consult Sanskrit lexicons for derivation of names in Hindi. That done, I naturally turned to the identification of bird-names in Sanskrit, for the dictionaries rendered a good few of them as 'a kind of bird' only. Soon after this was completed, I was closely associated with my friend, the late Dr. Raghuvira, Director, International Academy of Indian Culture, in the compilation of his book, *Indian Scientific Nomenclature of Birds of India, Burma and Ceylon*, according to the trinomial system of the *Fauna of British India* by Stuart Baker (1922-1930). In my present work, I have followed the order of bird-families of S. Baker, and the absence of birds of certain families in Sanskrit books consulted by me has been noted under the related chapters.

II

1. The Ṛgveda, concerned chiefly with the mystic Soma cult, mentions only about twenty birds which, however, does not imply that the Vedic poets' knowledge was confined to those birds only. They must have been familiar with birds of their neighbouring forest. Their powers of observation, love of birds, and prejudice againt some may be briefly illustrated: RV 1.164.20 presents a beautiful picture of two birds—one of beautiful plumage (सुपर्ण e.g. the Golden Oriole) and the other a bird of prey (सुपर्ण—an Eagle)— sharing as friends a common tree for their abode, and while the former enjoys the sweet berries of the tree (Ficus religiosa) the other, not eating the berries, keeps a lookout (for prey) perched high up on the tree.[1] RV 2.42 and 43 describe the welcome pleasant notes of the auspicious Grey Partridge (कपिञ्जल) and the poet lovingly blesses the bird that it may not fall prey to a hawk or to a bow-man. Further, he pays it high compliment by describing its sweet notes as a सामन् (song of praise). On the other hand the Rock Pigeon (कपोत) and the Hooting Owl (उलूक) are condemned as birds of ill omen in RV 10.165.4.

1. It is not necessary to bring out here the highly mystic transfer of the picture to a particular aspect of the mystic Soma cult in the next two verses of the hymn (consisting of

2. The Atharvaveda also shows familiarity with birds of prey like the Laggar Falcon or the Red-headed Merlin who hunt in pairs (श्येनौ संपातिनौ, AV 7.70.3). The mutual attachment of a pair of the Brahminy Ducks (चक्रवाक) who keep together during the day and move apart during the night in search of food among water plants but keep in touch with one another by mutual calls is the basis for pronouncing a blessing for mutual love upon a newly married couple in AV 14.2.64.

3. By the time the Saṃhitās of the Yajurveda came to be composed (c. 1000 B.C.) the Indo-Aryans had become familiar with many more birds and able to teach the Hill Myna and the Parrot (शारि and शुक)[2] to repeat human speech, and the priests at the horse-sacrifice dedicated them to सरस्वती, the goddess of speech, and to सरस्वान् (VS 24·33). They had also observed the parasitic habit of the Indian Koel laying its eggs in the nests of crows, and allotted it under the name of अन्यवाप to the half months because it assigned the work of brooding on its eggs and bringing up the young to others (VS 24.37). The Yajus Saṃhitās mention about sixty birds in all in the litany of the horse-sacrifice.

4. The broad V-form of a flight of Demoiselle Cranes was copied by the Pāṇḍavas in their war against the Kauravas for the arrangement of a squadron under the name of क्रौंचव्यूहं (MBh 6.51.1) and this formation has been well-defined in शुक्रनीति ch. 4, sec. 7. 297: "As the flight of cranes across the air assumes a regular formation, so should the state's army (देशबल) be arranged when at war like the क्रौंचव्यूह." Like the Crane, the Barheaded Goose (कादम्ब हंस) is also a winter visitor in India and a flock takes to wing in V-formation, and the Monkey-force of Rāmacandra, assuming the form of Geese in the air (हंसावली इवाम्बरे) attacked the demon-force of Rāvaṇa (Rām. VI. 69.36-37). The return of the geese to the Indian lakes and tanks in winter has been very compassionately mentioned in Viṣṇu Purāṇa, V.10.9: "Like an imperfect योगिन् who naturally suffers from worry and many an obstacle, the Geese (हंसाः) who had deserted the tanks and

---

riddles). The single verse, detached from the other two is differently interpreted in the much later मुण्ड. उप., श्वेता. उप. and the निरुक्त : the tree as the human body and the birds as the individual and the Supreme spirits.

As for the two birds sharing a common tree for their abode in RV 1.164.20 compare the story of two bird-friends, both woodpeckers, one quite strong and the other quite weak. The latter wanted to share the hardwooded tree occupied by the former, but despite the strong one's advice against the idea, tried to peck a hole in the tree and lost its life (Jātaka, II. 162). The two birds were the Goldenbacked and the Rufous Woodpeckers; the latter does not dig a hole in a tree but nests into the leafy bowls of tree-ants, and as it feeds on the ants it even shares it with them. The Jātaka of the Pali Text Society contains many bird-stories, and the story of three birds in V. 109 clearly shows that the ancient Indian gained knowledge of birds from the indigenous tribes (निषाद) as well.

2. For these birds TS 5.5.12 has श्वेतशारिः and श्वेतशुकः where we must render the word श्वेत as 'bright' or beautiful, for there is no white Myna or Parrot in India at all.

lakes earlier, have come back again to them (and run the risk of being killed by archers for food)." In Raghuvaṃśa XIII.55 flocks of the कादम्ब हंस are said to visit India from the Mānasarovara lake, and the Himālayan passes through which these birds and the cranes fly over to India are called हंसद्वार and क्रौंचरंध्र respectively.

5. By the time AV 20.135 came to be composed, the prejudice against the pigeon had disappeared, for in verse 12 of the hymn, Indra is said to have helped a wounded pigeon with food and water; and we also note it as a pet bird (गृहकपोत) in मालविकाग्निमित्र 4.17. We have seen above how as early as the age of the Yajus Saṃhitās, Parrots and Mynas were trained to talk, and we may not be surprised if the practice of keeping numbers of pretty birds had become common with kings and the rich, for we find in Act IV of मृच्छकटिक that the courtesan वसन्तसेना maintained a large variety of birds in her palace including a parrot which could repeat even verses from the Veda. Pet birds were also common in all hermitages.

6. Love of the calls of certain birds explains the comparison of the tones of music with the pleasant voices of birds like the Peacock, Hawk-cuckoo, Sarasa Crane, and the Kokil in संगीतरत्नाकर I.3.46. On the other hand, the silly pride of a physician went so far as to compare the pulse-beats of certain patients with the gait or steps of Geese, Peacock, Dove, Pigeon, Cock, Quail, Partridge etc. in the book नाडीप्रकाश where the author proudly declares that he has indicated the best method of judging ailments for the ignorant physicians:

7. Some popular maxims have also been coined after the ways of birds, e.g. काकतालीय न्याय, खलेकपोत न्याय, अण्डकुक्कुटी न्याय[3], काकाक्षिगोलक न्याय etc. The last of these is based upon a wrong belief that the crow has only one eye-ball because the bird, when looking down from a high perch turns its head both right and left. The नीरक्षीरन्याय is clearly reflected in the शाकुन्तल VI. 28, where the हंस (Goose) is credited with the habit of sucking up only pure milk from a mixture of milk and water. This, however, seems to be poetic extension of the Vedic picture of the Sun as a Swan or Goose (हंसः शुचिषद्, RV 4.40.5) who sucks up pure water (क्षीर, RV. 1.164.7) with his rays from even muddy pools.

8. In the Bh. P. X.15.11-13 fondness of Śrī Kṛṣṇa for sweet notes and songs of birds and the dance of the Peacock, is said to be so great that he learnt to imitate them quite correctly. In the Gītā (10.30) he identifies himself with वैनतेय, the best of the birds—वैनतेय was the one who robbed the सोम or अमृत well-guarded by the मरुत्s in the सुपर्णाख्यान.

9. The slow and graceful gait of pretty young women has often been poetically compared to that of a domestic Goose, e.g. in रघुवंश 8.59; कुमार. 1.34; ब्रह्मवैवर्तपुराण II.2.37; किरातार्जुनीय 8.29; मृच्छकटिक 4.28.

---

3. Comp. the rendering in Sanskrit of the first half of the Ardha Magadhi Nyaya verse quoted in अभिधानराजेन्द्र, the Ardha Magadhi lexicon: "यथा च अण्डप्रभवा बलाका। अण्डं बलाकाप्रभवं च" (the same as "Egg first or the hen first").

10. The authors of the original Epics would seem to have presented a more accurate picture of the wild scenery including animals, birds and trees, of palaces known to them, but we cannot say the same of the later interpolations,[4] e.g. the extravagant description of the गन्धमादन area of the Himalayas in महाभारत III. 158.44-45 where the tropical trees, coconut and the jack-fruit (नारिकेल and पनस) are said to grow; verses 43-47 of this chapter of the महाभारत have been copied with slight changes in the मार्कण्डेय पुराण ch. VI. 10-22 to describe the jungle surrounding the holy city of द्वारिका so that the Himalayan bird चकोर and the tree देवदार appear to be natural there.

11. The practice of divination from the ways, movements etc. of birds (and animals) was common to all primitive cultures (*Ency. Rel. and Ethics*, s.v. Augury; Divination; Omens) and India was no exception to it. Books like the षड्विंश ब्राह्मण, वसन्तराज शकुन and also Purāṇas (e.g. अग्नि पुराण chs. 230-232, मार्कण्डेय chs. 51.66-72) deal with the subject.

12. The कौटिलीय अर्थशास्त्र recommends the protection of auspicious and even other pleasant and cheerful birds and animals in pleasure grounds and the practice of sending information about the enemy by letters tied to homing pigeons carried with him by the king's spy is commended and it is also referred to in बृहत्कथामंजरी.

13. We have a good example of sympathetic magic in the पारस्कर गृह्यसूत्र where the first solid food commended for a six-month-old baby-boy is, 1) flesh of the female Skylark (भारद्वाजी) if his father wants him to be a fluent speaker; 2) the flesh of the auspicious Grey Partridge (कपिञ्जल) associated with field crops for abundance of food; or 3) the flesh of the Little Ringed Plover (कृकषा) for long life; or 4) the flesh of the Black Ibis (आटि) for holy lustre ब्रह्मवर्चस्. The Black Ibis (a holy bird in Egypt)[5] wears a triangular patch of crimson warts on the crown of its bare black head, a picture of a conical pile of red embers (अग्नि) indicative of its holiness.

14. India being rich in birds, their place in Indian drama is well indicated in the नाट्यशास्त्र of भरतमुनि. Chapter II of the book refers to the indication of the features of birds like the Goose, Cock, Pigeon, and the Eagle by an actor or actress with special movements of the hands and fingers; Ch. XI. 58 tells us that the presentation of birds (रूपणम्) by gesticulation is very interesting to watch, and the birds to be indicated in this manner are named in Ch. XXVI, while Ch. XXXII deals with the topic of repetition of a particular voice as a sort of burden, and its modifications in pitch, tune, or quality (sweet, soft, or coarse) are indicative of different call-notes of certain birds and copied by characters of high, middle, or low social status. The महाभारत XII.103.10 mentions an expert bird-catcher who invites birds with their call-notes to catch or trap them.

---

4. In महाभारत III the तीर्थयात्रा पर्व consisting of Chs. 80 to 156, would seem to be a later interpolation by its priestly author for the benefit of his own class.

5. Ibis was "the sacred bird of the God Thoth (God of Wisdom) who was believed to have the form of that bird" (*Ency. of Rel. and Ethics*, VI, pp. 650b, 651 b).

I have briefly indicated above that the ancient Indians closely observed and studied the ways, calls and songs of birds in nature, and utilized their knowledge to enhance the quality of their literature and drama. They also used them for purposes of secret news transmission. The कौटिलीय अर्थशास्त्र, II, अध्याय 34 mentions the use of royal homing pigeons for carrying news. Apart from different and alternative meanings often noticed in Sanskrit lexicons, e.g. कारण्डव, तित्तिरी and भास in the अष्टाङ्गहृदयकोश or the absurd equation 'चक्राङ्गसारसी हंसे' in the शब्दार्णवकोश I may refer to the variant renderings of bird names like कङ्क, किकिदीवि, चाष and पुष्करसाद mentioned in the *Vedic Index* of MacDonell and Keith, which clearly point to the difficulty in identifying the names with their proper owners. कङ्क is said therein to mean usually a 'heron', but in the same passages it also denotes 'some bird of prey', and in support of the latter references to the तैत्तिरीय and वाजसनेयी संहिता are given. The truly mystic shape of the sacrificial Fire-altar in the form of a particular श्येन (a Hawk) has been vainly extended by the priests to the कङ्क and even श्मशान (crematorium) in तैत्ति. संहिता V.4. 11.3. This कङ्क is really the Fishing Eagle, Bird No. 1779 in S. Baker's *Fauna of British India—Birds* still called कंकम् in Nepal. It is also a carrion eater, including the flesh of soldiers killed in war as is clearly stated in सामवेद II. 1214, where कङ्क, सुपर्ण (the Imperial Eagle, No. 1747, ib.) and गृध्र (Vulture) are said to find their food on the battlefield. कङ्क is one of the birds of prey in सुश्रुत I. 46, V. 74 and as a sharp-billed, bold and cruel flesh eater in राजनिघण्टु XVIII. 107. The common Pond Heron[6], the fish eater, is also a कङ्क (ib. v. 119), and another water-bird, the दीर्घपाद कङ्क (शब्दकल्पद्रुम) is the Adjutant Stork who "often consorts with kites and vultures to feed at carcasses" (Salim Ali's *Book of Indian Birds*) and stands about 4 ft. high.

In the *Vedic Index* किकिदीवि and चाष have been treated as two different birds, the former 'perhaps the blue jay', but according to the commentator 'a partridge', and the latter the 'blue woodpecker', but in point of fact, however, both चाष and किकिदीवि are one and the same bird, viz. the blue jay, किकिदीवि being its epithet in Ṛgveda 10.97.13, with reference to the bird's indistinct calls like ' 'कि-कि' and its playful flight in the air. That is why the bird is mentioned simply as चाष in VS 24. 23; 25.7; MS 3.14.4; 15.9; and as किकिदीवि in TS 5.6.22.1, and काठक संहिता (अश्वमेध) 10.2. Again, चाष of the phrase, 'चाषेण किकिदीविना' of RV 10.97.13, has been replaced with श्येन in the parallel 'श्येनेन किकिदीविना' in TS 4.2.6.4, where the श्येन is the Himalayan Kestrel, a winter visitor to the plains, whose flight and calls are described by Salim Ali: "Chiefly distinguished for its spectacular method of hunting. Checks itself in flight now and again and remains poised and stationary in mid-air on rapidly hovering wing tips for many seconds. Call: A sharp कि-कि-कि or त्तित्त... uttered on the wing, some-

---

6. The Heron does not fly very high, and keeps his eyes fixed down on the water for fish, and does not suit the context of TS and VS.

times when hovering." Now we also have the name रङ्गण (sporting, playful, or dancing) as a name for a bird of prey in कल्पद्रुकोश p. 327, verse 90 so that a Kestrel should be the रङ्गश्येन with which the चाष of the Ṛgveda has been replaced by the sporting श्येन with कि-कि as its call in the TS. Finally, it is interesting to quote both S. Baker on Bird Nos. 1516-17, and Salim Ali on the Roller or Blue Jay: The Kashmir Rollers "spend much of their time performing acrobatic feats in the air, first twisting one way, then the other and often making a complete turn...accompanied by much harsh creaking and shrieking..." (S. Baker); "Has a variety of loud raucous creaks and chuckles. Indulges in a spectacular courtship display, somersaulting and nosediving in the air to the accompaniment of harsh grating screams" (Salim Ali). We thus see the correctness of the derivation of the name or epithet, किकिदीवि for the चाष and both 'partridge' and 'blue woodpecker' have nothing to do with it. The अमरकोश, अभिधानचिन्तामणि of हेमचन्द्र and राजनिघण्टु treat चाष and किकिदीवि as synonyms, and the last named lexicon also stresses the auspicious nature of the bird with the epithet of पुण्यदर्शनः in its सिंहादिवर्ग, v. 157.

In the *Vedic Index* पुष्करसाद 'sitting on the lotus' is the name of an animal at the horse sacrifice in TS, MS, and VS and the authors do not accept Zimmer's rendering of it as a 'snake' but are inclined to accept either the suggestion of Roth as a 'bird', or of the commentator as a 'bee' (TS 5.5.14.1). It is, however, the name of the bird, the Indian Whiskereds Tern which places its nest on top of tangled floating water-plants and also upon leaves of the lotus as is clearly stated by S. Baker in Vol. VI, p. 112, of his *Fauna—Birds* : The Whiskered Terns make their nests "of reeds and rushes which are built partly or wholly supported by lily leaves and other water plants—in large colonies". The female is 'पुष्करशायिका' in सुश्रुतसंहिता and with 'पुष्करशायिन्या in the कल्पद्रुकोश as a water-bird, the following verse presents a beautiful picture of the females nesting in a colony amongst the lotuses under the diminutive name of कुररिकाः—in contrast with their larger cousins, the River Terns कुररी which make no nest and always lay their eggs in deep hollows scratched in sand (Bird No. 2080, in S. Baker), a fact which brings out the full significance of the epithet or name, पुष्कर (पत्र)-साद or पुष्कर-शायिका, who are gathering back with their wings their half-fledged younglings sprawling away from their beds on the lotus leaves:

अर्द्धाभ्युद्गतपत्रकं परिलुठन् पत्रेषु पङ्केरुहाम् ।
प्रायः पोतकजातकं कुररिकाः पक्षैः समूहन्त्यमूः ॥

Thus the guess of Roth was correct, and not the 'bee' of the commentator, nor the 'snake' of Zimmer.

The short notes on a few bird-names from the *Vedic Index* given above should make it clear that if one wants to know with a fair degree of certainty the particular kind of bird meant in a given context, one cannot always go by the dictionary meanings of the names, or by the published commentaries or translations, but must try to examine the overall context in each case with reference to the period of the composition of a work (Vedic, Epic or Classical), the geographical setting, the picture an author wants to present, and the object he has in view. This however, is easier said than done, for many an example in the Purāṇas would be found to be extremely vague, and it is perhaps true to say that the authors have striven in their compositions more after general effect and word sympathy than faithfulness to Nature. At the same time it cannot be denied that there is a considerable volume of hight class poetry which is quite as close to Nature as poetry can be

Turning to the commentaries, we must note that they are generally of a much later date than the original texts and cannot always be accepted as correct, for the commentators themselves are not quite sure of their own renderings of many a name of wild birds or animals, as is evident from the advice given by उव्वटाचार्य in his note on VS XXIV. 20, which mentions six different birds dedicated as symbolical victims to the six Vedic seasons of the year: "When the victims cannot be identified one should seek help from etymology, commentary of उव्वट on निघण्टु grammar, उणादिसूत्र lexicons, and from the people of the forests." The same advice is also given by Ācārya Mahīdhara, the second commentrator of VS, as a preliminary to his notes on the formulae 21-40.

The चरकसंहिता and सुश्रुतसंहिता divide the birds empirically into four groups: प्रतुदः (the peckers), विष्किराः (the scratchers), प्लवाः (the water-birds), and प्रसहाः (the birds of prey), but I have tried in this book to follow the scientific classification of Indian birds and to identify their names in Sanskrit; I have tried to do my best by a comparative study of their names in Prakrit, Pali, Hindi, Punjabi, Bengali, and at times even in South Indian languages. I may well have gone wrong with a number of both obscure and possibly corrupt terms for lack of sufficient material, and otherwise too, a situation not uncommon even with the best of scholars who have dealt with ancient culture and literature.

III

The probable usefulness of this book on birds for students of Sanskrit has been anticipated by my friend, Prof. Dr. V. M. Apte, in the following rather highly colourful words: "It will be a study—the fascination of which will be matched only by its utility. Scholars intellectually constituted with a purely theoretical bias and studying Nature not in the open but through books, have not a leg to stand on in this field and we will feel highly indebted to a scholar who introduces the ancient (and also modern, because surviving still) Birds in Vedic and Classical Sanskrit Literature to us in such a way as to make us feel that we can actually admire their colourful plumage and appreciate the effusions of their vocal chords".

IV

I owe a great debt of gratitude to my friend, the late Dr. Raghuvira who encouraged me in my work and also lent me some important books from the rich library of the International Academy of Indian Culture. I also acknowledge my deep obligation to my friend, Padma Bhushana, Dr. Siddheshwar Varma, who went through my work with great interest from the point of view of a general reader, and offered many a valuable suggestion both with reference to the presentations of particular topics and the grammatical derivation of some of the Sanskrit and vernacular bird-names. I was a member for a few years of the Bombay Natural History Society and am thankful to it for some factual information furnished to me regarding certain birds and animals.

Finally, I am grateful to the Ministry of Education, Government of India for the financial support it has given to the publication of this work.

Jabalpur, K. N. Dave
July 25, 1980

Postscript

The author passed away on the 6th of November, 1983 and could neither see his work in print, nor revise this introduction.

I wish to place on record our debt of gratitude, on his behalf, to the great ornithologist Dr. Salim Ali and the Oxford University Press for their permission to use the picture plates of birds that greatly enhance the readability of this work. The Oxford University Press deserve our special thanks for printing the plates.

Our thanks are also due to the publisher, Motilal Banarsidass for bringing out this valuable contribution to the study of Sanskrit literature.

A considerable labour of love has been put into the publication of this work by my brother, P. K. Dave and my wife, Smita.

New Delhi A. K. Dave
June 15, 1984

WORKS READ/CONSULTED IN THE PREPARATION OF THE PRESENT VOLUME

I. The Ṛgveda, Atharvaveda, and Saṃhitās of the Yajurveda—the Taittirīya and Vājasaneyī, with translations in English by Griffith, Wilson, Macdonell, M. Muller (hymns to the Maruts), H. Oldenberg (hymns to Agni), Whitney (AV), and Keith (TS).

II. The Epics; Rāmāyaṇa of Vālmīki and the Mahābhārata together with the Harivaṃśa.

III. The Purāṇas: Vāyu P. (Anandasrama Press, Poona); Matsya P. (do.); Mārkaṇḍeya P. (Syamakasi Press, Mathura); Śiva Mahāpurāṇa (do.); Kūrma P. (Venkatesvara Press, Bombay); Padma P. (do.); Brahmavaivarta P. (do.); Brahma P. (do); Skanda P. (do.); Varāha P. (do.); Brahmāṇḍa P. (do.); Nāradīya Mahā. (do.); Liṅga P. (do.); Bhaviṣya P. (do.); Garuḍa P. (do.); Bhāgavata P. (Gita Press, Gorakhapur); Viṣṇu P. (do.); the Jaina Mahā P. (Ādi P. and Uttara P. by Jinasenācārya and Guṇabhadrācārya, Syādvāda Granthamālā, No. 4).

IV. All the works of Kālidāsa and Bhavabhūti; Anargha-rāghava of Murāri; Prasanna-rāghava of Jayadeva; Prabodha-candrodaya of Kṛṣṇa Miśra Yati; Veṇīsaṃhāra of Bhaṭṭa Nārāyaṇa; Mṛcchakaṭika of Śūdraka; Subhadrā-Dhanañjaya and Tapatī-saṃvaraṇa of Kulaśekhara Varmā; Śiśupāla-vadha of Māgha; Saundarananda of Aśvaghoṣa; Kirātārjunīya of Bhāravi; Naiṣadha-carita of Śrīharṣa; Gīta-govinda of Jayadeva; Bhartṛhari's Śatakatrayam; Nāṭya-śāstra of Bharata Muni; Bāla-Rāmāyaṇa of Kavi-śekhara; Rāmāyana-mañjarī & Bhārata-mañjarī of Kṣemendra; Amaru-Śataka, Kādambarī Pūrva-bhāga; Pañcatantra; Hitopadeśa; Āryāsaptaśatī of Govardhana; Vikramāṅkadeva-carita of Bilhaṇa; Bhojaprabandha of Ballāla; Buddhacarita of Aśvaghoṣa; Kauṭilīya Arthaśāstra; Mudrā-rākṣasa of Viśākhadatta; Works published in Kāvyamālā series Nos. 3-7, 9 & 14; Subhāṣita-ratna-bhāṇḍāgāram (Venkatesvara Press, Bombay) and quotations under Bird-names in Śabda-kalpadruma; Yaśastilaka-campū of Somedeva Sūri; Nala-campū of Trivikrama; Bṛhatsaṃhitā of Varāhamihira, and Vasantarāja-śākuna, for birds of augury; Kathā-sarit-sāgara; Kauśika Sūtra, edited by M. Bloomfield, JAOS Vol. XIV; Samādhirāja-Sūtra (Gilgita Mss. Vol. II); Smṛtīnāṃ Samuccayaḥ, Poona; Yājñavalkya Smṛti; Dharm-shāstra-saṅgraha, Vol, 1; Āpastamba Dharma-Sūtra;

Manusmṛti; Mṛga-pakṣi-śāstra of Haṃsadeva, translated by M. Sundarācārya.

V. Protection of birds:

The fifth Pillar Edict of Emperor Aśoka prohibits the killing of about ten birds; and so do several Smṛti works, e.g. Manusmṛti, ch. 5. 11-14; Viṣṇusmṛti, ch. 50. 32—38, and ch. 51. 29-31, prescribes expiation for eating them; the Parāśarasmṛti or saṃhitā, ch. 6. 2-8, provides expiation for the killing of different birds numbering about thirty-six in all.

VI. Prākrit and Pāli works :

Lalita-vistar, Dr. Rajendralala Mitra's edn.

Supās-nāhacariam (Supārśvanāthacaritam) of Lakṣmaṇa-gaṇi.

Oyavaiya-suttam (Aupapātika Sūtram), edited by N.G. Suru, Poona.

Panhavāgarnaim (Praśnavyākaraṇam), the tenth Aṅga of the Jaina canon, ed. by Amulya Candra Sen (Wurzburg), Section 3, ch. 1, mentions over fifty-birds.

Sutta-Nipāta; Digha-Nikāya; Aṅguttara-Nikāya; Majjhima-Nikāya, of the Pāli Text Series. Sandeśa-Rāsaka of Abdur-rahamāna Singhi Jaina Mālā, No. 22, ed. by Shri Jina Vijaya Muni. Verses, 140 & 144, mention the pleasant notes of certain birds during the rainy season; others in 164 & 165, during autumn; and others in 217, during spring.

The Jātaka: quite a number of Jātaka stories have bird-titles, e.g. Tittiri Jātaka; Kukkuṭa J.; Haṃsa J.; Baka J. etc., and more than fifty different birds are mentioned in them.

VII. Medical works:

The Māṃsa-Varga of the Saṃhitās of Caraka and Suśruta classify the birds empirically under four groups and describe the properties of their flesh for use as medicine, but while the book Hastyāyurveda does so for the treatment of the wounds and diseases of the elephant, it also recommends the keeping of the royal mount in the jungle and near water during the spring, rains, and autumn, where he is expected to improve his health and also poetically to enjoy the company and the music of the birds—also the roar of the tiger. The Bhela-Saṃhitā, said to be older than the Caraka, prescribes the flesh of the various birds more often than Caraka and Suśruta for the treatment of various human diseases.

VIII. Sanskrit, Pāli, Prākrit and other lexicons:

Amarakośa; Abhidhāna-cintāmaṇi and Anekārtha-saṃgraha of Hemacandra, the latter with the comm. of Mahendra, ed. by Th. Zachariae (Vienna); Abhidhāna-ratnamālā of Halāyudha; Rāja-nighaṇṭu of Harihara Paṇḍita; Bhāvaprakāśa-nighaṇṭu of Śrī Bhāva Miśra; Viśva-prakāśa of Maheśvara Sudhī; Anekārtha-kośa of Śāśvata; Trikāṇḍaśeṣa of Puruṣottama; Viśvalocana or Muktāvalikośa of Śrīdhhara-senācārya; Aṣṭāṅga-hṛdaya-kośa compiled by K.M. Vaidya (Trichura); Kalpadrukośa of Keśava (Baroda); Vācaspatyam of Tārānātha Bhattāchārya; Abhidhāna-Ratnamālā of Halāyudha; Ratnasamanvayakośa of Raja Sābaji; Vaijayantīkośa of Yādava Prakaśa; Mankh kośa, ed. by T. Zachariae; Medinī-kośa; Śabdārtha-cintāmaṇi-kośa; Dhanvantari-nighaṇṭu; Madanpāla-nighaṇṭu; Śabda-Kalpadruma of Rādhākānta Deva; several Uṇādi Sūtras; and Hindī Śabda-Sāgara; Pāia-sadda-mahannavo (Prākrit-śabda-mahārṇava; a comprehensive Prakrit-Hindi Dict. with Sanskrit equivalents); Deśīnāma-mālā of Hemacandra; Pāialachhi-nāma-māla of Dhanapāla; Abhidhāna-rājendra; Ardha-māgadhī-kośa; Abhidhānappadīpikā by Muni Jina Vijaya; Bird-names extracted from tho Pali Dictionary compiled by the Pali Text Society; Mundāri-English Dict. by N.B. Bhāduri; Mahā-vyutpatti-kośa (Bibliotheca Buddhica, XIII).

A Sanskrit-English Dictionary, and English and Sanskrit Dictionary, by M. Williams; Practical Sanskrit-English Dict. by V.S. Apte; Sanskrit Worterbuch (by Otto Bohtlingk & Rudolph Roth) from which references for about fifty bird-names were extracted; Dictionary of Kashmirian Language, by Sir G.A. Grierson.

IX. Books on birds:

Fauna of British India—Birds, 1st ed. by E.W. Oates, and 2nd ed. by S. Baker; Birds of India, by T.C. Jerdon; Popular Hand-book of Indian Birds, by H. Whistler; Indian Birds or Avifauna of British India, by James A. Murray; Game Birds of India, 1. by Hume and Marshall (Vols. 2 & 3), 2. by S. Baker; Indian Ducks and Their Allies, by S. Baker; Book of Indian Birds, by Salim Ali; Birds of Prey of Punjab, by C.H. Donald (Bombay N.H.S., vol., XXVI); Bāz-Nāmā-i-Nāsiri, by Hussain and Lt. Col. D.C. Phillot; Birds of the Indian Garden, by T. Bainbrigge; Birds of Darjeeling and India, by L.J. Mackintosh and C.M. Inglis; Common Birds of India, by Douglas Dewar and Yeats; Cambridge Natural History, Vol. IX., by A.H. Evans; Several Vols. of ornithology of the Naturalists Library, and also of Stray Feathers by A. O. Hume & others, Cassell's Book of Birds edited by T.R. Jones; Hume's Nest and Eggs of Indian Birds; and few others. Vedic Index of Names and Subjects, by Macdodell & Keith, for birds in Vedic literature; Encyclopedia of Religion and Ethics; Encyclopedia Britannica, 11th and 14th edns.

LIST OF COLOUR PLATES

PLATE I

PLATE II

PLATE III

PLATE IV

PLATE V

PLATE VI

PLATE VII

PLATE VIII

PLATE IX

PLATE X

PLATE XI

PLATE XII

Plates I to VI placed immediately after Chapter 50;
Plates VII To XII immediately after Chapter 60

समीक्षध्वं महारण्य वशं बहुमृगद्विजम् ।

[Do please observe well the area full of wild animals and birds in this great forest.]

इदं च रमणीयं ते प्रतिभाति वनस्पते ।
यद् इमे विहगास्तात ! रमन्ते मुदितास्त्वयि ।।
एषां पृथक् समस्तानां श्रूयते मधुरः स्वरः ।
पुष्पसंमोदने काले वाशतां सुमनोहरम् ।।

MBh 12.150. 14-15

[This magnificent picture of thine is very charming indeed, O Lord of the forest, when these birds are happily enjoying themselves upon trees, O dear ! and their sweet musical notes are distinctly heard as they sing beautifully during the season of fragrant flowers (the Spring).]

1

CROWS & THEIR ALLIES

A. RAVENS & CROWS

1. In the Crow tribe we find "bird brains at their highest", and recognition of the virtues and vices of the common Crow is writ large in Sanskrit literature, the Jātaka-Stories and Folk-Tales. The काकोलूकीय of the पञ्चतन्त्र for examlpe, is fully illustrative of the wisdom and shrewd cunning of our friend, the House-Crow. Popular tradition places him on a footing of equality with that universal character, the barber :

नराणां नापितो धूर्तः पक्षिणां चैव वायसः

—Subhā. 159, 279.

2. Among Indian birds, the Crow enjoys the distinction of having the largest number of names and adnouns or epithets in the Sanskrit language. The शब्दकल्पद्रुम has collected no fewer than 36 synonyms for the common Crow and yet the list is by no means exhaustive. The expression काकजाति used in हारीतसंहिता, ch. 11, stands for the 'the Crow family or Corvidae, and both काक and वायस are in general use for any Crow. The poets, however, have often used synonyms like करट, ध्वाङ्क्ष, बलिपुष्ट, etc., to suit their verse.

3. Generally speaking, Indian Crows may be placed in the following seven easily recognizable categories :-

(i) The all black Punjab and Tibetan Ravens (length 26" 28") which are quite as large as, though lighter than, the Common Pariah Kite (शकुनि), and they are the कृष्णशकुन or कृष्णशकुनि[1] of the Vedas and द्रोणकाक (द्रुण् हिंसार्थे) of literature.

(ii) The Brown-necked Raven of Sind (22") of an umber-brown colour, more so on the neck and shoulders, is the रक्तद्रोण of मार्कण्डेय पुराण and probably दग्धकाक of the lexicons.

(iii) The Carrion and Jungle Crows (19"), entirely black, heavier than the House-Crow but much smaller than the Raven is the कृष्णकाक, काकोल or simply the काक proper in a specific sense. They are also the ध्वाङ्क्ष of AV. 11.9.9 and 12.4.8.

---

1. These and other Sanskrit names in this para are discussed later on.

(iv) The Rook (19″) is wholly black but the adult bird has the basal third of its bill almost white. It is the सितनीलचञ्चु काक or the Black-and-white-billed Crow of वसन्तराज and probably the नशाक काक of the lexicons.

(v) The Eastern Hooded Crow (19″) has the entire head and neck, the central part of the upper breast, the wings and tail glossy black. The upper and lower back and underparts are drabgrey. It is the नीलास्य काक, the 'Black-faced' Crow of वसन्तराज.

(vi) The House-Crow (17″) which appropriates the daily पक्षिबलि of the twice-born, and the offerings to the dead is the बलिपुष्ट काक or वायस. It bears the distinctive name of भस्मच्छविकाक after its grey neck and breast in वसंतराज. It the ग्रामीणकाक of the lexicons.

(vii) The Jackdaw of Kashmir (13″), migrating in winter to the near-by plains, is the चौरिकाक (thieving Crow) of Mahābhārata and पञ्चमकाक of वसन्तराज.

4. As a preliminary to a detailed consideration of these varieties, a workable classification of Crows may be referred to here. The महाव्युत्पत्तिकोश mentions three kinds of Crows, viz., (a) द्रोणकाक, the Raven, (b) काक, the all black Crow like the Carrion and Jungle Crows, and (c) वायस, the House-Crow. The षड्विंशब्राह्मण, 6. 8. also distinguishes between काक and वायस, and the distinction has been observed in the Mahābhārata and the Purāṇas where punishments based upon the doctrine of re-birth are provided for petty larceny. Persons stealing fish or flesh, for instance, are destined to be reborn as the carrion-eating काक[1] while those filching iron goods would become वायस.[2] Again, the punishment for theft of milk is rebirth as an all-white Egret (बलाका, बलाकिका)[3] based upon a similarity of colour, or a काक[4] by way of a complete contrast of colour. Similarly, in poetic comparisons between the Crow and the Indian Koel the former is invariably a काक, and not a वायस, thus emphasizing the jet black of the plumage common to both. Speaking generally, however, this distinction between the काक and the वायस has faded away both in the lexicons and the popular mind. Even Varāhamihira and others have not observed it.

5. अमरकोश has द्रोण and काकोल for the Raven, and काक, ध्वांक्ष, ध्वायस, etc., for other species including the House-Crow. अभि० चिन्तामणि, कल्पद्रु० and राजनिघण्टु have adopted this two-fold division but give additional names under each of them. The common names for a Crow need not detain us but the so-called synonyms for the Raven require some consideration. These are :—

(a) वृद्ध, द्रोण, दग्ध, कृष्ण, पर्वतेभ्यस्त्वसौ परः (each of these epithets followed by the word काकः) वनाश्रयश्च काकोलः

—अभि० चिन्तामणि

---

1. M. Bh. 13.111,123; Brahma P. 217, 108.
2. M. Bh. 13.111, 102; Mārk. P. 15,; Garuḍa P. 1.226,25; Brahma P. 217, 107. अपो- in the last two is clearly a w.r., for अयो० (iron).
3. M. Bh. 13.111, 110; Mārk, P. 15, 22; Garuḍa P. 2.2,80; Brahma P. 217, 98.
4. Manu, 12, 62; Yājñavalkya, 3, 214.

(b) अथ पलप्रियः । अरण्यवायसो द्रोणः काकोलो
घनवागपि । द्रोणकाको महाप्राणः स प्रोक्तः क्रूरवागपि
—कल्पद्रुकोश.

(c) द्रोणस्तु द्रोणकाकः स्यात् काकोलोऽरण्यवायसः ।
वनवासी महाप्राणः क्रूररावी फल (पल?) प्रियः[1] ॥
—राजनिघण्टु.

The वैजयन्ती has a mixed list :

(d) द्रोणः सकृत्प्रजोऽरिष्टो ध्वाङ्क्षः करट इत्यपि ।
कृष्णकाको वृद्धकाक ऐन्द्रिः[2] काकोल आसुरः[3] ॥

An examination of the above synonyms for the Raven shows that lexicographers have treated all black Crows including the Raven as varieties of a common type. Nevertheless, some at least of the above names, based as they are on some characteristic of each bird, offer the best clue to the identity of their respective owners. The lexicons, as is well known, were prepared as help to the poets to enable them to pick out words that would suit the metre in hand, and this has resulted in a mix-up of names of allied forms everywhere. The point is that some of the apparent synonyms for द्रोणकाक are really specific for other black Crows while a number of descriptive epithets like महाप्राण, क्रूरवाक्, etc., have been converted into adnouns or substantive names. It may well be that when the Indo-Aryans spread beyond and away from the Punjab the Jungle Crow (ध्वाङ्क्ष or कृष्णकाक) replaced the Raven in their minds and thus came to be equated with it in the lexicons. At the same time the Brown-necked Raven, the Rook and the Jackdaw were forgotten or lost their identity.

6. हंसदेव, author of an alleged book of the 13th century entitled मृगपक्षिशास्त्र, perhaps available in translation only, has arbitrarily selected twelve names for describing as many varieties of the Crow and given fanciful descriptions of them. His treatment of other birds also, with exceptions here and there, is equally fanciful but even his absurd classification[4] makes it

---

1. For the पलप्रिय काक See Section C of this article.

2. The name, ऐन्द्रि (lit. son of Indra), is based upon a story related in Padma Purāṇa, Uttara Khaṇḍa, Ch. 242, Nṛsiṃha P., Ch. 43, and in the interpolated chapter, between chs, 95 and 96, of Ayodhyā Kāṇḍa of Vālmiki Rāmāyaṇa (Bombay ed.). Jayanta, the son of Indra, assuming the form of a crow, insulted Sitā and Rāma punished him by depriving him of one of his eyes. Since then crow is supposed to have only one eye which, however, moves from one eye-socket into the other, for does not the crow turn his head from side to side when he looks at things below from a high perch ? This story is also the basis of the rule of logic known as काकाक्षिगोलकन्याय.

3. आसुर here simply means demon-like and आसुर काकोल (the devil of a crow) can only be the Raven. No lexicon gives आसुर or असुर for a crow.

4. He postulates twelve varieties of crow under the names—1. काक, 2. करट, 3. बलिपुष्ट 4. सकृत्प्रज, 5. ध्वांक्ष, 6. आत्मघोष, 7. परभृत, 8. वायस, 9. चिरजीविन्, 10. मौकुलि, 11. द्रोणकाक, and 12. काकोल.

clear that he was aware of the fact that all Crows did not fall into two classes only, and, undoubtedly, this awareness must have been shared by the more widely travelled lexicographers though unfortunately they did not care to connect particular names with particular birds.

7. वसन्तराज शाकुनम्, a treatise on augury describes five different kinds of Crow according to the five-fold division of the Hindu society, viz., विप्र, क्षत्रिय, वैश्य, शूद्र and पञ्चम ...a method of classification which was much in favour during a certain period of Indian literary history.[1] The descriptions, however, are sufficiently clear and enable us to identify the species intended by the author :

(i) बृहत्प्रमाणो गुरुदीर्घतुण्डो दृढस्वरः कृष्णवपुः स विप्रः ।
(ii) पिङ्गाक्षनीलास्यविमिश्रवर्णः स्यात्क्षत्रियो रूक्षरवोऽतिशूरः ।
(iii) आपाण्डुनीलः सितनीलचञ्चुः नात्यन्तरूक्षो रटितैश्च वैश्यः ।
(iv) भस्मच्छविः भूरिककारशब्दः शूद्रः कृशाङ्गः च पलोतिरूक्षः ।
(v) विरूक्ष सूक्ष्मास्य तनुः विशङ्कः यः कन्धरां दीर्घतरां [2]बिभर्ति
स्थिराननः स्थैर्यसमेतबुद्धिः काकोऽन्त्यजातिः स तु पञ्चमोऽत्र ।

—Varga, 12. 3-5

(i) describes the all-black Crow of large size, possessing a long and heavy bill. It is clearly the Raven later on called by him the द्रोणकाक. It is the वृद्धकाक (बृहत्प्रमाण) of वैजयंती.

(ii) refers to a black-faced Crow of different colours (evidently, black and drab-grey) and brown eyes. It is the Hooded Crow—— the नीलास्यकाक.

(iii) describes a Crow of black colour but with a different shade and with a black and white bill. It is the Rook——the सितनीलचञ्चुकाक.

(iv) contains a description of the slim, partly ash-coloured and very noisy Crow. It is the House-Crow——the भस्मछविकाक of Vasantarāja, गृहकाक of अग्निपुराण and the बलिपुष्ट of the lexicons.

(v) defines the self-possessed and confident looking bird with a not unpleasant voice (विरूक्ष, रूक्ष with वि as privation prefix; cf. रूक्षरव of the second and नात्यन्तरूक्ष of the third variety) and a small bill and body. This is the Jackdaw——the सूक्ष्मास्य काक of Vasantarāja, and the चौरिकाक of Mahābhārata.

8. The Punjab and Tibetan Ravens are entirely black and have powerful bills. They are the boldest among Crows and attack birds, weak mammals including freshly dropped lambs and the eyes of lambing ewes, young puppies, etc., wherein probably lies the germ of these birds being regarded

1. See घोटक, द्रुम, and हस्ती in शब्दकल्पद्रुम. Even gems have been so classified in युक्तिकल्पतरु.

2. This 13″ bird with a bill of 1.5″ and tail a little over 5″ as against the 17.5″ House-crow with a bill of 2″ and tail of 7″ has been supposed to have a comparatively long neck, i.e., as compared to its size, unless the text is corrupt.

as evil and inauspicious by the Vedic Indians who had a pastoral and agricultural economy. "With all the Raven's solemnity of voice and stateliness of carriage, the great bird is an enemy." This "magnificent felon" is, most prabably the कृष्ण शकुन of Rv. 10. 16, 6 and Av. 12. 3, 13, कृष्णशकुनि of Av. 7. 64, and गौतम स्मृति, ch. 17, and simply शकुनि of तै. आरण्यक, 4.35.[1] The terms शकुन and शकुनि in these names imply the large size of the bird as explained in M.W. and the Vedic Index of Names and Subjects. Later names for the Raven are द्रोणकाक, आसुर-काकोल (the devil of a Crow), दण्ड काक (दण्डः यमः : bird of the god of Death), and वृद्धकाक (the great Crow) as found in the lexicons (e.g. द्रोणः वृद्धवायसे—महीप.). The name वृक (—काक) for a Crow should also belong to it as वृक is the lamb-killing wolf.

9. The Brown-necked Raven has been named most appropriately as the रक्तद्रोण. This name occurs in what appears to have been the original reading of the 9th verse of ch. 15 of the मार्कण्डेय पुराण as quoted by Sāyaṇa in his commentary on the पाराशर धर्मसंहिता, प्रायश्चित्त काण्ड-2. ch. 12, Bom. Sansk. Series, Vol. 64, p. 265 :

परदाराभिगमने रक्तद्रोणस्तु जायते ।

It also points to दग्धकाक (दग्ध, of a brown colour) of the lexicons as another name for it. M. Williams renders दग्धकाक as an inauspicious Crow or a Raven which is partly correct. The शब्दकल्पद्रुम explains the term दग्ध as दग्ध इव, as if burnt, but goes on to specify the colour as black and then identifies the name with द्रोण which again is partly correct. पालकाप्य in his हस्त्यायुर्वेद describes hay that has changed into a brown colour through long keeping or otherwise as श्यावं दग्धनिभम् (p. 164). Again, the body of sage Nārada browned by penance is described as दग्ध in the स्कन्द पुराण, ब्रह्मखण्ड, 2, 1, 48 :

तपसा दग्धदेहोऽसि विष्णुभक्तिपरायणः ।

It will thus be seen that the word दग्ध in दग्धदेह stands for 'fire-scorched or sun-burnt' and hence for a brown colour, and accepting this meaning of the epithet I would identify दग्धकाक as the Brown-necked Raven.

10. The Rook is black all over with a purplish blue gloss (आपाण्डुनील) on the head, neck and lower parts and violet purple on the back. The base of the bill and face are white and devoid of feathers and the rest of the bill is black. It feeds chiefly in ploughed fields and grasslands on insects, seeds and grain. One of the names for a Crow is मौद्‌गलि, descendant of मुद्‌गल, from मुद्‌ग a kind of pulse-grain, and it may belong to this bird as he is more of a vegetarian than his cousins (cf. मुद्‌गभोजी for a horse), unless it is the same as मौकलि[2] for which see Para 12 below.

---

1. It is however more than likely that the कृष्णशकुन of post-Vedic literature refers to the Carrion and Jungle crows.

2. The त्रिकाण्डशेष gives मौद्‌गलि as v.l. for मौकुलि.

नशाक is yet another name for a kind of Crow which, if from root नश्[1] 'to disappear' may belong to the Rook because he is only a winter visitor to the North-West of India including the Punjab and Kashmir.[2] It must however be admitted that the etymology and correct significance of the names, मौकुलि, मौकलि and मौद्गलि, are not at all clear.

11. The names for the Hooded and the House Crows have already been given, but two other excellent names for the latter may be mentioned. They are ग्रामीण काक (the Crow of civilization) and गृहकाक (House-Crow). The last name occurs in अग्निपुराण, 317, 37 as a substitute for गृहकारी of Manu, 12, 66. It may also be stated that it is the House Crow which is the commonest victim of the Koel (Art. 37) and hence the epithet परभृत् for it.

12. Turning to names like अरण्य - or वन काक, पर्वत काक, कृष्णकाक, ध्वांक्ष,[3] and काकोल and also perhaps मौकुलि and मौकलि it would appear that they are more appropriate to the jet black Carrion and Jungle Crows than to the Raven. These all-black birds have been distinguished by वराहमिहिर as अन्यभृतपक्षकाक (black-plumaged like the Koel), ch. 94. 11, and by वसन्तराज as श्यामगलकाक (black-necked in contrast with the grey-necked or भस्मच्छवि), ch. 12. 6, as a sub-class of the Raven. According to Vasantarāja the best Crow for purposes of augury is the Raven and the next in order of preference is श्यामगल. This term includes not only the Carrion and Jungle Crows but also the Hooded-Crow, while the House Crow comes as the last but one of his series (ch. 12. 6-8). The बृहच्छार्ङ्गधरपद्धति, however, follows the lexical division of Crows into two groups and places the Raven and other black Crows in the काकोल group and the House Crow in the other :

कार्यकालेषु काकोलः प्रशस्तः स्याद्यथा किल ।
न तथा वायसो ज्ञेयो ग्राह्यस्तु तदभावतः ॥

pp. 393-394

The वैजयन्ती, however, is helpful in a proper subdivision of the black birds into two types, for the Raven is equated with "काकोल आसुरः" or आसुर काकोल, and it follows that the others are simply काकोल. This fits in admirably with the name लोहतुण्डकाकोल for the jet black Red-billed Chough discussed in the next section. The following verse maintains a clear distinction between

1. नशति पलायति नशाकः See, for similar formations, दशपाणाद्युणादिवृत्तिः, 3.34.

2. Poet Jyotirisvara of Bihar compiled his book Varṇa-Ratnākara early in the fourteenth century. It is a collection of items and suggestive phrases for the use of poets and story-writers under various heads. One of these is चौरवर्णना (description of a thief) in the eighth Kallola, p. 66. It contains the phrase "नष्टकाक अइसन चकितदृष्टि", i.e. a thief should be described as possessing eyes like those of the नष्टकाक or the नशाक variety of crow, for both these names are from root नश् to disappear or fly away (Apte's Dictionary) and would seem to refer to the Rook. In the alternative these names may well belong to the jackdaw, a resident bird of Kashmir but a winter visitor to the Punjab.

3. Synonyms like काकनीला, काकजम्बू and ध्वाङ्क्षजम्बू for the deep blue-black fruit of Eugenia Jombolana support the view put forth here.

the smaller black Crows like the Jungle or Carrion Crow (काकोल) and the Raven (नीलखग, the same as कृष्ण शकुन) on the one hand and between these and the House Crow (वायस) on the other :—

गृध्रः कपोतः काकोलो वायसो वाऽपि मूर्द्धनि ।
क्रव्यादो वा खगो नीलः षण्मासायुः प्रदर्शकः ॥
—Mark. Purāṇa, 40. 8.

The name नीलखग is evidently coined after the Vedic कृष्णशकुन. The mention of three different types of Crow in this verse agrees exactly with the three types named in the महाव्युत्पत्ति, viz., द्रोणकाक, काक and वायस (Sec. 213). काकोल, कृष्णकाक,[1] ध्वाङ्क्ष and काक are therefore synonymous with one another for the Carrion and Jungle Crows, but in literature they are mentioned simply as काक or ध्वांक्ष :—

शुष्कवृक्षस्थितो ध्वाङ्क्ष आदित्याभिमुखस्तथा ।
मयि चोदयते वामं चक्षुर्घोरमसंशयम् ॥ —मृच्छकटिक, 9.11

मूर्खं ध्वाङ्क्ष न लज्जसेऽप्यसदृशं पाण्डित्यमुन्नाटयन् ।
—Bhoja-prabandha, 269.

कार्ष्ण्ये कोकिलकाकयोः किल यथा भेदो भृशं भाषिते ।
—Kāvya-mālā, pt. 7, Vairāgyaśataka, 98.

काके[1] कार्ष्ण्यमलौकिकं धवलिमा हंसे ।
—Subhāṣita. 222, 38.

काकः कृष्णः पिकः कृष्णः को भेदः पिककाकयोः ।
—Ibid . 225. 120,
also 225, 122; 221, 205.

The औणादिकपदार्णव of पेरुसूरि has a list of items of a black colour in Section, 3 and काक, but not वायस is one of them. This distinction between the two is further strengthened by the following :—

गृध्रः शृगालः काकश्चाप्युलूको वायसस्तथा
—Bhela Saṃhitā, p. 100

Turning to the names अरण्यकाक, पर्वतकाक, or काकोल, it is not possible to allocate any of them to a particular species as both the Eastern Carrion Crow and the Himalayan Jungle Crow are found in the Himalayas, the former in Kashmir and the latter from Afghanistan to Bhutan, while the Indian Jungle Crow occurs throughout India south of the Himalayas, and since it is not easy to distinguish the three varieties in the field these names must be regarded as synonymous with कृष्णकाक and काक for them. काकोल in

1. कृष्णः काके पिके—हेमचन्द्र, both being jet black. The flag of यम consists of a huge ध्वाङ्क्ष or black crow made of iron कार्ष्णलोहमयो ध्वाङ्क्षो यमस्याभून्महाध्वजः—स्कन्दपुराण, कौमारिका खण्ड, Ch. 16.

the following example, placed with the vulture and jackal in a battle-field, presumably in the plains of North India, is the Indian Jungle crow :—

शृगालगृध्रकाकोलाः सदस्यास्तत्र पत्रिणः ।

—म० भा० 12, 98, 16.

13. The case for मौकुलि[1] (v. l. मौकलि ?) is perhaps a little different. Hemacandra equates it with काकोल which shows that it is a black Crow, and when we find that a flock of Crows (मौकुलिकुल) has been placed in the forest near the Godavari in South-India by poet Bhavabhūti it is but reasonable to conclude that it is the southern variety of the Jungle Crow. This, according to Whistler, is a highly gregarious species and large numbers collect to roost in special patches of forest, though never so many together as in the case of the House Crow. मौकुलि like वनकाक is thus found to be specific for the Jungle Crow :—

गुञ्जत्कुञ्ज-कुटीर-कौशिक-घटा-घूत्कारवत्कीचक-
स्तम्बाडम्बरमूकमौकुलिकुलः क्रौञ्चावतोऽयं गिरिः ।

—Uttara Râmacarita, 2, 29

14. The brief description of the सूक्ष्मास्यकाक given by वसन्तराज is fully borne out by what Whistler has to say about the Jackdaw. They are "as tame and impudent as the House Crow ...The call is more musical ...The whole demeanour is pert and knowing ... though the irresistible attraction which small bright articles have for the Jackdaw often makes it a nuisance about a house when tame enough to be allowed out of its cage" The last trait, described elsewhere as "a notoriety for thieving" helps us to appropriate the name चौरिकाक to it :—

लवणं चोरयित्वा तु चौरिकाकः प्रजायते ।

—महाभारत 12. 111, 123 (Cal. Ed.)

The Bombay edition reads चिरिकाक which, however, is the Green Magpie, and in a way both are equally correct, for both the birds are champion thieves of glittering trinkets and other small objects lying about the house. The propriety of the punishment lies in the fact that a person who steals salt—a most precious thing in olden times—is condemned to be a thief for all his life in the next birth.

15. Albinism is not unknown in crows and a completely white bird of the House Crow variety is occasionally met with. The Museum at Nagpur has a specimen. It is known as श्वेतकाक or शुक्ल काक and is always considered inauspicious. वसन्तराज calls it धवल वायस at 12.127 :—

---

1. This name may be from मुकुल, a half open bud, after the bird's semi-erectile feathers of the head.

The white Ibis also has been occasionally mentioned as a श्वेतकाक. i.e. the white water-crow (Art. 80).

काको मैथुनसक्तश्च श्वेतस्तु यदि दृश्यते।
राजा वा म्रियते तत्र स च देशो विनश्यति ॥

—मत्स्यपुराण, 237, 11

यद्वीक्ष्यते खलानां माहात्म्यं क्वापि दैवयोगेन ।
काकानामिव शौक्ल्यं तदपि हि न चिरादनर्थाय ॥

—आर्यासप्तशती, 465.

16. All Crows including the Raven were regarded as inauspicious and evil throughout the Vedic period and contamination of sacrificial or ceremonial objects, food, and the human body by one was a dreaded thing, but with the development of the science of augury (शकुन ज्ञान) there came about a slight change in their status for the better. Books on the subject contain chapters upon the interpretation of their behaviour and voice for good or ill, and instances are not wanting even in ancient literature where the sight or call of a Crow has been held to be auspicious[1] :—

यत आगच्छति काकः तत आगच्छति वरः

—Kauśika Sūtra, 34. 24

वायसः पादपगतः प्रहृष्टमपि कूजति
* * * * * *
पक्षी मां तु विशालाक्ष्याः समीपमुपनेष्यति

—Rāmâyaṇa, 4.55, 56
See M. Bh. 6.3.67

अमेध्यपूर्णवदनः काकः सर्वार्थसाधकः

Agni Purāṇa, 223, 13.

Finally, even the best of us has something to learn from the wily but sagacious bird, for in the chapter on राजधर्म in अग्नि पुराण, 225, 30 a king is advised always to be on his guard, i.e. suspicious, like a Crow :

"काकशङ्की भवेन्नित्यम्"

"Timid like a crow" for काकशङ्की in M. Williams is perhaps a little in correct. See also verse 402 at page 162 of सुभाषित where no fewer than five good points of the bird have been commended.

B. CHOUGHS

Choughs resemble the true Crows and are of a glossy black colour but differ from them all in having the bill and feet brilliantly coloured. The bill is fairly long, slender and pointed, with a gentle curve throughout.

1. The crow and particularly the Raven and their voice are regarded as unlucky—occasionally auspicious as well—in many parts of the world. See Ency. Religion and Ethics, Vol. 10, p. 367.

The Red-billed Chough, known in England as the 'Red-legged Crow', has vermilion-red bill and legs while its cousin, the Yellow-billed Chough, is characterized by a yellow bill but vermilion legs. Both are very social and noisy birds, haunting human camps and the wilds alike. They nest on rocky cliffs and are found throughout the Himalayas from 5,000 ft. in winter to 16,000 ft. above the sea level in summer.

2. If the adjective पर्वत in पर्वतकाक is in apposition to अरण्य or वन in अरण्य- or वन-काक for the Jungle Crow as also to the plains of the Punjab and Uttar Pradesh next below the Himalayas, the name पर्वतकाक may well belong to these denizens of the Himalayas. In any case they are the Crows designated as सुवर्ण वायसा: in the story related in Mahābhārata, 6.6, 14-15. Here the Vulture, सुमुख, proud of his noble descent from the great सुपर्ण, regrets that Mount Meru does not observe any distinction of high and low, and offers equal hospitality to the mean Crows merely because they too, like him, have gold on their bodies, and decides, therefore, to quit the place permanently :—

विहगः सुमुखो यस्तु सुपर्णस्यात्मजः किल ।
सर्वं विचिन्तयामास सौवर्णान् वीक्ष्य वायसान् ।।
मेरुरुत्तममध्यानामधमानां च पक्षिणाम् ।
अविशेषकरो यस्मात्तस्मादेनं त्यजाम्यहम् ।।

Now सुमुख is the Black Vulture with red head and neck (Art. 51) and the Golden Crows are indeed the Coughs with red or golden bills and red feet contrasting beautifully with their glistening black plumage. They occupy the central Himalayas while the Black Vulture does not rise higher than the outer and lower ranges and is quite at home in the plains below. The story is thus a mythical explanation of these facts of nature and gives us the beautiful name of सुवर्ण वायस[1] for the Choughs.

3. The Red-billed Chough (17.5″) with its fiery looking, conical, and pointed bill reminds one of the लोहतुण्ड काकोल or—वायस—red-billed Crows—who torture sinners in hell according to statements in some of the Purāṇas :—

लोहतुण्डैश्च काकोलैः हन्यमानः सुदारुणैः
Padma P., Uttara Kh. 250, 13

आप्लुत्याप्लुत्य दुर्दंष्ट्रकाकोलैः लोहतुण्डकैः
Sk. P., Kāśi Kh. 5, 75

भक्ष्यन्ते कृमिभिः तीक्ष्णैः लोहतुण्डैश्च वायसैः
Śiva P. 5. 9, 11

1. सौवर्णवायस. lit. the beautifully coloured bird. We thus have सुवर्ण for gold and red-ochre, and सुवर्णा for turmeric, while the female lac-insect has been described हिरण्यवर्णा golden, after the light orange red of the body and the rich red fluid it contains in AV 5.5. See Lac and the Lac Insect in the Atharva-Veda by the author (The International Academy of Culture, Nagpur, 1950).

The name काकोल is fully justified for these birds as they are as black as the Jungle or Carrion Crow. We thus have the following three types of काकोल or jet-black Crows :—

(i) काकोल—the Jungle and Carrion Crows;
(ii) लोहतुण्ड काकोल—the Red-billed Chough;[1]
(iii) आसुर काकोल—the Raven.

4. The authors of the above Purāṇas must have visited sacred places like Amarnāth, Badrināth, Gaṅgotrī, etc., in the Himalayas and seen the Choughs which are common in those parts. The Yellow-billed bird is comparatively small (16″) and his ineffective looking yellow bill has helped to exempt him from Satanic duties in hell, but if by any chance his services were needed, one may be sure, he would have been summoned under the name of स्वर्णतुण्ड काकोल.

C. NUTCRACKERS

The Nutcrackers are smaller than the House-Crow being about 15 inches in length. They have a chocolate-brown plumage with head and neck streaked white, and back and breast marked with oval white drops. The Larger-spotted Nutcracker is the darker bird, more profusely marked with white than the Himalayan Nutcracker. The former occurs from Kashmir to Sikkim and the latter from Nepal eastwards. As the name indicates, they subsist largely on the seeds of the pine, cedar, fir, spruce, etc., also fruits and insects.

Names like फलप्रिय-, सारङ्ग-, and द्वीप्य-(काक)are given merely as synonyms for a Crow in some of the lexicons but they clearly belong to these fruit-eating and spotted members of the Crow family. सारङ्ग (मृग) is the spotted deer and द्वीपिन् the (spotted) leopard, and these help to fix the identity of the birds as above. M. Williams does not mention all the birds that go under the name of सारङ्ग but the Hindi Śabda-sāgara gives it for a Crow as well. The महाव्युत्पत्तिकोश para. 213, gives द्वीपि towards the end of its bird-list where bats and some insects are named and it is therefore doubtful how far the name द्वीपि corresponds to द्वीप्य of M. Williams. It is however quite probable that the name द्वीपि is shared by animal, bird and insect having spotted bodies or wings.

D. MAGPIES

Magpies are an interesting group within the Crow family some species of which occur practically throughout India and some are confined

1. The अयस्तुण्डनामानो वायसा: of Mahāvyutpatti Kośa, 2.15.21 is no other than the लोहतुण्डवायस काकोल and clearly points to these names being specific. The substitution of अयस for लोह must be taken in the sense of copper-red.

to the outer Himalayas and the valleys to the south including Nepal. They are long-tailed birds of arboreal habits, and their attitude when perched on trees or the uncommonly long tails of some of them drooping in a gentle curve probably suggested to the highly imaginative ancients the striking resemblance which their body-lines bear to the shape of the village-plough or its long shaft, or perhaps to a long-shafted hammer (कूट; cf. their Hindi name महलाठ, fr. महा great, and यष्टि—, लाठ लट्ठि— a stick or pole) and they gave them the common name of कूट or कूटपक्षी,[1] and differentiated three principal types as under :—

(i) कृशकूट (M. W.) —the Indian, the Bengal and the Himalayan Tree-pies, the smallest of the series.

(ii) कालकूट (Matsya P.)— allied forms like the Kashmir and Black-rumped Magpies; and

(iii) पूर्णकूट (Varāhamihira) — the Red-billed and the Yellow-billed Blue Magpies, having the longest tails.

2. The treatment of these noisy birds by Varāhamihira and Vasantarāja from the point of view of augury goes to show that their sight or calls have the same value and this accounts for a mix up of the names of at least two different Magpies in the synonymy given in the बृहत्संहिता and in the terms used by Vasantarāja at several places in his work :—

भष, कूटपूरि, कु-रवक, करायिका, पर्णकूटसंज्ञाः स्युः
—Var. Br. S., 87, 4.

करायिका, कुरुकुञ्चिता भष, कूटपूर, सोमटिका[2] and दुर्गा
Vasant. 4.21, 56-65; 11.2 & 5

It will be seen that names like भष, कुरवक, कुरुकुञ्चिता and करायिका (कु-राविका?) are after the harsh call-notes of the birds and have their analogues in करियो को and करियावन of the Hill-men for the Himalayan Tree-pie (F.B.I.). These names belong to the Tree-Pies which are the commonest members of the group found all over North India and elsewhere too. करायिका of वसन्तराज is clearly an incorrect reading of the earlier करापिका of the Saṃhitā. सोमटिका, on the other hand, which may be rendered as 'the bird marked with a crescent' should be a Common name for all magpies (कूटपक्षी) as the white, lilac white or rufous red of the lower break has a sharp crescentic outline against the black upper breast in everyone of them

1. कूट also means a trick or anigma, and कुटपक्षी may well imply a mysterious bird, particularly as a bird of omen.

2. The Hindi and Urdu names corresponding to this are चाँद and महताब both mean- 'the Moon'. If the name करापिका is by any means the same as कलापिका which again means कलापक (कलां पाति) i.e., चन्द्रक the moon, it would be the same as सोमटिक and it is possible that करायिका is a scribe's error for करापिका, prakrit for कलापिका, meaning a little moon or part of a moon.

showing up a three quarters crescent of the moon.[1] That leaves the name दुर्गा which may be explained in two ways : (a) 'approached or seen with difficulty' and hence, found in inaccessible places; and (b) having the dark or bluish complexion of the goddess of that name, described as "अतसी-पुष्पवर्णाभा" in कालिकापुराण, quoted under दुर्गा in Śabdakalpadruma. The expression means, 'of the colour of the linseed flowers, i.e., of a light blue colour. दुर्गा for a Magpie, therefore, should properly belong to the Blue Magpies of the Himalayas. दुर्गा is also the Blue Rock Thrush (Art. 10).

3. The classification of the कूट— series may now be considered further :—

(i) The Indian and the Himalayan Tree-pies belong to genus Dendrocitta and closely resemble one another. They have sooty black head and neck, and buffish-brown upperparts with a tail of eight to eleven inches. Being the smallest of the group they are the कृशकूट (कृश small), कुरवक, भष (barking like a dog),[2] करायिका etc., as noted above. In the commentary on Vasantarāja it is described as लम्बपुच्छा उपरिश्यामवर्णा and the position in which its movements and voice are to be studied for augury is when the bird is बहिः तरुस्था (ch. 11, 3), i.e., when it is perching on a tree outside the village or on an outer or exposed branch of a tree. Its voice is syllabified by Varāhamihir as कोटुक्ली and by Whistler as 'kokli' or 'googely'. These particulars are more than sufficient to identify करायिका with the Tree-pie.

Superstition surrounds the Magpie not only in India but also in England and Europe even at the present day. The Britannica, eleventh edition, refers to it in the following words : "Superstition as to the appearance of the pie still survives even among many educated persons, and there are several versions of a rhyming adage ... (which) all agree that the sight of a single pie presages sorrow". The authors of "Our Bird Book" (1947) also mention the common saying, "one for sorrow and two for joy" and add that in the former case people take off their hats to ward off the evil effect. In Indian literature too there is an occasional reference to the unlucky nature of the birds :

यथाऽशुभः कूटपक्षी सर्वशोकैः समुद्गतः ।
गृहं स प्रविशेद् यस्य तस्य नाशो भवेद् ध्रुवम् ॥
—Padma P., Bhūmi Kh., 103, 70.

On the other hand Vasantarāja mentions certain situations where the birds prove auspicious to the observer.

1. Cf. चन्द्रकान्त for the white-breasted kingfighter—Art. 41.

2. वान्ताद (a dog from its habit of eating its own vomit) in the list of प्रसह birds in चरक is the same as भष of the बृहत्संहिता. वालाद in M. W. is incorrect. In the first part of the list of प्रसहाः in चरक the dog is mentioned as श्व as one of the animals of prey.

(ii) The Kashmir and the Black-rumped Magpies of genus Pica have the head, neck, upper breast, and upperparts black, and the wings are partly white and partly black, brilliantly glossed with blue. The tail also is black with a green and purple gloss. On the whole, therefore, the black colour predominates in their plumage and they should be the कालकूट (काल black) birds of the Himalayan hermitage described in the Matsya Purāṇa :—

कुररान् कालकूटांश्च खट्वाङ्गाल्लुब्धकांस्तथा ।
—118, 50

(iii) The Red-billed and the Yellow-billed Blue Magpies of the Himalayas belong to genus Urocissa and are characterized by very long blue tails measuring 18-19 inches. In these as in others the head, neck and breast are black: the back is purplish blue or ashy; the wings have purplish blue on them; and the lower plumage from the breast downwards is greyish white or lilac-tinged with blue or purple. The long tail accounts for their Hindi name दिग्गदल (दीर्घदल; दल a feather; i.e., long-tailed; cf. रज्जुदल for the long-tailed Paradise Flycatcher, Art. 11). They are clearly the पूर्णकूट marking the nearest approach to a कूट in shape. The Variants कूटपूरी and कूटपूर given in para. 2 above are Prakritisms of पूर्णकूट.

4. The Green Magpie of genus Cissa differs very considerably in extremal character and plumage from others, and not having a long tail, stands outside the कूट series. Its body plumage is generally green and the wing coverts are red. Bill and legs are a coral red, the former of a deeper colour. Its Sanskrit name is चिरिकाक (Parrot-Crow, fr. चिरि a Parrot) after its red bill and green plumage. It must have been a cage bird in former times as it makes an excellent pet and can be trained to talk. It is known as सिरिगंग in Hindi and Bengali which is perhaps a Prakrit form of चिरिकाक.[1] In certain dialects the letter च is often replaced by स, and क by ग, while in the present instance the nasal has been inserted for the sake of euphony; cf. Hindi कंकर for Sansk. कर्कर for lime-stone nodules. The nasal also helps to maintain the value of the long vowel of the penultimate का in चिरिकाक. The name occurs in the Southern recension of the Mahābhārata :—

लवणं चोरयित्वा तु चिरिकाकः प्रजायते ।
—13. 111, 123; also Brahma P. 217, 108.

The Bengal recension reads चोरिकाक which has been identified with the Jackdaw in Section A of this Article. The reason for the punishment also

1. चिरिकाक→सिरिगाग→सिरिगंग→सिरपंग

Cf. सञ्चान—चचान, चिचान for the Shikrā Hawk चरइ—सरइ a bird; चोखा-सोका rice in corrupt Gujarati; चीर्णपर्ण—शीर्णपर्ण—Azadirachta indica, the Neem tree. Sansk· कीर, चिरि and Talegu किलि or कीलि for a Parrot appear to be allied forms.

has been hinted at there. The Jackdaw, no doubt, loves thieving, "still, he is not the champion sneakthief that his first cousin the Magpie is" (Our Bird Book, pp. 64-65).

5. Manu Saṃhitā in its present editions reads चीरीवाक[1] at 12.63 in the same context as the Mahābhārata and Brahma Purāṇa, which is evidently a wrong reading of चिरिकाक. There is ample authority for this presumption, for we find Sāyaṇa Mādhavācārya quoting Manu, 12, 63 with the reading of चीरीकाक in his commentary on the पराशर धर्मसंहिता published in the Bombay Sansk. Series, No. 59 (1888), where the learned editor has pointed out in a foot note at p. 254 of Vol. 2, Pt. 2 that two MSS. of the commentary have चीरीकाक in the verse in question. It would therefore appear that the writer of the Bengal recension of the Mahābhārata substituted चौरिकाक for चिरिकाक which is also the reading in the ब्रह्मपुराण. The Verse does not suffer in sense as both the jackbird and the green magpie are noted thieves. On the other hand, it is quite likely that both चिरिकाक and चौरिकाक belong to one or the other of the two birds.

E. JAYS AND ROLLERS

"The Jays are birds of bright plumage, the wing especially being marked with vivid blue. They inhabit woods, have harsh cries, are rather shy, and live on all kinds of food". Two varieties of the bird occur in the Himalayas ranging from 3,500 feet in winter to 8,000 feet in summer. The Black-throated Jay (13″) has a black crested head, black wings closely barred with bright blue, vinous grey body and a blue tail barred with black. The Himalayan Jay (12″) lacks the black head and crest of the former and is of a rich vinaceous fawn-colour all over including the head except for a good bit of white both above and below the tail. Both are very noisy and live on fruits, insects, small mammals, birds and reptiles and other birds' eggs. During flight they often indulge, like the Rollers, in wing-flappings and contortions. Their cousin, the Siberian Jay, of the pine forests of Northern Furope and Asia is considered a lucky bird by the people of those parts (the Britannica, 11th Edn). The Rollers have a more plumage, their wings and tail consisting of various shades of blue, from pale turquoise to dark ultramarine, tinted in parts with green. They are, however, entirely insectivorous and also include mice, small reptiles, frogs and harmless snakes in their dietary, and are for this reason placed in the प्रसह group of birds in सुश्रुत and चरक. Both the Jays and the Rollers were formerly placed

1. Verse 13 of ch. 44 of the Institutes of Viṣṇu (विष्णुस्मृति) edited by Julius Jolly (Calcutta, 1181) read चीविवाक् in the same context. The original heading of चिरि or चीरीकाक would seem to have been corrupted through scribal error to चीरीवाक् in some copies of मनुसंहिता or विष्णुस्मृति and the error has been repeated and shortened to चीरी in याज्ञवल्क्य स्मृति 5.215.

with in the Crow family even by systematists but the latter have now been separated as a family under a different suborder. That Rollers were regarded as a kind of Jay is also clear from the fact that M. Williams renders their Sanskrit name, चाष, as "the Blue Jay". In India also both Jays and Rollers were looked upon as varieties of चाष and the former were distinguished simply as वनचाष, for the Hindi name बनसर्रा for the Black-throated Jay is apparently a corruption of वनचाष—वनचाषड़ा—बनसासरा—बनसर्रा ?

The common Sanskrit name for a Roller is चाष (V. L. चास), but as it is one of the most auspicious birds of India and one whose form god Śiva loved to assume on occasion it has earned for itself several complimentary epithets. Some of these like महायोगी and नीलकण्ठ are from the list of attributes of god Śiva contained in the शिवसहस्रनाम section of the Śiva Purāṇa, 3-koṭi-rudra Saṃhitā, ch. 35, 118. Epithets descriptive of the bird's plumage, voice and habits, though apparently set down as synonyms for चाष, are really applicable not to any particular species but to different species taken separately, while a third set of epithets emphasizes their lucky aspects as birds of augury. The following brief description of the three species of Roller found from Kashmir to Nepal would help to allocate the adjectives appropriate to every one of them.

(1) The Kashmir Roller (12″) has the whole head, neck and lower parts under wing-coverts and auxillaries pale blue, darkest and streaked with brilliant small-blue on the breast and throat; back rufous-brown; rump blue; and tail bluish-green. The bill is black. Its local name is 'Nila krosh'[1] (नीलचाष, the same as नीलाङ्ग-चाष) from the predominance of the blue colour in the bird's plumage not only on the wings and tail as in others but also on the head, neck and lower parts. It is confined to Kashmir and the North-West.

(2) The Broad-billed Roller has a dark brown head tinged with olive (yellowish-brown); tail and wings black suffused with deep blue; the back and lower parts greenish-brown with the centre of chin, throat and foreneck deep purple-blue. The bill is deep vermilion. It is a much quieter bird and of more crepuscular habits than the others. "All through the hotter hours of the day it may be seen perched quietly high up on the loftiest tree of that particular bit of forest, or on the topmost branch of a dead tree in a clearing. As it is motionless its head sunk into the puffed out feathers of its shoulder and breast, it seems to be fast asleep except for a harsh croak, uttered every quarter of an hour or so." But it is quite wide-awake all the time; cf. महायोगी below. It is the नील-or मणि-कण्ठ proper and therefore sacred to शिव who occasionally loved to assume its form—see Mahābhārata, 13. 15, 146.

This Roller occurs in the foot hills of the Himalayas and the adjacent plains, and also in the hills and nearby plains of the West coast from Wynad southwards and in Ceylon.

---

1. Grierson's Kashmir Dictionary. Nila Kias in F.B.I. is incorrect.

(3) The Indian Roller (13″) is a bird of the plains and fields and is commonly seen in the more thickly inhabited parts. It is bluish-green on the crown and nape and purplish red marked with broad creamy shaft-stripes on the throat and upper breast, fading into rufous-brown further down. The back is greenish-brown, and the remaining parts, including the tail and wings, consist of various shades of blue. The point to be noted is that there is no yellowish brown on the head nor any blue on the throat or fore-neck. The bill is blackish brown. The Rollers, when at rest, appear to be rather sombre coloured and not at all conspicuous but when on the wing they give us a most "vivid display of colour". The courtship exhibitionism is much the same in all species but the Indian Roller is not only the noisiest but also the most demonstrative of all three. The male "indulges in a series of fantastic acrobatics, rocketing into the air, somersaulting and nose-diving to the accompaniment of harsh grating screams and with the brilliant plumage flashing in the sun" (Salim Ali).

Now, since everyone of the above three is an auspicious bird (स्वस्तिक) and fulfils the requirements of augury, the names and epithets of all of them have been mixed up in the so-called synonyms for चाष :

(a) स्वर्णचूड, मणिकण्ठ, विशोक, स्वस्तिक, अपराजित, etc. in वसन्तराज

(b) किकिदीवि, चित्रवाज, महायोगी, नीलाङ्ग, पुन्यदर्शन, etc. in कल्पद्रुकोश.

(c) नीलकण्ठ, चलपुच्छ, माजल, राजविहङ्गम, किकी, etc. in M. W.

(d) हेमतुण्ड, नीलग्रीव, etc. in the verse quoted at the end.

The truly descriptive adjectives in the above lists are चित्रवाज (having variegated wings); नीलाङ्ग (blue-bodied), मणिकण्ठ, नीलकण्ठ or नीलग्रीव (blue-throated; cf. मणिकण्ठक[1], in the same sense as the name of the Peacock of Purūravas in Vikramorvaśīya, 5. 54 where मणि stands for 'a sapphire'); स्वर्णचूड (gold-headed, i.e., with a yellowish-brown head); हेमतुण्ड (golden, i.e., red-billed); किकिदीवि (calling 'ki ki' aloud during a sportive flight, or calling, and shining beautifully on the wing); and माजल (frequenting, or resident in dry waterless areas). It will be seen that all these cannot be true of any single species of Roller and must be allocated to their respective owners. In a general way, नीलाङ्ग and चित्रवाज would seem to apply to all the three species but since the lower parts of the Kashmir Roller are blue throughout the first epithet would seem to be specific for it, particularly as चित्रवाज for any Roller does stand in some contrast to नीलाङ्ग (see below). मणिकण्ठ and its variants apply to the Kashmir and the Broad-billed varieties but not to the Indian Roller. The epithets स्वर्णचूड and हेमतुण्ड clearly belong to the broad-Billed species and to no other. Lastly, किकिदीवि[2] (if it is really

1. मणिकण्ठक is also the common cock after its red Lappets.

2. कि कि इति शब्दं कुर्वन् दीव्यति क्रीडति. It appears that the names किकि and किकिदीवि are shared by (i) a noisy kingfisher which is a water bird and (ii] the Indian Roller

one of these birds), can only be the Indian Roller, the most playful and noisy member of the series. भाजल too must be the same as it occurs in the drier areas of the Punjab and Rajasthan. पालकाप्य also enumerates this चाष as one of the birds common in arid places (III. 6, p. 397). चलपुच्छ refers to the slow up and down movement of this Roller's tail every half minute or so when perched upon a branch or telegraph wire. The Indian Roller being the commonest, the epithet perhaps belongs to it. The remaining epithets are shared in common by all the species as birds of happy augury. Some of these, like स्वस्तिक, महायोगी, and विशोक are also applied to the domestic Cock who by his morning crow is supposed to herald a prosperous day. नीलाङ्ग, again, is descriptive of the body-colour of a Peacock, one of the Cranes and the Blue Heron; and नीलकण्ठ is shared by the Peacock, the Magpie Robin, the white Wagtail and others.

Finally, a few examples of the Roller in literature : The beautiful Broad-billed Roller with its deep vermilion bill would seem to be the bird dedicated to the deities, अग्नि and सोम :

"अग्निषोमाभ्यां चाषान्" —Vāja. Saṃhitā, 24.23.

In the Ṛgveda asthmatic cough is transferred from the patient to either the किकिदीवि-चाष, or to चाष and किकिदीवि birds both of which seem to delight in their raucous calls and would be glad of a further reinforcement:

"साकं यक्ष्म प्र पत चाषेण किकिदीविना"

10. 97. 13

Here किकिदीवि is either a simple epithet of चाष referring to its ki-ki cries (root-दीव्) or a different bird as held by सायणाचार्य and Griffith, the latter taking it for a Kingfisher. (Art. 41).

The ease and surety with which a Roller catches an insect have served as an excellent simile :

"पतङ्गं हि ग्रसेच्चाषो यथा क्षुद्रं बुभुक्षितः
तथा द्रोणोऽग्रसच्छूरो धृष्टकेतुं महाहवे"

—Mahābhārata, 7. 125, 39.

The proverbial beauty of the Jay's wings, so well admired in Europe, has not been lost on Sanskrit poets too :

"प्रेङ्खद्भूरि मयूख मेचकचयैरुन्मेषि चाषच्छद-
च्छाया संवलितैर्विवर्तिभिरिव प्रान्तेषु पर्यावृताः"[1]

—Mālatī-mādhava, 6.5.

---

which does not frequent water and has therefore been distinguisbed as माजल—मा+जल ? See Art. 41. The formation of माजल is perhaps analogous to मावल for a steady and plucky variety of dog named in the Vedic Index of Names and Subjects, and मास्थाल for a bat which does not descend to the ground, स्थल.

1. The reference is to the glittering jewellery of the gaily dressed hetaerae seated on tall royal elephants moving in a procession. The elephants carried clanging bells as part

"प्रेमरम्यमुभयोः समं दिशोः
कामिनां यदिह चाषपिच्छवत्
एकतस्तु न चकास्ति साध्वपि
श्यामपृष्ठमिव बर्हिणश्छदम्"

—Bāla-Rāmāyaṇa, 5.15.

The shining blue steel of an excellent sword has been compared with the deep blue of the Roller's wing :

"षण्डो नम्रे द्विषत्यप्यनमति परुषः पुष्टचाषच्छदश्रीः"

Khadga-śatakam, 29;
Kāvya-mālā, Pt. 11.

Recitation of the following eight names of the Roller, at the sight of one, is said to ensure not only the object of one's desire but also a good dinner.

"अशोकश्च, विशोकश्च, नन्दनः पुष्टिवर्धनः,
हेमतुण्डो, मणिग्रीवः, स्वस्तिकश्चापराजितः
अष्टौ चाषस्य नामानि चाषं दृष्ट्वा तु यः पठेत्
अर्थसिद्धिर्भवेत्तस्य मिष्टमन्नं वरानने"

शब्दार्थचिन्तामणि under चाषः

But a visit to an aviary will not do the trick !

---

of their trappings. This picture is compared with the sporting and joyfully crying flights of a number of चाष birds the glorious beauty (छाया) of whose expanded (उन्मेषि) wings as they turn and roll in the air (विवर्तिभिः) exhibits rainbows as it were (व्यक्ताखण्डल कार्मुका इव). The cries of the birds match the clanging of the bells—झण झण झङ्कार of the preceding passage.

The crow family—काकवंश

Crow, choughs & Nutcrackers	Magpies	Jays—वनचाष
1. The Raven—द्रोण-or वृद्धकाक:	1. Tree Pie—कृशकूट	Rollers*—चाष
2. The Brown-necked Raven—रक्तद्रोणकाक	2. Kashmir and Black-rumped Magpies—कालकूट	1. Kashmir Roller—नीलाङ्गचाष
3. The Hooded Crow—नीलास्यकाक	3. Red-billed and Yellow-billed Magpies—पूर्णकूट	2. Broad-billed Roller—हेमतुण्ड-or स्वर्णचूड-चाष
4. The Jungle and carrion crow—कृष्ण-or वन्काक, काकोत	4. Green Magpie—चिरिकाक	3. Indian Roller चाष
5. The Rook—नशाक or नष्टकाक, सितनीलचञ्चु-काक		
6. The House Crow—गृह-or भस्मच्छवि-काक, वायस		
7. The Jackdaw—चौरिकाक, पङ्कचम-काक		
8. The Choughs—सुवर्णकाक		
9. The Nutcrackers—फलप्रिय or सारङ्गकाक:		

*The Rollers, though placed in a separate family by scientists, were regarded by the ancients as allied to the jays and have therefore been included here.

2

TITS

1. The great majority of Tits are small sparrow-like birds four to six inches long, some with and others without a crest. All the species are very much alike in their habits and behaviour. Extremely active and sprightly, they spend much of their time on trees, clinging to twigs and flowering stems in a variety of acrobatic postures often hanging upside down like little bats, in search of their insect food. They also eat buds and small berries. The males have a cheerful, loud, and clear whistling song during the breeding season from spring to autumn. Most of the species occupy the outer Himalayas but the Grey and the Yellow-cheeked Tits are resident in the plains. The Grey Tit is bluish and black above and white below with a black neck and a broad black stripe running down from the throat to the abdomen and a white cheek-patch. The Yellow-cheeked species is a greenish and yellow bird with a pointed black crest and a black band (पट्टि or पट्टि) down the lower parts as in the Grey Tit. Both are of arboreal habits.

2. The only vernacular names available for any of these birds, other than in the Hill dialects of Assam, are (i) Sabzaroshan ('the light or charm of the green trees') in Urdu and (ii) Rāma-gangrā (राम: सुन्दरे, श्यामवर्णे + गुञ्ज शब्दे—'the beautiful voiced'?) in Bengali for the Indian Grey Tit. The first name is used by bird-fanciers in Central India and the second is noted in F.B.I. and this last would seem to agree in sense with Sanskrit क्षुद्र वल्गुलि (the little sweet-voiced bird, वल्गु—मधुरभाषणे)[1] which occurs only in its Pali form खुद्दक वग्गुलि in the Commentary on the Dhamma-pada edited by H.C. Norman, Vol. 3, p. 223. The Pali-English Dictionary (P.T.S. edition) renders the name as 'a small song-bird'. वल्गुलि also means a bat and क्षुद्र वल्गुलि should be a small bat or a pipistrelle, and having regard to the behaviour of the little Tits of often hanging upside down described above it would seem that they are the खुद्दक वग्गुलि of the Commentary.

The expression पब्बहारे ओलंबंता used for the खुद्दक वग्गुलि by the commentator refers to their penduline attitudes when engaged upon a search for insects

---

1. Since वल्गुलि means both a little bat and a bat-like bird and as both these roost and nest in holes it is perhaps better to derive the name from वल, a hole : cf. वल्गा and खलीन for a bridle which goes into the hollow (वल, खं) of the horse's mouth.

along the rough and broken roof of an open mountain cave. वल्गुली of the प्रतुद list in सुश्रुत should be the same.

3. सट्वा,[1] (Hindi, सट्टा, सटा or सटैला from सट, सटा a crest) is another Sanskrit bird-name which may well belong to a crested Tit like the Yellow-cheeked Tit. The term also means a musical instrument, probably a child's whistle so named after the little bird's whistling call (cf. Hindi सीटी, a whistle).

4. If the equation, पट्टिः वल्गुलौ, of the विश्वलोचन-कोश refers to वल्गुलि as a bird it gives us a third name for such of the Tits as have either a tiara i.e. an ornamented crest or a broad black band stretching from the neck to the abdomen, and these like the Grey and the Yellow-cheeked Tits would be पट्टिवल्गुलि. For पट्टि in the above sense see पट्टि, and उरः पट्टिका under तलसारिका, in M. W. and cf also वक्त्रपट्टे तु तलिश तलसारकम्—अभि. चिन्तामणि. हेमचन्द्र has श्यामावल्गुलौ which has been illustrated by his commentator महेन्द्र with "श्यामेव (श्यामैव?) लम्बते प्लक्षे"—'the श्यामा is in a pendant attitude in the ficus infectoria tree.' No lexicon equates श्यामा with 'a bat' and the term, therefore, refers to the वल्गुलि (bat-like birds), viz. the Tits.

5. The largest member of the Tit family is the eight inch long Sultan Tit of Nepal and Eastern Himalayas. The cock-bird is shining black with a beautiful brilliant yellow crest and deep yellow lower parts. It has a variety of shrill calls, the commonest being 'chip-tree-tree', and an occasional plaintive high-pitched 'pway, pway, pway'. Now a certain bird named स्वर्णशिख or स्वर्णचूल (v.l. सुवर्णचूल) figures in a story related in कथासरित्सागर, 10. 9 where a young prince playfully snatches away a musical instrument called पिञ्जरक[2] from his sister and she thereupon curses him to be immediately transformed into the स्वर्णचूल bird, presumably because of a close similarity of the sound of the instrument with the bird's voice. M. Williams conjectures that the bird is probaly the Blue Jay or the Indian Roller because one of the names for it is स्वर्णचूड, but the voice of the Roller is anything but musical. N.M. Penzer[3], on the other hand, identifies स्वर्णचूल with the Hoopoe but the crest of this bird is practically of the same rufous-fawn colour as the head, neck and breast, and is also tipped black. As against this, the name clearly implies a sharp contrast with the colour of the adjacent parts, and it is submitted that the Sultan Tit with its brilliant and entirely golden-yellow crest, worn jauntily on a shining black head, has a much better claim to the name.

6. We have therefore सट्वा and वल्गुली or क्षुद्र वल्गुलि as common names for the Tits as a group, श्यामावल्गुलि or वल्गुलि-श्यामा for the dark coloured Grey Tit, and स्वर्णशिख or स्वर्णचूल for the beautiful Sultan Tit.

7. It is possible, as suggested in the article on Bulbuls (Art. 6), that Tits possessing white ear-coverts, e.g. the Grey Tit, the Black-Tits and other allied forms were regarded as little Bulbuls of the श्रीकर्ण type. The identifications in this article should thus be regarded as tentative rather than conclusive.

1. सट्वा may be from सट+वत् contaminated by सटा or imitative of the bird's call.
2. Means also 'yellow orpiment' which is significant.
3. See Penzer's Ocean of Story, Vol. 5 foonote at p. 160.

3

PARROT-BILLS AND SUTHORAS

1. The striking feature common to this curious group of birds is their bill which resembles a parrot's. I have not been able to find a name for one in Sanskrit but from the fact that some of them are known in Hindi as सुठोरा I am satisfied that they certainly had a name in Sanskrit though it has not been preserved in the lexicons that are extant. The name सुठोरा (Suṭhorā) is evidently derived from Sanskrit शुकतुण्ड which is synonymous with शुकत्रोटि (शुक, a parrot, and त्रोटि, a bill), thus : शुकतुण्ड—सुक+ठोर =सुठोर+अ=सुठोरा, ठोर from तुण्ड meaning a beak, in Hindi.[1] Certain plants are also known as शुकानना and शुकनास, and I would not be surprised if at least one of these was also a name for the birds in question just as the words भृङ्गराज and किङ्किरात mean both a particular plant and a particular bird—the Racket-tailed Drongo and a parrot or cuckoo respectively—Arts. 15, 37 & 38. धन्वन्, कन्दली, रज्जुवाल, etc. are other names which have similar double meanings.

2. According to अनेकार्थसंग्रह of हेमचन्द्र and the विश्वप्रकाशकोश, "त्रोटि" means a kind of bird, and it appears to me that owing to a misunderstanding of an older text which gave something like 'शुकत्रोटिः खगे' the compound name शुकत्रोटि was split up into शुक and त्रोटि, and each was taken for a kind of bird. Once this was done others followed in the wake and त्रोटि by itself became a kind of bird. The Hindi name सुठोरा thus clearly points to शुकत्रोटि as a name for this group of birds, unless त्रोटि by itself is established as a specific name for a particular bird. That compound bird-names have occasionally been misunderstood and split up may be seen from the example of किकिदीवि mentioned by पेरुसूरि in his औणादिक पदार्णव :—

"एके तु किकिदीवी तु नामनी द्वे न्यरूपयन्"—Part 4, 168.

Similarly the name घोष्ठ-कुक्कुट for the Neophron Vulture has been wrongly split up into (i) घोष्ट and कुक्कुट in M. W. as discussed under Vulture No. 6, Art. 51. A mistake of this kind, once made, is copied and re-copied by subsequent compilers of lexicons and obtains a fictitious authority.

कङ्कत्रोटि is a kind of fish having a mouth resembling the bill of the Common Heron and this offers the strongest argument in support of the name शुकत्रोटि for the Parrot-Bills and Suthoras, formed in the same way, while we have very probable synonyms in शुकानन and शुकनास as well.

---

1. Hindi Shabda Sāgar. सुठोरा = शुकतुण्ड = शुकत्रोटि.

4

NUTHATCHES

1. The Nuthatches of North and Central India are small birds, not over 6 inches long, and have similar habits. In colouration also all are blue-grey or bluish above, and different shades of chestnut below. They are birds of mango-topes and other trees and keep to tree-trunks or branches and feed on insects and worms and also nuts if available. They are more often heard than seen, and it is their sharp notes and the sound of hammering on the bark of a tree or on hard seeds or nuts which help to locate them. All have black-bills except the velvet-fronted Blue Nuthatch which has a coral-red bill. They are known as सिरसी or सिरी in Hindi, चोर परकी (the invisible Little Dove in Bengal) and सिध्यी फिप (the 'सिध्यी' bird)[1] in Assam, and I think they should be connected with some of the Sanskrit bird names like शिलीन्ध्री, कन्दली, करक, कवक, कपोती or कपोतिका occurring as below :—

(1) "शिलीन्ध्रं कदलीपुष्पे कवकत्रिपुटाख्ययो:
शिलीन्ध्री विहगी" —हेमचन्द्र

(2) "शिलीन्ध्रं कदलीपुष्पे करकत्रिपुटाख्ययो:
— — — शिलीन्ध्री विहगीभिदि" —विश्वप्रकाश

(3) "कन्दली मृगपक्षि विशेषयो:" —मेदिनी

(4) "पारावत: कपोत: स्यात् कपोतो विहगान्तरम्"[2] —शाश्वतकोश.

(5) "कपोत: पारावते स्यात् कवकाख्यविहङ्गमे"[3]—हेमचन्द्र, विश्वप्रकाश.

(6) कपोत: स्यात्कलखे कवकाख्यविहङ्गमे" —विश्वलोचनकोश

The following subsidiary equations should help in construing the above :—

---

1. फो and फिप in Hill dialects mean a 'bird'. Cf. Sanskrit फुक, a bird. The local names given above are from F.B.I.

2. कपोत as a homonym in this synonymy means (i) a Dove or Pigeon—कवते इति कपोत: (M.W. उणादि) and (ii) क ईषद् क्षुद्रो वा पोत: पक्षिशावक: क्षुद्रपक्षी, a small bird.

3. The Nuthatch is called a कवक because when holding an to a tree-trunk, it resembles a mushroom jutting out from a tree in a similar position; cf. also कौति कवते कूयते वा कवाक:-दशापाद्युणादिवृत्ति: 3.34. By giving these derivations I do not at all imply that they are correct. They are merely suggestive and given as mere possibilities.

"गोमयच्छत्रिकामाहुर्दिलीरं च शिलीन्ध्रकम्" —हारावली
शिली = गण्डूपदी, a kind of worm —हेमचन्द्र, अमर
शिली = स्तम्भशीर्ष —मेदिनी
करक = पक्षिभेद —हेमचन्द्र
कवक = Mushroom—M. Williams.
"कन्दलं त्रिषु उपरागे नवाङ्कुरे कलध्वनौ, शिलीन्ध्रपुष्पे" —मेदिनी
"कपोतं अञ्जनेऽपि स्यात्" —विश्वप्रकाश

Now शिली being both 'a worm' and 'the top of a column' offers a reasonable derivation of शिलीन्ध्री from the two different senses of the word शिली with root धृ 'to hold.' As a catcher of worms शिलीन्ध्र would be a bird, and as resting on or holding the top of a column शिलीन्ध्रम् would be छत्राकम् a mushroom. If the bird also is in the habit of holding on to the trunk (column) of a tree it could be properly called a शिलीन्ध्र, and its small size would justify the form शिलीन्ध्री just as विहगी should mean a small bird[1] in addition to being the feminine of विहग (any bird).

2. "कन्दली" means 'a new shoot' (प्रवाल) which is often of a delicate shade of red and hence also 'a light red colour' (उपराग). The propriety of this name for a particular bird should depend on these senses. The red colour of the bill (resembling a new shoot) of the Velvet-fronted Nuthatch, when it is resting face up against a tree-trunk— quite a common attitude for it —with the body colour merging with the dark colour of the tree, would seem to justify the name कन्दली for it. The orange-red bill of सारिका (Indian Grackle) has been compared with कन्दली (a red shoot) by क्षेमेन्द्र :-

"................. श्यामाङ्गी सारिकाऽब्रवीत्
चम्पकस्येव कलिकां बिभ्राणा चञ्चुकन्दलीम्"

बृहत्कथामञ्जरी, 9·201

This seems to strengthen the above identification.

"शिलीन्ध्रम्" is also the flower of the banana which has a maroon red calyx when open. The Cinnamon-bellied Nuthatch, which has deep chest-nut lower parts, can well claim the name for itself. For similar reasons कन्दली as a मृग[2] would be the large Red Flying Squirrel.

3. "कलन्दक" according to M. Williams is either a squirrel or a bird, but in view of the equations :

---

1. This is according to the rule— स्त्री स्यात्काचिन्मृणाल्यादिर्विवक्षापचये यदि" —अमरकोश, 3.5. स्त्रीलिङ्गशेष: verse 7.

2. कन्दली and कदली are alternative readings in अभि. चिन्तामणि, and शब्दरत्नाकर has बिलशायिनि कन्दली कदली हस्तायामा. See also वैजयन्ती कोश which includes कदली among animals that yield useful skins. These large squirrels live in holes in trees and also underground. They are of the पर्णमृगा: group as living on trees and बिलेशया: group as living in holes.

"कन्दलं शिलीन्ध्रपुष्पे" — मेदिनी, and
"कन्दली मृगपाक्षिविशेषयोः" — विश्वप्रकाश

it would appear that कन्दलक and कन्दलीक (both with स्वार्थे कन्) became कलन्दक and कलिंदक in Pali by metathesis, and both the latter like the former mean a kind of squirrel and a kind of bird. The bird is of course, the Nuthatch, and as for the squirrel it appears to be the Large Indian Squirrel (Sciurus indicus maximus) of the plains, which is maroon-red above and buff below, or the Large Red Flying Squirrel of Kashmir and Nepal which is chestnut above and pale below. They have a soft fur and are of a good size to yield a useful skin. It is suggested that these are the कन्दलीमृग of the lexicons, and one of these, probably the Large Indian Squirrel, gave the name of कलन्दक निवाप (v. l. कालिन्दक निवाप) to a Buddhist Grove in वेलुवन where the life of a certain prince, sleeping under a tree and on the point of being bitten by a snake, was saved by the local sprite assuming the form of a squirrel and screaming a warning to him. That कलन्दक is definitely a squirrel is also proved by a little story in मिलिन्दपञ्ह[1] where one is described as frightening away its enemy by raising its puffed out tail. On the other hand, trustful of man as the Nuthatches are, it is equally probable that the निवाप derived its name from the कन्दली or कन्दलक birds. The resemblance of the bird's movements on a tree-trunk, including its ability to scuttle quickly down a tree-trunk head foremost, sideways or upside down along a branch, to those of a squirrel accounts, perhaps better still, for the name कन्दली for the Nuthatch group as a whole. The voice of these birds is a 'chwit-chwit' or a sharp 'tsit' and करक as a musical instrument must have been a small soft-toned whistle for children named after the call of a Nuthatch.

4. Again, the कन्दगलक bird in the कन्दगलक जातक (v.l. कलन्तक in ललितविस्तर) is no other than the कन्दली or कन्दलक bird, viz. the Nuthatch, the Chestnut-bellied or the Cinnamon-bellied variety. It is necessary to state, before setting out the story, that Nuthatches resemble Woodpeckers in the way they hunt and creep all over the trunks and branches of trees for insects, that they have hard-pointed bills with which they bore holes in the hardest of nuts for their contents, and that they breed in natural holes in trees, and one of them, the Velvet-fronted Nuthatch, selects a nest-hole deserted by a Barbet or a Woodpecker or enlarges a small natural crevice in a tree with its bill. The story is that a Woodpecker (रुक्ख कोट्ठक सकुन i.e. वृक्षकुट्टक or काष्ठकूट) living in खदिरवन[2] and a कन्दगलक were friends and the latter happened to pay a friendly visit to the former. He was entertained with plenty of succulent and soft worms so that he was tempted to shift permanently from his soft-wooded forest to the Catechu-forest. The Woodpecker advised

1. VII· ओपम्म कथा No. 3.
2. Forest of catechu trees.

him not to, for accustomed as he was to work upon soft-wood only, he could not bore into the hard Catechu wood for insects, but he would not listen, and actually broke his bill and neck at the first attempt against a Catechu tree-trunk and died. This interesting story leaves hardly any doubt as to the identity of कन्दगलक and supports the identification of कन्दली with a Nuthatch.

5. Synonymy No. 4, taken by itself, would appear to mean that पारावत or Pigeon is a kind of कपोत or Dove, and कपोत (Dove) is a different bird. In other words, कपोत is a larger category which includes both Pigeon and Dove as varieties within itself. Such an interpretation seems reasonable enough but the next two equations which run almost parallel to the first show that the latter half of the first, viz. "कपोतो विहगान्तरम्" actually refers not to कपोत in the sense of a Dove but to कवक (=करक) as a different bird altogether. We have also seen that कवक or करक is the same as the small bird known as शिलीन्ध्री. It follows therefore, that शिलीन्ध्री is also known by the name of कपोत including the feminine forms कपोती or कपोतिका which would be a diminutive of कपोत and therefore comparable with the name शिलीन्ध्री as विहगी, a little bird.[1] The aptness of the name कपोतिका becomes apparent when we recall the blue-grey of the upper parts of all Nuthatches, resembling the colour of the Blue Rock Pigeon. Cf. कापोताञ्जन for collyrium.

6. Lastly attention may be invited to the vernacular names given above which do seem to have some connection with Sanskrit शिलीन्ध्री—particularly the name सिध्यी which is perhaps a corruption of it. सिरी is also an abbreviation of सिरीन्धी (शिलीन्ध्री).

The विष्किर birds drawing out worms from the barks of trees referred to by भवभूति in :—

"शाखापस्किरमाणविष्किरमुखव्याकृष्टकीटत्वचः"

उत्तररामचरितम्, 2.9.

are either Nuthatches or Woodpeckers. They have been called विष्किर[2] as they dig out their insect-food from the bark or soft rotten wood of various trees like the common fowl on the ground. The alternative reading of छाया for शाखा is incorrect and goes ill with 'त्वचा' (bark).

1. Campare the Bengali name of 'the invisible dove' for a Nuthatch quoted above.
2. From वि with कृ to scatter, cleave, split, etc.—M. W.
विकीर्य भक्षयन्त्येते यस्मात्तस्माद्धि विष्किराः—भावप्रकाश, मांसवर्ग.

5

LAUGHING THRUSHES & BABBLERS

A. BIRDS EQUAL IN SIZE TO OR LARGER THAN THE COMMOM MYNA.

1. The members of this group have powerful legs and feet and short rounded wings which means that they are not good fliers. They are mainly terrestrial in their habits and feed on the ground on berries and insects for which they turn up leaves and other rubbish. Their gregarious and noisy habits have secured for them a place among the well-known birds of augury. Some of the Babblers are also birds of the plains. The White-Crested Laughing Thrushes indulge every few minutes "in an outburst of cackling and laughing calls in which each member tries to out-shout the rest." Similarly the Rufous-necked laughing Thrushes burst "every now and then into a perfect babel of shrieks, laughs and expostulations" and the noisiness of the Common and Jungle Babblers of the plains is a matter of common knowledge. In short, they "are all one blood."

2. Properly speaking they belong to the "peckers" or प्रतुद class and appear to be the वाक्कार[1] (वाचां करोति, i.e. noisy or cacophonous) of चरक and फाकार of कल्पद्रुकोश[2] but as they also scrape the ground with the bill and sometimes with the feet in search of food (Jerdon) they have been placed in the विष्किर class in सुश्रुत under the name of कुरुबाहुक (very noisy). Local names of these birds often emphasize their noisy character e.g. the Himalayan White-Crested Laughing Thrush is राविल काह्री in Hindi (cf. 'कहकहाराव'), and Nepali or Hindi भियाकुरो for the Rufous-necked and Slaty-headed Scimitar Babbler is evidently the same as कुरुबाहु, for भूयस् is भिय्यो or भिय्य in Pali and कुरो is the

---

1. Cf. वाग्गेयकार (वाक्कार+गेयकार, one who recites) in मानसोल्लास Vol. 2, 105 and Hindi बकबक for garrulity.

2. "फा शब्दकारी फाकारो"—where फा (निष्ठुरोक्तौ—शाश्वत) refers to the harsh calls and noisy nature of the birds and is in contrast with the sense of कल or मधु in names like कलरव, मधुक etc. अष्टाङ्गसंग्रह 1.7 gives पार्कार while Parādkar's edition of अष्टाङ्गहृदय (N. Sagar, 1939) quotes an alternative reading of फेत्कार in a foot-note at p. 95, both giving the same sense.

same as कुरव (harsh voice). Both these occur in Nepal where the influence of Pali and Buddhism was predominant in ancient times. वाक्कार, कुरवक, and कुरुबाहु are therefore, common Sanskrit names for these noisy birds. It may be added that कुरुबाहुक is a better reading in सुश्रुत than कुरवाहक though both mean the same thing. M. Williams gives the former as कुरुबाहु[1] and डल्हणाचार्य renders it as कुरुकुरुक, noisy.

The वाणीवाद birds of the following extract should be the Himalayan White-Crested, the Indian Black-gorgeted, the Indian Necklaced, and the White-throated, Laughing Thrushes of the Western Himalayas ranging between 2,000 and 5,000 ft. and common in the foot-hills of the Punjab, Garhwal, Nepal, etc. All these are allied forms and have similar habits. Some four or five birds get on the path or open space and begin to dance with lowered wings and spreading their tails, threading in and out amongst themselves in the most complicated figures while the rest of the mob watches and applauds from every branch of the surrounding bushes or trees in the heartiest and jolliest fashion (Stray Feathers, 6,286, and S. Baker in F.B.I.):—

"वाणीवादाञ्छुकांश्चैव सारिकान् भृङ्गराजकान्"- M. Bh. 13,54,10

The name वाणीवाद would seem to be connected with वाणी, sound of a hand-drum, वाणिनी, a dancer, वाण्य: a choir of musicians, and वाद sounding or playing a musical instrument; cf. पाणिवाद clapping the hands in approbation. Our birds certainly dance, sing and applaud one another. The Red-headed Laughing Thrush of Nepal is neither noisy nor gregarious and some of its louder notes are quite mellow and sweet. It should be the कुङ्कुमचूडक bird of a Himalayan hermitage described in मत्स्य पुराण, Ch. 118. This Thrush has a chestnut head and the adjective कुङ्कुम signifies the same colour in the plumage of the Brahminy Kite described as "कुंकुमारक्त" (Art. 52-E).

3. Names for members of the Starling group and for the Common, the Large Grey, and the Jungle Babblers (with yellow feet and, therefore, पीतपादा like the सारिका or Myna) have been mixed up in कल्पद्रुकोश, राजनिघंटु and other lexicons. The reason for this seems to be their apparent similarity to the common Myna in size, noisiness and the habit of feeding on the ground. That this confusion prevails in the popular mind as well may be seen from the fact that the Bengal Jungle Babbler is known as पेंगामैना or फेंगा in Hindi and the हिन्दीशब्दसागर defines पेंगिया मैना, फैंगा and गंगइ[2], names for the Bengal Jungle Babbler and the Large

1. वार्घ्रीणस (the Hornbill) is also a very noisy bird and कल्पद्रु कोश applies the epithet कुरुबाहु i.e. very noisy to it. बृहत्संहिता (87.4) calls the noisy Magpies as कुरवक (करवक in M.W.)

2. These Hindi names are from Sanskrit roots पिञ्ज्—पिजि—पिङ्ग and गुङ—गङ्गय to make a sound, all, more or less, of onomatopoetic origin. Another name for the सारिका is मदन सारिका which is shortened to मदना in Prakrit and this last again becomes मयना-मैना in Hindi.

Grey Babbler, "as a bird of the Myna tribe, commonly known as the Seven Brothers" (cf. the popular name 'Seven Sisters' for them). The Large Grey Babbler is also मैंना in Hindi and the Jungle Babbler is भुसारिण in Marathi, both these names going back to भूसारिका of राजनिघंटु :—

भूसारिका = भूमदना —भुइं मैंना—मैंना (H. मदना–मयना- मैंना)

4. Names like गोराटी, गोकिराटी or गोकिराटिका have again been regarded as synonymous with सारिका by हेमचन्द्र and others, but they are perhaps easy to distinguish and allocate between their respective owners. The Common Myna is noisy in day-time only when excited or quarrelling with others of its kind, but when roosting in the evening on trees in large numbers as usual they are very noisy and "the fuss and commotion accompanied by endless harsh chattering must be seen and heard to be appreciated" (F.B.I.). The name गोराटी (गां वाचं रटति) is, therefore, perfectly true of it and equally so of the Babblers. The names गोकिराटी and गोकिराटिका, however, seem to have a different derivation, गवि भूमौ किर इव अटति—a bird that moves (and works) on the ground like a pig, and this admirably describes the habit of the Babblers which turn up dead leaves and refuse for insects, berries, etc. Wilson gives this derivation, and perhaps correctly. Curiously enough the Tamil name for some Babblers like the Large Grey Babbler is पंदिजित्ता 'the Pig-bird'[1], which is an exact equivalent of गोकिराटी. In the alternative, the name may be derived from गो+किराती, गवि भूमौ वाचि वा किराती इव i.e. working on the ground or talking like women of the किरात tribe living in the forests. The occupation of digging out medicinal roots has also been attributed to किरात girls:

"कैरातिका कुमारिका सका खनति भेषजम्"

अथर्ववेद, 10.4.14.

The language of the Kiratas was nothing better than the chatter of these birds to the Indo-Aryans and this may well have been an additional reason for the name गोकिराती as suggested above. It was perhaps subsequently changed, under the influence of Prakrit, to गोकिराटी.[2] The epithets कुत्सिताङ्गी and कश्मलाङ्गी (for सारिका) in राजनिघण्टु refers to the dirty-grey, and untidy plumage of these Babblers.

5. Lastly, हृहोलिका (hysterically noisy; cf. हाहाकार) is one of the names in the कल्पद्रु synonym for the Myna-group and corresponds to Hindi गँगइ (गुङ्र अव्यक्ते शब्दे to shout) and पैंगा (पिञ्ज् अव्यक्ते शब्दे), and Gujarati भड़भड़ियां (भण भण्ड् to call) for the Common and Jungle Babblers. हृहोलिका must therefore refer to these birds who start shouting hysterically at the slightest provocation. S. Baker[3] devotes a whole paragraph to a description of the noisy

1. Per Jerdon in "The Birds of India".
2. Cf. कैरात, Prakrit गेलाट, for the Malkohas, Art. 37-B.
3. F.B.I. 2nd Edition Vol. I. 192.

habits of the Seven Sisters. For a remotely possible reference to these birds as सप्त स्वसारः in the Rg Veda see Art. 13.

6. मणितुण्ड (red-billed; cf. मणितारक, the Sarus, whose eyes are red, Art.62) is a familiar bird in the garden of Indra in the Himalayas:

"नानावर्णैश्च शकुनैः नानारत्नतनूरुहैः
सुवर्णपुष्पैश्चानेकैः मणितुण्डैर्द्विजातिभिः"

वायुपुराण, 39, 18.

It probably refers to the beautiful and sweet-voiced Coral-billed Scimitar Babbler which does not shun observation, unless the Grey-winged Black-bird with a red bill is intended. The red-billed Black Bulbul cannot be meant as it has very harsh notes and does not deserve a place with the beautiful and multicoloured (नानारत्नतनूरुहैः) little gems of the bird-world—the Sun-birds, Art. 30. It is however possible that the name मणितुण्ड as a homonym in the plural refers to both the above Babbler and the Black-bird.

B. BIRDS OF THE SIZE OF A SPARROW

1. Coming to the smaller members of the family there is, first, the widely distributed Iora[1] of the road-side trees, groves and gardens of the plains and lower hills, wandering up to the outer Himalayas. It is black and greenish-yellow above and deep yellow beneath, duller and greenish below the breast. The wings have two white bars. The male has a variety of pleasant and powerful whistling notes some of which resemble the सू (soo) and others the सी (see)call, uttered as a single or multiple whistle, up to eight notes in succession. It has besides a long drawn wee-e-e-e-tu or see-e-e-e-u-whistle. It is mentioned as a bird of augury under the name सूकरी or सूकरिका (सू इति शब्दं करोति) in बृहत्संहिता, 85.37;87.9 where it is described as a small Sparrow-like bird ("जात्या चटिका च सूकरिका"). वसन्तराज also mentions it at 4.51. Hindi सौबिगा for the bird is from Prakrit सूबिगा for Sans. शुकिका, incorrectly rendered as the मैना (starling) in पा० स०, महण्णवो. शुकिका is thus another name for the Iora. But the most beautiful and fully appropriate names for it are मधुक and श्रीवद, descriptive of its sweet whistling notes, given in देशी नाममाला where महुओ (मधुकः मधुना मधुरं वा कायति) is defined as "श्रीवदाख्यः पक्षी, श्रीः इति वदति वाश्यते".

2. The Black-headed Sibia of Nepal has a "Loud" ringing call Tit-teree, titteree, tueeyo" and its local name सिब्या (सीबय?) is clearly reminiscent of श्रीवद, the titteree note being the श्री call. If so it would be simply श्रीवद and the far sweeter Iora, मधुक-श्रीवद.[2]

---

1. Probably from Latin Io—a cry of joy.
2. For other birds bearing the name श्रीवद see Art. 10, 13.

3. The beautiful Red-billed Liothrix[1] of Nepal has an excellent song during the breeding season and is a favourite cage bird for its song and beauty. Its Nepali name recorded in F. B. I. is नंचुरा (नन्द चिड़ा from नन्दि चटक, a pleasing or excellent Sparrow?). On the other hand the रोचिष्णु bird of अश्वघोष is almost certainly the Liothrix (cf. रुक्मत् for a bright fire):—

"रोचिष्णवो नाम पतत्रिणोऽन्ये
दीप्ताग्निवर्णोज्ज्वलितैरिवास्यैः ।
भ्रमन्ति दृष्टीर्वपुषाऽऽक्षिपन्तः
स्वनैः शुभैरप्सरसो हरन्तः ॥"

सौन्दरनन्द, 10,31.

This verse is from a description of Himalayan scenery, apparently somewhere in Nepal, an important centre of Buddhism, and the brief pen-picture of the poet sufficiently declares the bird's identity. The verse may be freely translated:

"The रोचिष्णु birds with their fiery-red aspect and bills, song sweeter than the nymphs', and so attractive to look at, are sporting here and there." The Liothrix has a brilliant orange-red bill and bright orange-yellow throat and breast, and to quote Whistler, "It is a very lively cheerful little bird.. going about in parties. In the breeding season the cock has a delightful song of some variety and compass." I need not add a word more, for no other bird matches the beautiful description of अश्वघोष.

4. The same author portrays another beautiful bird in the following verse:—

मनःशिलाभैर्वदनैर्विहङ्गा
यत्राक्षिभिः स्फाटिकसन्निभैश्च ।
शादैश्च (V L श्यावैश्च) पक्षैरतिलोहितान्तैः
माञ्जिष्ठकैरर्धसितैश्च पादैः ॥ Ibid. 10.28

The Silver-eared Mesia[2], closely allied to the Liothrix described above, makes the nearest approach to the poet's description. The Cock-bird's golden-yellow forehead, orange-yellow chin and throat, and yellow-ochre bill, red-brown iris, wing-coverts edged with green, wings brown edged with crimson, crimson upper and lower tail coverts, the former showing up close to the folded wing-tips, and legs and feet fleshy-yellow, answer fully to the colour pattern described in the above verse. The only apparent difficulty is as regards the colour of the eyes which are said to resemble स्फटिक, ordinarily supposed to be colourless and transparent, but reddish and dark-coloured rock-crystals described as अशोकपल्लवच्छाय, लोहिताकार and कृष्ण were also known varieties of स्फटिक (शब्दकल्पद्रुम quoting युक्तिकल्पतरु) so that it is not incorrect to describe the red-brown eyes of the bird as

1. From Greek leios, 'smooth' and thrix, 'hair', after the sleek plumage of the bird.
2. Greek mesos, 'middle'?

स्फटिक सन्निभ. It has clear loud whistling notes and a party of these pretty little birds "form a wonderful spectacle of bright colour in front of heavy green bushes and undergrowth" (S. Baker in F. B. I.). Like its cousin, the Liothrix, it is also a favourite cage-bird of North India.

5. The last bird of the group to have a Sanskrit name is the Chloropsis[1], known as हरेवा (fr. हरित, green) in Hindi. Corresponding Sanskrit names are पक्षगुप्त and पत्रगुप्त which clearly imply that the bird is effectively camouflaged or rendered invisible in the foliage as the colour of their plumage merges with that of the trees in which they live. This is perfectly true of the Chloropsis. "The green Bulbul (i.e., the Chloropsis) is a bird of talent and it is a wag. It mocks a King-Crow, now a Sparrow-Hawk and now a Sun-bird. You stare into the tree and see none of them.............Not till he flits across to another tree will you find out who has been fooling you. For this reason few even of those who take an interest in birds know how very common the Green Bulbul really is".[2] This reminds one of what Wordsworth has said about the Cuckoo in England.

"No bird but an invisible thing,
A Voice, a Mystery."

The पक्षगुप्त of महाव्युत्पत्ति, Section 213 and the auspicious पत्रगुप्त of ललितविस्तर, Ch. 5, are, therefore, no other than the golden-fronted and the Orange-bellied Chloropsis both of which occur in the outer Himalayas. It is also interesting to note that the Green Finch which invariably nests in the trees has been called 'brother of the leaves'.[3] For a possible reference to these birds as हरिताः in the अथर्ववेद see Art. 34.

---

1. Gr. chloros, light green; opis, appearance.
2. EHA in the Common Birds of Bombay.
3. "Adventures in Woodcraft," p. 68.

6

BULBULS

1. The Bulbuls constitute a large and widely distributed family of small birds, and every part of India claims at least a few varieties as familiar denizens of towns, gardens, or the forest. They are arboreal by habit, keeping to the trees and bushes, and are fairly bold. Having short, weak legs they do not often descend to the ground. They have pleasant notes and are "extremely cheerful birds, always in an optimistic frame of mind and any garden is the richer for their lively, restless presence and constant gay notes". Sanskrit names are available for three distinct groups of Bulbuls common in North India, viz.: (i) the dark-grey and black-headed Red-vented Bulbuls; (ii) those with contrasting colours about the region of the ear, e.g. the White-cheeked, the White-eared, and the Red-whiskered Bulbuls, all of a grey-brown colour; and (iii) the Black Bulbul with noisy and discordant notes. The following lexical information is available about these birds:—

(1) "पेचस्तु मेचको[1]ज्ञेयो पुच्छान्तर्भागलोहितः"—धन्वन्तरिनिघण्टु;

(2) "अथ गोवत्सा पुच्छाधो रक्तवर्णका
पर्यंटिका कर्णिकिका रक्ता लट्वाऽपरा च सा
पुच्छाधः पीतवर्णोऽथ फेञ्चः पोटियकः पुनः
श्रीकर्णो नीलचटक इत्यादयः"[2] —कल्पद्रुकोश

(3) "कृष्णचूडः कृमिरिपुः वुल्वुलो नीलपिङ्गलः"[3]—पञ्चतत्त्वप्रकाश

Of the above names चरकसंहिता mentions लट्वा alone but furnishes an additional name अङ्गारचूडक[4] for the black-headed and black-crested Bulbuls taken together (अङ्गार charcoal, hence 'of a dark or black colour';

1. मेचक is descriptive of the generally dark colour of the plumage of these birds.

2. Subject to the alternative readings of गोवत्सक and कर्णियक for गोवत्सा and कर्णिकिका every name in this list stands for a particular bird or insect in वसन्तराज.

3. नीलपिङ्गल is descriptive of the generally 'brown' body-plumage of the black-headed or black-crested Bulbuls. Persian 'Bulbul' has been Sanskritized into वुल्वुल !

4. In the Marathi notes on चरकसंहिता (नि. सागर प्रेस,. 1922) अङ्गारचूडक has been correctly rendered as Bulbul.

चूडा crest, top or head). सुश्रुतसंहिता also mentions the लट्वा[1] and the बृहत्संहिता has श्रीकर्ण and रला which last is not a bird but an insect and the name has been listed in कल्पद्रु by mistake. To my knowledge वसन्तराजशाकुनम् is the only major work on augury which mentions all the bird and insect-names listed in the above extract from कल्पद्रु. It is really a mixed list for Bulbuls, other birds and a couple of noisy insects, and I believe that the author of कल्पद्रुकोश has drawn a good deal upon वसन्तराज for compiling his long list of birds. The above names occur in वसन्तराज, 8. 46-52 (pp. 247-250).

2. The commonest Bulbuls of North India, viz., the Central Indian and the Bengal Red-vented Bulbuls were probably the first recipients of the now popular name of 'Bulbul' at the hands of the Muslims who, wanting to find an Indian substitute for their favourite Bulbul, the Persian Nightingale, immortalized in song by great poets like Hafiz and others, chose these cheerful birds for the compliment. The name has stuck so well that the people have almost forgotten their old Hindi name, कलसिरी ('black-headed', the same as अङ्गारचूडक of चरक, and its later equivalent, कृष्णचूड of पञ्चतत्त्वप्रकाश). It is worth noting that the F.B.I. also records 'बुलबुल' as a Hindi name against the above named Red-vented Bulbuls and no others.

3. The author of कल्पद्रुकोश has given either his own emendations or alternative readings of गोवत्सा, कर्णिकिका, and पर्यण्टिका for गोवत्सक, कर्णियक, and पर्यन्दिका respectively of वसन्तराज where रला and कर्णियक are mentioned together:—

"शस्तौ रलाकर्णियकौ च वामौ सवल्गुला चर्मचटौ प्रयाणे" —1.8.47.

If कर्णियक like रला is also some noisy insect, as there is reason to believe, कर्णिकिका also will have to be excluded from the bird-list of कल्पद्रु (see last paragraph). The name श्रीकर्ण corresponds to Hindi कानधरा or कनधरा (wearing an ear-ornament, probably by association with कर्णधारा, the name of a beautiful Apsarā) which has been incorrectly recorded as 'Kandghara' and 'Kangdhara' in F.B.I. against the White-cheeked and White-eared Bulbuls through a phonetic error. Similarly Hindi कनेरा for the Bengal Red-whiskered Bulbul is from Sanskrit कर्णिकार which is common to several plants including Nerium odorum, having beautiful flowers worn by women in their ears for ornament and hence the name (cf. कर्णिका an ear-ornament and also the name of a certain अप्सरा). कर्णिकार is कण्णेर in Prakrit and कनेर in Hindi so that the name कनेरा for the Red-whiskered Bulbul is fully significant.

---

1. The name लट्वा as a homonym has been applied to several birds e.g., (i) fr. लट्व 'a curl of hair on the forehead' it is the White-cheeked Bulbul as explained later on; (ii) fr. लट्व 'a dancing boy', लट्वा 'a dancing girl', it is the Fan-tail Flycatcher, Art. 11, and in the same sense (iii) the Short-toed Lark, Art. 27.

4. It is clear from the first two synonymies given in para. 1 that पेच (v. 1. फेञ्च ?) and गोवत्सा (M.W. and वसन्तराज have perhaps the more correct form, गोवत्सक) refer to Bulbuls with red under-tail coverts, and लट्वा (लट्व—भ्रमरक a curl on the forehead) is the White-cheeked Bulbul which alone has a long and pointed crest curling forward and yellow under-tail coverts (पुच्छाधः पीतवर्णा). It will thus be seen that चक्रदत्त on चरक and डल्हणाचार्य on सुश्रुत have erred in rendering लट्वा as the फेञ्चाक or फेञ्जातक described by them as having a red patch under the tail (रक्तपुच्छाधोभागः). On the other hand, कल्पद्रुकोश rightly differentiates गोवत्सा (v.l. गोवत्सक), the Red-vented, from लट्वा, the yellow-vented White-cheeked Bulbul, and by extension the latter term would include the crestless but yellow-vented White-eared Bulbul as well. The terms, पेच, फेञ्च (केञ्च in M.W. and in the foot-note in कल्पद्रु, should be a w.r. of this), फेञ्चाक, and फेञ्जातक[1] seem to be allied forms which according to चक्रदत्त and डल्हणाचार्य, supported by धन्वन्तरि, denote the Red-vented Bulbuls. Now फेञ्च and गोवत्सक are two different birds according to वसन्तराज, and they should therefore be two different species of Bulbul with red under the tail, and these are (i) the familiar sub-crested forms, the 'Central Indian' and 'Bengal' Red-vented Bulbuls, and (ii) the much smarter looking and fully crested 'Bengal' and 'Southern' Whiskered Bulbuls. With these preliminary observations I proceed to allocate the above names, together with the pretty name पुष्पावतंसक of the Rāmāyaṇa amongst the commoner Bulbuls of North India, the name अङ्गारचूडक being of course a common name foı all of them. उद्गारचूडक in M.W. is a graphical error.

5. (1) The Bengal and Central Indian Red-vented Bulbuls are the पेच and फेञ्च of the lexicons and फेञ्चाक and फेञ्जातक of the commentaries on चरक and सुश्रुत.

(2) The White-cheeked, the White-eared, and the Red-whiskered Bulbuls should share the name श्रीकर्ण as they all have beautiful ears, as it were ("श्रीः शोभा कर्णे यस्य. श्वेतस्य कृष्णसन्निकर्षे शोभाधिक्यात्तथात्वम्"— शब्दस्तोममहानिधि). This name may also refer to the white-cheeked Grey Tit which looks like a miniature Bulbul—Art. 2. The Red-whiskered Bulbul[2] would seem to claim the name पुष्पावतंसक for itself in a special sense:

"विनिष्पतद्भिः शतशश्चित्रैः पुष्पावतंसकैः",

रामायण 5.15.7.

---

1. These appear to be Sansk. adaptations from names like 'Phaki-pho', 'Chinchiok-pho' or 'Chichiam' used by the Hill-tribes of outer Himalayas, e.g. for Bulbuls Nos. 386. 394 and 397 in F.B.I. The forms पेचक (पेच with स्वार्थेकन्) and पेञ्चाक (the same as फेञ्चाक) have occurred in literature also; see the last paragraph of this article.

2. This Bulbul has the "hinder parts of cheeks and ear-coverts white surrounded with black; a tuft of crimson-scarlet feathers under the eye and extending over the lower ear-coverts" (F.B. I. 2nd Edn.). It is therefore a Red and white -eared Bulbul rather than a Red-whiskered one.

The name refers to a beautiful (चित्र) bird which is wearing as it were a pair of floral ear-tops, and this Bulbul with what looks like a spray of red and white petals of Nerium odorum, the कर्णिकार (Hindi कनेर), stuck in front of the ear answers best to this pretty name which also agrees very well with Hindi कनेरा for it. The following parallels for पुष्पावतंसक (wearing a floral ornament in the ear) should prove interesting:

"अमी शिरीषप्रसावावतंसाः"—रघुवंश, 16.61

"कर्णावसक्तकुसुममञ्जरी"—कादम्बरी, p. 230

"रामदामोदरौ...वन्यपुष्पावतंसकौ"—ब्रह्मवै. पुराण, 184.53.

The Red-whiskered Bulbul, as already stated, is a much smarter looking bird than the common Red-vented variety and this is not merely because it wears a beautiful floral ornament in its ears but chiefly because it has a stylish, upright and pointed crest and a broad, dark band across the almost white breast more or less broken in the centre. It is this sprightly and trim appearance of the bird that has won for it the additional Hindi name of सिपाही बुलबुल (the Soldier-Bulbul). Besides it shares the crimson patch under the tail with its cousins. The गोवत्सक of वसन्तराज, defined under the name of गोवत्सा in कल्पद्रु is this bird. The etymology and the propriety of the name is not at all apparent though a suggestion or two may be risked with, however, hardly any chance of probability:

(i) गवि भूमौ वत्स इव — (a) 'like a toddler on the ground', in reference to the weak legs of the bird;

(ii) गो 'hair', वत्स 'chest'—after the divided dark-brown band appearing to descend from the neck like pendent locks of hair falling on the breast[1];

(iii) गवि पृथिव्यां वत्स इव—after the Vedic singer वत्स who successfully passed through a fire ordeal to establish his honourable Brahmanic parentage. This vain and confident looking Bulbul also with its sweet and cheerful notes remains unscathed despite fire (the red patch) under its tail. वत्स the sage is now in heaven but the bird acting his part on earth is still with us. See Manusmṛti, 8.166 and पञ्चविंशब्राह्मण, 14.6.6.

(3) लट्वा from लट्व a 'curl on the forehead' is specific firstly for the White-cheeked Bulbul with a yellow vent as defined in कल्पद्रु and secondly, by extension for the White-eared Bulbul, also with a yellow seat. The Black-crested Yellow Bulbul

1. Cf. श्रीवत्स, the tuft of hair on the chest of विष्णु.

too, having a long crest and bright yellow lower parts, should share this name.

(4) The Himalayan Black Bulbul (10″) is distinctly larger than the common Red-vented Bulbuls (8″). It has orange-red bill and feet, a decidedly forked tail and loud discordant notes, and as it keeps to the tree-tops "it is frequently mistaken for a Drongo".[1] It "goes about regularly in flocks all through the winter, ...and they have a curious follow my leader style when flying from one tree to another. It is a very bold bird. . . .but it is naturally restless . . . . (and) soon flits away out of sight" (F.B.I. 2nd Edn.) This Black Bulbul should thus be the पर्यंण्टिका (परि with अट्? the wanderer: v.1. पर्यंदिका in वसन्तराज 8.2.46). The name has been incorrectly rendered as a Drongo (भुजङ्ग) in the commentary on वसन्तराज where फेण्ट for the Drongo has not been explained at all (Art. 15). The कल्पद्रु has apparently amended पर्यंदिका into पर्यंण्टिका and the name fully suits the wandering habit of this Bulbul. Its harsh notes are also quite useful for purposes of augury. Its names in Hindi are दुकंल ((दुःकल, 'harsh-voiced') and बनवकरा (wild goat) after its wandering habit and harsh call-notes.

6. Finally, a few words about रला and कर्णियक of वसन्तराज and कर्णिकिका of कल्पद्रुकोश. It has already been suggested above that the latter has taken all these names from the former but in doing so the author has modified गोवत्सक and कर्णियक into गोवत्सा and कर्णिकिका probably under a mistaken belief that the terms were synonymous and were common to a female calf (गोवत्सा-कर्णिकिका 'a heifer') and a particular bird or birds. The बृहत्संहिता mentions रला with छुच्छु at 85.37 and again at 87.6. छुच्छु is छुछुन्दरी, the common 'mole' and रला is defined as follows:

"कलहकारिका च रला।
भृङ्गारवच्च विरुवति निशि भूमौ द्व्यङ्गुलशरीरा ॥" ibid., 87.6.

It is thus a kind of ground insect, a little over an inch long, and noisy like a cricket at night. This description, I venture to suggest, refers to the Mole-Cricket of the genus Gryllotalpa or Scapteriscus which is about the same length and is very noisy at night in wet ground. वसन्तराज who must have had the बृ. संहिता before him when he compiled his work on augury, seems to have added one more noisy insect, the कर्णियक (deafening, fr. कर्णि piercing or कर्णं कायति क्रन्दति) to his list of creatures that are noisy in the evening, for the science of augury must include omens for journeys begun at the close of day or at night. The half verse quoted in para. 3 above also includes, in addition to रलाकर्णियकौ,

1. The White-bellied and the Bronzed Drongos of North India are under 9 inches and therefore smaller than the Black Bulbul. The Commentator of वसन्तराज would seem to have made the same mistake as pointed outs a few line lower down.

the वल्गुला, either the Flying Fox or the Stone Plover bird, both noisy at night, and चर्मचट, a bat. The great majority of birds have diurnal habits and consequently कणियक, placed as it is with रला and other nocturnal animals, should be some other insect, probably the Cicada fly (also झिल्ली in Sansk.) noted for the prolonged shrill notes of the male. It is generally heard till late in the evening and often at night during the summer; cf. कर्णदुन्दुभि for insects that may accidentally enter a person's ear and make a buzzing noise inside. Both रला and कर्णिकिका are therefore out of place in the bird-list of कल्पद्रुकोश. It is also interesting to note that the commentator of वसन्तराज does not explain रलाकर्णियकौ and contents himself with the remark that they are known in other parts of the country (परदेशप्रसिद्धौ).

7. It may be noted that the little Bulbul has also contributed something to princely vanity as its bright red under-tail coverts were used to embellish royal jewellery and to set off the neck-bands of riding and polo ponies made from white beads:

"पेचकापिच्छसंयुक्तं बाहुसन्धिविभूषणम् ।
सुवर्णोपरि विन्यस्तं नानारत्नविराजितम् ॥"—मानसोल्लास, 2, p. 93.

"पेञ्चाकपुच्छपिच्छैश्च लोहितैर्भ्राजिता भृशम् ।
शङ्खजैर्मणिभिर्वृत्तैः क्वणत्कनकशृङ्खलैः॥— Ibid. 2, p. 221.

अङ्गारचूडक

BULBULS WITH A BLACK HEAD OR CREST

- The Black Bulbul: पर्यंष्टिका
- Common Red-Vented Bulbuls of North India: पेच, फेञ्च, फेञ्चाक, फेञ्जातक
- Bulbuls with a white or white and red patch in the ear-region: श्रीकर्ण
  - with a long crest and yellow under the tail: लट्वा
  - with a pointed crest, red under the tail, and a white and red cheek-patch — The Red whiskered Bulbul: गोवत्सक, पुष्पावतंसक

7

TREE-CREEPERS

Tree-creepers are inconspicuous grey-brown birds of the size of a common Sparrow. They are wholly insectivorous and spend their entire life hunting for insects on the trunks of the larger trees, working in zigzags up the bole "rather like a jerky brown mouse". They never perch on the twigs and may frequently be seen working along the under-side of a bough with their backs parallel to the ground. After working in this manner at one tree, from the lower bole upwards, they fly from the top of one trunk down to the lower part of another. They are resident birds of the Himalayan forests but come down to the nearby plains in winter. An allied form seeks its food in a similar way from perpendicular rock-faces, boulders, etc. and it is for this reason named the Wall-Creeper. This is a foreign bird and visits India during the winter.

Sanskrit चिकुर[1], means 'a little mouse', 'a kind of bird' (i.e. चिकुरचटक 'a mouse-bird'), and a kind of tree, and from the fact that the Tree-creeper is known as चूआ सराई, or Mouse-bird in Assam there is hardly any doubt that the name चिकुर (चटक) refers to this particular bird. The Wrens, with similar mouse-like habits on the ground, also share the name.

A particular bird named गोधक (from गोधा, a lizard, with अल्पार्थ कन्, and therefore meaning 'a little lizard') is mentioned in वेस्संतर जातक[2] and it is most probably this bird, for what Whistler has described as 'the movements of a jerky brown-mouse' appeared to the ancient Indians as the zig-zag movements of a lizard, and they very aptly named it गोधा or गोधक, cf. गोलत्तिका (लत्तिका a lizard) for the Yellow Wagtail.

The Tree-creeper, the female of the Black Drongo (कालका)[3] and the Woodpecker have been assigned to the deity presiding over the larger trees at the Horse Sacrifice:

---

1. चिकुरः पक्षिवृक्षभिदोः—हेमचन्द्र, विश्वप्रकाश and मेदिनी
2. Verse 2009.
3. Commentator उव्वटाचार्य renders गोधा and कालका as particular birds—पक्षिविशेषाः though his rendering of दार्वाघाट (the woodpecker) as सारस is incorrect. कालका is proabably the same as कालिका, the female of the अङ्गारक bird in पतञ्जलि महाभाष्य 6.3.34. अङ्गारक is the Black Drongo (Art. 15) and, as अङ्गारिका means a fire-pan and the black and red bird of the पलाश tree, it is possible to explain the separate name of कालिका (the black one; अंगारक also means 'black') for the female as some sort of a necessity.

"गोधा कालका दार्वाघाटस्ते वनस्पतीनाम्।" वाज.संहिता, 24.35.

The permanent association of the Tree-creeper with large trees (वनस्पति) is a well-known fact. Monitor Lizards (गोधा) are mostly ground creatures and climb trees occasionally in search of food and cannot have been intended here. The Drongo nests in the leafy crown of a tall tree and during the nesting period drives off all the large predacious birds like the Crows, Tree-pies, Kites, Hawks etc. from its vicinity and, indirectly as it were, keeps watch over the tree. The female is mentioned as she is naturally more zealous in these respects. The Woodpecker is of course permanently wedded to a tree-life, and herein lies the propriety of the Vedic allocation of the three birds to the Deity of the Trees.

8

WRENS

The Wrens are very small brown birds of the densest under-growth in the ever-green hilly forests. They live entirely on insects which they pursue with great energy, scrambling over mossy boulders and fallen trees. "Great skulkers and very shy, they are loath to take flight and prefer to creep away silently, if disturbed". The Brown Wren of Nepal is "a dark brown bird that creeps about under-growth like a mouse; the under-parts, which one seldom sees are white with blackish markings. Its ordinary note is a single 'zip' uttered at long intervals; in the breeding season it attempts a little song. If forced to fly it rises with a sharp 'chick' 'chick', 'chick' (Smythies). The Wrens of Kashmir and Nepal thus appear to be another group of little birds with mouse-like ways known as "चिकुर' ('चि' इति कुरति— —making the 'chi' or 'chick' sound) in Sanskrit, and the propriety of the name would seem to be highly probable.

9

DIPPERS

The Dippers are curious little grey-brown birds not over nine inches long. Their short, rotund and stout bodies are specially fitted for an aquatic life. They have a dense and waterproof plumage with even the eyelids covered with feathers. Two or three species of them are found in the Himalayas from Kashmir through Nepal to Assam. They live on water-insects and their larvae which are captured by wading, swimming and diving. They even possess the faculty of walking on the bed of the stream under water and are as perfectly at home on the most turbulent Himalayan stream as on a placid pool of water. The Brown Dipper is a common bird in Kashmir and Nepal as in other parts of the Himalayas and must have been observed by the curious ancients and named by them. Now वञ्जुल is the name of a bird that can walk or move under water: "वजति चलति जले वञ्जुल:"[1] and as the most striking characteristic of the Dipper is its power of walking under water—not possessed by any other bird—the name वञ्जुल should belong to it by right. It is known as जलकर in Hindi, perhaps a mistake in F.B.I. for जलचर, the same as वञ्जुल as explained above. The Dabchick or the Grebe is also वञ्जुल because of its love of reeds and cane-brakes, known as वञ्जुल, amongst which it places its nest and skulks about in case of danger. It is from this habit of the Grebe that the water-cane is named also वञ्जुलप्रिय (beloved of the वञ्जुल bird). The Grebe too swims under water and can well claim, its name in the etymological sense of the word वञ्जुल as brought out in the commentary of the Uṇādi Sūtra as quoted above.

1. उणादिसूत्राणि with प्रक्रियासर्वस्व of नारायण, I.93.

10

THE THRUSH FAMILY

1. This family includes the Chats, Indian and Magpie Robins, Blackbirds, Rock and Ground Thrushes, etc. of which the Chats, Robins, and Rock Thrushes are of a comparatively small size. They are active little birds and Whistler's characterization of some of them is typical, at any rate of the majority of birds constituting the family. The Indian Bush Chat, he says, is very restless and fairly shy, and is incessantly flirting its wings and tail. The Stone Chat also behaves in a similar way. The flight of the Pied Wheatear is strong and fast and always low over the ground, and perching or hopping, the carriage of the bird is very spry and upright. The Black bird hops and runs, while the Red-Start shivers its tail and bobs its head like the Brown Rock-Chat and the Blue Rock-Thrushes. The demeanour of the Indian Robin again, is very sprightly, hopping about with the head held stiffly high and the tail cocked well forward over the back These points in the behaviour of this bird have also been emphasised as prognosticating attitudes by वसन्तराज :—

"वध्वागमाभीप्सितकार्यसिद्धिं, करोति पुच्छं पुनरुत्क्षिपन्ती।
नृत्यन्त्यभीक्ष्णं परममप्रमोदान्महोत्सवं मङ्गलमादिशन्ती॥" 7.76
"लुठंत्यवन्यां[1] गुलिकेव तारा या याति पद्भ्यां गुलिकिर्मता सा॥" 7.115.

2. M. Williams renders "अश्वक" as a sparrow and a toy horse, and the term also means a small pony. Apparently a particular class of birds of the

---

1. तारा is a descriptive epithet of पोतकी when it shoots off in different directions like a meteor or shooting star (तारा) —Ibid. 7.107.9.

"लुठंति" refers to the Robin's fast tripping movement on the ground, like a rolling little ball (गुलिका, a Prakritism) and it is called the गुलिकि: when executing such a movement. Other styles of the bird are named दर्दुरवत् उत्प्लुति (hopping or leaping), स्खलित (faulty gait), गोमूत्रिका सर्पवत् (zig-zagging on the wing) and शरवत् अच्छिन्नवेग (straight arrow-like flight) —ibid. 7.113-16. These clearly exhibit a certain amount of parallelism with the प्लुता, स्खलित (a defect) and धारा types of motion in a horse as described in अश्वचिकित्सा of नकुल Ch. 8, cited in शब्दकल्पद्रुम under घोटक, and in शुक्रनीतिसार, 4.7.144-49, Jeevanand's Edn. (1898).

size of a common sparrow was named अश्वक by reason of a certain fancied similarity of habits with a frisky little colt. The latter is active and handsome, carries its neck and head high, flicks its tail now and then, and has otherwise a sprightly demeanour. In the avian fauna of North India no other birds, except perhaps the White Wagtails, make a nearer approach to this picture of a little colt than the Chats and Robins, and it must be a happy inspiration of some observant sage which gave them the name of अश्वक.[1] It seems to be a very ancient name and though its true significance was forgotten in later times the name itself was happily preserved in some of the manuscript lexicons for a "Sparrow" as 'अश्वक-चटके' even though a particular type of it may well have been intended, just as हेमचन्द्र gives क्रौञ्च, गोरङ्कु, वर्तक, etc. for खगे instead of "खगान्तरे" or पक्षिभेदे and yet they are names of particular birds. It is the same with other lexicons and उणादि lists. The name अश्वक, however, gives us very much more information as to the sort of sparrow it is than a brief and vague lexical definition like the above. It is also interesting to note that the Northern Indian Stone-Chat is known as पिद्दा or कालापिद्दा; the White-tailed Bush Chat as खरपिद्दा (खर a thorny plant on which the bird often perches); the Red-Spotted Blue-throat as नीलकण्ठी पिद्दा all in Hindi, and it is suggested that the name पिद्दा has something to do with Sanskrit पिद्व (probably the Goral Goat known as पिज in Kashmir) or पैद्व (the mythical horse). Hindi पीदड़ी[2] for any insignificant bird is related to Prakrit पिरिडि or पिरिली for the White-throated Munia and allied forms. It would seem, therefore, that the term अश्वक denotes a particular type of Sparrow-like birds and that type is represented by certain members of the Chat and the Robin group. The name, based on certain habits, may well include the smart and active Wagtails which are known as 'दीवाली घोडा' (winter-pony) in Gujarat. In this name दीवाली signifies the time when Wagtails are plentiful in the country and 'घोडा' their smartness, power of running on the ground and their tail-wagging habit. देशीनाममाला of हेमचन्द्र gives us a specific bird-name आसक्ख or आसक्खओ (अश्वाख्य, अश्वाख्यक; Cf आसक्खंध for अश्वस्कन्ध) which goes a great way to strengthen the above hypothesis regarding the type of sparrow-like birds indicated by the term अश्वक (see below).

3. The Indian Robin is a common plains bird, about the size of a sparrow, with blackish brown upper parts, glossy black head and breast, a small white patch on the shoulder and a conspicuous chestnut patch under the tail which is often flicked and spread out and carried erect. The female is dark brown all over and has a chestnut patch under the tail. It is mentioned as श्यामा and कपोतकी in बृहत्संहिता,[3] and पोदकी (v.l. पोतकी) in वसन्तराज[4]. The

1. क: प्रतिकृतौ; अश्वक: अश्वकं रूपम्—हैमशब्दानुशासन, 7.1.154. अश्वक—a sparrow, M. W. Prakrit आसक्ख (अश्वाख्य) has been defined more clearly as we shall see presently.

2. हिं. श. सा. equates पिदड़ी and पीदड़ी with पिद्दी, feminine of पिद्दा. This is perhaps questionable as no masculine form of पिदड़ी or पीदड़ी like पिदड़ा or पीदड़ा is known.

3. Ch. 87.5.

4. Ch. 7.4.

description of a pair of पोदकी given by the latter leaves no doubt in regard to the identity of the bird.[1]—

"ग्राम्येण तुल्यश्चटकेन नीलो योऽसौ पुमान्पाण्डुर पुण्ड्पक्षः ।
लघ्वी ततो धूमनिभा च नारी तत्पोदकी युग्ममुदाहरन्ति ।।"

Trans:—Equal in size to the House-sparrow the cock-bird is of a black colour and has a white wing-patch. The hen is smaller and of a smoky-brown colour. This is how a पोदकी pair is identified.

The prayer formula to be addressed to the bird at the time of putting a question to it for purposes of augury contains not only names that really belong to it but also of other birds of the same group and several flattering epithets consisting of names of goddess पार्वती[2]

"श्यामा वराही शकुनी कुमारी, दुर्गा च देवी चटका तथोमा ।
त्वं पोदकी पाण्डविका त्वमेव, त्वं कृष्णिका त्वं सितपक्षिणी च ।।
त्वं ब्रह्मपुत्री शकुनैक देवी, धनुर्धरी पान्थसमूहमाता ।"

It has also been called कृष्णशकुनि and कृष्णपक्षी respectively[3]. The name पोतकी is evidently connected with Pali and Prakrit पुत्तक and पोतक for 'a litte child, a young bird or animal', cf. ,'पोइय—पोतित, इतस्ततः स्पन्दिते" presumably like a frisky young goat or colt; 'पोआई—पोताकी, शकुन्तिकायाम्"— अभिधान-राजेन्द्र. पोतकी, देवी, चटका (the Sparrow par excellence),[4] कृष्ण पक्षी, कृष्णिका and श्यामा are names that properly belong to it while the others are merely intended for its glorification and to stress its exceptional importance in augury. It shares the names श्यामा and कुमारी with the Shama proper, and the name कृष्णपक्षी (कृष्णपत्रिन्) with the Blue-headed Rock-Thrush. The term सितपक्षिणी though of the feminine gender like the others, refers to the male which has a white wing-bar. The popular Hindi name काली चिड़ी for it is the equivalent of कृष्ण पक्षी.

4. The Shama and the Magpie Robin are the two of the best songsters of India. The head, neck, breast, and upper plumage of the male in both are glossy black; both have a black and white tail; but as against the chestnut under-parts of the Shama those of the Magpie Robin are pure white. The latter has also a broad white wing-bar in addition while the Shama has a longer and a graduated tail. Because of the black head and neck both are the कालकण्ठ—कलविङ्क of the lexicons, कलविङ्क proper of the poets and

1. 7.25.

2. 7.23-24. In the same way पिङ्गला, an Owlet, has been called ब्रह्मपुत्री in मानसोल्लास, 1, pp. 107, 108. Names of goddess पार्वती include श्यामा, कृष्णा, कुमारी, कृष्णपिङ्गला, तारा, उमा, देवी, and बराही.

3. 7.19; 7.344.

4. Cf. शकुनैकदेवी, viz., the chief Bird-goddess of augury, and देवचकली, from देवचटक, its name in Gujarat.

authors of the Purāṇas, and Pali करवीक of the जातक. For different types of कलविङ्क see Art. 23A.

5. Hemachandra defines आसक्ख i.e. अश्वाख्य as the श्रीवद पक्षी (bird with an auspicious song, or श्रीरिति वदतीति, uttering श्री or सी— like whistle). श्रीवद may also be rendered as a song-bird—श्री शोभनं वदतीति. Now it is well-known that the Magpie Robin has, in addition to its beautiful song, a long whistling call, principally heard during the non-breeding season. It is a bird of the अश्वक group, so that अश्वाख्य and probably also अश्वक are specific for it according to the rule of Hemachandra "सामान्योऽपि विशेषे वर्तते" —अभिधानचिन्तामणि,[1] i.e. as the particular or typical अश्वक.

6. The Magpie Robin is mentioned as दहियक in वसन्तराज[2] which corresponds to Hindi दहियर or दहिंगल for it. The 'संस्कृत व प्राकृत कोश' of Godbole, Poona (1872) equates कालकण्ठ with "दय्यर", the same as Hindi दहियर. Other Hindi names for the bird are ग्वालिन and महरी, both meaning 'a milk maid' or seller of milk and curds (दधि, दही) while महरी in Prakrit also means a songstress. दहियक, for ought one can say, may be a Prakrit form of Sanskrit दाधिक (seller of curds), or दध्यच्-दध्यञ्च् (दधिना अञ्चितः), दध्यक्त (दधिना अक्तः), and the idea underlying the name is perhaps the supposition that the original black plumage of the bird has been splashed over with curds as it were. That the idea is not foreign to the Indian mind may be seen from the लोलजातक (274) where a Crow is deprived of its feathers and painted white with curds as a punishment for stealing food from the kitchen of a Brāhmaṇa. The Magpie Robin is दहिय in Prakrit as well:—

"जं लावय तित्तिर दहिय मोरं, मारंति अद्धोस विन्के वि घोर

कुमारपाल प्रतिबोध (427)

7. श्यामा means, among other things, (i) of a dark or bluish colour; (ii) 'a pretty young woman possessing by implication a beautiful voice as well'; and (iii) musk or कस्तूरी. As a bird-name the term applies to the Shama (Turdus Macrourus)[3] and the Indian Robin, and there is reason to believe that other blue or brown song-birds also went by this name with qualifying epithets, e.g. the Brown Rock Chat is known as मटिया श्यामा (मटिया earthy brown) in Hindi and the Blue Rock thrush is श्यामा in the North and पाण्डु in the South and must have been known in Sanskrit as पाण्डु श्यामा because of its light blue colour. पाण्डविक for 'a kind of Sparrow' in M. Williams and पाण्डविका appropriated by वसन्तराज to the Indian Robin, should be the same. Again, the name दुर्गा[4] if not purely honorific, would also seem to be a misappropriation, for it implies a bird of a blue colour; Cf. the complexion of goddess दुर्गा described as blue like the linseed-flower:—

---

1. 404.
2. 8.2,52.
3. Now renamed Kittacincla macroura in F. B. I. 2nd Edn.
4. See Para 3.

अतसीपुष्पवर्णाभां सुप्रतिष्ठां सुलोचनाम् ।

—शब्दकल्प० under दुर्गा

Both दुर्गा and उमा like पाण्डविका should, therefore, be the Blue Rock Thrushes as both mean also the flax or अतसी plant : "उमा दुर्गाऽतसी स्मृता"—उणादिसूत्रवृत्ति (उज्ज्वलदत्त) :1.143; अतसी नीलपुष्पी च पार्वती स्यादुमा क्षुमा—धन्वन्तरि. Later on, however, some of the birds that bore the name of श्यामा came to be known by the synonymous term कस्तूरी[1] and thence as कस्तूरा. Thus we have कस्तूरी or कस्तूरा for the Black-birds and कस्तूरा for the Himalayan Whistling Thrush. The Blue-headed Rock Thrush is कृष्णपत्ती (कृष्णपत्रिन्) in Nepal and was probably कृष्णिका applied later by वसन्तराज to the Indian Robin.

8. We have seen that वसन्तराज has कुमारी (one of the names of goddess पार्वती) as one of the names for the Indian Robin, but there is reason to believe that it was originally a name for the Shama. The male Shama is black above and down to the lower breast, chestnut below and has a prominent white patch above the base of the tail which is black and white. The conspicuous colour pattern of the bird is fully comparable with the description of the goddess कुमारी created by the combined energy issuing from the eyes of ब्रह्मा, विष्णु and महेश according to a statement in the वायुपुराण[2] :—

"त्रिवर्णा च कुमारी सा कृष्णा शुक्ला च पीतिका।"

कुमारी as a bird-name, therefore, may well belong to the Shama, the best Indian songster, in her own right and would appear to have been appropriated by वसन्तराज as a compliment to the Indian Robin. It may be that the description of the goddess कुमारी herself was taken over from the bird bearing the name. It must, however, be conceded that the male Robin also is almost black throughout, has a white wing-patch, visible in flight, and a little chestnut under the tail. The white and chestnut are not, however, half as conspicuous as in the Shama and the Robin is almost a black bird by comparison and has been rightly named कृष्णपक्षी.

9. रक्तकण्ठ is 'a small song-bird' ir M. Williams, and should mean the Ruby-throat which is "a robin-like bird ashy-slate above with a white forehead, chin and throat bright crimson bordered with black" (S. Ali—Indian Hill Birds). "It runs and hops about on the ground,....wings partly drooping, tail cocked and switched over the back now and again.... In all its movements and behaviour it is extremely reminiscent of the familiar Blue-throat of the plains in winter, and in some ways also of the Indian Robin....In the breading season the cock utters a lively pleasant song" (ibid). It is quite common in the North-Indian plains during winter. रक्तकण्ठ (having a red throat) for a small song-bird should therefore belong to it, for no other song bird with a contrasting red throat or neck is known in India. रक्तकण्ठ as a homonym is also an epithet of the

1. राजनिघण्टु.
2. Ch. 90.23.

cuckoo in the sense of a bird with a passionate call—रक्त affected by राग or love and कण्ठ voice. Similarly श्यामकण्ठ 'a kind of small bird' in Wilson's Dictionary may well be the Red-spotted Blue-throat, another winter visitor of the same area. Its Hindi name नीलकण्ठ पिद्दा is fully synonymous with श्यामकण्ठ. It may be added that श्यामकण्ठ is also an adnoun for the Peacock while the Magpie Robin, the House Sparrow and the White Wagtail amongst the smaller birds share the adnoun नीलकण्ठ (नील black) but not श्यामकण्ठ.

10. कपेक्षुक is a bird of augury in वसन्तराज[1] and if it is from कप्—कम्प्[2] to tremble and इक्षु a kind of grass, it should be the Black Redstart which "has the ague in its tail" like a blade of grass trembling in the breeze. Its Hindi name is थरथरकंपा or simply थिरथिरा (स्थिर+अस्थिर ?). धन्वन्तरि distinguishes between खञ्जन and खञ्जरी and defines the latter as "खञ्जरी चलपिच्छकः" i.e. खञ्जरी is a bird with a trembling tail, and this and चलपिच्छक (चल-कम्पने) seem to be other names for the Redstart,[3] unless they refer to the Pippits (Art. 26 B).

11. The Grey-winged Black-bird is a well-known and familiar bird of its class and goes under the Hindi name of कस्तूरी and कस्तूरा (कस्तूरी = श्यामा, the dark coloured). The male, being black with grey patches on the wings is about eleven inches long. It has a coral red to deep orange bill and is "one of the finest and best known songsters of the Himalayas." For this reason it is a favourite cage-bird. Allied forms occur in the central parts of the country and in the Nilgiris. डल्हणाचार्य on सुश्रुत explains कलविङ्क as "कालचटकः भृङ्गराजाद् भिन्नः". It follows that, like the Magpie Robin (कालकण्ठ कलविङ्क) this bird too was regarded as a kind of कलविङ्क and was known as कालचटक (Black-bird or Black-sparrow) which is the same as काल or कृष्ण कलविङ्क, for चटक is synonymous with कलविङ्क in a special sense—"चटकः कलविङ्कः स्यात्"—अमर. The name कालचटक, it may be noted, is applied in certain parts of the country to the Common Black Drongo[4] or the Himalayan Whistling Thrush because all three have a black plumage. It is not to be wondered at if in a vast country like India names based on colour are applied to different birds in different parts of the country. वसन्तराज (8.2.50) also mentions the Blackbird by the name of कालचटक.[5]

12. माणितुण्डक ('red-billed') as a Himalayan bird may well be the Grey-winged Blackbird unless it is the coral billed Scimitar Babbler as suggested in Art. 5:—

---

1. 8.2.51.

2. Words like कपि and कपना are traced to root कपि-चलने in M. W. and Uṇādi. Compare also alternative forms like कपिल्वलक and कम्पिल्लक.

3. The name खञ्जरी is evidently coined after खञ्जरीट for the Wagtail. The Wire-tailed Swallow is known as "Leishra" (?) in the Punjab from the resemblance of the tail-wires with the 'Leishra'-grass (Jerdon).

4. भृङ्गराज mentioned by डल्हणाचार्य and the Black Drongo are allied forms within the same family, Dicruridae (Art. 15).

5. वसन्तराज mentions the Black Drongo under the name of फेण्ट (Art. 15).

"नानावर्णैश्च शकुनैः नानारत्नतनूरुहैः ।
सुवर्णपुष्पैश्चानेकैः मणितुण्डैर्द्विजातिभिः ॥
वायुपुराण, 39.18.

Blackbirds belong to the sub-family containing the true Thrushes which, unlike the Shama, the Magpie Robin, Chats etc. which are purely insectivorous, include small fruits and berries as well in their dietary. They feed a good deal on the ground, turning over the leaves and digging with the bill in soft soil for worms, grubs, etc. The Magpie Robin also feeds on the ground but entirely on insects. कलविङ्क placed in the विष्किरवर्ग by सुश्रुत and प्रतुदवर्ग by चरक and कुलिङ्गक (प्रकारार्थे प्रशंसार्थे वा कन् प्रत्ययः) as its synonym apparently refers to these two song-birds of the size of a sparrow (कुलिङ्ग):—

"कलविङ्कः स्मृतो ग्रामचटकेऽपि कुलिङ्गके"[1] —विश्वप्रकाश

13. It has been stated above that the names श्रीवद and श्यामा are shared by more than one bird and it is perhaps advisable to bring them together:

(I) श्रीवद
 i) श्रीवद—the Whistling Thrush (para. 15 below).
 ii) श्रीवद—the Sibia (Art. 6);
 iii) मधुक श्रीवद—the Iora, (Art.6);
 iv) अश्वक श्रीवद—the Magpie Robin.

(II) श्यामा :—
 i) देवी श्यामा—the Indian Robin;
 ii) कुमारी श्यामा—the Shāmā;
 iii) पाण्डु श्यामा or पाण्डविक—the Blue Rock Thrush;
 iv) मणितुण्ड श्यामा—the Blackbird.

14. The Magpie Robin, the Shama and the Grey-winged Blackbird sing morning and evening from the top of a tree and they are the कलविङ्क[2] of literature in the following examples though the probability in favour of the Magpie Robin is the greatest as it is the most common bird both of the plains and the outer Himalayas. The pleasant conversation and handsome looks of Lord Buddha have been compared with those of the कलविङ्क :—

---

1. I.e. कलविङ्कः स्मृतो कुलिङ्गके ग्रामचटकेऽपि. The name कलविङ्क properly belongs to the कुलिङ्गक bird and also by extension or courtesy to the House Sparrow. This seems to be the force of अपि in the synonymy. For कुलिङ्ग see Art. 23A.

2. Altogether there are seven different types of कलविङ्क—(i) रक्तशीर्ष कलविङ्क, the Rose Finch, (ii) पीतमुण्ड कलविङ्क the Yellow headed Weaver-bird, (iii) सेव्य कलविङ्क the Red Munia, (iv) तिलककण्टक कलविङ्क the crested Lark, (v) श्यामा कलविङ्क the Shāmā, (vi) कालकण्ठ कलविङ्क, the Magpie Robin, and (vii) मणितुण्ड कलविङ्क, the Blackbird (see Art. 23 A.) Of these only the last three are the true songsters of India. The Magpie Robin is common in the plains and hills, the Blackbird is common in the outer Himalayas and occurs at high elevation here and there, and the Shāmā is a bird of deep forests. The कलविङ्क of the passages quoted is most probably the beautiful magpie Robin. The plain looking crested Lark and its cousin, the Skylark (भरद्वाज) do not sing from tree tops and neither of these can be intended (Art. 27).

"कलविङ्को यथा पक्षी दर्शनेन स्वरेण वा"---

ललितविस्तर, Ch. 12.

"कलविङ्करुतेन स्वरेण वल्गुना मनोज्ञेन"— Ibid., Ch. 21.

"इति वाक्यमिदं निशम्य राज्ञः
कलविङ्कस्वर उत्तरं बभाषे"—

बुद्धचरित, 5.34.

A very handsome tribute is first paid to the कलविङ्क for his beautiful song and yet it is said that he is far from attaining the sweetness of the Lord's Voice:—

"द्विजगण कलविङ्कमञ्जुघोषाः
सुरुचिरप्रेमणीयाः सुगीतशब्दाः ।
शंखपटहभेरिवीणशब्दाः
कलमपि न लभन्ति बुद्धशब्दे[1] ॥

A number of them welcome with a chorus the sun rising from the ocean:—

"कृतकलकलविङ्कालापकोलाहलाभिः ।
जलनिधिजलमध्यादेष उत्तार्यतेऽर्कः ॥

सुभाषितरत्नावलि, Verse 2185.

and like the Thrush of Robert Burns the कलविङ्क also 'sings drowsy day to rest' :

"मदकलकलविङ्की काकुनान्दी करेभ्यः
क्षितिरुहशिखरेभ्यो भानुमानुच्चिनोति"

अनर्घराघव, Act 2, 45.

It may be noted that it is the male which sings but the poet's partiality for the gentler sex is responsible for the use of the feminine. European poets also make the Cock Nightingale, which alone sings, of the feminine gender.

In the description of a Himalayan scene the Magpie Robin or the Shama is mentioned with the Black-headed Oriole which too is noted for its sweet fluty notes:—

"सुग्रीवकाञ्चनरवैः कलविङ्करुतैस्तथा ।
कूजितान्तरशब्दैश्च सुरम्याणि च सर्वशः ॥

वायुपुराण, 36.4.

and the महाभारत too places the कलविङ्क with other sweet-voiced birds of the Himalayas:

"चकोरैः शतपत्रैश्च भृङ्गराजैस्तथा शुकैः ।
कोकिलैः कलविङ्कैश्च हारितैर्जीवजीवकैः ॥ 3.158.52-53.

This and the verse following it have been copied into the मार्कण्डेय पुराण, 6.13-19.

---

1. कलमपि—कलामपि, not in the slightest. समाधिराजसूत्रम्, Gilgit manuscripts, Vol. 2, edited by Dr. N. Dutt. 1941, 14th परिवर्त, 29. See also verses 53 and 84 ibid.

A good description of the charming song of कलविङ्क (Pali करवीक) is contained in verse 39 of the नलिनिका जातक[1] where the amorous voice of the princess नलिनिका in the garb of a ऋषिकुमार is compared with that of the bird:

"अकक्कसं अगलितं मुहुं मुहुं
अनुद्धतं अचपलंऽस्स भासितं।
रुदं मणुञ्जं करवीक सुस्सरं
हृदयंगमं रंजयतेव मे मनो॥

The "करविया" (करवीका:-कलविङ्का:) of the वेस्संतर जातक again are these birds and to translate करवीक as 'a Cuckoo' is clearly incorrect.[2] For Magpie Robin as a nominal victim for god त्वष्टृ at the अश्वमेध see Art. 23A.

15. The Himalayan whistling Thrush is a deep blue-black bird, brighter on the wings and tail with black legs and eye-rim which latter distinguishes it from the not much smaller Blackbird in which these parts are yellow. Another race of this Thrush, the Malabar Whistling Thrush occurs in the Indian Peninsula south of the Satpuras. The call is a loud melodious whistle, Blackbird-like in tone but more powerful and resembling the human whistle, hence it is nick-named 'the whistling school-boy' by the European residents of the country. It is known as सीकारम् (making a 'see' or श्री like whistle) in Telugu and is evidently the same as Sanskrit श्रीवद (श्री—इति वदतीति). Its Hindi names कालजित and कस्तूरा correspond to Sanskrit कालचटक and श्यामा respectively for the Blackbird because both are of a black colour and have a similar whistling call.

16. The black and white Fork-tails of the Himalayan streams resemble the Wagtail in general outline and have also the tail-wagging habit so that they are likely to be "mistaken for a Wagtail". They are actually known as खञ्जन in Kashmir and seem to be the bird खञ्जनाकृति rendered as 'a kind of Wagtail' by M. Williams, Wilson and शब्दार्थचिन्तामणि. The name itself implies a bird that is not a Wagtail proper but has the shape of one.

17. The Golden Bush-Robin of Nepal with a beautiful plumage of olive-green, black and bright orange goes by the name of मनसिल फो (मन:शिल चटक) in Assam. 'फो' in the Himalayan dialects means 'a Sparrow', (Cf. Sansk. फुक for a bird). We have the term मन:शिल (native red arsenic) used to describe the plumage of a bird in the following verse which makes it highly probable that this bird was known as मन:शिल चटक in Sanskrit as well though the name has not been preserved in the current lexicons:—

"मन:शिलाभैर्वदनैर्विहङ्गा....." —सौन्दरनन्द, 10.28.

---

1. Story No. 526 which is probably based upon the story of ऋष्यशृङ्ग and वेश्या in M. Bh. 3.111-112.

2. I refer to the English translation of the Jātaka by H.T. Francis, edited by E. B. Cowell, and the Pali Dictionary (P.T.S. edn.). Since wrting the above I have had occasion, through the courtesy of Dr. Lokesh Chandra, to glance through Asia Major. New Series Vol. II, Part I, 1951 where at p. 38 H. W. Bailey has traced करवी in a Khotanese Buddhist document to कलविङ्क—करविंक.

11

FLYCATCHERS

1. This family of birds contains a large number of species and is well-represented in India, but quite a few of them are only winter visitors with us. There is no mistaking a Flycatcher as all of them catch their insect food on the wing. Some species carry on their operations from a fixed perch while others return to a different perch after every sally into the air at flying insects. They are weak in the legs and rarely descend to the ground but when they do so they generally do not walk or hop about. The smaller and rather plain coloured birds like the Flycatcher Warblers, would pass for a चटिका but the larger and more strikingly plumaged birds, like the Blue, the Fan-tail and the Paradise Flycatchers, have distinctive names in Sanskrit.

2. लट्वा is a प्रतुद (pecking) bird in चरक and सुश्रुत and it is mentioned with नीलचटक in वसन्तराज.[1] The blue-coloured Niltava Flycatcher is known as नीलतवा or नीलट्वा in Hindi (F.B.I.). This last name is probably from Sanskrit नीललट्वा[2] and is the same as the नीलचटक or 'Blue Sparrow'. लट्वा is, therefore, a Flycatcher which is not of a blue colour, and as लट्व means 'a dancing boy', लट्वा should be the Fantail Flycatchers considered in paragraph 3 below and the white-spotted Fantail of the Peninsula. "For liveliness and grace", says Whistler, "it is not to be surpassed. It is never still, and the whole livelong day it dances and pirouettes, filled with an inimitable joie de vivre, it turns from side to side with restive jerky movements; like a ballet-dancer it tries new steps and attitudes. ....Never was bird better named." The Fantail rises and falls perpendicularly in the air, opening the fan-shaped tail or completely tumbles over.[3] The bird also combines a pretty little song of some five or six loud whistling notes with its dancing movements, and it is hardly necessary to add that the movement of its tail recalls the expanding skirt of a dancing girl during a performance. The लट्वा of वसन्तराज

1. 8.2.49-50.

2. लट्वा in a general sense means a sparrow and has been rendered as ग्रामचटक, the House Sparrow in शब्दकल्पद्रुम, but the name applies to particular birds (by the rule साधारणोऽपि विशेषे वर्तते, अभि. चिन्ता.) e.g. the short-toed Bush-lark (लट्वाका) (Art 26.) and probably also the Red Munia. नीललट्वा—ललोप:—नीलट्वा, नीलटवा—नीलतवा.

3. Cambridge Natural History, Vol. IX.

is, therefore, this Flycatcher, and, provided this identification is reasonably correct, one can say with Whistler, "never was bird better named" in Sanskrit. For लट्वा (fr. लट्व a curl on the forehead) as the White-cheeked Bulbul see Art. 6 and for लट्वाका, the Red Munia, Art. 22-B.

3. विहार ("विहारस्तु परिक्रमः—क्रीडार्थं सञ्चरणम्—रामाश्रमीटीका on अमर) according to शब्दकल्पद्रुम and शब्दार्थचिन्तामणि is the बिन्दुरेखक (बिन्दुविशिष्टा रेखा यत्र) bird. विहार also means 'sport or play' and 'a grove', बिन्दु is a 'spot or drop', and रेखा or लेखा is a 'row or series', 'border or edge'. These make it clear that the bird meant is of sporting or playful habits, frequents groves, and has a row or line of spots in its plumage. These characteristics obtain in the White-browed and the White-throated Fantail Flycatchers both of which have their tail feathers tipped white, and the tails when expanded exhibit a prominent border of white or white spots. They are, as we have already seen, of sportive habits and frequent groves of trees in garden or woodland. विहार and बिन्दुरेखक may well thus be the names for the above two Fantails within the larger लट्वा group of Fantail Flycatchers.

4. The most striking member of the present family is the Paradise Flycatcher (21″ inclusive of 16″ of central pair of tail feathers), sometimes called the Ribbon Bird. The crested head of the male and female is black. The young cock-bird is chestnut above and carries a pair of thin ribbon-like central tail-feathers of the same colour up to about two years of age after which it acquires the adult plumage which is pure white except for the head and the wingquills which are black. The female is chestnut above with a grey breast like the young male and sometimes grows the long central tail-feathers of a chestnut colour. They are most beautiful birds and their presence definitely adds to the charm of every grove, garden or hermitage. It must be their grace and beauty which moved the law-givers like मनु and याज्ञवल्क्य to include them in the list of birds prohibited as food, for otherwise they are so small that few would be tempted to kill them for the pot.

5. मनु calls it रज्जुवाल[1] and याज्ञवल्क्य, रज्जुदालक.[2] The commentators have missed the identity of the bird, and while some have rendered it as a Woodpecker others have held it to be some water-bird, but the names themselves hardly leave any room for doubt. रज्जु is 'a cord or string' and वाल 'a tail' (Cf. कृष्णवाल—'black-tailed'). दल is a 'leaf' or पत्र and therefore stands for a feather. दालक, from root दल, to split may also

---

1. 5.12. रज्जुरिव वालं पुच्छमस्य रज्जुवालः. In the commentaries on मनुस्मृति मेधातिथि frankly remarks that the birds in question should be identified with the help of fowlers (रज्जुदालादयः शाकुनिकेभ्यः उपलब्धव्याः), कुल्लूक and नन्दन are silent. रामचन्द्र accepts the मिताक्षरा on याज्ञवल्क्य while सर्वज्ञनारायण calls it a kind of water bird (जलचरपक्षिभेदः) which again is incorrect.

2. 1.174. दलं-खण्डम्; रज्जुदलाभ्यां, द्विदलारज्जुभ्यां, द्विदलाकृता, दारिता, रज्ज्वा वा युक्तः रज्जुदालः. The मिताक्षरा on याज्ञवल्क्य renders it as वृक्षकुट्टकः, a woodpecker. cf रुक्ख कोट्टक for the same in Pali (Art. 34). M.W. does not give this word but has an entry for वृक्षकुक्कुट, rendered as a 'tree-fowl, wild cock' which seems to be not quite correct.

refer to the two central tail-feathers as if they were the 'split' or separated strands of a cord. The रज्जुवाल (string or ribbon-tailed) is therefore no other than the Paradise Flycatcher.

6. सृजय is one of the birds assigned for the sun in his friendly aspect in the वाज.संहिता[1] :—

"शार्गः सृजयः शयाण्डकस्ते मैत्राः"।

शार्ग is the Bee-eater (Art. 40) and शयाण्डक the sun-loving Lizard (शयण्डक), both of insectivorous habits.[2] सृजय too should therefore be an insect-destroying bird—all three being friendly to the crop or fruit-farmer. Now सृज् means 'to let go or fly' or 'to cast or let go (a measuring line)'—M. Williams. श्वेतवनवासिन् has "सृज्यत इतिरज्जुःगुणमयी", उणादि, 1.10 and bearing these in mind it would seem that सृजय also is the Paradise Flycatcher which during flight appears (i) to have been tied to a string and let go like a paper kite, (ii) as leading away a measuring string, or (iii) as carrying a pair of strands as if to twist them into a cord (रज्जुं सृजति सृजयः)[3]

7. The bird अर्जुनक in the following passage would again seem to be this beautifully white Flycatcher:

"समीक्ष्यमाणौ पुष्पाढ्यं सर्वतो विपुलद्रुमम्।
कोयष्टिकैश्चार्जुनकैः शतपत्रैश्च कीचकैः॥
एतैश्चान्यैश्च विहगैर्नादितं तु वनं महत्।

—रामायण 3.75, 18-19.

The word अर्जुन is indicative of the whiteness of several things including 'milk' and it also means 'straw or a blade of grass' (अर्जुनस्तृणे—उज्ज्वलदत्त),[4] Our bird is milk-white (cf. its Hindi name, दूधराज[5]) and appears also to carry a couple of pieces of straw in its tail. It may be added that अर्जुन also means a Peacock which, however, has always been mentioned in the Rāmāyaṇa by the well-known names of मयूर and बर्हिन्, and has actually been so named a few lines below the verses quoted above. Moreover the

---

1. 24.33, Hindi सेछागुन if from स्वच्छ+गुण (a white thread) or स्वेच्छा+गुण (growing a cord at will), may well be this bird (हिन्दी शब्द-सागर).

2. See Art. 71 para. 10.

3. Compare "न रज्जुं सृजेत्"—वसिष्ठ स्मृति, 5.7 prohibiting a woman in a state of 'impurity' from making a rope, lest her womb gets twisted and becomes unfit to conceive a baby.

4. उणादिसूत्रवृत्ति, 3.59. The Wire-tailed Swallow is known as 'leishra' ('a kind of grass' according to Jerdon) in the Punjab as the tail-wires look like pieces of straw. The अर्जुन tree, Terminalia arjuna, is so named from its white trunk and the अर्जुन variety of grass too must be one of a whitish colour. सृजया according to वैजयन्ती is also a kind of lizard, apparently with a long thread like tail, probably, the Long-tailed Green Calotes (C. ophiomachus) having a body of five and tail of twenty inches. This lizard does not occur in North India and can not have been intended in the passage from the वाजसनेयी संहिता where the commentator takes सृजय for a particular bird.

5. दूधराज fr. दुग्ध milk with root राज् to shine, or दुग्ध-राजि a white streak or line.

name अर्जुनक for a forest-bird has occurred only once and that in the Râmâyaṇa and nowhere else except perhaps in the Atharva Veda, 4.37.5 in association with large trees which this bird always frequents with other insect eating birds. (see Art. 34).

8. Pali चेलकेदु[1] is a Himalayan bird in the वेस्संतर जातक[2] and looking to the "streamers of white satin ribbon" worn by the Paradise Flycatcher in its tail, the name should belong to it; Cf. चेलावक (चेलबक) of कुणालजातक for the Large Egret (Art. 82). The original sense of the word चेल was probably 'a strip of white cloth', as may be seen from the alternative reading of "श्वेतकण्ठिनः", per M. Williams in "कलशाश्चैल-कण्ठिनः"—हरिवंश,[3] where the piece of cloth wound round the neck of a ceremonial jar of water was of a white colour as is the Brāhmaṇical practice even today. This would, therefore, seem to suggest that चेलकेदु has the sense of श्वेतकेतु which makes its identification with our bird more certain. We have therefore रज्जुवाल, सृजय and अर्जुनक in Sanskrit and चेलकंदु in Pali for this strikingly beautiful bird.

9. Finally, all small Flycatchers, like the little Warblers, are simply चटिका ("चटिका : क्षुद्रपक्षिका:"—अभिधानरत्नमाला of हलायुध) as may be seen from the fact that the Eastern Red-breasted Flycatcher and the Blue-throated Flycatcher are actually known as चटकी in Bengal. Both चटिका and चटकिका are diminutive forms from चटक (a sparrow) and apply to all tiny birds of a non-descript character.

The personal names, उद्दालक आरुणि and श्वेतकेतु आरुणेय occurring in the Śatapatha Brāhmaṇa and the Upaniṣads, like other names based upon the names of birds, e.g. कापोति, हारीत, मयूर, etc. etc., are to be traced to the Paradise Flycatcher which begins to breed when still in its immature chestnut (अरुण) plumage.

---

1. चेल—चीर, a narrow strip of cloth. चीर is rendered as कच्छाटिका i.e. कोपीन in शब्दकल्पद्रुम. केतु a streamer, cf. उदक्षिपन् पट्टदुकूलकेतून्—भट्टिकाव्य 3.34. चेलकेदु is thus the same as चीरकेतु चेलं चीरमिवोत्क्षिपति चेलकेतुः a bird which carries aloft a streamer as it were.

2. verse 2099.

3. 2.50.72.

12

SHRIKES

The Shrikes "are in many respects very closely allied to the Flycatchers both in habits and structure"—F.B.I., 2nd edn. Most of them are cast in a common mould and resemble one another not only in general appearance but also in habits. A majority of them are a little heavier than the common Sparrow but with decidedly longer tails. Clad in shades of grey, black, chestnut, white, etc., they are smart and pretty looking birds, often seen perched on an outer branch of a bush or low tree on a keen lookout for insects, butter-flies and grasshoppers. They are of crepuscular habits and, like the flycatchers, begin their activities early at dawn and continue to catch insects till late in the evening. In view of these characters the ancients placed them with the Flycatchers (लट्वा) and named them लटूषक (लट्व-लट्+उषस्+क?). उषस् means both 'morning and evening'--उष: सन्ध्याप्रभातयोः—हेमचन्द्र, and the form उष also, rendered as 'dawn or day-break' by M. Williams and Wilson, should have both the above senses of ऊषस्. लटूषक, therefore, is a bird that begins to hunt for insects early in the morning and is active till after sunset.

Both लट्वा and लटूषक are प्रतुद birds in चरक, and चक्रदत्त regards them as allied forms of Bulbuls--लट्वा फेञ्चाको रक्तपुच्छाधोभागः, लट्वकोऽपि तद्भेदः"[1] Here the identification of लट्वा with the Red-vented Bulbul is perhaps slightly incorrect, for it is the yellow-vented White-cheeked Bulbul (Art. 6). लट्वा is a homonym and means not only the last-named Bulbul but also a Flycatcher (Art. 11) and it is in the latter sense of the term that लटूषक should be regarded as allied to लट्वा (तद्भेदः i.e. लट्वाभेदः). The common Hindi names for the Shrike are लहटोरा, ल्हटोरा and लटोरा, probably from लटूषक—लषटूक—लहटोर—ल्हटोरा—लटोरा.

1. The लटवा is the Red-vented Bulbul and लटूषक is a variety of it'—See Art. 6 for the Bulbuls.

13

MINIVETS

1. The Minivets are small Sparrow-like birds (6″-9″) with comparatively long tails and of colourful plumage with red or yellow conspicuous in most cases. Some have glistening black and scarlet as part of their dress. They are usually met with in parties and keep to tree-tops where they search for their insect food in the foliage. Constantly uttering their soft cheeping notes, a party keeps together flitting from tree to tree "in follow-my-leader-fashion". This trait has given them the pretty names of सजनी or सहेली (little girl friends) and सात सायली (the seven girl friends or sporting girls) in Bengali.

2. Hymn 191 of the first Maṇḍala of the Ṛgveda is a charm against the poison of snakes, scorpions, insects etc. where शकुन्तिका (verse 11), विष्पुलिङ्गक (verse 12), and मयूरी with सप्तस्वसारः (verse 14) are invoked for protection or cure. शकुन्तिका and मयूरी are of course birds but some translators have not accepted Sāyaṇa's suggestion that विष्पुलिङ्गक also is a particular bird, while सप्त स्वसारः has been rendered as the 'seven rays of the sun' or 'seven rivers' of the Punjab.

3. The numbers 'three', 'seven' and 'three times seven' are evidently supposed to have some magical significance and have been greatly in favour with ancient peoples, but in the present context they appear to have, in addition, a somewhat real, though necessarily vague, reference to actual numbers as well.

4. Sāyaṇa has explained शकुन्तिका as a कपिञ्जली which may mean either the female Grey Partridge (कपिञ्जल) or more probably a Quail (cf. "वर्तीरोऽल्पकपिञ्जलः"—कल्पद्रुकोश). In RV[1] as also in खिलसूक्त[2] the कपिञ्जल has been called a शकुन्त or शकुन्तक which would justify Sāyaṇa's interpretation, but the diminutive form "शकुन्तिका" seems to point to a smaller bird of the Partridge kind. However that may be, I must refer to a treatment for snake-bite sometimes practised in the Indian villages with the help of a fowl. The open (i.e. forced open) cloaca of a live chicken is pressed on the site of a bite and the poison is supposed to be sucked up

1. II.42 and 43.

2. No. 4.

by the gradually closing organ of the bird, and a similar treatment with Quail or Partridge in place of the chicken would seem to be indicated in verse 11 of the hymn. This is merely by the way and has nothing to do with the Minivets.

5. The विष्पुलिङ्गक of verse 12 is, according to Sāyaṇa, a kind of bird but has been translated too literally as "sparks of fire" by Griffith. I consider Sāyaṇa's hint of a bird to be correct, and most probably it is the Scarlet Minivet or its smaller cousin, the Short-billed Minivet. In both the head and the upper parts are glossy black, and the lower parts, rump, most of the tail and a bar on the wing bright scarlet. They are entirely arboreal and move from tree to tree in flocks which sometimes number as many as thirty to forty birds. "Feeding in the trees or flitting one by one across a patch of open the scarlet and black of the males and the yellow of the females is so conspicuous and so attractive in the sun-light" that not much of imagination is required to compare the picture with a series of scintillating sparks of fire, and who will say that the name विष्पुलिङ्गक is inappropriate for them ? During the great fire in the खाण्डव forest the flying sparks are described by क्षेमेन्द्र :—

"स्फुलिङ्गनिचया वह्नेर्विचेरुस्तरलत्विषः" (भारतमञ्जरी)[1]

and need one be surprised at the Scarlet Minivet being named विष्पुलिङ्गक ?

6. These birds kill and eat various kinds of insects that haunt the trees and were naturally supposed to enjoy immunity against insect poison. The idea is somewhat analogous to the virtue attributed to goat's milk as a protection against injury because the animal eats all kinds of herbs:—

अजा ह सर्वा ओषधीरत्ति सर्वासामेवैता—
मेतदोषधीनां रसेनाऽऽच्छृणत्ति। (शत. ब्राह्मण)[2]

Jerdon named this Minivet 'the Fiery Red Bird' which happens to be a very good rendering of the Vedic name. The very ancient practice of burning the site of injury by any poisonous agency with a live charcoal could also suggest these Minivets which resemble in a way a piece of half-glowing charcoal, partly black and partly bright red.

7. The Peahens, as snake-eaters, certainly deserve a place in the hymn but what are the सप्तस्वसारः the Seven Sisters ? Are they too not some kind of bird ? The Rosy and Small Minivets, moving as they do in small parties of six or seven are known in Bengal as सात सायली पाखी (the seven companion birds) and सजनी or सहेली in Hindi, and as their habits are similar to those of the Scarlet Minivets the reference may well be to them. The fact, however, that they come along with ground-birds like the Peahens makes for their identity with birds of the Jungle or Common Babbler type which kill and eat lizards, frogs, spiders, etc., and hunt for centipedes and insects in the grass and under-growth in semi-open jungle

---

1. आदिपर्व 1369.
2. 6.5.4.16.

where they seem not to be afraid of noxious vermin. Significantly enough they go by the traditional names of सात बहिनें or सात भाई, 'Seven Sisters or Brothers' in North India. If therefore these humble-looking birds are the सप्त स्वसार: they can certainly claim high Vedic recognition !

8. The Minivets and Babblers mentioned above are all denizens of the lower Himalayas from the Sutlej valley eastwards and therefore well within the geographical limits of the later Ṛgvedic culture.

9. I may finally quote an interesting Hindi verse of Jamāl, a Muslim poet, which is based on the same ideas of sympathetic magic as underlie the above hymn. A love-lorn young woman attemps to practise a charm against her tormentors, the Cuckoo, the bright Moon, the gentle breeze and finally the God of Love:

"वायस, राहु, भुजंग, हर, लिखति त्रिया तत्काल
लिखि लिखि मेटैं सुन्दरी कारन कौन जमाल ?"

Trans: "The pretty lady figures (upon the ground) the Crow, the Planet Rahu, the Python snake, and God Shiva, but immediately rubs them off, Jamal asks, why ?

10. The answer is that the figures are meant to spite the enemies—the Crow to silence the Cuckoo; Rahu to swallow up the Moon; the Python (वायुभक्ष) to suck up and stop the breeze; and God Shiva to suppress कामदेव the God of Love. But no sooner the figures are completed she realizes her folly, for she would want them all when her husband returns home, and lest the charm becomes perminently effective she hastens to erase the drawings.

14

SWALLOW-SHRIKES

The Ashy Swallow Shrike is the only bird of this family which occurs in India. It is of a plain grey-brown colour and of the size of a Sparrow. It has very long wings and resembles a Swallow in its method of hunting for insects on the wing. "They are most elegant birds when on the wing and but for their constant harsh cry and their comparative slow sailing through the air, might be taken for a bevy of large Grey Swallows on the wing" (S. Baker). They often nest at the base of the leaves of palms (ताल) or palm-ferns. Now चटक in Sanskrit means a Sparrow and also a Swallow or Swift so that the name 'ताल चटक', by which the Ashy Swallow Shrike is known in Bengal, should also be a Sanskrit name for it, and it very naturally shares this name with the Palm-Swift (Art. 45).

15

DRONGOS

The Drongos (Drongo Shrikes or Fork-tailed Shrikes) are a well known family of Indian birds defined by their black plumage and long forked tails. They are entirely insectivorous, and being weak in the legs they are incapable of any progression on the ground or even along the branch of a tree so that their movements are entirely aerial and they sally forth from a fixed perch after flying insect, picking them off from the tree trunks as well. Some, like the Black Drongo, descend to the ground to pick up a morsel while its larger cousins, the Racket-tailed ones, are entirely arboreal and hunt in the air from high or low vantage points. They are the bravest of our birds, dashing headlong at and driving away any unwanted intruder, including Hawks, Kites, Crows etc., from the vicinity of their nests or young, but allowing harmless birds like the Oriole to build their nests on the same tree. The Drongos share in common the Sanskrit name, भृङ्ग, after their black colour like that of the large Black Bee (भृङ्ग), and, Hindi भुजङ्ग (भुजं वक्रं गच्छति), after their agile swoops turning and twisting dextrously in the air like a serpent on the ground. The larger Racket-tailed Drongos, however, go by the name of Bhṛṅga-rāja. The main characteristics of important species and their names in a few of the Provincial vernaculars, given below, should serve as a brief introduction to them.

1. The Common Black Drongo is one of the most familiar birds of the Indian plains: Entire plumage black glossed with blue but with a small white spot close to the angle of the gape. It has "cheery loud notes", described also as "harsh scolding or challenging calls". It rides on the backs of grazing cattle and takes toll of insects disturbed by the animal's movements through the grass—hence its Sanskrit epithet, गोप्रेरक, and as its food consists of insects it is highly beneficial to agriculture (Salim Ali; Douglas Dewar) which fully explains its another epithet, धनसू (producer of wealth, i.e., valuable food crops—M.W.'s Dict.). Approaching nectariferous flowers for insects, it also feeds on floral nectar (S. Ali). These birds also turn up for a real feast in front of advancing clouds of smoke emerging from a forest fire particularly in open grass lands, or fired grass patches. Large numbers of grasshoppers and other insects are put up at the time and the plucky birds snap them up as they rise low in the air. This behaviour of the Drongo, known to the ancients and recorded by modern bird observers like Salim Ali and witnessed by me too, accounts for

its name धूम्याट in Sanskrit (धूम्यायां अटति). No other bird in nature can put up with smoke rising from such a fire and so close to it. The name धूम्याट is equated with कलिकार in Viśva-prakaśa, and the latter is explained in Śabda-kalpadruma: कलिं चिचि कुचीति शब्देन कलहं करोति—descriptive of the bird's pugnacity and challenging calls. It is in this very sense that the bird has been given the names of कलिङ्ग (कलहं गच्छति) and कुलिङ्ग (कुत्सितं लक्षणं यस्य having bad or wicked characteristics), and in MBh. I. ch. 61.9, the brave Duryodhana is said to have adopted the ways of the Kuliṅga bird (the Black Drongo) to worry the Pāṇḍavas and drive them away from the kingdom.

It is also known as कोलसा (black like charcoal) in Hindi, which is just synonymous with Skt. अङ्गारक (black like charcoal) for the male, and कालका (Kāla, black) for the female (see M. W., s.v. kālakā). In वाज० संहिता 24.35, गोधा (iguana, an arboreal lizard), कालका (the female Drongo), and दार्वाघाट (woodpecker bird) are quite properly associated with and allotted ritually to वनस्पति. The Bengali name for the bird, फिङ्गा, is a Prakrit derivative from the root पिङ्, पिञ्ज्, to make a sound, or from भृङ्ग, and the Punjābi जपल-कालचिट for it would thus seem to be from जल्पक काल-चटक, the prattling black bird.

2. The Himalayan and the Indian Grey Drongos: The whole upper plumage is indigo-blue with a high gloss and the lower plumage dark grey. Their ways are those of the Black Drongo. They have a very large vocabulary of notes, some harsh and some sweet, and a very musical song uttered almost throughout the year. In addition to this they are also excellent mimics (S. Baker). Both are known as नील फिंगा in Bengal.

3. The White-bellied Drongo: Upper plumage deep glossy indigo with greenish reflections in certain lights; breast brownish grey; belly, posterior flanks, vent and undertail coverts white. Song sweeter than that of the preceding two, and habits those of the family; found in the Himalayas and the greater part of India except the Punjab, Sind and Rajasthan. It frequents plantations and cultivated lands for its insect food. It is known as धौरी भुजंगा (Sk. धवल, white) in Hindi.

4 The Northern Bronzed Drongo: Whole plumage black glossed with bronze, shining green or lilac in certain lights; bill flatter, less carinated, than that of other members of the family. It is a bird of the outer Himalayas from Mussoorie to Assam. "Although like the rest of the family it has many discordant cries, it has a sweet song and many pleasant call-notes as well. It is as plucky in defence of territory, nests or young as are all the other genera of this family." (S. Baker). It is known as चपट्या (Sk. चिपट, flat) after its flattish bill, in Nepal, and छोटा भुजंगा, from its small size, in Bengal.

5. The Indian Hair-crested Drongo: Whole plumage black with blue gloss on head, neck, and breast, inclining to bronze on wing and tail. About half a dozen long hairs spring from the posterior crown lying over the neck and back. The tail is nearly square. Voice louder and more diversified

than any except the next two. It occurs from Mussoorie to Assam. It is locally known as केसराज and केसिया (Sk. केशराज, केश्य) after the hairs on the head. Its name in Telugu, Yentikā passālā poligadu, also means the 'Haired Cattle-Tom-bird' (Jerdon). Its second Nepali name, जोबराज (Sk. युवराज) seems to be complimentary in recognition of its vocal powers as next to those of भृङ्गराज, the Large Racket-tailed Drongo.

6. The Indian Lesser Racket-tailed Drongo (26"): Black glossed with blue-green; under wing-coverts and axillaries with small white tips. Has no crest but the feathers of the forehead form a curious flat pad over the base and covering the greater part of the beak. This gives the bird an unfavourable aspect as compared with the smart bright look of the next. The lateral pair of tail-feathers run up to 21 inches of which the middle 12 inches is bare shaft and the terminal 4 to 5 inches is equally webbed on both sides. It is distributed over Northern India from Eastern Nepal to East Assam and is a bird of the forest. It has many and most varied notes, very full and melodious, and is an excellent mimic though not so good as the next. It is known as भीमराज (the fearful king of the Drongos; but more probably a corruption of भृङ्गराज).

7. The Assam Large Racket-tailed Drongo (26"): Is a denizen of the outer Himalayas from Nepal to Assam and the forests of Madhya Pradesh and South India. The whole plumage is black glossed with blue, the under wing-coverts and axillaries frequently tipped white. It wears a full, erect, and beautiful crest of long plumes, up to two inches, on the forehead, curving backwards, each feather resembling a bow, curved sword or sickle. The outer pair of tail-feathers measure up to twenty inches of which the middle eleven or twelve inches is bare shaft and the terminal four inches is very narrowly webbed on the inner but broadly on the outer side and the broader web is twisted upwards. The two tail feathers, therefore, resemble an axe with a long shaft. It has been very properly named भृङ्गराज (King of the Black Drongo family) in Sanskrit and Hindi in recognition of its handsome appearance and musical talents.

The terms, भिंग (कृष्ण, black), भिंगार and भिंगारक in Prakrit[1], and भिंकार in Pali as names for पक्षिविशेष (a particular bird) may belong to members of the Drongo family or to this bird (Sk. भृङ्गार, or भृङ्गराज).

A few extracts from certain Sanskrit lexicons pertaining to these birds as also from others that give different meanings (अनेकार्थ) of the same words are given below:

(i) कलिङ्गः भृङ्गः धूम्याटः—अमरकोश, अभिधानचिन्तामणि.
भृङ्गः कलिङ्गः धूम्राटः (? धूम्याटः)
राजभृङ्गस्तु बुद्धिमान्—वैजयन्तीकोश.
गोप्रेरको भृङ्गराजो द्विपुच्छाग्रो वनप्रियः

1. The harsh cry of Bhṛṅgarāja is described as भिंगार रवंत भेरव रवे,, and its softer notes as भिंगारक दीण कंदिय रवसु, in पाइय सद्द मरण्णवो, s.v. भिंग and भिंगारक—कुणालजातक, P.T.S. ed., vol. 5, p. 416.

सुचूडशीर्षो वाचाल: सत्यवाक् स्याद् अथापर:
भृङ्ग: कलिङ्गो धूम्याटोऽपि—कल्पद्रुकोश.

(ii) भृङ्गराजो मधुकरे (bee) मार्कवे (plant) विहगान्तरे—हेमचन्द्र, विश्वप्रकाश.
कलिङ्गो पूतीकरञ्जे (plant) धूम्याटे (bird)—हेमचन्द्र.
भृङ्गराजो भृङ्गरजो मार्कव: (plant) केशरञ्जन: (plant)—अभिधान चिन्ता०.
कलिकार: करञ्जे स्याद् धूम्याटे पीतमस्तके[1]—विश्वप्रकाश.

We may now refer to the great compliment paid to the Large Racket-tail in the litany of the Horse-sacrifice in VS. and TS. It is dedicated to Bṛhaspati, the singer (RV 10.36.5), in VS. 24.34 (*bṛhaspataye vācaspataye paiṅgarājaḥ*), and to Vāk, goddess of speech, in TS. 5.5.13 (*vāce paiṅgarājaḥ*). The name Paiṅgarāja is probably derived from root पिज्, पिञ्ज् to sound, and thence पिङ्ग and पैङ्गराज (?) in Prakrit for Bhṛṅgarāja.[2] Again, in TS. 5.5.17, शित्पुट is allotted to Bṛhaspati (बृहस्पतये शित्पुट:), and शित्पुट, according to वैजयन्ती कोश is a synonym for षट्पद, a bee (भृङ्ग), and M. Williams also renders it as a 'large black bee', so that it is difficult to say whether शित्पुट[3] of TS. stands for the large buzzing bee, or one of the sweet voiced Drongos, but cf. Marāthi शेपूट, a tail.

The merits of the softer notes of the Black Drongo and the many musical calls merging into an excellent song of the Large Racket-tailed Drongo as a perfect mimic have been fully recognized in the Epics and the Purāṇas:

(1) The Black Drongo, भृङ्ग, with other birds and humming bees by the thousand, glorifies the वृन्दावन forest:

मत्तकोकिलभृङ्गाद्यै: कूजत्कलमनोहरम्
कपोतशुकसङ्गीतम् उन्मत्तालिसहस्रकम् ॥

Padma P., V. Ch. 69.64

(2) In addition to a very harsh metallic cry the भृङ्गराज has an excellent repertoire of musical calls and whistles, and is justly reputed as a firm mimic imitating all the birds of the locality. Writing about it in the *Fauna of British India,* 2nd edn., S. Baker remarks: "Their notes are most musical, and, though they have no really connected song, one mellow whistle follows another in such rapid succession that it is much the same in

1. A better reading, more easy to understand, of this half verse could well have been: कलिकार: स्याद् धूम्याटे करञ्जे पीतमस्तके, the second quarter relating to a plant bearing yellow flowers at its top. The reading, as it is, has apparently misled the compiler of the Śabda-Kalpadruma to render कलिकार as the धूम्याट bird with a yellow head. (M.Williams renders पीतमस्तक and पीतभृङ्गराज correctly as certain plants.) Similarly, the compiler of the हिन्दी-शब्द-सागर equates भृङ्गराज with भीमराज which, however, has been described quite incorrectly—that it catches and swallows small birds as well.

2. Comp. पिंगल (पिङ्गल), पिंगुल (पिङ्गुल), names of a particular bird (पक्षिविशेष) and पिंगलिअ (पैङ्गलिक) in पाइय सद्द महण्णवोप. For प and भ changed into फ in Prakrit, cf. फणस for पनस; फकवती for भगवती; रफस for रभस; रम्फा for रम्भा in Hemcandra's Prakrit Vyākaraṇa, VIII. 4.325.

3. Sāyaṇa's rendering of Śitpuṭa as a 'cat' does not suit the context at all.

effect. . . .a fine male bird, for many years the unconfined pet of the Sepoys in one of the North Cachar stockades, sounded the reveille, every morning with absolute correctness and punctuality." The reveille, sounded on an army bugle, consists of three parts, each made up of 20 or 21 notes. The first and the third parts are identical in composition but the notes of the second are differently arranged. The reveille is full toned and very melodious, and the ability to repeat it to perfection combined with a time-sense bespeaks both considerable intelligence and wonderful powers of imitation for the bird. No wonder, it has been described as बुद्धिमान् (intelligent) in the Vaijayantī Kośa, and as सत्यवाक् (a perfect mimic) in Kalpadru Kośa. It was held in great esteem by the ancient Indians and is still a valued pet with the aristocracy and bird-fanciers—fearless and most amusing with its imitations of noises about the house and garden (Whistler).

The Large Racket-tail, भृङ्गराज, is clearly mentioned as a mimic, and a beautiful song-bird in the following verses:

विहगो भृङ्गराजोऽयं शालस्कन्धसमास्थितः
सङ्गीतमिव कुर्वाणः कोकिलस्यानुकूजति ॥

Rāmāyaṇa, II.95a.13[1].

एवं विचित्राः पतगा नानारावविराविणः
* * * *
भृङ्गराजप्रमुदिताः सौमित्रे मधुरस्वराः ॥

Ibid. IV. 1.26-27.

भृङ्गराजाधिगीतानि ... वनान्युपवनानि च.

Ibid. VI. 39.11.

चकोरैः शतपत्रैश्च भृङ्गराजैस्तथा शुकैः
कोकिलैः कलविङ्कैश्च हारीतैर्जीवजीवकैः
प्रियकैश्चातकैश्चैव तथा ऽन्यैर्विविधैः खगैः
श्रोत्ररम्यं सुमधुरं कूजद्भिः ... ॥

M.Bh. III. 158.52-54.

शुकैश्च भृङ्गराजैश्च चित्रकैश्च समन्ततः
* * * *
कूजितान्तरशब्दैश्च सुरम्याणि च सर्वशः ॥

Vāyu P. Ch. 36.2-4.

The highest compliment has been paid to the bird in the following verse, in which recalling how a noisy congregation becomes still the moment a devotional song is begun, the poet says:

पारावतान्यभृतसारसचक्रवाक—
दात्यूहहंसशुकतित्तिरिबर्हिणां यः ।
कोलाहलो विरमतेऽचिरमात्रमुच्चैः
भृङ्गाधिपे हरिकथामिव गायमाने ॥

Bh. P. III. 15.18.

1. This is from an interpolated chapter.

The discordant uproar of all other birds is hushed (i.e. no one cares to listen to them) as soon as the *Bhṛṅgarāja* begins to sing, as it were, the story of the Lord. The bird has been named *Bhṛṅgādhipa* due to exigency of the metre but clearly as a synonym for *Bhṛṅgarāja*. Commentators, and following them M. Williams, have rendered Bhṛṅgādhipa as the large Black Bee and the reason for this bias lies in the fact that the Indo-Aryans became lovers of the Giant Honey-bee (Apis dorsata) some time after their arrival in India (RV mentions it as Saraghā) and the Black Bee became an obsession with the later poets. In point of fact the humming of the Bees has no place at all in comparison with the loud sonorous notes of the birds named in the verse. The misinterpretation is also due to *bhṛṅga* meaning primarily the Black Bee, and, by transfer after its shining black colour, the Black Drongo. Anyway, the real beauty of the above passage has often been lost to many readers of the Purāṇa. Finally, it is a pity that not a single member of this family, not even the Bhṛṅgarāja (v.l. Paiṅgarāja), finds a place in the works of the great Sanskrit poets.

16

WARBLERS

1. A great majority of the birds of this family are very small and plain coloured. "In fact most of them fall in the category of 'small brown birds without distinguishing features'.... It is impossible to identify many of these birds even with a plate and a good field description" (Smythies). They are all covered by the Hindi common name of फुटकी or फुदरी[1] which may well be from Sanskrit फुक[2], फुट्कारी, or फत्कारी (M. W.) all of which, at least the last two, seem to be after the little birds' single or double call notes (फुट्, फत् इति शब्दं करोति; cf. 'फो' for 'a bird' in some Himalayan dialects). फुट्कारी and also perhaps फुक् therefore seem to be common Sanskrit names for all non-descript Warblers. In addition diminutives in the feminine gender[3] like चटिका, चटकिका, पतङ्गिका, पुत्तिका (पुत्रिका, e.g. पुत्रिका इव पक्षिषु) etc. formed from common names like चटक, पतङ्ग for a Sparrow, generally signify all insignificant small birds (Cf. "चटिका-क्षुद्रपक्षिका"—हलायुध).

2. Flycatcher Warblers like the Eastern Red-breasted and the Blue-throated Flycatchers are known as चटकी in Bengal corresponding probably to Sanskrit चटिका which, besides being a term for any small bird, would also seem to be specific for the small-sized Warblers as a group according to the rule, "सामान्योऽपि विशेषे वर्तते" —अभि॰ चिन्तामणि, and the name perhaps refers to the चट् sound produced by the bird's bill whenever it snaps up an insect in the air.

3. The noisy and clever little Tailor-bird is probably टुण्टुक[4] from its 'towit, towit' or 'tuk-tuk' voice, and पुटिनी or पोटियक from its habit of placing its nest in a leaf-packet made by stiching up one or more leaves of low bushy plants. The names are from पुट, पुटिका, 'a leaf packet' (cf. पत्रपुट and Hindi पुड़िया). Its Hindi name पतिया is from पत्र, a leaf and

---

1. The हिन्दी-शब्द-सागर explains फुदकी as an onomatopoetic name and derives the verb फुदकना from the hopping habit of these little birds. But it is most probably from Sansk. फुत्, onomatopoetic for a weak sound or call, e.g. of a small bird.

2. फुनाऽस्पष्टवाक्येन कायति शब्दायते इति—शब्दकल्पद्रुम. फुः तुच्छवाक्यम्—ibid.

3. Diminutives in the feminine gender are formed in certain cases according to the "स्त्री ·स्यात्काचिन्मृणाल्यादिर्विवक्षाऽपचये यदि—अमर, 3.5.7.

4. टुण्टु इति अव्यक्तेन शब्देन कायति शब्दायते—शब्दकल्प. The streaked Fantail Warbler frequenting grass-fields goes by the name of तुन्तुनिया in Hindi. It is thus probable that

टुनटुनी (onomatapoetic) in Bengali. Compared to its size it has a very loud note and its occurrence in the wayside bushes and hedges has secured recognition for it as a bird of augury. वसन्तराज mentions the bird as पुटिनि at 4.21 and as पोटियक at 8.2.46.

4. The pretty little Ashy Wren-Warbler of our gardens, in towns and villages, dark ashy above and a beautiful shade of buff below, with a long graduated tail and a voice similar to that of the Tailor-bird, would also be टुण्टुक. The पुरल्लिका of वसन्तराज 4.56, rendered as पिदिडी in the commentary, should be the Ashy Wren-Warbler if the etymology of the name from Prakrit पुरिल्ल (पौर) पुरभव (पा.स.म) whence 'पुरेभवा—पुरल्लिका' is correct. Sansk. पौरक is a garden in a town to which the term पुरिल्लक should correspond. If so, पुरल्लिका should be a little bird of a garden in a town. Pali परिल्लक for a kind of bird would aiso be the same. In a general way, however, it would certainly be looked upon as a tiny bird or पिदिडी as noted in the commentary on वसन्तराज. Strictly speaking, however, पिदिडी is a particular Munia (Art. 22).

5. Among the Reed-Warblers Blyth's Reed-Warbler is known as टिकटिकी after its call note (F.B.I.) and as it is less aquatic than others of its class and is found in the long grass of the plains during the winter it has another Hindi name, पूदना (probably from पूततृण ? a kind of कुश grass which it frequents). The Black-throated Weaver bird of reed beds is शरबया or 'Reed Weaver-bird' in Bengal so that if back-formations from vernacular names of some of the Warblers are permissible, the Reed-Warblers must have been known as शरचटक. Indeed, the Indian Great Reed-Warbler goes by the name of 'Boora Jitti' (Boora—reeds, and Jitti or Jitta—the same as चटक) in Telugu. Similarly Warblers that frequent grass are known as 'Grass Sparrows' in different parts of the country. The Streaked Fantail-Warbler is known as घासकी फुदकी in Hindi and the Rufous-fronted Wren-Warbler is चीह्रो-चीहू (fr. चीही, a kind of grass—देशीनाममाला) in Sind. All such birds must therefore have been तृणचटिका or तृणफुट्कारी in the past just as we have तृणमयूर and शाड्वलि for the Floricans (Art. 57), and सुनार and सेव्य (kinds of grass) for the Red Munia (Art. 22). cf. names like 'Grass-finch' and 'Grass quit' for certain American birds.

---

these and others like them went by the name of टुण्टुक and तिन्तिडीक or तिन्तिडी given as a bird name in दशपाद्युणादिवृत्ति: 3.39.

The old scientific name for the Tailor-bird was Sylvia sutoria. It has a dark horny bill and has been incorrectly entered by M. Williams under पीततुण्ड (yellow-billed). This last is an adnoun for the Mallard Duck—See Art. 84, Section C.

17

GOLD-CRESTS

These tiny and inconspicuous birds keep to the higher branches of conifers in the Himalayas and are obviously very difficult of observation, and even if known they would simply be put down as चटिका or चटकिका.

18

THE FAIRY BLUE-BIRD

This is "one of the most beautiful birds known" and could certainly not have escaped observation by the ancients. The male is shining ultra-marine-blue above and black in other parts including the sides of the head and the fore-neck. It occurs in Eastern Himalayas and South India, and from its size and colour the term नीलचटक would include it. M. Williams, however has नीलच्छवी (–च्छवि ?) for 'a kind of bird' and the कल्पद्रुकोश defines it as below:

"नीलच्छवि कृष्णगलः स ग्रामचटकाकृतिः"

i.e., the नीलच्छवि ('Blue Beauty' fr. छवि beauty or splendour) has a black throat and is as big as the common Sparrow. These particulars and the significant name are fully descriptive of the bird and नीलच्छवि should be specific for it. It may be added that the second half of the verse in the lexicon:—

"ककुभः ककुभाकारः स्थलजो रक्तपर्णकः"

relates to a much larger bird (ककुभाकार), viz., the Coucal or the Crow-Pheasant, which is larger than the Common Crow and it would be absurd to describe it as ग्रामचटकाकृति. Nevertheless some commentators have cited the entire verse or its variant to explain the bird-name कुक्कुभ. See Art. 37-B for a further criticism of this half verse.

19

ORIOLES

1. The Orioles are beautiful birds of golden-yellow and black plumage except for the Maroon Oriole which is maroon and black. Three varieties of the Oriole, the Golden, the Black-headed and the Maroon, occur in the North India, the last in the Himalayas only. They are strictly arboreal and keep to the tree tops, rarely descending to the ground. They are very active birds and, though shy and secretive, indulge in aerial games, following each other from tree to tree and darting through the foliage with their bright plumage flashing in the sun. Their voice is a loud mellow whistle of several notes which is heard "alike in garden and forest, greeting the dawn and saluting the parting day." The yellow Orioles of both the species "often build in the same tree as holds a nest of the Black Drongo. That this is by design rather than accident can scarcely be doubted, considering how frequent the occurrence is. It is certain also that by this means the birds must enjoy a degree of protection against marauders like crows and tree-pies—inveterate stealers of other birds' eggs. The King Crow will tolerate the proximity of his harmless dependents with complacency, but a crow has only to show himself in the precincts of the nest-tree to be furiously set upon and beaten off by the valiant, 'kotwal' and his wife" (Salim Ali). They eat fruits, chiefly the berries of Peepul, bunyan and other fig trees.

2. The oldest names for the Golden Oriole are to be found in the Ṛgveda—(i) सुपर्ण which it shares with the Golden Eagle, and (ii) probably also हारिद्रव. The "द्वा सुपर्णा" in the following well known verses are no other than the Golden, or some other Eagle and the Golden Oriole, nesting together on a fig tree, the Oriole, of course, for protection:

"द्वा सुपर्णा सयुजा सखाया समानं वृक्षं परिषस्वजाते
तयोरन्यः पिप्पलं स्वाद्वत्त्यनश्नन्नन्यो अभिचाकशीति ॥
यत्रा सुपर्णा अमृतस्य भागमनिमेषं विदथाभिस्वरन्ति
इनो विश्वस्य भुवनस्य गोपाः स मा धीरः पाकमत्राविवेश ॥
यस्मिन्वृक्षे मध्वदः सुपर्णा निविशन्ते सुवते चाधिविश्वे
तस्येदाहुः पिप्पलं स्वाद्वग्रे तन्नोन्नशद्यः पितरं न वेद ॥

RV 1.164, 20-22.

On the high probability of a pair of Orioles sharing a bunyan or Peepul tree with a pair of Eagles I cannot do better than reproduce Col. D. Radcliff's remarks quoted by Hume in his book, *Nests and Eggs*, 2nd. ed.—"It is always the case with the larger Falcons that their fellow tenants of a rock or a tree are safe from molestation and in the breeding season actually look to them for protection." That birds of prey permit smaller birds to nest in close proximity to themselves including even those on which they normally prey is now acknowledged to be almost a universal fact (S. Baker on the Laggar Falcon in F.B.I. 2nd Edn.). The Golden Eagle has been known occasionally to place its nest on a tree but there is reason to believe that in the long past he did more often than now, for one of his oldest names is शाल्मल or शालमलीस्थ (nesting on Bombax malabaricum):—

"सु शू पर्वण्यवसानं महाद्रौ कृत्वा नीडं शल्मलौ तं महान्तम्
गरुत्मन्तं गरुडं वैनतेयं पतत्रिराजमवसे जोहवीमि ॥"

Suparṇādhyāya, 31.1

The Imperial, the Steppe and the Tawny Eagles breed as a rule on trees including the Peepul in the plains of North India and everyone of them is a सुपर्ण in the wider sense of the word. It is, therefore, more than probable, nay, almost a certainty, that the author of the above verses had not only seen a pair each of Eagles and Orioles nesting together in a peepul but had also observed how the Eagles kept away all marauders from the tree and the Orioles were happy under the protection thus afforded to them. These facts combined with the grandeur of the tall, leafy tree laden with fruit brought to his vivid imagination the similar situation obtaining before weak and dependent humans and their heavenly protector, and he, therefore, proceeded to illustrate the great spiritual truth with a parable drawn from nature.

3. With the growth of the civilisation and culture of the city as against the earlier life of farm and village even the learned Brāhmaṇas lost touch with nature and forgot the names and identity of many of the birds so beloved of their early ancestors. This divorce between the city, which now became the principal seat of learning, and the village was completed long before the time of महर्षि यास्क (c. 700 to 1000 B.C.), for he too does not say what exactly were the two particular birds mentioned in these verses. He and his successors, commentators including सायणाचार्य, undoubtedly knew that सुपर्ण was an Eagle, but their difficulty was about the second fruit eating सुपर्ण and they, therefore, intepreted the verses in the best way they could. The air was already thick at the time with Upaniṣadic speculation and philosophy of the आत्मन् and परमात्मन्, and the verses describing the two birds sharing a common tree came in very handy to illustrate that philosophy. Accordingly Sāyaṇa begins their exposition with—

"अत्र लौकिकपक्षिद्वयदृष्टान्तेन जीवपरमात्मानौ स्तुयेते"

without pausing to explain the actual physical basis of the verses. As late as 1935 V. K. Rajwade of Poona also wondered what bird it could be that refused to eat fruit, and as he could not think of two Suparṇas with such divergent habits in nature, he also agreed that the two birds were simple poetic imagery only for आत्मा and परमात्मा (See p. 1157 of his Marathi translation of the निरुक्त, Poona, 1935). In the absence of any guidance from Indian commentaries the Western interpreters of the Ṛgveda also had to content themselves with guess work and tried, each in his own way, to extract some sort of a hazy but always unsatisfactory meaning from the verses. In these attempts सुपर्ण in the singular, dual and plural has been variously interpreted as the Soma, the priests, day and night, stars, metres, Sun and Moon, rays of light, and so on. Ludwig goes so far as to say that the verses have scarcely anything in common except the word सुपर्ण which alone is responsible for their being placed together; and Griffith remarks in sheer desperation, "A generally satisfactory explanation is scarcely to be hoped for" (see his foot-note to verse 21). Hymn 164 of which these verses form a triplet is full of riddles and it is quite likely that this also constitutes one, but looking to the fact that the second and the third verses based upon the picture presented in the first, expound a moral, it would appear that the first verse is, if at all, a very thinly veiled riddle while there is nothing mysterious about the other two. However that may be, an attempt is made here to offer a rational interpretation of the verses based upon the habits of the birds as described above.

4. In the first verse the word सयुजा means 'in pairs,' i.e. with their mates, while the phrase "समानं वृक्षं परिषस्वजाते" clearly refers to the two pairs of birds having their nests on the same tree. The use of the verb सुवते (are born) in the third verse confirms this sense while the verb अभिचाकशीति (looks around) is best understood by the behaviour of the female Golden Eagle at the nest as described by Seton Gordon quoted in the *World Digest* for July 1946. "As she approaches and alights on the eyrie, then looks around her fiercely and defiantly before assuring herself that all is well, she makes a magnificent picture." Bonelli's Eagle also "proudly looks round" when on the nest. This verse, therefore, contains a statement of what the poet actually saw, viz. a pair of Eagles and a pair of Golden Orioles nesting together in friendly association on a Peepul tree and that while one kind of सुपर्ण ate the sweet berries of the tree the other merely looked around. The Oriole is a fruit eater and the Eagle is not.

5. In the second verse the poet attributes human sentiment of thankfulness to the Orioles and a consciousness on their part of the protection received from the larger bird.[1] It means that in the fig tree every discerning (विदथा) Oriole ceaselessly sings his grateful acknowledgment of his share of good things ("अमृतस्य भाग" refers to स्वादु पिप्पल and also hints at

---

1. The reader will kindly note here what Salim Ali says about the Oriole building designedly under the protection of a fighting bird, and I am sure he cannot help admiring the keen and correct observationof the Vedic poet of nearly 4000 years ago.

freedom from untimely death) in these words—"Weak as I am, the wise and powerful Lord and protector of the World (of birds, viz., पक्षिराज गरुड) has graciously admitted me into this safe tree (अत्राविवेश)."

6. At this stage the poet recalling to his mind the entire dependence of man for food and protection upon the heavenly सुपर्ण, the Sun, moulds the picture into a metaphor and proceeds to teach a moral in the third verse, viz., that men like the Orioles should be grateful to their heavenly protector for all the benefits received from him. Here सुपर्णा (plural) stands for 'the people', the fig tree for the Tree of Life or the mundane world, and the पिता for the Sun. The poet means to say that those, who live, multiply and prosper on the tree of Life but do not know (i.e. do not gratefully acknowledge) the protector, cannot really enjoy the sweet fruit high up on the tree (gifts of life). By implication they are worse than the Orioles who know and appreciate the truth. The idea is that a gift is fully appreciated when one knows the giver and is duly grateful to him for it. There can be no feeling of gratefulness and no true enjoyment of an anonymous gift. In a word, the gifts of life are enjoyed all the better for the consciousness that they are a boon from the heavenly Father. The feelings of dependence and hopefulness go together and unless one is thankful for what one has received one has no right to expect further favours, and if there is no hope for the future one cannot enjoy what he has which is as good as if he has it not (तत् न उत् न). We have indeed, good reason to be thankful to the majestic Eagle and the beautiful little Oriole who have inspired such wonderful poetry.

7. "वय: सुपर्णा" in the following verse rendered as "birds of beauteous wing" by Griffith should again be no other than the Golden Orioles who greet the dawn with their sweet notes:—

"वयः सुपर्णा उपसेदुरिन्द्रं प्रियमेधा ऋषयो नाधमानाः
उपध्वान्तमूर्णुहि पूर्धिचक्षु मुमुग्धस्मान्निधयेव बद्धान् ।।"

RV 10.73, 11.

The sacrifice-loving sages (प्रियमेधा ऋषय:) eager to perform their morning worship pray to Indra like the Orioles *greeting the dawn with their song*; Dispel the darkness, fill our vision with light, and deliver us from the snares (imposed by darkness and which prevent us from getting busy with the sacrifice).

8. The identification of हारिद्रव either as the Golden Oriole or the Yellow-headed Wagtail would seem to turn upon the correct meaning to be given to the word वन occurring in the second passage below:—

(1) "शुकेषु मे हरिमाणं रोपणाकासु दध्मसि
अथो हारिद्रवेषु मे हरिमाणं निदध्मसि ।।"

RV 1.50, 12.

(2) "हारिद्रवेव पतथो वनेदुप
सोमं सुतं महिषेवावगच्छथः ॥"

RV 8.35, 7.

The second verse refers to the habit of हारिद्रव and महिष of eagerly taking to वन which they apparently love. Now वन, according to सायण, is 'forest or water', but according to the Vedic Index of Macdonell and Keith, 'Vana' in the Ṛgveda and later denotes the forest and they do not mention 'water' as सायण does. It is probably a meaning acquired by the word in later times. If, therefore, वन stands for 'forest' हारिद्रव would be the Golden Oriole, for it is a bird which delights and sports amongst trees of the forest and grove. The wild buffalo also lives in deep forest and if surprised in an open glade would immediately take to it. In this view the Oriole, clad in brilliant yellow, would be the bird par excellence to which along with the पीतभद्रशुक the Red-breasted Paroquet having yellow wing patches and yellow-wattled Hill Myna, the yellowness of the skin caused by jaundice can best be transferred. If on the other hand वन must be taken in the sense of 'water' both हारिद्रव and महिष must be held to be fond of that element, and in this case the former would be the Yellow-headed Wagtail, the yellowest of Yellow Wagtails, which is constantly associated with water and is rarely found at any distance from it. The buffalo too is known to be a water-loving animal, for he loves to wallow in tanks and pools during the hot hours of the day.

9. The first verse above occurs with slight modifications in the अथर्ववेद (1.22, 4) where Sāyaṇa translates हारिद्रव as the गोपीतनक bird, and Dārila in his commentary on the कौशिकसूत्र, 26,18 renders it as गोपीतिलक. Allowing for corruption in the कौशिक text as it has come down to us both the above synonyms for हारिद्रव are the same as the later गोपीत or गोपीतक for the Yellow Wagtails in the बृहत्संहिता (Art. 26), and looking to the traditional treatment for jaundice with ceremonial washings it is just possible that हारिद्रव is the Yellow-headed Wagtail. But the interesting historical fact adduced by Griffith in a note to RV 1.50, 12 that the Romans too had a fanciful notion that jaundice was cured if the patient looked at the Icterus bird, and the bird probably belonged to the Starling family, supports the identification made in the preceding paragraph. The article on 'Icterus' in the Ency. Brit. 11th edn., shows that the Icterus of classical authors is generally identified with the European Golden Oriole. The name Oriole is from the French 'Loriot' L'oriol, from Lat. oriolum-aurum, gold. James Moray Brown also makes the statement : "Loriot, a bird that, being looked upon by one that hath the yellow jaundice cures the person and dies himself". (*Stray Sport,* vol. I, p. 158, William Blackwood and Sons, 1893). The belief would thus appear to be part of the common heritage of both branches of the Indo-Germanic peoples unless it travelled from one to the other after their separation. If, therefore, हारिद्रव was originally the Oriole, it is probable that by the time of दारिल the name had come to be transferred to or mistaken for the Yellow Wagtail.

10. Turning to some Pali and Prakrit sources including lexicons, which I have consulted, we have the following series of closely related names for the Orioles:—

(i) पिलग (पिलक), a kind of bird in अर्धमागधी, which stands very close to Hindi पीलक for the Oriole, and Sansk. पिपीलक in the following:

"पिप्पलस्तैलहरणात्, फलस्तैन्यात् पिपीलकः।।
भारतमञ्जरी, शान्तिपर्व, 1676.

This means that a person stealing oil would be reborn as the पिप्पल bird and one stealing fruit as the bird (पि-पी-लं इति कायति ?). It may be repeated that the Orioles are "great fruit eaters".

(ii) In the story of king ब्रह्मदत्त, who was a सर्वरुतज्ञ, i.e., who understood the language of birds and beasts, related by क्षेमेन्द्र in the हरिवंश section of the above work the male and female birds whose conversation the king overheard bear the names पिपीलक and पिपीलका.

(iii) पिपीलिय, a kind of bird in the Jain प्रश्नव्याकरण 3.1 is evidently the same as पिपीलक.

(iv) अंबक मद्दरी, a bird in the अंगुत्तर निकाय, महावग्ग, III.64.6 (P.T.S.):
"सेय्यथापि......अंबक मद्दरी फुस्सक रवितं रविस्सामि।"
Here फुस्सक is the Cuckoo and अंबक मद्दरी (अंबक the mango tree; मद्दरी fr. मर्दल, a little drum) the 'little drum of the mango tree' which is obviously identical with Tamil मामकोइल (आम्रकोकिल, Mango-Cuckoo) and माम्बल कुरवी (Mango-bird) for the Black-headed Oriole of Ceylon. The common Indian Oriole with identical habits and call-notes does not occur there.

(v) अंबाकपीलिक (v.l. अंबाकपिलिक, अंबाकिपिलिक) occurs as the last item in a series of bird-names (including जतु a bat, regarded as a bird both in India and Persia) contained in the Fifth Pillar Edict (Delhi Topra) of Emeperor Aśoka published in *Corpus Inscriptionum Indicum*, Vol. I, pp. 125 127 & 224. The name has been incorrectly syllabified and misunderstood by the various translators including Dr. Sir R. G. Bhandarkar, Shri Michelson and Prof. B. M. Barua.[1]

11. The names in (iv) and (v) above clearly establish the identity of the first element अंबाक of अंबाकपीलिक and माम or माम्बल of मामकोइल or माम्बल कुरवी with अंबक of अंबक मद्दरी, and अंबाक, therefore, simply means the 'mango tree'. Similarly the second element पीलिक of अंबाकपीलिक is the same as अर्धमागधी, पिलग and पिपीलक of क्षेमेन्द्र and Hindi पीलक for the Oriole. अंबाक पीलिक is thus a shortened form of or corruption from अंबाकपिपीलक, i.e., a

---

1. *Inscriptions of Aśoka*, Pt. II (1943).

bird that utters a triple पि-पी-लं note from a mango tree, and in this sense it is fully parallel to अंबक महुरी.

12. The Indian Orioles are local migrants, and finding the winter of the Punjab and the Uttar Pradesh too severe, disappear from these areas in October. The Black-headed variety continues to live in U. P. but it is silent during the winter (*A bird Calendar for India*—Douglas Dewar). "With the ripening of the mangoes in spring the Indian Oriole arrives in Northern India. To that circumstance, combined with the greens and yellows of the two sexes to the fruit and leaves of their favourite tree, is due the popular Anglo-Indian name of Mango-bird" (Whistler). A bird of entirely arboreal habits, the Oriole naturally takes to the dense foliage of mango trees and sings its melodious notes from there and hence the ancient names of अंबक महुरी and अंबाकपीलिक for it. I need hardly add that this association of the bird with the mango tree is not a recent Anglo-Indian discovery but was a well known fact in North India and Ceylon more than two thousand years ago, and it is highly probable that the Anglo-Indians got the name from South India or Ceylon. For the still unsolved bird-names in the Edict of Aśoka see Art. 37-B for गेलाट, and Art. 84 for अलुन and नन्दीमुख.

13. We may now take up the जृम्भ bird of the Rāmāyaṇa and the question of the confusion caused by the similarity of the name पिपीलक with पिपीलिक (an ant). The later scribes of the महाभारत and the authors of हरिवंश, मत्स्यपुराण and पद्मपुराण, having missed the identity of पिपीलक (fem. पिपीलका) as a bird, changed the spelling to पिपीलिक (fem. पिपीलिका). The authors of the above Purāṇas also recast the story of the pair of जृम्भ birds hinted at in the Rāmāyaṇa into one of a pair of ants! The earliest version of a सर्वरुतज्ञ king occurs in a brief reference to the father of queen Kaikeyī in the Rāmāyaṇa:—

"सर्वभूतरुतं तस्मात् संजज्ञे वसुधाधिपः
तेनं तिर्य्यंग्गतानां च भूतानां विदितं वचः ॥
ततो जृम्भस्य शयने विरुताद् भूरिवर्चसः
पितुस्ते विदितो भावः स तत्र बहुधाऽसत् ॥" 2.35, 19-20.

जृम्भ (having a far-reaching voice; cf. "सुखश्रवाः मङ्गलतूर्यनिस्वनाः व्यजृम्भन्त" रघुवंश 3.19) has been rendered differently by the commentators: (i) पिपीलिका विशेष, a kind of ant, by Govindarāja apparently misled by the later version of the story in the Purāṇas and हरिवंश, and (ii) जृम्भकाख्य पक्षी by Rāma in his तिलकव्याख्या commentary (Bombay Edn.) and he explains भूरिवर्चस as सुवर्णकान्त, of a golden colour. The use of the expression विरुताद् makes it clear that जृम्भ had an audible call, and this together with the fact that it belonged to the class of birds or beasts (तिर्यग्योनि) at once puts out of court the suggestion that it was an ant, for ants have no voice at all and belong to the कीट or सरीसृप class. Moreover, no lexicon gives जृम्भ for an ant. Nevertheless the interpretation of जृम्भ as पिपीलिका (masc. पिपीलिक) is particularly significant in view of what the terms पिपीलिक and

Prakrit पिपीलिय are now found to mean, viz., the Golden Oriole. It follows that the oldest synonym of जृम्भ was the पिपीलक bird. Poet क्षेमेन्द्र has spelt the masc. and fem. forms of the word correctly as already stated above but others mistaking them for ants proceeded to embroider the old story with minute details of a love quarrel between a pair of sugar-loving ants. This later version is found in ब्रह्मदत्तचरितम् in हरिवंश, 1.24 where the female is described as 'an angry little ant' (क्रुद्धा सूक्ष्मा पिपीलिका), and in the मत्स्यपुराण, ch. 20 where the pair becomes कीटमिथुन and the female is:—

"सुवर्णवर्णा सुश्रोणी मञ्जूका चारुहासिनी
सुलक्ष्यनेत्ररसना गुडशर्करवत्सला ॥"

The पद्मपुराण also has a similar story about king विक्रान्त in सृष्टिखण्ड ch. 10.

14. In the following verse from the Mahâbhārata पिपीलिकाः is clearly a mistake for पिपीलकः :—

"फलं वा मूलकं हृत्वा अपूपं वा पिपीलिकाः".... 13.111, 100.

Here the unnecessary plural is worth noting. क्षेमेन्द्र had the correct reading before him and he gives पिपीलकः (singular). The गरुड़पुराण also has the correct spelling : पूपं हृत्वा पिपीलकः" (see शब्दकल्पद्रुम under कर्मविपाक). The name, as suggested above is probably after the bird's call-notes but in view of the fact that its other names like चामीकर and काञ्चन are based on the golden colour of its plumage, it is quite likely that पिपीलिक for 'a kind of gold' has something to do with the change of spelling from पिपीलक to पिपीलिक (cf. Prakrit पिपीलिय) and this in turn helped the sordid ant to displace the glorious Oriole in the later forms of the original story. पिलग or पिलक in अर्धमागधी and पीलक in Hindi are the direct descendants of पिपीलक with one of the first two letters cut out, and the apparent affinity of the surviving form with Hindi पीला for 'Yellow' would seem to be accidental.

15. The Orioles are mentioned in Purāṇa literature under the names, काञ्चन, चामीकर, and सुग्रीव-काञ्चन in reference to their golden yellow or maroon-red plumage. Of these the first two are for the Golden Oriole and the third for the Black-headed (also black-necked) Oriole and the black-headed Maroon Oriole of the Himalayas and the adjoining plains. The epithet सुग्रीव refers to their black throat and neck in the same way as god शिव (of the black throat, because of the poison stored in it) bears the same name. Dried lac of a reddish-brown colour is described as हिरण्यवर्णा in AV 5.5, 6 and the dark brown Golden Eagle is हिरण्यपक्ष (Art. 52-A) so that the Maroon Oriole also very properly shares the name सुग्रीव काञ्चन[1] with his brother the Black-headed (yellow) Oriole. काञ्चन is one of the birds at a hermitage in पद्मपुराण:—

1. Cf. also काञ्चनी-हरिद्रा, काञ्चनाह्व-गैरिकम्, the red ochre, and काञ्चनार Bauhionia Variegata with pink and purple flowers.

"पक्षिणः काञ्चनप्रख्यान् नानाशब्दसमाकुलात्" —उत्तर खण्ड, 16.23

The मत्स्यपुराण mentions it as the sweet voiced चामीकर, and also describes its behaviour at the sight of poison:—

"खगैर्मधुररावैश्च चारुचामीकरप्रभैः" ... 136, 15;
"चामीकरोऽन्यतो याति, मृत्युं कारण्डवस्तथा" ... 220, 20.

The Black-headed Orioles (maroon or yellow) occur in the Himalayas according to the वायुपुराण:—

"सुग्रीवकाञ्चनरवैः कलविङ्करुतैस्तथा" ... 36, 4.

The शब्दरत्नसमन्वयकोश gives पिञ्जोला for 'a kind of bird', and looking to its derivation from पिञ्जलं (हरिद्राभे—विश्वप्रकाश) or पिञ्जालं, 'gold', it can only be the Oriole. The name seems to be allied to Hindi पिरोला and पियरोला for the Black-headed variety.

Our classical poets have been more than partial to birds like the कोकिल, चातक, and मयूर, and it is a pity that the common and charming Orioles should have been completely ignored.

20

GRACKLES OR HILL-MYNAS

1. The Grackle is popularly known as the Hill- or the Talking Myna. Apart from its glossy black plumage its distinctive features are fleshy yellow wattles on the head, bare yellow skin on the sides of the face, and orange yellow bill and legs.

2. In the Ṛg-Veda (1.50,12) it has been called रोपणाका from रोपण, 'causing a cicatrix' (also perhaps a cicatrix or healed wound) in reference to the wattles and the bare skin that characterize the bird. These features are supposed to be healed scars as it were. Its later name वरण्डा is also derived from वरण्ड, a boil or pimple on the face. There are other bird-names as well formed on the same lines, e.g., the Black Ibis is called कचाटुर from कच, a scar, because of the bare and pimpled head of the bird and the Red-wattled Lapwing सदालूता (लूता चर्मव्रणे—धन्वन्तरि— carrying permanent pimples on the face):— "टिट्टिभी पीतपादश्च सदालूता नृजागरः" धन्वन्तरि-निघन्टु.

3. रोपण also means an arrow i.e., शलाका which latter has formed the basis for its name मदनशलाका or simply शलाका in the Lexicons. The name means 'the dart of the god of Love' because the bird was taught by professional trainers (cf. शुकसारिका प्रलापन as one of the 64 Fine Arts) to repeat little 'bons mots' and love-phrases to remind a busy aristocrat or king, passing through his अन्तःपुर or harem, of the undying love for him of its (bird's) lady-patron, or to invite him to a particular queen. I doubt if the Vedic name was derived from रोपण in the sense of 'an arrow', but मदन-शलाका is certainly comparable with "कामशल्यामिषुं" in AV. 3,25,2.

4.. The Grackle or Talking Myna was also known in Sanskrit by the name 'मदनसारिका'. Names like कादम्बरी (कद्+अम्बर, black-plumaged) and the allied couples like, दूती and यासा ('love messenger', and 'one exerting for a lover' respectively), कञ्जक and कञ्जन (giving pleasure), सूक्ता and वचा (a good talker) for the bird are merely lexical pedantry. They seem to have been invented for use in a double sense in puzzles (प्रहेलिका) and puns (श्लेष).

5. It shares also the name शारिका (v.l सारिका) with the Common Myna (Art 21), and which of the two birds is intended in a given passage must be made out from the context. शारिका as a talking cage-bird is the

Grackle, but as a bird of ill omen, or a noisy one, it is the Common Myna. To cite but one example of each from the रामायण :—

"नूनं हि लालप्यते सीता पञ्जरस्थेव शारिका"—5.13, 16
"वीचीकूचीति वाश्यन्तः शारिकावेश्मसु स्थिताः
पतन्ति ग्रथिताश्चापि निर्जिताः कलहैषिणः"—6.35.33

The second passage is a perfect picture of the कलहप्रिया सारिका, the noisy or quarrelsome Common Mynas often given to fighting with their own kind.

6. The beautiful Grackle learns to speak with great facility and accuracy and was naturally a favourite cage bird of the ancients. The पुरुषवाक शारि of वाज. संहिता is the Grackle :

"सरस्वत्यै शारिः पुरुषवाक"— 24.33

Classical literature is full of references to its power of speech. One, for example, is represented as preaching to her Parrot-friend about the greatness of God Śiva:

"पठन्ती सारिका सारं शुकं सम्बोधयत्यहो
अपारावारसंसारसिन्धुपारप्रदः शिवः"

स्कन्दपुराण, काशीखंड, 1.8.72

It was also taught to repeat didactic and religious catch phrases:

"शिक्षापदोपदेशदोषोपशमशालिनीभिः सारिकाभिरपि धर्मदेशनां दर्शयन्तीभिः..."

हर्षचरित, उच्छ्वास, 8

For another example, see Art. 38. The मेधाविनी सारिका of the रत्नावली drama of श्रीहर्षदेव is made to play an exaggerated role and is represented as possessed of an extraordinary memory and able to repeat a long conversation overheard by her but once — all of which is simply poetic fiction. Lexicons have perhaps borrowed the name मेधाविनी for a Grackle from this work.

7. Another bird of this group is the Spotted-winged Stare, resembling the Mynas in shape and habits. It occurs in flocks and associates with the Grackles and other Mynas, the birds of a flock keeping up a constant chattering twitter. They are very restless and are always on the move. They breed in the lower and outer Himalayas as far east as Nepal and visit the adjacent plains in the winter. This Stare is known as पुली or पुलि in Hindi. It is the पुलीका (v. l पुलिका) of मैत्रा. संहिता, 3.14.5 and पूली (मूली appears to be a misprint) and शरभी of the कल्पद्रुकोश. The name is probably derived from the Dravidian पुलि (cf पुल्ली, a Panther—देशीनाममाला) because of its spotted plumage, and it is from this sense that I hold शरभी (शरभ, a tiger)

to be another but later name for it. Being a noisy bird it has been very properly named for the female relations of the gods implying a subtle satire upon their garrulous, fidgety and quarrelsome habits: —

"पुलीका देवजामिभ्यः"—मैत्रा संहिता, 3.14.5.

The वाज. संहिता, 24.24 reads कुलीका in place of पुलीका and as कुलि also means a Panther or Tiger in another South-Indian language (the Kannada) कुलीका too must mean the Spotted-winged Stare.

21

STARLINGS AND MYNAS

1. These birds are closely allied to the Grackles, a fact recognised by the ancients who gave them all the common name of सारिका. Even the Common and the Jungle Babblers have been regarded as varieties of the Myna and this accounts for the mixed synonyms found in धन्वन्तरि, कल्पद्रु and राजनिघण्टु where names found in different earlier MSS have been put together, but a close study of the names shows that they are not synonyms for one or two birds only. All Starlings and Mynas are gregarious and noisy by habit.

2. Starlings are glossy black birds, looking as if oiled and more or less spotted finely with buff. The whole plumage is iridescent with a high gloss of red, purple, green and blue (Whistler). The oldest names for them are पारुष्ण or पारुष्ण (spotted) and तैलपक (as if smeared with oil and, therefore, glossy). पारुष्ण is one of the birds required at the Horse-Sacrifice and has been named for the God of Fire:—

"अग्नये गृहपतये पारुष्णान्"—V.S. 24.24

Fire is कृष्णवर्त्मन् ('whose way is black', as a forest-fire leaves a black track) and Whistler's description of a flock of these black birds moving on the ground fully explains this selection: "The chief characteristic of the flocks is hurry; they feed on the ground . . . ., and all the time the flock advances with a bustle and hurry, not hopping but with a quick purposeful step the birds in the rear frequently flying over to settle in front of the leaders". No further comment is necessary.

3. According to मनु an oil-thief becomes a तैलपक खग or Starling in his next birth ("तैलं तैलपकः खगः" मनु, 12-63). This तैलपक appears as तैलपायी in याज्ञवल्क्य ("तैलहृत्तैलपायी स्यात्" 211) and in महाभारत[1] 13.111,111. सारिका and तैलपायिका in the following are the Grackle and Starling respectively:—

"गृहे पारावता धन्याः शुकाश्च सहसारिकाः
गृहेष्वेते न पापाय तथा वै तैलपायिकाः"

M.Bh.,13.104, 114.

---

1. तैलपायिका at 13.104, 114.

परोष्णी and तैलपायिका signify the spotted Cockroach, which feeds on oil, as well as the Spotted Munia (Art. 22B). In Hindi the Starlings are known as तिलोरी or तेलियामैना (Oily Starling). Both पारुष्ण and तलपक therefore denote the Himalayan and Finsch's Starlings which are common in North India.[2]

4. The name शारि (from शार, spotted, or a colour combination—"नीलपीतारुणश्शारो..." .... वैजयन्ती; cf. पारुष्ण) is again the above while the Common Myna, which is unspotted, is सारिका. This latter has earned additional epithets like कलहप्रिया, कलहाकुला etc. and वैजयन्ती has "वाचाला मुखरा शारि:" because of their quarrelsome and noisy nature, and it is for this reason that they are held to be inauspicious birds in वसन्तराज 8.17. A verse descriptive of the quarrelsome nature of सारिका has already been quoted from the रामायण in Art 20. Adnouns like पीतनेत्रा, चित्रनेत्रा, पीतपादा etc. are merely descriptive and apply equally to the Common Myna and the Grackle, and the last even to the Red and Yellow-wattled Lapwings. The Bank Myna is similar to the Common Myna except for the red of the bare skin round the eye. It is often found in company with the latter and would naturally go by the same name, viz., सारिका, though in Hindi it is distinguished as गंगा मैना as it lays its eggs in holes made in earthen banks over running water. It may well have been गाङ्गसारिक in Sanskrit.

5. The यक्षकुणपी of मैत्रायणीसंहिता, 3.10.3 is the Common Myna according to सायणाचार्य. कुणपी is the विट्सारिका or the Pied Myna in मेदिनी and त्रिकाण्डशेष, but this bird is not known to enter human dwellings, so that यक्षकुणपी cannot be this Myna. The Common Myna, on the other hand, is the "commonest and most familiar bird about human habitations—whether in the heart of a bustling city or far out on the countryside" and fitted "admirably for life of commensalism with man" "(Salim Ali). "Always perky and self-confident", it is the only bird, next to the House Crow, most likely to enter the sacred precincts of the यज्ञशाला and befoul the floor or peck at offerings arranged there for a sacrifice. कुणपी being a contemptuous name for the Pied Myna, the Common Myna has been very appropriately called यज्ञकुणपी. The name गोराटी for the Common Myna has already been considered in Art. 6, under Babblers.

6. The beautiful Brahminy Myna has the "top of the head, including a long bushy crest, black; the sides of the head, the whole of the neck and the entire lower plumage rich buff." It is, therefore, the गौरिका ("गौर: स्यात्पीतलोहित:" वैजयन्ती i.e. reddish fawn or buff) and कवरी (केशविन्यास:) of the कल्पद्रु list. This Myna is known as पवई in Hindi for which a respectable

2. The equation परोष्णी तलपायिका of अमरकोश is evidently a homonymous one applying to (1) the starling birds and (2) the cockroach insect, as is clear from the fact hat कल्पद्रुकोश repeats it in its lists of both birds and insects.

ancestry can be traced to शङ्करा for 'a kind of bird' in Sanskrit :—

"शङ्करा नाम परिव्राजिका शङ्करा नाम शकुनिका तच्छीला च तस्यां उभयं प्राप्नोति—"पतञ्जलि महाभाष्य[3]

परिव्राजिका is पव्वाइया in Prakrit and hence पवइ, for this smallest of Mynas. When we recall its black head and crest and the fawn colour of its body-plumage we are reminded of the काषाय वस्त्र of a बालश्रमणा or कात्यायनी and cannot but admire the imagination of the first man who gave this excellent name to the bird.[4] शङ्करा is thus a very old name for the Brahminy Myna which is a local migrant (परिव्राजिका तच्छीला च). The name also indicates that unlike the common Myna it is an auspicious bird and the English name 'Brahminy Myna' for it is very expressive. It has a soft voice and pleasant song.

7. The Rosy Pastor is of a rose-pink colour with a black head ornamented with a long bushy crest. The upper breast, wings and tail are also black. This Starling moves in flocks and the birds feed on insects and berries, and "are invariably present on silk cotton flowers ganging themselves on the sugary nectar they exude, and are truculent towards all other species visiting the tree on the same quest" (Salim Ali). It is, therefore, the मधुसालिया (Skt. मधुसारिका) explained as सुवण्ण सालिक (Skt. सुवर्ण सारिका, the beautifully coloured myna) by the commentator in किंचिद जातक, No. 511. The name मधुसारिका refers to the birds' love of the nectar (मधु) of flowers. Again, if the name कवरी does not belong to the Brahminy Myna, the Rosy Pastor is the only other bird of the present group to claim it in its own right, or it may be a name common to both the birds possessing a long black crest.

8. जाण्ट (perhaps, connected with जटा or झुण्ट) is a kind of bird according to उणादि भोजीयानि and झण्टी in Prakrit means 'short and erect hairs' (लघूर्द्ध्वकेशाः—देशी नाममाला). The Jungle Myna is झोंटी मैना in Hindi and जाण्ट सारिक, therefore, appears to be its Sanskrit name in reference to the tuft of short erect feathers on its forehead. झोंटा in Hindi means "dishevelled hair" so that all these words seem to be allied to झुण्ट or a bush.

9. The साल्विक is described as 'short-crested, dirty-feeder and frequenting damp reedy places' :—

"शरमल्लो क्षुद्रचूडो गूयलक्तश्च साल्विकः ।" —शब्दकल्प.

It is known as गुये सालिक in Bengal, the name being derived from 'गूयलक्त साल्विक. It is clearly the Pied Myna for which चित्राङ्गी (pied) in कल्पद्रु., कुणपी and

3. 3.2.14.

4. The name पवइ is in line with ग्वालिन (milk-maid) for the Magpie Robin, धोबिन (washer-maid) for the White Wagtail, and तेलिन (oil-maid) for the black Red Starling—all in Hindi. Tne dress of a कात्यायनी (परिव्राजिका M.W.) is of a fawn or buff colour : "वदन्ति कात्यायनिकां धृतकाषायवाससम्"—quoted in the commentary at p. 67 of हर्षचरित.

विट् सारिका (compare विट्चर for the tame Pig) in त्रिकाण्डशेष are other names. The epithet कलहप्रिया is on a par with गोराटी and हह्लोलिका and all these are equally applicable to the Starling, the Common Myna, the Pied Myna and the Babblers.

10. A kind of Myna, named श्येता शारि, is a victim for Goddess सरस्वती according to the तैत्ति. संहिता:[5]—

"सरस्वत्यै शारिः श्येता पुरुषवाक्"

श्येत means 'reddish white' and the only Myna that can be so described is the Grey-headed Myna. This is dark Grey above and rufous below, palest towards the throat and deepest towards the tail (Whistler) . It could probably be trained to talk. The पुरुषवाक् शारि of the वाज. संहिता[6] is evidently the Grackle.

5. 5.5.12.
6. 24.33.

22

WEAVER-BIRDS AND MUNIAS

A. WEAVER-BIRDS

1. Weaver-Birds are very Finch-like both in size and appearance and the males are gaudily dressed in rich yellow particularly at breeding time. They are rather noisy birds and have a twittering call ending with a whistle. Their beauty and the art of building fine weather-proof nests account for their being regarded as a kind of कलविङ्क in Sanskrit (See Art. 23A), and the correct name for them is पीतमुण्ड कलविण (yellow-headed sparrow "कलविङ्कस्त्वसौ पीतमुण्ड: "—वैजयन्ती). M. Williams has, however, mixed up पीततुण्ड (–कारण्डव), the Mallard Duck, with पीतमुण्ड, the Weaver-Bird. "Weaving is a passion with these birds, and a pair of them work in complete co-operation, the male outside (the partly built nest) passing the ends of the grass through the wall of the structure to the female inside, who threads them back to him, till the beautifully woven structure is complete; it is secured by the serrated edges of the strips of grass and is almost too tough to be torn apart by the hands" (Smythies). The nest is a retort-shaped structure of woven grass with a long tubular passage opening downwards. This description of the habits of the bird fully justifies the following names for it:—

(1) कौलीक from कौलिक, a weaver or कुलिक, an artisan, corresponding to Hindi बया from वय् to weave;

(2) चञ्चुसूची or सूचीमुख (Prakrit सुईमुह) from the bird's beak being used like a needle; and

(3) सुगृह (v.l. स्वगृह ?) i.e. having an excellent and well protected nest. 'सुगृह' (Prakrit सुहर) has been defined by हेमचन्द्र in देशीनाममाला as a kind of sparrow which builds a nest opening downwards ("यस्या अधोमुखं नीडं भवति"). कल्पद्रुकोश has—"सूचीचञ्चुः पीतशीर्षः सुगृहश्च".

The habit of these cheerful birds of keeping up all day long their conversational chatter has won for them the epithet of कलिकार (कलिं कलहं करोति——noisy; "कलिकारः धूम्याटे पीतमस्तके"— विश्व., हेम. and मेदिनी. पीतमस्तक i.e. पीतमुण्ड).

2. As the best architect among birds, it is dedicated to त्वष्ट्रा, the Divine Architect, under the name of कौलीक in : "त्वष्ट्रे कौलिकान्" वाज. सं. 24, 24— unquestionably the best selection for this deity.

3. The पञ्चतन्त्र mentions it as सूचीमुख in वानरयूथसूचीमुखकथा told in the मित्रभेद section and कथासरित्सागर at 10.4,200. कावृक is yet another name for it and it may have something to do with the male bird's donning a yellow cap on his head (कं शिरं आवृङ्क्ते आवृणोति) during the breeding season, or again with his habit of suspending the nest from the branch of a tree where it overhangs water (कं जलं). The Black-throated Weaver-Bird which nests in tall grass or reeds is शरबया (Sanskrit शरकौलीक) in Bengali.

4. The name गृहकारी[1] in मनुस्मृति, 12, 66 and विष्णुस्मृति, 44, 36, if correctly interpreted as 'a kind of bird' by commentators, रामचन्द्र and सर्वज्ञ नारायण, appears to be the same as सुगृह (कर्ता) for the Weaver-Bird which uses various materials in the construction of its nest. This fits in very well with the punishment awarded to a person who steals miscellaneous petty goods. Otherwise also the context would seem to demand a bird. गृहकारी as an insect is the Solitary Wasp (genus Eumenes) commonly known as the Mud or Potter Wasp which uses only mud for its nest. The सिगिल (?) bird (v.l. सुहिल, cf. प्राकृ. सुहर) of किंचिद जातक, 321 which had a rain-proof nest was apparently a Weaver-Bird, as the story is the same as the one from Pañcatantra noted above.

B. MUNIAS

The Munias are small birds, and like the majority of Warblers would go by the general name of चटिका, पुत्रिका, or पुत्तिका (cf. Pali and Prakrit पुत्तक, पोतक, a little child and a young or small bird) but some have indeed specific names given to them. For example, the Spotted Munia is परोष्णी (fr. परुष, spotted, a little spotted bird; "चटिका विशेषः"—शब्दार्थचिन्तामणि. cf. पृष्णि, परुष्णी, a speckled cow) The equation—"परोष्णी तैलपायिका"—अमर, is said to refer to the spotted Cockroach only but it may well be a homonymous equation referring to the Cockroach as well as the spotted little bird—both of an oily brown colour. In any case the names have been extended to this bird as well, as it is known in Hindi under the name of तेलिया मुनियां. It may also be recalled here that similar names obtain for the spotted Starling, viz., पारुष्ण, तैलाक and तैलपायी (Art. 21). वसन्तराज gives us yet another name for this bird, viz., पुष्पभूषी (ch. 8, 46), and the commentator explains it as a small dark-coloured bird with white spots ("कृष्णवर्णा लघुचटिका श्वेतबिन्दुयुक्ता") which agrees very well with the White-spotted chocolate-brown of this Munia. पुष्प in पुष्पभूषी means 'a spot.'[2]

2. The White-throated and the White-backed Munias are पिरिलि or पिरिली (बृहत्संहिता, 85, 20 & 44; वसन्तराज, 4, 56) in Sanskrit (?) corres-

---

1. Commentator शूलपाणि on याज्ञवल्क्य, 3.214 also renders गृहकारी as a particular bird.

2. cf. "कुसुमैश्चित्रिता मृगाः" for the spotted deer, Rāmāyaṇa, 2.93,13. where कुसुम is synonymous with पुष्प and means a white spot.

ponding to पिरिडी in Prakrit and पिदड़ी, पीदड़ी, in Hindi. These appear to be Prakrit words related to परिअडि, a hedge (from Sanskrit परि and वृति, a hedge) and have been applied to these birds because they frequent hedges in villages. The name may well be from Prakrit पिरिली, a cluster, from the bird's habit of moving in flocks. They are also चिड़क्का, or चुड़क्का (from Skt. चटकिका) in Hindi.

3. The Red Munia appears to be सुनार कलविङ्क (from सुनाल with ल changed to र, see शब्दकल्पद्रुम. "सुनारः कलविङ्कः"—विश्व. and मेदिनी) and सेव्य which latter is one of the names for Sparrow-like birds listed in the वैजयन्ती :—

"चटको वर ग्राटकः
बलिभुक् कलविङ्कश्च सेव्यस्तिलककण्टकः"

Now both सुनाल and सेव्य are varieties of Andropogon grass growing near water, and it is chiefly in these and similar tall grasses that the Red Munia roosts and breeds. सुनाल again, in the sense of a red water-lily, may refer to the red colour of the male bird. These facts make it highly probable that सुनार and सेव्य in the sense of a कलविङ्क or चटक, are no other than the beautiful Red Munia. सेव्य has an additional significance attached to it, viz., the birds so named are worth keeping as pets, and these birds are indeed in great favour throughout the country as cage-birds, a number of them being kept together in a single cage. The pretty male is known as लाल ('red' and also 'a little boy') and the female मुनियां (मुन्नी a little girl, fem. of मुन्ना) in Hindi, names which fully correspond to Sanskrit पुत्रक and पुत्रिका for small children and birds; cf. पोतः शिशुः; पोती पक्षिणां स्त्र्यपत्ये"—शब्दार्थचिन्तामणि; पोतकी, the Indian Robin —Prakrit पोआई from पोताकी, a little bird; and Pali पुत्तक, a young bird. Although no Sanskrit dictionary gives पुत्रक or पुत्रिका for a little bird, we have numerous instances of expressions like चातक पोत, चातक शिशु, or शकुन्त बालक in literature. पुत्तिका or पूतिका in the following stands for a tiny bird:

"पुलाका इव धान्येषु पुत्तिका इव पक्षिषु"—म.भा. 12,181,7
"पुलाका इव धान्येषु पूतिका इव पक्षिषु
मशका इव मर्त्येषु येषां धर्मो न कारणम्"—पञ्चतन्त्र, काकोलूकीय, 97.

The mention of मशक, a winged insect, in the last verse considerably strengthens the meaning of पुत्तिका or पुत्रिका as a tiny bird, and the Pali form पुत्तिका (fem. of पुत्तक) appears to have been purposely used in a contemptuous sense for पुत्रिका, a little bird. It is highly improbable that the expert author of पञ्चतन्त्र should have drawn upon two equally insignificant insects, the white ant and the mosquito, for two out of three similes. Again, कुलिङ्कक as an alternative reading for कुलिङ्गक is possible only through Prakrit लिंक, a child, and the term corresponds in formation to गोवत्सक for a Bulbul (Art. 6).

4. We have already considered लट्वा for the Fan-tail Flycatcher in reference to its dancing habit (Art. 11) and, as the active little Red

Munias, when caged as pets, keep on dancing as it were within the cage, they have been given the name of लट्वाका, a diminutive of लट्वा. लट्वा as a musical instrument, probably a boy's whistle, is perhaps so named because of the whistling notes of the birds that go under the names of लट्वा and लट्वाका ("लट्वा क्षुद्रचटका"—उणादि भोजीयानि. कटका is a misprint). लट्वा also means the deep orange-red safflower and the little Red Munia may well have been so named after the colour of the male. In the लटुकिका जातक (No.357), a small bird, called लटुकिका (Pali for लट्वाका),[3] figures prominently. It placed its nest on the ground in grass-land and when the nest was in danger of being destroyed by a roving herd of wild elephants the little mother-bird lifting her wings in salutation makes a pathetic appeal to the leader not to kill (inadvertently or otherwise) her still unfledged young ones (पुत्तके). (This verse is quoted in Art. 45.) Again, a लटुकिका, singing freely or fearlessly in its cage (कुलायिका), is mentioned in a proverb in दीघनिकाय :—

"लटुकिकापि खो अंबट्ठ सके कुलावके कामलायिनी होति"

P.T.S. Edn. 1.91.

The Red Munia frequently builds its nest in tall grass very low or even on the ground (Whistler). It is thus more than probable that लटुकिका of the Jātaka, i.e. लट्वाका, is the Red Munia. The root word being 'लट्' or लट्व (लट् बाल्ये, लड-लल-लालन; लट्वा a dancing girl) the name लट्वाका perhaps stands close enough to Sansk. सेव्य (लालन योग्य) and Hindi लाल (the red colour and a little boy, cf. Sansk. लालक).

3. The name लट्वाका was also used for the Rufous Short-toed Lark—Art. 27, and as none of the short-toed Larks is a breeding bird of India proper the Jātaka story mentioned here cannot refer to any of them.

23

FINCHES AND BUNTINGS

A. FINCHES

1. This family includes a very large number of birds recognizable from their short massive bills, more or less forked tails, and the general resemblance they bear to the common House Sparrow. Many species are to be found in the higher Himalayas though quite a few of them are forced down to lower levels in winter.

2. The basic terms, चटक, कुलिङ्ग, and कलविङ्क which are applicable not only to birds of the present but of other families also, have been treated in the Glossaries as synonymous, but चरक mentions कलविङ्क and कुलिङ्गक separately, and सुश्रुत distinguishes कुलिङ्ग, गृह-कुलिङ्ग and कलविङ्क but places the last in the विष्किर group. भावप्रकाश, मांसवर्ग, includes कलविङ्क, कुलिङ्ग and कालकण्ठ within the meaning of चटक but distinguishes between चटक and कलविङ्क in the अर्शोऽधिकार section. चटक, besides being specific for Swallows and Swifts (Art. 25), is a wider and more general term for, (i) 'a bird in general' e.g., in compound bird-names like मयूरचटक, मृगेन्द्रचटक, कालचटक, etc. and (ii) any bird of the size of a common Sparrow, and it is from this latter sense of the term that diminutives like चटिका, चटकका, or चटकिका have been formed for the still smaller birds like the Warblers, White-eye, Munias, etc. Grammarians derive the name from the root चट्, 'to break or kill' but it is probably of onomatopoetic origin in reference to their twittering notes, or the snapping sound made by the bill of a bird like the smaller Flycatchers when catching insects (Art. 11). The term कुलिङ्ग (कौ पृथिव्यां भक्षणार्थं लिङ्गति गच्छति) refers to the habit of Sparrows moving about on the ground in search of food, while the name कलविङ्क (कलं मधुरास्फुटं वङ्कते रौति) applies to several song-birds of the size of a Sparrow which are also beautiful to look at. Both these are also specific for particular types of song birds.

3. The House Sparrow is गृहकुलिङ्ग or ग्रामचटक as against the Tree-Sparrows, plain looking Buntings and other wild Finches which go under the common names of कुलिङ्ग, वनचटक, वनकुलिङ्ग, etc. The House Sparrow being under every-day observation has won for itself several poetic adnouns, e.g., कामुक, कामचारी and वृषायण after the male's amorous behaviour towards the female; चित्रपृष्ठ for its variegated back; गृहनीड from its nesting in human

dwellings; and नीलकण्ठ or कालकण्ठ from the black patch on its fore-neck. These so-called names are merely descriptive epithets, some of which have been applied to other birds as well:

"कामी स्यात्कामुके चक्रवाके पारावतेऽपि च"—मेदिनी,
"कालकण्ठस्तु दात्यूहे कलविङ्के च खञ्जने"—विश्वप्रकाश.

कलविङ्क on the other hand shares the epithet कलानुनादिन् (singing beautifully) with the large black Bee, the Hawk-Cuckoo and the Grey Partridge, the last two being कपिञ्जल :—

"कलानुनादी रोलम्बे कलविङ्के कपिञ्जले"—विश्वप्रकाश.

Everyone of the three best songsters of India, (i) the Magpie Robin, (ii) the Shama (श्यामा), both of which are also कालकण्ठ कलविङ्क as they have black head and neck, and (iii) the Blackbird, is a कलानुनादी कलविङ्क. In literature they are mentioned simply as कलविङ्क. Poetic courtesy, however, has extended the term (कालकण्ठ-) कलविङ्क to what was merely the गृहकुलिङ्ग or ग्रामचटक simply because of its black throat and upper breast:

"कलविङ्कः स्मृतो ग्रामचटकेऽपि कुलिङ्गके"—विश्वप्रकाश,

where the use of the term 'अपि' is perhaps significant. मेदिनी, however, reads कलिङ्गक. If कुलिङ्गक is the correct reading it would refer to the Grey-winged Blackbird or the Magpie Robin (Art. 10), but if with कलिङ्गक (के मूर्ध्नि लिङ्गं चूडा यस्य), supported as it is by the विश्वलोचनकोश, the bird meant would be the तिलककण्टक कलविङ्क i.e., the Crested Lark (Art. 27). श्रीहर्ष mentions the House Sparrow by the name of कलविङ्क in a rather vulgar reference in नैषधचरित, 18.16.

4. The वैजयन्ती has listed several Sparrow-like birds as types of चटक:—

"चटको वर आटकः
बलिभुक् कलविङ्कश्च सेव्यस्तिलककण्टकः
कलविङ्कस्त्वसौ पीतमुण्ड:"

चटक as a common name for a sparrow is probably intended to serve as a base for the qualifying epithets that follow it. Thus:

(i) वर चटक (वर कुङ्कुमे श्रेष्ठे and, therefore, of 'a red colour' and 'excellent') refers probably to the Scarlet and Rose Finches, the रक्तशीर्ष कलविङ्क of डल्हणाचार्य;

(ii) आटक चटक ('wandering Sparrow') are the Buntings, one variety of which, the Crested Bunting, is चिरिटीक in चरक;

(iii) बलिभुक् चटक is the House Sparrow, the same as गृहकुलिङ्ग;

(iv) कलविङ्क are the Magpie Robin, the Shama, and the Blackbird (Art. 10);

(v) सेव्य चटक is the Red Munia, the same as सुनार कलविङ्क, (Art. 22 B);

(vi) तिलक कण्टक is the Crested Lark (Art. 27);
(vii) पीतमुण्ड चटक also called पीतमुण्ड कलविङ्क, is the Weaver-Bird (Art. 22-A).

5. The पशु to be sacrificed to the personified deity of Summer must have white in its body-colour (वाज. संहिता, 24, 11), and the कलविङ्क in "ग्रीष्माय कलविङ्कान्—" (Ibid., 24, 20) is no other than the beautiful Magpie Robin which, with black head, neck, and upper part, is pure white below with a good deal of white on the wings and tail. No other Sparrow has so much and such pure white in its plumage. Moreover, this bird is in full song in Summer. कलविङ्क, again, is a victim for god त्वष्ट्रा in :—

"कलविङ्को लोहिताहिः पुष्करसादस्ते त्वाष्ट्राः"— Ibid., 24.31

and is probably the same, for one is said to have come out of the सुरापीथ head of विश्वरूप, the son of त्वष्ट्रा, and the bird's powerful and spirited song is attributed to its peculiar birth from a drunken head:

"ततः कलविङ्कः समभवत् तस्मात् सोऽभिमाद्यत्क इव वदत्यभिमाद्यन्निव हि सुरां पीत्वा वदति"—शतपथ ब्राह्मण, 5.5.4,5

In the alternative, the bird may be the beautiful पीतमुण्ड कलविङ्क, the Weaver-Bird, some sort of a whistler, and the best bird-architect of India, in reference to त्वष्ट्रा being the expert artisan of the gods. This goes well with the nest-making skill of the Whiskered Tern, which alone of the Indian Terns, constructs a nest on a lotus leaf by winding round and round water-weeds upon it, and hence called पुष्करसाद (Art. 69), and लोहिताहि, the beautifully marked red Coral Snake of genus Callophis.

6. डल्हणाचार्य on सुश्रुतसंहिता is uncertain as to the identity of कलविङ्क and offers several alternatives, one of which:—

"अन्ये तु रक्तशिरसं कृष्णग्रीवं ग्रामचटकाकारं कलविङ्कमाहुः,"

is significant and would seem to refer to the Gold-headed Black Finch or the Gold-fronted Black Finch. It is possible that the statement has mixed up the descriptive terms (i) रक्तशीर्ष for the Rose and other Finches having red on the head, and (ii) कृष्णग्रीव (i.e., कालकण्ठ कलविङ्क) for the Magpie Robin and the Shama, as different kinds of कलविङ्क or Song-Sparrows. In any case रक्तशीर्ष कलविङ्क refers to the Rose-Finch, and रक्तशीर्ष कृष्णग्रीव कलविङ्क to the Gold-fronted and the Gold-headed and Gold-fronted Black Finches, the Red-headed Bull-Finch, etc., beautiful Himalayan birds found in Kashmir and Nepal and some of which migrate to the plains in winter. In short all pretty looking Finches with a sweet voice are कलविङ्क and many of them have been favourite cage-birds in Nepal and elsewhere from time immemorial.

7. कालपुच्छ चटक or black-tailed Sparrow) is a kind of Sparrow in M. Williams and निघण्ट रत्नाकर and the name probably belongs to the Bull-Finches which have entirely black tails. The Red-headed Bull-Finch

is known as कोबिन in Assam and this name is perhaps a corruption of कलविङ्क कलबिन—कोबिन as under the influence of Bengali कल is pronounced as कोल. The Bull-Finches are, therefore, the कालपुच्छ चटक or कलविङ्क of the lexicons.

It must be added in conclusion that the term कलविङ्क as used in स्मृति and धर्मशास्त्र literature, in connection with the ban against the killing of birds for food, is co-extensive in meaning with the term चटक and covers all Sparrow-like birds just as the terms बक and हंस imply all Storks, Ibises and Herons, and all Swans, Geese and Ducks, respectively, and so on with other generic bird-names.

B. BUNTINGS

1. The Buntings form a well-defined group within the Finch family, but those resembling the common Sparrow in outward appearance and habits would, as individuals, pass for a कुलिङ्ग or वनचटक. Some species, however, like the Black-headed and the Red-headed Buntings which are very gregarious and move in large flocks or swarms and cause considerable damage to winter-crops, were named very early. Thus we have अन्नदूषक (grain-robber or crop destroyer) for them in the प्रतुद class of birds in सुश्रुत. These birds breed beyond the Indian limits and visit the plains of India during the winter from the foot of the Himalayas southwards, and from Sind in the west to Bihar in the east. The Black-headed Bunting has the entire lower plumage deep yellow but in the Red-headed this colour is confined to the lower breast, flanks, and the abdomen. Other Sanskrit names for them are based on this and other features:—

(i) "भोरिटः श्यामचटकः शैशिरः कणभक्षकः
गृहकर्तृक्षमो भीरुः कृषिद्विष्टः कणप्रियः" —कल्पद्रुकोश

In the राजनिघण्टु the two halves of the above verse have been slightly displaced:—

(ii) "भारीटः श्यामचटकः शैशिरः कणभक्षकः
धूसरोऽन्यो ऽति सूक्ष्मः स्याच्चटको धान्यभक्षकः
गृहकृत्यक्षमो भीरुः कृषिद्विष्टः कणप्रियः"

Here the first and third lines constitute a connected verse and the second line refers to a different bird, viz., the Finch Lark (Art. 27) and is clearly out of place. The authors of both these lexicons appear to have borrowed from an old manuscript, probably of धन्वन्तरिनिघण्टु, the present printed edition of which, however, contains only the second slightly corrupt line of the original as below:—

(iii) "गृहकर्ताऽक्षमो भीरुः कृषिद्विष्टः कणप्रियः"

and the first line was probably similar to what we have in the other two lexicons. The readings गृहकर्तृक्षम (perhaps more correctly गृहकर्त्रक्षम = गृहकर्तृ +

अक्षम) and गृहकर्ताऽक्षम in (i) and (iii) above are most probably incorrect readings or inadvertent variants of गृहकृत्यक्षम (गृहकृति + अक्षम = गृहकृतौ अक्षमः, unable to build a nest, or one that does not build one), the original reading of धन्वन्तरि or other lexicon correctly reproduced in (ii). The expression means that the भारीट birds do not nest in the country. If on the other hand it is split up into two separate words, गृहकर्तृ or गृहकर्ता and क्षम or अक्षम, they hardly make any sense so far as these birds are concerned. They do not breed in India and cannot be described as गृहकर्ता, while क्षम or अक्षम (competent or incompetent) can hardly be a bird-name. The misunderstanding and the consequent confusion is not difficult to explain. गृहकारी is an independent bird-name in मनु, 12.66, for सुगृह the Weaver-Bird (Art. 22-A) and lexicographers, missing the significance of the adjective गृहकृत्यक्षम, read into it गृहकर्तृ or गृहकर्ता as synonyms of गृहकारी and substituted what each believed to be the correct reading. In doing so one retained the negative अ before क्षम and the other omitted it. It is this negative, अ, happily preserved in the current edition of धन्वन्तरि, that helps to dissolve the expression गृहकृत्यक्षम correctly as indicated above. क्षम for a kind of Sparrow in M.W. is, therefore, incorrect. The Black-headed and the Red-headed Buntings are (i) श्यामचटक (श्याम—हरिद्वर्ण, the yellow sparrow, cf. श्यामा-हरिद्रा) and (ii) भारीट (v.l. भोरिट, भारिट—भरेण समूहेन अटति, going in flocks). The epithets, कणभक्षक and कृषिद्विष्ट correspond to अन्नदूषक of चरक and mark them out as enemies of cultivation. भीरु[1] means 'dreadful or awful' (Wilson) while शैशिर describes all the Buntings as winter visitors.

2. The Grey-necked and the Ortolan Buntings, both migrating to India in flocks, have no yellow in their plumage and are not श्यामचटक but they are certainly शैशिर चटक or भारीट. They go by the name of जमजोहरा (fr. Sansk. याम, यामन् moving, marching, or यम god of death, and यवहर grain-robber) and the Red-headed variety as दलचिड़ी in Hindi. Both the names mean 'a bird that moves in large flocks' or in the alternative 'the crop-destroying host of death (यम)'. Other local Hindi names are भर्रा and बुर्रा (fr. भारीट); cf. "हारन में बुर्रा हजारन लागे"—'Buntings by the thousand are attacking the crops.'

3. चिरिटीक (v.l. चिरीटीक) is a प्रतुद bird in चरक, 1.27 and is evidently the same as चिरटा in Hindi for the Crested Bunting. It is a bird of solitary habits and wanders a good deal. तिरीट means 'a head ornament and also a kind of sparrow'. This Bunting has an upright crest (किरीट) and would seem to be the तिरीट (चटक) of M. W. Perhaps the terms किरीटी, चिरीटी and तिरीटी are closely allied. The second, viz., चिरीटी occurs as a bird name in कल्पद्रु—"चिरीटी तु चिरिण्टिका" which appears to be a wrong reading of 'चिरीटी तु चिरीटिका or चिराटिका'. If, on the other hand, चिरिटीक is from चिर+टीक्, चिरंटीकते, the name would correspond to the आटक चटक of वैजयन्ती, and would then refer to the Buntings as a class.

---

1. Also means a panther or tiger in राजनिघण्टु.

24

WAXWING

This family is represented by a single Species, Bombaycilla. It breeds in the Arctic region, is a rare winter visitor to the extreme North-west, and has been observed at Bannu and Kohat on a few occasions only. Except for a single plaintive note, uttered occasionally, it is a silent bird and no Sanskrit name is possible for it.

25

MARTINS AND SWALLOWS

1. The Swallows resemble each other very closely in structure, differing only in the shape of the tail, which, however, is different in almost every species and cannot be considered a generic character. They have, therefore, been classified according to their colour-pattern and habits. Even in Europe at the present day people confuse a Martin for a Swallow and vice versa.

2. Swifts at a distance resemble Swallows and in common parlance both are known as अबाबील in Hindi but the former belong to a different Order of Birds (Art. 45). The chief difference between the two is that while Swallows have the first toe directed backwards and the remaining three forwards Swifts have all the four toes directed forwards. This results in different perching habits for the two kinds of birds. Swallows can freely perch on trees, telegraph wires, buildings and on the ground but Swifts cannot do so except on their nest, and once a Swift finds itself on the ground it cannot get back into the air except with the greatest difficulty. Because of this weakness they have been named कृश and दुर्बल or दुर्बलिक in Sanskrit. Swallows and Martins with the exception of the Sand-Martin build cup or retort-shaped nests of mud and have therefore been termed भाण्डीक (fr. भाण्ड in what must have been its original sense, viz., an earthen pot or vessel; Cf. कौलालकं घटादि भाण्डम्—हेम शब्दानुशासन).[1] Nevertheless they came to be confused with the Swallows at a very early date as may be seen from the statement "दुर्बलिको भाण्डीकः प्राच्यानाम्" in the बृहत्संहिता, 88.7.

3. In spite of the confusion in the popular mind and even on the part of the writers like वराहमिहिर, the धन्वन्तरि-निघण्टु has curiously enough distinguished three different kinds of these birds:

"चटी चटक इत्युक्तो, भारद्वाजो, नहिः कुटिः।
चटकोऽन्यश्चतुर्थस्तु खञ्जरी चलपिच्छकः॥

viz. (i) चटी or चटक (ii) भारद्वाज and (iii) नहिः कुटि.[2] The equation "खञ्जरी चलपिच्छकः" refers either to the Pipit or to the Redstart. धन्वन्तरि has भारद्वाज

1. 6.3.194.

2. निघण्ट रत्नाकर has the incorrect reading of अहिकुटी which is equated with भरद्वाज पक्षी.

and व्याघाट separetaly for Larks. Small Swallow-like birds are mentioned by the name of चटक in the प्रतुद group of birds in चरक independently of कुलिङ्गका: for the Sparrow-group, as चटक is interpreted by the commentator चक्रपाणिदत्त as "चटकस्तु देवकुलचटक: स्वल्पप्रमाण:." The expression देवकुलचटक would include the Common House Swift, the Indian wire-tailed and Striated Swallows all of which nest in cliffs, caves, under bridges, houses and temples (देवकुल). The now extant हारीतसंहिता also mentions चटक as one of the जलेचरविहङ्गा: and the reference is to (i) the Sand Martins which nest in sandy cliffs and banks in the vicinity of running water and spend the greater part of their waking hours hawking insects over the surface of the water, placid or running, and out of the breeding season roost in the reed-beds bordering water; (ii) the Wire-tailed Swallows which again are essentially birds of the neighbourhood of water, skimming over the surface for insects; and (iii) the highly gregarious Cliff Swallows which nest in colonies and hawk for insects in big flocks in the near vicinity of water. It will be noted that all these belong to the Swallow group and the synonyms चटी and चटक like भाण्डीक must refer to the Swallows proper. The term चटक, in the sense of a small bird, is also used for a Swift (Art. 45). The name भाण्डीक, on the other hand, excludes the Sand Martins, which tunnel a long hole for their nest in a Sand-bank and do not construct a nest of mud stuck to a wall or rock-face.

4. The next name in धन्वन्तरि is भारद्वाज (भरन् धारको वाजोऽस्य—borne high on wings). भारद्वाज is also the Skylark which again flies strongly and very high. Now कृश and दुर्बल are synonymous terms, and when the latter means 'a Swift' (Art. 45) the former too must be another name for it. कृश as a bird in the कौशिक सूत्र[3] has been explained differently by the two commentators : (i) as गोमेणक (गवि आकाशे मिणमिणति ?), a black and long-tailed bird (कृष्णवर्णा दीर्घपुच्छा), referring probably to the Wire-tailed Swallow, and (ii) as भारद्वाज. If the identity of कृश and भारद्वाज with दुर्बल is accepted, all three would mean a Swift and the reference to the Wire-tailed Swallow by one of the commentators must be held erroneous.

5. The third variety in धन्वन्तरि is नहि: कुटि: (नहिकुटि: ?) (कुटि, a hut or a nest; cf. कुटिदूषक, a destroyer of a nest, in the title of the Kuṭi-dūsaka Jātaka), a name which has survived in Bengal as नकुटि[4] for the Indian Sand Martin, and would seem to apply to the Crag Martin

3. 11.1.2 at page 313 of the Notes. The अष्टाङ्गसंग्रह, 1.7, also mentions कृश as a bird of the प्रतुद class, and the expression "कृशा गृहा:" occurring there probably means the कृश birds living in human habitations.

4. This appears, probably by metathesis, as कुनटी in the list of edible birds in the हारीत संहिता Ch.11— "पोतकी भृङ्गिका क्षुद्रा तथा च कुनटी स्मृता । एते तुल्यगुणा ज्ञेया:". The little भृङ्गिका is the same as भृङ्ग mentioned earlier (ib.) as a water-bird, both referring to the steel-blue swallow which hawks insects over water; Cf. भृङ्ग: the large black-bee and a Drongo, and भृङ्गरोल for the Purple Sun-Bird of a deep blue-black colour.

as well. These birds do not nest in buildings or houses and "never associate with man" and the name probably is after this habit of the two Martins. The first element नहि: in the name certainly implies an emphatic negative, and नहि: कुटि: means 'a bird that does *not* nest in a shop or house'. It is really interesting to note that, despite the confusion that obtains in the popular mind all over the world, the ancient Indians had distinguished three main types amongst these seemingly similar birds with a very fair degree of accuracy.

6. The Swallow and the Swift are known in Marathi as पाकोली which is capable of more than one derivation : (i) पाका, पुत्रिका, and अवली —little birds living or moving in groups or parties (ii) Prak. पाकुल (प्र+आकुल) very confused, referring to the erratic flight of a party of such birds; and (iii) as bearing a close affinity to the first of the correlated expressions, "उत्पत्यपाकला" and "निषण्णश्यामा", explained as a bird which looks white when high up on the wing and black when settled on the ground or the nest:

> "उत्पत्य आकाशे भूत्वा या पाकला पाण्डुर्भवति सा उत्पत्यपाकला. निषण्णा सती श्यामा जाता निषण्णश्यामा—" गणरत्नमहोदधि, 122-23.

The birds referred to in the above statement are evidently the Common and Wire-tailed Swallows and the House Martins which are black above and white or pale-white below. They have very short tarsi, less than half an inch, and therefore sit very low, so that in this position they look black (निषण्ण श्यामा) but when they are high in the air they appear to be white (उत्पत्य पाकला).[5] The Hindi Śabda-Sāgara gives कृष्णा as one of the names for a Swallow (under अबाबील) perhaps from some Sansk. lexicon and this name seems to be an analogue of निषण्णश्यामा as पाकोली may be of उत्पत्यपाकला.

7. The शब्दार्थ चिन्तामणि has इल्वल and M. Williams इल्लल for 'a kind of bird'. If the names are connected with the root 'इल्-स्वप्ने क्षेपणे'—'lying down and going up' they would seem to correspond in meaning to the correlated expressions considered above. इल्वला: are five stars in the head of Orion and इल्वल perhaps implies the idea of shining high in the air or sky which is true of the birds under discussion. On the other hand the name इल्लल may be imitative of the bird's call and therefore identical with अलिल, and if so, it would apply to the Swift (Art. 45) and इल्वल would be a wrong reading of the former.

---

5. Cf. terms like कृष्णपाक and पाकशुक्ला implying change of colour from green to purple on ripening and from dark to white on burning, respectively.

Prakrit वाउप्पइया (वातोत्पतिका) for a kind of bird is clearly allied to this word. It probably refers to the Swifts which spend most of their time in the air and never descend to the ground (Art. 45).

8. A certain, small Sparrow-like bird named पूजनी शकुनि (चटका इति भरतः—शब्दकल्पद्रुम) is mentioned in the story of king ब्रह्मदत्त in महाभारत[6] while it appears under the name of पूजनीया शकुनिका in हरिवंश,[7] where it is said to frequent tanks and rivers and is described as below:—

"शितिपक्षा शोणशिरा शितिपृष्ठा शितोदरी।"

Commentator नीलकण्ठ explains शितिपक्षा as "white-winged"[8] and शितिपृष्ठा as "black-backed" and lets शितोदरी severely alone. Looking, however, to the fact that the little bird is in the habit of visiting tanks and rivers, and further that the term चटक means also a Swallow, it seems more reasonable to interpret शितिपक्षा as "having black and white wings", i.e. black above and white below; शितिपृष्ठा as "black above" and शितोदरी as 'having white lower parts'. This would also fit in with a clever and yet punning or mystifying use of the word शिति by the poet in three different senses. Subject to the correctness of this interpretation, the Indian Wire-tailed Swallow fully stands up to the description given in the verse. It has a chest-nut red head, black wings with a white lining to them, and white under-parts. It visits water regularly for insect food, builds an open cup-shaped nest from which the young ones can be gently taken out and replaced. This Swallow would thus seem to be the पूजनी bird and the physical basis of the story where the other details are of course imaginary and intended to heighten the effect and lead up to a moral. The name पूजनीया is happily conceived inasmuch as the black and white bird appears to have been worshipped with कुङ्कुम on the head, for it has no red elsewhere on its body. Alternatively the names also imply that the bird is one that has to be respected or treated with hospitality, i.e., to be allowed to nest and breed in one's house and therefore protected. Swifts also are to be treated in a similar way and a person who does so is known as चीरल्लि पोषक (Art. 45). These birds often establish themselves at one place and continue to breed from generation to generation if not disturbed. This has given rise to a belief that the family owning and occupying the house would also continue to prosper in the same way.

6. 12.139.
7. 1.20
8. 1.20.81.

26

WAGTAILS AND PIPITS

A. WAGTAILS

1. Wagtails are small dainty birds with a compact plumage, walking, running or trotting about with great speed on the ground and constantly wagging their long tails up and down. "The gait is a brisk walk or run, with a back and forward motion of the head" (Smythies), reminding one strongly of the name अश्वक (a little pony) for a kind of sparrow. The common name for a Wagtail is खञ्जन, and खञ्जखेट (खञ्ज: विकलगतिक:, खेट: घोटक:, or खेट इव खञ्जति—'a dancing little pony'; see शब्दकल्पद्रुम for खेट) is one of its many synonyms. In Gujarat it is known as दीवाली घोड़ा (winter-pony) as different varieties of it arrive in the country after the rains are over. This analogy with a pony occurred to Gilbert White also who remarks in his letter No. 60 to Thomas Pennant that "the tail of the Wagtail when in motion bobs up and down like that of a jaded horse."

2. Wagtails may be divided for the purpose of this article into three groups—(i) White Wagtails; (ii) Yellow Wagtails and (iii) the Large Pied Wagtail. Birds of the first group are the खञ्जन proper of works on augury like the बृहत्संहिता and वसन्तराजशाकुन, as also of the poets who compare the dark, sparkling and longish eyes of beautiful young ladies with the shapely body of these smart and active birds. बृहत्संहिता, ch.44 refers to the White Wagtails as खञ्जन, or खञ्जनक but they are also named possibly as श्रीक in 47, 6 but certainly as श्रीकण्ठ in 85, 38. भट्टोत्पल regards these names as synonymous but does not equate them with खञ्जन. श्रीकण्ठ in वसन्तराज 4.52, however, has been rendered as खञ्जन by the commentator which appears to be correct, for the black-throated god Śiva also is श्रीकण्ठ. Like नीलकण्ठ the name श्रीक also would appear to be a homonym, applicable, with different derivations, to two birds—(i) श्रीरिव कायति शब्दं करोति—श्रीक:, the Himalayan Whistling Thrush (Art.10), and (ii) शोभायुक्त: भद्रो वा श्रीक:, a 'beautiful bird'— from the black patch on a white breast, or 'a lucky bird'—the White Wagtail, in either case. Persian 'Sareecha' for a Wagtail is perhaps identical with Sanskrit श्रीक: as क is often changed to च in Persian, e.g., अश्वक—अस्पचा (aspacha), a small pony. If this is correct श्रीक: would be a very old name for a White Wagtail.

खञ्जन, though often derived from खजि—गतिवैकल्ये, may well be a later name analogous to Prakrit खंजण meaning (i) mud, (ii) lamp-black, and (iii) black grease from the axle-hole or hub of a cart-wheel. The idea in each case is that of a thing produced in or from a void, sky, or hole (खं), and as applied to these birds the term should refer to their coming to the earth from the skies ((खात् आकाशात् जननं उत्पत्तिरस्य—खञ्जनः) at the end of the rains; cf. दिवौकस् and त्रिशङ्कु below, also खलीन for the bit of a bridle which rests in the hollow of the horse's mouth. Two other synonyms for a खञ्जन are तण्डक and तातन both referring to its active movements like those of a dancer (शब्दकल्पद्रुम). For खञ्जनाकृति see Art. 10, and for खञ्जनिका, Art. 71.

3. The Yellow Wagtails also are variously known, e.g. as गोपीत, गोपुत्र, गोप or गोपापुत्र*, गोपीतिलक (गोपीतलक ?), or गोपीतनक; and the Large Pied Wagtail, having black head, neck and upper breast like the Magpie Robin, is कालकण्ठ—नीलकण्ठ, and काकच्छदि-खञ्जन (having black upper plumage like a Crow's; काकच्छर्दि is incorrect). The Large Pied Wagtail being resident throughout the country is not a bird of augury. One variety of the White Wagtail and several Yellow Wagtails breed in the Himalayas. The remaining species, listed in the Fauna of British India, breed outside India and are only winter-visitors to the plains.

4. All migratory Wagtails are birds of augury according to वसन्तराज and बृहत्संहिता. The former divides the White Wagtails into five varieties and places all Yellow Wagtails into a single group called गोपुत्र or खञ्जरीट. The latter distinguishes only three kinds of White Wagtails and calls the Yellow ones as गोपीत खञ्जन. The interesting explanation of वसन्तराज (10.1-9) for the mysterious disappearance of the birds and their sudden reappearance, and the names given by him to different varieties are as under:—

"त्वं योगयुक्तो मुनिपुत्रकस्त्वं, अदृश्यतामेषि शिखोद्गमेन
विलोक्यसे प्रावृषि निर्गतायां, त्वं खञ्जनाश्चर्यमयो नमस्ते"

(1) समन्तभद्र, (2) प्रभद्र, (3) अनुभद्र, (4) अम्बर भद्र, and (5) गोपुत्र (गोमूत्र is a misprint) or खञ्जरीट; cf. भद्रनामा below. The गोपुत्र or Yellow Wagtail is defined as under:—

"स्याद्यो हरिद्रारससंनिकाशो गोपुत्रनामा स तु खञ्जरीटः"

The classification in the संहिता is as below:—

"स्थूलोऽभ्युन्नतकण्ठः कृष्णगलो भद्रकारको भद्रः
आकण्ठमुखात्कृष्णः सम्पूर्णः पूरयत्याशाम्
कृष्णो गलेऽस्य बिन्दुः सितकरटान्तः स रिक्तकृद्रिक्तः
पीतो गोपीत इति क्लेशकरः खञ्जनो दृष्टः"

बृहत्संहिता, 44.2-3.

*भेलसंहिता, 1.27 mentions गोपापुत्र as one of the edible birds.

In the above extracts the first verse refers to their migratory habit and the traditional belief that they grow a crest towards the end of spring which renders them invisible during the hot weather and the rains, then the crest is lost and they become visible again just as the star Canopus, called अगस्त्य, rises above the horizon some time in August-September. The name मुनिपुत्रक, therefore, poetically represents the bird as the child of sage अगस्त्य. It is listed as ऋषिपुत्र in विष्णुधर्मोत्तर, 1.151.46. It is interesting to note that the absence of the Large Pied Crested Cuckoo, the सारङ्ग चातक or दिवौकस for a period of about six months, October, November to June, July, is explained by the belief underlying the name, दिवौकस् (living in heaven or high up in the sky, Art. 37). This चातक is also त्रिशङ्कु but त्रिशङ्कुक for a Wagtail in M. Williams on the authority of Galanos is most probably incorrect (see Ibid).

5. All White Wagtails are extremely tame and make themselves at home in gardens and on open spaces in towns and villages and near about country-huts and houses. The different species visiting India consist of adult and immature birds and their plumage in winter varies a great deal, so much so, that it is impossible to differentiate the species in the field. The classifications in बृहत्संहिता and वसन्तराज are more or less superficial, based principally on the character of the plumage of the birds at the time of observation. All Yellow Wagtails are गोपुत्र or गोपीत. हारिद्रव as the name of a particular bird occurs twice in the Ṛgveda, 1.50.12 and 8. 35. 7, and once in the Atharvaveda, 1.22.4 which is the same verse as RV 1.50. 12. It also occurs in the कौशिक सूत्र 26, 18. सायणाचार्य in his commentary on RV 1.50. 12 has rendered हारिद्रव as a kind of tree (Sk. हरिद्रु, Hindi हलदू, Adina Cordifolia, which occurs in sub-Himalayan tracts from the Jumna east-wards. Chloroxylon Swietenia, another tree with a yellow wood, does not occur north of the Nerbudda), but on RV. 8.35. 7 as a kind of bird (पक्षिविशेषः) as the reference to the action of flying forced him to adopt that meaning. It is worth noting that he does not give here any synonym for the bird. The commentators of the कौशिकसूत्र have described हारिद्रव as हरिद्रवर्णाः पीताश्चिटकाः (चटकाः) at p. 76, f.n., and equated it with गोपीतिलक at p. 326, i.e. a Yellow Wagtail. Sāyaṇa or his collaborator must have seen this commentary before he commented on the अथर्ववेद, and he, therefore, rendered हारिद्रव in AV. 1.22.4 as the गोपीतनक bird but failed to revise his notes on the Ṛgveda. Both गोपीतिलक and गोपीतनक (गोपीतलक in each case ?) are evidently the same गोपीत खञ्जन of the बृहत्संहिता. But हारिद्रव is, more probably, the Golden Oriole—See Art. 19.

6. The half verse cited above from वसन्तराज (10.9) would seem to show that खञ्जरीट stands for any Yellow Wagtail and this finds support from मत्स्यपुराण, 118, 50 and 53 where खञ्जरीटक stands for the Yellow and प्रभद्रक for the White Wagtails. Similarly अग्निपुराण, 232, 14 and 16 gives खञ्जन, and खञ्जरीटक as different birds. The Yellow Wagtails alone perch on trees and the following cited by महेन्द्र in his commentary on अनेकार्थसङ्ग्रह of

हेमचन्द्र clinches the point in favour of खञ्जरीट being the Yellow Wagtails:—

"कुजेषु खञ्जन्ति च खञ्जरीटाः"—(कुजेषु—on trees).

Poets and Lexicons have, however, obliterated the distinction between खञ्जन and खञ्जरीट and both these terms have been used for the White Wagtails which are a standard of comparison for beautiful eyes in literature.

7. Names like गोपुत्र, गोपपुत्र or गोपापुत्र ('dear to the Cows or Cowherds') denote the Grey-Wagtail, the Black-headed and the Yellow-headed Wagtails which "hover round grazing cattle for insects" (Hume) or "assemble in parties and feed among cattle" (Cassall's Book of Birds). The equation "गोपपुत्रस्तु लोपाको" in the bird section of कल्पद्रुकोश is indicative of their disappearance from the country in summer. गोपपुत्र is mentioned in विष्णुधर्मोत्तर, 1.151.48.

8. वैजयन्ती कोश gives गोलत्तिका for खञ्जरीटी i.e. a female Yellow Wagtail and one of this type is prescribed as a victim for the Spirits of the Waters:—

"रोहित् कुण्डृणाची गोलत्तिका तेऽप्सरसां"—वाज. संहिता, 24.37.

Now these three sacrificial creatures must be closely connected with water and रोहित् should be the fish of that name or at best the swamp-deer; कुण्डृणाची, rendered as a kind of lizard, must be a water-lizard of the Varanus group, probably the Kabara Goya, a large slender species of water lizard of India which is "equally at home on land or in the water where it swims by means of the flattened tail, the limbs being closely pressed against the sides."—Enc. Brit. 14th. Edn. Vol. 14, 247. This Lizard is found in Nepal and reaches a length of 7 ft.—ibid., 11th Edn., Vol. 16, 827.* Turning to गोलत्तिका (गो, earth or water and लत्तिका a lizard; moving on land or near water like one) there can hardly be any doubt that it is Hodgson's Yellow-headed Wagtail, "the most aquatic of all Wagtails", which chiefly frequents marshes, and edges of rivers, tanks, etc. If the difficulty of distinguishing the male and female of these birds is borne in mind, it would be better to treat the name in the feminine as an instance of a जातिवाचक संज्ञा like many other bird-names in Sanskrit, and it would then be a specific name for the above-named Wagtail. I may add that the selection of a water-lizard and a water-Wagtail makes it highly

*This rendering of कुण्डृणाची would perhaps help to explain the movement of a storm crashing upon a forest with the zigzag, turning and twisting motion of a large water-lizard first on the land and then throwing itself into the water with a loud splash, referred to in the Ṛgveda:—

"पताति कुण्डृणाच्या दूरं वातो वनादधि"—1.29. 6.

Cf. कुड्रीची, the गुडूची creeper, which climbs upon a tree (List of New Words in the Introduction to कौशिक सूत्र).

probable that रोहित् is a fish and not a deer as taken by the commentators. All three water creatures are of very active habits, befitting the nature of Water-nymphs.

9. A few of the so-called lexical common names of the bird may now be explained. The adnoun गूढनीड (whose nest is not visible) for खञ्जन can only refer to the White and Yellow Wagtails which do not breed in the plains of India. सूत्रकण्ठ refers to a particular phase in the plumage of the White and White-faced Wagtails in which the black on the breast is reduced to a narrow crescent in summer. This corresponds to अम्बरभद्र of वसन्तराज :—

"कृष्णा भवेत् कण्ठगतेव रेखा यस्य त्वसौ चाऽम्बरभद्रनामा"—10.7.

The रिक्त खञ्जन of बृहत्संहिता and आकाशभद्र of वसन्तराज is the immature White-faced Wagtail or a young Hodgson's Pied Wagtail in both of which the black patch on the breast is a small one. कर्कराक्ष (कर्कर, a mirror; holding a mirror to an excellent eye, i.e. resembling one); कर्कराङ्ग (कर्कर, hard, having a neat and compact body); कणाटीन (moving on the sands); कलाटीन and खञ्जखेल (cf. तण्डक; tripping beautifully); मिथुनिन् (going about in pairs). मीनाम्रीण (surpassing the fish in agility and beauty of form, both fish and bird being used as comparisons for beautiful eyes); भद्रनामा (auspicious named; cf. भद्र of बृहत्संहिता and names ending in भद्र in वसन्तराज); and रतनिधि (abounding in love or passionate—"प्रचुररतमन्मथविकारवत्त्वात्" as the male bird not only displays before the female but also sings lustily during consummation and after the act). This last name, रतनिधि, derived differently (रतस्थलगर्भे निधिः धनं यस्य) and therefore, misunderstood, gave rise to the belief that there is wealth underneath where the birds mate:—

"तस्मिन्निधिर्भवति मैथुनमेति यस्मिन्"—बृ. संहिता, 44.12.

However eager or ardent, the bird will not mate except where there is wealth underground:—

"अङ्गेषु जीर्यति परं खञ्जनयूनोर्मनोभव प्रसरः
न पुनरनन्तर्गर्भितनिधिनि धरामण्डले केलिः"—आर्यासप्तशती, 7.

वराहमिहिर also adds that there is likely to be coal underground where the bird voids, and advises the curious actually to dig for wealth or coal at such places:

"तत्कौतुकापनयनाय खनेद्धरित्रीम्"—44.12.

In literature the खञ्जन (the White or the White-faced Wagtail) is a standard of comparison for (i) the light, sportive gait of a young lady, and (ii) dark, beautiful, sparkling and longish-looking eyes:

(1) खञ्जन for the playful gait of a goddess:

"क्षेमा क्षेमावती चैव खेलत् खञ्जनगामिनी"—पद्मिनीस्तोत्र.

(2) Lover, willing to stake his life for the sake of a maiden possessing eyes like a खञ्जन :

"युष्मत्कृते खञ्जनगञ्जनाक्षि ! शिरोमदीयं यदि याति यातु"—उद्भट.

(3) A pair of White Wagtails, supposed to face each other, as it were, at the root of the nose of the beloved—the contrasting black breast-patches of the birds representing the black of the eyes.

"अन्योन्यचञ्चुपुटचुम्बनखञ्जरीट-
युग्माभिरामनयना शयने स्मरामि"—बिल्हणकाव्य

(4) The almond-shaped long eyes of Śrīkṛṣṇa :—

"कर्णोपान्त चरन्नेत्र खञ्जरीट मनोहरम्"—वायुपुराण, 104.46

(5) The river Gaṅgā personified as a young woman with a pair of white Wagtails for her eyes:

"तन्वी शरत् त्रिपथगा पुलिने कपोलौ
लोले दृशौ रुचिरचञ्चलखञ्जरीटौ" —अमरुशतक

B. PIPITS

Pipits are small brown birds, whitish or pale—fulvous below and streaked on the breast. On one side, they are related to the Wagtails like which they run on the ground and wag their tails up and down but more sedately, and on the other to the larks which they resemble somewhat in plumage and other characters. According to their habits, they are called Tree-Pipits, Ground- or Indian-Pipits and Water-Pipits. In the breeding season, the males suddenly rise in the air, uttering their song and after reaching the highest point (which is not very high) come down in an abrupt curve, with stiff partly extended wings. They are known as चचड़ी (from Sanskrit चर्चरी—हर्षक्रीडा) in Hindi and स्फोटिका* in Sanskrit after the manner of their flight and song. Other Sanskrit names are तुलिका or डुलिका (तुल्-उन्माने; "तुलिका स्फोटिका समे-" त्रिकाण्डशेष, from their tail wagging habit). The equation, "खञ्जरी चलपिच्छकः" of धन्वन्तरि if not applicable to the Red-start as suggested in Art.10 would certainly apply to these birds which are closely allied to Wagtails.

*Cf. "स्फोटः चट चटा शब्दः"—Com. on कामन्दकीय नीतिसार, 7.16.

27

THE LARKS

1. The Larks of India proper are small grey-brown birds closely resembling the Pipits. They are less nimble and have a more crouching gait. Not all the members of the family are good singers, and only the true Sky-Lark, the Crested Lark and the Singing Bush-Lark are appreciated for their song and favoured as cage-birds in India. The others have only a few sweet notes which can hardly be dignified by the name of a song. The rhapsody of the Sky-Lark is world -famous and it is not to be wondered at if one of the ancient Vedic singers has been named after this bird—भरद्वाज v. l., भारद्वाज. Next comes the Crested Sky-lark which sings high up in the air like the true Sky-lark and takes the notes of several other birds in its sweep. The singing Bush-Lark also has a full and sweet song but not at all comparable with that of the Sky-Lark or even the Crested Lark. It sings both on the wing and on the ground. About the song-flight of the Sky-Lark, Smythies remarks: "In the song-flight the bird mounts vertically or obliquely with a vigorous fluttering action to a great height in the air, the song commencing a few feet from the ground. The bird remains poised, head to wind, the wing beats momentarily interrupted at intervals. It presently sinks gently down with wings inclined upwards till it suddenly completes the descent by an abrupt drop to the ground....The song..may be heard from October to April at all times of the day but specially at dawn long before it is really light."

2. भरद्वाज (fr. भर, 'song of praise', or 'what is carried away' and वाज, strength, power of wings, i.e. a bird which sings during flight, or which is carried high on wings), भारती and ब्राह्मी चटी (धन्वन्तरि निघंटु) referring to its beautiful song as a prayer, are names for the Himalayan and Indian Sky-Larks. Its song high up "at Heaven's Gate", is well described by वसन्तराज :

"प्राप्य स्थिरत्वं चिरमन्तरिक्षे, नानाप्रकारं मधुरं स्वनन्ती"—8.55

3. The excellence of the sustained, varied, and vigorous song of the Sky-Lark has been well recognized in पारस्कर गृह्यसूत्र which lays down that a baby-boy six months old should be given solid food at a special अन्नप्राशन ceremony at which the first feed should consist of the flesh of certain birds according as the parents desire him to develop certain qualities in his adult

life. Thus he should be given the flesh of the भारद्वाजी or the Sky-Lark, if he is to excel in eloquence:—

भारद्वाज्या मांसेन वाक्प्रसारकामस्य, 1.19.7

Compare— "स्वरवैचित्र्यं सर्वं भारद्वाज्याः शुभं प्रोक्तम्" —बृहत्संहिता, 87.15. The following half verse from त्रिकाण्डशेष with alternative readings would seem to refer to two different birds, a Quail and a Sky-Lark. Both the readings are set out below:—

(1) फालखेला गरुदयोधी भारती व्योमलासिका

(2) फालखेला गरुद् गोधा भारती व्योमनासिका

Now फालखेला (frequenting cultivated land) is certainly applicable both to a Quail and the Sky-Lark, but it is very doubtful how far भारती for a Quail si correct, and here lies the main difficulty. हेमचन्द्र, मेदिनी and विश्वप्रकाश give भारती for only one kind of bird, which is evidently the Sky-Lark, and no other lexicon, to my knowledge, gives भारती for a quail except probably on the basis of No. 2 above. The epithet गरुद् गोधा (winged-lizard) is clearly a wrong reading for गरुद् योधा (fighting with wings), since the Quails, when they fight, strike each other with their wings. Similarly, the epithet व्योमनासिका, though it may refer to the Quails' habit of roosting on the ground at night with the bill pointing upwards, would seem to be a wrong reading of व्योमलासिका (sporting, dancing, in the sky) which is perfectly true of the Sky-Lark. गोलासिनी in Prakrit for 'a kind of bird' (from गो, the sky, and लास, dancing) is clearly the same as व्योम-लासिका, and, therefore, the Sky-Lark. It would be seen, therefore, that the original synonymy of त्रिकाण्डशेष was the one set out as No. 1 above, and in this the first half "फालखेला गरुद्योधी" — refers to a Quail, and the second half—"भारती व्योमलासिका"—to the Sky Lark. It is incorrect, as the commentators have assumed, to treat all the four terms as relating to a single bird.

4. The Rufous Short-toed Lark belonging to genus Calandrella is known as बघेरा and बघेरी in Hindi which at once reminds one of Sanskrit व्याघ्राट. It is also the वार्तीक of चरक and सुश्रुत, which has been explained by डल्हणाचार्य with a quotation from some Glossary: "वार्तीकाः वर्तिचटकाः स्वल्पाः संघातचारिणः, बगेड़ा इति लोके"; comp.—"वर्तीको वर्तिपटको वार्तीकश्चैव स स्मृतः" (भावप्रकाशनिघण्टु).

Now the Rufous Short-toed Lark as a resident bird occurs here and there in small numbers, but in the winter these are greatly augmented by very large flocks migrating from outside into the plains of North India and they are then netted in large numbers for food. Thus this Lark is व्याघ्राट in Sanskrit and बघेरा in Hindi, and the synonymy of भरद्वाज with व्याघ्राट is not quite correct. The शब्दार्थचिन्तामणि equates वर्तकी, वर्तिका, वर्त्तक, and वर्त्तका, with व्याघ्राट and gives भारइ as the vernacular equivalent of वर्त्तक, and भारइ of भरद्वाज. The शब्दकल्पद्रुम also has confused these names and equated वर्त्तक and वर्त्तिका with the vernacular भारई. This mix-up is due to the fact that the Rufous Short-toed Lark is व्याघ्राट, वार्तीक, and also वर्तिचटक (Quail-like sparrow).

It was regarded as a Quail-like sparrow because it was plentiful during the winter with flocks of migrating Quails and was largely netted along with them, and this seems to be the reason why it has been placed with the Quails in चरक and सुश्रुत संहिता as already stated. They are also the मास वर्तिका (fr. मास a month and, therefore, a Quail-like bird that visits the country for a short period or a season only) and पोथवर्तिका (fr. पुथ to kill, the birds being killed in large numbers for food).

The धन्वन्तरिनिघण्टु includes in one synonymy, three names of three different birds of the Lark family:—

भरद्वाज क्रुकराटो व्याघ्राटः पुन्यदर्शनः ।

क्रुकराट is ऋकराट in other lexicons, but instead of being a synonym for the Sky-Lark, it is the same as Hindi चरचरा (कस्य चः) for the Bush Larks, other than the Singing Bush Lark, which have hardly a song and this fact is recognised in the imitative names ऋकराट and चरचरा.

The Singing Bush Lark is known as अगिन in Hindi and अगिन जित्ता in Telugu, and these names are probably traceable to कण्ठाग्नि, the same as अग्निकण्ठ, which means simply 'a bird' according to the lexicons but should have been rendered, as I strongly suspect, as 'a kind of bird.' A perusal of the various Unadi Sutras and lexicons shows that many specific bird-names have been briefly rendered simply as 'a bird' so that it is most likely that the term कण्ठाग्नि or अग्निकण्ठ, was also so dealt with, and the bird's identity having been lost, the expression came to mean just 'a bird'. An absurd etymological explanation also has been offered for कण्ठाग्नि :— कण्ठे कण्ठाभ्यन्तरे अग्निः, पाचनरूपाऽग्निरस्य—शब्दकल्पद्रुम, for everybody knows, and the etymologist certainly knew, that the 'digestive fire' (जाठराग्निः) is in the stomach of all creatures including birds and not in the throat or neck. If on the other hand the lexicographer had to interpret it as a specific bird-name, he would have derived it in some such way:—

कण्ठदेशे अग्निः शब्दरूपाग्निरस्य; comp. मुखाद् वाग् वाचोऽग्निः (ऐत. उप. 1.4), and अग्निर्वाग् भूत्वा मुखं प्राविशत् (ibid. 2.4.)

The singing Bush-Lark is very vocal and has a powerful voice—a caged bird often singing for the better part of twenty four hours of the day during the season and hence the name, अग्निकण्ठ or कण्ठाग्नि. This derivation finds support from the fact that the name is on a par with मधुकण्ठ for the Cuckoo and readily explains the Hindi name अगिन for the singing Bush-Lark, otherwise it is very difficult to see why the bird should have been named अगिन and अगिन जित्ता (अग्निचटक) i.e. fire, and fire-sparrow respectively in Hindi and Telugu. Compared with the other Bush-Larks with harsh notes (ऋकराट), the singing Bush-Lark would pass for a good and powerful songater, and though, nowhere in comparison with the Sky-Lark or the Crested Lark, it is nevertheless a popular cage-bird of India.

The धूसर चटक and अरण्य चटक are names of a particular bird which is described as कुब्ज (crouching), भूमिशय (roosting and breeding on the ground), कुज (ground-born), and स्वल्पसञ्चर (walking little or in short spurts) in धन्वन्तरिनिघण्टु, राजनिघण्टु and कल्पद्रुकोश. These characters agree very well with the habits of the Finch Larks. Salim Ali says about the Ashy-crowned Finch Lark—"This little Lark affects flat, open cultivated country and semi-barren waste land. It is usually met with in pairs or parties which run along the ground, body held low, in short zig-zag spurts, facing this way and that, in search of food. Its colouration is remarkably obliterative and matches the ground to perfection...The nest is a tiny, neatly made saucer-like depression in the ground ....in open country." In regard to their obliterative colouration, Whistler mentions another trait of the birds: "On the ground their colouration renders these Larks very inconspicuous, and an observer walking along is often astonished at the numbers which rise one by one around him and then fly away in a dense flock from the ground which was apparently empty of life." They are called दुरी and दबकचिड़ी the same as कुब्ज चटक (crouching or squatting sparrow) in Hindi.

Lastly we have तिलककण्टक included by वजयन्ती in its list of song-sparrows. As the name implies, it is a bird which wears a sharply pointed crest on the fore-crown like a तिलक or upright sectarian mark on the forehead. It is clearly the Crested Lark. This bird is spread to the west and central Asia also; compare, Khār-i-sar, having a thorn i.e. a crest of pointed feathers on the head) for a Lark in Persian. The Hindi name for this bird is चंडूल, which may be from Sanskrit चूडाल (having a crest) or कण्डोल, a basket, referring to the little cage in which it is confined as a pet. The cage being covered with at least two folds of cloth, the bird is not distracted and continues to sing even when it is carried about along a busy thorough-fare.

28

THE WHITE EYE

The White Eye is a small arboreal bird chiefly olive-green and pale yellow in colour, and easily recognised by a conspicuous white ring round the eye. A tiny and pretty bird like this would simply pass for a पुत्रिका* or चटकिका in Sanskrit, and indeed its Hindi name बाबुना (a little child) shows that it was just a पुत्रिका in Sanskrit. Its short pretty song, rather nasal in tone, should claim for it the name सरङ्ग (a kind of bird—M.W.) for it. सरङ्ग means 'having colour'and also 'a nasal tone' and admirably suits the White Eye in both the senses.

---

*For पुत्रिका in the sense of a small or dear little bird, see Art. 22 B.

29

THE RUBY-CHEEK

The tiny Ruby-cheek does not occur west of Sikkim, and we cannot expect a Sanskrit name for it. It is a brilliant metallic green bird with coppery-red about the face, and stands very close to the Sun-birds in size and habits and would ordinarily pass for one. Its twittering call notes resemble those of the White Eye.

30

THE SUN-BIRDS

1. The Sun-birds are of small and delicate make and the majority of the males are clothed in resplendent metallic plumage, and they are therefore easy of recognition as a group. They are found solitary or in pairs and being entirely of arboreal habits they feed on minute insects and the nectar of flowers. The males have a short but pretty song in the breeding season. The birds of the Aethopyga genus are brilliantly dressed in metallic green or blue, crimson, yellow and purple. They have metallic green or crimson tails, the middle pair of feathers prolonged. Certain varieties like the Indian Yellow-backed Sun-bird, the Fire-tailed Yellow-backed Sun-bird, and the Nepal Yellow-backed Sun-bird are common in the Himalayan valleys of North India and Nepal. They are evidently the सुवर्णपुष्प (Golden- flower) of the garden of Indra described in the वायुपुराण, ch. 39, 18:—

"नानावर्णैश्च शकुनैः नानारत्नतनूरुहैः
सुवर्णपुष्पैश्चानेकैः मणितुण्डैर्द्विजातिभिः"

These tiny Sun-birds of multicoloured and shining plumage are comparable with the still smaller Humming Birds of America described as "jewels on wings", and it is interesting to note that their Indian counterparts too have been portrayed as possessing 'a be-jewelled plumage'— "नानारत्नतनूरुह" in the above verse. They have been beautifully described by अश्वघोष under the name of शीञ्जिरिका (शिज्शिञ्ज् to tinkle or jingle, referring to their sweet jingling song):—

"मनः शिलाभिर्वदनैर्विहङ्गा यत्राक्षिभिः स्फाटिकसन्निभैश्च
शादैश्च (v.l. श्यावैश्च) पक्षैरतिलोहितान्तैः माञ्जिष्ठकैरर्धसितैश्च पादैः
चित्रैः सुवर्णच्छदनैस्तथान्यैः वैदूर्यनीलैर्नयनैः प्रसन्नैः
विहङ्गमा शीञ्जिरिकाभिधाना रुतैर्मनःश्रोत्रहरैः भ्रमन्ति"

सौन्दरनन्द, 10.29-30.

2. The Purple Sun-bird, common throughout India, is भृङ्गरोल and मधुकर, (the Bee or Honey-Bird, cf. Urdu, शकरखोरा for it), so named from its small size, glistening black plumage, and the habit of collecting honey from the flowers. It is mentioned as मधुकर in वायुपुराण, 36.5:—

"मदोत्कटैः मधुकरैः भ्रमरैश्च महालसैः
उपगीत वनान्तानि किन्नरैश्च क्वचित् क्वचिंत्"

It is known in Hindi as फुलचुही which is synonymous with पुष्पंधय (flower-sucker), the same as मधुकर or मधुप. Gorressio's edition of the Rāmāyaṇa also mentions the bird as मधुपखग at 2.56.11 according to the St. Petersberg Dictionary.

31

FLOWER-PECKERS

The Flower-peckers are tiny Himalayan birds (3.2" to 4.5") resembling the Sun-birds in habits, but beyond a twitter they have nothing in the way of a song. Brightly coloured species like the Indian Scarlet-backed and the Fire-breasted Flower-peckers would ordinarily pass for a variety of सुवर्णपुष्प considered in the preceding article but not as a शीञ्जिरिका, for they have no song. Others like the Plain-coloured and Tickell's Flower-peckers would, from their small size, simply go by the common name of चटिका for any small bird.

32

PITTAS

Three varieties of Pitta are found in India. The Indian Pitta is found all over the country, the Blue-naped Pitta occurs in the outer Himalayas from Nepal eastwards, while the Blue Pitta of Bhutan is found in Assam and further east. They are coarsely built birds (7″-9″) with a short tail and long and powerful legs. Terrestrial by habit they feed chiefly on insects, lizards and occasionally mice. Their stumpy shape and upright carriage are distinctive. The male has a "magnificent double whistle" as well as a song.

The Indian Pitta has a plumage variegated with blue, green, black, white, fulvous and crimson, and is very aptly known as नौरंग (bird of nine colours) in Hindi. The Blue-naped Pitta is tawny rufous, washed with grass-green on the back, rump and tail, and bright blue on the nape and hind neck. The Blue variety is blue above and has a blue wash on different parts of the body, some red on the head and nape and yellow on the breast. The name पद्मपुष्प (shaped like a lotus flower prior to opening out), if correctly equated with पिकाङ्ग (पिक Cuckoo and अङ्ग a bird, i.e., a bird with a double call-note like the Cuckoo) in शब्दार्थचिन्तामणि and शब्दकल्पद्रुम should properly belong to the Pitta. If पिकाङ्ग is rendered as 'having a body like the Cuckoo's' it would refer to a bird like the Large Cuckoo-Shrike which is a dark grey bird and can by no means be described as पद्मपुष्प.

Another probable name for the beautiful Indian Pitta is चित्रक (चित्रम् नानावर्णंरञ्जि तम्—a painted bird), corresponding to Hindi नौरंग, mentioned with other song birds of the Himalayas.:

"शुकैश्च भृङ्गराजैश्च चित्रकैश्च समन्ततः।
सुग्रीवकाञ्चनरवैः कलविङ्करुतैस्तथा।
कूजितान्तरशब्दैश्च सुरम्याणि च सर्वशः॥ वायुपुराण, 36,2-4.

सुचित्रक (beautifully painted) is the Common Kingfisher, a little jewel of a bird in its own class (Art. 41). It is, however, quite possible that चित्रक and सुचित्रक are synonymous with each other and refer to the common Kingfisher alone.

33

BROAD-BILLS

The Broad-bills, as their name indicates, are characterised by very broad and flattish bills. They are small birds (not over 10″) but possess a beautiful plumage of striking colours—green, blue, black, and yellow. They are denizens of deep ever-green forests and insectivorous by habit. The Long-tailed Broad-bill is found throughout the Himalayas and Hodgson's Broad-bill is confined to the Eastern Himalayas as far west as Nepal. They build gigantic pear-shaped nests which are suspended from the end of a branch over-hanging a stream or pool of water. They are unwary birds and show no fear of man. They have a whistling call and are known as राइसुग्गा (राजिशुक) in Hindi though the name is more appropriate to the Long-tailed Broad-bill which is principally green and blue with some yellow and orange-yellow on the chin and throat. It has also a blue collar (राजि) and a pointed and graduated blue and green tail somewhat resembling the Parrot's. Its climbing habits when engaged in searching for insect food are very Parrot-like, and being familiar birds of the forests of Nepal and its foot-hills it must have had a Sanskrit name. I have, however, not come across any for these birds, but the name शुकपुच्छक for a certain plant could well have signified the Long-tailed variety, as birds and plants often share names between them. That it had a name after a Parrot is clear enough from the Hindi name of राइसुग्गा (राजि-शुक) from the collar consisting of a single blue stripe as against the two-or three-coloured collar of the Large Indian Parrot described as त्रिवर्णराजि by poet दण्डी in:—

"तुण्डैराताम्रकुटिलैः पक्षैर्हरितकोमलैः
त्रिवर्णराजिभिः कण्ठैरेते मञ्जुगिरः शुकाः"—२.६.

The Parrot-bills were thus probably known as राजिशुक or शुकपुच्छक.

34

WOODPECKERS

1. Woodpeckers are well-known Indian birds more than one species of which occur in every part of the country. Most of the species are adorned with a crimson crest in strong contrast with a pied and darker body-colour.

दार्वाघाट and काष्ठकुट्ट (v.l. काष्ठकूट) in Sansk. and रुक्खकोट्ठक, कोट्ठ or कोट्ठसातक (fr. Sk. वृक्षकुट्टक, कोष्ठ, or कोष्ठसाद) in Pali are common names for all Woodpeckers. If the element आघाट in दार्वाघाट has anything to do with the Vedic आघाटि for 'a musical rattle', this name should be regarded as primarily applicable to the 'drumming Woodpeckers' like the Great Slaty, the Scaly-bellied Green and the Yellow-fronted Pied Woodpeckers which produce a vibrating noise, "louder than a watchman's rattle", with quickly repeated blows of their beak on a branch or bamboo, and thence by extension to any Woodpecker. In its original sense, therefore, the name दार्वाघाट would mean, 'one who makes music on wood or bamboo'. Generally speaking, however, no such distinction is observed and both the names are commonly applied to all birds of the family. One of them figures as काष्ठकूट in the चटकदम्पती story in the मित्रभेद section of पञ्चतन्त्र; as सतपत्त (शतपत्र) in the कुरंगमिग जातक (206) and as रुक्खकोट्ठकसकुण (वृक्षकुट्टक शकुन) in the कंदगलकजातक (210). वृक्षकुक्कुट in M. Williams is perhaps a mistake for वृक्षकुट्टक, cf. Pali रुक्खकोट्टक for a Woodpecker.

2. The Great Slaty Woodpecker of the Himalayan Terai and nearby plains is a magnificent bird (20 inches) of an ashy grey plumage with a pale crimson patch below the eye and saffron-yellow, tinged with red, throat and foreneck. It is not a shy bird and moves in parties of four to ten or twelve, and is very noisy. The call is a peculiar and quite distinctive whinnying note, and the drumming noise it makes "starts with slow very resonant taps which get faster and faster, finishing off with a series of rolling reverberations which can be heard at a great distance" (S. Baker). शतपत्र means (i) the Large Indian Parrakeet, (ii) the Peacock, and (iii) a Woodpecker. Evidently the term is both an epithet and a substantive specifying the largest bird in each group. मत्स्य पुराण[1] mentions शतपत्र and काष्ठकुक्कुट (incorrect for काष्ठकुट्टक as the Jungle fowl is separately mentioned as कुक्कुट) as different and the former is clearly meant for this grand Woodpecker.

1. 118. 49 & 53.

It has been regarded as one of the auspicious birds of augury and its call or resonant drumming was a very welcome sound.:

"मङ्गल्यार्थप्रदैः शब्दैरन्ववर्तन्त सर्वशः ।
सादसाः शतपत्राश्च हंसाश्च मधुसूदनम्" ॥

—महाभारत[2]

"चकोरैः शतपत्रैश्च भृङ्गराजैस्तथा शुकैः ।
श्रोत्ररम्यं सुमधुरं कूजद्भिश्चाप्यधिष्ठितम् ।"

—मार्कण्डेयपुराण and महाभारत[3]

3. The beautiful Golden-backed Woodpecker (11″) is one of the best known in the whole group as it is found all over the country from the Himalayan foot-hills downwards. Its pied plumage, bright crimson crest, rich golden yellow back and the loud call never fail to attract the attention of persons with eyes and ears to see and listen. The कल्पद्रु synonymy includes two additional adnouns दारुण (having a very powerful call) and कर्बुराङ्ग for a Woodpecker and these are not found in M. Williams and other lexicons. कर्बुर means 'variegated' and 'gold' so that the name or epithet कर्बुराङ्ग means 'having both a variegated and a golden body' and it is submitted that the name applies to this common bird. The subject of the following descriptive verse of अश्वघोष is most probably this Woodpecker:—

"रक्ताभिरग्रेषु च वल्लरीभिर्मध्येषु चामीकरपिञ्जराभिः ।
वैदूर्यवर्णाभिरुपान्तमध्येष्वलङ्कृता यत्र खगाश्चरन्ति" ॥

—सौन्दरनन्द[4]

The red crest (रक्तवल्लरी) in front, golden-yellow in the middle, and brown elsewhere in the plumage hardly fits any other bird, and the poet appears purposely to have avoided the rather harsh sounding common names for it, and he certainly knew that the name शतपत्र belonged to a different variety of Woodpecker.

4. The Speckled Piculet (4 inches) and the Rufous Piculet (3.5 inches) are tiny Woodpeckers. The first is found throughout the Himalayas and the adjoining plains and the second from Nepal Eastwards. They haunt bamboos and bore holes in them for nests, the entrance hole being bored just below a node (Smythies). कीचक means 'bamboo and also a kind of bird' in M. Williams, and the कीचक birds of Rāmāyaṇa and some of the Purāṇas are the beautiful little Piculets whose voices are a quaint little piping imitation (or querulous miniature) of their larger brethren (S.

---

2. 5.83-25.
3. 6.18-19;3.158, 52-54. See also महाभारत 3.108.8; 3. 159, 86; पद्मपुराण, सृष्टिखण्ड 42.64.
4. 10.30.

Baker). The following verses help to bring out the difference between कीचक as a bamboo-clump and कीचक as a bird:—

"कोयष्टिकैश्चार्जुनकैः शतपत्रैश्च कीचकैः।
एतैश्चान्यैश्च बहुभिर्नादितं तद्वनं महत् ॥" (रामायण)[5]
"कीचकैश्च सुधोषैश्च कूजितं भ्रमरैरपि।" (स्कन्दपुराण)[6]
"तटे कीचकगुल्मैश्च तथा वृक्षैश्च शोभितम्।" (Ibid)[7]
"झिल्लीशब्दैश्च केङ्कारैः कीचकानां रवैस्तथा" (Ibid)[8]
"रवैः कीचकवेणूनां मधुरीकृतकाननम्।" (ब्रह्माण्डपुराण)[9]

Commentators and many lexicographers have missed the meaning of कीचक as a bird simply because their mind was obsessed with the dry bamboos of Kālidāsa in which holes had been bored by the black bees and which when blown over by a high breeze produced whistling sounds:—

"शब्दायन्ते मधुरमनिलैः कीचकाः पूर्यमाणाः" (मेघदूत)[10]

5. Finally, I may be forgiven for the wild guess I offer below in respect of a couple of verses in the अथर्ववेद—

"यत्राश्वत्था न्यग्रोधा महावृक्षाः शिखण्डिनः
तत्परेताप्सरसः प्रतिबुद्धा अभूतन
यत्र वः प्रेङ्खा हरिता अर्जुना उत
यत्राघाटाः कर्कर्यः संवदन्ति
तत्परेताप्सरसः प्रतिबुद्धा अभूतन" (AV.)[11]

In an attempt at interpreting the above verses the following may well be borne in mind:—

"क्रिमिर्जिन्वत्पृथिवि। यद् यदेजति प्रावृषि..." (AV.)[12]

where insects and other creeping things so much in evidence in the wet season, are mentioned, and

"ये गन्धर्वा अप्सरसो ये चारायाः किमीदिनः।" (AV.)[13]

where certain malignities are described as गन्धर्वाः and अप्सरसः. In English translations of these Sūktas, the terms गन्धर्व and अप्सरस् are

5. 3.75.12.
6. वैशाखमाहात्म्य 18.19.
7. 18.22.
8. 18.27.
9. मध्यम भाग 22.50.
10. 56.
11. IV.37. 4-5.
12. XII.1.46.
13. XII.1.50.

taken too literally whereas the Hindi rendering[14] regards AV. IV. 37 as a charm or as prescribing means against the swarms of various tropical insects which invaded the homes of the Indo-Aryans in the evening during the watery (rainy) season. This, it is submitted, is probably the more correct interpretation, having particular regard to the general tenor of this and other similar sūktas of this Veda. It must however be stated that my agreement with the मण्डल ends here, as my own rendering follows a line different from theirs.

The nuisance of insect-pests must have been very great indeed in Vedic times when the country around was full of jungles and marshes which are the great breeding grounds of all sorts of insect life. Stinking bugs and flies (Pentatomidae and genus Chrysopa respectively) are evil-smelling and seem to have been euphemistically addressed as गन्धर्वाः,[15] and the buzzing (singing) mosquitos, beetles and other insects and moths, swarming and dancing around light and fire, as अप्सरसः. These were driven off or were kept away with the strong-smelling herbs and incense named earlier in the same Sūkta. The terms हरिता, अर्जुना, and आघाटा would seem to be insect-destroying birds—हरित (Hindi हरेवा) the beautiful Chloropsis; अर्जुन ('the white', Hindi दूधराज, i.e., milk-white and अर्जुनक, the White bird in the verse from Rāmāyaṇa quoted above), the white Paradise Flycatcher and आघाट (दार्वाघाट) the drumming and rattling Woodpecker. All three frequent large trees in search of insect food and have musical or semi-musical voices (कर्कयः—कर्करी a musical instrument); Cf. RV. I1.43.3. where the root वद् in संवदन्ति is used in association with कर्करी as a bird's voice as in the above verses from the AV. Again the dipping and undulating flight of the Woodpeckers and the brilliantly white Paradise Flycatchers with their long trailing ribbons gives an impression as if the birds are moving on swings (प्रेङ्खा). In short the charm draws an inviting picture of the large fig trees, and asks the various insects with the flattering epithets of गन्धर्व and अप्सरस् to be well advised (प्रतिबुद्धा अभूतन) to visit the trees where swings and music await them (to be, of course, gobbled up there by the birds). The principles underlying the charm are deceit and flattery:—

"प्रियवाक्यप्रदानेन सर्वे तुष्यन्ति जन्तवः।"[16]

6. This digression is just intended to secure, if possible, a most ancient literary pedigree to a Woodpecker (आघाट). At any rate the basic idea of the charm put forth by the स्वाध्याय मण्डल is worth investigation at the hands of Vedic Scholars.

---

14. Published by the Svādhyāya Mandala of Satara.

15. In the same way they have been ironically given the names of sweet-smelling herbs and herbal products, औक्षगन्धि, प्रमन्दनी etc. In the alternative these drugs also were used with the strong-smelling अजशृङ्गी to drive off the insects—evil beings—as assumed by सायणाचार्य who renders गन्धर्वाप्सरसः as उपद्रवकारी or malignant beings, and according to him the words हरिताः and अर्जुनाः qualify प्रेङ्खाः.

16. Compare also— आराध्यमानो नितरां कपोतोऽपि हि तुष्यति—परिशिष्ट पर्वन्, 3.6. कपोत according to tradition is an inauspicious bird—See Art.

35

BARBETS

1. The Barbets are essentially birds of the tree-tops, from whence they utter their loud monotonous call-notes for hours on end; but owing to their green or greenish plumage blending with the foliage they are difficult to see, and for this reason few people know them by sight. All nod their heads in a peculiar manner in the act of calling. Sanskrit पिप्पल for 'a kind of bird', if derived from its habit of eating पिप्पल (figs and other fruits), may well apply to the Barbets as a group of fruit-eating birds, but if the name is after the bird's call it would be specific for a particular Barbet.

2. The Great Himalayan Barbet (13″) is olive-brown streaked with greenish-yellow above, and roughly the same colour below, striped yellow and brown on the sides, blue down the centre with a scarlet patch under the tail. Seen from a distance it appears to be a dark dully-coloured bird. Purely arboreal, it is best known by its call, 'a loud melancholy mee-ou or pyillo' (Whistler), and according to Hume "a fine plaintive call, till-low, till-low, till-low...uttered in a chorus, striking and pleasant".[1] Stuart Baker on the other hand, renders the call as a triple 'pio-pio-pio'. It is well-known how difficult it is to render bird-voices into human syllables and no two persons agree in their syllabification. Bearing this fact in mind and the nature of the bird's call as syllabified above it is not at all difficult to see that Hindi पियोली, त्रैहो and चैपला, and Sansk. पिप्पल for this Barbet are of an onomatopoetic origin as indeed the following Hindi verse would show:

"कहत 'पीपलौ पीपलौ' नितहि चैपला श्राई"—रसनिधि

Hindi त्रैहो, from त्रि and आह्वा a call, clearly refers to the triple 'pio- pio-pio' rendering of S. Baker, while Sans. पिप्पल is a happy blend of the bird's call as well as its fruit-eating habit.

3. In भारतमञ्जरी, शान्तिपर्व (Verse 1676) क्षेमेन्द्र says that an oil-thief is reborn as a पिप्पल bird ("पिप्पलस्तैलहरणात्") which would seem to be in keeping with the bird's olive or yellow-brown plumage...the colour of oil. It is one of the birds that were eaten in the long past:

1. "Stray Feathers", Vol. VIII.

"चटकान् भृङ्गराजांश्च तथा पिप्पलकानपि"—भेलसंहिता, p. 46

The वटहा of चरक (वट a fig-berry and हन् to destroy; Prakrit वडभा—वट+भक्ष?) appears to be the same as पिप्पल. मञ्जुलीयक of कल्पद्रुकोश ("मञ्जुलीयक मञ्जुनादो") and अष्टाङ्गसंग्रह, 1.7, and मञ्जुलीतक of मत्स्यपुराण, 118, 55, refer like पिप्पल in a dual sense to the bird's habit of keeping to dense foliaged tree-tops (मञ्जु—a bower +ली to disappear or conceal) and its sweet call-notes (मञ्जु—pleasing). Hindi मियोली for this Barbet is very close to these names —मंजुली - मंयुली - मियोली.

4. The Northern Green Barbet (10.5") and the Lineated Barbet (11") are generally of a green colour and both have a similar call—kutur-kutur-kutur—and they go by the name कुटुर in the North as well as in the South and in Ceylon. These are undoubtedly the कुटरु birds of the वाज. संहिता where one of them forms a trio of very noisy birds dedicated to the deities presiding over horse-races:—

"क्वयिः कुटरुर्दात्यौहस्ते वाजिनाम् ।"—24.39.

क्वयि is the Screech Owl or the Noisy Common Owlet and दात्यौह the White-breasted Water-hen, and the noisy character of all three is typical of the tumultuous applause and commotion attending a horse-race. The Blue-throated Barbet (9") with its 'took-a-rook', 'took-a-rook' is known as कुतुरुरु in the vernacular and would be included in the कुटरु group. This noisy Barbet has, as it were, the fire in its throat and has therefore been consecrated to अग्नि[2] :—

"अग्नये कुटरून्"—V.S. 24, 23.

5. The Crimson-throated Barbet (6") is a thick-billed, gaudy and dumpy looking green bird of the size of the Common Sparrow. It has a loud, monotonous ringing call tuk, tuk, tuk,....., as of a distant coppersmith hammering on his metal (Salim Ali), heard during the hotter parts of the day. The regular beat of its notes combined with its head-movements, now in one direction and now in another is very suggestive of a little drummer-boy playing alternately on a pair of small drums and that is how it is called डिण्डिमाणवक in सुश्रुत and डिण्डिमानक (v.l. दण्डिमाणक) in चरक from डिण्डिम a drum or in Prakrit 'bell-metal- ware' and 'Worker in Brass'[3] and माणवक a small boy. Prakrit णंदमाणक and Pali दिदिम (दिंदिम ?—डिण्डिम) refer to it. Hindi तंबायत or तमेरा (coppersmith) corresponds to the meaning of the word डिंडिम in Prakrit, whence its popular English name, 'the Coppersmith'.

6. The showy appearance of this little green bird, with patches of red, yellow and black about the head and breast accounts for its selection for the next birth of a jewel-thief in मनुस्मृति under the name of हेमकर्तृ, a gold-smith:

---

2. See para 6, Art. 27.

3. पाइय सद्दमहण्णवो.

मणिमुक्ताप्रवालानि हृत्वा लोभेन मानवः।
विविधानि च रत्नानि जायते हेमकर्तृषु॥ 12.61

Similarly the हेमक (cf. हैरण्यक a gold-smith) of the following is this Barbet:

जीवंजीवकनादैश्च हेमकानां च नादितैः। वायुपुराण, 36.4

Both these names are very close to Hindi तंबायत (Copper-smith) for the bird though the former gives it a higher status.

36

HONEY-GUIDE

A single species of this bird, the yellow-backed Honey-Guide, occurs in the Himalayas at two places only, viz., in Sikkim and near Murree and Abbotabad where, again, it is very rare. No Sanskrit name is available for it.

37

CUCKOOS

The birds of this family are divided into two groups, the one arboreal and parasitic, and the other terrestrial and non-parasitic.

A. PARASITIC CUCKOOS

1. The parasitic nature of Cuckoos has long been known in India as we find one named as अन्यवाप in the वाज. संहिता, 24.34. Other common names are परभृत् or परपुष्ट. These are usually applied to the Himalayan Cuckoo and the Koel but the expression परपुष्ट जाति evidently includes the चातक group as well:—

"धन्यं धिनोति वचनैः श्रवणानुकूलैः
अन्यं दुनोति परुषैः परपुष्टजातिः"

भिक्षाटनकाव्य, 27.4, काव्यमाला, Pt. 12.

In this verse a love-sick person complains principally against the Cuckoo but generalises against the whole tribe including the Hawk-Cuckoos, the Pied Crested-Cuckoo, etc. whose calls are not welcome to a separated lover. Cuckoos other than the Black Koel cuckold small birds of different kinds, e.g., Babblers, Chats, Pipits, Wagtails, etc., and knowledge of this fact on the part of the ancients is fully reflected in the names given above, and in the half verse from शाकुन्तल given below:—

"प्रागन्तरिक्षगमनात् स्वमपत्यजातं
अन्यैर्द्विजैः परभृताः खलु पोषयन्ति"—5.22.

The Koel of the plains on the other hand victimises the common House-Crow and occasionally the Jungle-Crow, and is therefore called काकपुष्ट. The male bird's loud call of 'कुहू कुहू' has given us names like कुहूकण्ठ, कुहूमुख etc., for it and the name कुहू[1] for the night of the New-moon which is supposed to be as black as the bird itself. Sanskrit काकपुच्छ appears to have been formed on a false analogy with the Prakrit काय

1. AV.7.47.1. For other derivations of कुहू see यास्क, 6.11.23.

पिउच्छा though, independently of the latter, it can stand by itself as "Crow-tailed" which, however, is quite colourless and uninteresting. काय पिउच्छा (काकपितृस्वसा — the Crow's father's sister) for the female Koel, on the other hand, seems to be an excellent name based upon the bird's parasitism. In India a sister often leaves her little children with a brother for rearing them and this is exactly how the female Cuckoo deals with her supposed brother, the Crow, and hence her nick-name, 'the Crow's aunt'. The Koel shares the names कोकिल and पिक with the European and the Asiatic Cuckoos which breed in the Himalayas and, very sparingly, on the hills in certain parts of the country. It is therefore difficult to say whether a given reference is to the Cuckoo proper or to the Koel.

2. अन्यवाप in "अन्यवापोऽर्द्धमासानाम्"—V.S., 24.34. would be the Cuckoo if the Saṃhitā was compiled in the North-West, for the Koel is non-existent in the extreme North-West and rare in the Punjab, but if the compilation took place in the मध्यदेश, it is more probably the Koel. The reason for the dedication of the bird to the deity presiding over the Half-months is apparently the fact that the bird performs only half its part in reproduction and the particular name chosen emphasises this.

3. The poets of Kashmir and others describing Himalayan scenery (e.g. in the Purāṇas and other literature) have mentioned the Cuckoo by names like कलकण्ठ, पिक, परभृत्, परपुष्टा, and पुंस्कोकिल and these names in the particular context refer to the European or the Asiatic Cuckoo both of which have a similar and very sonorous call of two notes 'ku-koo'. In "कामाय पिकः" V.S., 24.29 पिक is one of these and the name, used purposely (साभिप्राय), must refer to the sweet amorous voice of the bird in the Spring. Poetic names like मधुघोष and गन्धर्व would again seem to refer to these two birds as their voice is more melodious than the Koel's; Cf. "पुण्णमुखो नाम फुस्स कोकिलो...अतिवियमधुरगिरो"—Kuṇāla Jātaka, where the extremely pleasant and full-throated voice of the फुस्सकोकिल (Cuckoo with spotted or variegated plumage; पुष्प a spot, cf. फुस्सरथ for पुष्परथ, v.l. पुष्यरथ) is mentioned. Both the birds are grey above and barred or spotted white below and have been distinguished from the Koel (काल, कृष्ण or श्यामकोकिल) as श्वेतकोकिल :—

"भास्करोदयकालोऽयं गता भगवती निशा।
असौ सुकृष्णो विहगः कोकिलस्तात कूजति"—रामायण, 2.52.2
"देवलोकोद्भवाः[2] श्वेता विलेपुः कोकिलास्तदा"—हरिवंश, 2.88.69

In the आवश्यक सूत्र, a Jain work by मलयगिर्याचार्य, two Cuckoo birds ('दो कोइला') are one of the ten different items seen in a dream, and the scholiast explains the birds to be a श्वेत कोकिल and a विचित्र कोकिल. श्वेत कोकिल being the same as फुस्स or चित्र कोकिल in Pali the latter विचित्र कोकिल is either a mistake for कृष्ण कोकिल or is to be rendered as वि not चित्र, variegated i.e. of a uniform colour viz. black, or again it may

2. "देवलोकोद्भवाः i.e. bred in the Himalayas, देवलोक.

refer to one of the Malkohas which have a variegated plumage. In the Kuṇāla Jātaka, the Koel is called काल कोकिल and the Asiatic Cuckoo फुस्स कोकिल फुस्स[3] is Pali for Sansk. पुष्य and has taken the place of पुप्फ (i.e. पुष्प) due to an erroneous substitution of पुष्य for पुष्प, e.g. in पुष्यरथ. चित्र कोकिल is a synonym for it in the Pali-English Dictionary (PTS. Edition). Hindi फुफु, पुफु or पुहुपु fr. पुहुप—पुष्प a flower, for the same bird is a more correct form of पुप्फ (पुष्प).

4. The Himalayan Cuckoo, breeding in the Himalayas from Kashmir Eastwards, resembles the Asiatic Cuckoo in coloration and size but has a different voice. The male has a spring-song consisting of four dull booming notes, 'hud-hud-hud-hud' similar in tone to the call of the Hoopoe (Smythies). This Cuckoo would therefore seem to be the दुन्दुभि, a प्रतुद bird of चरक. "दुन्दुभि: दुन्दुभिध्वनि:" is the definition given for it in the कल्पद्रु कोश, and दुन्दुभि is also a small child's drum in Prakrit. The name is thus fully descriptive of the bird. This is apparently the Cuckoo whose voice has been described by जिनसेन as "कोकिलानकनिस्वन:" (like the sound of a drum) in (जैन) आदि पुराण 33.89. In the preceding verse he uses the common classical expression कोकिलालाप for the Koel. The name दुन्दुभि may also apply to the Indian Cuckoo which too has a similar call of four melodious notes, "bo-ko-ta-ko", capable of being syllabified as "pu-pu, pu-pu" as well. मद्दालक (from मर्दल, a drum) is a kind of Himalayan bird in वेस्संतर जातक verse 2099 and from the similarity of the name to दुन्दुभि it may also be for the Himalayan Cuckoo. Two other bird-names have been derived from the names of different kinds of drum डिण्डिमाणवक (डिण्डिम–माणवक), the Little Barbet, and पाणविक (पणव), the Stone Plover—See Arts. 35 and 64.

5. No description of वसन्त in Sanskrit literature, but refers to the Sweet Song of the "thrice welcome darling of the spring"—the Cuckoo or the Koel, the वसन्त दूत of India.:—

> "कुसुमजन्म ततो नवपल्लवास्तदनुषट्पदकोकिलकूजितम् ।
> इति यथाक्रममाविरभून्मधुर्द्रुमवतीमवतीर्य वनस्थलीम् ।।
>
> रघुवंश, 9.26.

I give below just a few examples to illustrate the knowledge of the ancients regarding some of their peculiarities, e.g.—

(i) Cuckoos do not pair for the breeding season like other birds and promiscuity is very common with them (Jerdon) and this fact not only underlies the Prakrit adnoun पंसुल (Sk. पांसुल a libertine) for the male Cuckoo but also the punishment prescribed for a man who has insulted his brother's wife. He is to be reborn as a पुंस्कोकिल so that he may

---

3. Is it possible that फुस्स कोकिल is the Pali rendering of Sansk. पुंस्कोकिल? If so, the latter would be specific for the Himalayan Cuckoo though the later poets extended the term to the male of the Koel as well.

suffer the torture and humiliation of seeing his own sweetheart being pursued by others:—

"भ्रातृभार्यां तु पापात्मा यो धर्षयति मोहितः।
पुंस्कोकिलत्वमाप्नोति सोऽपि संवत्सरं नृप॥

महाभारत, 13.111.76

(ii) Those who have listened to the first broken and incomplete notes of the Cuckoo in early spring will appreciate the following :—

"कण्ठेषु स्खलितं गतेऽपि शिशिरे पुंस्कोकिलानां रुतम्।"

शाकुन्तल, 6.4

"गायन्तो गलरागमङ्कुररसश्च्यूतस्य चञ्चुक्षते-
श्च्योतद्भिः शिशिरोपरोधशिथिलं पुष्णन्ति पुंस्कोकिलाः।"

सुभद्राधनञ्जय, 2.9

"प्रथममन्यभृताभिरुदीरिताः
प्रविरला इव मुग्धवधूकथाः।" रघुवंश, 9.34

As the season advances the voice becomes fuller and sweeter

"चूताङ्कुरास्वादकषायकण्ठः
पुंस्कोकिलो यन्मधुरं चुकूज" कुमारसंभव, 3.32

adding character to mountain scenery:—

"प्रमत्तपुंस्कोकिलसंप्रलापैर्हिमालयोऽतीव तदा रराज।" ब्रह्मपुराण, 36.116.

No poetic embellishment however can match the following simple statement about the peculiar charm that the Cuckoo lends to sylvan surroundings

"कोकिलानां रुतैः पुण्यैः सर्वत्र मधुरायते।" पद्मपुराण, भूमिखंड, 24.38

6. Cuckoos whose calls are different from those of the birds mentioned above are : (i) the Hawk Cuckoo, the Common and the Large; (ii) the Plaintive Cuckoo; (iii) the Banded Bay Cuckoo; (iv) the Violet Cuckoo; (v) the Emerald Cuckoo; (vi) the Drongo Cuckoo; (vii) the Pied Crested Cuckoo and (viii) the Red-Winged Crested Cuckoo. The first three and No. (vii) go under the common name of चातक in Sanskrit, as their notes are plaintive in character. The breeding time for these often runs into the rainy season and the males are then very vocal. This coupled with the fact that they derive all the moisture they need from their soft food consisting of caterpillars and various kinds of figs etc. and are therefore not seen to visit the water, has given rise to the popular fiction that they drink only rain-drops and that ground water is harmful to them ——" धरणीपतितं तोयं चातकानां रुजाकरम्."[4] Hence also the conceit that their persistent calls are an appeal to the rain-cloud for a few drops to cool their parched throats. This interesting belief has given us some very beautiful अन्योक्ति type of poetry.

4. Quoted by M. R. Kale in his notes on रघुवंश, 5.17.

7. पंपका are certain birds in the वेस्संतर जातक. पम्पा in Prakrit means पिपासा or thirst; and पम्पा is the name of a lake and a river. The word पंपक would thus appear to have some connection with water or the desire for it, and पंपका is probably the Pali equivalent of चातका: which are supposed to be ever thirsty. No other name for the चातक appears in the long lists of birds occurring in the Jātaka and it is far too important a bird to be omitted.

कल्पद्रुकोश gives a mixed list of synonyms for the चातक :—

"अथ चातकः

घनाखश्च वापीहः सारङ्गो मेघजीवनः ।
वर्षप्रियः त्रिशङ्खः स्यात्स्तोको बभ्रुर्हरीतकः
कपिञ्जलोऽपि हारीतः तञ्जलो,.........."

and looking to some of them, like सारङ्ग, बभ्रु, कपिञ्जल, हारीत, etc. which clearly indicate the colour of the plumage, it is impossible to say that they all belong to only one kind of bird. The list certainly includes the names of several kinds of चातक. Thus घनाख, वापीह (Hindi, पपीहा), कपिञ्जल[5], and बभ्रु (Cf. भ्रो for it in Bengal) are clearly for the very noisy Hawk Cuckoos which are of a grey-brown colour (बभ्रु, पिञ्जर); वर्षप्रिय, वरिषाप्रिय (M.W.) and त्रिशङ्ख (having a triple note) are for the Plaintive Cuckoo which is known as पौस्या or पाउस्या in Marathi (from Prakrit पाउस and Sanskrit प्रावृष्, प्रावृषिक) and has a triple call of 'whe-whe-ew' or 'pi-pi-yu'; सारङ्ग (Pied or variegated) is the larger form of the Pied Crested Cuckoo (Clamator jacobinus) and finally हारीत and हरीतक (of a green colour) clearly point to the Emerald Cuckoo, for हारीत is also a name for the Emerald Dove and the Green Pigeon. Its call, according to S. Baker[6] is "a shrill but not unmusical succession of three notes". The Violet Cuckoo occurs in Assam but not to the west of it. It is generally a silent bird and has no Sanskrit name for itself.

8. शब्दार्थचिन्तामणि has "राजपट्टिका चातकखगे" and the name राजपट्टिका (adorned with bars or stripes) clearly refers to the Banded Bay Cuckoo which is barred brown and rufous all over including the head and the face. The call notes of this bird are not unlike those of the Plaintive Cuckoo but it also has another call resembling the Cuckoo's 'Bo-ko-ta-ko', though much higher.

9. The following verse from the महाभारत mentions the bird प्रियक with चातक :—

"प्रियकैश्चातकैश्चैव तथान्यैर्विविधैः खगैः।" 3.158.53

Now प्रियक also means 'a black bee' or भृङ्ग and भृङ्ग is also the Drongo. The Drongo Cuckoo "is remarkable for its extra-ordinary resem-

---

5. कपिञ्जल-क ईषत् पिञ्जर वर्णः ?
6. Second Edition of F.B.I.

blance, both in structure and coloration, to the common Black Drongo. It differs from all other Cuckoos in the shape of the tail, which is very long and forked......"[7]. "Its call is a most human whistle of six notes in ascending scale and it also utters a very plaintive double note, sounding like "wee-whip" and very like a breeding call of the common Black Drongo. Its flight also is generally dipping and buoyant, much like the flight of that bird...." (Ibid). प्रियक (प्रियं मधुरं कायति शब्दायते), therefore being a synonym of भृङ्ग, would seem to have been very appropriately chosen for the Drongo Cuckoo. It also means a musical instrument, perhaps some sort of a whistle, so named after the bird's voice: cf. लट्वा and सट्वा, both as birds and musical instruments.

10. The Hawk Cuckoo is one of the commonest birds of India and some of its names, given in the कल्पद्रुकोश have already been mentioned above. The older names for it are अत्यूह and दात्यूह as seen in the list of प्रतुद birds in चरक and सुश्रुत respectively. The name दात्यूह is of frequent occurrence in Puranic and other literature and at times it becomes difficult to say what bird is exactly meant, for the term also means at least a couple of water-birds. The Lexicons also give quite a number of so-called names for the Hawk Cuckoo which are really in the nature of descriptive epithets, and दात्यूह qualified with one of them at a time should be specific for a particular bird. In poetry, however, where 'brevity is the soul of wit' or, perhaps, of mystification, the epithets are dropped and the bare homonym is given. ("मादक दात्यूहे"—माद्यति वर्षागमे हृष्यतीति—शब्दकल्पद्रुम) is one of such epithets and as it means 'exhilarating, gladdening', it should refer to the Hawk Cuckoo whose voice is appreciated in India and therefore figures very largely in erotic poetry.[8] Referring to these birds calling all around in the Himalayas Herbert Stevens characterises the chorus as a "pandemonium which reigns all day long and throughout the long hours of the night"[9] which may be contrasted with a healthy appreciation of the same by the hardy ancients of India:

"दात्यूहव्यूहकेलीकलितकुहकुहा रावरम्या वनान्ताः।"

बालरामायण, 1.63

"सलीलदात्यूहसमूहनिस्वनाः।" विक्रमाङ्कदेवचरित, 11.15

The voice of the Hawk Cuckoo never caused 'brain-fever' to the nature-loving except, of course, the love-lorn:

"अशंकितैः पक्षिगणैः प्रगीतैरिव च प्रभो।
केकाभिर्नीलकण्ठानां दात्यूहानां च कूजितैः" म. भारत, 15.27.9

7. F.B.I. 2nd Edition.
8. Other epithets are considered in Art. 58: Cf. मदालापी for the Koel.
9. Journal of B.N.H.S.; XXH.680.

"प्रमत्तदात्यहरुतैश्च वल्गुभिः"—मत्स्यपुराण, 68.1
"एष दात्यूहको इष्टो रम्ये मां वननिर्झरे।
प्रणदन् मन्मथाविष्टं शोचयिष्यति लक्ष्मण॥" रामायण, 4.1.24

It was also a favourite cage-bird as सीता is represented in the बाल रामायण, wishing an affectionate goodbye to her pet-birds including a दात्यूही (Act.6.27); Cf. also the idiomatic phrase, "कक्षा पञ्जर दात्यूह" (Act.8.72) for a person completely under one's control.

11. वर्षाहू is a bird in "वर्षाहू ऋतूनाम्" वाज. सं. 24.38 and the name means 'rain-invoker'. It is evidently one of the Cātakas. An alternative form 'वर्षाभू' occurs in the bird-list quoted from पाराशर by भट्टोत्पल in his commentary on बृहत्संहिता 85.28. This name is on a par with names like वर्षप्रिय and घनाख्य considered above, and all three remind one of वृषारव probably a bird answered back by another bird, चिच्चिक in the अरण्यानी hymn of RV.:—

"वृषारवाय वदते यदुपावति चिच्चिकः[10]
आघाटीभिरिव धावयन् अरण्यानिर्महीयते।" RV. 10.146

वृषारव also would therefore appear to be a kind of चातक, and having regard to the loud and persistent call of the Hawk Cuckoo, it is probably entitled to claim all these names (except वर्षप्रिय) in its own right.

12. From amongst the different birds going under the name of चातक only two appear to be the favourites of Sanskrit Poets, the Hawk Cuckoo, always mentioned as चातक and rarely as वापीह, and the larger Pied Crested Cuckoo, called more correctly as सारङ्ग than as चातक though it is the चातक of many a verse in अन्योक्ति and other poetry. To the poets any चातक is simply a चातक and they do not seem to worry what particular kind of bird they are actually referring to. In this way even the name सारङ्ग has lost its identity. कालिदास, however, would seem, for once at least, to have observed the distinction. Two examples from the मेघदूत should suffice:—

(i) "मन्दं मन्दं नुदति पवनश्चानुकूलो यथा त्वां
वामश्चायं नदति मधुरं चातकस्ते सगन्धः।" (v.l. सगर्वः)

(ii) "नीपं दृष्ट्वा हरितकपिशं केसरैरर्धरूढैः
आविर्भूतप्रथममुकुलाः कन्दलीश्चानुकच्छम्।
दग्धारण्येष्वधिकसुरभिं गन्धमाघ्राय चोर्व्याः
सारङ्गास्ते जललवमुचः सूचयिष्यन्ति मार्गम्॥"

In the first example चातक is most probably the Hawk Cuckoo with its powerful and persistent call justifying the use of the epithet सगन्धः or

---

10. For चिच्चिक see Art. 45.

सगर्वं: which would be out of place for the plaintive calls of other Cātakas. In the second, सारङ्ग is clearly the Pied Crested Cuckoo, at least for purposes of the last verse where the cloud is called जललवमुच् to suit the 'drop-craving' bird—'स्तोकक'. सारङ्ग has three other specific senses—"सारङ्गश्चातके भृङ्गे कुरङ्गे च मतङ्गजे—" विश्वप्रकाश, and it would appear that the term is to be taken in all its four senses—one for everyone of the four lines. The नीप or कदम्ब tree is also called भ्रमरेष्ट or भृङ्गवल्लभ, 'beloved of the large Black Bee', two varieties of which are known as सारङ्ग (variegated) viz. (i) Xylocopa aestuans and (ii) X. basalis, as both of them have white or yellow pubescence on their backs. The first is found throughout India and the second in North India. The Bee-lines making for the नीप trees are supposed to lead the way for the Cloud. कन्दलीप्रिय is a kind of deer, probably the Spotted Deer (हिन्दी शब्द सागर) which is सारङ्ग in Sanskrit, and a herd of these, advancing to feed upon the newly risen कन्दली (kind of lily plants which sprout up with the first showers), are the सारङ्गा: understood in the second line. The third refers to elephants, with reddish-white marks (पद्म or पद्मक) on their bodies and hence called सारङ्ग, sniffing their way in search of new grass; Cf. the following references to this same habit of elephants:—

"त्वन्निष्यन्दोच्छ्वसितवसुधागन्धसम्पर्करम्यः
स्रोतोरन्ध्रध्वनितमधुरं दन्तिभिः पीयमानः।"

मेघदूत, 44.

"तदाननं मृत्सुरभि क्षितीश्वरो
रहस्युपाघ्राय न तृप्तिमाययौ।
करीव सिक्तं पृषतैः पयोमुचां
शुचिव्यपाये वनराजिपल्वलम्॥" रघुवंश, 3.3.

चारित्रवर्धनाचार्य adopts this interpretation of the verse in his commentary on मेघदूत and I submit, correctly. The plaintive wail of Rāma for Sītā is likened to the persistent call-notes of the सारङ्ग:—

"एवमादिनरश्रेष्ठो विललाप नृपात्मजः।
विहङ्ग इव सारङ्गः सलिलं त्रिदशेश्वरात्॥"

रामायण, 4.30.13

The smaller form of the Pied Crested Cuckoo is permanently resident in Ceylon and part of the Madras Presidency. The larger form, which is migratory, occurs in the rest of India, and "there is reason to believe that it winters in Africa" (Whistler). Salim Ali also remarks that "the larger '*Pica*' is a rains (breeding) visitor to the rest of our area (i.e. excluding Ceylon and South India), presumably from Africa". He adds further that "The arrival in our midst of the larger migrant race coincides with the onset of the S-W Monsoon". The सारङ्ग चातक thus moves northward in India with the Monsoon and the poetical suggestion of the birds acting as guides to the Cloud in his north-bound journey is based on this observed fact of nature. The bees, deer and wild elephants are introduced to complete the picture.

13. These birds leave the country with their young after they have been reared by their foster parents by the end of October and are not seen again in the country for nearly six months, i.e. till about June. They were therefore supposed to spend this time out of sight and hence the name दिवौकस् (one living in heaven, Himalayas or the sky). Belief in the invisibility of the white Wagtail for a period of five months, April to August, due to its growing a crest offers a good parallel to the above (Art. 26). कालिदास has incorporated this belief regarding the सारङ्ग चातक in the following verse where king दुष्यन्त's sky-going chariot encounters the birds above the clouds:—

> "अयमरविवरेभ्यश्चातकै र्निष्पतद्भिः
> हरिभिरचिरभासां तेजसा चानुलिप्तैः।
> गतमुपरिघनानां वारिगर्भोदराणां
> पिशुनयति रथस्ते सीकरक्लिन्ननेमिः॥" शाकुन्तल,[11] 7.7

It is worth noting in this connection that the whole of the action of the Sixth Act, the immediately following journey of king दुष्यन्त to इन्द्र's heaven, his brief stay there and return (Act 7) take place in the spring season, and the existence of the चातक birds in the region beyond the clouds coincides with the absence of the Pied Crested Cuckoos from the country below. Additional support for this view is found in another mythological name for the चातक, viz., त्रिशंकु (शब्दकल्पद्रुम and शब्दार्थचिन्तामणि) based on the Purāṇic story of a king of that name who being unable to go straight to heaven was changed into a constellation and remained suspended midway between heaven and earth through the power of sage विश्वामित्र. त्रिशङ्कु is also the migratory Wagtail according to M. Williams. The Mt. Everest Expedition of 1922 saw this Cuckoo in the Himalayas at an elevation of 14000 feet.[12] It is a दिवौकस् indeed and कालिदास had good reason to place it there.

14. The Red-winged Crested Cuckoo is resident in the Himalayas and in South India. Its voice is a very loud, harsh scream, utterred constantly during the breeding season (May and June in the Western Himalayas) and fairly often at other times. Since its call is neither sonorous nor plaintive in character it cannot be termed a चातक. किङ्किर means

---

11. Kālidāsa seems to have borrowed the idea of the birds' passing between the spokes of a fast-moving wheel from the महाभारत (I.33.4) where गरुड is said to have reduced himself in size and got through a fast-moving wheel to bring away the strongly guarded अमृत.

12. J.B.N.H.S. XXX, 682.

'a Cuckoo' and also the 'red colour'[13] and it is suggested that because of the presence of red in the wings and the shape of the body and parasitic habits being those of a Cuckoo, the name किङ्कुर suits this bird more than any other Cuckoo.

15. चातक in the well known verse of भर्तृहरि beginning "रे रे चातक सावधानमनसा"—can only be the Hawk Cuckoo which calls aloud and incessantly. Similarly the चातक of the following verse is again the same, as the सारङ्ग चातक visits North India only during the rains:—

"ग्रीष्मे ग्रीष्मतरैः करैर्दिनकृता दग्धोऽपि यश्चातकः।
त्वां ध्यायन् घन वासरान्कथमपि द्राघीयसो नीतवान्॥"
भामिनीविलास, 1.33.

I may here point out a slight error of interpretation of the following half verse:—

"तत्किं प्रोषितभर्तृवध्य पटहो हा हा हताशः बकः।
प्रावृट् प्रावृडिति ब्रवीति शठधीः क्षारं क्षते प्रक्षिपन्॥
मृच्छकटिक, 5.18

Here the guilty bird calling "प्रावृट्" "प्रावृट्" is of course a चातक for which the poet has used "बक" as a term of contempt and abuse, but Prof. R. B. Karmarkar holds too literally that the "wretched heron'' ('Stork' per R. B. Raddy and V. G. Paranjape) is calling "प्रावृट्" "प्रावृट्". बक—Stork, Heron or the white Ibis—is in the first place too mean a bird to be seriously mentioned in describing the noble sentiment of love. Secondly, the Storks are voiceless; no Heron calls loudly enough or persistently, and the White Ibis just booms. It is only the birds belonging to the "भद्र" or "मङ्गल्य पक्षिणः like the Swan, Goose, Flamingo, Peacock, Cuckoo and चातक that have been referred to in love-poetry. Again, S. P. Pandit, quoted with approval by M. R. Kale in his notes on रघुवंश 5.17 is categorical that the Crested Cuckoo has a long bow-shaped crest, pulled back and held fast by an arrow-like attachment which prevents any downward movement of the bird's head and bill, and it is therefore impossible for it to drink any but rain-water. I need hardly add that the idea is fantastic in the extreme, and the चातक birds have as free a neck and head as any other bird and there is nothing in their bodily structure to prevent them from drinking ground-water if they want to. Pandit was possibly misled by a verse like the following:—

"नीलाब्जपुञ्जरजसारुणितान्विमुच्य
स्वच्छान्सुधाधिकरसानपि वारिराशीन्।

13. See derivation of किङ्कुरात and other terms with the same base in शब्दकल्पद्रुम. The word also means the Aśoka tree which bears red flowers, and the red or yellow amaranthus.

यश्चातकः पिबति वारिधरोदबिन्दून्
मन्ये तदानतिभयाच्छिरसोऽभिमानी" ॥

सुभाषितावलि, 679

Not only Pandit but a lesser poet[14] also has misunderstood the above verse when borrowing from it.

Like the कोकिल there is ample poetic coinage for the चातक as well, e.g. मेघचिन्तक, वनतोल, ककुञ्जल, धाराट, तञ्जल, etc.

B. NON-PARASITIC CUCKOOS

1. This group includes the Coucal (Crow-Pheasant), the Malkohas and the Sirkeers, commonly known as Ground-Cuckoos as all of them are of terrestrial habits. The Coucal has a shining black body and chestnut-red wings; the large Green-billed Malkoha has a green gloss on the upper plumage and a hooked green bill; and the Sirkeers also have green in the plumage but have red and yellow parrot-like bills. All have long heavy tails.

2. The Coucal is one of the best known birds of the country with a characteristic call, a deep and rather sonorous hoop-hoop-hoop, heard at all times of the day but more often early in the morning. As the calling progresses, the number of hoops frequently increases and sometimes as many as twenty-five hoops are uttered at a stretch. The oldest name for it is कुक्कुभ placed in the विष्किर group of birds in चरक as it hunts mostly on the ground for insects, caterpillars, grasshoppers, lizards, small snakes etc. Whistler notes that due to its heavy build, slow gait and the habit of feeding on the ground it is often mistaken for a game bird (विष्किर). Other names for it are—कुलालकुक्कुट, कुलालकुक्कुम, कुम्भकारकुक्कुट, कुलाल, कुकुभ, and कुम्भ. Lexical synonymies are as under:—

(i) "कुम्भकारकुक्कुटस्तु कुक्कुभः कुहकस्वनः"—कुम्भेति शब्दं करोति कुम्भकारः स कुक्कुट इव कुम्भकारकुक्कुटः। कोकतेकुक्कुभः; कु कु शब्देन भाति इति वा। कुहक इति स्वनोऽस्यकुहुकस्वनः।" अभिधानचिन्तामणि.

(ii) "कुलालो घूक पक्षिणि कुक्कुभे"—हेमचन्द्र.

(iii) "कुलालं कुक्कुटं प्राहुः कुक्कुभं कुहकस्वरम्"—हारावली.

(iv) "कुलालः कुम्भकारे स्यात् ककुभे (कुकुभे?) कौशिके"—पेरुसूरि.

(v) "कुकुभः पक्षिविशेषः"—उणादि भोजीयानि.

The word "कुक्कुट" in the above compound names simply means a 'bird' in general as in प्रासादकुक्कुट for a Pigeon. कुलाल or कुम्भकार means 'potter' and the sound of tapping or blowing into an empty earthern jar seems to

14. Author of verses 1746 and 1786, in सुभाषितावलि.

have offered an excellent parallel for the voice of two birds— (i) a particular kind of hooting owl, known as कुलाल and कुम्भोलूक (Art, 49) and (ii) the Coucal, named कुम्भ in मत्स्यपुराण 118, 51; cf. रिक्तकुम्भ, 'voice of an empty vessel'—M.W.

3. The identity of कुलालकुक्कुट and कुलालकुक्कुभ together with the splitting up of the former into "कुलालं कुक्कुटं "in the हारावली has led to an incorrect synonymy of कुक्कुट with कुक्कुभ though these two names standing by themselves are altogether different, कुक्कुट being the Common or the Wild Cock and कुक्कुभ the Coucal; Cf. जलकुक्कुभ for the Water-Cock which too has a booming call. None of the important lexicons like अमरकोश, अभिधान चिन्तामणि, त्रिकाण्डशेष, कल्पद्रु कोश धन्वन्तरिनिघण्टु and राजनिघण्टु mentions कुक्कुभ as a synonym for कुक्कुट, a cock. On the other hand there is literary evidence to show that कुक्कुभ is quite a different bird from the Jungle Fowl (कुक्कुट):—

"कोकिलांच्छतपत्रांश्च सकोयष्टिक कुक्कुभान्।
मयूरान्कुक्कुटान् हंसान्सारसांश्चक्रसाह्वयान्॥"

महाभारत, 13.54.10-11

The वेस्संतर जातक also clearly distinguished between कुक्कुट and कुक्कुह (कुक्कुभ):—

"चंकोरा कुक्कुटा नागा अञ्जमञ्जपकूजिनो"— Verse, 2098

"करविया च सग्गा च उहुंकारा च कुक्कुहा"— Verse, 2100

Thus कुक्कुभ in the following is the Coucal and not a cock:—

"वीरुन्नीडकपोतकूजिमनुक्रन्दन्त्यधः कुक्कुभाः"

मालतीमाधव, 9.7.

The full verse describes a mid-day scene in the hot weather and the idea in the above line is that while the Doves are continuously cooing high up in their resting places the Coucals are 'hooping' lower down in the trees. The word क्रन्दन implies 'continuous calling' and suits the Coucals better than the wild cocks that go to rest and sleep and ordinarily do not crow during the hot hours of the day. The onomatopoetic explanation of the name कुक्कुभ given in अभिधानचिन्तामणि and the Marathi name for the Coucal, कुंभार कुकड़ी (from कुम्भकार कुक्कुट) leave no doubt whatever about its identity, and the rendering of "Phasianus gallus" i.e. the wild cock, in M. Williams is incorrect.

4. Each of the two lines of the following verse from the कल्पद्रुकोश is descriptive of a single bird, the first deals with नीलच्छवि the Fairy Blue-Bird (Art. 18) and the second with the Coucal:—

"नीलच्छविः कृष्णगलः स ग्रामचटकाकृतिः।
ककुभः ककुभाकारः स्थलजो रक्तपर्णकः॥"

Two other variants of the verse are as below:—

"नीलच्छविः कृष्णगलः स्याद्ग्रामचटकाकृतिः।
कुक्कुभः कुक्कुभारावः स्थलजो रक्तवर्त्मकः॥"

Quoted in the gloss on अष्टांगहृदय, Paradkar's edition, N. S. 1939.

"सितपुच्छो नीलगलः स्याद् ग्रामचटकाकृतिः।
कुक्कुटः कुक्कुटारावः स्थलजो रक्तवर्णकः॥"

Quoted by Tripurari on मालतीमाधव, 9.7, Niraṇaya Sāgar edition, 1926, and M. R. Kale in his Notes on the same, Poona.

A descriptive synonymy for the bird known as ककुभ occurs separately in the कल्पद्रुकोश : "चित्रवर्णस्तु ककुभो". K. M. Vaidya in his अष्टांगहृदयकोश renders कुक्कुभ as a variety of the Red Jungle Fowl; a large type of cock per चक्रदत्त or according to some (इति केचित्) even the Turkey-Cock (?).

5. With कुक्कुभ as a certainty for the Coucal and रक्तवर्त्मक for Pheasants having red orbital skin it is difficult to resist the conclusion that the correct original reading of the second half of the above verse was as under:

"कुक्कुभः कुक्कुभारावः स्थलजो रक्तपर्णकः।"

and the descriptive words ककुभः ककुभाकारः belong to a different synonymy for the bird named ककुभ which besides being a heavy plump bird resembling in outline the gourd fitted to a guitar or वीणा as a sound box (ककुभो वीणाङ्गे। अर्धाबद्धालाबूमय भाण्डे—वाचस्पत्यम्; वीणा प्रसेवे—हेमचन्द्र, कल्पद्रु) had also a variegated plumage (चित्रवर्णस्तु ककुभो), and I have identified this truly ककुभाकार bird with the Himalayan Snow Cock (Art. 55). The epithets रक्तवर्णक and रक्तवर्मक are evidently wrong readings inserted by ignorant scribes. The Coucal being a black bird with chestnut-red wings has a better claim to the attribute of रक्तपर्णक than to the others. Similarly the incorrect reading of कुक्कुटारावः is due to the confusion between कुक्कुभ and कुक्कुट. The epithet स्थलज (land-born) really distinguishes it as स्थलकुक्कुभ from the Water-Cock which is जलकुक्कुभ (Art. 58), the call of both being of a booming variety (कुक्कुभारावः). The red glow of sun has been compared with the chestnut-coloured wings of the coucal:—

"कुम्भकार कुक्कुटपक्षविच्छाय मनाक्तमोनुविद्ध संध्यारागः।"

नलचम्पू, 5, after verse 76

The Hindi name for the Coucal is महोक which it is difficult to derive though it may be from मुहुः+क, मुहुर्मुहुः कायते or मही with ओकस्, or again from मधुक, a sweet-calling bird, with a secondary reference to मधुक, 'a bard' or मागध who wakes up royalty with soft music in the morning. The Coucal too begins its hooping call at dawn; cf. the following:—

"प्रबोध्यते मागधसूत पूगैर्नित्यंस्तुवद्भिः स्वयमिद्रकल्पः।"

महाभारत, 3.236.10

6. Malkohas and Sirkeers frequent undergrowth and forest or scrub-jungle and are seldom seen in the open. Their food chiefly consists of insects, grasshoppers etc. and also berries for which they hunt in bushes and trees. They are *great skulkers* and prefer to seek safety by foot rather than by wing and are expert in threading their way through tangled scrub and dense bushes. They are generally silent birds and their voice is a soft chuckle or a croak. चरक mentions three names for birds of the Cuckoo family together.... कैरात, कोकिल, and अत्यूह (Hawk Cuckoo) in the प्रतुद class. कैरात means a 'forester and a dwarf (वामन) and is a most appropriate name for Malkohas and Sirkeers. The Small Green-billed Malkoha of South India is 'वामन काकी' in Telugu, so that the allied bird of the North, viz. the Large Green-billed Malkoha should be the कैरात of चरक. The following description of the natural secretive instincts of किरात and कुब्ज is fully applicable to the birds in question:—

"पर्यन्ताश्रयिभिर्निजस्य सदृशं नाम्नः किरातैः कृतं
कुब्जा नीचतयैव यान्ति शनकैरात्मेक्षणाशङ्किनः।"

रत्नावली, 2.3

किङ्किर according to the lexicons means a Cuckoo or a Koel, and किङ्किरात 'a Parrot as well as a Cuckoo'. Now the Sirkeer Cuckoos are known as जंगली तोता in Hindi and 'Adavi chilluka' in Telugu, both names meaning 'Jungle-Parrot' from their green upper parts and red curved bills. Again, the Large Himalayan Green-billed Malkoha goes by the name of बन कोकिल (Jungle Cuckoo) in Bengal. A comparison of these local names with किङ्किरात (of the nature of a किरात) in its two senses makes it abundantly clear that the name किङ्किरात like कैरात of चरक really belongs to these birds of the Cuckoo family and not to the Cuckoo proper or the Koel. It is also a synonym for the red-breasted Paroquest or पीतभद्र शुक in शब्दार्थचिन्तामणि.

7. Finally, the term 'गेलाट', name of a particular bird in the Fifth Pillar (Delhi-Topra) Edict of Aśoka would seem to be the same as कैरात[1], and evidently refers to the Malkohas and Sirkeers. It is also highly probable that the अंगहेतुक, a forest bird of the Himalayas, named in the वेस्संतर जातक, Verse 2099 , is the Larger Himalayan Green-billed Malkoha or one of the two Sirkeer Cuckoos, the Punjab Sirkeer and the Bengal Sirkeer Cuckoo, the latter of which also occurs in Nepal and Bihar, or all three taken as a group of skulking birds. Etymologically the name should mean one who is anxious about his personal safety and therefore conceals himself —in short a skulker, from अङ्ग plus हेतु or हित; Cf. गुहाहितम् concealed in secret (RV.4.5.8). The Pali name would thus seem to correspond to आत्मेक्षणाशङ्किनः descriptive of the कुब्ज people in the quotation from रत्नावली given above.

1. कैरात—गेलात—गेलाट– cf. Marathi आमटा for Sk. आम्नात, and Prakrit केटा for क्रेता, किरात—किराड. ड in Prakrit is often replaced with ट.

38

PAROQUETS OR PARROTS

1. The Parrots of North India have been divided into two genera, one of which is represented by five and the other by a single species. They are all of a predominantly green colour and differ little in their habits. Though normally arboreal they are attracted in large flocks to ripening crops like paddy and sorghum (juar) to the great despair of the cultivator and have been regarded with birds like the Buntings (अन्नदूषक) as one of the natural calamities (ईतयः) befalling a country. All the same, their brilliant plumage, quaint habits, "sedate and knowing demeanour" and, above all, their teachability to talk and perform tricks have endeared them to the people and made them one of the most favourite cage-birds of India from very ancient times.

2. "The Parrots rank as among the most intelligent of birds. The mere talking to which they can be trained is nothing. The wisdom of the bird judged by this standard, is inferred from the degree of appositenees with which it utters its phrases." (Harmsworth Popular Science, p. 2978). The European students of Indian bird-life do not, however, credit any of the Indian species with ability to talk beyond a few words; nevertheless, Sanskrit literature attributes considerable ability to them in this respect and whole verses have been placed in their and the Hill-Maina's mouths. A couple of such examples are reproduced below:—

A Parrot to his beloved Maina:—

"आलिङ्ग प्रतिवाचमुद्गिर सुधाकण्ठि ! क्व भूयो वयः ।
कोपं मुञ्च मयि प्रसीद सुभगे ! नैवं विधास्ये पुनः ।।" भाव-शतक 54

The following half verse may well have been taught to a royal Parrot in the ordinary way though the next two lines (not reproduced here) give it a topical setting. On the defeat of his royal patron, the bird, released from his cage, is supposed to address a painting of his master in the royal Picture-gallery:

"राजन् ! राजसुता न पाठयति मां देव्योऽपि तूष्णीं स्थिताः ।
कुब्जे ! भोजय मां कुमार सचिवैर्नाद्यापि किं भुज्यते ।।"

काव्यप्रकाश 10.94

If such examples had not been true a compliment like चाटु-गाथा-समुच्चारण contained in the following beautiful passage would not have been paid to a pet bird. The poet describes goddess पार्वती as playing with her pet bird—

"सर्वविद्याविशेषात्मकं, चाटुगाथासमुच्चारणं,
कण्ठमूलोल्लसद्वर्णराजित्रयं, कोमलश्यामलोदारपक्षद्वयं,
तुण्डशोभातिदूरीभवत्किंशुकं, तं शुकं लालयन्ती परिक्रीडसे ॥"

काव्यमाला 1, श्यामला–दण्डक 5

nor would poet कुसुमदेव have written :

"शुक: श्लोकान् वक्तुं प्रभवति न काक: क्वचिदपि"

काव्यमाला, 14, दृष्टान्तकलिकाशतक, पृ॰ 86

Compare also:

"नित्याकर्णनया शुकेन च पदं साम्नामिदं गीयते"

नागानन्द 1.10

3. शुकसारिकाप्रलापन was one of the arts practised in India by professional men like the trainers of Song-finches, Canaries, Thrushes, etc. in Europe today, and no one need be surprised at the performances of exceptionally talented Parrots and Mainas recorded in Indian literature,[1] barring, of course, poetic exaggeration in attributing to them human intelligence and capacity to make impromptu replies or even to carry on a conversation. I have myself heard a Rose-ringed Paroquet repeat the following Hindi verse without a hitch though the articulation was certainly not equal to that of the Maina—

चित्रकूट के घाट पै भइ संतन की भीर।
तुलसीदास चन्दन घिसैं तिलक देत रघुबीर ॥

i.e., "In the midst of a gathering of saints at the waters near Chitrakoot Tulsidas prepared the sandal-paste and god Ramachandra applied it to his forehead."

4. Literary tradition has regarded a talking Parrot (शुक) as the mate of a talking Hill-Maina (सारिका), and it is on this supposition that वच is a Parrot and वचा a Maina, and if he is मेधावी she is मेधाविनि which, by the way, is also the name of a most intelligent Maina in रत्नावली, 2.5.6. Even Keśava, the commentator of the कौशिकसूत्र, would seem to have succumbed to this tradition, for he renders रोपणाका of AV. 1.22.4 as काष्ठसुक[2] and, following him, Sāyaṇācārya also has translated रोपणाका (loc. cit.) as काष्ठशुकाख्यपक्षी and again as शुकां or female Parrot in his notes on तैत्तिरीय-संहिता 3.7.6 although in his commentary on RV. 1.50.12 he correctly explains the term to mean a सारिका.

---

1. Parrots taught to repeat Lord Buddha's maxims have been described as शाक्य शासन कुशल in हर्षचरित, 8.

2. M. Bloomfield's edition, 1890, p. 326. The insertion of मु in काष्ठमुसुकं and the masculine gender would seem to be clerical errors.

5. Common names for all Parrots, except the Loriquet are शुक and कीर, but there is reason to believe that the larger members of the group were designated as शुक and the smaller varieties like the Blossom-headed and the Slaty-headed Paroquets, which have a much softer voice than the former, as कीर (कीति अव्यक्तं शब्दं ईरयति). Names like चिरि, चिमि, and चिमिक for a Parrot are also indicative of softer notes and must belong to them. This distinction still obtains in their vernacular names, e.g., सुग्गा or तोता for the large and टुइयां for the small Parrots in Hindi, and पोपट or राघू and कीर in Marathi. The mention of both शुक and कीर in the following extracts from (i) the Skanda Purāṇa, Vaiṣṇavakhaṇḍa and (ii) Padma-Purāṇa, Uttarakhaṇḍa are clearly based upon the above distinction and fully support it :

(i) मयूर-कीर-गरुड-शुक-सारस-संकुलान्

Veṅkaṭācala Māhātmya 5.52

(ii) हंसैः कीरेषु पाण्डित्यं कुर्वाणैः सङ्कुले शुकै"

Ch. 180.21

In literature and lexicons, however, the difference between शुक and कीर has been entirely done away with. Adnouns like त्रिकेतु, रक्त–or वक्र–तुण्ड, प्रियदर्शन, etc., apply to all Parrots but the epithet दण्डी belongs to a pet bird as 'always holding on to his perch-rod', and also, humorously, to his leading 'an ascetic and celibate life by compulsion'; cf. कान्तां विना सीदतः said of one in सुभाषितरत्नभाण्डागार p. 228, verse 222. मञ्जुपाठक is true of only such birds as are able to talk.

With these preliminary remarks I proceed to a consideration of individual names for the six species of Parrot found in North India.

6. The Large Indian Paroquet (21″) is marked on the wing with a large maroon-red patch. The bill is wholly red as compared with others whose lower mandible is differently coloured, and the legs and feet are of a dirty-flesh colour. Being the largest Parrot of India it is the राजशुक or शतपत्रशुक of the lexicons—

"अन्यो महान् राजशुकः शतपत्रो निगद्यते" धन्वंतरि

No Indian Parrot has red legs and the epithet रक्तपाद for one may be rendered as 'red-marked' (पादः चिह्नः अङ्कः—वैजयन्ती and विश्व) and in this sense it should belong to this bird after the conspicuous red wingpatches rather than the colour of the feet. The Blossom-headed Paroquet also has a small and inconspicuous red spot on the wing but is better named कृष्णाङ्ग शुक after its deep purplish-red head. Other poetic names for this bird are प्राज्ञ, वाग्मिन्, नृपप्रिय, etc.

7. The Rose-ringed Paroquet (16″) is the commonest and by far the most numerous of all and, as it moves in large flocks, it is the one that is responsible for a major part of the total damage caused to the crops by all the Parrots put together. It is the बाहुज शुक (बाहुल्येन अतिशयेन जातः, very prolific?) of the lexicons but its proper name is काष्ठशुक (wild or inferior) both

according to वसन्तराज, हंसादिप्रकरण 15, and केशव and सायणाचार्य as already pointed out in para 4 above. Its Hindi name, कठल सुआ is an exact rendering of काष्ठ शुक.

8. The Blossom-headed Paroquet (15″) is कृष्णोत्तमाङ्ग or कृष्णांग शुक in कल्पद्रुकोश and Monier Williams respectively, from the colour of the head in the male. It also shares the name of कीर with the next.

9. The Slaty-headed Paroquet (16″) is the पतिचञ्चुशुक of कल्पद्रु after the colour of the bill. The upper mandible is orange-yellow and the lower yellowish. In the Blossom-headed variety the lower mandible is black.

10. The Indian Red-breasted Paroquet (15″) is पीतवर्ण शुक (Monier Williams) or पीतभद्र शुक (well-marked with yellow) referring to the yellow patches on its wings, and also किङ्किरात शुक (किङ्किरं रक्तवर्णत्वं अतति— शब्दकल्पद्रुम; पीतभद्रः किङ्किरातशुके—शब्दार्थचिन्तामणि) from its red breast. A common synonymy obtains for bird and plant in this as in the case of भृङ्गराज the Large Racket-tailed Drongo (Art. 15):—

किङ्किरातो हेमगौरः पीतको पीतभद्रकः—भावप्रकाश, पुष्पवर्ग.

The similarity of the Hindi मदन गौर for it with हेमगौर in the above equation is also worth noting. The श्येत शुक of the तत्ति. संहिता. 5.5.12

सरस्वते शुकः श्येतः पुरुषवाक्

is evidently this Parrot as the adjective श्येत signifies the reddish colour in the bird's plumage, and the name corresponds to किङ्किरात.

11. Lastly, the Indian Loriquet (5.5.″), which is no bigger than a Sparrow, is the पत्रशुक of वसन्तराज, हंसादिप्रकरण, 16, पर्णशुक of कल्पद्रु and भेदाशी of सुश्रुत, rendered as पुत्रशुक by डल्हणाचार्य. The first two names imply the colour assimilation of the bird with the green foliage of a tree; cf. पत्रगुप्त for the Chloropsis in Art. 5 B. Salim Ali makes the following observations about these tiny birds: "On account of their small size and the wonderful obliterative effect of their colouration when clambering about among the foliage of tall trees, the birds are seldom seen except when flying accross from one tree to another." The name पुत्रशुक, on the other hand, indicates its tiny size; cf. पुत्रक and पुत्रिका for very small birds in Art. 22 B, and their habit of breaking open the hardest of nuts is reflected in the name भेदाशी. It has a short tail and no collar, and is therefore not a त्रिकेतु.

12. The flight of Parrots is very swift and a flock flying to or from rich crops in the open, or hurtling through the forest, swerving gracefully to avoid trees and branches, is always a fine sight. A selection of verses in appreciation of their beauty at close quarters and high up on the wing should prove interesting—

"तुण्डैराताम्रकुटिलैः पक्षैर्हरितकोमलैः ।
त्रिवर्णराजिभिः कण्ठैरेते मञ्जुगिरः शुकाः"

काव्यादर्श 2.9

Parrots descending upon a paddy-field—

यत्र शालिवनोपान्ते खात्पतन्तीं शुकावलीम् ।
शालिगोप्योऽनुमन्यन्ते दधतीं तोरणश्रियम् ।।

Ādi-Purāṇa of Guṇabhadra, 4. 61

And pretty peasant-girls, dressed in green, driving them away—

शुकाञ्छुकच्छदच्छायैं रुचिराङ्गी स्तनांशुकैः ।
छोत्कुर्वतीः कलक्वाणं सोऽपश्यच्छालिगोपिकाः ।।

Ibid. 35.36

A Yakṣa describes to Arjuna a flight of Parrots, many carrying golden ears of paddy in their bills—

मुखैरसौ विद्रुमभङ्गलोहितैः
शिखाः पिशङ्गीः कलमस्य बिभ्रती ।
शुकावलिर्व्यक्तशिरीषकोमला
धनुश्रियं गोत्रभिदोऽनुगच्छति ।।

Kirātārjunīya, 4.36

Poet माघ also presents a similar picture—

हरितपत्रमयीव मरुद्गणैः
स्रगवनद्धमनोरमपल्लवा ।
मधुरिपोरभिताम्रमुखी मुदं
दिवि तता विततान शुकावलिः ।।

Śiśupāla-vadha, 6.53

39

ROLLERS

The Rollers were formerly classed with the Jays by ornithologists who named them as Blue Jays; but they have now been separated and placed in a separate family of birds. In India also both Rollers and Jays appear to have been regarded as an allied group, going under the common name of चाष. Sanskrit nomenclature for both has, therefore, been considered in Art 1-E.

40

THE BEE-EATERS (शार्ङ्गाः)

1. The Bee-eaters with their bright green, blue, bronze, and chestnut plumage are among "the most resplendent birds of the world" and their place in the Fauna of British India (Birds) is between the Rollers (चाषाः) and the Kingfishers (मत्स्यरङ्काः). All of them have about the same habits. They feed on insects including bees and even wasps which they capture in the air and after each sally return to their perch, uttering pleasant whistling notes on the wing. A party of them hawking insects over water is a pretty sight indeed. They often live in colonies and excavate almost horizontal tunnels about two inches in diameter and several feet long in the banks of rivers, streams, bridle paths, etc. and even on level ground, and it is at the far end of such a hole that a rounded chamber is made for eggs and young. Sometimes they utilize deserted rat holes as well.[1]

2. They are represented by no fewer than seven species in different parts of India and four of them, which are the subject of this article, occur within the territories called ब्रह्मर्षिदेश and मध्यदेश as defined in Manu-smṛti, 2.19 & 21, i.e. from East-Punjab to about Allahabad, including the outer Himalayan valleys to the north and the Vindhyas to the south. The best known of the series is the Common Indian Bee-eater (9" long) known as पत्रिगा[2] (from पत्रिन् 'arrow') in Hindi and वेदराघू (the 'Vedic or holy parrot'—'parrot' after its predominantly green colour) in Marāthi. It is a "most elegant little bird" and with its predominantly green, bronze or gold, and chestnut plumage, a long, slender slightly curved and pointed bill and the habit of catching its insect food on the wing from a perch on a tree or low bush, and its sweet 'tit tit' or 'tiree tiree tiree' call uttered on the wing it is easily identified.

3. The Blue-tailed Bee-eater is 12" in length and has a fully 2" long pointed bill. Though, like the Common Bee-eater, it is a plains species, it is partial to the neighbourhood of rivers, jheels and tanks. Its voice is a mellow rolling whistle or a chirp like 'teerp' or 'te tew, te tew' (cf. पिप्पका below). The Bearded Bee-eater, a magnificent bird, full 14" long, with a rather

---

1. G.F.L. Marshall in 'Birds' Nesting in India'.
2. पत्रिगा should be a semi तद्भव term fully comparable with शार्ङ्ग mentioned later.

heavy bill of over 2″, is the largest member of the family. It is entirely a forest bird, feeds little on the wing and lives mainly on insects and honey which it seeks among the leaves and flowers on tree-tops. It utters its harsh double notes first with the head held low and the long blue throat feathers puffed out; with each succeeding note the head is gradually raised and the last of the series is sounded with the head pointing straight up, perhaps reminiscent of the head movements of the उद्गाता ![1] The Chestnut-headed Bee-eater (9.5″) captures its food on the wing and its evolutions in the air are extremely beautiful accompanied by a most musical trill, uttered every few minutes. It nests in banks of rivers or, like the Common Bee-eater, in almost level sandy ground. These Chestnut-headed are amongst the earliest bird risers and their pleasant notes may be heard almost with the first glimmer of light in the morning, especially if their roosting place is one among the tall reeds of a river bank. The Common Bee-eaters on the other hand are late risers and stir out only when the sun is well up.[2]

4. The Common Indian, the European,[3] and the Blue-tailed Bee-eaters have the two middle tail feathers longer than the others, with their terminal portions narrow and a little separated from each other. In their very graceful sailing flight the outline of these birds resembles or recalls to one's mind the shape of a drawn bow with an arrow mounted on it ready to shoot. The long, thin and sharply pointed bill represents the pointed head of the arrow and the square part of the tail, showing equally on both sides of the central tail feathers, corresponds to the feathered part of the arrow, while the projecting central feathers separated towards the end resemble the split end of the shaft (कर्तरी) which rests on the bow-string where the bowman grips and pulls it hard towards himself before letting the arrow go for the target. A good look at a Bee-eater during its sailing flight would bear out the picture suggested above. The Chestnut-headed and the Blue-bearded varieties have even tails, i.e. they lack the projected central tail feathers.

5. A majority of these birds include in their dietary a large proportion of honey-bees and hence the common English name of Bee-eater for them all.[4] The oldest and the most-picturesque Sanskrit name for them, based upon their shape in flight and upon their surety of aim in catching flying insects (like a good marksman hitting the target with his arrow) is शार्ग (शर arrow) or शाङ्गं (Viṣṇu's bow; शृङ्गस्य विकारः शाङ्गं:, तद्वत् रूपं आचरणं वा अस्य). The करञ्ज tree (Pongamia glabra) when in blossom, is visited by large numbers of bees and the latter in turn attract the Bee-eaters. The tree

1. Cf. उद्गातेव शकुने साम गायसि—said of the कपिञ्जल bird in RV 2.43.2. The Bee-eaters have been described as ब्रह्मवादिनः, 'prayer-singers' in MBh.; see below.

2. F.B.I. (Birds), second edition and 'The Book of Indian Birds' by Salim Ali where three of them are illustrated in colour.

3. This allied form (10.5″) is confined to the extreme North-West of India including Kashmir.

4. They are a regular pest at all apiaries.

is therefore also known as शाङ्गेष्ट (beloved of the Bee-eater) just as the शिरीष (Acacia sirissa) is शुकेष्ट and the निम्ब (Melia azadirachta), काकेष्ट. Pali सग्ग as a bird-name in Vessantar Jātaka, verse 2100, is the same as शार्ग.

6. According to the वैजयन्ती कोश the terms शाङ्गं, कीर्शा and पिप्पिका are synonymous, which however is open to doubt as we shall presently see. The name कीर्शा (v.l. कीर्षा) is perhaps derived from root कृश् to 'draw or bend a bow' and corresponds in meaning to शाङ्गीं or शार्ङ्गिका, the feminine of शाङ्गं; cf. कृशानु (कृष्-कृश्, कर्षति धनुम्), the archer who guards the Soma in heaven or atmosphere according to the Ṛgveda. पिप्पिका (v.l. पिप्पीका, पिप्पका), feminine of पिप्पिक (पिप्पीक or पिप्पक) is apparently an imitative name after the call note of a particular Bee-eater.

7. These beautiful birds have secured a place of honour with others at the Aśvamedha ritual:

(1)	शार्गः सृजयः शयाण्डकस्ते मैत्रा—	वाज.सं.,24.33.
		मैत्रा.सं.,3.14.14.
(2)	कृकलासः पिप्पका शकुनिस्ते शरव्यायै	वाज.सं.,24.40.
		मैत्रा.सं.,3.14.21.
		तैत्ति.सं.,5.5.19.
		काठ.सं.,5.7.9.
(3)	ब्रह्मणे शार्गः —	तैत्ति.सं.,5.5.19.
		काठ.सं.,5.7.9.
(4)	इन्द्राण्यै कीर्शा (कीर्षा in काठ.सं.)—	तैत्ति.सं.,5.5.20.
		काठ.सं.,5.7.10.

It will be seen that पिप्पका the female of the पिप्पक Bee-eater has been dedicated to शरव्या,[1] the female deity presiding over 'marksmanship' or the 'art of archery' in all the four Saṁhitās; the male शार्ग is assigned to ब्रह्मन्, the 'lord of prayer' or prayer personified, in the TS and to मित्र, the sun in a friendly aspect, in the VS; and the female कीर्शा is named for goddess इन्द्राणी in the TS and KS. The names शार्ग and कीर्शा derived from शर and कृश् respectively, have apparently a similar significance and the male and female birds with these names, being dedicated to male and female deities, it would appear that they belong to the male and female of the same species of Bee-eater. In short, both these names correspond to शाङ्गं (and शाङ्गीं or शार्ङ्गिका of the Mahābhārata; see below). The TS and KS mention all the three names in connection with different deities and it follows that पिप्पका and शार्ग (including कीर्शा as shown above) are two different species of Bee-eater and the synonymy in वैजयन्ती is not wholly correct.

---

1. This dedication to शरव्या supports the derivation of शार्ग from शर given above. M. Williams regards शार्ग as a w.r. of शाङ्गं—but both appear to be correct Sanskrit forms.

8. The commonest of the 'bow and arrow' shaped Bee-eaters is the Common Indian Bee-eater found all over the country, and this should be the शार्ग and कीर्शा of the Saṁhitās. In his commentary on the TS Sāyaṇācārya renders पिप्पका and शार्ग simply as पक्षि विशेष and अरण्य चटक: respectively which does not help at all, but he gives कुलाली शकुनिका as a synonym for कीर्शा, and if कुलाली can be explained as कौ भूम्यां लालयति पालयति शावकान् 'a bird that brings up its young on or under the ground,'[1] the name कुलाली शकुनिका would be fully descriptive of the breeding habit of a Bee-eater particularly as the term शकुनिका implies a 'small bird' which the Common Bee-eater certainly is.

9. This Bee-eater also figures as a bird of augury in Varāhamihira's Bṛhatsaṁhitā under the names of दिव्य or दिव्यक and धन्वन (दिव्यो धन्वन उक्त: —Ch. 87.9: "the shining bird is the 'bow-bird'"), and the rendering of धन्वन as a 'kind of animal' by M. Williams requires correction. The Pārāśara Saṁhitā quoted by Bhaṭṭotpala in his commentary on Bṛhatsaṁhitā, Ch. 85.28, also mentions धन्वन as the bird which breeds during the rainy season. The Common Bee-eater "generally prefers a lower perch than the larger species"[2] and this habit of perching on low bushes has been particularly mentioned in the Bṛhatsaṁhitā which says that the sight of one, on one's left, perched at a height of only one cubit is auspicious and fulfils one's desire:

शस्तं वामे दर्शनं दिव्यकस्य
सिद्धिर्ज्ञेया हस्तमात्रोच्छ्रितस्य । 87.18

10. The Mahābhārata[3] furnishes quite a few interesting facts about these birds, e.g., the standard or war-flag of the brave prince Abhimanyu was quite appropriately emblazoned with the figure of a 'Golden Bee-eater' (हिरण्मय शार्ङ्ग—the golden 'bow-bird'):—

अभिमन्योः कुमारस्य शार्ङ्गपक्षी हिरण्मयः ।
रथे ध्वजवरो राजंस्तप्तचामीकरोज्ज्वलः ॥—
Mbh 7.23.89.

11. It is also interesting to note that, like some other birds, the Bee-eater too has contributed to the mythical code of punishments for certain offences laid down in the great Epic and the Purāṇas. A person, guilty of calumny is doomed to be reborn as a Bee-eater:

---

1. Cf. कुलाल 'a potter'—कुं भूमिं मृत्तिकां वा लाडयति ?

See Śabda-kalpadruma also. कुलाल-कुक्कुट is a Crow-Pheasant, कुंभार कुकड़ी in Marathi, which places its large nest very close to the ground in a large bush and brings up its young in that situation. Similarly the term कुलालं for an owl in अनेकार्थसंग्रह of हेमचन्द्र and the विश्वप्रकाश (Benares editions) should refer to the Grass Owl of N. India which nests on the ground in high grass.

2. F.B.I. (Birds), 1st edition.

3. Oundh and Poona editions.

असूयको नरश्चापि मृतो जायति शार्ङ्गकः—

MBh 13.111.68.

Now a slanderer must have a foul tongue so that when eating bees and wasps in his next life he should be in constant danger of being stung by them on his tongue, a fitting retribution indeed ! But perhaps it was not known that the Bee-eater catches a bee head-foremost, squeezes out and jerks off the sting before swallowing it, and yet how much indeed did the ancients not know about these and other birds ? The later author of the Mārkaṇḍeya Purāṇa[1] appears to have missed the significance of the above punishment and has changed the offence so punishable into one of stealing wearing apparel, probably of a green or golden colour (Ch.15, verse 28). The Garuḍa Purāṇa[1], on the other hand, bearing in mind the following statement of शार्ङ्गिका complaining of desertion by her husband—

इत्येवमुक्त्वा प्रययौ पिता वो निर्घृणः पुरा—

MBh 1.232.10,

condemns a deserter of his wife to be reborn as a शब्दवेधी-प्राणी i.e. a शार्ङ्ग (शब्दवेधी an arrow, प्राणी creature):

धर्मपत्नीं त्यजन् शब्दवेधी प्राणी[2] भवेत् क्षितौ।—

Garuḍa P. II.2.70.

12. Finally, we have the rather detailed and circumstantial story of the bachelor-sage Mandapāla who, to secure his proper place in heaven, had to assume the form of a male Bee-eater (शार्ङ्गक) and beget progeny by a female bird (शार्ङ्गिका). Later on when the young had been born he, privately prayed to god Agni for their safety, and, after telling his bird-wife what his sons would do when grown up, left her. The four bird-sons of his bore the names of जरितारि, सारिसृक्व, स्तम्बमित्र and द्रोण :—

जरितारौ कुलं ह्येतज्ज्येष्ठत्वेन प्रतिष्ठितम्।
सारिसृक्वः प्रजायेत पितॄणां कुलवर्धनः॥
स्तम्बमित्रस्तपः कुर्याद् द्रोणो ब्रह्मविदां वरः।

MBh 1.232. 9, 10.

Soon after however a forest fire breaks out nearby and the lives of the young unfledged birds are in danger and the mother advises them to get into a rat-hole. Ultimately the young birds pray to god Agni who spares them. The mention of the rat-hole clearly shows that the author of the story knew the breeding habits of the birds though he had to place the young out in the open to deck out the story with a pathetic conversation between them and the mother. Now the names of the four birds and the fact of a forest conflagration have certainly been taken from the hymn to the fire-god in

---

1. Venkateshwar Press edition.
2. A deliberately mystifying paraphrase of the name—शार्ङ्ग

RV 10.142 as we shall presently see. For the present let us see if it is possible to distribute the four names among the four North-Indian species of Bee-eaters. जरितारि, the same as जरिता (जरिन्ट singer) of the Veda, is said to be eldest of the four and the physical basis for him should be the Blue-bearded species which is the largest of all. Next comes सारिसृक्व (सारि arrow, with सृक् to be pointed, or सृज् to let go; v.l. सृक्क and सृक्त) who should be the next larger, the Blue-tailed species. The name स्तम्बमित्र for the third शार्ङ्ग clearly implies a type that prefers a low bush for a perch, for स्तम्ब means a bush or clump. It is said to be a phonetic variation of स्तम्भ with probably a slight change in meaning. M. William gives also स्तम्भमित्र as v.l. for स्तम्बमित्र. The RV hymn is a late one and it is suggested that स्तम्ब has the same meaning there as in expressions like स्तम्बशः, 'by clumps or tufts' and स्तम्बिन्, 'bushy' occurring in TB and MS respectively (see M.W.). We have already noted the Common Bee-eater's habit of perching low and it remains to add that such perches are mostly in the open and fully exposed to the sun. The statement, "स्तम्बमित्रस्तपः कुर्यात्" in the verses quoted above from the MBh 1.232, therefore, clearly points to it as स्तम्बमित्र. Lastly, द्रोणो the fourth, is said to be the best of 'praise-singers'—ब्रह्मविदां वरः द्रोणो[1] and the basis for him can only be the Chestnut-headed species which roosts in flocks and begins its trilling chorus with the first glimmer of morning light. The only objection to this allocation of the names is that they are all said to be from a single nest but it will be readily seen that this is entirely due to the exigencies of the story as told in the MBh., for there is no such statement in the hymn or in the Anukramaṇī and so far as the hymn goes Jaritā alone appears to speak for all. The Anukramaṇī, however, attributes two verses each to the four joint bird-authors of the hymn. They thus sing there as adults and most probably represent the four different species of the bird known to the Vedic sage.

13. The story in Mahābhārata mentioned above is nothing more than a Purāṇic elaboration of the situation envisaged and briefly described in RV X.142. The author of the hymn would seem to have loved the birds for their beauty, graceful flight, pleasant call notes and their winsome ways. What is more, he also knew their breeding habits and the occasional danger to their young from a forest fire, and having witnessed their apparently wonderful escape from a conflagration he, in a spirit of thankfulness, attributed their safety to the mercy of god Agni and celebrated the event in the form of a beautiful prayer hymn. This he placed in the mouths of the birds themselves, for according to the Anukramaṇī each of the four birds contributed two verses to complete the hymn. जरिता, the eldest according to MBh, opens the prayer and is followed by the others. The general purport of the hymn is summarised below:—

1. Cf. the epithet ब्रह्मवादिनः for all four in MBh 1.131.16.

14. On behalf of all Bee-eaters and particularly the young in their underground nests Jaritā says in the first verse that he has always been in a special relationship with god Agni and that he has no other kinship, i.e. he does not expect help from any other quarter. He then pays the compliment of heavenly birth to Agni and reminds him that he is a helping friend to all living creatures, and assures himself that his prayer, moving fast like fleet horses to the god, would of themselves protect him as does a herdsman his herd. (The comparison with a fleet horse is very apt as the bird sees the advancing fire and hence the need for quick action, and a cow-boy leading his little herd into a dense jungle is better than one who follows it.)

15. In the third verse, describing the awful results of a conflagration, Jaritā humbly assures the god that he would never think of incurring his displeasure. The next two verses, the 4th & 5th, vividly describe the action and course of the forest fire, while verse 6 allows for a full play of the flames, both high up and low down, and expresses a fervent hope that other gods in their benevolent mood (वसव:) may be with god Agni at the moment so that their silent influence may persuade him to spare the little young in the nests.

16. The 7th verse refers to the waters of a river and a large tank or 'jheel' in the neighbourhood of which the nests are located, and requests god Agni to stop there and choose a different course (as in the very nature of things he must), and, finally, in the last verse of the hymn, after the fire has destroyed the grass about the nests and the place has cooled off, Jaritā looks around and, out of gratefulness to the god for having passed lightly over the nests and spared the young, prays for a fresh growth of green grass all about and continued existence of the waters and the lilies[1] as providing safe homes for the progeny of the future. The phrase आयने ते परायणे refers to possible future visits of the god and Jaritā's faith in his kindness at all times.

17. The above rendering gives a perfectly natural setting to the entire hymn and when so read one cannot miss its great poetic beauty and artistic composition. Griffith is certainly not right when he says that stanzas 7 and 8 belong to some other hymn and have been simply transplanted there. Similarly the opinon of Bloomfield (S.B.E., XLII, p. 515) that these two verses are independent of the hymn and have been "repeated with variants" both here and in AV 6.106 is not correct.[2] Both the verses, in fact, are not

1. The lilies typify all aquatic vegetation where insect-life of all sorts thrives and furnishes food to the Bee-eaters.

2. No blame whatever attaches to these and other scholars who have dealt with the hymn for the simple reason that they did not know what exactly was the Śārṅga bird. It has been identified for the first time by the writer of this article and it is only with the help of the life history of these birds and the MBh version that a proper understanding of the hymn has become possible.

only an integral but a most essential part of the hymn. They complete and round off the prayer beautifully upon a very optimistic note indeed. The AV and other Saṁhitās have utilized them, not at all improperly, for purposes of a charm against fire.

41

THE KINGFISHERS

1. Kingfishers are usually brilliantly coloured in blue, green, chestnut and white, and can be recognised at sight. They excavate tunnels in the bank of a river or stream from one to five feet deep and egg-chambers are hollowed out at the farther end.

2. The common names for a Kingfisher are मत्स्य-or मीन-रङ्क (greedy of fish), जलमद्गु (a diver) and झम्पाशी (plunging for food) but these have been mixed up in the glossaries with specific names for particular birds. Thus for example मत्स्यरङ्ग (dancing for fish) and मत्स्यरङ्क have been incorrectly regarded as synonymous through the influence of Prakrit where क is changed into ग (cf. जलरङ्क = कोरंक, कोरंग). The former is specific for the Pied Kingfisher (12″) as the very name shows —मत्स्य–fish, and रङ्ग dance ("नृत्ये रङ्गः"—मेदिनी, cf. रङ्गणश्येन for the Kestrel and व्योमलासिका, sky-dancer, for the Skylark). In all these names the hovering or playful flight of the birds is regarded as a kind of dancing movement. The Pied Kingfisher hovers over water at a height of ten to twenty feet and on sighting a fish dives straight for it. Its other names are काचाक्ष (brown-eyed; "कृष्णपीतस्तु काचः"—वैजयन्ती) and कपर्दिक (Hindi कौड़ियाला, spotted like a sea-shell), and its way of fishing is well described by the कल्पद्रु कोश :—

"काचाक्षः कपर्दिकः
आपाशे सुषिरं भ्रान्त्वा जले पतति लोष्टवत्"

No other Kingfisher dives for fish in this style. It is also named छत्रक (suspended high up like a parasol) fiom its hovering habit. मत्स्यरङ्क is also an epithet for a श्येन, i.e., Osprey or Fishing Eagles which are known as मछमंगा and मछरंगा, in Hindi (Arts. 50 & 52-C). All blue Kingfishers, some of which are considered in the following paragraphs are मत्स्यरंक.

3. The Common Indian Kingfisher (7″), "one of the loveliest bird-sights," and not much bigger than a sparrow, is a little beauty, a gem amongst Kingfishers, flashing like blue jewels across the gloomy water. It is described in the Natural History of the Birds of Great Britain and Ireland, Ornithology, Vol. X as follows:—The Common Kingfisher is "one of the most gaily tinted birds and when darting down some wooded

stream, and shone upon at times by the sun-beams it may give some faint idea of the brilliant plumage that sports in the forests of the tropics and that flits from place to place like so many lights in their deeply shaded recesses." It may well be called a gem or multi-coloured flower as indeed it has been in Sanskrit, viz., मणीचक, a Kingfisher (shining like a jewel or a flower—"मणीचकं प्रसूनं" and "मणी पुष्पमौक्तिकयोरपि"— वैजयन्ती; cf सुवर्णपुष्प for the brilliantly coloured Sun-birds, Art. 30; पुष्पशकुन, the beautifully ocellated, black and scarlet Tragopans, Art. 55-B; and मणिधनु, the rainbow). मणीचक in the sense of 'moon-stone,' which is entirely white, does not suit any Kingfisher. सुचित्रक (beautifully painted), again, for a Kingfisher, should be another name for this bird corresponding to नीका किलकिला (the beautiful Kingfisher) for it in Hindi.

4. The White-breasted Kingfisher (11″) is mainly a land bird and feeds largely on insects, lizards, frogs and such small fry, which it captures after the manner of a Roller, flying down to them on the ground from an elevated perch. The flight is strong and direct, and on the wing a loud screaming cry is uttered which is one of the familiar sounds of India (Whistler). It is found both near and away from human habitations and is by no means closely dependent on the presence of water for its sustenance. Its voice has been described by Salim Ali as a loud cackling call. This bird is evidently the चन्द्रकान्त (चन्द्रवत् कान्तं वपुरस्य, from its white breast): cf. its name in Marathi खंडू from Sanskrit खण्डेन्दु, a half-moon or crescent. This may be the किकिदीवि of the Ṛgveda—but see below.

5. The Brown-headed Stork-billed Kingfisher (15″) is a big bird as Kingfishers go, being a little smaller than a Pigeon, and can be readily distinguished from all other brightly coloured birds of the group not only from its size but also from its enormous pointed, red bill. A bird of well-watered and well-wooded country, it is found all over the sub-continent except the dry regions like the extreme North-West, Sind and Rajasthan. Its chief diet consists of fish, crabs, reptiles, etc., and its "hoarse explosive chattering call or 'laugh', ke-ke-ke-ke-ke-ke, repeated every little while, bears a general resemblance to the White-breasted Kingfisher's, but is louder and more raucus" (Salim Ali). It is evidently the कर्कट or कर्कटक (crab, crabby) of the lexicons wrongly identified with कर्करेटु in शब्दार्थचिन्तामणि perhaps because it stands nearest to the latter in sound. On the other hand, the name would seem to be after the crab-eating habit of the bird. A crab, before it can be eaten or swallowed, must be battered on a stone or a tree-branch and this habit of the bird has given it the name of कुट्टक (the thrasher) also in Sanskrit. Pali कुलीरक for a bird (Sanskrit कुलीरक, a crab) in the following, rendered as कक्कटक (कर्कटक) in the commentary, is clearly the same and strongly supports the above identification:—

"कुकुट्ठका कुलीरका कोट्ठ पोक्खरसातका"

वेस्संतर जातक, Verse 2104.

कुकुट्ठक is Sanskrit कुठाकु for the Hoopoe (Art. 43), and since the first two and the last names are in the plural it would be incorrect to separate कोट्ठ in the singular, and the proper way to treat the compound "कोट्ठपोक्खरसातका" is to analyse it as कोट्ठसातका and पोक्खरसातका. Both these, as *names of Water-birds*, would then be the Cotton Teal, which nests in holes in trees in the neighbourhood of water, and the Whiskered Tern, which nests on a lotus-leaf, respectively (Arts. 84-C and 69). If on the other hand कोट्ठ is to be taken by itself for a particular bird as in the Pali Dictionary (P.T.S.), it may be the same कोण्ठ of the वैजयन्ती कोश for a hooting or Large Owl, probably the Brown Fish Owl which nests and also often spends the day in a tree-hole.

6. The Stork-billed bird appears to be the Vedic किकिदीवि:—

"साकं यक्ष्म प्रपत चाषेण किकिदीविना"—
RV 10.97.13.

Here the cough of a person suffering from asthma is asked to quit the patient and go away with or to the चाष, the Roller bird, and the किकिदीवि, the Brown-headed Stork-billed Kingfisher, both of which have harsh croaking or screaming "ke-ke-ke-ke-" notes resembling a fit of coughing. The proximity of the two names in the verse has led almost all the lexicographers to treat them as synonymous, but सायणाचार्य commenting on it has held them to be two different birds:—

"चाषाख्येन पक्षिणा सह। तथा किकिदीविना पक्षिणा च सह"

At other places ((तैत्ति. संहिता, 5.6.22 and तैत्ति. ब्राह्मण, 2.5.8), however, he has rendered किकिदीवि as a तित्तिर or Partridge which is clearly incorrect. The important point is that he did not regard the two names as synonymous despite the lexical equations before him. The charm against jaundice in RV 1.50.12 mentions three different birds which makes it more than probable that चाष and किकिदीवि in the above verse are two different birds. Griffith in his translation of the Ṛgveda has correctly rendered them as the Blue Jay and the Kingfisher.

7. पेरुसूरि in his औणादिक पदार्णव mentions that some authorities have split up किकिदीवि into two words, किकि and दीवि, the first of which means a kind of bird and the second an animal of prey (द्वीपिन्?), and श्वेतवनवासिन् has accepted this and given किकि for a kind of bird. But "किकीति कुर्वन् दीव्यति किकिदीवि:" of उणादि भोजीयानि seems to be the only correct analysis of the name. Nevertheless किकि or किकी seems to have been in common use as an abbreviation, for we find किकी सकुन or किकी as a bird with a harsh and unpleasant voice in the सुजात जातक, and कल्पद्रुकोश has the equation "दीदिविस्तु किकीविक:" which agrees with किकिवि (the कि-कि call + वि —a bird) in the supplement of M. Williams. We thus have three more names for this noisy King-fisher—दीदिवि (the shining one), किकि or किकिवि and किकीविक (one calling out ki-ki, ki-ki) and they correspond to Hindi दलेला किलकिला (दलेल—दरेर, very noisy) for it.

8. The beautiful blue feathers of the Peacock, the Roller and the Kind-fishers (मत्स्यरङ्क) were often used for ornamenting royal flagstaffs:—

"केकी चासो मत्स्यरङ्कः त्रिविधानां महीभुजाम्
ध्वजाग्रेषु विधेयानि पक्षाणि श्रियमिच्छताम्"

युक्तिकल्पतरु, p. 70.

42

HORNBILLS

1. "The Horbills are a well marked family of birds. They are especially remarkable for their nidification......A hole in a tree is selected, and then the female, usually with the aid of the male, encloses herself and shuts up the orifice with the exception of a narrow vertical slit, by means of earth mixed with the bird's own droppings. She is thus enclosed before she begins to lay, and apparently remains in the hole till the young, which are naked when they leave the egg, are fledged, being fed all the time by the male through the slit....which just allows room for the bird's bill to be pushed through".[1] Four species of the Hornbill occur in the sub-Himalayan areas west of Assam including the Common Grey Hornbill which is found almost all over India.

2. Common names for all Hornbills are मातृनिन्दक (सुश्रुतसंहिता) from the more than maternal care taken by the male bird not only of the young but of the mother also; for the father puts the mother to shame, as it were, in the matter of parental care; प्रियात्मज (चरक सं., v.l. प्रियात्मक, per डल्हणाचार्य in his gloss on सुश्रुत); and वार्ध्रीणस (वार्ध्रीव नासिका यस्य or वृद्धि गता नासाऽस्य) from the casque upon the base of the bill regarded as an overgrowth of the nose.[2] The Rufous-necked Horbill of Nepal has, however, no casque but the basal portion of the upper mandible is thickened, and from the similarity of habits with others of the group it has been included within the general name of वार्ध्रीणस. In fact this bird and perhaps also the Great Hornbill are वार्ध्रीणस par excellence, and dear to God विष्णु as his favourite food, and they are also offered to the manes of the ancestors.

"कृष्णग्रीवो रक्तशिराः श्वेतपक्षो विहङ्गमः
स वै वार्ध्रीणसः प्रोक्तः पितृणां पुष्टिवर्धनः"[3]

वार्ध्रीणस is also the rhinoceros. The corresponding name in Hindi is धनेश (fr. वार्ध्रीणस). व्याग्घीनस as a bird in वेस्संतर जातक is corrupt Pali for it.

---

1. Blanford and Oates.

2. It is एकाङ्गवरक in मानसोल्लास, 2.276 from एकाङ्ग—head and वरक—covering, i.e. a bird having a sort of covering on the head.

3. Quoted by उज्ज्वलदत्त at 2. 27 of उणादिसूत्रवृत्ति.

3. The कल्पद्रुकोश in addition to explaining प्रियात्मज as the nourisher and regaler of his mate ("त्वपुषो [स्व्यपुषो?] रञ्जकस्तु प्रियात्मजः"), has two verses for two different varieties of the bird:—

"नीलग्रीवो रक्तशिराः शुक्लपक्षो वनेचरः।
कुरुबाहुः कुरुकुरुः स च वार्ध्रीणसोऽथ च ।।
स स्यात्कृष्णोदरशिरा वर्णतः कृष्णकर्बुरः।
पन्थालकः पुंसि भवेत् स्त्रियां स्यादवगण्डिका"।।

The first corresponds to the following verse from the कालिका पुराण quoted in the शब्दकल्पद्रुम:—

"नीलग्रीवो रक्तशीर्षः कृष्णपादः सितच्छदः।
वार्ध्रीणसः स्यात्पक्षीशो मम विष्णोरतिप्रियः ।।"

The verse below is also quoted by the same authority from some commentary on the मार्कण्डेय पुराण:—

"रक्तपादो रक्तशिराः रक्तचञ्चुर्विहङ्गमः।
कृष्णवर्णेन च तथा पक्षी वार्ध्रीणसो मतः ।।"

It will be seen that the colour-patterns of (i) the Great Hornbill which is principally a black and white bird with black head and neck and some yellow and orange on the bill and (ii) the Rufous-necked Hornbill with a rufous or Chestnut (red) head, neck and lower parts, yellow bill with chestnut grooves on it and naked skin, blue round the eyes and scarlet at the throat, have been mixed up in these verses but there is no doubt that they refer to these birds. The legs of no Hornbill are red. The quotations however make it sufficiently clear that the particular varieties of वार्घ्रीणस sacred to God विष्णु are the Rufous-necked Hornbill, and the Great Hornbill. The name पन्थालक for the latter given by कल्पद्रु appears to be a wrong reading for some other word, probably खट्वाङ्गक. यवगण्डिका for the female is with reference to the casque on her head being regarded as a sort of tumour or growth.

4. खट्वाङ्ग would seem to be specific for the Great Hornbill as the bird makes the nearest approach to the description of the mythological खट्वाङ्ग as a weapon of God Śiva. It is described as a staff the upper part of which resembles the human skeleton......cross pieces in the upper half for ribs and a skull at the top. The bird in flight, over four feet long, with its long tail, black and white wings and the head-assembly including the casque and the large massive bill, offers quite a comparable picture to Śiva's weapon. Vernacular names like कुडांग, कुड़ांग, and हिवांग (खिवांग) common in Assam are probable corruptions of खट्वाङ्ग. खट्वाङ्ग is one of the Himalayan birds listed in मत्स्य पुराण.[1] खट्वाङ्ग वन the name of a region in the Himalayas mentioned in the Purāṇas, e.g. हरिवंश,[2] is evidently named after the Great Hornbill which was apparently very common there.

1. 118.50.
2. 2.22.48.

5. The Common Grey Hornbill (24 inches) of the plains south of the Himalayas is a slim grey bird whose tail constitutes nearly half its total length. The small casque with a point in front has given it names like सेलगिल्ली ('a tip cat' on the head) or सिरखिली (a nail on the head) in Hindi and पत्तियल धनेश (पत्र वार्ध्राणस; cf. पत्रशुक for the smallest Paroquet, the Loriquet) in Bengal. It must therefore have been पत्र वार्ध्राणस in Sanskrit.

6. The flesh of the Great and Rufous-necked Hornbills is said to be very good eating ("far superior to any fowl or pheasant"—Hume), and hence their selection as offerings to God विष्णु and the manes of ancestors:

"वार्ध्रीणसस्य मांसेन तृप्तिर्द्वादशवार्षिकी।"

मनु[1]

The commentator has explained वार्ध्राणस as a very old and weak goat also called "त्रिपिब" i.e. with such long ears that when the animal bends down to drink, his ears and muzzle touch the water at the same time. A त्रिपिब variety of goat may be called वार्ध्राणस but why should the flesh of a wretched old goat be held in such high esteem when on all accounts it is very unpalatable and almost uneatable.[2] It is therefore suggested that वार्ध्राणस in the above context is no other than the Hornbill. If its flesh is dear alike to God विष्णु and man, why not to the manes of the departed as well? The विष्णुस्मृति indeed contains a statement by the manes themselves as to what exactly they would like to have at a श्राद्ध, and the menu includes the flesh of वार्ध्राणस rendered incorrectly as a Crane of that name in the S.B.E. Vol. 52.

"कालशाकं महाशाकं मांसं वार्ध्रीणसस्य च।
विषाणवर्ज्या (श्व?) खड्गास्तांस्तु भक्ष्यामहे सदा॥"[3]

The idea in Manu (3.271) therefore is that once fed with such a delicacy as the flesh of a Hornbill, the manes not only feel happy but would also not like to spoil their taste for a long time to come with anything inferior.

7. Finally it may be noted that alleged bird-names like "कृष्ण-कर्बुरवर्ण" and "कृष्णोदरशिरस्" given by M. Williams on the authority of Galanos' Dictionary are not substantive names at all but merely descriptive adjectives taken from the definition of वार्ध्राणस in the कल्पद्रुकोश or some other glossary.

---

1. 3.271.
2. "वृद्धानां दोषलं मांसम्"—भावप्रकाश.
3. 80.14

43

HOOPOES

The Hoopoes are closely allied to the Hornbills both in structure and nesting habits. They feed on the ground which they probe with their long, pointed bills for insects, grubs, and caterpillars. They nest in holes and the female sits very closely and seems never to leave the hole until the young are well grown and the male feeds her during all this period. The voice of the male is a double or treble "hoop" or "pooh" after which the bird has been named in many languages, e.g. हुदहुद in Persian and Hindi.

The Sanskrit names for this beautiful bird are derived from (i) its voice and love of progeny — पुत्रप्रिय ('pooh-pooh', पुत्र ! पुत्र !; v.l. प्रियपुत्र) and (ii) its habit of "quartering the ground methodically" and probing it for food—कठाकु ("कठाकु: खगशिल्पिनो:"—वैजयन्ती). Alternative forms of this last name are कुठाकु (M. Williams) and कठारु ("दरिद्र: पक्षी च" — उणादिवृत्ति, II, श्वेतवनवासिन्), names which correspond to सुतार in Marathi and खुट बढ़ई (a carpenter 'pegging' the ground, from खूंटी a peg, for a lay-out, as it were; cf. कुट, a mallet or hammer) in Hindi. These names are the same as शिल्पी, an artisan who, like the village carpenter, frequently combines the functions of a smith and a house-builder. The bird's habit of regularly quartering the ground and stopping every now and then to probe it for food very naturally invited the comparison with a village carpenter. Yet another name for it in Hindi is पत्थरफोड़ or stone-breaker, an adaptation from कुट for a hammer related to कुठार, an axe. It is known as कटकुटो in Sind which is the same as कठाकु. The Pali form of कुठाकु or कठाकु (कुष्यते छिद्यते भूमि ?) is कुकुट्ठक or ककुट्ठक in वेस्संतर जातक[1] and the first of these, कुकुट्ठक points to the correct Sanskrit spelling of कु-कुट्टक (कुं भूमिं कुट्टति छेदयति) 'one who pierces or breaks the ground with his bill' which agrees with the habit of the Hoopoe who pokes his bill deep into the ground for worms and insects. Moreover, with the folded crest and the long bill, the bird's head looks also like a toy pick-axe (E. H. Aitken).

पुत्रप्रिय again, is another happy name for the bird (cf. प्रियात्मज for the Hornbill). Fletcher and Inglis testify to the extraordinary love of the female for her eggs: "On one occasion, to inspect the nest, the hen

---

1. 547 Verses 2097 and 2104.

bird had to be pulled out of the hole and in doing so some of her tail feathers came out, but even this rather severe handling did not make her quit the place".[1] The male feeds the female during incubation to ensure proper hatching out of the young. No wonder the ancients loved and remembered these devoted birds in their epics:

"पुत्रप्रियोऽसौ शकुनिः पुत्र पुत्रेति भाषते।
मधुरां करुणां वाचं पुरेव जननी मम॥"

रामायण,[2]

"पुत्र पुत्रेति वाशन्ते यत्र पुत्रप्रिया खगाः।
यथा शिवप्रियाः शैवाः नित्यं शिव शिवेति च।"

स्कन्दपुराण[3]

"चकोरैरसितापाङ्गैस्तथा पुत्रप्रियैरपि।"

महाभारत[4]

1. Birds of an Indian Garden.
2. (Interpolated Canto) 2.96.12.
3. कौमारिका खण्ड 3.62.
4. 3.108.8.

Also ब्रह्मपुराण 41.46.
मार्क॰ पुराण 6.19.
मत्स्यपुराण 118.52.

44

THE TROGONS

These beautiful birds inhabit forests and from their perch on a tree they fly out from time to time in pursuit of insects, chiefly beetles, moths and cicadas. They are generally silent birds but have a low 'mew' or a soft 'too-too-too' call. As a North-Indian bird we are concerned with only one species, the Red-headed Trogon which occurs in the Himalayas upto about 5000 ft. elevation from Nepal to Assam and eastwards. "It is exclusively a forest bird and prefers the interior of the damp, dark, evergreen cover, where it sits very silent and quiet throughout the heat of the day," and is most common in the lower hills between 1,500 and 2,500 feet. It is deep crimson on the head, neck, and upper breast with the remaining lower parts bright crimson. Its back, scapulars and wing-coverts are ferruginous-brown, brighter and more rufous on the rump and upper tail-coverts; wings are black.

लोहपृष्ठ is the name of a प्रतुद bird in चरक (also a descriptive term for the Brahminy Kite, Art. 52-D) and लोह is a bird of some peculiar habits recommended as an object-lesson to a prince in the मार्कं० पुराण.[1]

"हंसकुक्कुटलोहानां शिक्षेत चरितं नृपः।"

A king is advised to acquire the power of distinguishing good from evil from the हंस; qualities of valour, early-rising etc. from the कुक्कुट; and other qualities from the लोह bird. Now if the Red-headed Trogon (लोह means 'red' and लोहपृष्ठ means "red or reddish-backed" bird) is the bird meant here, as I believe it is, it certainly possesses qualities which an enterprising prince should do well to cultivate. Out on an expedition, he must keep to cover in a forest, practise secrecy, talk only in whispers, and know how and when to sally forth suddenly against an unsuspecting enemy and return to cover again with the booty. The Trogon has all these and should be the लोहपक्षी of the Purāṇa and लोहपृष्ठ of चरक. लोह is also mentioned as one of the Himalayan birds in मत्स्य पुराण[2].

1. 25.18 (cf. verse 397, "सामान्य नीति" सुभाषित.)
2. 118.52.

45

SWIFTS

1. We have seen in Art. 25 that the common name चटक applies to both Swallows and Swifts, and while भाण्डीक is a general name for the former, the latter are generally known as दुर्बल, दुर्बलिक and चिरिल्ली or चीरल्लि. In this article an attempt is made to explain the latter terms along with other names for the Swift.

2. The Swifts, though similar in appearance and outline to the Swallows, are very different in structure and belong to a different order of birds. "They are the most aerial of all birds, spending the whole of their waking existence on the wing. The flight is very rapid and highly characteristic,......a Swift wheels and dashes through the air with frequent changes of direction, tilting now to one side, now to the other, with a succession of rapid wing-beats alternating with *long glides on extended wings*.. *It does not voluntarily settle on the ground*., the short legs with all the toes directed forwards being only adapted to clinging to rocks, masonry, etc." (Smythies). Should it be grounded, due to some accident, "it rises with great difficulty, the bird raising itself by repeated attempts and strokes upon the ground by the shoulders."[1] The Common House Swift is "highly gregarious, being usually found in flocks of fifty or more, which breed together in colonies, ...The nest colonies are found about buildings, whether these be the ordinary dwelling houses of an Indian village or town or ruined temples, shrines and forts.The birds occupy these nest colonies continuously, breeding rather irregularly, so that eggs or young may be found in some of the nests at any time, and at all times using the nests to rest or sleep in.... (Their voice is a) curious squealing call which so aptly seems to express the fierce joy of an aerial creature in its element. The flocks usually feed in loose open order, but at times, specially in the evenings, they collect together into a "ball", mounting high into the air as a squealing, careering mass" (Whistler).

3. Names like दुर्बल, दुर्बलिक, and कृश (=दुर्बल) are clearly in reference to the Swift's inability to rise from the ground; cf. the phrase "पङ्के गौरिव दुर्बला" for a cow that has got stuck up in deep mire and is too weak to extricate herself.

1. Birds of Great Britain and Ireland.

अश्वघोष refers to दुर्बल as a bird that loves to be constantly on the wing and makes use of its nest merely as a resting place:

"धारणार्थं शरीरस्य भोजनं हि विधीयते।
उपस्तम्भः पिपतिषो दुर्बलस्येव वेश्मनः।"
सौन्दरनन्द[1]

The बृहत्संहिता[2] mentions the Swift, दुर्बलिक, as a bird of augury. The Hindi names बंगनकुटी and बतासी for the House Swift are from Sanskrit व्यङ्गिन् कुटी (having a defective body) and वाताशिन् (living on the air, as the birds seem to eat nothing). The first corresponds to दुर्बल and the second to वायुभक्ष a certain type of ascetic.

4. The शब्दार्थचिन्तामणि defines अलिल as a kind of bird that is constantly flying in the sky (सततं गगनचारिणि शास्त्रप्रसिद्धे पक्षिविशेषे) and cites the following verse from some Vārtika on a treatise on Vedānta:

"अलिलः पक्षिणः पुत्रो गगनाद् याति भूतलम्।
स्वबोधाभावतः स्वस्य बोधे यात्यम्बरं पुनः॥"

The habit of the bird अलिल is used here to illustrate the nature of the 'ātman' who can enjoy a state of ecstatic happiness only in a high spiritual plane. Now the only bird whose habits fulfil the above description is the Common House Swift which not only takes its food, drink and nesting materials on the wing but even mates and feeds its grown-up young in the air.[3] It resorts to its nest either for a momentary rest during the day or to sleep in at night. It does not voluntarily descend to the ground and if by accident this does happen, it manages to fly back into the air. The name अलिल like चरिल्ली is most probably after the bird's call and Prak. अडिल्ल is merely a variant according to the rule डलयोरैक्यम्.

5. Prakrit अडिल्ल said to be derived from अटिल (अटल not moving?) is defined in अभि० राजेन्द्र as चर्मपक्षिभेदे" i.e. a kind of bat, probably the small house-bat, which also finds it rather difficult to take to the air once it has landed itself on the ground; Cf. मास्याल[4] (not coming to the ground) for the larger fruit-bats. Little bats, however, do not fly even half as high as Swifts and can certainly not be described as गगन-or अम्बर-चारी. Moreover, it is highly improbable that such an unclean looking thing as a bat, occupying stinking nest-holes and blind by day, should be chosen by the Vedāntic philosopher to illustrate one of their principal doctrines. Sansk. अलिल may therefore, stand apart

1. 14.13.

2. 87.7 & 28.

3. प्राणक जातक and प्राणिभूत are obscure bird-names in महाव्युत्पत्ति, Section 213. If प्राण—प्राणक means 'wind or air' the first may mean 'a bird that is begotten in the air', and प्राणिभूत may be an allied form 'begotten in the ordinary way'. This is, of course, pure guess-work.

4. गौतम स्मृति Ch. 17; आश्रम ग्रन्थावलि No. 61, Poona.

from Prak. अडिल in spite of their close affinity. Nevertheless, it is possible to reconcile and connect the two through two different meanings of the Marathi term पाकोली as given in the महाराष्ट्र शब्दकोश[1], viz., (i) a small bat and (ii) a kind of small bird, evidently the Swallow or Swift both of which are popularly known in Marathi by that name and are not distinguished one from the other. The Chief reason why the bat and the Swift share a common name seems to be the fact that in their daily routine of life they are complimentary, as it were, to each other. If the Swift is on the wing all day and returns to the nest for the night, the bat keeps flying all night and spends the day in its nest-hole. Both are however, seen flying at dusk and often returning to their nests to feed the young. This makes it easy to reconcile old survivals like चामचिकि ((चर्मचटी?) in Bengal for the Palm Swift and चमरू (bird with wings of skin, cf. Hindi पखेरू a bird) in Sind for the Pale Brown Swift as alternative names for them. It follows, therefore, that अलिल and अडिल are merely different forms of the same word, but while the former means the House Swift in Sanskrit the latter has been confined to the small bat in Prakrit.

6. The name चटक in the प्रतुद list of चरकसंहिता stands probably for both Swallows and Swifts, for चक्रपाणिदत्त renders it as देवकुलचटक: स्वल्पप्रमाण: i.e., little birds living in temples, and we know that both these build their nests there. चटक is also a common name for Sparrow-like birds but चरक has mentioned separately the House and other Sparrows as कुलिङ्गक[2] and song-Sparrows as कलविङ्क. The interpretation of the commentator must, therefore, be accepted as correct.[3] चटक, देवकुल चटक, and चिरिल्ली or चरिल्ली thus seem to be general names for both Common House Swallows and Swifts, but it must be remembered that strictly speaking चटक and चटी are the Swallows and भारद्वाज the Swifts according to धन्वन्तरि निघण्टु (Art. 25).

7. The औणादिक पदार्णव of पेरुसूरि, 4.163 gives the equation "जीवि: चटके" and the name जीवि (जीर् speedy or quick, and वि a bird) is an exact equivalent of "Swift" as a specific bird-name, and the aptness of the name for the Swift would be appreciated when it is recalled that the normal speed of a Swift on the wing is 75 miles as against 35 miles per hour of the Swallow. These speeds are very much higher when the birds are pressed by danger, and though hundred miles per hour for a Swift is definite, that accurate observer of bird-life, E.C. Stuart Baker, has actually timed a Swift with a stop-watch flying at the tremendous speed

1. Ed. by Y. R. Date (1933).

2. सुश्रुत has distinguished them as कुलिङ्ग and वेश्म-कुलिङ्ग.

3. Just as the common terms शकुन, शकुन्त, and पत्री mean both 'a bird' in general and particular birds of prey, the word चटक also means 'a sparrow' and 'a swallow or swift' according to the rule—सामान्योऽपि विशेषे वर्तते—अभिधानचिन्तामणि.

of two hundred miles per hour.[1] जीवि, therefore, is a most expressive and accurate name for it as the fastest little bird known. पिण्डीक of the list from पराशर quoted by भट्टोत्पल under 85.38 of the बृहत्संहिता is again the Swift which collects into a "ball" (पिण्ड) and mounts "high into the air as a squealing careering mass" at evening.

8. चरिल्ल in अर्धं मागधी means a kind of bird and is the same as चिरिल्ली or चरिल्ली, and the expression चरिल्ल पोसक means a person who gives protection to Swifts nesting in his house. It is an old belief commonly held both in India and China that the continuous nesting of these birds in a residential house is very auspicious, for it augurs well for prosperity and continuity of the family occupying it. If the nests are inconveniently situated, e.g., over a passage or stair-way, planks are fitted under them to catch the droppings. A similar belief obtains in England too.[2]

9. The Western Palm Swift of North India is known as तालचट in Hindi corresponding to Sanskrit तालचटक, and when it is rememoered that चटक implies also a swift, it is but natural to call a Palm Swift a तालचटक. This name does not occur in any currect lexicon but one can hardly doubt that the bird had it in Sanskrit as well.

10. The बृहत्संहिता mentions एकपुत्रक (having one egg or young) as a bird of augury and attributes to it the habit of swooping down on the surface of a stream or tank ("स्रोतस्तडागभेदि एकपुत्रक:")[3]. These characteristics agree very well with the habits and ways of the Crested Swift, an ashy grey bird with a deeply forked tail and resembling a Swallow in flight. It is a forest bird, freely perching on the top-most branches which are leafless or dead. The call is a loud and Parrot-like 'kia, kia, kia' (which may also be rendered as 'chia, chia, chia') frequently uttered either from a perch or on the wing. The bird is particularly noisy in the evening when preparing to roost. "Should there be a tank or pool of water or river near its haunts this Swift is fond of descending rapidly from the air to the surface of the water, touching it and mounting again in one graceful curve" (Whistler). It makes a tiny nest on the side of a horizontal branch, barely half an inch deep and so small as to be covered completely by two anna-pieces placed side by side. The single egg it lays completely fills the nest. It is clearly the एकपुत्रक of the Saṁhitā.

11. One of the most poetic hymns of the Ṛgveda is the अरण्यानी, and its second verse mentions two birds, वृषारव and चिच्चिक as playing music to the goddess of the forest:—

"वृषारवाय वदते यदुपावति चिच्चिक: ।
आघाटिरिव धावयन्नरण्यानिर्महीयते ॥"

Ṛgveda, 10.146.2

1. "Birds, Trees and Flowers", pp. 15 & 129.
2. "Adventures in Woodcraft", 52. See Art. 25 for a similar idea about the पूजनी or Swallow.
3. 87.6.

M. Williams explains वृषारव as a kind of animal and चिच्चिक as a kind of bird. सायण in his gloss on this Vedic verse takes the first for झिल्ली or the Cicada Fly and the second for another insect with a 'chi, chi' call, probably a cricket or green grasshopper which has such a call. Commenting on तैत्ति. ब्राह्मण II.5.5.6 where this verse occurs, he however renders both as birds:

"वृष्टिकाले रवः शब्दविशेषो पक्षिविशेषस्य सोऽयं वृषारवः
.........वृषारवाय पक्षिणे प्रत्युत्तरवादी चिच्चिकाख्योऽन्यः
पक्षी.........उक्तिप्रत्युक्तिरूपचिच्चिशब्दसहस्राणि—
कुर्वद्भिः सूक्ष्मैः पक्षिविशेषैः युक्ता इयमरण्यानिः शोभते।"

Apparently the commentator had good reason to revise his opinion by the time he came to annotate the Brāhmaṇa, and for one thing, he must have come to know that the descriptive title of शकुनसूक्त (Bird-hymn) had been applied long long ago to either the "द्वा सुपर्णा" verse of RV 1.164.20 or in the alternative to the verse quoted above. It is therefore submitted that the later interpretation of वृषारव and चिच्चिक as particular birds by सायण is correct. Further we have चिच्चिका in Prakrit and सट्वा and लट्वा in Sanskrit as names for musical instruments, probably 'whistles', each named after the bird whose call it imitated.

12. The name वृषारव (वृष् to rain, and आरव to call, i.e. some sort of a rain-bird) is probably the same as घनारव of the कल्पद्रुकोश— "घनारवश्च वापीहः", the Hawk-Cuckoo which is very vocal at the beginning of and during the rains. चिच्चिक is obviously an onomatopoetic name for a small bird (सूक्ष्म पक्षी) comparable with चीरल्ली for the House-Swift and Swallow. The Crested Swift, as we have seen, is a forest bird and has a loud 'chia, chia, chia' call. It hawks for insects in parties in a wheeling, graceful flight and is particularly noisy in the evening (Whistler). This, I submit, is probably the चिच्चिक of the hymn which has been happily conceived to answer back, as it were, to the loud and persistent call notes of the Hawk-Cuckoo.[1] The Hymn is apparently addressed to the goddess of the forest in the evening by a person who is late in coming home or has lost his way through the forest. The fifth verse is perhaps a pointer in this direction.

---

1. Z. A. Ragozin renders वृषारव and चिच्चिक as Owl and Parrot respectively in Vedic India, p. 273.

46

NIGHTJARS

1. The various species of Nightjar resemble each other very closely and are difficult to identify in the field except by their distinctive calls in the breeding season. The plumage is a mixture of mottled grey and brown with white, resulting in a remarkable protective colouration. "The bird seems to be conscious of the fact, only springing into life when the intruder comes within a yard or two." It spends the day resting quietly, flat on the ground, but as the evening approaches and dusk turns into darkness it becomes active hawking insects on the wing in open spaces near trees. While on the ground, it is incapable of any progression because of its long central toe. This toe has a pectinated nail (serrated like a comb) with which it probably removes insect-wings etc. sticking to the long bristles surrounding the extraordinarily wide gape. This wide mouth gave rise to a false belief in the western countries that the bird was capable of and actually given to sucking the milk of goats, and hence the name 'Goat-sucker' for it. It has a habit of sitting in the middle of the road at night and travellers by motor car often see it so doing.

2. It is known in Hindi as छिप्पक or छप्पा and अंधी चिड़िया, the names being in reference to the obliterative colouration of the bird on the ground. It is नप्तृका, a विष्किर bird in सुश्रुत and a night bird with a keen sight in कौटिल्य,[1] the corresponding Hindi names being नपता and नपरका. The Nightjar does not usually fly for many minutes together and between each circuit it rests on the ground (Dewar). It is incapable of walking or hopping and must therefore drop down to its resting place on the ground, to rise again after a minute or two. This trait of the bird would seem to justify the apt name of नप्तृका for it—न+पत् one that falls but not permanently like a stone, पतति न पतति च पुनरुत्पतनाय पतति(?). The बृहत्संहिता[2] and वसन्तराज[3] mention the bird under the प्राकृत name of छिप्पिका from प्रा. छिप्पिय 'fallen down' and Sansk. क्षिप् to throw. The name thus corresponds to Sansk. नप्तृका

1. II.14.2.
2. 88.2. and 35.
3. 4.62; 8.32.

3. It is also the bird selected as an offering to the deity of the Night at the अश्वमेध under the name सीचापू :—"रात्र्यै सीचापूः"—वाज० संहिता,[1] 24.25. The name सीचापू is most probably from शी-सी, शयने and चप् सान्त्वने; शयानं चपति, one that rests in a lying down posture. Hindi छप्पा and Marwari छापो for a Nightjar, also Sansk. छिप्पिका seem to be from the root चप्.

4. M. Williams gives दर्दू as a kind of bird in चरक, 1.27 but I have not been able to trace it in my copy. The name, however, seems to have some connection with दर्दुर a frog. The Nightjar is known as 'the frog-bird' both in Telugu and Tamil, apparently because when perching low on the ground, as is its habit, it looks like a frog. Its extraordinarily wide gape, when the bill is open, also has a striking resemblance to the wide mouth of a frog. दर्दू as a bird, therefore appears to be a Nightjar. Indian linen of old must have been of a coarse texture and of a rather grey-brown colour which explains the punishment proposed in the विष्णुस्मृति 44.27 for a thief of clothes made from it.—"क्षौमं दर्दुर" etc. and here दर्दुर is more probably a Nightjar than a frog as the name occurs as one of a series of bird-names for the next birth of different types of thieves. Again दर्दुर in the following may well be a homonym signifying both frogs and these birds:—

"स्तोककाः शिखिनश्चैव पुंस्कोकिलगणैः सह।
मत्ताः परिपतन्ति स्म दर्दुराश्चैव दर्पिताः॥"

महाभारत, 3.183.8.

In England also a Nightjar is popularly known as the Flying-toad. वर्षाहू as a bird in the bird-list quoted from पाराशर by भट्टोत्पल under 85.28 of बृहत्संहिता would seem to be this bird.

1. "This bird is most punctual in beginning its song exactly at the close of day"—Gilbert White, Letter XXII to T. Pennant. Compare also the English name 'Twilight Nightjar' in Cassells' Book of Bird.

47

FROGMOUTHS

These birds resemble small Nightjars and occur only near Sikkim and east of it and in the extreme south of India—Wynad and Travancore. The name दर्दुर probably from दर्दुर a frog, for a bird, has already been noticed in the preceding article.

48

THE BARN OWL

1. The Barn Owl is pale grey-brown and rufous ochre above, has a white face and, white under-parts, spotted with brown.[1] It is also known in English as the White or Screech Owl, looking "strangely white among the black trees". It is found all over India but not in forests. It haunts roofs of buildings, outhouses, wells and ruins. Its cry is a peculiar weird shriek or screech, and when perched during the day it makes a snoring sound (T. Regan), and at night as well. Sansk. घर्घरक (one who makes a guttural or snoring sound) for an owl clearly refers to it and the name perhaps corresponds to करेल in Hindi. Its other names in Hindi, Telugu and Tamil mean 'bad bird' corresponding to Sans. कुवि, कुवय or क्वयि[2] in वाज० संहिता (24.39) where it is placed with two other noisy birds, कुटरु and दात्यौह. The Larger Owls have been looked upon all over the world as birds of bad omen and the Barn Owl is no exception. The श्वेतोलूक of भविष्यपुराण (मध्यमपर्व 20.17) is clearly this Owl which is considered there to be an evil bird.

The चन्द्रक (white like the moon) Owl in the महाभारत story of a Rat, Cat and Mangoose would also seem to be the Barn Owl as he is described there as the enemy of rats :

"उलूकं चन्द्रकं नाम तीक्ष्णतुण्डं क्षपाचरम् ।"

महाभारत, XII 138.33.

चन्द्रकोलूक would be yet another name synonymous with श्वेतोलूक. This Owl has a fleshy-white or fleshy-horny bill and the adnoun रक्तनासक may belong to it if not to the Himalayan Wood-Owl with a fleshy-yellow bill.

2. The Grass Owl (14") also belongs to the present family and resembles the Barn Owl in the colour pattern of the body plumage, and if seen perched upon a tree it would pass for one. But its ways are very different and unlike the Barn Owl, which breeds in holes in buildings, wells, or trees, it always lays its eggs on the ground in fairly long grass and inhabits the long grassy areas of the Himalayan Terais, the adjoining plains, and in similar

---

1. Sometimes it is pure white below.

2. If क्वयि is not the Barn-Owl it would be the common Owlet which too is very noisy. The name कुवि occurs in राजनिघण्टु, and कुघि in कल्पद्रुकोश is a wrong reading of कुवि.

situations in Bihar, Madhya Pradesh and further south. Even where these Owls are common they are but seldom seen unless put up by beating through the grass. They come out in the evening when they often perch on trees. The following synonymy probably furnishes us with a name or epithet for this bird:

"कटप्रू: कीटके घूके[1] कामरूपिण्यपि स्मृत:"—पेरुसूरि'ऽग्रोणादिक पदार्णव 2.211.

कटप्रू is clearly a homonymous adnoun or epithet designating several objects, and as an epithet for an Owl it may be analysed as below:—कटं—तृणम् (श० कल्प०); प्रु गमने; कटे तृणे प्रवते कटप्रू, hence कटप्रू उलूक is an Owl that moves or lives in grass; cf. कट तीरं प्रवते इति कटप्रू नदीतरंग: in दशमाद्युणादिवृत्ति 10.2. कटप्रू also means a demon or राक्षस (M.W.) and should, in this sense, refer to one that hides and moves in tall grass or in the deeply dented banks of rivers. It is thus just possible that the name कटप्रू उलूक belongs to the Grass Owl.

---

1. घूक here simply means an owl that is not a क्षुद्रोलूक

49

OTHER OWLS

1. This family constitutes a well defined group of predacious birds easy of recognition. Most of them hunt for prey during the dark hours of the night but a few have diurnal or semi-diurnal habits. One particular species eats carrion in addition to the common fare of all Owls consisting of insects, small or large mammals and birds according to the size and strength of the different species (of Owl). The Fish Owls subsist mainly on fish though they kill other prey as well. All have broad rounded heads, flattened faces, and large eyes directed forwards which give the bird a fearful expression and a fixed gaze as it were (cf. जिह्माक्ष below). The feet are powerful and furnished with sharp, curved and cutting claws of great grasping power and it is with these that an Owl secures its food (नखाशी). The plumage is soft and downy enabling the bird to fly almost noiselessly.

2. The Indo-Aryans regarded the hooting Owls as birds of ill omen but this apparently did not prevent them from observing the birds and their ways. Early Buddhist monks who travelled widely to propagate the Gospel of Lord Buddha in countries like Kashmir, Tibet and further north used articles of dress like gloves, and perhaps also leggings and shoes, lined with or made from soft feathered-skins of Owls for protection against the bitter cold (see Art. 54). This involved the killing of a large variety of Owls and the people naturally came to know something about them and that perhaps accounts for the naming of individual species and groups of allied forms of a bird that is rarely seen during the day and has never been kept as a pet. That the ancients made a close enough observational study of these birds may be gathered not only from the works on augury now extant —and these difinitely mention earlier authorities—but also from a knowledge of the reactions of a bird when intruded upon or annoyed at the nest. All Owls hiss and snap their bills fiercely at an intruder and the larger ones quite loudly:—

उलूकाकारतां धृत्वा फूत्कारैरतिदारुणैः

स्कन्दपुराण, काशीखंड, I.20.48.

Some of the larger Owls like the Tawny Fish-Owl occupy the deserted nest of an Eagle for Laying their eggs and bringing up the young. This fact was known to the ancients, to wit, the story of a dispute between उलूक

and गृध्र for the possession of a nest related in the third canto interpolated between cantos 59 and 60 of उत्तर काण्ड of the Rāmāyaṇa. गृध्र has been used here in the general sense of a bird of prey including the Eagle. It is a poor story, badly told and the final judgment of Rāma is also incorrect, but that is immaterial for our present purpose.

3. The common names for an Owl are उलूक, कौशिक and पेचक. The first name probably refers to their noisy character (cf. उलुलि, उलूलि outcry), the second to their living and breeding in holes (कोश), and the third to the dark brown plumage of some of them.[1] The smallest Owls, viz. the Owlets, being known as क्षुद्रोलूक, उलूकचेटी, पिङ्गला or डुण्डुल the term उलूक has as a rule been confined to the larger hooting Owls both in the Ṛgveda and later literature while the names महाकौशिक and महापक्षी belong to the boldest and most powerful of them all, the Forest Eagle Owl (see below). On the other hand the so-called common names like नक्तंचर, तामस[2], क्रूरराविन्, दिवाभीत, दिवान्ध, नखाशी, हरिलोचन, घूक, घोरदर्शन etc. are merely in the nature of descriptive adnouns stressing a particular habit or character of an Owl. Complementary names like काकारि and कौशिकारि mean an Owl and a Crow respectively as mutual enemies, a particular large Owl overpowering and killing a Crow at night and the latter having the better of the former during the day.

4. Apart from the general classification based on the size of the birds there is another which subdivides the family according to (1) the colour of the plumage, e.g. ताम्रोलूक for the Bay Owl, श्वेतोलूक for the White or Barn Owl (Art. 48) and पिङ्गला for the Owlets; (2) the shape of the head, e.g. कुम्भोलूक for the larger hooting Owls with a large round head and a marked depression on the forehead which divides the head into two globes, as it were, resembling the prominences on the forehead of an elephant (कुम्भिन्) ; and (3) the way ear-tufts are carried, e.g. शशोलूक for one that has long aigrettes or ear-tufts resembling the long ears of a hare; ऊर्ध्वकर्ण for one that wears its ear-tufts always erect; and finally, प्रावारकर्ण or प्राकारकर्ण for those that have their tufts spread out sideways. Besides we have the name वायसान्तक उलूक for a particular species that kills and eats mainly Crows and श्येनोलूक far one having the ways of an eagle.

5. The following verse from the काकोलूकीय in पंचतंत्र is an interesting commentary on the epithet घोरदर्शनः—

---

1. धन्वन्तरि, राजनिघण्टु and कल्पद्रुकोश have listed the names of the larger Owls and the Owlets separately. धन्वन्तरि also has पेचस्तु मेचको ज्ञेयो for the dark coloured Bulbul (Art. 6) so that it is possible that पेचक and मेचक are allied forms meaning 'black or dark colour'. अभिधानप्पदीपिका, 1023 actually gives मेचक in the sense of Sansk. पेचक for हस्तिपुच्छमूलोपान्त.

2. तामस. malignant or loving the darkness तमस्.

"वक्रनासं सुजिह्माक्षं क्रूरमप्रियदर्शनम्
अक्रुद्धस्येदृशं वक्त्रं भवेत् क्रुद्धस्य कीदृशम्"[1] ॥

In the following passages उलूक and कौशिक are evidently the inauspicious large hooting Owls as distinguished from the Owlets which often nest near or actually in human habitations:—

"यदुलूको वदति मोघमेतद्—"
RV. 10.165.4.

"कपोत उलूकः शशस्ते निर्ऋत्यै—"
VS. 24.38.

"गृध्रः कङ्कः कपोतश्च उलूकः श्येन एव च
चिल्लश्च धर्मचिल्लश्च भासः पाण्डर एव च ॥"
शब्दकल्पद्रुम under पाण्डर.

"गुञ्जत्कुञ्जकुटीरकौशिकघटाघूत्कारवत्कीचकः"
उत्तररामचरित, 2.29.

One who kills his friend is reborn as a large Owl destined to kill innocent (i.e. friendly) birds all his life :—

"कौशिको मित्रहन्ता—" गरुडपुराण, 2.2.80.

These hooting Owls have been mentioned as उलूक, कौशिक or घूक both in बृहत्संहिता, 42.62; 85.49 and वसंतराज (pp. 245, 246). With these preliminary observations we may now proceed to a brief consideration of the various types of Owl, their Sanskrit names and some references to them in literature.

OWLETS:

6. The common Spotted Owlet of the towns, villages and gardens is the best known Owl in India. This is the शाकुनेय or bird of augury mentioned as पिङ्गला in बृहत्संहिता, 87.4 and as पिङ्ग, पिङ्गला,[2] पिङ्गेक्षण, पिंगचक्षु, and पिंगलिका in the 13th Varga of वसंतराज. In this work the bird's call-notes consisting of one to five syllables, its attitudes and movements have been described and interpreted in great detail for purposes of augury. The खर्गला (खर+गल, कण्ठ, noisy) of ऋग्वेद 7.104.17 and अथर्ववेद, 8.4.17 would seem to be this Owlet. Similarly the कृकालिका of the काकोलूकीय of पंचतंत्र who conducted the day-blind Owl to his nest-hole should be this bird which does not shun

1. रक्तनासिक (fr. रक्तनास) for an Owl in the lexicons seems to be a wrong reading of वक्रनास, for no Indian Owl has a red or reddish bill. The Himalayan Wood Owl, however, with its fleshy-yellow bill makes the nearest approach to the adnoun. This verse occurs in तंत्राख्यायिका in a slightly different form.

2. पिंगला may well mean yellow-eyed, and if so the name would correspond to हरिलोचन for the larger Owls.

day-light. The name उलूकचेटी (Owl's hand-maid) is perhaps based on a similar but more ancient story.

7. Smythies refers to certain calls of Owls as "having the character of 'songs', i.e. either one note or a simple combination of notes repeated at varying intervals" (p. 310). Thus the call of the Brown Wood Owl is said to consist of four deep musical syllables, who-hoo-hoo-hoo (ibid.). This reminds one of the story how the sage Nārada was advised to learn music from an Owl residing near the Mānasarovara lake on the Himalayas:

"उलूकं पश्य गत्वा त्वं यदि गाने रता मतिः
मानसोत्तरशैले तु गानबन्धुरिति स्मृतः ॥"
x x x
"गंधर्वाः किन्नरा यक्षास्तथा चाप्सरसां गणाः"
x x x
"गानविद्यां समापन्नाः शिक्षितास्तेन पक्षिणा" ॥[1]
लिङ्गपुराण, II.2.7-10

The point is that the ancient Indians also appreciated the musical calls of the hated bird ! Now the Western Himalayan Barred Owlet, occurring from Muree to Simla and from Garhwal to Eastern Nepal, is not only the most diurnal of all Owls but has also "a really very beautiful rippling call: a whistle consisting of notes running into one another and dying gradually away" (S. Baker in F.B.I., 2nd edn.). Similarly the Eastern Collared Pigmy Owlet of Nepal has a "rather metallic tonk-ta-tonk-tonk, high pitched (call), usually repeated many times. Often heard in the day-time" (Smythies, p. 311). The former goes by the name of बड़ा डुंडुल in Hindi which is the same as Sansk. डुण्डुल for a small Owl. डुण्डुल (डुं डुं इति शब्दं करोति) is probably an onomatopoetic word and would seem to be related to Prakrit डुंडुओ for जीर्णघण्टा, an old or perhaps a small and slightly damaged bell. The name therefore clearly refers to the bell-like notes of the above two Owlets, and both are डुण्डुल क्षुद्रोलूक.

8. The Scops Owl is practically the same size as the common Spotted Owlet but unlike the latter it is entirely nocturnal and possesses well developed aigrettes which are carried in an erect position. The call is a soft and musical too-whoo or too-whit. It should be the ऊर्ध्वकर्णोलूक mentioned in अभिधानराजेन्द्र under उलूक, after the erect ear-tufts of the bird.

9. The body-plumage of the Northern Bay Owl (11.5") is of a chestnut colour on the upper parts including the tail, and vinous pink below. It occurs in Nepal and further east in the Himalayan valleys. It is entirely nocturnal in its habits and in the day-time the most stupid and incapable of all Owls, allowing itself to be captured by the hand and, when released,

1. The bird of these verses would seem to be the Himalayan Brown Wood-Owl with a "deep musical call—who—hoo—hoo—hoo" (Smythies).

sitting dazed in the sunlight. During the breeding season it excels all other Owls in the appalling nature of its cries as if half-a-dozen cats are fighting (S. Baker). The adnouns दिवान्ध (blind by day) and क्रूररावी (having atrocious calls) found in the synonymies for the Owl are therefore more true of this than any other Owl. बिडाल for a kind of bird (the Cat-bird) in the following could well be for this bird except for the fact that पक्खि बिराल in Prakrit means the flying-fox or the large fruit bat:—

"बिडालोऽपि खगान्तरे"—विश्वप्रकाश.

The most fitting name for this Owl, however, is ताम्रोलूक (the reddish Owl) which was emblazoned on the flag of the यक्ष tribe and called ताम्रोलूक ध्वजा in Ch. 16 of कौमारिका खंड of स्कन्दपुराण. See also मत्स्यपुराण, 148.90.

10. The Indian Brown Hawk-Owl (12.5") is brown above and white marked with large drops of light brown below. It has no aigrettes and has a soft call of whoo-hoot repeated twice or thrice. It is known as कालपेचक in Bengal and the name corresponds to Sansk. कृष्णपेचक (M.W. under पेचक but not *sub voce*).

11. The Long-eared Owl (14.5") is distinguished by long tufts, usually borne erected (Ency. Brit. 11th edn.) and is most probably the शशोलूक which has served as a model for the face of a particular attendant of स्कन्द:—

"कूर्मकुक्कुटवक्त्रश्च शशोलूकमुखास्तथा।"

—M.Bh. 9.45.79.

Again, one of the 'mātris' of the same deity is said to have had a face like that of the शशोलूक :—

"शशोलूकमुखी कृष्णा कर्णप्रावरणा तथा"।

ch. 30

शतोलूक in the Venkateshwara edition is a misprint. This Owl breeds in the Himalayas and is found in the outer ranges from Kashmir to Sikkim.

12. The Short-eared Owl (15") is a winter visitor and prefers thick grassy plains of the Terai areas of North India. Its ear-tufts are so small that they are "hardly discernible even at close range" (Smythies). Its call is a shrill clear keaw, keaw (ib.) and the name काकरुक (काकस्य रुक् ध्वनिरिव ध्वनिर्यस्य—त्रिकाण्डटीका) for an Owl would seem to belong to it. The only other Owl having a call like the Crow's is the Snowy Owl (Para. 20 below). The correct form of the word is probably काकरूक as in हेमचन्द्र and मेदिनी, and like काकभीरु simply means an Owl in general. If so the short-eared Owl has no particular name in Sanskrit. It is however also possible that both the forms काकरुक and काकरूक existed and had different meanings but came later to be mixed up.

HOOTING OWLS:

13. If उलूक and कौशिक are common names for all large Owls irrespective of their calls, the name घूक (घू घू शब्देन कायति) is specific for

hooting Owls. पेच or पेचक[1] again, is a hooting Owl (पेचक: घूके— हेमचन्द्र) and if from root पच्, 'to burn or bake' the name may well refer to the darker coloured birds like the Brown Fish-Owl, "a large heavy brown" bird and the Indian Great Horned-Owl described as "a large dark brown owl" (Salim Ali). The name कुलाल (को भूम्यां लालयति शावकान्?, cf. कुलाली शकुनिका, Art. 40), on the other hand refers to the habit of laying the eggs and bringing up the young on the bare ground which is characteristic of Scully's Wood-Owl, the Himalayan Brown Wood-Owl and a couple of others. There is yet another classification of these Owls with respect to the presence or absence of ear-tufts. The Wood-Owls have no tufts on their large round heads and they are the कुम्भोलूक of the Mahābhārata, cf. कुम्भवक्त्रस्तु कुम्भकः, M.Bh. 9.45.75:—

"हृत्वा पिष्टमयं पूपं कुम्भोलूकः प्रजायते"

M.Bh. 13.111.101.

One may well ask, what exactly is the connection between पूप and the Owl? पूप is a pan-cake made from batter prepared with some flour and the cake on being fried in oil or ghee assumes a brown colour and is pitted all over in a lighter shade, thus resembling the mottled plumage of the bird, and hence the propriety of the sentence on the person guilty of stealing the cake.

14. Other members of the group possess long pointed ear-tufts which emerge outwards in a curve from the head. These are the Fish-Owls and the Horned-Owls one of which, said to be a resident of the Himalayas and given the fully descriptive name of प्रावारकर्ण, is mentioned in the Mahābhārata as a long-lived bird: अस्ति खलु हिमवति प्रावारकर्णनामोलूकः— 3.199.4. The काकोलूकीय section of पंचतंत्र, on the other hand, mentions the Crow-killing species of Owls, their king अरिदमन and the latter's minister प्राकारकर्ण. Now as there is only one particular species of Owl in India, the Dusky Horned-Owl, that kills and eats Crows, the very apt name of प्राकारकर्ण belongs to it. There is also a clear reference to the Crow-killing habit of this Owl in the Rāmāyaṇa. When after a break with रावण, विभीषण goes over to Rāma the latter's ally सुग्रीव warns him against the Owl-like tactics of the enemy:—

"निहन्यादन्तरं लब्ध्वा उलूक इव वायसान्।" 6.17.19.

Again, it was after seeing this Owl work havoc among the Crows at night that अश्वत्थामा determined to kill the पाण्डव's while asleep during the night (M.Bh. 1.2.296), and the Epic gives us an interesting description of the bird:—

1. I believe it is possible to deduce the meaning of 'the brown colour', the colour of charred or burnt material, in a secondary sense from the root पच् to bake or burn (M.W.).

"उलूकं घोरदर्शनम्
महास्वनं महाकायं हर्यक्षं बभ्रुपिङ्गलम्।
सुदीर्घघोणानखरं सुपर्णमिव वेगिनम्
सुप्ताञ्जघान सुबहून् वायसान् वायसान्तकः॥"

M.Bh. 10.1.36

The स्कन्दपुराण also relates the above incident and calls the Owl भास after भास, the powerful Bearded Vulture:—

"ततोऽपश्यत्समायातं भासं द्रौणिर्भयंकरम्
क्रूरशब्दं क्रूरकायं बभ्रुपिङ्गकलेवरम्॥
स भासोऽथ भृशं शब्दं कृत्वालीयत शाखिनि
सुप्तान्काकान्निजघ्नेऽसौ अनेकान् वायसान्तकः"॥[1]

ब्रह्मखंड, सेतुमाहात्म्य, 31.44-45

We have, therefore, प्रावारकर्ण or प्राकारकर्ण-उलूक for the Fish-Owls and Horned Owls as a group, and वायसान्तक-उलूक or भासोलूक for the Dusky Horned Owl. बृहद्रूप for a kind of Owl in M. W. may be one of these (cf. महाकाय above), or the name, more probably, refers to the next bird, the महाकौशिक:

15. The magnificent Forest Eagle Owl (24″) is one of the largest and the most powerful members of the entire family. It is dark brown above and fulvous barred dark brown below and wears long dark brown aigrettes like its cousin, the Great Horned Owl. The feathers on the face are bristly and the tarsus is fully feathered. It breeds in the outer Himalayas in the North and in the forests of the Nilgiris and Malabar in the South. It is bold and daring like an Eagle and preys much upon the same kinds of birds and animals as an Eagle does. "As soon as it is twilight it sallies off after its prey and when hungry does not hesitate to hunt by daylight. For this purpose it quits the heavy forest and takes to the open country, light scrub and bamboo jungle, or thin deciduous forest. This Owl is certainly the boldest of all Owls. It preys constantly on the largest pheasants, jungle-fowl and does not hesitate to attack pea-fowl...saw one feasting on a big civet cat which showed by the marks that it had been killed by the bird. The power of its grip is extraordinary and it will drive its claws half an inch deep into the leg or arm of a man. The usual note is a very deep mumble, and when, as was often the case, a pair perched on my house-roof at night, the noise sounded just like two old men conversing in very deep tones. It also has a loud caterwaul—a single note very seldom used but very piercing.[2] It eats fish, snakes and monitor lizards as well as game etc. and

1. The sources of adnouns like घोरदर्शन, हरिलोचन, and क्रूराविन् of the lexicons for an Owl are perhaps to be found in these passages. The Dusky Horned Owl has been compared to भास because of its very pale grey plumage resembling that of the Bearded Vulture.

2. Also a call of "two soft but resounding booms at about 3 seconds interval and audible from a great distance"—Smythies. Hence the Hindi name of हुहु for it.

will also devour carrion, for I once disturbed it eating the remains of a tiger and once that of a goat" (S. Baker in F.B.I., second edition). It is also "said to kill. . .young deer" (Blanford and Oates, F.B.I., first edition).

16. This Owl is the महापक्षी ('the great bird', महासउण in Prakrit) of the lexicons, the महाकौशिक (the Great-Owl) of Garuḍa Purāṇa, and श्येनोलूक the carrion-eating Owl of the Mahābhārata. वैजयन्ती defines it as under:—

"महापक्षी च कृष्णोऽसौ नक्तकः कृतमालकः।"

i.e. the great bird is of a dark colour and an Eagle of the night. कृतमाल is a homonym and means (i) the tree Cassia fistula, known also as सुपर्ण and सुवर्णक (beautiful leaved or gold-coloured), from its long drooping racemes of yellow flowers regarded as garlands (कृता माला येन); (ii) the spotted deer which occurs in flocks or in long lines when on the move; and (iii) one wearing a sort of garland or tuft of some thing. The last meaning is not given in the lexicons but in the present connection the adnoun कृतमालक, descriptive of a bird, is comparable with the Sansk. names मालक and मालिक for the Tufted Pochard (Art. 84, C.). In this sense the epithet would seem to refer to the long ear-tufts on the Owl's head. But it is also possible that the author of the वैजयन्ती wishing to describe the bird as 'a night Eagle' (नक्तकसुपर्ण) has used कृतमालक as a synonym or substitute for सुपर्ण due to the exigency of the metre which called for a longer word.[1] The phrase सुपर्णमिव वेगिनम् used in the Mahābhārata for the Dusky Horned Owl, quoted above, would seem to support this last interpretation. Be that as it may, the name महापक्षी for a kind of Owl in वैजयन्ती is fully appropriate to this great bird. In the same way महाकौशिक occurring as the title of a charm or मंत्र quoted in the Garuḍa Purāṇa, 1.134 refers to this bird. There the guttaral conversational notes of the Owl have been given a set form just as the various calls of the Spotted Owlet have been conveniently rendered for purposes of augury in वसन्तराज, 13. 25-33 and बृहत्संहिता, 87. 38-39.

17. The mythological story of the destruction of the sacrifice being performed by दक्षप्रजापति is related in the Mahābhārata, 12.283 where a dwarfish demon born out of a drop of Śiva's perspiration pursues and destroys the यज्ञ who having assumed the form of a deer was fleeing up a hill. The physical characteristics of the dwarf are said to resemble those of the श्येनोलूक (Eagle-Owl):—

"ह्रस्वोऽतिमात्रं रक्ताक्षो हरिश्मश्रुर्विभीषणः।
ऊर्ध्वकेशोऽतिरोमाङ्गः श्येनोलूकस्तथैव च॥
करालकृष्णवर्णश्च रक्तवासास्तथैव च।"

---

1. शाल्मली, the tree Bombax malabarica, is also a synonym for सुपर्ण, the Golden Eagle which is also सुवर्णाङ्ग; cf. सुवर्णक for कृतमाल; cf. also words like किङ्किरात, पीतभद्र, भृङ्गराज, वञ्जुल, i.e. which mean both a particular plant and a particular bird सुपर्णः स्वर्णचूडे च गरुडे कृतमालके—मेदिनी.

Here the reference is clearly to an Owl having the habits and courage of an Eagle. हरिश्मश्रु corresponds to the whity-brown bristly feathers on the face of the bird; ऊर्ध्वकेश to the long aigrettes; कृष्णवर्ण and रक्तवास to the dark brown and fulvous colour of the bird; and अतिरोमाङ्ग stands for its soft and downy plumage. It is also interesting to note that the demon, like the Eagle Owl, is made to kill a deer. The श्येनोलूक[1] would thus seem to be our Eagle Owl.

18. Again, the carrion-eating Owl of the same Epic cannot but be this bird:—

"गृध्रकाकबलोलूककङ्कगोमायुहर्षणम् (युद्धम्) ।" 7.167.83

and the Owl eating away the bodies of sinners in hell with other carrion-birds is the same:—

"काकैर्बकैर्वृ कोलूकैर्मशकैर्वृ श्चिकैस्तथा ।"

गरुडपुराण, 2.3.14.
(Venkateshwar Edition);
मार्कण्डेयपुराण, 12.9. (Ibid.)

19. The Eagle Owl goes under the name of हुहु or हुहु चील in Hindi and मिगदोरी (मृगद्रोही –मिगदोन्ही –मिगदोरी ?) in Bhutan. This is probably the same as the शुशुलूक of RV. 7.104.22 (शुशु—हुहु). The Bhutanese name, if it means 'enemy of deer', would also be significant. According to Sāyaṇācārya शुशुलूक means a शिशुलूक (?) an Owlet, i.e., a minor enemy. उलूक यातु would then be a more powerful enemy working at night and कोक यातु, an enemy couple moving about and working together like a pair of चक्रवाक birds, cf. "चक्रवाकेव दम्पती" (AV. 14.2.64).

20. The Snowy Owl is again a large bird with a length of twenty three inches and a wing-span of about five feet. It is a pure white bird with a few brown bars on the upper parts and is feathered to the toes for protection against the cold of the circumpolar region which is its breeding home. Its voice is "a cry harsh like the crow's". It is very bold and does not hesitate to attack the man who molests him—even dogs. It preys upon wild pigeons, ducks, ptarmigans, fish etc. in day-light but during winter it also hunts at night (Cassess's Book of Birds). In winter it moves down to Central Europe and Central Asia and has once been obtained in North-West Punjab. It is possible that in the long past this Owl bred more plentifully in its native haunts and was therefore seen more often in the Himalayas and the North-West of India. The शब्दकल्पद्रुम renders पाक as a large Owl (पेचक)[2]

---

1. Prakrit वीरल्ल सउण—उलूकजातीये हु-लापक पक्षिणि of अभिधानराजेन्द्र exactly corresponds to the name श्येनोलूक. वीरल्ल means श्येन. हु-लापक calling हु हु, clearly points to the Hindi name हुहु for this Owl. चील in हुहु-चील is a bird of prey, the Kite. The crested Serpent-Eagle is called डोगर चील (fr. Pr. डूंगर a hill; Hill-Kite) in Hindi. Although the Owl has brown eyes the demon's red eyes emphasize his fiery nature.

2. पेचक clearly implies that पाक is not a क्षुद्रोलूक.

and the name of a particular राक्षस by killing whom Indra received the title of पाकशासन (ibid.). पाक also means' 'a child' and the 'grey or white colour'. The term पाकोलूक may thus refer either to an Owlet (शिशुलूक of सायण) or a large white Owl just as पाकहंस means the all-white Swan (Art. 84-A).

21. Now it is quite possible that this powerful Owl capable of killing large birds and bold enough to attack man was the physical basis for the पाक Demon killed by Indra just as the gigantic Adjutant Stork (बक) is at the bottom of the mythological बकासुर[1] (Stork-Demon) killed by young Kṛṣṇa. We also have the various types of Demons (यातु) named after large birds like गृध्र, उलूक, सुपर्ण, etc. in the Ṛgveda, 7.104.17. Finally the adnoun कटश् means both an Owl and a demon (para 2, Art. 48). If the above conjecture has a certain amount of probability in it the name पाकोलूक may well belong to the Snowy Owl. The epithet of उलूक for Indra also may have something to do with his killing the 'Owl-demon', the पाक राक्षस.

---

1. भागवत, 10. 11.48 ff. Cf. also पूतना in bird form in हरिवंश, 2.6.22 and the two sons आडि and बक (Black and White Ibis) of अन्धकदैत्य in मत्स्यपुराण, 156, 11 ff.

PLATE I

1. Indian Grey Shrike
2. Indian Baybacked Shrike
3. Rufous backed Shrike
4. Indian White-bellied Drongo
5. Indian Golden Oriole
6. Crowbilled Drongo
7. White-breasted Swallow Shrike
8. Marshall's Iora
9. Grey Hypocolius or Shrike-Bulbul
10. Waxwing

PLATE II

1. European Tree Pie
2. Tawny Pipit
3. Redthroated Pipit
4. Central Asian Water Pipit
5. Upland Pipit
6. Blueheaded Yellow Wagtail;
   Head of Grey-headed;
   Head of Turkestan Blackheaded.
7. Indian White Wagtail
   Head of Masked Wagtail
8. Northern Yellow-headed Wagtail

PLATE III

1. Red-faced Malkoha
2. Sirkeer Cuckoo
3. Hawk-Cuckoo
4. Blossomheaded Parakeet
5. Layard's Parakeet
6. Ceylon Lorikeet
7. Violet Cuckoo
8. Banded Bay Cuckoo
9. Small Cuckoo
10. Drongo Cuckoo

PLATE IV

1. Changeable Hawk-Eagle
2. White-Bellied Sea-Eagle
3. Hodgson's Hawk-Eagle
4. Short-toed Eagle
5. Eastern Steppe-Eagle
6. Greater Spotted Eagle
7. Golden Eagle
8. Imperial Eagle

PLATE V

1. Rufousbellied Hawk-Eagle
2. Crested Serpent Eagle
3. Forest Eagle Owl
4. Crested Hawk-Eagle
5. Grey-headed Fishing Eagle

PLATE VI

1. Spotted Sandgrouse
2. Large Pintail Sandgrouse
3. Tibetan Sandgrouse
4. Coronetted Sandgrouse
5. Imperial Sandgrouse
6. Indian Sandgrouse
7. Painted Sandgrouse

50

OSPREY

1. The Osprey stands in a family by itself, being in some respects a link between the Owls and the diurnal raptores. It is a magnificent fisher, and dives from a great height for fish which is its principal food. It frequents large rivers and lakes and also the sea along the coast. Its voice is a short shrill musical whistle repeated a number of times at a stretch. Unlike the Fishing and the Sea Eagles it does not stoop to eating carrion. It is brown above and white below, with a whitish head. It is known as कुरल and मछरंगा in Hindi corresponding to कुरर and मत्स्यरङ्क (-श्येन) in Sanskrit. Recognition of कुरर as a bird of prey is to be found in the fact that it is supposed to be the progeny of भासी the sister of श्येनी :—

"श्येनी श्येनांश्च भासी च कुररानप्यजीजनत्"

पद्मपुराण, सृष्टिखण्ड, 6.64.

अमर and later lexicographers have treated कुरर and उत्क्रोश as synonymous and have therefore done away with the old distinction between the Osprey on the one hand and the Fishing and Sea Eagles on the other simply because they too like the former kill fish for food:—

"उत्क्रोशकुररौ समौ"—अमर[1]

"उत्क्रोशो मत्स्यनाशन. कुरर."—अभि. चिन्तामणि

"कुररो मत्स्यनाशनः।"—हारावली

चरक and सुश्रुत, however, have kept them apart, the former as कुरर and the latter as उत्क्रोश and the same distinction obtains in Buddhist and Sanskrit literature as well. डल्हण on सुश्रुत explains कुरर as "कुररश्चिल्याकारो नादोत्थापितमत्स्यः, हस्तमत्स्यग्राही, कुरल इति लोके"—and उत्क्रोश as 'कुररभेद' i.e. a bird resembling, or a kind of कुरर. This is as it should be, for the fishing

---

1. This equation is really a homonymous one covering the Osprey, Fishing Eagles, Gulls, Terus and the Curlew. For the last two it must be taken in the feminine gender—उत्क्रोशी कुररी समौ. See Art 68. For कुरर as the Demoiselle crane See Art. 62.

Eagles and the white-bellied Sea-Eagle have very loud and raucous calls and are therefore उत्क्रोश, whereas the call of the Osprey is a shrill musical whistle and it is for this reason कुरर. मत्स्यरङ्क is a common name for Kingfishers and has been extended to these large fishers both in popular nomenclature and in poetry. The fishing Eagles do not dive for fish but take it from the surface of the water or from the shallows. मत्स्यरङ्क in the following verse is therefore the Osprey diving in the sea for fish:

"मत्स्यरङ्कनिरातङ्क लवणाम्भसि मज्जसि।
इयं हि जाठरी ज्वाला व्याकुलीकुरुते न कम्॥" उद्भट

कुररा: in the following are either Gulls or Ospreys:

"अस्माद् हंसा जलक्लिन्नाः पक्षैः सलिलरेणुभिः
कुरराः सारसाश्चैव निष्पतन्ति पतत्रिणः"॥[1]
रामायण, IV.52.12.

'कुरर' with the descriptive epithet of पंक्तिचर is the Demoiselle crane which rarely, if ever, swims and never dives, so also the सारस, the Indian crane. Both these birds cannot therefore be intended and 'सारसा': must be understood to mean swimming and diving birds in general i.e., other than the Geese, Ducks and Gulls.

2. The वेस्संतर जातक, verse 2106, mentions उक्कुस (उत्क्रोश) and कुरर as different birds in the Himalayas and the commentary explains उक्कुस as कालकुरर 'dark-plumaged' and कुरर as सेतकुरर 'white-plumaged' which agrees very well with the dark-grey or brown body-colour of the Fishing Eagles, and the white head and lower parts of the Osprey respectively. There is an interesting play upon the word कुरर in its two different meanings of Osprey and Demoiselle Crane in a story of the महाभारत where the fish-eating bird कुरर, having, once upon a time, been punished with death for taking life by the vegetarian birds (Swans), is changed into a mainly vegetarian कुरर, the Crane:

"सामिषं कुररं दृष्ट्वा वध्यमानं निरामिषैः।
आमिषस्य परित्यागात् कुररः सुखमेधते॥"
12.179.9

This example of the virtue of giving up meat-eating is repeated in स्कन्दपुराण, नागरखण्ड (185.10), and the भागवत has the following:

"सामिषं कुररं जघ्नुः बलिनो ये निरामिषाः।
तदामिषं परित्यज्य स सुखं समविन्दत॥"
11.9.2

---

1. The Allahabad edition reads सलिलविस्रव: for सलिलरेणुभि: If the description—जलक्लिन्ना:. . . रेणुभि: is confined only to हंसा; it is possible to render कुरर and सारस of the second line as referring to the Demoiselle and सारस cranes.

बलिन: are the Swans—See Art. 84A. In the स्कन्दपुराण, however, कुरर, described as holding a snake in its talons, is not the Osprey which does not kill or eat snakes but the उत्क्रोश,White-bellied Sea-Eagle, which lifts up sea-snakes for food. The line dividing कुरर and उत्क्रोश is so thin that they are often confused both in the lexicons and literature.

"आकाशस्थं ददर्शाऽसौ सामिषं कुररं नृप।
भ्रममाणं गृहीताहि वध्यमानं निरामिषैः।"

रेवाखण्ड. 54.59.

—निरामिषैः i.e. हंसैः as in the verse from the भागवत. For Fishing and Sea Eagles see Art.52C.

51

VULTURES AND LAMMERGEYER

1. The Vultures of India have been distributed into five genera, four of which are represented by a single species and one by three. Two of these last, the Fulvus and the Himalayensis, look very much alike in the field and appear to be members of a single species as the colour of the plumage in both is variable in shades of fulvous, fulvous-brown and fawn. We have, therefore, six readily distinguishable species of Vulture, and including the Lammergeyer, seven. The following statement shows the genera, the species, their size, and common English and Sanskrit names:

GENUS	SPECIES	SIZE	ENG. NAME	SKT. NAME.
Aegypius	Monachus	42″	Cinereous Vulture	काल or श्यावगृध्र
Sarcogyps	Calvus	32″	Black V.	कुण्डली or रक्ताङ्ग सुमुख- or उद्दीपक-गृध्र
Gyps	i. Fulvus &) Himalayensis)	41″-47″	Griffon	पाण्डर गृध्र
	ii. Indicus	38″	Long-billed V.	शकुन गृध्र
Pseudogyps	Bengalensis	35″	White-backed V.	शितिकक्ष गृध्र
Neophron	Perenopterus	24″-26″	White Scavenger V.	भासक, शकुन्त, or गोष्ठ कुक्कुट
Gypaetus	Barbatus	48″	Bearded V.	भास, अलज, आज-गृध्र

2. The Bearded Vulture, with a fully feathered head and neck, occupies an intermediate position between the Vultures proper and the true Eagles but has been placed with the latter in the F. B. I. There is reason to believe that the ancient Indians also regarded him both as a Vulture and an Eagle. Later on, however, his affinity with the Neophron (भासक) was recognized under the names भास and महागृध्र, and he is therefore included in this Article. The term गृध्र, now a common name for all Vultures, originally applied to all birds of prey including the Eagles as is clear from its use in "श्येनो गृध्राणाम्"—RV. 9.96,6, and has been so used in classical literature as well. Thus the snake-lifting गृध्राः of दशकुमारचरित, ch. 5 can only be the Serpent Eagles while in बृहत्कथामञ्जरी, 15.212 and प्रबोधचन्द्रोदय,

4.3 गृध्र and गृध्री mean the Common Kite. धन्वन्तरि, indeed defines the Kite as a क्षुद्रगृध्री. Similarly the term शकुनि also in the sense of 'a large bird' is occasionally used for a Vulture, e.g. in :

"कार्यहेतोरिवायातः शकुनिर्वीर्यवान् महान्
गृध्रराजस्य सोदर्यः सम्पातिर्नाम गृध्रराट्"

रामायण, 5.35,62.

3. All birds of prey are mythologically descended from a common ancestor by different Bird-mothers like भासी, गृध्री, श्येनी, etc. which shows their close affinity and yet separates them into subfamilies :

"श्येनी श्येनांस्तथा, भासी भासान्, गृध्रांश्च गृध्रयपि"

विष्णुपुराण, 1.21.16.

The ancients were expert bow-men and had ample opportunities of studying and gaining knowledge about these and other large birds which they often killed for their quills with which to feather their arrows. The story of prince सोमदत्त is an instance in point :

"तस्य छित्त्वा ततः पक्षौ गृहीत्वा राजनन्दनः
बाणपक्षान्विधातुं च सोमदत्तो गृहं ययौ"

वराहपुराण, 137, 74-77.

The अथर्ववेद describes seven sages or singers as seven Eagles and mentions an equal number of Vultures;

"सप्तसुपर्णा कवयः....सप्तगृध्रा इति शुश्रुमा वयम्"

AV. 8.9, 17-18,

and curiously enough six species of true Eagles and roughly, six of Vultures occur in North India, and with the Bearded Vulture included in each group we have seven of each kind as stated above.

4. Vultures appear to have been divided into three groups, viz., (i) गृध्र, (ii) पाण्डर and (iii) भास, as the following verse from विष्णुधर्मोत्तर quoted in शब्दकल्पद्रुम under चिल्ल and पाण्डर would show :

"कङ्कः गृध्रः कपोतश्च उलूकः श्येन एव च
गृहे यस्य पतन्त्येते गेहं तस्य विपद्यते ।"

The name (i) गृध्र would seem to be confined to birds of a dark or brown colour (cf. the synonyms धूम्रपत्रा and गृध्रपत्रा—"गृध्र इव धूम्रवर्णं पत्रमस्याः"—शब्दकल्पद्रुम; and Kālidāsa's description of this darker group of carrion birds—"धूमधूम्रो-क्रव्यादगण" in Raghuvaṃśa, 15, 16); (ii) पाण्डर to those of a lighter colour; and (iii) भास to still lighter or almost white ones. Next we have names for the seven individual species falling within these three groups and they are considered below.

(1) The Cinereous Vulture (48") is a bird of immense size and of a uniform dark-brown colour with the neck naked. He is known as कालगिद्ध

in Hindi which is the same as कालगृध्र of ब्रह्मपुराण, 214, 93-94 named as one of the myrmidons of god Yama in hell, detailed to torture persons found guilty of certain offences. The श्यावगृध्र (dark-brown; cf. श्यावा, the night) of the following would also appear to be this bird :

"उदस्य श्यावौ विथुरौ गृध्रौ द्यामिव पेततुः"

AV. 7.95.1.

(2) The Black Vulture (32″) is distinguished by his red head and neck and red wattless behind the ears. He is a bird of solitary habits and confined to the outer Himalayas and the plains of India. At a carrion-feast other members of the fraternity often "hold this bird in wholesome respect and give way before its superior spirit and demeanour" (Whistler), and the red of his upper parts and the ear-lappets (कुण्डल) being distinctive account for his names like कुण्डली दीपक (flame-red; cf. Prakrit दीवओ = दीपक), and सुमुख in the list of names of the progeny of गरुड in महाभारत,, 5.101,9-12; रक्तोत्तमाङ्ग red-headed; रक्ताङ्ग in M. Williams; cf. रातंग and लालमाथाशकुनि in Bengali; and कर्णिक–or कर्णी–गृध्रः–

"रक्तोत्तमाङ्गः क्रव्यादो गृध्रः परमभीषणः" —M. Bh. 7. 175. 18.

"कङ्कगृध्राश्च कर्णिकाः"—ब्रह्माण्डपुराण, Pt. 2,7. 448.

"काक (कङ्क ?) गृध्राश्च कर्णिनः"—वायुपुराण, Ch. 69.327.

For the mythological explanation why this सुमुख गृध्र deserted the higher Himalayas the reader is referred to Art. 1-B.

The carrion-eating श्विङ्क्षाः of RV. 10.87.7, AV. 8.3.7, and T. Saṃhitā, 5.5.16, rendered as a particular bird of a reddish colour by सायण on AV. and as spotted kites (?) by Griffith would appear to be this Vulture. If, on the other hand, it is an animal, the name may possibly be the same as the later खिखि or खिङ्खिर for the fox or jackal. The interpretation of सायण or T.S. as 'the red-faced monkey' is impossible as no monkey is known to be a carrion-eater.

(3) The White-backed Vulture (35″) is of a dark leaden colour with a conspicuous large white patch across the rump, white lining to the wings and white flanks. He is clearly the शितिकक्षिन् of तैत्ति. संहिता, 5.5.20 from कक्ष 'arm-pit or waist, also flank'; cf. हिरण्यकक्ष, 'wearing a golden girdle'. कक्ष in the name refers either to the rump as the bird's waist or to his flanks. The name सुपार्श्व for a son of सम्पाति in रामायण, 4.59,8 also refers to him. This complets the list of गृध्राः as dark or brown coloured Vultures.

(4) The Griffon (Gyps fulvus, 41″-47″) occurs in India in three forms or geographical races, viz., the European, the Indian, and the Himalayan, but they resemble one another so closely that they are not ordinarily separable in the field (Whistler). The head, body and the front part of wings are a dirty white and the remainder of the plumage is brownish grey and black. In the Himalayan form (44″-49″) the contrast between

the whitish undeıbody and the black wings is conspicuous during flight. The bill is deep and laterally compressed. The Griffons are in the habit of congregating in large numbers at fixed resting places on rocky cliffs, but if a good meal is obtained in the plains they assemble on trees. They also breed in colonies on cliffs; cf. गृध्रवट for a fig-tree and गृध्रकूट, for a mountain on which Vultures cangregate or breed in numbers. They are evidently the पाण्डर or पाण्डुर (–गृध्र) of the verse quoted in para. 4 above, and the मेरुतुण्ड (having a high or deep beak) of कल्पद्रुकोश which also refers to their great size and gregarious habits :

"अपि सङ्घातचारी स्यात् मेरुतुण्डो महाखगः"

The Griffon is always well represented at a carrion-feast and this fact accounts for the punishment in store for a flesh-eating glutton in his next birth—"पाण्डुरः परमांसभुक्"—गरुडपुराण, 2.2,71. This vulture is the वायुवेग and मातरिश्वा of Mahābhārata, 5.101 and is also the basis for the mythological सम्पाति (flying or settling down together), brother of जटायु :—

"गृध्रौ द्वौ दृष्टपूर्वौ मे मातरिश्वसमौ जवे
ज्येष्ठोऽवितस्त्वं सम्पाते ! जटायुरनुजस्तव"—रामायण, 4.60, 19-20

(5) The Northern Long-billed Vulture (Gyps indicus, 38″) is again a pale coloured but much smaller bird than the Griffon. In general colouration he varies from dark to buffish brown, has no feathers at all on the head and scarcely any down on the neck, and differs in this respect from all the preceding birds. He is known as सागुन in Hindi corresponding to Skt. शकुन, 'rendered as a vulture or kite' in M. Williams. In the following equation from मेदिनी शकुन is specific for a particular kind of bird, and the नामचन्द्रिका commentary on the त्रिकाण्डशेष also renders शकुन as a Vulture and the name should therefore belong to this bird :

"शकुनस्तु पुमान् पक्षिमात्रपक्षिविशेषयोः"

In Bengal the name सागुन has been extended to the White-backed Vulture as well.

(6) The White Scavenger Vulture or the Neophron occurs in two sizes (24″ & 26″) in India. The larger Egyptian variety ranges from about Delhi to the extreme North-West and the smaller is common throughout the country but is rare in the territory of the former. Both haunt towns and villages and live largely on human excreta and dung and occasionally on carrion. The name भास really belongs to the Bearded Vulture but has been applied to this bird as well because of his white plumage. Strictly speaking, however, his size and habits fully justify the more correct name भासक (अल्पार्थे, कुत्सितार्थे-कन्) for him, as indeed he is called in the following verse :

"कङ्क गृध्र वट श्येन भास भासक बर्हिणः"

Bhāgavata. 3.10,23 (Bengal edition, cited in शब्दकल्प० under कङ्क).

Other names are गोष्ठ–, घोष्ट-कुक्कुट, गोष्ठचर, गोष्ठगोचर and शकुन्त. The first four emphasize his mean status and correspond to his European name, 'the Pharaoh's chicken' and the following synonymies connect them with the last name as also with भास:—

"भासो घोष्ट-कुक्कुटगृध्रयोः"—विश्वप्रकाश.

"भासस्तु भासि गृध्रशकुन्तयोः"

"शकुन्तो विहगे भासे"—हेमचन्द्र

The names based on गोष्ठ or घोष्ट (a village or settlement of cowherds) refer to the bird's habit of frequenting the neighbourhood of villages but the etymology of the name शकुन्त for this particular bird is not clear and even हेमचन्द्र contents himself by merely saying—"सामान्योऽपि विशेषे वर्तते"— अभि० चिन्ता०. It is however important to note that the bird goes by the name of गोबरगीध (Dung-Vulture) in Hindi and this may perhaps help to etymologise शकुन्त as शकं, गोमयं पुरीषं वा उनत्ति भेदयति; or शकार्थे उनत्ति गच्छति (?)[1], for he is also seen descending to farm refuse or cow-dung.

The power of flight of this junior भास in regard to speed and altitude has been rated above that of the Sparrows and the Crows and as equal to that of birds like the Storks, Ibises, Herons, etc. (क्रौञ्चाः) and the Fishing Eagles including the Osprey. Then come in order the commoner Eagles and Hawks, the large or true Vultures, the Swans and Geese, and finally, the Golden Eagle :

"आद्यः पन्थाः कुलिङ्गानां ये चान्ये धान्यजीविनः
द्वितीयो बलिभोजानां ये च वृक्षफलाशनाः
भासास्तृतीयं गच्छन्ति क्रौञ्चाश्च कुररैः सह
श्येनाश्चतुर्थं गच्छन्ति गृध्रा गच्छन्ति पञ्चमम्
षष्ठस्तु पन्था हंसानां वैनतेयगतिः परा"

Rāmāyaṇa, 4.58,24-27.

It is an admitted fact that the Golden Eagle (वैनतेय, सुपर्ण) soars to a greater height than any other bird (British Ency.—"Eagle").

The White Scavenger Vulture is apparently the most tame and harmless member of the group and soars high enough but not very high. The name शका in the following, rendered as शकुन्ति by the commentator, would seem to stand for this bird :

"आरण्योऽजो नकुलः शका ते पौष्णाः"

—Vāj. Saṃhitā, 24, 32.

शकुन्ति means भासपक्षी in शब्दकल्पद्रुम, and गोष्ठकुक्कुट in निघण्टरत्नाकर which therefore settles its identity. God पूषन् is regarded as the keeper of flocks and herds of goats, cattle, etc., and bringer of prosperity. Being toothless he lives on a kind of gruel and is therefore known as करम्भाद also. Of the three living things dedicated to this deity the first is his own mount, the second, an

1. cf. कुन्तः—कुं शरीरं उनत्ति भेदयति दारयति वा धातूनामनेकार्थत्वात् उन्द+बाहुलकात् तः। शकन्ध्वादिवत् साधुः।—शब्दकल्पद्रुम.

ichneumon which helps to protect herds of goats and farm animals against snakes and other vermin and must therefore have been a welcome tenant of the early settlements probably even before the cat was domesticated,[1] and the third, the innocuous Vulture being in attendance about the settlements, is indicative of their prosperity and well-being. Soaring low over them he typifies the supervising and protective function of पूषन्. It is not without reason that पूषन् has no teeth and is compulsorily a vegetarian, for the idea seems to be to place this guardian of the herds beyond the temptation of even killing any of his wards for what would otherwise be to him a dainty meat-dish, and the bird chosen for him is also one that rarely eats carrion and depends principally upon a very low type of soft food.

The name शकटार (v.l. शकटाल), again, for 'a bird of prey' would appear to be this Vulture, and the name may well have something to do with शक (dung) and टल्-टाल 'to disturb' and have the same sense as शकुन्त. Neither of these two names can be from शक्-शक्तौ as this bird has nothing to deserve a name indicative of strength, and I repeat that his Hindi name of 'Dung-Vulture' lends strong support to the derivations suggested above. If, on the other hand, the name शकुन्त is also applicable to the powerful Bearded Vulture, it must be treated as a homonym and derived from the root शक्-शक्तौ.[2]

This "base and degrading object" is clearly the दिआहमद (द्विजाधम, a mean or low bird) and कीबसउण (v.l. कीवसउण) from क्लीब शकुन,[3] impotent or weak Vulture) of Prakrit Lexicons. The शकुन्त birds, again, who, according to महाभारत, 1.72.12-13 protected the infant शकुन्तला were apparently a party of these harmless Vultures. He is also the सुपर्ण of a story related in the जैमिनीय ब्राह्मण, II. 438. The Asura-Panis who were the keepers of the cows of Indra and other gods stole and hid them in a deep valley. The gods therefore flatteringly addressed the bird as a सुपर्ण (having excellent or powerful wings) and commissioned him to discover the whereabouts of the cows. He actually discovered them but, accepting a bribe of दधि and आमिक्षा from the Panis, told a lie and betrayed the trust reposed in him by

1. Cf. "[illegible] गेहनुले"—हेमचन्द्र, for the pet Ichneumon sometimes acts treacherously and kills domestic poultry.

2. The synonymy "भासो भास समाख्यातो घोष्टकुक्कुटगृध्रयोः"—विश्वप्रकाश, has been inadvertently mis-interpreted both in शब्दकल्पद्रुम and M. Williams, for overlooking the dual termination of the compound घोष्टकुक्कुटगृध्रयोः. They have incorrectly split up घोष्टकुक्कुट (a single synonym for भास) into घोष्ट and कुक्कुट and rendered भा स as (i) a cow-pen, and (ii) a Cock ! The name simply means 'a bird of a cattle-settlement or of a village'. He is one of the village birds and animals (ग्रामवासिनः) in अग्निपुराण, 231.11. भास as a गृध्र in the synonymy is the Bearded-Vulture or the Lammergeyer.

3. Cf. क्लीब जीविका in महाभारत, 3.33.13. Prakrit गुत्थंडो for भास पक्षी in देशी नाममाला would refer to this Vulture if गुत्थंडो is from गूथ and स्थण्डिल open ground, or अण्डज a bird; cf. गूथलक्त as an adnoun for the Pied Myna.

the gods. Indra, suspecting what had happened, took the bird in his hand and proved his deceipt by squeezing out the आमिक्षा eaten by him. He then let him go with the curse, "May thy sustenance be of bad origin", and that is why the bird now feeds on what is found in the dirty outskirts of a village :—

"सुपर्णे इमा नो गा अन्विच्छेति । तथेति ।....
तस्मै हान्वागताय सर्पिः क्षीरम् आमिक्षां दधीत्येतद् उपनिदधुः ।.....
सुपर्णेष एव ते बलिर्भविष्यत्येतदन्नं मा नः प्रवोच इति ।.....तं ह तच्छ-
शापाऽश्लीलजन्म ते जीवनं भूयाद् यो नो गा अन्विद्य ता न प्रावोच इति ।
तस्य हैतद् ग्रामस्य जघनार्धे यत्पापिष्ठं तज्जीवनम् ।"

जैमिनीय ब्राह्मण[1] II. 338

Needless to say that the story is based upon the habits of the bird and fully supports his later names like गोष्ठ-कुक्कुट and गोबर गीध. The statement attributing the power of separating milk from water to this Suparṇa in the Vedic Index of Names and Subjects is incorrect.

7. The majestic Lammergeyer (Lamb-Vulture) or Bearded Vulture (48″) is a huge Eagle-like bird distinguished from other Vultures by a fully feathered head and neck, and a beard consisting of a tuft of long black bristles descending perpendicularly from the chin and similar bristles overhanging the base of the upper mandible (correspoding to moustaches in man). The head and throat are white speckled with black; neck all round, and lower parts white, tinged with ferruginous; upper back and small wing-coverts black; and the remaining parts including the wings deep silver grey. In flight he has a wing-expanse of about ten feet and is altogether the finest of all Vultures. He is a denizen of the Himalayas, keeps to rocky hills and mountains, and is usually seen beating regularly high over precipices and slopes with a steady sailing flight. He also occasionally soars at great elevation and was observed at the immense height of 24,000 feet during one of the Mt. Everest Expeditions (Journal of the B.N.H.S., XXX. 874-875).[2] "The Lammergeier eats carrion but prefers above all things, to feed on bones, swallowing the smaller whole and carrying the larger in his claws high up into the air and dropping them to shatter to pieces on the rocks below, where at its leisure it collects and devours the fragments", and birds on the sea-coast or rivers deal with tortoises in the same way. He is one of the birds "that have fired the imagination of mankind from the earliest days" and his name 'Lamb-eagle' is a relic of ancient days when confusion with the more courageous Golden Eagle credited him with depredations amongst sheep, goats and even children (Whistler).

1. Translated in J.A.O.S. 19, 97 ff.

2. This clearly shows that the भास of the Rāmāyaṇa quoted above cannot be this bird. The भास bird that was occasionally cooked on a spit and eaten (अङ्गारशूल्य-भास— चरक, 26,86) was evidently this vulture and not the filthy Neophron.

The oldest Sanskrit names for this bird are अलज in the Saṃhitās and आज noted in the additional list of Vulture-names in अभि. चिन्तामणि, and both probably derive from अज a goat. अलज, from अल्-भूषणे and अज, should mean 'ornamented like a wild goat, i.e., possessing a beard' while आज should be 'one resembling a goat in some particular detail, e.g., the beard'.[1] Once these names were given to the bird it would indeed not take long for the popular mind to forget the etymology, re-interpret the names and attribute to him the habit of carrying off kids, lambs, etc. It is also possible that the Indians took over the Central Asian tradition mentioned by Whistler. This may also explain the name मेषहृत् for one of the progeny of Garuḍa in Mahābhārata, 5.101, although the Golden Eagle is better entitled to the name as he actually lifts young lambs from villages and young of the Tahr, Barhel, etc. in the Himalyas.

His size and soaring habit has won recognition for him in Vedic ritual, for he is dedicated to the deity of the sky or the intermediate space between heaven and earth : "अलज आन्तरिक्ष:"—Vāj. Saṃhitā, 24.34.

Two of the fire altars in तैत्ति. संहिता 5,4,11 are to be constructed in the shape of the अलज and कङ्क birds. Sāyaṇa regards them as varieties of Eagle, "कङ्कालजौ श्येनस्येवावान्तरजातिभेदौ", and distinguishes the two from the shape of the head and claws, and it may be added that this Vulture has, like other members of the family, blunt claws whereas कङ्क, Palla's Fishing Eagle, is armed with very sharp ones. In his notes on the same Saṃhitā, 5,5,20, he renders अलज as भास, viz., this bird, which again is quite correct. The name भास is after his grey-white head, neck and underparts. It is this भास who is mentioned as one of the nobler birds possessed of great powers of flight :

"हंसभासश्येनसुपर्णादय: पतत्त्रिप्रवरा: ।

Bhāgavata, 5, 24, 6.

He is listed under the names of भास and वट in भागवत, स्कन्दपुराण, महाभारत, etc. with other carrion-birds. वट, as we know, is the न्यग्रोध (न्यञ्च् to hang down and रुह् to grow), the Indian Fig-tree (Ficus benghalensis), which throws out tufts of aerial roots from its branches and is for this reason also named जटाल and भूकेश ("भूकेश: शैवले वटे"—त्रिकाण्डशेष, 'having hair growing downwards') and the similarity of the pendant beard of the big bird to the aerial roots of the fig-tree may well be responsible for the name वट[2]. Moreover when the tree is जटाल the bird is जटायु. In the alternative, the name may be from वट्-विभाजने with reference to the bird's habit of breaking bones by dropping them on the rocks, and in this sense the name would correspond to his Hindi name हड़फोड़ा (bone-breaker). In the following examples भास and वट refer to this Vulture :

---

1. "As it sails past on a level with the observer on a mountain top....its absurd little black goatee stands out in clear profile"—Salim Ali, *Indian Hill Birds* (1949) p. 161.

2. If वट is Prakrit from वृत्, the name may be indicative of the wide expanse of his wrings; cf. नभोवट.

"भासामिषादानुसृतैः श्येनैश्चामिषगृध्नुभिः" (वृतं देशम्)

Harivaṃśa, 2. 5. 20.

"कङ्कवटादिभिश्चेतस्ततस्तिग्मतुण्डैराहन्यमाना आत्मशमलं स्मरन्ति"

भागवत, 5.26.32.

"गृध्रकङ्कवटश्येनश्वसृगालादनीकृतान्"

M. Bh. 11. 16. 29

"व्याघ्रव्यालाननै रौद्रैः काककङ्कवटैस्तथा"

Sk. P. Avantī Kh. 6. 33

Yet another name for him is कम्बालायिन् (कम्बल a dew-lap; a little incorrectly rendered as 'a Kite' by Wilson but doubted as a bird name by M. Williams) after his beard hanging downwards like a dew-lap.

The Vulture that dropped a bone into a tank from the air was probably this :

"पुरा गृध्रेण केनापि नभोमार्गेण गच्छता
अस्थिखण्डं स्वकात्तुण्डात् पातितं क्वापि वारिणि"

Padma-purāṇa 8. 181. 64.

The possibility of this bird being the mythological भेरुण्ड is considered in Art. 81.

जटायु according to हेमचन्द्र and विश्वप्रकाश is 'a kind of bird' (खगान्तर) evidently in reference to his being the महागृध्र of the Rāmāyaṇa. The name clearly implies 'one possessing tufts of hair' which, as we have seen, is perfectly true of the Bearded Vulture with long narial bristles on the face and a beard on the chin; cf. जटिल for a person with plenty of hair on the face. Mythologically जटायु is the son of अरुण and brother of सम्पाति. These names are certainly founded upon the characteristics of three different Vultures. Thus the physical basis of (i) अरुण is the Black Vulture with red upper-parts :

"अरुणो गरुडभ्राता जपापुष्पचयप्रभः"

Harivaṃśa 3. 37. 20;

(ii) सम्पाति, the Griffon of gregarious habits; and (iii) जटायु, the Bearded Vulture. Both गरुड and अरुण, described as birds, were given authority by their father कश्यप to rule over other birds:

"एतौ सर्वपतत्रीणामिन्द्रत्वं कारयिष्यतः"

M. Bh. 1. 31.29,

whence the Hindi name of राजगिद्ध for the Black Vulture or अरुण.

The description of the dying जटायु in the रामायण leaves no doubt whatever as to his identity with the grand Lammergeyer. First we have a reference to his dark-grey back and white breast :

"तं नीलजीमूतनीकाशकल्पं सपाण्डुरोरस्कमुदारवीर्यम्"— 3.51.45,

and then to his red eyes and large body :

"तं गृध्रं प्रेक्ष्य ताम्राक्षं गतासुमचलोपमम्"—3.68.19.

The colour pattern of the bird has already been given above, and as for the eyes, his irides are of a pale orange colour and the sclerotic membrane is blood-red. No other Vulture has red eyes, much less such strikingly red ones, and I need hardly add how very faithfully the great Vālmīki has described जटायु. He has also truly called him गृध्रराज, महागृध्र, and पक्षिप्रवर in the chapters quoted from and elsewhere in the work. I conclude with a highly poetic description of his powerful flight:

"पर्यायात्क्षणदृष्टनष्टककुभः संवर्तविस्तारयोः
नीहारीकृतमेघमोचितधुतव्यक्तस्फुरद्विद्युतः
आरात्कीर्णकणात्कणीकृतगुरुग्रावोच्चय श्रेणयः
श्येनेयस्य बृहत्पतत्रधुतयः प्रख्यापयन्त्यागमम्"

Mahāvīracarita, 5. 1.

The verse is put into the mouth of Sampāti who, listening to the distant sound of his younger brother's wing-beats, anticipates his visit to himself :

'With rythmic beats alternately covering and uncovering parts of the sky; scattering the clouds and thereby exposing flashes of lightening to view; and breaking down the rocky cliffs of the mountain ranges into pebbles and powder, the mighty vibrations of the vast wings of Jaṭāyu proclaim his arrival from a great distance.'

Lastly, the monkey-eating habit attributed to a vulture in the following passage of the Rāmāyaṇa is clearly based upon information furnished by sea-faring Indians visiting the eastern Pacific Islands where the Harpy Eagle of the Philippines, is said to live chiefly on monkeys :—

"ते प्रायमुपविष्टास्तु दृष्ट्वा गृध्रं प्लवङ्गमाः
चक्रुर्बुद्धि तदा रौद्रां सर्वान्नो भक्षयिष्यति"

Ram. 4.51, 2.

52

EAGLES, FALCONS AND ALLIED BIRDS

The Fishing and Sea-Eagles, and the Lammergeyer belonging to the present group have already been dealt with, the former with the Osprey and the latter with the Vultures for reasons stated in the respective articles. The remaining birds of the group are considered here. In the second Edition of the *Fauna of British India* (Birds), the Falcons are placed before the Eagles but as the latter are the largest members of the family, I give them precedence in this article.

A. TRUE EAGLES

1. In English, the name Eagle is ordinarily confined to the larger diurnal birds of prey which are not Vultures. Seven or eight species of them are known to exist in Europe, and six in India. As a rule the female Eagle is visibly larger than the male. They are "remarkable for the power and stateliness of their flight which is largely soaring-in type, i.e. the wings are not flapped, but kept stretched out, and the bird appears to float through the air". The voice of an Eagle is a "not unmusical trilling scream" of several notes. They kill their prey like mammals, birds, reptiles, frogs, etc., on the ground, and all, with just one solitary exception, feed on carrion as well. That exception is the Golden Eagle of the Himalayas (Aquila chrysaetos daphnea) while the western sub-species (A. C. chrysaetos) is known to be a carrion-eater. The older belief of scientists that the Himalayan bird also feeds on carrion was recorded in the first edition of the *Fauna of British India* (Birds) but it has since been definitely contradicted by that keen observer of the Raptores of the Punjab and Himalayas, C. H. Donald, F. Z. S., who after a prolonged and accurate study of these birds, has established the fact that the Himalayan subspecies never stoops to carrion, and the earlier statement has now been omitted from the second edition (1922) of the *Fauna* in justice to the great bird who inspired the sages of the Ṛgveda in a most wonderful way and played no mean a part in the evolution of Vedic thought and imagery, including even the later Vedānta Philosophy. I must, therefore, record here our grateful thanks to Mr. Donald for his vindication of the honour of the truly noble Suparṇa, the Himalayan Golden Eagle.

2. All the birds of prey are descended from the primeval Garuḍa according to the mythological statement in the Mahābhārata, 5. 101 where the opening verses give a fairly long list of the names of the Raptores of North India. That a majority of the names are actually after the physical or mythological characteristics of the different birds is hardly open to doubt, though it is not always easy to identify the individual birds with their respective names in the list. The reason is that several names refer to the same bird either according to his different mythological aspects or to actual habits and colour of its plumage. An attempt, will, however, be made to identify some of them, at least tentatively. The Raptores in their totality, are गारुडाः, गरुडात्मजाः or गरुडान्वय (the Garuḍa family) :—

नैकेर्महापक्षिगणैर्गारुडैः शीघ्रविक्रमैः ।
संपूर्णवीर्यसम्पन्नैर्दमनैरुरगारिभिः ॥ वायुपुराण, 40.3

A further division, indicative of an ancient classification into different groups, e.g. श्येनाः (a comprehensive term for the Falconidae, inclusive of the Eagles, Falcons, and Hawks), भासाः (the Bearded and Neophron Vultures) and गृध्राः (other Vultures) is to be found in another genealogy[1] reproduced in the Purāṇas with slight modifications.[2] The चरकसंहिता, 1.27. 34-35 appears to confine the term श्येन to the Eagles as it separately mentions other birds like कुरर (Osprey and Fishing Eagles) शशघ्नी (Hawk-Eagles), मधुहा (Honey-Buzzard), धूमीका[3] (the Shaheen Falcon), कुलिङ्गका (Sparro Hawks), भास (Bearded and Neophron Vultures) and गृध्र (other Vultures). सुश्रुत, 1.46.74 adds चिल्ल for the Kites, but omits मधुहा and धूमीका.

3. Apart from being the names of the primeval bird the terms गरुड, तार्क्ष्य and वैनतेय are also synonymous with सुपर्ण as a specific name for the Himalayan Golden Eagle. But it must be remembered that सुपर्ण and श्येन have often been used synonymously in the Ṛgveda both for the Golden and other Eagles, and श्येन for the Falcons. Nevertheless the difference between the majestic Golden Eagle, the Eagle *par excellence*, and the others was well understood as may be seen from the following examples where the former is either distinguished as the foremost, the strongest and the fastest Eagle or is called the Suparṇa proper (प्रश्येनः प्रकर्षेण श्येनः the best of all Eagles) as against the smaller members of the group called श्येन :—

"प्रश्येनः श्येनेभ्य आशुपत्वा.... सुपर्णो",

(Ṛgveda[4])

---

1. In Mahābhārata 1.66.59.

2. See the typical verse on the subject cited in Art. 51.

3. Also धूमाका a bird of prey—M. W. It is red as the King-crow (फिङ्गा or धूम्याट) in शब्दकल्पद्रुम and in अष्टाङ्गहृदयटीका apparently by confusion with धूम्याट, but see in Section D., paragraphs 9 and 10.

4. 4.26.4. For सुपर्ण the Golden Eagle and the Golden Oriole, see Art. 19.

"मा त्वा श्येन उद्वधीन्मा सुपर्णो......." (Ibid[1])
"वयसां ग्रोजिष्ठं बलिष्ठं यच्छ्येनः ...."(श. ब्रा.)
"श्येनसदसि गृध्रसदसि सुपर्णसदसि"
(Tait. Saṃhitā[2])
"तद्यथाऽस्मिन्नाकाशे श्येनो वा सुपर्णो वा ....."
(Brah. Up.[3])
"हंसभासश्येनसुपर्णादयः पतत्रिप्रवराः"
(Bhāgavata[4])

In the following examples "श्येनाः" are the carrion-eating Eagles :—

"गृध्राः श्येना बकाः कङ्का वायसाश्च सहस्रशः ।" (महाभारत[5])
"भासामिषादानुसृतैःश्येनैश्चामिषगृध्नुभिः ।" (हरिवंश[6])

Similarly the name गरुड has often been used for the Sea-Eagle (Art. 50). The flesh and bones of गरुड are ingredients in the preparation of a certain medicated oil in a recipe for the treatment of rheumatism, in भावप्रकाश[7] but it is difficult to say what particular bird is meant. If the author belonged to North India it may well be the Golden Eagle but if he was from the South the bird would be the White-bellied Sea-Eagle of the Indian Coast, or again the term may refer to the common Tawny Eagle.

4. As alreay observed in Art. 51 the अथर्ववेद speaks of "Seven Eagles":—

"सप्त सुपर्णा कवयः......इति शुश्रुमा वयम्" (अ. वे. 8.9.17-18)

and it has just been stated that at least six species of true Eagle are at present known to occur in India, where however as in the West the lammergeyer also has sometimes been regarded as a kind of large Eagle. It is the 'gier eagle' of the Bible, Leviticus, ch. 11,18 and Denteronomy, ch. 14,17. We have already seen in Art. 51 that the Lammergeyer stands midway between the Vultures and the Eagles so that by including it in the सुपर्ण or Eagle group we have seven Eagles representing the seven sages mentioned in the verse from the Atharva-Veda. The तैत्तिरीय संहिता[8] places the अलज,, viz., the Lammergeyer, on a footing of equality with श्येन and कङ्क for diffierent fire-altars and सायणाचार्य in his commentary actually regards अलज as a kind of श्येन or Eagle:—

---

1. 2.42.2 and Śata. Brāh. 3.3.4.15.
2. 4.4.7.
3. 4.3.19.
4. 5.24.6.
5. 7.7.36; 7.97.13.
6. 2.5.20.
7. Verse 304 in the Chapter styled वातव्याध्यधिकार.
8. 5.4.11.

"कङ्कालजौ श्येनस्यैवावान्तरजातिभेदौ" ।

There cannot, therefore, be any objection to the inclusion of अलज as the seventh member common to both the groups, Eagles and Vultures.

5. The original physical basis for गरुड as the नागाशी (snake-eater) was most probably the Sea-Eagle who picks up sea-snakes from the sea or sand-beach and devours them on a nearby tree, and the ancients must have obtained this knowledge either from their own maritime residence prior to their entry into India as a second wave along the Persian Gulf or from their maritime experiences along the Makran-Sind-Kathiawar-coast-line. The Sea-Eagle is certainly the bird who is the गरुड of Acts 4 and 5 of the Nāgānanda Drama of Śrīharṣa. Here the old tradition of गरुड as a snake-eater is fully preserved and we find the Eagles taking snakes from the sea and eating them at fixed perches so that large heaps of bleached bones of snakes have formed under particular trees.[1] This habit of the powerful Sea-Eagle was later transferred to the सुपर्ण (Golden Eagle) of the Himalayas, who does not, however, kill or eat snakes. Support for the above view is to be found in the following verse where सुपर्ण clearly refers to the Sea-Eagle:—

क्रममाणं समीक्ष्याथ भुजगाः सागरंगमाः ।
व्योम्नि तं कपिशार्दूलं सुपर्णमिव मेनिरे ॥ (रामायण[2])

And yet a knowledge of the true habit of the Golden Eagle not killing snakes is clearly reflected in the story of कृष्ण granting a boon to the great Cobra of the Jumna whom he subdued that the सुपर्ण would no more eat snakes marked with his foot-print, viz., the spectacled Cobras and incidentally any snake:—

द्वीपं रमणकं हित्वा ह्रदमेतमुपाश्रितः ।
यद्भयात्स सुपर्णस्त्वां नाद्यान्मत्पदलाञ्छितम् ॥ भागवत (10.16.63)

6. नाग means both a snake and an elephant, so that the name नागाशी (elephent-eater) for गरुड came to be interpreted as 'the eater of snakes and elephants', though we must not overlook the possibility of an Imperial Eagle actually feeding, on rare occasions, upon the carcass of a dead elephant, as a probable event in support of the name. More probably however, the idea of गरुड eating an elephant was taken over from a belief common in Persia and the neighbouring countries of western Asia regarding the fabulous Roc or Rukh of immense size carrying off elephants to feed his young[3]. Similarly the habit of the Lammergeyer, regarded as a

1. इत्येष भोगपतिना विहतव्यवस्थो यान् भक्षयत्यहिपतीन् पतगाधिराज ।
मास्यन्ति यान्ति च गताश्च दिनैर्विवृद्धिं तेषाममी तुहिनशैलरुचोऽस्थिकूटाः ॥ Act. 4.6.
2. 5.1.73. For further evidence on the point see section C of this Art.
3. Article on Roc., Ency. Brit., 11th Edition.

kind of Eagle, of eating turtles was also attributed to गरुड. All these attributes, touched up with a little anthropomorphism, helped to raise गरुड to the status of a semi-divine being (नराङ्ग) destined to play a great role in Hindu mythology:

पक्षिजङ्घो नराङ्घ्रिश्च तुङ्गनासो नराङ्गकः।
द्विबाहुः वक्षयुक्तश्च कर्त्तव्यो विततासुतः ॥
नारदपञ्चरात्र in शब्दकल्पद्रुम, 2.8.811, col.1.

We have again the picture of गरुड or तार्क्ष्य holding both an elephant and a tortoise as food:

यस्य हस्तिनमादाय महाकायं च कच्छपं ।
भक्ष्यार्थं गरुडः शाखामाजगाम महाबलः ॥ —रामायण[1]

and sage कश्यप advising his son गरुड to live on both these in Mahābhārata.[2] The अग्निपुराण also describes the semi-human form of तार्क्ष्य in these words:

पुनर्ध्यायेन्महाताक्ष्यं द्विपक्षं मानुषाकृतिं ।
द्विभुजं वक्रचञ्चुं च गजकूर्मधरं प्रभुम् ॥
असंख्योरगपादस्थमागच्छन्तं खमध्यतः ॥ 33.22-23.

This composite bird is the गरुड of mythology and the vehicle of God विष्णु. It is quite possible that the difference between the Golden Eagle and the Lammergeyer was well understood, and certain traits or habits of some of the important birds of the group were deliberately attributed to the primeval गरुड, their progenitor, so as to account for them in the progeny on grounds of heredity. This is perhaps going too far, but this much is fairly certain that the actual physical basis for the conception of गरुड as पक्षिराज and even of his composite form, is no other than the Golden Eagle. This is clear from the description of the the plumage of गरुत्मत् or सुपर्ण and his Himalayan home given in महाभारत and elsewhere:—

हृष्टानि सर्वभूतानि नाम चक्रुर्गरुत्मतः
सुरूपं पत्रमालक्ष्य सुपर्णोऽयं भवत्विति ॥ महाभारत 1.33,23.

---

1. 3.35.28. Cf. Mahābhārata 1.29.43.

2. 1.29.13. ff. It is also possible to explain these mythological facts differently: The etymological meaning of पन्नग is "what moves low on the gound'; कच्छ is 'land by the side of water or a hill' so that कच्छप-कच्छेष्ट is 'what lives in such places'; and निषाद 'what squats on the ground'. The terms may well therefore simply refer to the normal prey taken by सुपर्ण in different situations. Now if we remember how mythology has grown up from forgotten metaphors, polynymy, use of equivocal words and false etymology it is not impossible to see how the mythical सुपर्ण came to have attributes like पन्नगभोजन, नागाशन, etc. and is said to have eaten serpents, tortoises, elephant and even the human निषाद. Or, are these statements illustrative of the principle परोक्षप्रिया हि देवाः according to which facts must be dressed up in mystifying language as in a riddle ?

पक्षिराजो गरुत्मांश्च यं नित्यमधितिष्ठति[1]— म. भा. 12.327.7.
सुवर्णस्वर्णवपुषा सुपर्णं खेचरोत्तमम् । मत्स्य पुराण, 1.174.47.

The देवकूट mountain in the Himalayas is mentioned as the breeding place of सुपर्ण—

जन्मक्षेत्रं सुपर्णस्य वैनतेयस्य धीमतः । —वायुपुराण, 40.2.

and another where a certain medicinal herb was known to grow—

सुपर्णसुवने गिरौ जातं हिमवतस्परि— अथर्ववेद, 5.4.2.

The easy, effortless and graceful soaring flight, as also the courage and power to carry off heavier prey of the Golden and incidentally of other Eagles have been fully recognized:—

प्र सु ष विभ्यो मरुतो विरस्तु प्रश्येनः श्येनेभ्य आशु पत्वा
अचक्रया यत्स्वधया सुपर्णो हव्यं भरन् मनवे देवजुष्टम् ॥ (ऋग्वेद, 4.26.4)
अयं लोकः सुपर्णानां पक्षिणां पन्नगाशिनां ।
विक्रमे गमने भारे नैषामस्ति परिश्रमः ॥ महाभारत, 5.10.1.

The epithet अचक्र refers to the soaring flight of the Eagle with wings held stiff on a level with the body, and the real significance of the term becomes clear when we recall the adnoun चक्रपक्ष for the Swan or Goose which must fly with a rotary motion of the wings and cannot soar.

7. Finally, types of demons and robbers, active during the day and night, have been named after certain birds of prey in RV (VII. 104. 22) where सुपर्णयातु is one who robs forcibly even the strong during day-time; गृध्रयातु, one who robs the weak in the day, and so on. वाज.संहिता (11.79) also names different kinds of thief.

8. The following six true Eagles of genus Aquila are, everyone of them, a सुपर्ण or श्येन in a general sense, and no individual names for them, with the solitary exception of the Tawny Eagle, are available though I have ventured to offer a couple of guesses based on vernacular names which however need not be taken seriously at all.

(i) The female Golden Eagle measures up to 40 inches and has a wing-expanse of over 7 feet. The male is 4-5 inches shorter. The colour of the plumage is brown becoming darker with age, and the feathers of the head and neck are pointed and of a golden-red hue. With powerful feet and long claws the birds are mighty hunters and live on Snow-cock, Monal, other Pheasants, Pigeons etc., and on mammals like young antelopes, sheep, and Musk-deer. These Eagles often hunt in pairs,[2] and taking advantage of this trait Falconers used to train them in pairs to hunt

---

1. The carrion eating Imperial is a tree-breeding Eagle of the plains and lower hills in the outer Himalayas, Sind and Baluchistan and has no right to the title of पक्षिराज or गरुत्मान्.

2. Cf. AV. VII. 70.3 cited in Section D of this Art.

gazelles etc. in their natural way. They also carry off lambs and kids from the sub-Himalayan villages. They are to be met with along the Sutlej water-shad, from Kotgarh to the Kailas range in suitable localities, also in parts of Kashmir, Chamba, Simla district and in Tehri-Garhwal as far up as Hursil (हरशिला) within two marches of Gangotri[1]. C.H. Donald remarks that the Golden Eagle in flight "shows a large expanse of chest" and this fact has been beautifully recorded by the great poet भारवि. Describing the magnificent flight of a number of Golden Eagles soaring higher and higher, he says that the sky, being pushed back as it were by their broad chests, appears to be retreating before them :

मनःशिलाभङ्गनिभेन पश्चात्
निरुध्यमानं निकरेण भासाम् ।
व्यूढैरुरोभिश्च विनुद्यमानं
नभः ससर्पेव पुरः खगानाम् ॥ (किरातार्जुनीय[2])

In the preceding verses the poet has named the birds तार्क्ष्यं, गरुत्मत् and सुपर्णं which is perfectly correct.

The Golden Eagle, the noblest of all Eagles, is also called महावीर ("महावीरस्तु गरुडे" —मेदिनी) probably for two reasons: (i) for his mythological exploit in successfully bringing away the सोम from heaven and (ii) as a compliment to his courage and boldness in a state of nature and also as a trained bird in capturing fawns, gazelles, wild goats, etc., for his keeper. The Chinese practised the art of falconry so far back as 2000 B.C.,[3] and even at the present day the nomads of Central Asia train a certain species of Eagle to take large game, such as antelopes and wolves, and tribes in the neighbourhood of Yarkand use the Golden Eagle for hawking purposes and so too the Kirghiz Tartars.[4] A Golden Eagle returning to the fist of his master is illustrated in the *Encyclopaedia Britannica*.[5] That the ancient Indo-Aryans also were equally familiar with this sport and actually trained the Golden Eagle for the chase is clearly stated in the letter-press to the illustration of the bird opp. p. 822, Vol. 7, Ibid. It runs, "It is the largest bird of prey trained for falconry, and has been used in Asia, especially in India, for taking bustards, antelopes, hares, foxes, and, it is said, even larger animals, such as wild goats and wolves." It is, therefore submitted that many of the metaphors and similes in which सुपर्ण or श्येन figures

1. C. H. Donald. F.Z.S., in the Journal of B.N.H.S. Vol. XXVI, 247 ff.

2. 16.45.

3. "Falconry", Enc. Brit. 14th Edn. The Golden Eagle is still trained in Eastern Turkistan "for hawking and flown at deer, hares, wolves, and even wild boar; and as one can imagine, the eagle's dash and courage is magnificent"—F. Martin Duncan in *Birds, Trees and Flowers* (Odhans, London, 1947).

4. "Eagle" and "Falconry". Enc. Brit. 14th Edn.

5. Opp. p. 44 of Vol. 9, 14th Edn.

in the Ṛgveda are actually based on the practice of the art. Pāṇini mentions the art of Falconry as "श्यैनम्पाता" in 4.2.58 and Manu (3.164) debars Brahmans living by falconry or dealing in Falcons from ceremonial feasts.[1] H. Kirke Swann, E. Z. S., has also traced in *A Monograph of the Birds of Prey*, Part I the art of falconry back to 1700 B.C. in Persia and earlier still in China[2]. Thus the commonest picture of श्येन bringing away सोम (rendered at places by सायण as food or अन्न) from the mountain heights unaided (RV. IV. 26. 4-7) would seem to be based on a trained Golden Eagle capturing a mountain goat or fawn and holding it down until his keeper took it from him. The pictures depicted in RV. IV. 26.4-7 and IV· 27 would seem to be based on the performance of a trained Eagle. Take again similes like the following:—

> सीदंछ्येनो न योनिमा—RV. 9.61.21.
>
> श्येनो न योनिमासदत्— RV. 9.62.4.
>
> श्येनो न वंसु षीदति— RV. 9.57.3.
>
> श्येनो भूत्वा परापत यजमानस्य गृहान् गच्छ तन्नौ संस्कृतम्—वाज. संहिता 4.34.

and several others which compare सोम, flowing into its proper vessel, with a श्येन getting back to the wooden perches (वंसु) or stands meant for hunting Eagles and Falcons in their master's house. The Lugger Falcon, for instance, released for the chase, returns to his master's fist.[3] The पञ्चविंश ब्राह्मण[4] relates a story that once यज्ञ left the gods and kept flying high up as a सुपर्ण or Golden Eagle and returned to them only when he was invited back with the सौपर्ण साम. This is clearly based upon the art of falconry where a bird flown from the wrist often returns to his master when called back. A tame Golden Eagle will at once perch on the arm extended for him, and he frequently alights on the trees and follows his master from tree to tree keeping him in sight.[5] The female of an Eagle or Falcon is larger and more powerful than the male and it is she who is always the more efficient hunter. For this reason it is invariably the female that is preferred and trained for the chase. This fact has been recognized in गायत्री as the female and गायत्र as the male Eagle :—

> यद्गायत्री श्येनो भूत्वा दिव. सोममाहरत् तेन सा श्येन:—शत. ब्राह्म. 3.4.1.12.
>
> गायत्रीं हरिणीं ज्योतिष्पक्षां. . . . Ibid. 11.4.1.8.
>
> गायत्रचितं पक्षिणं चिन्वीत स्वर्गकाम:—कपिष्ठल कठसंहिता 21, 19.

---

1. Sale of Eagles (सुपर्ण) and Hawks (श्येन) and theft of these, presumably trained, birds is mentioned in चतुर्वर्गचिन्तामणि of हेमाद्रि Vol. 4, pp. 176 & 244, respectively.

2. See C. H. Donald on the Monograph in the *Journal of the Bombay Natural History Society*, Vol. XXX, p. 895.

3. Jerdon; See also section B of this Art.

4. 14.3.10.

5. *British Birds*, Part I. Vol. IX, Birds of Prey.

For the reason why the female गायत्री becomes the श्येन (masculine) see section D, para, 3, of this article. It will be seen that the term श्येन really stands for the female bird.

The highest compliment to the courage of this Eagle is paid when it is said that, during a drinking bout, the courage of god इन्द्र flowed out of his heart in the form of a श्येन—"हृदयात्त्विषिरस्रवत् स श्येनो ऽपाष्ठिहा भवद् वयसां राजा"-शत. ब्राह्मण.[1]. The significance of the epithet अपाष्ठिहन् (killing with the claws) would be clear when it is remembered that the powerful hind claw of the Golden Eagle with which, backed by the impetus of the swoop, the prey is struck down, is as large as three inches and more round the curve as against two inches of the Imperial and still less of the other Eagles. No wonder, therefore; at the well-deserved epithet or name of महावीर for him. This reminds one of the name महामुक्तक for a kind of bird included in the list of birds quoted from the old पाराशर संहिता (probably no longer extant) in the भट्टोत्पलटीका on बृहत्संहिता.[2] मुक्तक means a missile like a javelin (cf. करमुक्तम्) and the term has probably been extended also to Falcons and Hawks discharged from the hand to strike or bring down other birds. Expressions like हस्तमोक and मुष्टिमोक (from root मुच्) used in the श्यैनिक शास्त्र[3], lend strong support to this supposition. Applied to other birds the qualifying adjective 'महा' clearly signifies their large size in their own class, e.g. क्रौञ्च and महाक्रौञ्च; हंस and महाहंस. महामुक्तक., therefore, would seem to be a Golden Eagle trained to hunt for his master. The simile of 'a great bird sent forth or cast away'—'शकुनो यथा हितो' in RV.[4] is probably based upon the use of a large bird of prey for hawking. In वाज.संहिता, 24.25 this Eagle has been called a महासुपर्ण to distinguish it from the Smaller Imperial or Tawny Eagle called simply सुपर्ण (Kaṇḍikā 37 of the same chapter)[5], and the almost reverential respect paid to this great bird may be seen in references like :

वैनतेयश्च पक्षिणाम्—भगवद्गीता 10.30.
सुपर्णोऽहं पतत्रिणाम्—भागवत, 11.16.15.

where Lord श्रीकृष्ण identifies himself with him.

A few of the other names attributed to this Eagle may now be considered. स्वर्णपक्ष, golden-winged, is after the light rufous-brown on shoulders of the dark-brown wings. The equation "चिरात् गरुडे"—'eating for a long

1. 12.7.1.6.
2. page 1018.
3. 4.2-3.
4. 9.86.13.
5. In this kaṇḍikā the imposing Blue-bull or Nilgao, the beautiful Peacock and the lordly looking Tawny Eagle (सुपर्ण) are offered to the handsome गन्धर्वाः. These latter are also very noisy (hence named हाहा, हूहू) singers and the three victims selected for them are also noisy. The तै. सं. 5.5.16 substitutes श्येन for सुपर्ण.. In classical litrature also the Tawny Eagle is referred to as श्येन, see para. (iv) below.

time or taking long over one's meal'—would seem to refer to the snake-eating birds like the Serpent-Eagles or the White-bellied Sea-Eagle; or again it may be a purely mythical name referring to गरुड taking a long time to finish off an elephant ! शिलानीड is the Golden Eagle who builds as a rule on cliffs and only occasionally on a tree; cf. the description of the sun at dawn as a reddish Golden Eagle who has no nest i.e. who knows no rest and is ever soaring in the heaven :—

अरुणः सुपर्ण आ यो महः शूरः सदानीकः" RV.[1]

उरगाशन and its synonyms, e.g. नागाशी, are truer of the Serpent and Sea-Eagles than this and must be treated as epithets based on a mythical assumption only. The name शाल्मली refers to the Eagle perching for preference on a large tree of that name or occasionally nesting on it. Names like गुरुभार, वज्रविष्कम्भ (mythical, with reference to Indra's bolt made ineffective by सुपर्ण), विशालाक्ष, विष्णुधर्मा (mythical, being the vehicle of God विष्णु) etc. in the महाभारत -list belong to him. The name मेषहृत् is perfectly true of him but may also be shared by the Lamb or Bearded Vulture according to popular belief though the latter is wholly incapable of lifting a lamb or kid.

(ii) The Imperial Eagle is a sluggish heavy bird, some 5-6 inches smaller than the Golden Eagle. He is of a glossy blackish-brown colour with the lanceolate feathers of the head, back of the neck and sides tawny buff, the head being very much lighter than the Golden Eagle's. The plumage of an adult Imperial is very like that of an adult Golden but a young Imperial has the whole upper plumage tawny buff, wing-quills blackish to brown and the lower parts pale fulvous-buff. The young of both take several years to acquire the adult plumage. In strength, courage, method of flight and of obtaining food they are poles apart. If the Golden Eagle is the most powerful and the boldest of the larger birds of prey, living on Snow cocks, Pheasants, Pigeons, Tahr, Barhel (species of Himalayan goats and sheep) and Musk-deer, the Imperial is inferior in every respect, can hardly kill anything for himself and is content for the most part with carrion and is a constant attendant at slaughter houses. He is also more of a plains bird and places his nest always on trees. He is found throughout the Punjab. Because of his outward similarity with the Golden Eagle the latter has frequently been credited by less expert observers with the ignoble habits of the Imperial Eagle (Donald). This and other Eagles are the carrion-eating (क्रव्याद) सुपर्ण and श्येन of the अथर्ववेद, महाभारत, etc. :—

मर्माविधं रोरुवतं सुपर्णैरदन्तु दुश्चितं मृदितं शयानम्—अथर्ववेद[2]
सर्वानदन्तु तान्हतान्गृध्राः श्येनाः पतत्रिणः—Ibid[3]

---

1. X.55.6.
2. XI.26.
3. XI.10.24.

अतीव हृष्टाः श्वसृगालवायसा,
बकाः सुपर्णाश्च वृकास्तरक्षवः । —महाभारत[1]
तान् सुपर्णाश्च गृध्राश्च कर्षयन्त्यसृगुक्षिताः । Ibid[2]

The Imperial and the next two Eagles breed on trees and any of them, more probably the first, is one of the "द्वा सुपर्णा" of the Ṛgveda.[3] The Golden Eagle also breeds occasionally on trees.

(iii) The Steppe Eagle is a uniform brown to umber brown bird, a few inches smaller than the Imperial Eagle. He is a winter visitor to North India but has been known to breed in India. His habits are very similar to those of the Imperial Eagle and is, therefore, a सुपर्ण or श्येन like him.

(iv) The Indian Tawny Eagle is again a uniform brown varying from pale brown to dark umber, sometimes whitish on the head and body. He is "a fine lordly looking bird and has plenty of courage,...chasing and robbing falcons and hawks of their booty." He goes under the name of रागर in Hindi which is evidently the same as रागपक्षी (jealous of other birds of prey who have secured food) of the निघण्टु रत्नाकर which equates it with रणपक्षी, and the latter is defined by the धन्वन्तरि कोश and राजनिघण्टु in a half verse common to both :

रणपक्षी पिच्छबाणः स्थूलनीडो भयङ्करः ।

The कल्पद्रुकोश also gives the same description with रणमत्तः for रणपक्षी. पिच्छबाण means a bird whose quills are used to feather arrows with. The epithet स्थूलनीड refers to the large nest of sticks and thorny twigs that he makes and भयङ्कर to his shrill screams and habit of robbing other birds of their prey. It is this last trait which has given him the names रणमत्त (–श्येन), रणपक्षी and रागपक्षी. उद्दीपक[4] (one easily excited) as a bird of prey in Mahābhārata, should be this Eagle as the name corresponds to रागपक्षी. Its entry into a residence was considered unlucky :

उद्दीपकाश्च गृध्राश्च कपोता भ्रमरास्तथा ।
निविशेयुर्यदा तत्र शान्तिमेव तदा चरेत् ॥

M.Bh. 13.104.115

He exhibits several traits of the jackal and therefore shares the names शृगाल and गोमायु with that animal. See para. 13, section D of this Article.

---

1. 7.50.9.
2. 11.16.827.
3. RV. I. 164.10

4. The term दीपक rendered as 'a kind of bird of prey' by M.W. is incorrect. This is based upon a misunderstanding of the following lexical definition:—

पक्षिणा येन गृह्यन्ते पक्षिणोऽन्ये स दीपकः । —अभि० चिन्ता० and कल्पद्रुकोश,

दीपक is a pet decoy-bird used to attract wild ones with the object of trapping or killing them. We thus have दीपक कक्कर, दीपक तित्तिर, दीपक मृग, etc. in the जातक and दीपमृग in मानसोल्लास. The underlying idea is that of a light (दीपक) attracting moths & insects to itself.

He is much the most common and most widely distributed Eagle of India but is confined to the drier areas. He is a methodical hunter and preys upon small mammals and birds but attacks even larger birds when pressed by hunger. He also freely devours dead animals even when putrid (F.B.I. 2nd Edn). The carrion-eating brown-plumaged and noisy श्येन in the following examples is apparently this Eagle :—

आधोरणानां गजसंनिपाते शिरांसि चक्रैर्निशितैः क्षुराग्रैः ।
हृतान्यपि श्येननखाग्रकोटिव्यासक्तकेशानि चिरेण पेतुः ॥ रघुवंश, 7.46
श्येनपक्षपरिधूसरालकाः सांध्यमेघरुधिरार्द्रवाससाः । Ibid 11.60

विभिन्नं धन्विनां बाणैर्व्यथार्तमिव विह्वलम् ।
ररास विरसं व्योम श्येनप्रतिरवच्छलात् ॥ कुमारसंभव, 16.12·

गृध्राः कङ्काः बकाः श्येनाः वायसा जम्बुकास्तथा ।
बहुशः पिशिताशाश्च तत्राऽदृश्यन्त मारिष ॥ महाभारत, 7.97.13.

In the last example the first four of the carrion-eaters are Vultures, Pallas's Fishing Eagles, Adjutant Storks, and Tawny Eagles respectively.

(v) The Greater Spotted Eagle (27″) is a dark almost blackish brown bird though in the younger phase the upper back and the smaller wing-coverts are spotted. He is known as कलिजंग in North India and as जियाधर in Bengal. The exact meaning of कलिजंग is not clear but it may refer (कलि-कलह) to the bird's wild clanging cry, jeb-jeb-jeb, compared to a high pitched barking of a small dog by Smythies. जियाधर means one who catches living creatures. "This is a rather sluggish Eagle, often sitting for hours on a perch on some lofty tree" (S. Baker). His food consists in great part of frogs though he also catches fish and kills small birds and mammals for food.

(vi) The Smaller Spotted Eagle (25″) is also a dark chocolate brown bird differing from the preceding bird in minor details of the body plumage but particularly in the tail which shows some traces of a paler barring while the tail of the Greater Spotted Eagle is merely tipped paler. This Eagle goes by the name of जियाधर in the north corresponding to Sanskrit जीवान्तक or जीवहर (?), a catcher or killer of living things. He is not so lethargic as his larger cousin but otherwise the habits of both are similar. He is however more of a thief and plunderer of other birds and their nests. His call is a "very high-pitched cackling laugh" (S. Baker). The Indian Black Eagle (Section B, para 3) also is in the habit of plundering birds' nests for their young or eggs which reminds one of the powers of observation exhibited by the great बाणभट्ट who mentions Eagles that pull out nests of small birds :—

क्वचिच्छकुनिकुलकुलायपातिनः श्येनाः ।

हर्षचरित, p. 82.

(vii) The Lammergeyer or Bearded Vulture, as the seventh Eagle of ancient tradition, has been considercd in Art. 51. This completes the list of सप्त सुपर्णाः, the seven Eagles of India.

B. HAWK-EAGLES, SERPENT-EAGLES & BUZZARD-EAGLES

1. "The Hawk-Eagles are birds of more slender build with smaller bills, longer and more slender tarsi, and longer tails than the true Eagles" (F. B. I. 1st. Edn.) but of similai habits and are members of the larger श्येन group. Almost all of them kill hares for food in addition to other prey consisting of reptiles and birds. They aie the शशघ्नी (= शशाद, शशघाती) of चरक. A young Bonelli's Eagle is brown above and rufous underneath while the adult has umber-brown upper parts and a white body mottled with brown. The Crested, the Changeable, and Hodgson's Hawk-Eagle also have the upper parts umber-brown or brown with a coppery tinge. All these hunt hares, birds, etc. and being of a fairly large size (27-29 inches) they are the शशाद-श्येन defined by सुरेश्वराचार्य in his वार्तिक on the बृहदारण्यक as a large ruddy-brown bird living on hares :—

"श्येनः शशादो विज्ञेयो बृहत्कायश्च रोहितः"—4.3.1160.[1]

The शब्दार्थचिन्तामणि also in its definition of श्येन as शशाद describes the bird as of large size but slow of speed :

महाकायो मन्दवेगः इति व्याख्यातारः

The truth of this statement is confirmed by H. C. Donald who says that though it is easy to train Hawk-Eagles like the Crested Hawk-Eagle, they do not all come up to what may be expected of such large and powerful birds. On the other hand सायण माधवाचार्य commenting on पराशर-संहिता[2] distinguishes the Pigeon-hunting smaller Falcons like the Peregrine and Shaheen (श्येन) from the शशाद :

श्येनः कपोतादीन् पक्षिणो निहन्ति न तु शशमत्ति
अतः श्येनशशादौ भिन्नजातीयौ

Thus we have श्येन, for the true Eagles and the Falcons, and शशाद for the Hawk-Eagles. It may be stated here that the Hawk included under the name of शशाद in the list of Falcons in the श्यैनिक शास्त्र, 4·20 is the Female

1. मन्दवेग slow in hunting; cf: क्षिप्र श्येन, the Perequine Falcon.
2. Ch. 6.5. Bom. Skt. Series. No. 59; Vol. II. Pt. 1; 1898.

Goshawk trained to capture hares (Section F of this Article). It will be seen that while all शशाद's are श्येन, all श्येन's are not शशाद and to this extent the lexical synonymy of श्येन and शशाद is subject to modification, and चरक is right in mentioning श्येन (true Eagles) and शशाद (Hawk-Eagles) as different categories in his list of the birds of prey. Some of these शशाद Eagles have specific names as well and they are considered below.

2. M. Williams renders वर्तुलाक्ष (fr. वृत् दीप्तौ to shine) as a "brown Hawk" and the name clearly implies some peculiar quality of brilliance in the eye of the bird meant. Now the eye of Bonelli's Eagle, whose body-plumage is brown as already described "is peculiarly brilliant and fiery in its glance indicating fierce boldness" (Cassel's *Book of Birds*). If, on the other hand, the term is rendered as 'round-eyed' it will have no significance as all Eagles and Hawks have round eyes. वर्तुलाक्ष श्येन should therefore be this Eagle. One of the Hindi names for this Eagle is मोरंगी as it often kills Peacocks in nature and the name is from Sank. मयूरघ्नी (Cf. शशघ्नी) which may well have been its name in Sanskrit though not preserved in the lexicons now extant.

3. भल्लक and भल्लूक mean a bird of prey as well as the black bear :

भल्लूकः प्लवः शकुनिः हिंस्रमृगश्च—उणादि, श्वेतवनवासिन्

The name भल्लूक for a bird of prey therefore clearly points to the Black Eagle (female, 31", male 27") which is brownish black or black throughout. It is found in the Himalayas in the North and Nilgiris in the South. It is mentioed in the भागवत पुराण

"कङ्कगृध्रवटश्येनभासभल्लूकबर्हिणः" 1.10.24.

It is in the habit of carrying off the nests of small birds and examining them for young or eggs, a trait noticed by बाणभट्ट in his कादम्बरी.

4. The Indian Crested Hawk-Eagle and Hodgson's Hawk-Eagle possess long crests (पिच्छ which also means the tail). M. William has नीलपिच्छ for a 'black-tailed hawk' and the name may refer to these birds after their black crests and as a homonym to the Black-crested Baza with both a black tail and a black crest. The Indian Crested Hawk-Eagle is the बाजराज of श्यैनिकशास्त्र 4.39 corresponding to शाहबाज in Persian. The practice of training the Hawk-Eagles for the chase has been considered in Section F on Hawks. The Changeable Hawk-Eagle is known as शदल (fr. शशादन?) in Bengal.

5. The Short-toed Eagle and the Crested Serpent-Eagles in two sizes kill snakes including the poisonous varieties. They are known in Hindi and Bengali as सांपमार and सर्पचर which are the same as Sanskrit सर्पारि, सर्पान्त or नागाशी. One carrying off a black cobra is mentioned by सोमदेव :-

"तावद् गृहीत्वा कृष्णाहिं चञ्च्वा पादयुगेन च ।
श्येनः कुतश्चिदागत्य तरौ तस्मिन्नुपाविशत् ॥—कथासरित्सागर. 87.43.

The M. Bh. list includes नागाशी and सर्पान्त for types of Eagles and these names can apply only to these or to the White-bellied Sea Eagle. Another name, मालाय, in the list is probably in reference to the spotted and broad nuchal crest (माल) covering the whole nape of the crested Serpent-Eagles (cf. मालक for the Tufted Pochard—Art. 84c).

6. The Indian White-eyed Buzzard Eagle is the sole representative of its genus in India. The iris of adult birds is almost white or pale yellow and the name पुण्डरीकाक्ष (white-eyed) for a kind of Hawk in हिन्दी शब्दसागर is for this bird as no other Hawk or Eagle has eyes of that colour. The Buzzard-Eagle (12″-18″) is "no bigger than a Crow" and the name द्रोणक (द्रोण the Raven) of the कल्पद्रुकोश may refer to it or to the Black Eagle which is a little larger than Raven.

C. SEA-EAGLES & FISHING-EAGLES

1. The white-tailed Sea-Eagle is a winter visitor to the north-west of India while the White-bellied Sea-Eagle is a bird of the Indian sea-coast. Both live on fish and the latter also largely on sea-snakes. The white-bellied Sea-eagle is very voracious and seen incessantly returning to one of the big trees on the coast carrying sea-snakes, five to six feet in length, in his claws and devouring them at ease.[1] Both again, do not refuse carrion if available.

2. "The Sea Eagles are among the noblest looking of all birds" and the White-bellied sea-Eagle of the Indian coasts is undoubtedly the bird referred to as the सुपर्ण (गरुड) diving to the sea to seize serpents in the story of the Prince अयोगृह in the जातकमाला of आर्यशूर :—

पक्षानिलैर्लडितमीनकुलं व्युदस्य
मेघौघभीमरसितं जलमर्णवेभ्यः ।
सर्पान्हरन्ति विततग्रहणाः सुपर्णा
मृत्युं पुनः प्रमथितुं न तथोत्सहन्ते ॥ Verse 32.

Simiarly the bird belonging to the family of गरुड (पक्षी गरुडवंशज:) led by his love of carrion to pick up a bundle of elephant-hide containing a living person floating on the sea, is this Eagle :—

तत्र दृष्ट्वा च तच्चर्म निपत्यामिषशङ्कया ।
हृत्वाब्धेः पारमनयत् पक्षी गरुडवंशजः ॥ कथासरित्सागर 12.113

The White-bellied Sea-Eagle, again, is mentioned as the king of birds (अधिपः पतत्रिणां = गरुड) catching snakes in the sea :

"फणावतामुद्धरणेषु वारिधि-
प्रवाहसिक्तावुदयाचलस्थितः ।
वितत्य पक्षावधिपः पतत्रिणां
व्यशोषयन्नप्रतिसूर्यमायतम्" जानकीहरण, 5.20

1. "Stray Feathers". IV. 423.; Cf. चिरात् (चिरं अत्ति) for गरुड—शब्दकल्पद्रुम.

He is known as कोहासा (उत्क्रोश) and सांपमार (सर्पान्तक) in Hindi. The first name is after the bird's call which is, "a very loud clanging cry of many notes" (cf. सप्तराव of the M. Bh. list) and the second explains itself. The White-tailed Sea-Eagle has merely "a querulous chatter, insignificant for so large a bird" and is therefore not उत्क्रोश, but being a powerful bird he has been designated as बल in the Mahābhārata—see below, and cf. सुबल included in that progeny of गरुड in the Mbh list.

3. The Ring-tailed Sea Eagle of Jerdon, belonging to the same genus, Haliaetus, as the two Sea-Eagles considered above, now goes under the name of Pallas's Fishing Eagle. In North India he is undoubtedly a resident inland bird but out of India his range extends to the Caspian and Black Seas and the Persian Gulf. He is the largest Fishing Eagle of North India and is sub-equal in size to the white-tailed Sea-Eagle. He is fulvous white on the head, neck and upper back including the scapulars, also on the upper neck and breast and dark brown on lower back, rump and the remaining parts. Generally speaking, therefore, the colour-pattern of this Eagle resembles that of the much smaller Brahminy Kite (लोहपृष्ठ कङ्क) with white and chestnut where the other is fulvous and dark brown. From his brown-back this Eagle is the कालपृष्ठ कङ्क and from habit of fiercely defending his young at the nest he is also the प्रियापत्य कङ्क of the lexicons (see section E of the article). He is actually known as कंकम् in Nepal (See Sectlon E). It is this कङ्क which is described as a kind of श्येन by सायण in his gloss on तै० सं० 5.4.11. He is मछरंगा or मछमंगा (Sansk. मत्स्यरङ्क) in Hindi, and मछकोरल (मत्स्यकुरर) and बल in Bengal. Now बल (powerful, strong,) as a carrion eating bird, mentioned with कङ्क, Pallas's Fishing Eagle, at several places in the महाभारत most probably refers to the white tailed Sea-Eagle, and both occur in North India. M. Williams renders बल merely as a 'Crow' but in the St. Petersburg Dictionary it is (i) a Crow and (ii) a bird of prey. The passages given below mention बल with काक or वायस and leave hardly any doubt as to its identity :

सम्पतन्तश्च दृश्यन्ते गोमायुबलवायसाः (6.100.27)
बलानां वायसानां न पुरस्तात्सव्यसाचिनः (7.00.4)
गृध्रकाकबलोलूककङ्कगोमायुहर्षणम् (7.107.49)
गृध्राः कङ्का बकाः श्येना यातुधानास्तथा वृकाः (5.143.19)

Here बल is the white-tailed Sea-Eagle, कङ्क Pallas's Fishing Eagle, श्येन the Tawny Eagle, and बक the Adjutant Stork—all carrion eaters. The following again from the महाभारत clinches the point :

गृध्रकङ्कबलैश्चासीदन्तरिक्षं समावृतम् (7.129.19)

Here कङ्क and बल are said to be soaring high in the sky in company with the Vultures and they are the above two Eagles as a Crow is not commonly known to fly, much less to soar, so high whereas the White-tailed Sea-Eagle and Pallas's Fishing Eagle are undoubtedly high-soaring birds. The northern version of the Rāmāyaṇa also mentions बल as a carrion-bird :—

कङ्कगृध्रबलानां च गोमायुगणरक्षसाम् ।
नित्यं भक्ष्यप्रदं युद्धे यमरूपं भयावहम् ॥ (6.171.11.)

and the commentator Govindarāja translates बल as a kind of गृध्र or Vulture, which, though strictly speaking incorrect, is significant and strengthens the above identification. बल and कङ्क again, are compared to महानक्र (the long-snouted Gavial or Gharial and महाग्राह (the crocodile) in a metaphor where a battle-field running with blood and strewn over with dead bodies, weapons etc., is pictured as a river. The comparison evidently implies the great size of the birds feeding on dead bodies :—

बलकङ्कमहानक्रां गोमायुमकरोत्कटाम् । M.Bh. 7.146.35.
कङ्कगृध्रमहाग्राहां नैकायुधझषाकुलाम् । Ibid. 7.131.120.

4. As carrion-eaters, again, the last viz. the white-tailed Sea-Eagle and Pallas's Fishing Eagles would seem to be the अलिक्लव and जाष्कमद respectively of the passage below :—

अलिक्लवा जाष्कमदा गृध्राः श्येनाः पतत्रिणः ।
ध्वांक्षाः शकुनयस्तृप्यन्त्वमित्रेषु समीक्षयन् रदिते अर्बुदे तव ॥ A.V. 11.9.9.

अलिक्लव[1] is apparently a difficult word to solve but if the element अलि in the sense of a bee per Sāyaṇa on अलिंश in AV. 8. 6 .1 is the same as अरि, it may well mean 'one that is terrible to or is feared by the enemy, and the term would qualify the carrion-birds named as an adjective. सायणाचार्य also takes it that way though he explains it as " "अ+विक्लव. The second name जाष्कमद, is perhaps derived from जष[2] or झष, a fish, and refers to a carrion-bird that owes its great strength to eating fish or has an ardent desire for fish-food. In this sense the name corresponds to मत्स्यरङ्क and the only carrion-bird that fulfills this character is Pallas's Fishing Eagle.

5. The Grey-headed Fishing Eagle occurs in two sizes in North India. The large form is not found west of Delhi and the smaller variety is confined to the outer Himalayas and descends as far south as Lucknow only, during winter. None of them would seem to be comprised within the term बल though like the others they too eat carrion. Finally, all the Eagles considered above with the exception of the White-tailed Sea-Eagle, are very noisy and have strident calls and the name उत्क्रोश belongs to them in common. The name महाउत्क्रोश occurs in the title of Jātaka No. 486, the महा उक्कुस जातक, and must belong to Pallas's Fishing Eagle as the largest of the three

---

1. अलिक्लव is mentioned again with गृध्र in A.V. 11.2.2.

2. The form जष occurs in Taitt. Sam. 5.5.13 corresponding to झष in Kāṭhaka Sam. 5.7.3. जष also occurs with water-animals like शिशुमार, पुरीकय, and मत्स्य in A.V. 11.2.25.

Fishing Eagles of North India. The epithet महा clearly implies lesser birds going under the name of उत्क्रोश.

6. Although the Osprey and the Fishing Eagles have been named differently (Art. 50), their proper status as श्येन has been clearly recognised. Thus the punishment of God Viṣṇu by the bird-form (शरभ) of God Śiva is described after the manner of the White-tailed Sea-Eagle or Serpent Eagles stooping again upon a sea or other snake that has slipped out of his talons in mid-air, missing it in the first attempt, and shooting down a second time to catch it :

श्येन इवोरगम्
उत्क्षिप्योत्क्षिप्य संगृह्य निपात्य च निपत्य च[1]

The Osprey or the Fishing Eagle is called a श्येन in the वाराह पुराण[2] and they would therefore be मत्स्यरङ्क श्येन as indeed their Hindi names like मछरंगा and मछमंगा show.

Turning to names in the M. Bh. list it would appear that if by any means सारस, सरिद् द्वीप and पङ्कजित् refer to the Osprey which dives for fish, the Fishing Eagles which take fish from the surface, shallows or mud-shelves of rivers, and the Harriers which pick up frogs etc. from the marshes respectively, the name दैत्यद्वीप should point to a foreign bird like the White-tailed Sea Eagle which visits the country during the winter only. The Himalayan Grey-headed Fishing Eagle is particularly noisy on moonlight nights during the breeding season and may be the basis for the name निशाकर in the list. दिवाकर would then be either an Eagle which is noisy during the day or the Golden Eagle as an emblem of the sun (दिवाकर) which has often been pictured as a सुपर्ण in RV.

D. FALCONS AND HAWKS

I. INTRODUCTORY

1. Falcons and Hawks are two readily distinguishable groups of medium and small sized birds of prey within the family Falconidae differentiated not only by certain physical characters but also by their different methods of attack. The Falcons have as a rule a rather plump looking body, a ring of bare skin round the eyes making for better vision, and long and pointed wings. They have stout beaks armed with a tooth on either side of the upper mandible, and a sharp and powerful hind claw. They attack their quarry in the air and pursue it if missed in the first attack. The Hawks, on the other hand, have a compact body, a long neck, a small head, short rounded wings, a very long tail, and high tarsi. The beak is less vaulted

1. शिवपुराण 3rd रुद्र संहिता 12.15. लिङ्गपुराण 1.25.95.

2. 122.21 ff.

and more compressed at the sides. It has no tooth like the Falcon's but has instead a well pronounced festoon. The bare circle around the eye is entirely wanting. They are more arboreal, hunt low in the woods and hedgerows and pounce upon the quarry on the ground and do not pursue it if missed. A Falcon kills by tearing open the back of a bird with its powerful hind claw but a Hawk overpowers with a formidable grip of its claws and does not immediately kill the quarry. Both have fine large and expressive eyes but their colours are different. A Falcon has brown eyes while the Hawk's are yellow. Both these groups are distinguished in Sanskrit nomenclature as well despite the fact that the term श्येन as a general name for all birds of prey other than Kites and Vultures, is, like the English term Hawk, very comprehensive. Falcons are श्येन in a restricted sense and Hawks प्राजिक (v. l. प्राजि, प्र+आजि contest?), वाजि–, प्राजि-पक्षी, वाजी and वाज. The विश्वकोश and हेमचन्द्र give पालङ्क as well for a Hawk (प्राजि, वाजि, पक्षिणि) but if the word is from पाल् रक्षणे as in शब्दकल्प० it should signify a pet Hawk trained for catching birds.
Derived from roots श्यै, and वज् signifying 'motion' all the names refer to the fast and powerful flight of these rapacious birds.

2. As already pointed out in section A, the art of Falconry, श्येनम्पाता, had been practised by the ancient Indo-Aryans from time immemorial and there are references to it in the Dharma-śāstra and classical literature as well. The magical sacrifice called श्येनयाग in षड्विंश ब्राह्मण, 4.2 performed with the object of killing or injuring a particular enemy is clearly based upon the practice of Hawking where a trained Falcon brings down the intended quarry; compare also 'श्येनेनाभिचरन् यजेत्'—आप. श्रौ. सू., 22.4.13 ff. मनुस्मृति, 3.164 mentions a Brāhmaṇa practising Falconry or dealing in Hawks as श्येनजीविन्. क्षेमेन्द्र describes a princely young man bearing on his left hand the scratch marks made by the claws of a Falcon :

श्येनाङ्घ्रिग्रहदारितोत्तरकरः ....

औचित्यविचारचर्चा, का. मा. Pt. 1, p. 152,

The नैषधचरित gives a highly artificial and forced concept of श्येनम्पाता in 4.20.21 but the much later सुदर्शनचम्पूकाव्य mentions the flying of Falcons and Hawks (श्येनादि) at large birds as quarries :

स हापयत्येव करस्थितेन श्येनादिना पक्षिवराणि भूयः[1]

का. मा. Pt. 14, p. 66.

मानसोल्लास, an encyclopaedic work of the first half of the twelfth century from South India contains a chapter on Falconry (श्येन-विनोद, Vol.2, 267) and although the text is corrupt at places it gives a fair idea about the various species of Hawks caught and trained for the chase, the methods of

1. Has the English word "Hawk" any connection with Sansk. forms like हापन, हापित from root हा in the sense of a bird that is discharged from the hand to catch another bird ?

catching and training them, their respective merits, the different styles of releasing them after the quarry, and the different kinds of birds a particular Falcon or Hawk is capable of killing. Some of the names for the Falcons and Hawks, current in South India, appear to be of Prakritic origin :

सद्यः श्येन विनोदोऽयं कथ्यते कौतुकावहः ।
शालिवा, जावला, लग्नः प्राजिको लङ्गणस्तथा ॥
संजाणा, वेसरा, गृध्रास्तथा यवलकण्ठिकाः ।
चण्डी यावावहाः श्येनाः श्येनानां जातयस्त्विमाः ॥
विनोदेषु प्रयुंजन्ते ततोऽन्ये जातिमात्रकाः ।
तोणकश्चेति विख्यातः पुमानल्पशरीरकः ॥

Verses 1329-1331.

The author of कल्पद्रुकोश would seem to have incorporated the above names in his list of the birds of prey at page 327 :

शालियाजावडाश्चैव लङ्गवः प्राञ्जिका अणिः ।
रङ्गणाश्चैव संवाणा गृध्रा अपिच वेसराः ॥
अचण्डिका कंविकाश्च द्रोणकाश्चावहावकाः ।
पापर्द्धि रसिकैर्ज्ञेया गन्धमादनसम्भवाः ॥

Here too the text is partly corrupt. शालिवा has been misread as शालिया, सञ्चाण as संवाण, कण्ठिका of यवल-कण्ठिका has been separated as कंविका, and the corrupt चण्डी यावावहा has been read and broken up into अचण्डिका and अवहावका. All these make no sense for me at least. लङ्गण would seem to have been rightly corrected to रङ्गण.तोणक, v.l. द्रोणक has been correctly rendered as द्रोणक. Non-Sanskrit names have been underlined above. If शालिव is a corruption of शालि+वि, it may mean 'the noble bird' or 'the noble falcon'. All brown-eyed falcons are known as 'the noble falcons' and the yellow-eyed Hawks as 'ignoble falcons' in English.

3. A later but more comprehensive treatise on the subject is the श्यैनिकशास्त्र by Rājā Rudradeva of Kumaon who seems to have lived in the 16th century A.C. In this book the term श्येन, like the English 'Hawk', has been used both in the title and elsewhere in the body of the book in the inclusive sense for both Falcons and Hawks, and श्यैनिक for the Falconer. Sanskrit names of quite a few of these birds, which must have been current in ancient times, had apparently been forgotten due chiefly to the influence of the Jaina and Buddhist doctrine of अहिंसा and the effective check exercised by it on the sport of Hawking[1] and the authors of both the above works were forced to use local vernacular names in a Sanskritised garb for some of them. Following the practice of Muslim Falconers Rudradeva classifies the sporting Hawks (श्येन) into two classes : (i) the 'brown-eyed' Falcons as कृष्णाक्ष श्येन corresponding to स्याहचश्म वाज of the Persians and (ii)

1. पापर्द्धि as a synonym for मृगया should be traced to the same influence.

the 'yellow-eyed' Hawks as पाटलाक्ष श्येन, the गुलचश्मबाज, and enumerates them as under :-

(i) Female Falcons—

अतोऽनुवक्ष्ये श्येनानां पृथग्जातिविवेचनम् ॥
कृष्णाक्षा पाटलाक्षा च जाती द्वे प्रस्फुटान्तरे ।
तयोश्चावान्तरा भेदा लक्ष्यन्तेऽन्येऽपि भूरिशः ॥
तेषां नामानि कथ्यन्ते जातानां जातिमुख्ययोः ।
कुही, शशाद, चरक, वहरी, लगरास्तथा ॥
तथान्या पक्षकलिका तथा तुरमती परा ।
पुंव्यक्तयश्च तत्संख्याः कृष्णाक्षाजातिजो गणः ॥ Page 18.

The male birds are just referred to in the last line but their names are not given in the book.

(ii) Female Hawks :

वाजा, वासा, वेसराश्च सिचानाश्च चतुर्विधाः ॥ Page 19.

(iii) Male Hawks :

जूराश्चटाः धूति, टुनास्तथा पुंव्यक्तयस्त्वमी ॥
उभयोर्गणयोश्चैषां स्त्रीणां प्राधान्यमूर्जितम् ।
संस्थाने, साहसे, मूल्ये पक्षपातादिसौष्ठवे ॥
वाजाद्याश्च प्रधानत्वात् पुंलिङ्गे व्यपदेशिताः ॥ Page 20.

The last three lines stress the well known fact that the female of these birds is definitely superior in size, strength, speed, and sporting qualities and are therefore always preferred to the males for purposes of hawking. This superiority is the foundation of a convention among Falconers according to which the name of the female bird is always in the masculine gender. This, incidentally, explains why गायत्री, the famle Golden Eagle (the सुपर्ण,), is supposed to be a श्येन (masculine) when she goes up to bring down the सोमः—

यद्गायत्री श्येनो भूत्वा दिवः सोममाहरत्तेन सा श्येनः। शत० ब्रा० 3.4.1.12

and if this explanation is correct the above tradition is very ancient indeed.

4. Foreign birds were often imported by Indian Falconers during the Muhammadan period and these were what are known as "the great northern" Falcons (Hierofalco, the sacred falcons), viz., (i) the Gyrfalcon of Scandinavia, resembling in colouration the Blue Hawk (the Peregrine) but of a much larger size; (ii) the Icelander from Iceland with a paler colouring and a decidedly longer body; and (iii) the Greenland Falcon with a predominantly pure white plumage. Among Indian Hawks the female Goshawk stands out as the most powerful and the largest of all the Falcons and Hawks taken together though the Peregrine and the Shaheen excel in dash and speed. The Peregrine and the Shaheen which head the

list of Falcons in size do not exceed 18 or 19 inches in length whereas the Goshawk measures up to fully 24 inches. The "great northern" Falcons which come nearer in size and strength to the Goshawk were naturally looked upon by the author of श्यैनिक शास्त्र as foreign varieties of the Hawk and he accordingly placed them with the adult and young Goshawks in a separate group, the वाजिनः i.e. the Hawks *par excellence*.

वाजिनः पञ्चधा तेषां पृथक् लक्षणमुच्यते ।
कृशाकृतिर्बलाकाक्षः श्वेतःकृष्णकर्पादिकः ॥ 34
भवत्यङ्गे तथोर्वोश्च सुखसाध्यः प्रकीर्तितः ।
यश्चक्रवाकसंस्थानश्चक्राङ्गः स च कीर्तित : ॥ 35
प्रलम्बः कृष्णसंस्थानः कङ्काभः[1] कालकः स्मृतः ।
चिराद्विश्रम्भमभ्येति सुरक्तोऽपि विरज्यते ॥ 36
यः सर्वाङ्गे हिमप्रख्यो हंसवाजः स कथ्यते ।
स यत्र पूजितस्तिष्ठेत् कल्याणं तत्र जायते ॥ 37
तं प्रयत्नेन रक्षेत्तु वाखेटादिषु योजयेत् ।
तस्य स्पर्शेन नश्यन्ति ज्वराश्चातुर्थिकादयः ॥ 38
यस्याश्वत्थदलप्रख्या लेखा पुच्छच्छदादिषु ।
जायते वाजराजोऽसौ महारावणसंज्ञकः ॥ 39

Ibid. p. 20.

The second line of verse 34 and verse 35 in the above passage refer to the slim looking (because of its very long tail), yellow-eyed or the powerful Goshawk[2] with a black and white spotted plumage (कर्पादिक fr. कपर्द a spotted sea-shell; cf. कर्पादिक for the pied Kingfisher, Art. 41). It is the बलाकाक्षवाज. The चक्राङ्गवाज of the fourth line is a young Goshawk with rufous lower parts (चक्रवाक संस्थान having a body resembling that of the Brahminy Duck). The third line refers to the ease with which the Goshawk can be trained. The कालक वाज of verse 36 and the महारावण वाज of verses 39 and 40 appear to be the Gyrfalcon and the Icelander respectively. The former has an elongated body (प्रलम्ब) and more of the bluish colour than in the Blue Hawk (the Peregrine) so that the descriptive phrase कृष्णसंस्थान also suits it better[3]. The हंसवाज of verses 37-38 is almost certainly the practically all-white Greenland Falcon. This was considered to be a great possession and as the risk of its loss could not be taken it was never to be used for hawking. No wonder, a superstition grew around it, viz., the mere touch of it cured

1. कङ्क in the context is the Grey Heron.

2. Cf. the technical term "Red Hawk" for a Hawk of the first year in young plumage —Ency. Brit., 11th edition, vol. 10, p. 143a.

3. The three 'great northern' Falcons "are very difficult to back to the hood and to manage in the field".—Ency. Brit., ibid., p. 145ff. This goes to support what is stated about the कालक वाज in verse 36, viz. that it takes longer to train and even though well disposed towards its owner it often becomes wild.

a patient of fevers. This would seem to be the white Falcon, 'Taighoon', mentioned in the Memoirs of Jehangir (*Tuzuk-i-Jehangiri*, trans. by A. Rogers, Vol. 2, pp 10-11). It has not been possible for me to find out the Persian names of the other two 'great northern' Falcons. The smaller Sparrow Hawks have been described in the book under the names वासा, वेसर and सिचान. These and their males will be discussed in the section on Hawks.

5. The following lists of vernacular names of the different Hawks and Falcons current in North India and Bihar should prove very useful in the elucidation of the Sanskrit and other names given in paragraphs 2 and 3 above :

बहरी, कुही, लगर, जरकटी, बाज, जुर्रा, बांसा, शाहीन, तुरमती, सचान
चरखा, टोना, बेसरा —हिन्दी शब्दसागर[1]

पाझि, सारिम, नगल, बेसर, वेसरि, ठरङ्गल, ओरङ्गल, जुराटी, छुरिकार,
छुरिआरी, जाओल, टुनिजा, मुरछली, चिचुकार, सइचान
—वर्णरत्नाकर, p. 36.

A comparative study of the Sanskrit and vernacular names supplemented by similar information from the F.B.I. (Birds), Vol. V. leads to the following identifications and they are given here as a preliminary to a more detailed consideration of these birds in the sections that follow.

1. Hawks and Falcons in मानसोल्लास :—

शालिव—the Peregrine Falcon; वहरी of श्यै. शा.; बहरी, बिहिरी in Hindi; Bhyri in F.B.I.; सारिम in वर्णरत्नाकर :

जावल— the Shaheen F.; जावलूम्, in Telugu, कुही, and शाहीन in H. per हि. श. सा. and F.B.I.; कुही in श्यै. शा.; जाओल in वर्णरत्ना.

लग्न:— the Luggar F.; लगर, लग्घड़ in H. and F.B.I.

प्राजिक—the Goshawk; वाजि, वाजी, वाज, in Sansk,; बाज in H. and F.B.I.; पाझि in वर्णरत्नाकर.

लङ्गण—the Kestrel; रङ्गण in कल्पद्रुकोश; but if the root word is लङ्ग 'association' it may be the male of लग्न i.e. Luggar F.

सञ्चाण—the Shikra Hawk; सचान, सिचान in H.; सञ्चान of lexicons including M. W.; सइचान in वर्णरत्नाकर

वेसर— The Besra Hawk and its allies; बेसरा in H. and F.B.I.; वेसर, वेसरि in वर्णरत्नाकर.

(viii) गृध्र—शशाद of श्यै. शा. is a Hawk-Eagle :

(ix) अवलकण्ठिक—जमलकंठी of F.B.I. is the Crested Goshawk :

(x) तोणक (v.l. द्रोणक; कोणक is a w.r.)—द्रोणक in कल्पद्रु॰; तुम्रा, टोना in H. & F.B.I.; टुनिजा in वर्णरत्ना॰; is the male of सञ्चान, the Shikra :

1. "जुर्रा, बाज, बांसे, कुही, लगर, लौने टोने, जरकटी, त्यौं सचान, सानबारे हैं"—from "चिड़ीमारिन" a book of Hindi Poetry by Raghurāja, quoted in हि. श. सा. under 'लगर'. जरकटी and तुरमती are names for the Merlin F.

"बांसा बटेर लव औ सिचान । धूती रु चिप्पिका चटक भान"—सूर, quoted in ibid. under चिप्पिका.

(xi) चण्डी यावावहा and its v. 11 is a corrupt compound the original of which is very difficult to determine. The कल्पद्रु separates it into अचण्डिका and अवहावक. It therefore seems probable that the first element is चण्डिक which may refer either to the Merlin or the Cherrug Falcon. The second element might be for the Basha Sparrow Hawk or the Hobby Falcon. All the four birds were used for Hawking and it is highly probable that at least two of them were included in the compound which has been corrupted.

2) Falcons and Hawks in श्यैनिक शास्त्र :—

(i) कुही—the same as जावल in (1) above :

(ii) शशाद—"गृध्र in (1) (viii) above :

(iii) चरक—चरख of हि. श. सा.; चरग of ibid; and is the Saker or Cherrug Falcon of F.B.I.

(iv) बहरी—the same as शालिव in (1) (i) above :

(v) लगर—लग्न in (I) (iii) above :

(vi) पक्षकलिका—is probably the Hobby as discussed later :

(vii) तुरुमती—तुरमती in H.; तुरुमती in F.B.I. (जरकटी of हि. श. सा. and जेलकट in F.B.I. are the same); it is the Merlin Falcon:

(viii) वाज—the same as प्राजिक in (1) (iv) above :

(ix) वासा—बांसा in H. and बाशा in F.B.I. is the Asiatic or the Indian Sparrow Hawk :

(x) वेसर—the same as वेसर in (1) (vii) above :

(xi) सिचान—सञ्चान in (1) (vi) above :

(xii)-(xv) जूरा is the male of Goshawk; चेटा, the male of the Sparrow-Hawk; घृति, the male of the Besra Sparrow-Hawk; and टुना the male of the Shikra as in (1) (x) above :

All the names noted in this paragraph and others will be considered later with the individual Falcons and Hawks in sub-sections II and III of this section.

II. FALCONS

1. This sub-section deals with the Sanskrit nomenclature of Falcons which, for their size, constitute a most remarkable group of birds. Bold and predacious by nature they possess an extraordinary keenness of vision, great strength, speed, and above all persistence. As trained birds they are loyal and greatly attached to their master whose voice and person they can recognize from a great distance and often utter a call of recognition long before returning to the master's fist. The best representatives of the group are the Peregrine and the Shaheen Falcons and they must be given precedence over others in the discussion that follows.

2. The Peregrine or the Blue Hawk (19") is the Falcon *par excellence* and for this reason is simply known as 'Falcon' amongst British falconers. "For its size it is perhaps the most powerful bird of prey that flies, and

its courage is as great as its power". It is bluish grey above and white below with brown or black spots (bars in old birds) on the lower breast and abdomen. It is the नीलच्छद श्येन as defined in the कल्पद्रुकोश :

नीलच्छदस्तु करणो लम्बपर्णो रणप्रियः

Where नीलच्छद (having a blue cover) is descriptive of the colour of the upper plumage, करण of its perfect aptitude for training and its expert performance, and the other adjectives refer to its long wings and love of the chase. चरकसंहिता mentions it as the धूमीका (v.l. धूमिका or धूमाका? M. W.) in reference to its bluish or foggy colour. In Hindi it is known as वहरी (v.l. बिहिरी)[1] which appears as वहरी in the श्यैनिक शास्त्र, 4.20. Hindi बहरी or विहिरी may be from वि-हर्तु, वि-हारि or वि-हन्त्री (one that carries away or kills birds), or again from वि-हरि (वीनां वीषु वा हरिरिव, a lion among birds; cf. पक्षिसिंह for गरुड, the Golden Eagle). हरि (a lion) is the name of one of the descendants of गरुड, in the Mahābhārata list where the name is comparable with शरभ (a tiger) and पुण्डरीक (a panther) for the Pelican (Art. 71) and is very appropriate for the bold and fearless Peregrine. विहरि is again on a par with मृगेन्द्र चटक (a lion-sparrow, hence a comparatively small but very courageous bird of prey) :

मृगेन्द्रचटको घातिपक्षी ग्राहकमारकौ—हारावली

हरि or बिहरि would thus seem to account for Hindi बहरी or बिहिरी for this Falcon.

3. In the wild state it takes both land and water-birds from a Lark to a Duck to which last it is very partial. If by any chance it has not succeeded in securing its staple diet in the course of the day it will attack a Crow-colony late in the evening. This very important trait of the Falcon had happily been noted by the ancient Indians and now helps us to identify it with the क्षिप्रश्येन of Vedic literature :

क्षिप्रश्येनाभिपन्नानां वायसानामिव स्वनः
बभूव पाण्डवेयानां भृशं विद्रवतां स्वनः ॥
M. Bh. 7.26,64.

The terrific speed of this bird during a 'stoop' has been estimated as high as 150 miles per hour which, despite some exaggeration, means that no bird can escape its devastating attack and it is in recognition of this fact that the ancients gave it the distinctive name of क्षिप्रश्येन. Now if the 'fast bird', तक्ववी[2], of RV. 10.91.2 is the same as the क्षिप्रश्येन I would suggest that the expression वने वने in the verse has the same meaning as the word

1. "बिहिरी कहुं निबहत सुनौ लगर झगर हित बेस" quoted under 'बेसरा' in हिं. श. सा.

2. तक्ववी can also be the Shaheen Falcon, a species closely allied to the Peregrine and almost as good for purposes of hawking. Being a resident bird it is preferred by Indian falconers.

वंसु (वनेषु नीडकाष्ठोपरि) in RV. 9.57.3[1] as interpreted by me in Section A viz., wooden poles or posts in a house used as perches for tame Falcons. वन in the sense of 'wood' (timber) i.e. for things made of wood, e.g. a cart (विकारे प्रकृति शब्दः) has been used in the Ṛgveda (2.14.9; 3.1,13; 10.132.7; etc.) and there is no very great improbability against how I propose to interpret RV. 10.91.2[2]. The second पाद of the verse ('वने वने शिश्रिये तक्ववीरिव") compares अग्नि, the welcome guest, with the Falcon as a valued pet and guest of every tribe. It may be noted that when plants and trees have been directly mentioned as the food and source of अग्नि in verses 5-7 of the hymn, and particularly when *any bird* may be said to have its home in a tree there would seem to be no point in particularising the तक्ववी. On the other hand the parallel between the glorious अग्नि and the equally glorious तक्ववी as honoured guests makes an excellent simile. When the first, third and the fourth Pādas refer to the domestic fire as a guest the second Pāda also should naturally refer to the bird as another guest in the house.

4. At present the Peregrine is a winter visitor in India and is said to breed throughout Northern Asia but it is quite probable that in times long past it bred in the Himalayas as well and was more plentiful in the country than now. Even now it is found throughout the country in the cold season but in former times when the country had a far greater number of marshes and jheels bird-life of all kinds, serving as food for birds of prey, was also very much more plentiful than now, and consequently the raptores also must have been far more numerous then. The

---

1. स मर्मृजान आयुभिरिभो राजेव सुव्रतः । श्येनो न वंसु षीदति ॥

Trans: "He, the object of pious observances, cleansed by the priests, fearless as a king, sits on the waters like a hawk."—per Wilson, following Sāyaṇa's rendering.

"He, when the people deck him like a docile king of elephants, sits as a falcon in the wood."—Griffith.

2. स दर्शतश्रीरतिथिर्गृहेगृहे वनेवने शिश्रिये तक्ववीरिव ।
जनंजनं जन्यो नाति मन्यते विश आ क्षेति विश्यो विशंविशम् ॥

Trans: "Of manifest glory, he resorts as a guest to every house (of his worshippers) to every forest; friendly to man, like one repairing to all men, he disregards them not; kind to all, he dwells amongst all men," (he presides over every one). Wilson.

'"वनेवने........तक्ववीरिव "—"he lurks in every forest like a robber,"—per Langlois, vide Wilson's notes.

"He, excellent in glory, guest in every house, finds like a swift-winged bird a home in every tree. Benevolent to men, he scorns no living man: Friend to the tribes of men he dwells with every tribe." 'Swift-winged bird': or, bird of prey. 'Hunter' according to Ludwig.—F.N.—Griffith.

Cf. "वने निपूतं वने उन्नयच्वम्"— (सोम) purified in a wooden vessel, lift it up in a wooden चमस—RV. 2.14.9.

Sāyaṇa does not render तक्ववी as a bird and the idea of a Hawk or Falcon sitting on the water is impossible. The rendering as a fast bird or better still, as 'a bird of prey' suits best. That अग्निचयन for the अश्वमेध is in shape of a bird of prey supports the rendering of तक्ववी by Griffith, and as 'a fast flying bird' in the Vedic Index. Both 'robber' and 'hunter' are totally inappropriate for a deity like अग्नि.

passage from शत० ब्राह्मण considered in para, 7 below also supports the breeding of the Peregrine in the outer Himalayas about two thousand years ago.

5. An experienced old Peregrine knows well how to deliver its attack on a particular quarry. If it is a Heron, the Falcon, after tearing open the back of the bird with its hind claw, would contract its claws and lay hold of the bird's neck so as to avoid being struck by its sharp and powerful bill, but if the quarry happens to be the Demoiselle Crane, it keeps well on its back and escapes a blow from the sharp, curved inner claw of the Crane which often inflicts a severe wound. This cleverness on the part of the Falcon would justify the name दक्ष (clever, wise) for it as a descendant of Garuḍa in the Mahābhārata list.[1] The following verses in praise of a trained Falcon should prove interesting :

तज्ज्ञैः सुशिक्षिताः श्येनाः भवन्त्यानन्ददायिनः ।

श्यैनिक शास्त्र, 5.40

सम्यक् सुशिक्षितानां तु श्येनानां मरुतामिव ।
नाकार्यं विद्यते किञ्चिन्नासाध्यं योग्यवस्तुषु ॥ Ibid 6.8.

The following verses descriptive of sport with a Peregrine (वहरी) will be appreciated. Here कङ्क and दात्यूह as the birds flown at are flights of Grey Herons and Black Ibises respectively :

अतिदूरगतानां नु कङ्कदात्यूहपक्षिणाम् ।
लक्ष्ये मोको वहर्या हि जनयत्यद्भुतं रसम् ॥
यत्र वेगानिलस्वानभीषिताः खात्पतन्ति च ।
छिन्नपक्षनगाकाराः खगास्तस्मात् किमद्भुतम् ॥

श्यै. शा. 6.37-38.

The second verse refers to the first earthward flight of the birds frightened by the loud swish of the wings of the Falcon during a stoop from above. If the quarry is already at a good height its chance of escape from the marauder is "to keep above the enemy, and it often happens, therefore, that both birds may fly so high as to disappear entirely. Eventually, however, the—relentless pursuer will rise above his victim, and then in a few moments will come the savage and certain downward plunge, and the clutch of the merciless talons which means death in mid air." This method of escape is often attempted though not with much chance of success by large birds like the Black Ibis and Cranes, which incidentally explains the term खेगमन for the कालकण्ठ दात्यूह (M.W. and श. कल्प.) i.e., the Black Ibis (Art 80), for when not in danger it does not ordinarily fly very high. खेगमन (sky-going) for the Ibis, therefore, owes its origin to the practice of falconry.

1. M Bh. 5.101.9-15.

6. Returning to the name क्षिप्रश्येन it is to be noted that the Peregrine has also been described as the 'little Golden Eagle', सुपर्णक (सुपर्ण with अल्पार्थे कन्) for like the Eagle it has both courage and speed and like him again it breeds on inaccessible cliffs. As against the brief synonymy, "क्षिप्रश्येनः सुपर्णकः" in वैजयन्ती कोश the definition given by सुरेश्वराचार्य in his वार्तिक on the बृहदारण्यक is more specific in describing this small and yet powerful bird (a mere 19" in length compared with 36" to 40" of the massive Golden Eagle) though he calls it a सुपर्ण by way of compliment :

क्षिप्रश्येनः सुपर्णस्तु बलवानल्पविग्रहः—वार्तिक on 4.3.160.

सुपर्ण in the context must evidently be taken as synonymous with the more correct सुपर्णक in the वैजयन्ती, and it follows that the interpretation of सुपर्ण or गरुड as the क्षिप्रश्येन in the शाङ्करभाष्य on बृहदारण्यक, 4.3.19 and by Sāyaṇa elsewhere is not to be taken too literally but in the sense of a small (अल्पविग्रह) bird possessing the excellent flight and speed of the true सुपर्ण. The high esteem in which this Falcon was held may be judged from the fact that no other bird, not even the सुपर्ण proper, has been deified and considered worthy of an individual offering at the अश्वमेध at which a Quail is assigned to it—"क्षिप्रश्येनाय वर्तिका", वाज. संहिता, 24.30.

7. The female Peregrine, again, would seem to be the अमृतवाका bird of the शतपथ ब्राह्मण, where she is said to give birth to a क्षिप्रश्येन (fast Falcon). According to a statement in the ब्राह्मण a man desirous of a brave son should not join his wife at meal-time but allow her to eat by herself, and it is in support of this proposition that the example of the अमृतवाका bird doing so and begetting the fast and courageous क्षिप्रश्येन is cited :

> जायाया अन्ते नाश्नीयाद् वीर्यवान् हास्माज्जायते वीर्यवन्तमुह सा जनयति यस्या अन्ते नाश्नाति । तदेतदेव व्रतं राजन्यबन्धवो मनुष्याणामनुतमाङ्गोपायन्ति तस्मादुतेषु वीर्यवाञ्जायतेऽमृतवाका वयसां सा क्षिप्रश्येनञ्जनयति[1]...
>
> शत. ब्रा., 10.5.2.9-10.

Sāyaṇa comments on the above as follows :

> वयसां पक्षिणां मध्ये अमृतवाका नाम पक्षिजातिः एतद्व्रतम् गोपायति अतः सा क्षिप्रम् शीघ्रगामिनम् श्येनं नाम पक्षिणम् जनयति ।

Now most of the Eagles and only two among the Falcons, the Luggar and the Merlin, are known to go about and hunt in pairs and share the spoils in common, but the Peregrines, male and female, hunt independently as a rule and each kills and eats its own prey. Taken young, the Peregrine is easily the best of all the hawking birds. A trained bird is very much devoted to and shows great affection for its keeper, and during a hunt when the bird is returning to its master from high up in the air it utters a

1. This passage shows a close observation of the habits of falcons in nature which in turn lends strong support to the proposition that the ancient Vedic Aryans practised falconry.

clear drawn out plaintive cry as a call of recognition (Smythies). This call is the अमृतवाक् (sweet voice) of the bird so cheering and welcome to its keeper. Stuart Baker also records his personal experience regarding a pair of Serpent Eagles kept by him. They would recognize their master from high up when they were still invisible to the human eye, and come down with their screaming calls and actually alight on his shoulder (see also the article on Falconry in Ency. Brit. 11th and 14th editions). The meaning of अमृतवाका as explained above is greatly strengthened by the accepted sense of the term अच्छावाक for the welcome sound of the wheels of a wagon returning home laden with the barley crop in शत. ब्रा., 5.4.5.22 (see also Eggling's trans. in the S.B.E. series). That the voice of such a bird is appreciated elsewhere may be seen in names like the "Singing Hawk" or "Chanting Falcon" for an African bird. Finally, like the name दक्ष (wise or clever), the name सुस्वर of the MBh. list corresponds to अमृतवाका and may well refer to this Falcon.

8. The Shaheen Falcon (18"), a very close relative of the preceding, is the best indigenous and breeding bird of India. Its breeding places on the cliffs in different parts of the country have been known to the people from time immemorial (Jerdon). It is a darker bird than the Peregrine, the head being almost black, and the under parts more rufous. The definition of the नीलच्छद श्येन quoted from कल्पद्रुकोश in support of the Peregrine would seem to be equally applicable to it. In a state of nature it preys upon a variety of game birds including Pigeons and Quails, but it is partial to Paroquets. The Peregrine, as we have seen, prefers water-birds but the most important difference between the habits of the two is that when the hungry Peregrine wends its way to a Crow-colony in the evening the Shaheen turns to the bats in similar circumstances. Despite the admitted superiority of the former the Indian falconers have always shown a preference for the latter (Shaheen) and they train it for what is known as the "standing gait" and is not slipped from the hand like the Peregrine i.e. when released it keeps circling high in the air over its master and party, and as the game is started it makes its stoop with amazing speed, faster than an arrow, which is a very sure and deadly way of hunting.

9. It is known as कुही in Hindi and जावलुम् (Jowalum ? in F.B.I. due to a phonetic error perhaps, and there are many such errors in recording the Indian names of birds) in Telugu. कुही may be from (i) कुह्-विस्मापने, because when domestic Pigeons are flown high for their daily exercise it frequently appears suddenly over them to the great consternation of the Pigeon-fancier, or (ii) by direct substitution of Sansk. कुही (fog) as a synonym for धूमीका (v.l. धूमिका) :

धूमिका स्यान्नभोरेणुपर्यायाऽपि कुहीति च—कल्पद्रुकोश.

If, as is more probable, the second explanation of the name कुही is correct, it would be purely a Sansk. name, indicative of the colour or the upper plumage of the Shaheen like the terms नीलच्छद and धूमीका. The name कपोत of the MBh. list may well refer to it after its small size, bluish colour, and the habit of killing Pigeons. Like its elder cousin, the Peregrine, it was trained to kill a variety of birds including even such large ones as the Sarus and other Cranes :

कुह्या मोकः सारसेऽथ क्रौञ्चे रौद्ररसावहः
सपक्षयोः पर्वतयोरिव यत्राऽनुधावनम् ॥
निपत्य नखराक्षेप क्रूरकेङ्कारकूजितम्
परावृत्योग्रचञ्च्वा च प्रहारो रौद्रसङ्गरः ॥ श्यै. शा. 6.35-36

The reference to the Crane's counter-attack with its bill is interesting.

10. The Laggar (19″) is one of the commonest Falcons of India frequenting dry open country and areas adjoining cultivation. Dark to grey brown above and predominantly white below it is not difficult of identification in the field specially as pairs are seen together. An important feature about the bird is that nearly always it hunts in pairs. English 'Laggar' is derived from the Hindi लगर and लग्घड़ for the female Falcon. The male goes by the name of झगर in Hindi from झकटकं[1]—झगड़ा a dispute, because a pair when attacking a quarry in co-ordination appear to be carrying on a dispute as it were. The लग्न and लङ्गण of मानसोल्लास should be the female and male respectively of this bird as Hindi लगर and Sansk. लग्न are from root लग् to adhere, and लङ्गण, if not the same as रङ्गण, may be a South-Indian variant of लग्न used for the male Falcon. The second Hindi name लग्घड़ and even लगर may also have something to do with Vedic रघट (रघ्, रङ्घ, लघु ? speedy, hence a Falcon[2]—*Vedic Index*, where रघवो, swift is suggested as an alternative)—रघट—लघट—लग्घड़ - लगड़—लगर; Telugu लगड्ड for this Falcon also points in the direction of रघट-लघट. Sansk. लगुड, for a handy missile, seems to be an allied word. रघट is one of the bird-names in the following verse :

या सुपर्णा आङ्गिरसीर्दिव्या या रघटो विदुः ।
वयांसि हंसा या विदुर्याश्च सर्वे पतत्रिणः ॥ AV. 8.7.24.

Derived as suggested above the name रघट is comparable with लघुविक्रम as descriptive of the quick action of a warrior and a Falcon :

शैनेयः श्येनवत् संख्ये व्यचरल्लघुविक्रमः । —MBh. 7.120.36.

We thus have लग्न and probably रघट as Sanskrit names for this Falcon

The Luggar and his mate usually hunt together with complete cooperation between them as already stated, and the following simile pictured after a pair of Falcons or Eagles (श्येनौ) acting together against a common objective is fully reminiscent of the behaviour of a pair of these Falcons or some Eagle :

---

1. कलहं झकटकं—com. on यशस्तिलकचम्पू, p. 357.
2. Per Bloomfield in *Hymns of the Atharvaveda*, p. 43.

अजिराधिराजौ श्येनौ सम्पातिनाविव
आज्यं पृतन्योपहतां यो न कश्चाभ्यघायति ॥ AV. 7.70.3.

11. The Saker (Arabic, al-saqr) or the Cherrug Falcon (22″) has a whitish head and brown upper parts. The lower parts are white often marked with brown drops. The bill is pearl or ivory white. It is a desert form frequenting open lands, deserts and wide uncultivated tracts. Next to the Peregrine it is a very fast and courageous bird and was formerly trained to capture gazelles, fawns, hares, Cranes, Bustards, etc. In nature, however, it lives on small mammals and principally on lizards. It is known as चरग or चरख in Hindi, and चर्ख़ or चर्ग़ in Persian while श्यै. शा. mentions it by its Hindi name of चरख and refers to its frightful attack and perseverance when let go after a fawn :

हारिणं शिशुमादाय सान्त्राण्यङ्गानि भक्षयन्
अनिवार्यो हि बीभत्सं चरखो जनयत्यलम् ॥ —6.39.

The Hyena is also चरग or चरख in Hindi and जरख in Prakrit, and these names are from Sansk. तरक्ष or तरक्षु. The कल्पद्रुकोश mentions तरक्षक as a bird of prey and defines it as मणितुण्ड ("मणितुण्डो तरक्षकः") where मणि means 'a pearl' and तुण्ड 'a beak' so that the white-billed तरक्षक (तरक्ष with स्वार्थे कन् or to fill the metre) is no other than the Cherrug Falcon which alone has a white bill. चरेल्लग (fr. चरक a wanderer) is a kind of bird in अर्धमागधी and probably corresponds to Hindi चरग for this Falcon. चरग (fr. चरक) again in the same dialect, is defined as a class of mendicants who obtain their food by violent means. In Persian, too, 'charkh' not only means this Falcon but also a 'faqeer' or mendicant who goes out on his rounds at night. Evidently, therefore, Ardhamagadhi चरग, Hindi चरग or चरख and Persian 'charkh' are identical and have their root in Sansk. तरक्ष which means (i) the hyena which prowls for prey at night and (ii) this Falcon which secures its food by violent means. दगतुंड is also a kind of bird in Prakrit where दग is synonymous with स्फटिक which means rock-crystal, alum, and camphor which are all of a white colour. It is thus a bird with a white bill and should refer to the Falcon under discussion.

12. The late Shri C.V. Vaidya, author of *Mahābhārata, A Criticism* in English, contributed a voluminous epilogue in Marathi to a nine-volume translation of Mahābhārata in Marathi published by G.V. Chiplunkar and Co., Poona, the epilogue, named उपसंहार being the tenth volume of the translation. This उपसंहार is based upon a very close, detailed and systematic study of the great Epic. According to Vaidya it was Souti who converted the original 'Bhārata' into the present 'Mahābhārata' about the second century B.C. by incorporating into it a very great amount of floating tradition, stories, moral teaching, and Brahmanical religious discourses and doctrines with a view to strengthen and consolidate the सनातन धर्म or Brahmanical religion against the persistent onslaughts of the heretical Jainism and Buddhism on it. In the process of augmentation of the

Epic he, says Vaidya, inserted a large number of कूट श्लोकाः or enigmatic verses throughout the body of the work, each chapter having its share of a few such verses (उपसंहार, ch. 1, pp. 37-40). The following verse from the उद्योगपर्व appears to be of the कूट type. I have picked it out just to see if the words मृग, शृगाल, and तरक्षु have been used in their usual meanings or in a कूट sense for particular birds, तरक्षु being the fast-flying Laggar Falcon. Here is the verse :

मृगाः शृगालाः शितिकण्ठाश्च काका गृध्रा बकाश्चैव तरक्षवश्च ।
सुवर्णपत्राश्च पतन्ति पश्चाद् दृष्ट्वा रथं श्वेतहयप्रयुक्तम् ॥
MBh. 5.48.104-5.

The commentators have taken the terms मृगाः, शृगालाः, and तरक्षवः to mean 'deer', 'jackals' and 'hyenas' respectively, and शितिकण्ठाः, Peacocks. These interpretations, barring the 'deer' do not suit the context at all.[1] Arjuna, the great warrior, makes in this verse a proud statement regarding the extra-ordinary speed of his war-chariot drawn by a pair of white horses, and bearing this in mind one must admit that the poor hyena with his limping gait or run is indeed no match for any much less a really fast horse. The very idea of a horse outstripping a hyena in a race is most incongruous and the comparison is simply ridiculous. The jackal, though a fast runner, is too mean a creature for Arjuna's boast. In the Ṛgveda the speed of horses has been compared with that of the wind and in literature with that of the Golden Eagle[2], the fastest of the tribe. The Peacock, again, is mostly a ground bird with a heavy and laboured flight. It is therefore submitted that all the names in the above verse represent large and fast-flying birds as suggested below :

मृग—fr. मृग् अन्वेषणे, one looking around for food; 'a large bird' in RV. 1.182.7; 10.136.6 (M.W.). It is probably either the Bearded Vulture (भास) or Pallas's Fishing Eagle (कङ्क), more probably the latter. Both, like the other birds of prey have to search for food from the air and both are carrion eaters and fast fliers. मृग as a carrion bird occurs in the हरिवंश :

अथ श्येना मृगाश्चैव कङ्का गृध्रास्तथाऽपरे ।
तुण्डैः शवान् विनिष्कृष्य भक्षयन्ति ततस्ततः ॥
3.122.20

मृग is thus different from श्येनाः, Eagles, कङ्काः, the Adjutants or Pallas's Eagles, and गृध्राः, the common Vultures (excluding the Bearded Vulture which despite its name is often regarded as a different bird). If कङ्क is taken for the Adjutant Stork, a great carrion eater, the two that would

1. Cf. नवाजिनं वाजिना हासयन्ति न गर्दभं पुरो अश्वान्नयन्ति । RV. 3.53.31

2. The Vedic horse दधिक्रा is compared to an impetuous Eagle in RV 38.2.40; 40.3, etc. Compare also expressions like, "हयाः सुपर्णेन समानवेगाः" in कर्णभारम् of भास, 13.

be left for identification with मृग would be either the Bearded Vulture or Pallas's Fishing Eagle.*

शृगाल—the same as गोमायु. Both these names, like क्रोष्टा, फेरव, घोरवासन, etc. for the jackal, refer to his extreme noisiness. सृकाल and सृगाल should be from root सृ 'to blow violently' (M.W.) and hence to make a noise. एकसृक is probably a Fox who is of a solitary habit and utters a single cry at a time (एकः सृक एक पदः सृगालः per com. on हिरण्यकेशी श्रौतसूत्र, 24.7.23) but सृक' in 'एकसृक' should mean 'cry or call' and the compound एकसृक should be rendered as an animal that utters a single cry at a time. This will help to distinguish सालावृक, the jackal, from एकसृक, the fox in the श्रौत text. गोमायु as a homonym may be explained as (i) गवि भूमौ मिमाति मायुः, one that makes a noise on the ground, and hence the jackal; and (ii) गवि आकाशे मायुः, one that is noisy in the sky or air, and therefore a noisy bird. शृगाल as a bird is thus the same as गोमायु in the second sense. Now गोमायु is listed as a particular bird in पालकाप्य at page 397 with other birds frequenting a dry region (जाङ्गल देश), while जम्बुक (जम्बु in the printed text is an error), the jackal, is also mentioned in the same passage as one of the animals found in the same zone. That the term गोमायु is applicable to a noisy bird like the Peacock, which has a loud call, is also clear from the following :

सृगालोऽपि मयूर उच्यते—"मयुः मयूरो गोमायुः सृगालश्चेति शब्दितः" इतिनामरत्नमालावचनात् ।

विश्वरूपटीका on याज्ञवल्क्यस्मृति, प्रायश्चित्ताध्याय, Verse 266 (Trivandram ed.).

The next question is what particular bird is this गोमायु of पालकाप्य or शृगाल of the Mahābhārata ? That it is a noisy bird is clear enough, and when we consider other characteristic names for the jackal indicative of his other habits, e.g. वञ्चक (a cheat) and कटखादक (carrion eater) we would be justified in expecting similar qualities in the शृगाल bird as well. Now all these traits are present in the Tawny Eagle in the fullest measure, for he is not only very noisy on the wing but also eats carrion and is always eager to cheat other birds of prey of their booty. He is a fast bird too (see para. 8 iv Sec. A of this Article). Hardly any other fast-flying bird fulfills all the conditions that the name शृगाल demands. Considering everything

*This Eagle prefers to build its large nest, lined with twigs and green leaves, on solitary cotton trees (Bombax malabaricum) which stand as landmarks in an Indian river-bed. During floods the tree is naturally surrounded by water on all sides. The picture of Aśvins securing भुज्यु holding on to such a tree in the midst of a flood like a large bird (मृग) carrying twigs & leaves in RV.1.182. 7 would seem to be based on the habits of this Eagle.

therefore गोमायु and सृगाल should be the Tawny Eagle.* There are several other animal-names as well that are shared by birds, e.g., पुण्डरीक and शरभ (Pelican), भष (Tree-Pie), भल्लूक (Black Eagle), तरक्ष (Cherrug Falcon), etc.

शितिकण्ठ—fr. शिति 'black' and white', and the word interpreted in both the senses should mean birds with black as well as with white necks, and, looking round for large sized birds with great wing-power, the Black-necked and the White-necked Storks at once present themselves, and both these must be included for purposes of the कूट verse. The Black-necked Stork is mentioned elsewhere in the Epic as the 'fearful black-necked and red-legged bird'—"कृष्णग्रीवाश्च-शकुना रक्तपादा भयानकाः" MBh. 5.143.25. The शितिकण्ठाः (note the plural) are therefore these big Storks and not the Peacocks.

बक—the Adjutant Stork; cf. the frequent use of the term for this bird, a fast flier that soars high with Vultures.

तरक्षु—the Cherrug Falcon.

सुवर्णपत्र—the same as स्वर्णपक्ष, the Golden Eagle, the fastest of all others in the verse.

It will be noticed that सुवर्णपत्र is placed the last with an emphatic 'च' and the sense is that 'even the Golden Eagles fall behind my chariot'. The significance of the principal sentence, (एते पक्षिणः) रथं दृष्ट्वा पश्चात्पतन्ति, is that these birds with great power of wing at the very sight of Arjuna's fast-moving chariot fall back of their own accord since they know that they cannot compete with it, much less outstrip it, even if they tried their best. It is an excellent poetic thought based upon the indifference of the birds of the sky to what does not concern them below.

13. The Indian Hobby is a small Falcon (11.5"), black above and light ferrugineous below. The European species, known as the Hobby, is slightly larger and has the lower parts white. It is very fast and active on the wing and of rather crepuscular habits. पक्षकलिका is one of the "brown-eyed" Falcons in the श्यै. शा. 4.21. Harprasad Shastri translates the name as "having short wings" but does not identify the bird. The wings of the Hobby, like those of other Falcons, are of course long and it cannot be described as a short-winged bird. Formerly it was trained for hawking small birds like the Hoopoes, King-crows, Larks, etc., and writing about its performance on the wing, H.C. Donald says that its wonderful evolutions in the air cannot help attracting attention and if watched for a few seconds it will be seen to constantly change direction and turn and twist

---

*The three Eagles, two of whom are calling loudly (मायू), in the higher regions, mentioned in the following verse should be the Tawny Eagles under discussion:—

"त्रयः सुपर्णा उपरस्य मायू नाकस्य पृष्ठे अधि विष्टपि श्रिताः ।
स्वर्गा लोका अमृतेन विष्ठा इषमूर्जं यजमानाय दुह्राम् ॥

AV.18.4.4.

in the air in a most amazing way in pursuit of insects, on which it mostly preys. It does not usually make its appearance till late in the afternoon and may be seen circling, stooping, rising vertically and playing extraordinary tricks in the air, some time after all diurnal birds have gone to rest (J.B.N.H.S.XXVII). It therefore seems to me that the beautiful name पक्षकलिका (पक्षकलावती) should be rendered as a small Falcon which exhibits पक्षकला, the art of flying, in a variety of ways. That the term कलिका is also related to कला (art) is clear from the technical meaning of कलिका as an artistic style of composition :

कला नाम भवेत्तालनियता पदसन्ततिः ।
कलाभिः कलिका प्रोक्ता तद्भेदाः षट् समीरिताः ।। श. कल्प. under कलिका

Moreover, the Hobby would be the only "brown-eyed" Falcon trained for Hawking that would seem to have been left out by the author of श्यै. शा. if पक्षकलिका is some other unkown Falcon. The probability of its being the Hobby is therefore of the highest degree.

14. It is very active early in the morning and again late in the evening, and thus seems to be the चिरान्तक (staying till late in the evening, or absenting oneself during the day) of the MBh. list; cf. निशान्तक as an adnoun for a particular Heron in कल्पद्रु. See also Art. 82.

15. The Merlin occurs in two forms in North India : the Red-headed Merlin (14″) of the Himalayas and the North Asian Merlin (12″) with a whitish head. Both are bluish grey above and white, barred or streaked with black, below with a rufous tinge in the smaller variety. The old opinion giving the palm to the Merlin for courage and speed is no longer held and it is now definitely known to be slower than the Peregrine and even the Hobby. Nevertheless its "flight is very swift and graceful...and the bird stoops at its quarry with wonderful skill and speed, a most finished performer" (Whistler). It was trained to capture Mainas, Quails, Rollers, etc. and sometimes also to work in pairs. Its Hindi name तुरमती (fr. तुर् to be speedy) should be the same as the वेगी of कल्पद्रुकोश—

वेगी खगान्तकः क्रूरः एतद्भेदा अनेकशः ।

वायुवेग of the MBh. list is a name comparable with वेगी. The श्यै. शा., however, contents itself with the Hindi name तुरमती.

16. The European as well as the Himalayan Kestrel (14″) are winter visitors to North India. The head is ashy-grey and the upper parts brick-red with black arrow-shaped black spots while the lower parts are of a vinous colour. The Himalayan species is darker. Its Hindi name, खैरमटिया (खदिर+मृत्तिका, reddish-brown) in the North and नारजी, (Persian 'nār'—fiery) in the South of India are after its body-colour. It is a plains-bird, and while beating over grass lands it is often seen "hovering with a quick motion of the wings above a spot where it has seen or suspects it has seen its prey, on which it drops quietly." This habitual hovering is the most characteristic feature of the Kestrel to which it owes its popular

English name of 'Windhover'. "When watching for food from a perch the head is incessantly turning and bobbing" (Smythies). From its hovering habit it should be the रङ्गण* (रङ्गः नृत्यम्) of कल्पद्रुकोश; from its reddish colour, the अनल (fire), from its habit of turning its head in different directions the दिशाचक्षु, and from the quick fanning movements of wings the निमेष (winking of the eyelids) of the MBh. list. It may be stated here that out of a total of 47 names in the list as many as ten refer to the Golden Eagle and four or five each to some of the commoner birds of prey found in North India. They are mostly in the nature of descriptive epithets apparently invented by सौति who gave the Epic its final comprehensive and bulky form. No kite or Falcon lays such deep red eggs as the Kestrel and the adnoun लोहाण्डी or full name लोहाण्डी शकुनि of ग. महोदधि should also belong to it :

लोह इवाण्डमस्याः लोहाण्डी नाम शकुनिः ।

Commentary on verse 44.

17. The call of the Kestrel is a shrill scream, kee, kee, kee, and therefore good enough for purposes of augury. The Prakrit work, सुपासनाह चरिअं mentions a bird of augury by the name of आगास जोइणी (Sk. आकाश योगिनी) :

"आगासजोइणीए निसुओ सद्दो वि वाम पासम्मि"—

p. 185, verse 202

The particular bird it is must be determined with reference to the meaning of the name itself, for the Dictionaries explain it merely as a kind of bird (पक्षिविशेषः). The name literally means 'a fairy or female magician of the sky', and योगिनी taken by itself may well be from योग defined as "चित्तवृत्तिनिरोधः", ध्यान, and वपुःस्थैर्यम् (अमर, मेदिनी, etc.). In its habit of hovering at a point high up in the air longer than any other bird and of close concentration upon a possible quarry below, the Kestrel may indeed be said to be a magician of the sky or to exhibit यौगिक power, and the charming name of आकाश योगिनी may well belong to it (cf. खकामिनी for the Brahminy Kite in the next Section).

18. Two other probable names for the Kestrel appear to be खभ्रान्तिः and कण्ठनीडक of the following synonymy which also includes two names for the Common Kite :

चिरम्भणस्तु चिल्लः स्यात् खभ्रान्तिः कण्ठनीडकः । —त्रिकाण्डशेष

Annotators take all the four names for the Kite and they may be right but it must be remembered that the त्रिकाण्डशेष purports to give us a supplement to the अमरकोश, i.e. additional synonyms for (i) objects already named there and (ii) objects not mentioned at all, and naturally new names falling within the first category could not be numerous. It is therefore highly

*If रङ्गण is the same as लङ्गण of मानसोल्लास the name would indicate the Laggar Falcon and not the Kestrel—see para. 10 infra.

probable that the first quarter of the above half verse gives only चिरम्भण (calling for long) as an additional name for चिल्ल (the Kite) and the second refers to a Kite-like bird not mentioned by अमर, viz. the Kestrel. That annotators have differed among themselves along the above lines (i.e. in the way I do) is proved by the remarks of महेश्वर at several places in his अमरविवेक commentary on the अमरकोश[1] (Bombay, 1907).

19. The Pied Kingfisher "flies over the water at a height of some ten or twenty feet above the surface, and suddenly, catching sight of a shoal of fish below, checks itself dead in mid-air and hovers with the wings vibrating rapidly and the bill pointing perpendicularly downwards, as if taking aim" (Whistler). This action of the bird has been described in कल्पद्रुकोश as below :

"कपर्दिकः ।
आकाशे सुचिरं भ्रान्त्वा जले पतति लोष्टवत्" ॥

The point to be noted is the use of a derivative of root भ्रम् to describe the act of hovering in the air. I therefore suggest that खभ्रान्ति (hovering in the sky; भ्रान्तिः अनवस्थितिः—हेमचन्द्र and विश्व.; quivering—M.W.; cf. Windhover) is the Kestrel. Salim Ali also speaking of the hovering flight of certain Indian birds remarks that the Kestrel and the Pied King-fisher are the foremost exponents of it—*The Book of Indian Birds*, 4th edn., page 268. The Brahminy Kite which flies in circles like the Common Kite is named खकामिनी (loving the sky) which is certainly different from खभ्रान्ति as explained above. Turning to कण्ठनीडक I fail to see how this term can apply to a Kite unless it is translated as 'a bird that cries or calls at the nest' which however is a trait common to all the birds of the family. On the other hand the term may very appropriately mean— "कण्ठे पर्वतकण्ठे नीडं करोति योऽसौ"[2] i.e. a bird that builds its nest in rocky cliffs, and the Kestrel regularly does so. "The eyrie" of a Kestrel "is in our area (India) almost invariably in holes and rocky ledges of cliffs" (Whistler). It is submitted therefore that the very striking peculiarity of our bird has won for it several interesting and aptly suggestive names.

20. The Himalayan Red-legged Falconet (7″), the 'White-naped Pigmy Falcon' of Jerdon is a mere midget amongst Falcons, and yet it is a bold little bird, has the carriage and the wonderful eye of the fiercest Eagle, and preys in the wild state upon small birds and at times those bigger than itself. It can also be trained for hawking as we have it from Jerdon that it was so used by the Raja of Rangpur (Assam) and F.B.I.,

---

1. Referring to 16 synonyms for गृह, and 4 for वास he says विंशतिर्नामानि गृहस्येत्यन्ये——page 73; regarding the two synonymies, "गर्भागारं वासगृहमरिष्टं सूतिकागृहम्"—we have चत्वारोऽपि पर्याया इत्यन्ये —p. 74; on "अजमोदा तूग्रगन्धा ब्रह्मदर्भा यवानिका" we have यवानी द्वयस्य द्वे द्वे नामनी इत्यपि मतम्—p. 112.; again we have at p. 204 चत्वारि धूल्याः, द्वे पिष्टस्य । षडपि रजस इत्येके; and so on in several other synonymies.

2. Substituted for "कण्ठे प्रासादवृक्षादीनां शिरोभागे नीडमस्य" given as an alternative explanation of कण्ठनीडक in श. कल्प.; cf. also कुण्डकीट—कुण्डे नरककुण्डे कीट इव—ibid.

first edition, also records a similar report. It is known as मुट्ठी in Hindi (fr. Sansk. मुष्टि closed fist) according to Jerdon. This name not only emphasizes its small size but probably also the fact that when trained for hawking it was held in the fist and tossed like a stone towards the intended quarry. This style of throwing a Falcon is adopted with the Shikra as well and is described as मुष्टिमोक in श्ये. शा., 6.29. It is therefore highly probable that this Falconet was known as मुष्टि or मुष्टिक in Sanskrit as well. वामन as a descendant of Garuda in the MBh. list should refer to members of the Falconet (Microhierax) group.

21. It is recorded in F.B.I., second edition, about the Eastern Red-legged Falcon (12″) that it is a migratory bird and moves south in vast flocks from its breeding grounds in Siberia and Mangolia in winter. One of their routes passes through Cachar in Assam and as they roost in large numbers on the bamboos for the night the Hill Tribes manage to catch them for food and also for sale. The भावप्रकाश also prescribes the flesh of a certain type of small Falcon, श्येनक (ह्रस्वः श्येनः श्येनकः) for a patient suffering from piles in अर्शोऽधिकार, 2.5.121. It would thus appear that the term श्येनक stands for the Red-legged Falconet of North India as the counterpart of the small Siberian Falcon eaten by the Hill Tribes of Assam.

III. HAWKS

Hawks—वाजि-पक्षिणः

- Genus Astur
  - Goshawk — वाज, वाजी, प्राजिक,
  - Crested Goshawks — चूलाङ्क वाजि
    - The Crested Goshawk — माणिक or अधम वेसर
    - Northern Crested Goshawk — मध्यमवेसर, यवलकण्ठिक
  - Shikras — सञ्चान-वाजि
- Genus Accipiter
  - (i) Asiatic & Indian Sparrow-Hawks | वासा वाजि ओरञ्जन,,
  - (ii) Southern Besra Sp-Hawk... शुद्ध वेसर
  - (iii) North Besra Sp. Hawk— धावन वाजि
  - (iv) Japanese, Pale Eastern, Indo-Chinese Sp. Hawks | प्रतिष्ठान वाजि

Note—The Shikras and Hawks of genus Accipiter are the कुलिङ्गकाः of चरक-संहिता.

1. All Indian Hawks have been designed by nature on a more or less the same pattern and their body-plumage is ashy or slaty-grey to grey-brown above and white or rufescent below marked with brown or rufescent bars or streaks. Unlike the Falcons the bill is furnished with a festoon instead of a 'tooth'. They have been classified in the *Fauna of British India (Birds)*, 2nd Edn. under two main genera, the Astur and the Accipiter.

The former includes the magnificent Goshawks, the Crested Goshawks and the Shikras, and the latter contains all the Sparrow-Hawks. It may be added that the Shikras also are just Sparrow Hawks and nothing more. In Sanskrit the term श्येन is often used in a wider sense to include the Hawks as well, for both मानसोल्लास and श्यैनिकशास्त्र apply the term to all hawking birds, viz., Falcons and Hawks (cf. श्येनो वाजिकः-भट्टोत्पल on बृ० सं० 85.38). But they also have different names for the several types of Hawks trained for sport. The Goshawk, which occurs in two forms, is वाज, वाजी, वाजि, or वाजिक[1]; the Crested Goshawks, the चूलाङ्क; the Shikras, the शिकारा; and the Sparrow-Hawks, the वासाः and the वेसराः

2. The terms वाज and वाजी do not occur in the lists of the birds of prey given in चरक or सुश्रुत and it appears that while powerful Hawks like the Goshawk were supposedly included in the term श्येन by both, the चरकसंहिता separately mentions the weaker and smaller Sparrow-Hawks including the Shikras as the कुलिङ्गकाः (कुलिङ्ग a sparrow, hence 'sparrow-killers').

Sanskrit lexicons give वाजिन्-वाजी merely as a common noun for 'a bird' in general but not in a specifie sense for a particular bird (पक्षिविशेष). The word वाज has nowhere been rendered as 'a bird or a particular bird' but from the use of these two words for the Goshawk in the श्यै. शा. it is clear that they had this sense though the lexicographers have overlooked it. The अमरकोश includes शकुनि, शकुन, शकुन्त, पत्री, विष्किर, and गरुत्मत् in the list of synonyms for 'a bird' in general and yet each of these terms also signifies a particular bird and we have :

चिल्लः शकुनिरातापी—अभि.चिन्ता. Here शकुनि also means a 'Kite'.
शकुनस्तु पुमान् पक्षिमात्रपक्षिविशेषयोः—मेदिनी, शकुन a kind of Vulture
शकुन्तः भास पक्षिविहङ्गयोः—ibid., शकुन्त, another Vulture
पत्री श्येने पत्ररथे— ibid., पत्री a Hawk
विष्किराः तित्तिरमयूरकुक्कुटादयः—शब्दकल्पद्रुम
गरुत्मत् सुपर्णः सुधाहृत् (the Golden Eagle)—अभि.चिन्ता.

This is according to the rule "सामान्योऽपि विशेषे वर्तते" quoted in अभि.चिन्ता., 404 and श्यं. शा. too has the following:

श्येने पत्रीति वाजीति शब्दो वैशिष्ट्यसूचकः—4.31

There is thus hardly any doubt that the terms वाज and वाजी also connoted a particular bird, i.e. the Goshawk. पत्री in the sense of a श्येन or a fast bird has been explained as "अतिशयितं प्रशस्तं वा पत्रमस्य" in the रामाश्रमी टीका on अमर by भानुजी दीक्षित, and it should not be incorrect if वाज and वाजी for 'a speed bird' are also explained in the same way: प्रशस्ता वाजा पक्षाऽस्य वाजः वाजी च.[2]

1. v.l. प्राञ्जि and प्राजिक in मानसोल्लास. Compounds like वाजिपक्षिन् and प्राजिपक्षिन् (M.W.) would seem to be common names for Hawks in general.

2. The synonymy "वाजी बाणाश्वपक्षिषु"—मेदिनी, refers to two speedy items, बाण and अश्व so that it is possible to render the third, पक्षी also as 'a fast bird'.

3. It has been stated in the Introductory sub-section that it is the more powerful and larger females of these birds that are preferred for hawking. It is therefore easy to understand that where we have a name for individual female Hawks used for the chase the male of every such female has not been named individually. Thus the male of the Goshawk (वाज in Sansk. and बाज in Hindi) is जुर्रा in Persian and Hindi and जूरा in श्यै. शा. In मानसोल्लास the male of any Hawk or Falcon is simply a द्रोणक (or तोणक) i.e. a 'petty or little Crow', from द्रोण, a Crow. It is a contemptuous name signifying the poorer killing power of the male as compared with the female:

द्रोणकश्चेति विख्यातः पुमानल्पशरीरकः ।
द्रोणका स्वल्पकायत्वादधमा लघुमारकाः ॥ Vol. 2,267

The श्यै. शा. confines the terms टुना or टोना (the same as तोणक) to the male Shikra alone, the term धूति to the males of the Besra Hawks and चेटा to the males of the Asiatic and Indian Sparrow-Hawks. These terms are current in Hindi as well and in the same senses.

4. The श्यै. शा. divides the smaller Hawks into three categories; (i) वासाः, (ii) वेसराः, and (iii) सिचानाः The first are said to be of four kinds, the second of three and the third of several (नैकधा). The वासा type of Hawk thus consists of औरङ्गनाः, धावनाः, प्रतिष्ठानाः, and शिकाराः (the Shikras) *. The वेसरा's are of three kinds: माणिक वेसर, चूलिकाङ्क (v.I. चूलाङ्क in 5.5) वेसर, and शुद्ध वेसर. Lastly the सिचाना's (सञ्चानाः), said to be of different kinds according to differences in size, habits and country of origin, have been barely mentioned but not classified to save space (विस्तारभयान्न प्रदर्शिताः—4.50). The different species of Hawk and their nomenclature will now be considered in the following paragraphs.

5. The adult and the juvenile Goshawk, called the बलाकाक्ष वाज and the चक्राङ्ग वाज have been mentioned in para. 4 of the Introductory sub-section. It is the largest and the most powerful of the Hawks and is trained to strike down the largest variety of game like Grouse, Pheasants, Partridges, Quails, Ducks, Bustards, Storks, Ibises, Spoonbill, Peafowl, Jungle Fowl, and even Kites and Vultures, Hares and Rabits both in Europe and Asia. Not that a single Hawk is trained to kill all these, but one can be trained to kill any five or six included in the above list. In nature, however, it preys upon Pheasants, Partridges and Pigeons with a partiality for Hares. Because of its all-round excellence, and being second only to the Peregrine and the Shaheen, it is called by courtesy the "gentle Falcon" (Astur gentilis). Its courage, flight and technique have always been admired:

एवं लक्ष्यानुसरणात् बहुशः परिधावनात् ।
अतिविश्रम्भणाद् वाजा गताः श्रैष्ठ्यं पतत्रिषु ॥

---

*These, i.e. the Shikras, really belong to the सिचानाः group and have been wrongly placed with the वासाः as will be explained later.

उत्प्लुत्योत्प्लुत्य पतनैः परिगृह्यावपातनैः ।
मल्ला इव विदग्धानां हरन्ति प्रसभं मनः ॥
श्यै. शा., 6. 48-49

6. The term पदेक means a Hawk or Falcon according to M.W., and if it is the same as एकपद्, it should prove to be an excellent adnoun or epithet for the Goshawk. It means 'limping' or 'moving on one foot'. Now the Goshawk, despite its versatility, is "chiefly trained to catch hares and for this purpose she is booted or furnished with leather leggings to prevent her legs being injured by thorns as the hare generally drags the Hawk some yards after being struck. She strikes with one leg, and stretches the other one out behind to clutch at grass, twigs or anything on the ground, to put the drag, as it were on the hare" (Jerdon). It is thus highly probable that the adnoun पदेक refers to the Goshawk because she seems to 'limp' on the ground after striking her favourite quarry, a hare. If my interpretation of the term is correct it speaks volumes for the nature-study and power of observation of the ancients.

7. Hawks other than the Goshawk are listed with their names below for easy reference:

(i) The Shikra (Astur badius): Four sub-species of this occur in India proper, the Indian Shikra being the commonest. The female is शिकारा and the male, टुना and टोना in श्यै. शा. corresponding to शिकरा and टोना respectively in Hindi. The female is recorded in F.B.I 2nd ed. as तुन्ना (?) in Nepal but she is सञ्चाण (सञ्चान) and the male द्रोणक or तोणक in मानसोल्लास.

(ii) The Crested Goshawk (Astur trivirgat us trivirgatus) of South India is known as गोर बेसरा, कोटेसरा or मानिक बेसरा[1] in Hindi. This is probably the माणिक or अधम वेसर of श्यै. शा. as it lives principally on frogs and lizards and is hardly, if ever, fancied for hawking.

(iii) The Northern Crested Goshawk (A.t. rufitinctus): This is known as चुरियारी and जमलकंठी in Nepal corresponding to Sansk. चूलिकाङ्क and यवलकण्ठिक in श्यै. शा. and मानसोल्लास respectively. This is the मध्यम वेसर of श्यै. शा. छुरिकार and छुरियारी of वर्णरत्नाकर appear to be the same as चुरियारी.

(iv) The Asiatic Sparrow-Hawk (Accipiter nisus) two sub-species of which are known : The female and male of both are known as बाशीन and बाशा respectively in Hindi. The Himalayan sub-species is the 'Indian Sparrow-Hawk'. They are perhaps the औरङ्गन variety of the वासा in श्यै. शा., and औरङ्गल of वर्णरत्नाकर. The name औरङ्गन seems to be from Persian औरंग meaning 'intelligence'.

---

1. गोर-गौर probably refers to the Hawk's white breast streaked with rich rufous while मानिक-माणिक्य refers to the reddish streaks.

(v) The Southern and Northern Besra Sparrow-Hawks are two subspecies of Accipiter virgatus occurring in the country, the latter being a little smaller than the former. The Hindi names for the female are बेसरा, खंड बेसरा, or खंडेसरा (fr. षण्ड a forest) corresponding to शुद्धवेसर of श्यै. शा. The male is धूति both in Hindi and Sansk. (श्यै. शा. 4.32).

(vi) The Japanese, the Pale Eastern and the Indo-Chinese Sparrow-Hawks (A. gularis): The first is only an occasional winter visitor to India and the other two occur in Burma. No Indian name for them is known and they may well have passed as varieties of the Basha type of Sparrow-Hawk.

8. Two series of Indian (Hindi) names for different kinds of the Besra Hawk, taken from two different books on Indian Falconry (in Hindi or Urdu—not mentioned) have been quoted by Jerdon in his *Illustrations of Indian Ornithology*, 1847 and they are :

(a) खंडेसरा, चतीसरा, सखुरता, and बेसरा (proper);

(b) खंडबेसरा, खरबेसरा, जूतेसरा, भगुरीना, खोड खुर बेसरा and मानिकबेसरा*.

He adds that the last three names in (b) may be different names for the same Hawk, and that while the Northern Crested Goshawk goes by the name of गोरबेसरा in South India it is known as चुरियाली in the Eastern Terai (Bihar, and Assam?). In the same way, referring to the Indian nomenclature for the Shaheen Falcon and the Red-capped Falcon, both used in India for hawking, he observes that several varieties are enumerated, viz., the Red, the White, the Blue, and the Black Shaheens but these are merely differences of shade in the colours and in the more or less distinctness of the body markings. It is therefore highly probable that the classification of the बेसरा group of Sparrow-Hawks in the श्यै. शा. is not in accordance with the real species of the Hawks as now separated by scientists but is based mainly on their colour features and partly on size and behaviour as trained birds. Insofar as the Shikras (शिकारा) have been included in the वासा group the classification is definitely incorrect. The Shikra belongs to the सिचान (सञ्चान) group of Sparrow-Hawks and is not a वासा at all. With these preliminary remarks on the nomenclature of the smaller Hawks I proceed to a brief discussion of the various Hawks and their Sankskrit and other names.

9. The basis for the वासा type of Hawks are evidently the Asiatic and the Indian Sparrow Hawks known as बाशा and बाशीन in Hindi. The श्यै.शा. divides them into four categories:

---

* Like खंडेसरा (खंडबेसरा) the names चतीसरा and जूतेसरा seem to be corruptions of जूटबेसरा—(the crested Goshawk, of the कोटेसर) and खरबेसरा (the true Besra) is the शुद्ध वेसर. भगुरीना, खोड and खुर बेसरा are extremely doubtful. कोटेस्वर (in F.B.I.) should be कोटेसर or कोटेसरा corrupted from कूट बेसरा for the crested Goshawk.

औरङ्गना धावनाश्च प्रतिष्ठानास्तथैव च ।
शिकाराश्चेति वासानां चतुर्धा जातिरुच्यते ॥
4.41

Eliminating the शिकाराः (the Shikras) we are left with the औरङ्गन, धावन, and प्रतिष्ठान Hawks each of which is supposed to be of more than one variety according to their flight, courage or dash and colour. The औरङ्गना, i.e. the वासा proper would seem to be the two kinds of Sparrow-Hawks named against (iv) above while the धावन and प्रतिष्ठान types are rather difficult of identification. The ओरङ्गल and ठरङ्गल of वर्णरत्नाकर would seem to correspond to औरङ्गन and धावन of the श्यै. शा. and from the delicate build and small size but excellent speed of the धावना described in श्यै. शा. 4. 43 they seem to be the Northern Besra Sparrow-Hawk which is smaller than even a Shikra but very speedy on the wing. The प्रतिष्ठान type described as very weak and timid and coming from वाजदेश would seem to refer to some foreign Hawks, e.g. the Japanese, the Pale Eastern, and the Indo-Chinese Sparrow-Hawks not used for hawking.[1]

10. The name वासा for the Asiatic and Indian Sparrow-Hawks seems at first sight to be a Hindi corruption from Persian Bāshā but it is more than probable that like the Pers. Bāz (fr. Sansk. वाज) 'Basha' too is from Sansk. वासा from वास (नीड ?, a nest) after the practice of falconers to prefer young birds taken from the nest as they can be more easily trained than the adults captured in the ordinary way. This practice is referred to in the following verse:

ये श्येना नीडनिलया लब्धाः प्राग्बन्धपोषिताः ।
सुशिष्या इव ते श्येनाः शिक्षां गृह्णन्ति सत्वरम् ॥—श्यै. शा. 6.6.7
सच्चाणा वेसरा ग्राह्या नीडस्थाश्च करग्रहैः—मानसोल्लास,
Vol. 2, p. 267.

On the other hand the term may be from root वाश्-शब्दे, to make a sound—"वास्यन्ते रुवन्तीति वासाः पक्षिण इत्यन्यः"—गण. महोदधि, verse 296. As compared with the Goshawk the Sparrow-Hawk is a rather noisy bird, a point stressed in श्यै. शा.:

"वासा मधुरवाग् धन्यो, वाजी मूकोऽतिशोभनः"—4.54

In this second sense also the name वासा would be a purely Sanskrit name for the above mentioned Sparrow-Hawks.[2]

11. The कल्पद्रुकोश lists वेसर as one of the birds of prey and it obviously refers to the Hawks mentioned as वेसराः both in मानसोल्लास and श्यैनिक शास्त्र. The latter distinguishes three different kinds of the वेसर Hawk:

---

1. In the alternative the प्रतिष्ठानाः may be the Harriers. See next sub-section.

2. The मानसोल्लास does not mention the वासा Hawks, which it probably includes in the वेसर type and these it recommends, as we have seen, to be taken from the nest. On the other hand, unlike the श्यैनिक शास्त्र it keeps the crested Goshawks in a separate category as the यवलकण्ठिकाः.

वेसरास्त्रिविधास्तेषां पृथङ्‌नामाभिधीयते ।
स्थूलोऽधमो माणिकस्तु चूलिकाङ्कस्तु मध्यमः ।
शुद्धस्तु वासाप्रतिमः पक्षाधिकोऽपि साहसे ॥ —4.47-48

(i) माणिक वेसर, probably the Crested Goshawk of South India which is गोर- or मानिक बेसरा in Hindi. It is described as स्थूल i.e. dull or stupid, and also as अधम (mean, low, worthless), because of its low teachability for the chase as in nature it prefers to take frogs and lizards though it also kills small birds, rats, etc. (ii) चूलिकाङ्क or चूलाङ्क वेसर occupies an intermediate position (मध्यम), and it should be the Northern Crested Goshawk known as चुरियारी in Hindi, the same as चूलाङ्कित, from Sansk. चूडा, चूड, चूल, a crest. It is a bolder bird and kills Partridges, Green Pigeons and even larger birds. Another Hindi name for it is जमलकंठी corresponding to यवलकण्ठिक of मानसोल्लास. This name would seem to refer to the dark shafts on the neck-feathers looking like dark यव or barley markings. (iii) The third is the शुद्ध वेसर, said to be as good as the वासा ("वासाप्रतिम") and therefore the best of the series. It is most probably the Southern Besra Hawk, known not only as the speediest of all Sparrow-Hawks (Jerdon) but also a bold bird, and for this reason a favourite with falconers for small birds like Quails and Doves. The epithet वासाप्रतिम may also refer to its very noisy habit. Just as the terms वाज and वाजी mean both a spirited horse and the powerful Goshawk, the name वेसर (वेगसर speedy) also is common to the mule and these lower grade Sparrow-Hawks. The Besra series are also more difficult to train for sport (Jerdon) and the name वेसर for them perhaps implies their 'mulish' nature as well.

12. The सिचान[1] type of Hawks are said to be of several kinds with differences in size, body-colouration and habits, and breeding in different parts of the country. In a word different species of the bird are indicated :

अनेकदेशजन्मानस्तेन देशस्वभावतः ।
नानासंस्थानचेष्टाभिः सिचाना नैकधा स्मृताः ॥
श्यै. शा. 4.49

The generio name सिचान (Hindi सचान; सिचान of poet कबीर quoted in हिं. श. सा.) is a Prakrit form of Sansk. सञ्चान —श० कल्प० (सम्यक् चानयति, excellent killer[2]), defined as a brave Hawk:

"महावीरस्तु गरुडे सञ्चानविहगेऽपि च"—मेदिनीकोश

---

1. cf. "बांसा बटेर लव औ सिचान । धूती रु चिप्पिका चटक भान" —quoted in हिं. श. सा. under चिम्पिका. चिपका, चिप्पक is Hindi for the male Shikra in F.B.I. In the verse therefore सिचान is the female & चिप्पिका the male Shikra; cf. SK. प्राचिका for a female Hawk falcon; also "वाजिका पक्षिजातिः स्यात्"—अनेकार्थध्वनिमञ्जरी, verse 185.

2. The Shikra is a noisy bird and has a loud double call—tui tui—which may also be rendered as चुइ चुइ. चिचुकार of वर्णरत्नाकर may be this Hawk and it is likely that a non-Sanskrit imitative name like चिचान-चचान for it has been Sanskritised into सञ्चान with a plausible etymology; cf. Hindi चिचियाना—to shout.

According to the शब्दकल्पद्रुम 'सञ्चान' is the Shikra. It is one of the best known Hawks of India, a small, stout bird, grey above, rusty below with whitish bars and a fierce golden yellow or orange eye. It is a favourite with Indian falconers as it begins to catch small birds for its keeper within ten days of being caught. Stuart Baker describes it as "a most plucky little Hawk" which is fully supported by the श्यै. शा. :

सुशीला जवना हिंस्राः शिकाराश्चण्डसाहसाः ।
च्योतन्त इव पीयूषं दृशोः संस्थानसौष्ठवैः ॥ श्यै. शा., 4.45

The epithet महावीर is thus seen to be a fitting tribute to the most powerful Eagle on the one hand and a compliment to the pluckiest of small Hawks, the Shikra, on the other. Thus the शिकारा proper of श्यै. शा., incorrectly placed in the वासा group, is the common Indian Shikra while the सिचानाः are the other forms or sub-species of the Shikra occurring in the extreme North-West, the extreme South, and North-East (Assam) of India.

13. The female Shikra is the सञ्चाण of मानसोल्लास where the male is named as द्रोणक or तोणक,, the same as टुना or टोना of श्यै. शा. 4.32. In Nepal however it is the female that is known as तुम्रा which occurs as टोना in Hindi poetry (see quotation in f.n. to para. 5 of the Introductory Sub-section). Finally, the Shikra and the Black-crested Baza feed on flying termites and these, particularly the former as the commoner bird, should be the वाल्मीकि (fr.वल्मी, वम्री white-ant) of the Mahābhārat List (5.101.11).

E. KITES, HARRIERS, & BUZZARDS

1. The Brahminy Kite is "a bright chestnut bird of prey with black wing-tips and a white head and breast, found near water." In flight and habits it resembles the Common Pariah Kite and lives on fish caught by itself or on fish-offal to be found near fishing villages, crabs, frogs etc. It is also given to robbing Crows and Common Kites of their food. Its oldest name is कङ्क or more correctly लोहपृष्ठकङ्क corresponding to the name, "the Maroon backed Kite", given to it by Jerdon because of its chestnut upper parts. The name कङ्क, however, belongs to several other birds with of course appropriate descriptive epithets and it has been a matter of some difficulty to separate them, especially because the lexicons have lumped together the different epithets in a common synonymy. Some of the lexical equations relating to different kinds of कङ्क are reproduced below :—

1) "कंकस्तु कर्कटस्कन्धः पर्कटः कमनच्छदः
दीर्घपादो प्रियापत्यो लोहपृष्ठश्च मल्लकः"—वैजयन्ती

2) "कङ्कस्तु कमनच्छदः
लोहपृष्ठो दीर्घपादः कर्कटः स्कन्धमल्लकः"—अभि. चिन्तामणि

3) "कङ्कस्तु लोहपृष्ठः स्यात्संदंशवदनः खरः ।
रणालङ्करणः क्रूरः स च स्यादामिषप्रियः"—राजनिघण्ट

4) "लोहपृष्ठस्तु कृकरः संदंशवदनः खरः
रणालङ्करणः क्रूरः कृकरश्चामिषप्रियः"
"उपचक्रः श्वभ्रतनुः (शुभ्रतनुः ?) कृशचञ्चुर्मंदाविलः"—कल्पद्रुकोश

5) "कङ्को लोहपृष्ठे"—मेदिनी, हेमचन्द्र, अमर, विश्वप्रकाश etc.

6) "जलाटनः कङ्कखगे"—हेमचन्द्र

7) "जलाटनो लोहपृष्ठः"—विश्वप्रकाश

8) "कोलपुच्छस्तु कङ्कः"—हारावली

9) "कालपृष्ठस्तु कङ्कपक्षिणि"—विश्वप्रकाश, हेमचन्द्र. etc.

10) "दीर्घपादस्तु कङ्कः स्यात्, गलेगण्डस्तु मर्कटः"—त्रिकाण्डशेष

11) "बकः कङ्को बकोटश्च"—राजनिघण्ट, कल्पद्रु.

12) "अरिष्टः काककङ्कयोः"—विश्वप्रकाश

2. The following five different birds, all going under the name of कङ्क (के जले, जलोपरि, जलसान्निध्ये वा अङ्कति गच्छति) are indicated in the above extracts and everyone of them is a जलाटन and आमिषप्रिय i.e. keeps to the neighbourhood of water and lives on animal food :—

i) The Brahminy Kite is लोहपृष्ठकङ्क,, कमनच्छदकङ्क, रणालङ्करणकङ्क, अरिष्टकङ्क

ii) The Common or Grey Heron—कृशचञ्चु-or संदंशवदन-कङ्क or कङ्क बक (Art. 82)

iii) The Adjutant Stork—दीर्घपाद-, गलेगण्ड-, मर्कट-, कर्कटस्कन्ध-(कर्कर–?),कोलपुच्छ-, स्कन्धमल्लक-, कङ्क (Art. 81).

iv) The Lesser Adjutant Stork—दीर्घपाद कङ्क (Art. 81)

v) Pallas's Fishing Eagle—प्रियापत्य–, खर–, क्रूर-कालपृष्ठ–, कङ्क where खर and क्रूर mean a noisy श्येन, Eagle, (Art. 52).

Equation 6 is true of all five, but Nos. 5 and 7 refer to the Brahminy Kite alone. No. 8 and the second half of No. 10 are applicable to the Adjutant alone and refer to its pendant pouch hanging from the neck and in front of its chest, while the first half of No. 10 is shared by it with the Lesser Adjutant as an allied form. No. 1 has equated कङ्क with the Brahminy Kite, the Adjutants and Pallas's Fishing Eagle. Similarly it will be seen that equations Nos. 2-4 have mixed up several of the above five birds. No. 11 refers to the Grey Heron and even the white Ibis (बक, बकोट Art. 80) as a kind of कङ्क, and No. 12 to the Black Crow or the Raven ((कृष्ण शकुनि) principally as a bird of evil omen, and the Brahminy Kite as a permanently auspicious bird, the term अरिष्ट as a homonym being understood in its two opposite meanings, viz., 'evil' and 'good'.

3. In this article we are concerned with कङ्क as the Brahminy Kite alone and for others the reader is referred to the Articles noted against them. The present Kite is कमनच्छद because of its beautiful plumage, and रणालङ्करण because it was commonly present over battle-fields along with Vultures, Ravens, Crows and Common Kites to snatch tit-bits from them,

and also because its presence over an army was supposed to presage victory to it. This belief was shared even by the Mussalmans who call it 'Ru-mubarik' or 'lucky-faced'. This also explains the name क्षेमङ्करी for it. The पद्मपुराण[1] relates that God शिव was once secretly enjoying the company of certain pretty women in the absence of Pārvatī and the latter divining the truth assumed the form of this Kite (क्षेमङ्करी), flew to the place and drove off her rivals. People wishing for good luck are therefore advised to greet the bird at sight and address the following prayer to it[2] :—

"कुङ्कुमारक्तसर्वाङ्गि कुन्देन्दुधवलानने ।
सर्वमङ्गलदे देवि क्षेमङ्करि नमोऽस्तु ते" ॥

The first half of the verse, it will be noticed, describes correctly the colour pattern of the bird's plumage. People in South India follow this advice but incorrectly call the bird Garuda. This name (क्षेमङ्करि) corresponds to अरिष्टकङ्क in a good sense as already indicated above.

4. Other names for this semi-sacred bird are धर्मचिल्ल, शंखचिल्ल, and कम्बातायिन् (कम्बु, a white conch, and आतायिन् a Kite), the last two in reference to its white head, neck and upper breast. As खकामिनी and चर्चिका are the names of Durgā or Pārvatī they would also appear to be additional names for the bird whose form she assumed :

"चर्चिका चिल्लदयिते खकामिन्यौ प्रकीर्तिते ।"—त्रिकाण्डशेष

The name चर्चिका for this Kite is perhaps after its persistent call notes or it may refer to its body which looks as if painted with white and red sandal (cf. चन्दनचर्चित), while खकामिनी (loving the sky) refers to its soaring habit. For गृत्स as a possible name for this Kite see Art. 81, (5) para 7.

5. There is some doubt as to the identity of प्रियापत्य (lover of one's progeny) as there are recorded instances of both the Brahminy Kite and Pallas's Fishing Eagle fiercely defending the nest, or young in the nest. E.H.N. Lowther, F.Z.S. speaking about this Kite says:—"there are few species more bold in the defence of their 'lares et penates' than is this species. Of the Brahminy Kite I think I can say, that always it has attacked us when we have climbed to its nest, or busied ourselves building a tower from which to photograph the bird; and always it has struck home and usually drawn blood"...[3]. Pallas's Fishing Eagle, which does not attack a stealer of its eggs, shows a different temper as soon as the young are

---

1. सृष्टिखण्ड Ch 53.

2. Ibid. 53.15. An alternative reading is quoted in शब्दकल्पद्रुम under क्षेमङ्करी—"कुङ्कुमारुणसर्वाङ्गि कुन्देन्दुधवलानने । मत्स्यमांसप्रिये देवि क्षेमङ्करि नमोस्तु ते" The statement in the F.B.I. that this kite is sacred to god विष्णु is incorrect and it is based upon an erroneous belief prevalent in certain parts of South India that it is the गरुड of mythology. The physical basis of गरुड is the Golden Eagle (Section A of this article) and the Brahminy Kite can only he said to be sacred to god शिव for reasons given above.

3. *Journal, Bom. Nat. His. Soc.*, Vol. 45. p. 6.

hatched out and it will then defend its young (अपत्य) with fierceness and determination. Hume writes from personal experience that once this Eagle attacked a man "with an unexpected ferocity from which nothing but my gun could have saved him". The female finding that the man was able to avoid her attack, gave a shrill cry which brought the male on the scene and both then charged together with rage and fierceness of despair, and he had to fire and wound both of them as they advanced, and but for this they would have certainly hurled the man down into the river. He adds that the birds are not offensive before the eggs are hatched. Now both the Kite and the Eagle are कङ्क and both may be described as प्रियापत्य, but perhaps, the Eagle has a better right to the epithet as it loves and defends *its young only* but not the nest or even the eggs.[1]

6. This Kite is always found near water and is seen flying back and forth or floating lazily in wide circles overhead. This habit of flying in circles and thus facing round in all directions won for it the distinction of being named as a victim for the deities presiding over the points of the compass in "दिशां कङ्को"—वाज.संहिता[2], and its method of picking up food from the surface of village tanks where water-nuts and lilies always grow, has furnished a name for a certain type of ascetics leading a hand to mouth life :—

"बिसशृङ्गाटकाहारास्ते कङ्का: साधका: स्मृता:" —स्कन्दपुराण[3]

A poet has pictured this Kite as the evening twilight :

"सिन्धो: सुधांशुशकलं परिगृह्य सन्ध्या-
क्षेमङ्करी निपतिताम्बरभूरुहाग्रे ।
चञ्चूपुटेन चपलेन तया विकीर्णा-
स्तारामिषेण पतिता इव पक्षखण्डा:" ।। —सुभाषित[4]

7. The Common Pariah Kite and allied forms are common everywhere. In literature they are mentioned by the names of शकुनि and गृध्री while the lexicons give चिल्ल, चिरम्भण आतायिन्, and क्षुद्रगृध्री (धन्वन्तरिनिघण्टु) as additional names. If the equation, "खभ्रान्ति: कण्ठनीडक:"—त्रिकाण्डशेष does not apply to the Kestrel as suggested in Section D, para 17, it would give two other synonyms for the Common Kite. In the Vaj. Sam. a kite is dedicated to the deity presiding over 'Marksmanship' or the Art of Archery : "कृकलास: पिप्पका

---

1. S. Baker holds the opposite view, viz. that this Eagle is a cowardly bird (F.B.I. 2nd ed.) though he refers to Hutton for a graphic description of a ferocious defence put up by a pair for their young.

2. 24.31. It may well share the name दिशाचक्षु of the महाभारत List with the Kestrel, and also be the चित्रकेतु (painted tail) of the same List from its chestnut tail. The last name can also be claimed by several birds with bars on the tail.

3. प्रभासक्षेत्रमाहात्म्य, 106.64.

4. 297.25.

शकुनिस्ते शब्यायै"—वाज. सं॰ 20.24 as it picks up scraps of food unerringly either from the ground or when thrown up to it in the air—even from the hands of a person carrying eatables in the open. The only other bird possible in the context of the Saṃhitā is the Brahminy Kite who is a past master at taking grasshoppers off the stems of growing rice, and the unerring aim with which it takes off the insect without seemingly so much as touching the stalk is really wonderful.

गृध्री in the imaginary picture below is no other than the Common Kite :—

> "श्येनावपातमवपत्य पदद्वये माम्
> आदाय धर्ममपरेण करेण घोरा
> वेगेन सा गगनमुत्पतिता नखाग्र-
> कोटिस्फुरत्पिशितपिण्डयुतेव गृध्री" । —प्रबोधचन्द्रोदय

8. The Black-winged Kite (13″) is light ashy-grey above with the lesser and median wing-coverts black, and white below. It occasionally hovers like the Kestrel and seen from below it appears to be a pure white bird with black wing-tips. It would therefore appear to be the कुमुद (white water-lily) of the Mahābhārata List. Seen from above or when sitting it is a small black and white Kite but being predominantly white it goes by the name of कपासी (cotton-white) in Hindi and may well have been known as कार्पासिका in Sanskrit though this name is nowhere recorded.

शकुनि being the larger Pariah Kite and its allied forms शकुनिका should be thus the smallest of Kites. M. Williams does not render शकुनिका as a Kite but देशीनाममाला equates Prakrit Kite-names like सउलि (शकुनि) and चिल्ला with शकुनिका; cf. चटक a sparrow, and चटिका or चटकिका a little sparrow.

9. This Black-winged Kite would seem to be the शबलिका as a bird of augury in वसन्तराज :—

> संमुखी शबलिकाऽथ वामिका श्रेयसी यदि च भास संगता ।
> तद्विशेषशुभदा तु सामिषा यस्य मूर्ध्नि पतेत्स भूपतिः ॥—8.37

None of the commentators gives any synonym, Sansk. or Hindi for शबलिका which, however, should not be the Common Pariha Kite since the बृ॰ संहिता does not include the ubiquitous Kite (शकुनि, गृध्री or चिल्ल) as a bird of augury. Moreover it is only with the rarest of incidents and uncommon combinations in bird-behaviour that the choicest of boons, e.g. kingship, can go as a prediction. In the above verse the mere sight of शबलिका in certain positions is auspicious, more so in association with भास, the Scavenging Vulture, but if by any chance it settles on the head of a person, the latter is destined for kingship. Considering everything therefore this black and white Kite should be the शबलिका of वसंतराज. The Common Kite is known as समड़ी or समळी in Gujarati and if these names are from Sansk. शबली, it may be an example of the transference of the name of a rather uncommon bird to a common and familiar one, for the name शबली (pied) would hardly fit the predominantly brown Kite of India.

10. The Harriers also known as Field-Kites,[1] are a well-defined group of Hawks, easily recognized by their flight and appearance. They make nests on the ground or amongst reeds in marshes. They never perch on trees and therefore, roost on the ground for the night, and here, they are sometimes surprised and killed by Jackals. Out of five varieties found in India only two breed in the country and the others are winter visitors. They fly low over the paddy plains, marshes and jheels and buoyantly quarter the ground for hours, poising for a moment almost motionless aloft, or glide in circles to great heights. They prey upon lizards, frogs, insects, mice, young or sickly birds, etc. but are simply incapable of catching even small healthy birds. The Pale and Montagu's Harriers are known as गिरगिटमार (lizard-killer, Sansk. कृकलासक ?) and पत्तई (Sansk. पत्री a Hawk), and the Pied Harrier as अबलक पत्तई (शबल पत्री—the Pied Hawk). These names would seem to show that the term पत्रिन्, पत्री, apart from being a common noun for 'a bird' is also a specific term for a Hawk-like bird, probably the Harriers with कृकलासक and सारस् for birds like Montagu's Harrier and the Marsh-Harrier respectively. The significance of the name पत्री for these Hawks seems to lie in the fact that beyond the powers of sustained flight, i.e. wing-power, they have hardly any claim to recognition as Hawks proper, i.e. as birds fit for the chase. In other words they possess a graceful flight but are absolutely useless for purposes of hawking. In this connection I would recall the प्रतिष्ठान type of Hawks considered in the preceding Sub-section,

"पत्रप्राया: प्रतिष्ठाना मन्दा वेगे च साहसे"—श्यै. शा. 4.43

It is thus quite possible that the प्रतिष्ठान (fr. प्रतिष्ठा foot, and hence the lowest ?—M.W.) are the पत्री ("पत्री श्येने"—हेमचन्द्र) type of Hawks, viz. the Harriers defined as पत्रप्राया:—पत्राण्येव प्रशस्तपक्षा एव सन्ति अस्य न तु शौर्यम्, a श्येन by appearance but not in action.

11. Reverting to the names कृकलासक and सारस् as probable names for some of the Harriers it is interesting to note that they occur with other bird names in the following verse :

हंसकाकमयूराणां कृकलासकसारसाम् ।
रूपाणि च बलाकानां गृध्रचक्राङ्गयोरपि ॥ MBh. 13.14.145

God शिव is supposed to assume at pleasure the forms of the birds named in the verse. कृकलासक, a garden lizard, is too mean a creature to be considered in the context and must be understood in the sense of a bird, and the formation of the word is analogous to that of कुलिङ्गक (one that takes or kills sparrows, discussed in the preceding Sub-section) for the Sparrow-Hawks.

1. Compare 'माठचील' in Bengali for the Marsh Harrier. The name means a 'field or medow Kite'.

कृकलासक should thus be the same as गिरगिटमार for, a Harrier (para 9 above). M. Williams on the other hand separates the last two words of the first line as कृकलास and कसारस्,, and renders the latter as 'a kind of bird', but this I have not met with it in literature or in any other lexicon. The term सारस् may be the same as सारस for the Crane or it may, placed as it is with कृकलासक, refer to the Marsh-Harrier which flies chiefly over water-logged areas in search of frogs, water-mice, sickly birds, insects, etc. for food.

12. The Buzzards are closely allied to the Eagles but due to extreme colour variation among them it is almost impossible to distinguish the different species in the field. They are comparatively sluggish birds with a heavy flight and feed upon rats, mice, frogs, lizards, large insects, etc. and go by the name of चूहामार बाज (rat-hawk) in Hindi corresponding to Sansk. गिरिशाल (गिरि, गिरिका a mouse, and शल् to move or शल a dart) for a kind of Hawk in हिन्दी शब्द सागर but not found in Sansk. lexicons none of which however claims to be exhaustive in any respect. The sentence, "अन्तर्हत्वा मूषिकां श्येनो गतः—"the Hawk went away taking hold of the mouse in सिद्धान्तकौमुदी, Basu's translation, supports the name गिरिशाल for a kind of Hawk.

13. The Indian Crested Honey Buzzard (27") is a brown Hawk with a dense body-plumage and the entire face covered with small scale-like feathers. Thus equipped by nature it is free to attack combs of wasps and bees and feed upon honey wax, larvae and even bees (Oates, *F.B.I.*, first edition). It is known as श्याम in Nepal and is the मधुहा* or मधुहन् (honey-thief) of चरकसंहिता. Two of the names for the progeny of Garuḍa in the Mahābhārata List, viz., मधुपर्क (मधुना पर्को सम्पर्को यस्य—शब्दकल्प०) and सोमभोजन (cf. "एतद्वै प्रत्यक्षात् सोमरूपं यन्मधु"—शत. ब्राह्मण, 12.8.2.15) probably refer to this Hawk.

14. The Indian Black-crested Baza is a very small Hawk (13"). It is a black and chestnut bird with a long black nuchal crest, black tail, and white breast with two broad white and chestnut bands separating the black neck and the white breast. The eyes are beautiful and lustrous. It is thus a very beautiful little Hawk and is aptly known as श्याम (beautifully dark, cf. श्यामसुन्दर for श्रीकृष्ण) in Nepal. The term is an adnoun for the Indian Koel but the lexicons do not give it for a Hawk. कुमार is a name of one of the descendants of the Mahābhārata List, and कुमार is also the name of god कार्त्तिकेय, represented as a beautiful youth. It is therefore suggested that the name may well refer to this handsome Baza. नीलपिच्छ for 'a bird

* मधुहा in the following verse probably refers to a human robber of a honey-comb:

सर्वथा संहितैरेव दुर्बलैर्बलवानपि ।
अमित्रः शक्यते हन्तुं मधुहा भ्रमरैरिव ॥—MBh. 5.33.70

But with a pun on मधुहा it can apply to man and Hawk both, for it is just possible that occasionally by a determined attack by a swarm of infuriated rock-bees even the Hawk is driven off.

of prey' has already been suggested in Section B, para 2 for the Crested Hawk Eagle but it can also apply to this bird as it has a black crest and a black tail, for पिच्छ means both 'crest' and 'tail' of a bird. नीलपिच्छ would then be a Hawk in which both these parts are black.

53

PIGEONS AND DOVES

A. INTRODUCTORY

1. No sharp distinction can be drawn between Pigeons and Doves both of which are members of the family Columbidae but the name Pigeon is exclusively given to the wild Pigeon and the name Dove is most commonly applied to the smaller members of the group. In general English literature, however, the two words are used almost indifferently. In Sanskrit literature also, the position is exactly the same, for though the terms पारावत and कपोत denote the wild Blue Rock Pigeon and Dove respectively in Caraka, Suśruta and some Law-books (धर्मशास्त्र), the poets have not always observed the distinction and the domestic Pigeon is गृह कपोत even according to Caraka and others. The lexicons, with certain exceptions like the Vaijayantī, have treated the terms as synonymous. Indeed, कपोत,[1] would seem to be the oldest name for both Pigeon and Dove, as according to Vedic scholars पारावत in the Ṛgveda does not mean a Pigeon and the term कपोत would seem to have been used for both. Thus कपोत in Ṛgveda (1.30.4) probably refers to a Pigeon. Here it is evidently regarded as an auspicious bird, for god Indra is requested to approach the cup of Soma juice offered to him with the warmth and eagerness of a Pigeon courting his mate. In the tenth Maṇḍala (165.1-5), however, which may well be separated in point of time from the first Maṇḍala by several centuries, the कपोत is a messenger of evil. If this was a particular kind of Dove, as is highly probable, it would appear to make the beginning of the prejudice against the Dove as a bird of evil omen. The belief, probably originated, as all superstitions generally do, with a few accidental coincidences of serious domestic calamity including death, with the entry of some particular Dove into the house. This old Ṛgvedic prejudice against the कपोत finds an echo in the Vājasaneyi Saṃhitā where a distinction between कपोत and पारावत has been observed for the first time. The पारावत as an auspicious bird is named for the auspicious day, "अह्ले पारावतानालभते, 24.25 while कपोत

---

1. The equation, कपोतः स्याच्चित्रकण्ठपारावतविहङ्गयोः— मेदिनी, shows that the term कपोत includes both Dove and Pigeons.

कपोत = Pigeon and Dove in the Ṛg Veda

- —पारावत— Pigeon
  - —भस्माङ्ग पारावत, नील कपोत — Blue Rock Pigeon
  - —रुचक-कपोत ,, पारावत — Wood Pigeon
  - —श्वेत पारावत Snow Pigeon
- —हारिद्रक, हरिताल हारीत, Green Pigeon
  - —हरिताल हारीत — Any Green Pigeon
  - —पट or वर्द्धमान कपोत — Imperial Green Pigeons
  - —कोकथु or कोकदेव — Pin-or White-tailed Green Pigeons
- —कपोत Doves
  - —धूसर कपोत—Little Brown Dove
  - —कुंकुमधूम्रकपोत—Do. & Rufous Turtle Dove
  - —अरुण or काण–कपोत —Red Turtle Dove
  - —चित्र–or चित्रपक्ष कपोत — Spotted Dove
  - —धवल कपोत—Ring Dove
  - —तुषार कपोत (Back formation from तुसाल) — Bar-tailed Cuckoo-Dove
  - —शुकच्छवि–or हारीत कपोत — Emerald Dove

(Dove) is placed in charge, as it were, of Mitrāvaruṇa, the deities who are the joint-upholders and guardians of the world, promoters of religious rites and *avengers of sin aad untruth*, "मित्रावरुणाभ्यां कपोतान्-24.23 and again said to belong to निऋति the goddess of Misery, कपोत उलूक: शशस्ते निऋत्यै-24.36. The association of उलूक, कपोत, and the crop destroying शश is worth noting. कपोत which was hiterto an inclusive terms came to be restricted to Doves, and Pigeons now came to be known as पारावत (coming from afar, i.e. from hills and mountains where they went back to roost and breed as against Doves which lived nearer home). That Pigeons have long been welcome birds is clear from the following in the Mahābhārata :-

गृहे पारावता धन्याः शुकाश्च सह सारिकाः
गृहेष्वेते न पापाय तथा वै तैलपायिकाः[1] ॥ —13.107.106

Given even a particular kind of Dove as a bird of ill-omen e.g. in RV and VS, it is an easy step for all Doves to be so regarded. This would seem to be the reason why बृहत्संहिता, 47.4-6 recommends such natural waters for princes to bathe in as are not only situated in beautiful surroundings but also have auspicious birds calling or singing in the neighbourhood, and the list of birds named purposely excludes कपोत (Dove) though it includes पारावत. Bhaṭṭotpala expands the illustrative list of "कौशिक गृध्र प्रभृतिः" by adding to it "काक कङ्क प्लव श्येन कपोताः. According to the संहिता, 87.12-13 all the three varieties of Dove common in North India are inauspicious. Kālidāsa and other poets do not refer to a Dove as such and both the terms कपोत and पारावत, when used by them, always mean a Pigeon, domestic or wild.

B. PIGEONS

1. Green Pigeons are well represented throughout India and despite differences in colour-pattern or size there is no mistaking a Green Pigeon as they are all cast upon a common model and the habits of all are similar. They are "comparatively small Pigeons which may be known at a glance by their beautifully soft green plumage, often mixed with maroon or lilac on the shoulders or back, and always with one, and sometimes with two, bold yellow bars across the wings. By ear, too, these lovely birds may always be identified . . . their musical whistling call being quite unlike the coo of any Dove or Pigeon of other groups."[2] They are entirely arboreal in their habits and live on wild fruits, figs of all kinds, berries, plums, etc., including such large fruits as the black-plum (जम्बू) and nutmeg (जातिफल) which are swallowed whole. They occasionally descend to drink

1. सारिका in the Verse is the Grackle or Common Myna and तैलपायिका the starling—Arts. 20, 21.

2. Stuart Baker, "*Indian Pigeons and Doves*."

at the river's edge but normally prefer to climb down overhanging canes and bushes until they are within reach of the water. They keep a firm foot-hold when moving about in thick foliage, and if a bird is shot at and killed it sometimes simply hangs downwards or if the twig gives way, it comes down with the twig still firmly held in its feet. The popular belief that a green Pigeon never sets foot on the ground except with a twig held in its feet has nothing more than the above facts for a basis. This fiction has furnished some beautiful similes in Hindi poetry, but, perhaps, not in Sanskrit.

2. All Green Pigeons are हारिद्रक (चरक, 1.26,86), हरिद्राङ्ग, हारीत[1] or हरिताल, corresponding to हारिल or हरियल in Hindi and Bengali, though a couple of species are known as कोकथु and कोकदेव in Sanskrit and कोकला in Hindi. Similarly, Imperial Green Pigeons of large size are वर्द्धमान कपोत, पट or पटाव in Sanskrit. The Green Pigeons of Malabar are the हारीत of Kālidāsa :-

मारीचोद्भ्रान्तहारीताः मलयाद्रेरुपत्यकाः—रघुवंश, 4.46

The black-plum ((जम्बू) is the favourite food of the Bengal Green Pigeon and the कपोत in the following is evidently this bird. The Wood Pigeons of the Himalayas also eat this fruit but they are not found in the Vindhyan country :

फलपुलकितजम्बूकुञ्जकूजत्कपोत—
प्रियशबरपुरन्ध्री बन्धवो विन्ध्यलेखाः —अनर्घराघव, 5.27

Their sweet whistling notes have often been appreciated. A jungle scene on the Tamasa river :

प्रहृष्टनानाविधपक्षिसेवितं
प्रमत्तहारीतकुलोपनादितम्
समन्ततः सुन्दरदर्शनीयतां
समुल्लसत्तद्वनमुल्लसन्महत्

God Śiva affectionately mentions a Green Pigeon who, by nesting in a branch overhanging his shrine and thus seeking his protection secured a place in heaven :

हारीतः कोऽपि सम्प्राप्तः शाखानीडो ममान्तिके[3]

Green Pigeons with other beautiful-voiced birds in a jungle-scene :-

कोकिलैः कलविङ्कैश्च हारीतैर्जीवजीवकैः
श्रोत्ररम्यं सुमधुरं कूजद्भिश्चाप्यधिष्ठितम्[4]

---

1. The Emerald Dove is also हारीत, perhaps more correctly.
2. Skanda Purāṇa, Ayodhyāmāhātmya, Ch. 9.30.
3. Skanda Purāṇa, Aruṇācalamāhātmya, Pūrvakhaṇḍa Ch. 9.
4. Mahābhārata, III. 158, 53-54; Mārkaṇḍeya Purāṇa, 6, 18-19.

3. The Pin-tailed and the Wedge-tailed Green Pigeons are also found in North India, the former from Kumaon eastwards and the latter throughout the Himalayas and the broken country below them. They must also be regarded as हारीत or हरियल, but from the orange-pink colour of their breasts they are known as कोकला in Hindi corresponding to कोकथु and कोकदेव and probably also चक्रकोक in Sanskrit. Their notes are sweeter than those of other birds of the class. In particular the notes of the Wedge-tailed bird are "fuller, richer, and more sweet than those of any other Green Pigeon" (S. Baker). For this reason this last bird is very much sought after as a pet. Both these species are generally seen either singly or in pairs, or in very small parties of a few birds only. In this also as in the colouring of their breasts they resemble the कोक or चक्रवाक birds. These two species stand midway in point of size between those considered earlier and the next group.

4. The largest among the Green Pigeons of North India are the Green Imperial Pigeon and Hodgson's Imperial Pigeon measuring up to 18 and 20 inches in length respectively. They occur in and east of Nepal. Both have the head, neck and the whole of the lower parts (except the tail-coverts) a beautiful pale dove-grey, vinous pink or vinous-grey with the upper parts green in the first and copper-brown in the second bird. The contrast between the darker upper plumage and the lighter head, neck and breast makes it appear as if the birds wear a light silken upper garment or scarf, thrown over the head and neck, and brought down in front upon the chest after the style of women in North India, and this accounts for their Hindi name of दुकुल from Sanskrit दुकूल for a fine upper garment; cf. 'पट" and "दुकूल" in the following from सौन्दरनन्द :-

> शनैर्व्रजन्नेव स गौरवेण पटावृतांशो विनतार्धकायः— 5.7.
> सात्रासयन्ती वलभीपुटस्थान् पारावतानूपुरनिस्वनेन
> सोपानकुक्षिं प्रससार हर्षात् भ्रष्टं दुकूलान्तमचिन्तयन्ती—6.8.

5. Now पट is one of the auspicious birds mentioned in Lalitavistara (ch. 21, p. 398) :-

> पटक्रौञ्चहंसकोकिलमयूराः अभिप्रदक्षिणं करोन्ति ध्रुवमस्य जयो भवत्यद्य ।

पटाक is also a kind of bird in शब्दार्थचिन्तामणि. दुकूल and पट are almost synonymous terms and both are frequently used in the sense of उत्तरीयम् or upper garment :

> दुकूलं सूक्ष्मवस्त्रे स्यादुत्तरीये सितांशुके—शब्दार्णव[1]
> चण्डालस्तिमिरावगुण्ठनपटक्षेपं विधत्ते विधुः—साहित्यदर्पण, 3, under verse 76
>
> दुकूलपटपल्लवेन. . . .कृतशिरोवेष्टनः—कादम्बरी[2]
> आरोप्य उत्तरीयपटादि—सहृदयलीला, अलंकारोल्लेख, का. मा. Pt. 5

1. *Śabdārṇava*, cited by Pathaka on Meghadūta, 65.
2. *Kādambarī*, Kale's edition, Pt. 1. p. 33.

पट (पटेन आवृतः इव), therefore, is either or both of these birds, and so also पटाक. All Pigeons and Doves are bad-tempered and quarrelsome but these are an exception, and as peace-loving birds, have been selected as one of the "मङ्गल्य पक्षिणः" to herald the coming of Buddha, the Prince of Peace in ललितविस्तर.

6. पालकाप्य mentions वर्धमान कपोत as a "high-flying bird" in हस्त्यायुर्वेद, 8.58, and भरतमुनि describes a particular method of salutation in which a person after producing a clapping sound with the palms of his hands holds them like the wings of a वर्धमान कपोत :-

"खटिका वर्द्धमानेन कपोताख्येन वा पुनः"—नाट्यशास्त्र, 28.70

All Pigeons and Doves make a clapping sound at the beginning of a flight, and this is what S. Baker has to say about the Green Imperial Pigeon : "When starting from a tree or suddenly frightened into diverting their course, the wings beat loudly against one another and make a sound audible at a great distance." खटिका in the sense of "clapping" refers to this sound so that it is incorrect of M. Williams to treat खटिका वर्धमान as a compound. वर्धमान must go with कपोत as an adjective. The epithet is indicative of the size as well as the auspicious nature of the bird, and as पट is the largest (and auspicious) of all the Green Pigeons, it would appear that the name वर्धमान कपोत also refers to these large and beautiful birds.

7. The wild or Blue-Rock Pigeon and similar forms are पारावत or नील कपोत (""भकाकः नीलकपोते"—शब्दार्थचिंतामणि)[1] and भूमिशय (M.W.) while the domestic Pigeon of similar or different colours and derived from the wild stock is the गृहकपोत of Caraka and the poets :

धूपैर्जालविनिःसृतैर्वलभयः संदिग्धपारावताः ।

— विक्रमोर्वशीय, 3.2

बन्धनभ्रष्टो गृहकपोतको बिडालिकालोके पतितः ।

मालविकाग्निमित्र, 4

The wild Pigeon has been nesting and roosting in high buildings in populous towns as a semi-domesticated bird from very ancient times and has been mentioned under the name of पारावत by Kālidāsa and other poets :-

तां कस्यांचिद्भवनवलभौ सुप्तपारावतायाम्—मेघदूत, 1.41

Garden set off with white-washed temples, and the latter with the Blue-Rock Pigeons :—

1. The lexical verses for पारावत and कपोत at p. 296 of धन्वन्तरिनिघण्टु have become disjointed and corrupt but the terms नीलाङ्गक and भस्माङ्ग clearly refer to the colour of the plumage of the Blue Rock Pigeon when on the ground or perching and during flight respectively. When on the wing the bird looks ash-grey chiefly because of the lighter colour of the under-surface of the wings. गृहस्वामी of the first verse (56) refers to the semi-wild birds taking possession, as it were, of the various parts of a building.

पारावतध्वनिविकूजितचारुशृङ्गैः ।
अभ्रंकषैः सितमनोहरचारुरूपैः ॥

मत्स्यपुराण, ch. 180

The blue-grey of their bodies and the iridescent purple of their necks taken together has offered an excellent comparison for the smoke arising out of sacrificial fires :

ऋषीणामग्निहोत्रेषु हुतेषु विधिपूर्वकम् ।
कपोताङ्गारुणो धूमो दृश्यते पवनोद्धतः ॥

रामायण, 2. 119, 6.

The behaviour of the cock-bird during courtship has been beautifully described :-

स्मरसमरसमयपूरितकम्बुनिभो द्विगुणपीनगलनालः (पारावतः)

आर्यासप्तशती, 597

सुकान्तकान्तामणितानुकारं, कूजन्तमाघूर्णितरक्तनेत्रम्
प्रस्फारितोन्नम्रविनम्रकण्ठं, मुहुर्मुहुर्न्यंञ्चितचारुपुच्छम् ॥

कुमारसंभव, 9.2.

8. Of the Wood-Pigeons the Eastern Wood-Pigeon or Ring-Dove is common in Kashmir and Nepal, and extends into the Punjab in winter. An allied form, the Ashy Wood Pigeon, occurs in Nepal and in Eastern Himalayas. The former wears a broad semi-collar of buff (dull yellow or yellowish-orange) glossed green or purple-copper, and the latter a similar but narrower collar. Sanskrit रुचक[1] means a gold ornament or necklace as well as Pigeon or Dove. The bird meant, must, therefore, seem to wear a yellowish collar and this requirement is fulfilled only by these Wood Pigeons and they are probably the रुचक पारावत.

9. The Snow Pigeon has a dark Grey head and neck, a white collar, light brown upper parts, white lower back, a broad white band on the tail and a pure white breast changing to dove-grey on the abdomen. It appears white when high up on the wing. It is a bird of the higher Himalayas but is found in Kashmir and Nepal. Pilgrims to the Amarnath cave which contains a "शिवलिङ्ग" often see these Pigeons, and a pair of them is said actually to live in the Cave itself. They are less shy than most Pigeons and are sometimes trapped in Nepal for the Calcutta market. As the bird has much white in its plumage and also looks white during flight, the श्वेत पारावत mentioned as a Himalayan bird in the Padma Purāṇa can only be this bird :

नदत्पारावतैः श्वेतैश्चकोरैः कलकोकिलैः
राजहंसैर्मयूरैश्च सदा रम्यः स पर्वतः ॥[2]

---

1. M. Williams and the Medini Kośa.
2. Padma Purāṇa—Uttarakhaṇḍa. Ch. 221. 20-21.

It is to be noted that the author is referring to wild birds so that the Mayūra stands for Mayūra-Kukkuṭa, the beautiful crested Impeyan Pheasant or Munal. The place is evidently some lake-country in the Himalayas probably in the Garhawal District which stretches right up to the Mana and Niti passes beyond Gangotri, Badrinath and Kedarnath.

C. DOVES

1. Doves are the smaller cousins of the wild Pigeons, lighter in build, more slender in form, and also dressed rather more plainly. They, therefore, go by the name of कपोत, पाण्डुकपोत or simply पाण्डु (cf. पाण्डू colour of natural wool) corresponding to Hindi पंडुक or पड़की. Other Hindi names like टुटरू, घुग्घी or घूघी are of an imitative nature recalling the notes of some of them.

2. The different species of Indian Doves and their Sanskrit names (to be discussed presently) are as under :—

(i) the Rufous Turtle Dove—कुंकुम-धूम्र कपोत.

(ii) the Little Brown Dove—कुंकुम -धूम्रकपोत, धूसर कपोत (?)

(iii) the Spotted Dove—चित्र-, चित्रपक्ष-कपोत.

(iv) the Ring Dove—धवल-, अपांडुर-कपोत; धवलपाण्डु,.

(v) the Red Turtle Dove—काण-, अरुण-कपोत.

(vi) the Emerald Dove—हारीत; शुकच्छवि-, रक्तकण्ठ-कपोत.

(vii) the Bar-tailed Cuckoo-Dove—तुषार कपोत.

3. The first four birds are members of the same genus and of these the Rufous Turtle Dove occurs in two forms differentiated as the Northern Indian and the Indian. The former breeds in Central Asia and the Himalayas as far as Nepal and thence through the lower levels up to Sikkim, while the latter is a bird of Eastern India, and it is only during the cold weather that both forms visit the areas to the south of their respective territories. They are grey-brown suffused with rufous above and vinous rufous below and would therefore share the name of कुंकुमधूम्र कपोत with the Little Brown Dove The Hindi name लाल पंडुक for the Northern Indian variety emphasizes the rufous or अरुण in the plumage while the name साम घूघू for the other, the Indian Rufous Turtle Dove, stresses the brown (धूम्र, श्याम) in the body colour. As this Dove is neither a permanent resident of the मध्य प्रदेश nor so common about towns or villages it does not find place in the list of birds of augury.

4. The next three Doves, Nos. 2-4, are the commonest and most familiar birds of India. The Indian Little Brown Dove, छोटी पड़की in Hindi, is again a greyish-brown bird with lilac-pink on the head and neck and chestnut to vinous-pink on the breast. "It is typically a bird of civilization, exceedingly common all round villages and towns and one of the tamest and most confidential of our Indian birds" (S. Baker in *F.B.I.*). It is the कुंकुमधूम्रकपोत of भट्टोत्पल and probably also the धूसर कपोत (the grey-brown

Dove) of the lexicons.[1] The Spotted Dove is blackish-brown and spotted white or rufous above and vinaceous-pink below. This also, like the preceding "is a most tame and confiding little bird, running about freely in gardens and villages...generally hunting in couples and constantly calling to one another in the softest and sweetest of coos" (Ibid.). It passes as चितरोख in Hindi and is the चित्रकपोत or चित्रपक्ष कपोत of the lexicons and literature. The fourth and the last of the series is the Ring-Dove, the lightest coloured member of the group, being lilac-grey on the head and neck, fawn-brown on the back and lilac to pale dove-grey on the breast. Some white on the tail and the silver-grey and greyish-white of the flanks, axillaries and under wing-coverts give the bird, when on the wing, a whitish look. It is धौर- or धौला-पंडुक in Hindi corresponding to धवल-पाण्डु in Sanskrit. Like the other two it also "haunts the vicinity of humanity and is most common in cultivated country round villages and towns, freely entering gardens" (Ibid.).

5. These three Doves of towns and villages (Nos. 2-4) have been mentioned as birds of omen (कपोताः त्रयः) in अग्निपुराण, 231, 15, बृहत्संहिता, 87,1 and वसंतराज, p. 247 though the relevant text in the last appears to be incomplete. Nevertheless it refers to the त्रिभेद कपोत, i.e. three different Doves, viz. the विपाण्डुर, the particularly whitish, the चित्र, spotted or variegated, and the धूम्र, the brown. This agrees very well with Bhaṭṭotpala's commentary on the बृहत्संहिता where he enumerates the three species as आपाण्डुर-, चित्र-and कुंकुमधूम्र-कपोत. These names belong respectivly to the Ring-Dove, the Spotted Dove and the Little Brown Dove.

6. All the races of the first three species listed above have chequered black patches on either side of or behind the neck and are comprised as miniature or half-pigeons within the lexical equation अर्धपारावतश्चित्रकण्ठे—मेदिनी, हेमचन्द्र, etc. (cf. 'Half-Snipe' for a small Snipe). The Ring-Dove, on the other hand wears a semi-collar of black edged white both above and below and is therefore the सूत्रकण्ठ कपोत of the lexicons. The Red Turtle Dove also has a black semi-collar behind the neck and it must share the epithet. Other names for the Ring Dove are धवल-पाण्डु and धवल-कपोत (see below).

7. So far we have dealt with names based upon the colour of the plumage but some of these birds have also been classified according to the nature of their call notes. Thus the Spotted Dove with a confluent or rippling call—a guttural 'croo' repeated several times in quick succession, is classed as the कलध्वनि[2] type and the Ring Dove (धवल कपोत) with its distinct triple "coo" call is a स्फुटध्वनि type of Dove; cf. छेद्य or छेद्यकंठ (छेद्य separation of syllables; interruption—M.W.) as a synonym for कपोत and पारावत in शब्दकल्पद्रुम. धन्वन्तरि has the following :

---

1. "धूसरो धूम्रलोचनः"—राजनिघंटु, सिंहादिवर्ग, 138.
The adnoun धूसर is descriptive of a donkey and camel as well; but see para. 8 below.

2. The Little Brown Dove with the call "Cru-do-do-do-do" would also belong to this type.

पाण्डुस्तु द्विविधो ज्ञेयः चित्रपक्षः कलध्वनिः ।
द्वितीयो धवलः प्रोक्तः स कपोतः स्फुटध्वनिः ॥

A third type, the घूघूकृत् includes the next bird.

8. In the Red Turtle Dove (अरुण कपोत) alone are the sexes differently coloured. The male is a warm vinous-red and the female brown. The chin and throat of the male are albescent contrasting with the dark ashy-grey head and the vinous-red breast. The eyes vary from hazel-brown to dark brown. Both have a black semi-collar on the hind neck which naturally attracts the adnoun सूत्रकंठ for this species as well. The call is a distinctive, "rolling groo—gurr—goo repeated four or five times quickly" (Salim Ali). धन्वन्तरि notes the call and the colour of the eyes of this Dove as under :—

"कपोतोऽन्यो घूघूकृद् धूम्रलोचनः"—p. 296.

It is possible that the brown female was looked upon as a different species and the equation, धूसरो धूम्रलोचनः, of राजनिघंटु, सिंहादिवर्ग, 138 refers to her as the धूसर कपोत. Being the smallest of the Doves it is the काणकपोत of चरक, 1.25.37-38 and सुश्रुत, 1.46.69. चक्रपाणिदत्त on the former explains the adjective काण (fr. कण little, small) as अल्पार्थवाची while डल्हणाचार्य on the latter renders the name as अरुणवर्णकपोत which has been adopted by K.M. Vaidya in his अष्टाङ्गहृदयकोश. The name अरुण कपोत corresponds to the bird's Hindi names इंटिया घूघू (इंट a brick; the brick-red Dove) and गुलाबी घूघू (the rose-coloured Dove). It is widely distributed in the country and is very numerous in the North-west but being a shy bird it keeps to well-wooded areas.

9. The male of the beautiful Emerald Dove or हारीत has a blue-grey head, metallic emerald-green upper parts and deep vinous-red neck, shoulders and breast. The female has the head also vinous-red. Even for a Dove it is rather a small bird, being only 10 inches in total length (i.e. only one inch longer than the Red Turtle Dove). It is found throughout the greater part of India including Kashmir and Nepal in forest country with a sufficient rainfall. These pretty birds are very terrestrial in their habits and are therefore, very active on the ground and frequent damp footpaths in evergreen forests. Like the entire Pigeon family they are fully vegetarian except for termites which they eat greedily. Another Dove which shares this habit is the Spotted Dove. "Their flight...is extremely swift, and at the same time wonderfully silent, and it is often quite startling the way these birds flit into sight and then disappear without a sound, twisting and turning so as to avoid bushes and other obstacles in their flight. Invariably they keep low down, and it is rare to see them rise twenty feet from the ground even when they dash across some opening in forest"... (S. Baker). They are not gregarious, but in some favourite spots half a dozen or more may sometimes be met with. "It has a curious habit of entering and passing through buildings, which, doubtless, it hopes will afford refuge from the glare of the sun; but finding the interior so different from what it expects, it passes straight through instead of resting."

(S. Baker). Other writers also have remarked upon this curious habit of the bird. Its note "is a soft but very deep and rather plaintive 'coo', and during the breeding season they may often be heard calling to one another for some minutes together" (Ibid). This agrees fairly well with Varāhamihira's description of the bird's call :

"हारीतस्य तु शब्दो गुग्गुः"

बृहत्संहिता, 87.15.

The voice of Green Pigeons, on the other hand, is, "a very pleasing full-toned rolling whistle." This bird is रक्तकण्ठ कपोत as well as हारीत, the latter being apparently due to its green wings. It has also been called अरुणकपोत by भास्कर on वाग्भट, though the name properly belongs to the Red Turtle Dove.

10. Green Pigeons are purely arboreal birds and do not descend to the ground except at the water's edge to drink, or at a salt-lick, whereas the Emerald Dove is very terrestrial picking up seeds and berries, etc. from the ground and from low bushes. God Śiva describes the beauties of an extensive garden in काशी and refers to a group of Emerald Doves ("हारीत वृन्द") walking here and there along the garden path :—

"हंसानां पक्षपातप्रचलितकमलस्वच्छविस्तीर्णतोयं
तोयानां तीरजातप्रविकचकदलीवाटनृत्यन्मयूरम् ।
मायूरैः पक्षचन्द्रैः क्वचिदपि पतितै रञ्जितं क्ष्माप्रदेशं
देशे देशे विकीर्णप्रमुदितविलसन्मत्तहारीतवृन्दम् ॥"[1]

11. The Bar-tailed Cuckoo-Dove of Kashmir and Nepal goes by the Hindi name of तुसाल ("तुषार कपोत, a Dove of the cold region). "Its deep booming 'Coo' calls one's attention from far away, and when the bird is finally located it is almost certain to be seated high up on some tree which stands well above those surrounding it" (S. Baker). A bird of such striking manners, different from others of its kind, would naturally invite attention and it is highly probable that the name कु-रव कपोत (having a distinct "coo" note) for 'a kind of Dove' (M.W.) is for this particular bird (Cf. कलध्वनि for the Spotted and स्फुटध्वनि for the Ring Dove)[2]. It is further permissible to say that the 'back-formation', तुषारकपोत, was also its name in Sanskrit.

12. In conclusion, an attempt must be made to determine the identity of the particular kind of कपोत which from the time of the Ṛgveda has been regarded as the messenger of Death and Misery, and otherwise a bird of ill-omen along with the hooting owl :

---

1. Matsya Purāṇa, ch. 180. This verse occurs in a slightly corrupt form in the Liṅga Purāṇa, 92.24. चरक 1.26.81 (Chowkhamba edition; 1.26.86 in others) mentions हारिद्रक, the Green Pigeon and हारीतक, the Emerald Dove. The Lahore edition reads हारिद्रक at both places in the same section which is incorrect.

2. Cf. also कण्ठीरव, a Pigeon, and कु-रवक, the Tree-pie.

यदुलूको वदति मोघमेतद् यत्कपोतः पदमग्नौ कृणोति ।
यस्य दूतः प्रहित एष एतत् तस्मै यमाय नमो अस्तु मृत्यवे ॥
ऋग्वेद, 10.165.4.

The hooting owl, again, is held to be as bad as the कपोत, the messenger of Death :—

मृत्युदूतः कपोतोऽयमुलूकः कम्पयन्मनः ।
प्रत्युलूकश्च कुह्वानैः अनिद्रौ शून्यमिच्छतः ॥
भागवत, 1.14.14.

This verse, it will be noticed, is a clear echo of the one from Ṛgveda. The allocation of inauspicious birds between Gods and others (सुरासुराः) is as below :—

श्येनं जग्राह मृत्युश्च, काकं कालो गृहीतवान् ।
उलूकं निर्ऋतिश्चैव जग्राहातिभयावहम् ॥
गृध्रं व्याधिस्तदीशोऽथ, कपोतं च स्वयं यमः ॥
मार्क. पु. 48.68-69.

It will be noticed that the Owl and कपोत have been distributed exactly in accordance with the Vedic tradition. With "गृहे पारावताः धन्याः" in favour of the Blue Rock Pigeon and the habit of the Spotted and the Little Brown Doves of frequently nesting inside human habitations it is evident that these birds cannot be the calamitous कपोत, nor should the Rufous Turtle Dove, the Red Turtle Dove or even the Ring Dove be that bird as they keep away from inhabited houses. According to the commentator of the आश्वलायन गृह्यसूत्र, however, it is apparently the Ring Dove (Dhavala Kapota) which, we shall see, is incorrect :—

कपोतश्चेदगारमुपहन्यादनुपतेद्वा—"देवाः कपोतः" इति प्रत्यृचं जुहुयाज्जपेद्वा—
—3.7.7

Commentary—"कपोतो रक्तपादः शुक्लवर्णोऽरण्यवासी" ।
As against this शौनक specifies the Emerald Dove as the guilty bird:

कपोतं विशेषयति शौनकः —
रक्तपादः कपोताख्यः अरण्यौकाः शुकच्छविः ।
स चेच्छालां विशेत् शालासमीपं च व्रजेद् यदि ॥
अन्येषु गृहमध्ये वा वल्मीकस्योद्गमादिषु ।[1]

The description of the Kapota as "शुकच्छवि" (of the colour of a Parrot) and the attraction it has for the termite ant-hill (वल्मीक) combined with its habit of occasionally entering human dwellings leaves no doubt whatever that the bird meant by शौनक is the Emerald Dove. The habits of the bird described earlier fully confirm the identification. It may be

1. Quoted in Śabdakalpadruma under "अद्भुतम्"

added that small Indian houses with a room set apart in them for worship of the sacrificial fire were not as open and spacious as modern bungalows which the Dove is known to enter at one end and pass out at the other without nesting so that once the bird entered the house or the sacrificial chamber, it would flounder and be forced to settle down somewhere... even near the fire-altar- ("यत्कपोतः पदमग्नौ कृणोति) though it might ultimately escape. Its low and fast but noiseless flight like that of an Owl at night was rightly regarded as typical of a secret messenger. With the clear authority of शौनक before us it is easy to see that correct reading of the commentary on the आश्वलायन सूत्र is "शुकवर्ण" and not "शुक्लवर्ण" and both, therefore, agree as to the identity of the offending bird. Additional evidence in support of the above identification is found in the भविष्यपुराण where the रक्तकण्ठ कपोत is placed in the list of birds and animals whose entry into a dwelling is considered ominous:—

द्रोणकाको बकश्चैव, उलूकद्वयमेव च ।
रक्तकण्ठः कपोतश्च, व्याघ्र एणश्च वा विशेत् ॥ 2.10.140.

With its maroon-red neck and breast and bright green wings the Emerald Dove is both रक्तकण्ठ (रक्तग्रीव—M.W.) and शुकच्छवि. It shares, of course, red legs and feet with all other Doves.

13. The bird, as it happens, possesses a good deal of red in its dress and would thus seem to have some esoteric affinity with fire. The कपोत whose form god अग्नि was compelled to assume to pick up the 'seed' of the god Śiva out of which कार्त्तिकेय was ultimately born should be this Dove:—

अग्निर्भूत्वा कपोतो हि प्रेरितः सर्वनिर्ज्जरैः ।
अभक्षच्छांभवं वीर्यं चञ्च्वा तु निखिलं तदा ॥
शिवपुराण IV. 2.158,32-35.

The Matsya Purāṇa (158, 32-35) has a different version according to which Agni acted similarly but in the shape of a parrot. Here the green colour of the bird is significant, and the author of the Purāṇa seems to have interpreted हारीत or शुकच्छवि पक्षी of some other Manuscipt as a Parrot, for in other versions the bird is a कपोत only. Again, the कपोत–form taken by Agni at the instance of Indra, who, became a Falcon, to test the moral virtue of उशीनर and शिबि would seem to be this low flying Dove which by landing itself into the lap of the two kings put them in great difficulty (i.e. निऋृंति)[1]. In yet another 'श्येन-कपोत' story, with king वृषदर्भ-उशीनर as the protector of कपोत, Agni and Indra do not figure but the कपोत is described as a beautiful bird with a blue head which must be assumed to be in effective contrast with the body-plumage:

नवनीलोत्पलापीड चारुवर्ण सुदर्शन !—महाभारत, 3.32,7

1. Mahābhārata. III. Ch. 131 and 197.

Our Dove has a blue-grey head and beautiful plumage and the above description fits it all right. The stories from the Mahābhārata and the Śiva Purāṇa referred to above clearly help to connect this Dove with the following synonymy for a kind of Kapota:—

अमङ्गल्यः स भवति द्विजो यस्तु यभो यतः (? यमो यतः)
दहनोऽग्निसहायश्च भीषणो गृहनाशनः ॥[1]

i.e. the bird which is under the control (यत) of Yama is inauspicious and is named 'fire' (i.e. destructive like fire), 'associate of Fire-god', 'fearful' and the 'house-destroyer'—all which is rather hard upon the pretty little Dove. All considered, therefore, the malignant bird of the Ṛgveda, Vājasaneyi Saṃhitā and later literature is the Emerald Dove.

14. Several Doves, and particularly the Spotted Dove mate for life and always go about in pairs. Stuart Baker who closely watched a pair of Spotted Doves regularly nesting in his verandah, describes them as "a most loving little couple", the cock-bird "very attentive to his little wife, often taking her up special dainties from the table below." It is indeed, a pleasant surprise to find that the physical features and habits of these birds had been carefully observed by the ancients more than 2,000 years ago. This is proved by the touching story of a pair of Doves purposely made very human and circumstantial in the telling, narrated in the Mahābhārata.[2] They are described as चित्रतनूरुह (=चित्रपक्ष) and चित्राङ्ग (Cf. चित्रकपोत) and as a greatly devoted couple. The characteristic description of the bird's eye furnishes a most helpful clue to its identity:

यदि सा रक्तनेत्रान्ता चित्राङ्गी मधुरस्वरा ।
अद्य नायाति मे कान्ता न कार्यं जीवितेन मे ॥[3]

The eyelids and the narrow bare orbital skin of the Spotted Dove are red (रक्त नेत्रान्त) and no other Indian Dove has this feature. Evidently the heroes of the story are a pair of Spotted Doves, held up as a model of conjugal fidelity for erring humanity. In the Western world, too, the Turtle Doves are "the time-honoured emblem of tenderness and conjugal love."

15. The कपोत, in हर्षचरितम्, 19.61 beginning—

"दाक्षीपुत्रस्य तंत्रे ध्रुवमयमभवत् कोप्यधीती कपोतः"

is the Indian Red Turtle Dove (Para. 8 above). Brahman boys at a Grammar School memorized the Sūtras of Pāṇini by constant

1. धन्वन्तरि p. 296, राजनिघण्टु मांसवर्ग, 138, Bhattacharya's edition (1899). Calcutta; कल्पद्रु, p. 332.

This seems to have been the original verse in some older lexicon but it has been corrupted and split up in the later compilations as in the current editions of धन्वन्तरि, राजनिघण्टु and कल्पद्रुकोश.

2. Mahābhārata, Śāntiparvan, chapters 143-149.

3. Ibid., 144, 7.

repetition and at the close of the day's lesson applied a little chalk to their throats to ensure a good memory. The male Red Turtle, the सूत्रकण्ठ कपोत, repeats his groo—gurr—goo's every morning and has besides a whitish throat. सूत्रकण्ठ also means a Brahman who is ready to repeat the Sūtras at call and this seems to have stimulated the poet's fancy. Describing a morning scene he refers to the male Dove's repetitive call, and humorously suggests that he would not keep on calling घु घु (the घुसंज्ञा सूत्र—काशिका, 1.1.20) unless he had attended a class of Pāṇinian grammar. His whitish throat, as if marked with chalk, is additional proof of the statement !

54

SAND-GROUSE

1. Sand-Grouse occupies an intermediate position between the Pigeons and the Partridges. This fact has been recognised in their Hindi name, भट तीतर (fr. भट, 'a fighter, तित्तिर, a Partridge) as all Sand-Grouses are known to be pugnacious among themselves; cf. भट कुक्कुट for a fighting Cock in Art. 55-B, para 1. The Common Sand-Grouse is known in North India as ककर, काकर (having a harsh call) which is apparently the same as ककर of वाज. संहिता:

"ककराञ्छिशिराय, विककरान् हेमन्ताय"— 24, 20

विककर (विशिष्टः ककरः) would then be a different species of Sand Grouse possessing some particular character, e.g. a distinctive plumage or a striking colour-pattern, and the Painted Sand-Grouse, beautifully marked with a triple band of white-black-white on the forehead and a tri-colour gorget of chestnut, buff and black on the breast, should be the विककर. Large numbers of Sand-Grouse of different kinds visit North-West India, a number spreading further to the east, in the cold season, and this explains the allocation of these birds to the personified deities of Winter-months.

2. The definition of क्रकर by हेमाद्रि qnoted in the अष्टाङ्गहृदयकोश is :

"पीतः कृष्णगलः कृष्णचञ्चुचरणः रक्तपृष्ठः"

This can only apply to the Large Imperial Sand-Grouse which visits North India in large numbers in winter. It has a good deal of pale and rich buff in its plumage including some yellow, a black patch on the lower throat, and bluish or plumbeous grey bill and feet. At any rate ककर is not a Partridge according to this authority. The synonymy" क्रकरकृकणौ समौ"—अमर, हेमचन्द्र, etc. would, therefore, seem to refer to these birds as allied to the Partridge, but as their exact identity had been forgotten lexicographers rendered the names as a Partridge, more specially the Swamp Partridge (कुतित्तिर = Prakrit, कायर) which, however, is incorrect; see Art. 55-C. वसन्तराज on the other hand mentions क्रकर as different from कृष्णतित्तिरि,, वृत्ततित्तिरि (Swamp Partridge, Art. 55-C, 9), and गौरतित्तिरिः—

"कृष्णतित्तिरिरितीह पतत्री, वृत्ततित्तिरिरिति प्रथितो यः ।
यश्च पक्षिषु मतोऽधिपमल्लो, गौरतित्तिरिसमः शकुनेन ॥
खगोऽत्र यो लावकनामधेयः, खगौ चकोरक्रकराभिधानौ" । 8.30-31

सुश्रुत too mentions क्रकर as different from तित्तिर, कपिञ्जल and कुतित्तिर, and पालकाप्य,, p. 569, has क्रकर with कपिञ्जल and तित्तिर. क्रकर is therefore the same as Vedic ककर, and the terms कृकर, कृकण and क्रकण are merely phonetic variants of the later क्रकर for a Sand-Grouse. They are all after the call notes of the birds syllabified as Katarr Katarr, ka ka, etc.

3. The pugnacious nature of Sand-Grouse was taken advantage of by the ancients who trapped the birds by enticing them to fight with a decoy called दीपक कक्कर (कक्कर जातक, No. 209). दीपक तित्तिर is mentioned in कपि जातक , No. 404 and other stories, which again shows that क्रकर and तित्तिर are different.

4. कृकल is either for a bird-form allied to क्रकर, a Sand-Grouse or just a variant of it. मार्कण्डेय पुराण,, 15, 26 reads क्रकर for कृकल[1] in the following half verse which it otherwise shares with महाभारत, 13.111,104 :—

"पत्रोर्णं चोरयित्वा तु कृकलत्वं निगच्छति"

Does पत्रोर्ण mean 'feather-wool or down and articles made from it'? Buddhist literature mentions articles of dress made from the soft downy feathers of Owls, and the Pali Dictionary has उलूक चम्म for shoes lined with such feathers; and उलूकपक्खिक for other things, probably gloves, etc., and even bigger items, cf. ""उलूक पत्तानि गंथेत्वा कत निवासनं", while हंसतूल is often mentioned in Sanskrit literature. The materials recommended in सुश्रुत, सूत्रस्थान, 18, 16 for dressing and bandaging surgical cases include पत्रोर्ण with linen, cotton, wool, fine cotton, silk (कौशेय), etc. but the notes of डल्हणाचार्य indicate uncertainty about the exact nature of पत्रोर्ण, and the synonyms श्योनाक and धौत कौशेय (washed or white Kosa-silk) in अमर are not convincing.[2] If therefore, पत्रोर्ण is 'feather wool', a very plausible identification of कृकल as a bird-name offers itself with reference to the punishment for theft of articles of dress made from that material provided in the above verse. They were apparently needed for wear in the extreme cold climate prevailing at places like Leh, Ladakh, etc. in Kashmir and Tibet in and across the Himalayas. The idea, therefore, seems to be that a person, who deprives another of this special kind of protective clothing, should be made to suffer the same inconvenience by being reborn in conditions of extreme rigour. Now the Tibetan Sand-Grouse is not a migratory bird and spends

1. क्रकर and कृकल for 'Ardea Virgo' in M. Williams seem to be mistakes.

2. The श्योनाक tree is rendered as पाडर or सोनापाठा in Hindi. It is described in detail in हिन्दी शब्द सागर under the name सोनापाठा but there is no mention of any woolly or hairy stuff obtained from it. It belongs to the order Bignaoniaceae and no member of this order produces any cotton or similar stuff in India. The seeds are light and have their wings (See *Indian Trees* by D. Brandis). They are used for lining present-day Sola hats and were probably used to stuff cushions in ancient times—hence the name स्योनाक from स्योन a bag. The buds of certain trees in this order are curved and hence the name शुकनास. The flowers of some e.g. of genus stereospermum, are thinly hairy or pubescent and the name पत्रोर्ण probably refers to this character. It is highly doubtful if such flowers could be used for dressing wounds. The meaning of पत्रोर्ण as feather wool has been lost.

the winter also on the snows, and is known as 'kaklingma or kakali' (ककलिमा or ककली) in Tibet. These names are very close to Sanskrit कृकर and कृकल, and it is highly probable that the Buddhists of Tibet borrowed कृकल from Sanskrit and made it into ककली; or it may be that कृकर underwent the change into ककली and travelled back as कृकल to India for the Tibetan Sand Grouse. कृकल would thus be an original or borrowed name for the bird which fits in very well with the idea underlying the above verse. Incidentally, it also helps to confirm the identification of ककर and क्रकर with the Sand-Grouse of India.

5. The Common Indian Sand-Grouse (क्रकर) and Chakor figure among the fowl served at a bacchanalian feast held by Rāvaṇa the end of which was witnessed by Hanumān when, in search of Sītā, he passed through the various halls of the palace :

"क्रकरान् विविधान्सिद्धांश्चकोरानर्द्धभक्षितान् ॥

Rāmāyaṇa (Alld. edition) 5. 11,17.

The Bombay edition of the Rāmāyaṇa has a different reading with कृकल for क्रकर.

55

PEAFOWLS, JUNGLEFOWLS, PHEASANTS, AND QUAILS

1. This family includes all birds properly classified by authorities like चरक and सुश्रुत as 'विष्किराः, though the partial lists of such birds given by them include just a few which according to the present-day scientific classification are outside the order Gallinae but which, from their habit of frequenting the ground either for food or otherwise appeared to belong to the 'विष्किर' group. For example the list in चरक includes the वार्तिक, the Short-toed Rufous Lark, and कङ्क, the Adjutant Stork, the former of which somewhat resembles the Quail in its habits and the latter seeks its food from refuse heaps like the Common Cock; also गोवर्द, the Great Bustard, and वारट, the Little Bustard—ground birds of Order Grallae which look somewhat like a Peacock without the train. सुश्रुत includes नप्तृका, the Nightjar, वार्तिक, the Short-toed Rufous Lark, कलविङ्क, the Magpie Robin and Blackbird, सारङ्ग, the Little Bustard, and कुरवाहक the Laughing Thrushes and Babblers. The Nightjar keeps to the ground during day-time and the others find their food chiefly on the ground. Subject to these exceptions the lists are fairly representative of the Gallinaceous birds of India.

2. अभिधानचिन्तामणि gives शिखण्डिक and चर्मचूड in the lists of names for a Cock, and मेदिनी and others have शिखी and शिखण्डी for both Cock and Peacock. शिखण्डिक and शिखी (both meaning 'one having a crest') are best interpreted with reference to the synonymy for शिखा :—

"चूडा केशी केशपाशी शिखा शिखण्डिका समाः"—हेमचन्द्र

Both the terms thus clearly apply to the Peacock and such Cocks as have a feathery crest contrasting with the Common Cock and Jungle-fowl who have a fleshy comb and are therefore the चर्मचूड कुक्कुट strictly so called. शिखी कुक्कुट are, therefore, the Cheer and Kalij Pheasants as a group as they have feathery crests. For the same reason the Peacock is शिखी, शिखावल, etc., and the Monal is शिखी and more specifically मयूरक or मयूर कुक्कुट. सुश्रुत has observed the distinction by naming मयूर, कुक्कुट, and यवालक (the 'White-crested Kalij') as representing three different types separately, and in a similar way चरक names बर्ही (Peacock), कुक्कुट, इन्द्राभ (Monal) and रक्तवर्त्मक (the Cheer and Kalij Pheasants) as a group as they have red skin surrounding only the eyes which distinguishes them from the Junglefowls which have the whole face

Phasianidae—विष्किरा:

- Pavoninae Peacock-मयूर:
- Argusianinae Peacock Pheasant जीवञ्जीवक:
- Phasianinae कुक्कुटा:
- Perdicinae तित्तिरवर्तकादय:
- Turmicidae लावा:

Phasianinae—कुक्कुटा:

- चर्मचूडा: ताम्रचूडा:
  - Red Jungle-fowl बादर कुक्कुट
  - Grey Jungle fowl यवग्रीव कुक्कुट
- शिखिन:
  - असितापाङ्ग
    - Impeyan Pheasant इन्द्राभ कुक्कुट, मयूर कुक्कुट, सुवर्ण मयूर,
  - रक्तवर्त्मक
    1. cheerPheasant—सरल कुक्कुट
    2. Kokras ,,—पालाश कुक्कुट
    3. White-crested kalij यवालक कुक्कुट
    4. Nepal kalij—कोणालक कुक्कुट
    5. Black breasted kalij मद्राग कुक्कुट

Perdicinae तित्तिर वर्तकादय:——

- —तित्तिरा:—
  - —Horned-Pheasants—वर्कर-, वल्गु-शकुन.
    - Crimson Horned Pheasant—पुष्प शकुन
  - —Blood-Pheasant—शारपद कुक्कुट
  - —Mountain Quail—गिरिवर्तिका
  - —Red Spur-fowl—सीरपादकुक्कुट.
  - —Black Partridge—तित्तिर, कृष्णतित्तिर
  - —Grey Partridge—गौर तित्तिर, कपिञ्जल
  - —Swamp Partridge—कुतित्तिर
  - —Hill Partridge—प्रियेश्वर तित्तिर
  - —Chukor—चकोर
  - —See-see Partridge—उपचक्र
  - —Himalayan Snow-Cock—वरिष्ठ तित्तिर
  - —Snow Partridge—ककुभ तित्तिर
- —वर्तका: True Quails
  - —Grey Quail—वर्तक
  - —Blue breasted Quail / Black-breasted Quail — वर्तिका
  - —Bush-Quails—वर्तीर, अल्प कपिंजल
    - Rock Bush Quail पांसुललाव
    - Jungle B.Q. गैरिकलाव
- —लावा: Bustard and Button Quails
  - —Bustard Quails—दर्भर लाव
  - —Button Quails—पौण्ड्रकलाव

(Bush-Quails and Bustard Quails: लावा: according to later classification)

and head covered with bare red skin and hence described as ताम्रवक्त्र (red-faced) in बृहत्संहिता, 62,1.[1] The महाव्युत्पत्ति, 213 mentions मयूर for the Monal, बर्हीं for the Peacock, शिखी for the crested Pheasants, जीवंजीवक for the Peacock Pheasant, and कुक्कुट for the Common or Junglefowl. पद्मपुराण[2] mentions कुक्कुट, शिखी (शिखिनः, crested Pheasants) and मयूर but permits only the last as food. शिखी, मयूर and कुक्कुट (crested Pheasants, Peacock and Cock respectively) are mentioned in three consecutive paragraphs of चरकसंहिता.[3]

3. जीवञ्जीवक, as we shall see, is strictly the Peacock Pheasant but the later Purāṇa literature seems to have grouped all the Himalayan Pheasants, principally those that occur in the Central and Western Himalayas as जीवञ्जीवक जाति (the Pheasant-tribe):—

मत्तक्रौञ्चमयूराणां नादैरुपघुष्टकन्दरे ।
जीवञ्जीवकजातीनां वी–रुद्भिरुपशोभिते ॥

—वायुपुराण, 54,33.

जीवञ्जीवकजातीनां विरावैरुपकूजिते ।

—ब्रह्माण्डपुराण, 1.25,28.

चातकैः प्रियपुत्रैश्च जीवञ्जीवकजातिभिः ।

—ब्रह्मपुराण, 68, 16

The common name for all Partridges is तित्तिर and for all Quails वर्तिका though quite a number of well marked species in both the groups have specific names in Sanskrit. These will be given under each group of birds.

A. PEAFOWL

India has only one variety of Peafowl within its limits but it also happens to be the most beautiful and gorgeous looking bird and, what is more, it is readily tamed. For these reasons the Peacock has been a favourite with the people, and the poets have given him a permanent place in literature, singing of his love for the clouds, his beauty and sonorous cries (sonorous by contrast with the thundering of rain-clouds), and the graceful dance with "the train expanded into a gorgeous fan" in which the bird proudly indulges during courtship and at other times to express his shear joy of living. No wonder, therefore, that such a popular bird should have been given many poetic names in addition to the common one of 'मयूर'. Only a few of them may be mentioned : सर्पारि (enemy or eater of snakes); नीलकण्ठ (blue-necked); सारङ्ग (variegated or painted); राजसारस (the shining crane-like bird); अर्जुन (shining, but if taken in the sense of 'white' the

1. Similarly the term ताम्रचूड distinguishes the wild Cock with a red fleshy crest from the others having a feathery crest.

2. आदिखण्ड, Ch. 56, 31-38.

3. सिद्धिस्थान Ch. 12., 38-40.

name may refer to an albino form of the white Peacock imported from China); सितापाङ्ग (having the orbital skin of a white colour); and शिखी (having a crest). He has also been called महामयूर to distinguish it from मयूरक or 'the little Peacock', the Impeyan Pheasant or Monal :—

"महामयूराञ्जयति स्वरेण
बलेन नागान्तुरगाञ्जवेन ।" —भेलसंहिता[1]

The snake-eating habit of the Peacock, implying the power of destroying snake-poison, has been referred to in the "विषघ्नोपनिषद् सूक्त" of the Ṛgveda[2] ("त्रिसप्त मयूर्यः" etc.). Like the Flamingoes flying high, in formation (बलाकपंक्ति) and the चातक birds calling from the tree tops, the Peacocks also have a permanent association with rain-clouds. Dancing to their mates in open forest glades, they add a peculiar charm to forest scenery :—

"घनानां शक्रचापेन वनानां शिखिताण्डवैः ।
परस्परप्रभापुञ्जस्पर्धेव समजायत ॥" —भारतमञ्जरी[3]

"क्वचित्प्रनृत्तैः क्वचिदुन्नदद्भिः
क्वचिच्च वृक्षाग्रनिषण्णकायैः ।
व्यालम्बबर्हाभरणैर्मयूरैः
वनेषु सङ्गीतमिव प्रवृत्तम्" ॥ —रामायण[4]

B. JUNGLEFOWLS AND PHEASANTS

Two kinds of Junglefowl, चर्मचूड or ताम्रचूड कुक्कुट, occur in India, the Red and the Grey. The former is common throughout the lower Himalayas and the Gangetic plain, and the latter in the Peninsula and as far north and west as Mt. Aboo. This last has been a celebrated place of pilgrimage for ages and is repeatedly mentioned in the Purāṇas. The Indo-Aryans, therefore, must have known and named both the varieties of wild Cock. The Cock has also been domesticated in India from time immemorial (See AV. 5.31.2) and several colour types of it including the red and the grey, have been mentioned in the बृहत्संहिता :—

"यवग्रीवो यो वा बदरसदृशो वाऽपि विहगो"
—62.2.

Cock-fighting too was very popular and one such fight is described in the दशकुमारचरित, where the combatant birds are described as नारिकेलाकृति, and

1. P. 170, 232. The हारीतसंहिता, Ch. 11, मांसवर्ग, also mentions नील मयूर and मयूरक
2. I.191.14.
3. हरिवंश. 570.
4. 4.28.37.

बलाकाकृति. The first is evidently the common domestic fowl, but the second, as its descriptive name shows, is the Aseel type of Game-Cock which too is a very ancient Indian breed. The name बलाकाकृति signifies a long-necked and long-legged bird which the Aseel certainly is and क्षेमेन्द्र calls it भटकुक्कुट (fighting Cock):—

"यत्क्लीबैर्भटकुक्कुटोत्कटरणक्रीडा समादिश्यते ।
यन्मूर्खैः सुखलीलया कविशुकालापश्चिरं चर्व्यते ॥"

—चतुर्वर्गसंग्रह[1]

It is doubtful whether the Aseel is a descendant of a larger wild species now extinct (Gallus giganteus of Temminck) or was evolved by selection from the existing Red Junglefowl. Probably it was imported very early into India from the Malay country. Anyway, the Common Cock has been a great favourite with the Indo-Aryans and no royal house-hold was without its Fowl-run, and even the Army carried a complement of Cocks during campaigns to strike the early hour, as it were, for everybody to get ready in time for the day's march or action. The very best birds were selected for breeding and their good points have been briefly stated by वराहमिहिर in his बृहत्संहिता, and what he says good humouredly and rather affectionately about a good hen would be welcomed as a flattering compliment by any pretty young lady proud of her charms:—

"कुक्कुटी च मृदुचारुभाषिणी
स्निग्धमूर्तिरुचिराननेक्षणा"

—62. 3.

2. Returning to the Junglefowl, adnouns like चर्मचूड, ताम्रचूड, चरणायुध, विष्किर, कालज्ञ, मणिकण्ठ, etc. would be common to both varieties of it, and if the colour epithets given above used in बृहत्संहिता are taken over, the Red bird would be the बादर कुक्कुट and the Grey bird, यवग्रीव कक्कुट. Apart from the differences in colour-pattern, however, the two can be told apart from their voices. The call of the Red Junglefowl resembles that of tame birds except for the concluding note of the Cock which is shorter. The Crow of the Grey Junglefowl on the other hand is quite distinct—"a broken and imperfect kind of crow quite unlike the call of the Red Junglefowl" (Jerdon). Now दीर्घनाद and पूर्णक are two names for the Common Cock and they evidently signify a bird with a full voice (पूर्णेन स्वरेण कायति).[2] As against these, there is स्वरभङ्गी for 'a kind of bird' which is probably the Grey Junglefowl. If so, पूर्णक कुक्कुट and स्वरभङ्गी कुक्कुट would be the most fitting names for the

1. 2.3 (Kāvyamālā Pt. 5). मानसोल्लास 2. p. 239 et seq. describes in detail the various kinds of domestic cocks, their maintenance, and training for the arena. It mentions the Aseel as गृध्रजाति कुक्कुट and it is interesting to note that this particular Cock is still known as "गिधाड्या मुरगा" in cock-fighting circles of Nagpur, Maharashtra.

2. See, पूर्ण in M. Williams.

two varieties of Junglefowl found in India. The great esteem in which the Cock was held by the Indo-Aryans may be seen from the epithet of मधुजिह्व (honey-tongued) applied to it in the शतपथ ब्राह्मण[1] with reference to its announcing the time for the morning sacrifice[2].

3. The Red Junglefowl is mentioned in literature under the names वनकुक्कुट, कृकवाकु (imitative name?), ताम्रचूड etc. The name शूलिक refers to its long and sharp spurs and it is possible that names like शूर, शूलिक, शौण्ड, दक्ष and particularly उद्रथ (ऊर्ध्वं रथं शरीरमस्य i.e. tall or standing erect) are meant for the fighting or Game-Cock known as असील in Hindi. Of a thinner build to look at, it is all muscle and a very popular bird, for cock-fights. Like the Peafowl the Cock too has numerous names in Sanskrit and they are mostly self-explanatory. मयूर चटक (petty Peacock) for the domestic Cock would seem to be a left-handed compliment to its gaudy plumage and proud strutting gait—a petty bird attempting to play the Peacock. The Rāmāyaṇa mentions the Junglefowl in its natural haunts:—

"लताकण्टकसङ्कीर्णाः कृकवाकूपनादिताः
निरपाश्च सुदुर्गाश्च मार्गा दुःखमतो वनम् ।" 2.28.10.

It is incorrect to translate कृकवाकु in this passage as the Peacock.

4. The Bhutan Peacock-Pheasant has the upper plumage light buffy-brown: the feathers of the mantle, almost all the wing-coverts and the inner secondaries have violet green-blue ocelli at their tips, each ocellus surrounded with a narrow brownish black band and a second broader one of white; and similar but larger and oval ocelli on the tail feathers. "The display of this Pheasant is very beautiful, both wings being fully expanded with tail, so that the whole looks like an ocellated fan. The wide tail is used as a screen for the young who move about under its shelter close to the heels of the parent" (Smythies). A fuller and graphic account of the display of this Pheasant is given by Stuart Baker in his *Game Birds of India, Burma and Ceylon* (3.117). In a small open space the pair "scratched about for insects and then, without a moment's warning, the Cock-bird began to display to the hen. At first he confined his attention to running round her with tail partially extended and slightly raised and both wings drooping and spread. In a minute or two, however, he ceased to run round and sank slowly to the ground until his breast rested on it. His tail and wings were then raised until the three were fully spread in the manner of a fan, the tips of the inner secondaries of the wings almost meeting above and in front of the tail, whilst the shoulders were brought down to the ground. The head was then withdrawn momentarily into the soft mass of feathers, but immediately protruded again on the hen moving".

5. The short extract from Smythies is sufficient to identify the bird with the Sanskrit वीजन (a fan) for a kind of Pheasant and जीवञ्जीवक (v.I.

1. I.1.4.18.
2. See also वाज० संहिता I.16.

जीवजीवक) defined as "मयूरतुल्यपत्रक", i.e., having ocelli in the plumage like the Peacock, by महेश्वर in his notes on अमर. The second name is from the hen-bird's habit of protecting her young under her tail when out feeding. सुश्रुत refers to the effect of smoke issuing from poisoned food placed on fire on the चकोर and this Pheasant and advises a king to keep them for testing his food:—

"चकोरस्याक्षि वैराग्यं जायते क्षिप्रमेव तु
. . . . म्रियन्ते जीवजीविकाः
सन्निकृष्टांस्ततः कुर्याद्राज्ञस्तान् मृगपक्षिणः'

The belief has been referred to in चरक[2] and in मत्स्यपुराण[3] where several other birds also are included. Despite the difference maintained in सुश्रुत and अमर later lexicons like विश्व and मेदिनी make the name जीवञ्जीव applicable to चकोर, ("जीवञ्जीवश्चकोरे च") apparently because चकोर like the other, helps to save life: Cf." "प्राणदोऽपि च जीवकः"—शाश्वतकोश.

6. The Peacock Pheasants are frequently mentioned with other birds in descriptions of Himalayan scenery, e.g. the tree-perching habit of these birds has been correctly referred to:

"रक्तपीतारुणाः पार्थ पादपाग्रगताः खगाः ।
परस्परमुदीक्षन्ते बहवो जीवजीविकाः ॥"

—महाभारत,[4] 3.159.87-88

The hermitage of दधीचि:—

"षट्पदोद्गीतनिनदैर्विघुष्टं सामगैरपि ।
पुंस्कोकिलरवोन्मिश्रं जीवञ्जीवकनादितम् ॥"

महाभारत, 3.101.14.

A pair of pet birds are described as perching on the top of a rock in a garden in the कादम्बरी:—

"विषमशिलाच्छेदोपविष्टजीवञ्जीवकयुगल . . ." p. 97.

The picture of the Peacock Pheasant drawn by अश्वघोष to illustrate a moral in सौन्दरनन्द based on actual observation of the Cock-bird's display before the hen, is simply unique and fully bears out what Stuart Baker says about it:

"अवशः खलु काममूर्छया प्रियया श्येनभयाद्विनाकृतः ।
न धृतिं समुपैति न ह्रियं करुणं जीवति जीवजीवकः ॥" —8.20.

The poet has not only seen the display, but what is more, the occasional

1. कल्पस्थान, 1.30-33.
2. 6.23.108.
3. 220, 18-21.
4. Also सुश्रुत, 5.1.30-32; पद्मपुराण, सृष्टिखण्ड 42, 65; and हरिवंश, 3.41.76.

tragic end of it. Just when the Cock mad with love forgets himself and all else about him, he is suddenly struck down by an Eagle from the air.

For जीवञ्जीवक as the Pheasant-tailed Jacana see Art. 60.

7. The Cheer and Kalij Pheasants have feathered faces with only the red orbital skin bare, and are the रक्तवर्त्मक (कालज्ञ) of चरक and रक्तवर्त्म of मत्स्यपुराण[1]. The name Kalij in English is borrowed from Hindi कालिज (कालज्ञ) for the birds. "Kalij Pheasants are not nearly such noisy birds as are Junglefowl but call, one can hardly call it crowing, pretty regularly during the breeding season. This call or crow seems to be uttered only during the mornings and evenings, never in the middle of the day. A Cock Kalij only calls on his roosting perch before he gets down from it in the morning, and after he has returned to in the evening before settling down for the night".[2] It will be seen that the Kalij series of birds are the कालज्ञ कुक्कुट i.e. birds 'who know the time when to call' as against the domestic Cock who crows at all times of day. Again, the Kalij are not such good fighters as the others. These differences fully justify the two separate synonymies for Cocks in धन्वन्तरिनिघण्टु which regards the common domestic and Aseel Cocks as दक्ष (expert fighter) and शौण्ड (proud of bearing), and separates the विष्किर, कालज्ञ, कृकवाकु and चरणायुध for the wild varieties:—

"कुक्कुटस्ताम्रचूडश्च दक्षः शौण्डोऽथ विष्किरः ।
कालज्ञः कृकवाकुश्च नियोद्धा चरणायुधः ॥"

The mixing up of the names of the wild varieties is understandable. The Kalij Pheasants as a group are, therefore, रक्तवर्त्मक-or कालज्ञ-कुक्कुट.

8. The Pine tree is known as चीर in Hindi and सरल or शरल in Sanskrit. The Cheer Pheasant (34"-40") also is चीर or हरल (from सरल) in Hindi so that Sanskrit सरल for 'a kind of bird' is no other than this Pheasant and M. Williams' rendering as 'Pavo Bicalcaratus' (the Peacock Pheasant) is incorrect. Another Hindi name for the Cheer is काहर which is the same as Sanskrit काहल (कुं भूमिं हलति) or रसाखन for a Cock. निघण्टरत्नाकर defines काहल as a very large cock. Sanskrit names for it are, therefore, सरल– or काहल-कुक्कुट.

9. The White-crested Kalij Pheasant, known as कालिज, कुकेरा or कलेसुर in Hindi, apparently derives these names from Sanskrit कलज, कालज्ञ (a Cock), कुक्कुट and कालशूर (काल black, and शूर a Cock) respectively. Perhaps कलज like कालिज is a Prakrit form of कालज्ञ for a Cock. सुश्रुत has यवालक (यव barley and, therefore, of a white or whitish colour, and अलक a lock of hair, a crest) for a kind of gallinaceous bird, and the white crest of this Pheasant contrasting with its black body fully supports the name यवालक (–कुक्कुट) for it.

10. The Nepal-, the Black-backed-, and the Black-breasted-Kalij Pheasants are closely related birds, principally of a dark or black colour and

1. 118.53.

2. Stuart Baker in *Indian Game Birds*, III. pp. 279-280.

with black crests. They are always found in the neighbourhood of water. The first two occur to the West and East of the Arun river in Nepal respectively, and the third further East in Assam. Prakrit कोण (from कृष्ण) means 'black' and कोणालक (कोण+अलक) is therefore 'black-crested'. With यवालक for the White-crested Kalij कोणालक is highly probable for these black-crested Pheasants. Their habitat near water would seem to justify the following reference to them though it may well be to the Water Cocks which also perhaps share the name as a homonym, i.e., through a different derivation :—

"नित्यमत्तविहङ्गानि भ्रमरैः सेवितानि च ।
कोणालकविघुष्टानि सारसाभिरुतानि च ॥"

—रामायण[1]

11. The Black-breasted Kalij is known locally in Assam as मदुरा or मथुरा which is from Sanskrit मदराग (मद musk and राग colour; 'of the colour of musk' i.e. black or dark-brown) for a (black) Cock. As all the three Black-crested Pheasants are allied, they are मदराग-कुक्कुट in Sanskrit.

12. One of these crested Kalij Cocks figures as "लंबचूल विहंगम" (bird with a pendant crest) in the कुक्कुट जातक[2], where a cock hunting cat offers to be his wife without any dowry if only he descends to her from his high perch on the tree, but the shrewd bird replies that no matrimony is possible between a two-footed bird and a four-footed animal, and finally advises her to seek another mate :

"सुचित्त पत्तच्छदन लंबचूल विहंगम
ओरोह दुमसाखाय मुधा भारिया भवामि ते ॥"

The Cock :

"चतुप्पदा त्वं कल्याणि द्विपदाहं मनोरमे ।
मिगी पक्खी असज्जुत्ता अञ्जं परियेस सामिकम् ॥"

13. The Koklas Pheasant has a fully feathered face and a triple crest consisting of a median anterior tuft and two very elongated lateral posterior tufts (one on each side of the head). The crest thus bears an obvious resemblance to the trifoliate leaf of the त्रिपर्ण or पलाश tree (Butea frondosa), and the bird is no other than the पलाश (-कुक्कुट) of the हिन्दी शब्दसागर. It is actually known as प्लास (पलाश) in Kashmir and in the neighbourhood of Simla. No Sanskrit lexicon gives the name but there can be no doubt that it was पलाश- or पालाश-कुक्कुट in Sanskrit as well, and the compilers of the Hindi lexicon had the name from some manuscript glossary. The other local name कोकलास is a palpable corruption of कुक्कुटपलाश or पलाशकुक्कुट.

---

1. All. Edn. 6.39.11.

For कोणालक as a Water-Cock see Art. 58 and for कुणाल as the Painted Snipe see Art. 61.

2. No. 383.

14. The अभिधानराजेन्द्र has कण्णतिय (कर्णंचिक, under चम्मपक्खि) for a kind of चर्मपक्षिन् and if चर्मपक्षिन् has been inadvertently used for लोमपक्षिन्, and it has certainly been so used for the जीवञ्जीवक and समुद्रकाक, the name clearly refers to this three-crested Pheasant as कर्णत्रिक (कुक्कुट).[1]

15. The noble Impeyan Pheasant, "the most magnificent" of all Indian Pheasants, is common in Garhwal, Kashmir, Kulu and Kangra valleys. It has a Peacock-like crest, a most brilliant body-plumage of metallic green, copper and purple, and a cinnamon-chestnut tail, and "when seen in sun-light the effect is indescribably beautiful". The orbital skin and cheeks are smalt blue to brilliant ultramarine-blue. In the Peacock this area is white (सितापाङ्ग). From its crest and brilliant plumage, it has been regarded as a sort of small Peacock and is known in Hindi as नीलमोर or मुनाल (Prakrit for मृणाल = पुष्करमूल, because the bird eats roots and tubers) and दतिया (दाति, दात्रम् a cutting or digging implement) after its powerful bill used for digging up roots for food. Sanskrit names for it are इन्द्राभ (having the colours of a rainbow), a विष्किर bird of चरक; असितापाङ्ग (having blue orbital skin); मयूरक ("मयूरप्रतिकृति"—शब्दार्थचिन्तामणि) a little Peacock; मयूरकुक्कुट (Cock resembling a Peacock); चित्रबर्हण or चित्रबर्हिण (a bird with a coloured or painted tail or a peculiar kind of Peacock); and probably also मयूक (short for मयूरक ? "मयूकश्चित्रपिङ्गलः" in वैजयन्ती appears to be significant). With its "great shovel mandibles" the bird is said to be "a great digger" for tubers and roots, and शूरणोद्भुज for 'a kind of bird' in M. Williams would seem to be a descriptive epithet for it from some old lexicon; Cf :—

"कन्दानि मूलसस्यानि विदुः कन्दांश्च सूरणान्" —शाश्वतकोश.

It is quite probable that the Hindi name मुनाल for it is from मृणाल (edible root of the lotus) as the bird perhaps digs up the tubers of ground lilies also for food, and hence the name. The terms बर्हिण and मयूरग in the Jain प्रश्नव्याकरण refer to the Peacock and this Pheasant respectively, while the महाव्युत्पत्ति, refers to them as बर्ही and मयूर or vice versa.

16. The following from the Mahābhārata refer to this Pheasant as बर्हिण or मयूर (cf. Hindi नीलमोर) and असितापाङ्ग :—

"महाद्रुमाणां शिखरेषु तस्थुः मनोरमां वाचमुदीरयन्तः ।
मयूरदात्यूहचकोरसङ्घाः तस्मिन्वने बर्हिणकोकिलाश्च ॥"—3.24.18[2]

"मयूरैः शतपत्रैश्च जीवञ्जीवककोकिलैः ।
चकोरैरसितापाङ्गैस्तथा पुत्रप्रियैरपि ॥" —Ibid. 3.108,8.

---

1. See ibid under 'चम्मपक्खि'.

2. चकोरसङ्घ on the trees must be the tree-perching Hill Partridges which have a white gorget upon a dark neck as against the black gorget of the चकोर. They have, therefore, been regarded as a kind of चकोर which however is entirely a ground bird. The Simla Hill Partridge is actually known as रामचकोर (beautiful or God Rama's चकोर) in Hindi, Cf. ईश्वरप्रिय for the same with the Hindi name.

Appreciation of this Pheasant, one of the most beautiful birds of the world is indicated by the fact that it was considered as a fit present for young कार्त्तिकेय :—

"सुपर्णोऽस्य ददौ पुत्रं मयूरं चित्रबर्हिणम् ।" —M.Bh. 13.86,21
"गरुडो दयितं पुत्रं मयूरं चित्रबर्हणम् ।" —स्कन्दपुराण[1]
"चित्रबर्हणनामानं स्वपुत्रं गरुडो ददौ ।
अरुणस्ताम्रचूडाख्यं बलिनं चरणायुधम् ।।" —शिवपुराण[2]

17. इन्द्राभ as a name for this Pheasant has been defined by हेमाद्रि as a particular bird resembling a कङ्क, the Brahminy Kite, and of a variegated plumage ("पक्षिविशेषःकङ्कसदृशो विविधवर्णः"—अष्टाङ्गहृदयकोश). Now this bird with a square tail, unlike most other Pheasants, and a large hooked bill does bear a certain amount of resemblace to the Brahminy Kite and for this reason has been considered as mystically related to गरुड as his son. The मयूर said to have been born out of the tip of a feather or सुपर्ण knocked out by the bolt of इन्द्र in सुपर्णाध्याय, 28, is obviously this Pheasant.

"छिन्नं त्रिधा तत्कुलिशेन पत्रं
तस्याग्रखण्डादभवन्मयूरः ।"

This clearly explains the relationship with Garuḍa and also the convertibility of the terms मयूर and बर्हिण for the Peacock and this Pheasant as already indicated above. चित्रबर्ह again in the महाभारत list of Garuḍa's progeny is evidently this bird, the चित्रबर्हण of the Purāṇas. One of the Nāga Kings of the Buddhist Literature was named after this bird as इन्द्रायुध शिखिन्[3], which simply means a Cock with feathery crest and body-plumage of the colours of a rainbow—cf. इन्द्राभ.

Goddess नारायणी, i.e., पार्वती, is said to live in the midst of मयूरकुक्कुट birds:—

"मयूरकुक्कुटवृते महाशक्तिधरे ऽनघे ।
कौमारी रूपसंस्थाने नारायणि नमोऽस्तु ते ।।" —मार्क. पुराण 88, 14

and the doubting commentator has fortunately reproduced the following alternative note on मयूर कुक्कुट from the commentary of शन्तनु चक्रवर्ती on सप्तशतिका :—

"मयूराः कुक्कुटा इव चित्रपुच्छवर्जिता मयूरकुक्कुटाः तैः वृते ।
यदभ्युधुः :— आरक्तनेत्रपिच्छाग्रो मयूरः कुक्कुटः स्मृतः ।
बर्हेण वर्जितो बर्ही यः स मयूरकुक्कुटः ।।"

1. I कौमारिका खण्ड Ch.30.
2. 2nd रुद्र सं०, कुमार खण्ड. 5.49.
3. महाव्युत्पत्ति 168.47.

The eyes of the Monal are brown and to this extent the above definition is incorrect but it would be equally so for the Peacock as well for there is no red in or about its eyes. It would be ridiculous to take the phrase "बर्हेण वर्जितो बर्ही" as the common Peacock devoid of its splendid train, for then the reference to पार्वती living in the midst of Peacocks shorn of their glory would be a most graceless one and there seems to be little doubt that what is meant is "a Peacock-like bird which does not possess a long tail like the Peacock's". The identity of मयूरकुक्कुट (a Cock resembling a Peacock without the latter's long tail) with the Monal or Impeyan Pheasant should thus be beyond doubt. Nevertheless, the compound name has been misunderstood and rendered as two different birds, viz., the Peacock and the Common Cock, in a later Purāṇa. A gift again to कार्तिकेय :—

"गरुडादतिसृष्टौ हि पक्षिणौ द्वौ प्रभद्रकौ ।
मयूरः कुक्कुटश्चैव, पताका चैव वायुना ॥" —ब्रह्माण्डपुराण.[1]

In this verse the singular "मयूरःकुक्कुटः" of the following would seem to have been mistaken for two different birds :—

"मयूरः कुक्कुटश्चैव पताका चैव वायुना ।" —वायुपुराण[2]

The मयूर as the mythological mount or vehicle of कार्तिकेय should therefore be this Pheasant and not the Peacock but here too the position has often been misunderstood.

The Monal has been mentioned as मयूरादिविया (दिव्य 'living in heaven, i.e., in the Himalayas' or 'shining') in verse 26 of किंचिदजातक[3] and as "सुवण्ण वण्ण मोर" or सुवण्ण मोर (सुवर्णमयूर) in मोरजातक,[4] described as :—

"दस्सनीयो पासादिको पक्खानं अंतरे सुरत्तराजि विराजिते ।"

It is said to pray to the sun morning and evening, referring to the whistling calls of the bird, quite unlike the केकाध्वनि of the Peacock related to thundering clouds. "पक्खानं अंतरे सुरतराजि" refers to the rather longish cinnamon-chestnut tail between the wings. The name सुवर्णमयूर has its analogue in Persian "Murgh-i-Zarreen", the Golden Cock, for this Pheasant.

C. TRAGOPANS, BLOOD PHEASANTS & PARTRIDGES

1. "The Horned Pheasants or Tragopans are amongst the most beautifully coloured of all game-birds, the males being more or less clad in red, with white or grey spots, and armed with a stout spur. The male has an

1. 2.10.47.
2. उत्त० 11.46.
3. No. 511.
4. No. 159.

occipital crest of lengthened feathers and two elongate erectile sub-cylindrical fleshy horns one from above each eye; these usually lie concealed by the crest, and are only erected when the bird shows off. There is also a brilliantly coloured apron-shaped gular wattle or lappet, that can be spread or withdrawn at pleasure." They have a bleating call in the breeding season (Hume & Oates).

The Crimson Horned Pheasant is mostly crimson above and below, spotted over with white black-edged ocelli. The horns are larger in the breeding season, at times over three inches in length. The Western Horned Pheasant generally resembles the crimson variety though it has less of red and more of black in its plumage. Its names in Hindi are सींग मुनाल (Horned Pheasant), जिगुरान (fr. Persian जेंगा a head-ornament, and राना beautiful : or by fusion from Sansk. जिगनु: fire and जुहुराण a goat; ("जुहुराण: अग्नि: छाग:"—उणादि श्वेतवनवासिन् 1.93), and फल्गुर (corrupted from वल्गु a goat, त्रिकाण्डशेष, मेदिनी). The bird is undoubtedly a विष्किर, and the Lahore Edition of the चरकसंहिता has वृकर for a kind of विष्किर bird, but there is no such word in the dictionaries. वाग्भट, 6.43 has बकर (a goat) instead, so that वृकर in चरक is evidently a mistake for बर्कर[1] (a goat). The Tragopan has not only a pair of horns but also the bleat of a goat, and बर्कर or बकर as a bird is no other than the Tragopan. The वायुपुराण mentions वल्गु as a Himalayan bird :

"जीवञ्जीवकनादैश्च हेमकानां च नादितै: ।
मत्तकोकिलनादैश्च वल्गूनां च निनादितै: ॥" 36.3.

It is also a bird of the woods on the banks of the Tamasā in the स्कन्दपुराण.

"विनादितं सारसमुत्कुलादिभि:
प्रमत्तदात्यूहकुलैश्च वल्गुभि: ।" —अयोध्यामाहात्म्य, Ch. 9.

In the latter case the term वल्गु can also mean 'sweet-voiced', but looking to the general sense of the passage it would appear to be a bird-name. Yet another possible name for it may be क्रतुयष्टि as a kind of bird given in कल्पद्रुकोश ("क्रतुयष्टिस्तु यज्ञार्हो") which is from क्रतु will, determination or संकल्प (कामनाधीनचित्तवृत्तिविशेष:—शब्दकल्पद्रुम sub voce क्रतु) and यष्टि a stick i.e. a horn in the case of a bird; cf. यष्टिक and कोयष्टिक for the Water Cock which carries a red, flat, horny shield projecting from the head. क्रतुयष्टि thus means a bird which can erect its horn-like appendages at will; cf. the meaning of क्रतु in :—

"स यथाकामो भवति तत्क्रतुर्भवति । यत्क्रतुर्भवति तत्कर्म कुरुते"—
—बृहदारण्यकोपनिषद्, 4.4.5.

Being a kind of Partridge or game-bird it has been declared fit for sacrifice (यज्ञार्ह:).

---

1. बर्कर as a bird-name occurs in विष्णुधर्मोत्तर, 1.151.43 where बर्कशान् is a clear mistake for बर्करान्

2. M. Williams renders पुष्पशकुन[1] as the Common Cock (Phasianus gallus) which appears to be incorrect, for Emperor Jehangir describes a bird under the name of फूल पैकर in his Memoirs[2] and his description fully agrees with that of the Tragopan. फूल पैकर means 'resembling a flower' and is evidently an extempore or off-hand Urdu rendering of Sansk. पुष्पशकुन (bird like a flower). This last name also means a spotted bird (पुष्प a spot, referring to the spotted body of the Crimson Horned Pheasant) but looking to the colour pattern of the bird the first may well be the intended meaning. पुष्परथ again, (पुष्प flower or spot and रथ body) a bird in the list quoted from पराशर in the बृहत्संहिता (भट्टोत्पल-टीका p. 1018) appears to be this bird just as उष्ट्ररथ of the same list is clearly the Ostrich which not only has long legs and neck like a camel but also only two toes like him. The Ostrich must have been known as an imported bird. It is evidently the Camel Crane of the Chinese Traveller, Ju-Kua, who mentions it in his description of the Chinese and Arab trade of the 12-13th century.[3]

3. The Blood Pheasant is noted for the unusually large number of spurs he wears on his legs—two to four and even five of them. The female also has two on each leg. शारपद of चरक (fr. शार. hurting or सार strong; cf. शरु for the Grey Partridge and शूलिक for the Cock) and सीरपाद[4] (having spurs resembling a plough-share; cf. सीरपाणि) of the list of Himalayan birds in मत्स्यपुराण, 118, 54 probably refer to this bird. His voice is 'a peculiar cry not unlike the squeal of the Kite' (S. Baker) and the vernacular names like चिलमिलि (cf. चिल्ल for kite) and सेरेमिन (cf. चिरम्भण for the Kite) seem to point to the bird's original Sanskrit names like चिल्ल-कुक्कुट or चिरम्भण-कुक्कुट which have now been lost.

4. Another bird to claim the names सारपाद and सीरपाद (कुक्कुट) is the Red Spur-fowl of the Nepal Teraï (and related forms occurring in other parts of the country) which too is armed with two to four spurs in the male and one or two in the female. It is known as 'Sārvā' in Tamil country. The propriety of these names would seem to lie in the fact that both the Cock and the hen of the Blood-Pheasant and the Red Spur-fowl are furnished with spurs whereas in the Common Junglefowl the male alone bears this character. The Peacock Pheasant, however, also carries two or more spurs but he is better named जीवञ्जीवक after the protection the hen gives to her chicks who walk under the cover of her broad tail. Again, the Red spur-fowl, though a member of the Partridge group, looks like a small fowl and might well have been known in Sanskrit as कुक्कुटक (अल्पार्थे, प्रकारार्थे कम्). Its Hindi name is indeed छोटी जंगली मुरगी (the small jungle fowl).

---

1. Presumably on the basis of a lexical equation like पुष्पशकुनः कुक्कुटे which, however, is correct in a way inasmuch as the horned bird is big enough to pass for a kind of Cock.

2. Tuzuk-i-Jehangiri; Vol. II. 221.

3. Penzer's *Ocean of Story*. Vol. I.

4. सीर = हल, and the latter term has actually been used for the Cock's spur in the expression "ताम्रचूडहल" in यशस्तिलकचम्पू at p. 296. But the corresponding passage of विष्णुधर्मोत्तर, 1.151, 42-48 reads शारपाद.

5. The Mountain Quail (10″) found only within certain areas in the outer Himalayas (e.g. neighbourhood of Nainital and Mussoorie) is the गिरिवर्तक (v.l. गिरिवर्तिका) of चरक and गिरिशा of सुश्रुत and कल्पद्रुकोश ("गिरिशा गिरिशायिका"—a bird breeding on the mountains; cf. पुष्करशायिका, कुशेशय etc. as bird names). डल्हणाचार्य equates गिरिशा with गिरिवर्तिक and gives पर्वतवाही (वासी ?) as an alternative. In its behaviour it closely resembles the Bustard-Quail as it refuses to fly until almost trodden upon, pitching into the grass again after a short flight, and would therefore appear to be the बृहल्लाव of भावप्रकाश, अर्शोऽधिकार 121. See Section D paras 5-10 for Bustard-Quails.

6. The Hill Partridges are confined to the Himalayas only and do not occur in the plains or the peninsula of India. Their call is a low soft whistle, single or double, quite unlike the call of the Grey and Black Partridges. Unlike these again, they normally perch on trees. The Common Hill Partridge and the Rufous-throated Partridge, as also some of the varieties of the Eastern Himalayas, are known in Hindi by the name पिउरा. M. Williams gives शङ्करप्रिय (शङ्कर = शिव = ईश्वर) and the वैजयन्ती has ईश्वरप्रिय for a Partridge, both obvious synonyms. Now the term प्रिय in a बहुव्रीहि may optionally stand first as गुडप्रियः or प्रियगुडः,[1] so that ईश्वरप्रिय would be the same as प्रियेश्वर and this latter would seem to have given us the bird's Hindi name, पिउरा (प्रिय-पिय-पिउ+ईसुर, पियेसुरा-पिहुरा-पिउरा ?). Apart from this inexpert playing with etymology there is a reason for this Sanskrit name to denote the Hill Partridge, viz., that both Lord Śiva and this bird, being permanent residents of the Himalayas, are supposed to be born companions. ईश्वरप्रिय (or प्रियेश्वर) may therefore denote the Hill Partridge.

7. The Chukar is a beautiful Partridge of an ashy and buff colour with a black gorget and red bill and feet. It is rather lucky in that it has been allowed practically to retain its Sanskrit name चकोर in English[2]. उपचक्र is said to be a bird resembling a चकोर ("उपचक्रश्चकोरभेदः"—चक्रदत्त on चरक). The Seesee Partridge stands nearest to the चकोर in physical characters and shares a common habitat in the hills of the Punjab even taday. In olden times it may well have ranged along the hilly country further east. It, therefore, appears to be the उपचक्र of चरक, सुश्रुत and महाभारत :—

"चकोरैरुपचक्रैश्च पक्षिभिर्जीवजीवकैः" 3.178.7.

उपचक्र and चकोर are again mentioned together in a very ancient work :

"उपचक्रचकोराणां हंससारसयोरपि"— भेलसंहिता , 174

उपचक्र is also the Sheldrake (Art. 84-C).

---

1. Pāṇini 2.2.35.

2. According to poetic tradition, based upon the bird's habit of roosting on open ground at night, the चकोर is said to be greatly devoted to the moon and to live upon moon-beams. The epithet चकोरनेत्र applied to a man or woman implies his or her intense desire to look constantly at the beautiful moon-like face of the beloved and has no relation to the shape of the eyes: सा च तेन समानाय रूपयौवनशालिने । दत्ता वराङ्गना नेत्र चकोरामृतरश्मये ॥ —कथासरित्सागर, 77.50; see also ib. 76.11 and 93.45.

8. The Black and Grey Partridges of north India are कृष्णतित्तिर or simply तित्तिर (v.l. तित्तिरि) and गौरतित्तिर or कपिञ्जल respectively, and have been well-known in Sanskrit literature from the Ṛgveda onwards. The former has given its name to the तैत्तिरीयसंहिता of the Yajur Veda (hence called also याजुष:) and the connected उपनिषद् and आरण्यक. The beautiful verses of the खिलसूक्त of the Ṛgveda addressed to the कपिञ्जल, a bird of the farmlands who 'sticks to the farmer as close as he can' have been given in the Introduction and need not be repeated here. पारस्कर गृह्यसूत्र (1.19.8) advises the flesh of the plump and contented-looking Grey Partridge (कपिञ्जल) to be fed to a baby-boy at his अन्नप्राशन ceremony if the parents want him to grow up in opulence as a well-fed and happy young man. Other names for the Grey Partridge are जाङ्गल ("जाङ्गलो निर्जलदेश:" and therefore a bird living in such country. In this sense, the term probably also means the Himalayan Snow Partridge, a bird of the snow-line, another type of जाङ्गल country), and कपिश तित्तिर (कपिश grey). The Black Partridge is also चित्रपक्ष (of veriegated or spotted plumage) and its spotted plumage is accurately described in the शतपथ ब्राह्मण[1]. The name चित्रपक्ष as an adnoun would also include the Painted Partridge which occurs south of the Gangetic plain.

9. The Grey Partridge or कपिञ्जल, being always associated with crops and his breeding season falling in spring (March-April), he is dedicated to the beneficent deities, the वसव: and to the deity presiding over the spring season :—

"वसूनां कपिञ्जल:" —VS. 24, 38; TS. 5.5.16.

"वसन्ताय कपिञ्जलानालभते" —Ibid. 24.20

The Black Partridge, तित्तिरि, continues to breed till July when the rains set in and Nothern Painted Partridge, and allied form, begins to breed with the break of the rains and this fact coupled with its black colour accounts for naming this bird either for the rain-deity or the रुद्रा:—

"वर्षाभ्य: तित्तिरीन्" — VS. 24, 20,

"रुद्राणां तित्तिरी" —TS. 5.5.16

As food for the prowling snake:—

"मण्डूको मूषिका तित्तिरिस्ते सर्पाणां" —Ibid. 24.36

10. The Kayah or Swamp Partridge occurs from the Gangetic alluvial plain eastwards. It is known as कयार in Bengal and कोडरा (कुतितरा-कुतित्तिर?) in Assam. It is brown above with buffy white bars and white to pale buff below. The male has only short blunt spurs but is the most pugnacious of all the Francolin Partridges. It is probably the कुतित्तिर of चरक as the brief description of it in कल्पद्रुकोश,

"यस्तु स्यात्पाण्डुकपिल: स कुतित्तिर:"

agrees very well with the colour pattern of the birds's plumage. वसन्तराज, 8,20 mentions three different Partridges according to the commentator

---

1. 5.5.4.6.

and a proper reading of the verse[1] gives the three names as (1) कृष्णतित्तिरि (2) वृत्ततित्तिरि, the great fighter (यश्च पक्षिषु मतोऽधिपमल्लो) and (3) गौरतित्तिरि and of these the first two are said to be of equal value with the third for purposes of augury. Now वृत्त, i.e., वृत्तगुण्ड is a kind of grass or water reed (दीर्घनाल—M.W.) and the name वृत्ततित्तिरि therefore points to the Swamp Partridge which keeps to and breeds in elephant grass, "nal", etc. either close alongside some swamp or water-course... (F.B.I 2nd ed.).

11. The Himalayan Snow-Cock is a huge Partridge with a variegated plumage of white, buff, black and chestnut. It is 28 inches long and often weighs upto six pounds, i.e. four times as much as the Common Grey Partridge or कपिञ्जल. It is thus not only the largest Partridge known but its flesh also is 'one of the best for the table' and far superior to that of the Grey and Black Partridges. It thus appears to be वरिष्ठ (तित्तिरि) of the lexicons for वरिष्ठ means 'the largest or best' and the Snow-Cock is both. In the following synonymy:—

"........... वरिष्ठस्तु तित्तिरौ ।
वरिष्ठं मरिचे ताम्रे वरोरुतमयोरपि ॥"

वरिष्ठ is clearly a descriptive epithet for the best or largest Partridge, the best kind of pepper and the best amongst the metals, viz. copper. The Napali name for the bird is बैरा or बएरा which like Hindi बरेठा for the 'washerman' are perhaps corruptions from वरिष्ठ. In Kashmir it is known as कबुक which is the same as ककुभ, described as a bird with variegated plumage:—

"चित्रवर्णस्तु ककुभो"—कल्पद्रुकोश

The name ककुभ is certainly for a kind of Partridge and probably belongs to the Snow-Cock as the lexicon gives it with other names for Partridges. ककुभ also means 'lofty or excellent' and is quite in line with वरिष्ठ for the bird. ककुभ is included with the Quail, Grouse, Grey Partridge and other birds in a medical formula for elephants in sickness by पालकाप्य in हस्त्यायुर्वेद.

12. The Snow-Partridge is known as जंगुरिया in Hindi, which is from Sanskrit जाङ्गल, an adnoun for the Grey Partridge of the Plains. This name indicates a dry region more or less poor in trees, and it is quite understandable that two different birds of the Partridge family inhabiting dry territory, one in the plains and the other above the snow-line in the Himalayas, should share a common name. Another Hindi name for it is तेर तीतर, probably from तेजल तित्तिर (तेजल-तेयर-तेर '?), a synonym for कपिञ्जल in the राजनिघण्टु and, therefore, of जाङ्गल also. तेजस् is 'fire and brightness' and the name refers to the bright red bill and feet of the Snow-Partridge (तेजो लाति-तेजल:).

D. QUAILS & BUSTARD-QUAILS.

1. Science recognizes two kinds of Quails, viz., (i) true or four-toed Quails belonging to the Order Gallinae, and (ii) the three-toed Bustard Quails,

1. Quoted under Art. 54.

placed in the Order Hemipodii, but as there is a general similarity of appearance common to both they have been distinguished and named separately in Sanskrit in accordance with their size and habits. चरक and सुश्रुत divide the true Quails into three varieties, viz., वर्तक, वर्तिका and वर्तीर or वर्तीरिक, and place the Bustard Quails in a single group as लाव (fr. लव small) since they are the "most diminutive of the game-birds". This point is made clear in the कल्पद्रुकोश :—

"तस्मिंल्लघुतरे पुंसि लवी लावो लवः पुनः ।"

The name वर्तक has variants like वार्ताक, वार्तक etc., and वर्तिका is similarly synonymous with वर्तका, वार्तिका, etc. Owing to this confused spelling mistakes have crept into some printed texts of the above two Saṃhitās. All the names seem however to be derived from root वृत् and probably refer to the quick running movement of these plump little, almost tailless, birds on the ground like a rolling ball.

2. The largest in the series of true Quails is the Common or Grey Quail (about 8″) and next to it are the Black-breasted or Rain Quail (about 7″) and the Blue-breasted Quail (5.5″). The first is the वर्तक and the other two are वर्तिका of चरक as explained by चक्रपाणिदत्त :—

"वर्तिका स्वल्पप्रमाणजात्यन्तरमेव .... अन्यथा स्त्रीत्वेन वर्तकाद् वर्तिकाया लाघवं स्यात् ।"[1]

It is thus clear that the feminine वर्तिका has been deliberately applied to the smaller Quails. डल्हण also holds वर्तक and वर्तिका to be different species, "वर्तिकावर्तकतद्भेदौ". अमरकोश has वर्तक and वर्तिका for different birds in the list of thirteen individual names for as many kinds of birds. भावप्रकाश and अष्टाङ्गहृदय also regarded the two as different. If the Grey Quail is बड़ा बटेर, the other two are चीना बटेर (fr. Telugu चिन्ना small) in Hindi.

3. The equations "फालखेलागरुद्योधी" and "वर्तिका विष्णुलिङ्गी स्यात्" of त्रिकाण्डशेष give merely descriptive epithets and if फालखेला is 'a bird that favours cultivated fields' it would apply to the Grey Quail which always prefers wheat and barley fields to grass or jungle. It also fights like others of the group with its wings and गरुद्योधी would thus apply to all fighting Quails (see Art. 27 for a further discussion of this equation). विष्णुलिङ्गी (having the sectarian mark of a वैष्णव) probably refers to the buff coronal streak and supercilia common to these birds. The equations are therefore not specific for any particular bird or birds in the Quail group.

4. The Bush-Quails (6″-7″) "resemble Quails in size, but differ widely from them, and, to some extent, agree better with the Partridges in structure and habits. ...armed in the males with a blunt tubercular spur" (Oates). They are great fighters and fight even with greater rancour and clamour than the Grey Partridge (Hume and Marshall). It is to be noted

1. Based upon the rule—"स्त्रीस्यात्काचिन्मृणाल्यादिर्विवक्षापचये यदि"—अमर. 3.5.7.

that the Grey, the Blue-Breasted and the Black-breasted Quails have no spur at all. These differences had certainly been noticed by the ancients and they therefore differentiated the Bush-Quails as वर्तीर or वर्तीरिक. डल्हणाचार्य describes वर्तीर as "कपिञ्जलाणकः" i.e. 'a little Partridge' and the lexical synonymy, वर्तीरोऽल्पकपिञ्जलः"—कल्पद्रुकोश, brings out the same fact. The expressions अल्प-कपिञ्जल and लघुजाङ्गल mean the same thing and the equation "लावको लघुजाङ्गल" —त्रिकाण्डशेष, fully corresponds to the one from कल्पद्रुकोश. But it shows that the Bush Quails came later to be looked upon as varieties of लाव (लावक—प्रकारार्थे कन्). The names वर्तीर and वर्तीरिक therefore belong to the Rock and Jungle Bush Quails of North India. As a result of their inclusion into the लाव group, however, they came to be distinguished as पांसुल-and गैरिक-लाव (see below). वाना and वनवर्तिका should be simply a wild as against a pet or domesticated Quail, as all, except the Rock Bush Quail, live in the Jungles.

The above four-fold division of these seemingly similar birds as noted in para 1 above is indeed creditable to the Indians of at least two thousand years ago, for they must have been distinguished long before चरक and सुश्रुत adopted the classification in their works.

5. The Bustard-Quails, including the species called Button-Quails, have only three toes and lack the hind toe. Outwardly they bear a close resemblance to the true Quails but are definitely smaller in size. They are the लाव of चरक and लोपा of the वाज. संहिता. The Bustard-and Button-Quails together with the Rock-and Jungle and Bush-Quails came later to be classified into four varieties of लाव as follows :—

"गैरिकः पांसुलश्चैव पौण्ड्रको दर्भरस्तथा ।
लावश्चतुर्विधः प्रोक्तः तित्तिरिः द्विविधस्तथा ॥

—डल्हणाचार्य on सुश्रुत

"लावा विष्किरवर्गेषु ते चतुर्धा मता बुधैः ।
पांसुलो गौरकोऽन्यस्तु पौण्ड्रको दर्भरस्तथा ॥"

—भावप्रकाश and धन्वन्तरिनिघण्टु.

The first question to be decided in this connection is whether the names are related to the colour-pattern—which is very variable in all members of the group—or to the habitat of the birds. Considering however the facts (i) that animals and birds have been divided into जाङ्गलाः and आनूपाः according as they occupy dry and wet zones respectively, and (ii) that their food values, from the point of view of medicine, are related to the habitat, it would appear that the above names also refer to the type of country favoured by these little birds. The name गौरक in the second verse has an alternative reading of गैरिक under "लाव" in the अष्टाङ्गहृदयकोश and also in मदनपाल निघण्टु (Bom. Edn.) and the latter (गैरिक) appears to be the correct reading. In the first place, the term गैरिक cannot be related to any particular type of country and can only refer to the colour of the bird's plumage, but in this case it would seem to come in conflict with पौण्ड्रक in a similar sense (i.e. of the colour of the pale variety of sugarcane). Secondly if पौण्ड्रक

is taken in the sense of 'having a पुण्ड्र mark on the head, the term would apply almost to all Quails which cannot have been intended. It is therefore suggested that the four names including गैरिक should be interpreted with reference to the type of land favoured by the birds. As all the Bustard-Quails have similar habits and confine themselves to grass-land or crops including sugar-cane, they would fall within the दर्भर and पौण्ड्रक groups and it is difficult to pick out birds which prefer hills (गिरि) or sandy areas to grass or crops. In other words no Bustard Quails can be classified as गैरिक or पांसुल and one is forced to include both the species of Bush Quails of North India in this so-called लाव group to complete the series. Bush-Quails are definitely smaller than the common Quail and therefore came to be treated as varieties of लाव. The equation "लावको लघुजाङ्गलः" fully bears this out and they are actually known as लवा in Hindi. This view finds further support from the fact that the generic names of चरक and सुश्रुत for Bush-Quails, viz., वर्तीरिक and वर्तीर, have been completely omitted from भावप्रकाश and धन्वन्तरिनिघण्टु. The following classification is based on the above considerations.

(1) पांसुल लाव—the Rock Bush-Quail (7″) which avoids forest hills and dense vegetation, and is chiefly found in sandy or rocky ground. It is one of the वर्तीर group and is the लावक of the equation "लावको लघुजाङ्गलः".

(2) गैरिक लाव—The Jungle Bush-Quails (6″) which frequents hills (गिरि), thick bush and forest. Another member of the वर्तीर group.

(3) पौण्ड्रक लाव—the Button-Quails (5.5″-6.5″) of the Indo-Gangetic plain and lower Himalayas found in young sugarcane (पुण्ड्र) and borders of cultivation (Stuart Baker).

(4) दर्भरलाव—The Bustard-Quails (6″-6.5″) chiefly found in grass or low bush. Their local names are after the names of grass, e.g., the Burmese Bustard-Quail is तिनिस्क (fr. तृण) in Nepal and Bihar; the Common Bustard-Quail is गुन्द्रा or दूर्वा (kinds of grass) in North India and Ratnagiri; and the Calcutta Bustard-Quail is also गुन्द्रा.

The only improvement that this classification makes upon that of the old authorities is that the original लाव group has been divided into दर्भर and पौण्ड्रक corresponding to the Bustard-and Button-Quails of Stuart Baker (in F.B.I.). Curiously enough डल्हण felt sure about the गैरिक and पांशुल but not about दर्भर and पौण्ड्रक which are the true लाव of चरक and सुश्रुत, for he says,

"गैरिकपांशुलौ प्रसिद्धौ, पौण्ड्रकदर्भरौ देशान्तरे लोकादवगन्तव्यौ" ।

6. The कल्पद्रुकोश gives a few additional and odd names, probably of Prakritic origin and also perhaps corrupt in spelling which need not detain us, but two of them कूणिः (कूणी ?) and कुमारकः are probably connected with the breeding habits of the Bustard-Quails. These live chiefly in grass and low bush but are seldom seen, except when disturbed. The bird then rises

at one's feet, flies for about ten or fifteen yards, and drops again into the grass, whence it can very seldom be flushed for a second time. They differ in another respect as well from the true Quails. The ordinary conduct of the sexes is reversed during the period of incubation and it is the females who "do all the courting; they fight with rival females, for the favour and possession of the males, to whom they relegate the care and incubation of the eggs and the up-bringing of the young. One hen will apparently go on laying eggs as long as she can find a supply of males to incubate them...". (Smythies, S. Baker and others).

7. In respect of the breeding habits of these birds Hume cites a statement by Jerdon that the Indians knew them, a fact which is clearly reflected in the names given to the female and the male birds in the कल्पद्रुकोश, viz. कूणि: and कुमारक: respectively. The first may mean (i) 'having a defective hand or limb' from कुणि or कूणि, "कुकरे"—अमर, and the name should refer to a Bustard Quail which is short of one toe, or (ii) as an abbreviation of कुलकूणि'[1]—'harlot' in reference to the breeding habits of the female. This is no doubt a little far-fetched and may not stand the scrutiny of grammar but the name for the male bird is very suggestive of this latter sense. कुमारक (with कुत्सितार्थे कन्; cf. "माणवक: कुपुंसि स्यात्"—हेमचन्द्र) is a half-witted, hen-pecked or servile youth and refers to the jilted male Bustard left in charge of eggs and young.

8. Finally, the skulking habits of Bustard-Quails as a group have given us the very ancient name of लोपा[2] for them. वैजयन्ती has "लोपालोपायिके समे" and the name is from root लुप्, लोप, 'disappearance'. The skulking habit after the first flight, is so persistent that they prefer to be caught by the hand or even hammered to death at the place of hiding rather than escape by taking wing again (Hume and others), and naturally they fall an easy prey to the prying fox. This peculiar trait of these birds and the employment of dogs to make them rise again, if possible, have been described in श्यैनिक शास्त्र :—

> "उत्थापयेयु: लावादीन् ढौकयेयुश्च तद्गती: ।
> यत्रैकवारं पतित: पक्षी कुर्यान्नचोत्प्लुतिम्
> स रज्जुना शुना तत्र मार्गयित्वा (—तुं ?) विसर्जयेत् ॥ (6.32-33)

The Indian Button-Quail is known as लोवा (लोपा, पस्य व:) in Hindi. The Indian fox is known to eat small birds so that लोपाश is (लोपाशिका a fox in त्रिकाण्डशेष) a fox that eats the लोपा birds. In the वाज. संहिता 'लोपाश'[3] is dedicated to the Aśvins, "लोपाश आश्विन:" 24.36 which helps to connect the story of the Aśvins saving the life of a Quail so often mentioned in the Ṛgveda (I.117. 16;118.8; etc.). The enemy of the वर्तिका was of course वृक but the term apparently included the fox, for मेधातिथि on मनु (8.235) explains वृक as "शृगालप्रभृति," and the वर्तिका of the Veda was most probably a Bustard-Quail. In

1. कुलकूणी तु कुलटा—कल्पद्रु.23. Cf. Prakrit कूणित—rotten.
2. This is a most appropriate name for these birds: cf. प्रसक्तस्यादर्शनं लोपसंज्ञं स्यात्—काशिका, 1.1.60, i.e. the disappearance of a thing previously observed is लोप:.
3. लोपा and लोपाश are mentioned in तै. संहिता, 5.5.18 and 21.

saving one from a fox, the Aśvins defeated the mischief of the latter, and, seen in this light, the propriety of naming the लोपाश for them with of course a touch of humour becomes quite clear.

9. Quail fighting, as a royal sport, is described in मानसोल्लास, 2,253 where three varieties of wild birds are named कच्छेल (from damp areas; cf. दर्भर), गरञ्ज (from the Vindhya territories, cf. गाञ्जीकाय for a Quail), and पांसुल together with three home-bred hybirds of the first and second degrees. As the wild varieties are said to interbreed in captivity it is highly probable that they all belong to the group of Bustard Quails, the females of which are great fighters. In any case it is not possible to fix the identity of the species particularly because the nomenclature has undergone considerable change under Dravidian influence—मानसोल्लास being a South-Indian work.

10. Like many other birds the Quails too have contributed their share to sacred and other literature. The वर्तिका has the distinction of being mentioned in the Ṛgveda with the Aśvins as their protectors, and in the Vaj. Saṃhitā with its enemy, the क्षिप्रश्येन. It has furnished a beautiful illustration to the logician in "अन्धकवर्तक न्याय", and a picture of helplessness against superior force in :—

> "श्येनावपातचकिता वनवर्तिकेव
> किं चेष्टसे ननु चिरात्कवलीकृतासि ।   —मालतीमाधव, 8.8.

Against this last may be set the resourcefulness of the little लापसकुण (Bustard-Quail) in the सकुणग्घिजातक (168) which not only successfully avoided the attack of the Falcon but, by a sudden manoeuvre, also brought about the latter's death. The वट्टकजातक (35) is a replica of the story of मन्दपाल and शार्ङ्गिका in the Mahābhārata with Quails as the principal actors. The story of the Quail and the Crow in the *Hitopadeśa* illustrates the evil consequences of keeping bad company (section 3, story 5).

56

MAGAPODES

No bird of this family occurs within India proper.

57

BUSTARD-QUAILS

These birds as a class are the लाव, लोपा, or लोपायिका, the females being कूणि and the male कुमारक in Sanskrit. Generally speaking they are regarded as smaller varieties of Quail and have, therefore, been considered in the combined article on Quails and Bustard-Quails —No. 55D.

58

RAILS, CRAKES, MOORHENS, WATERCOCKS AND COOT

- Waterhens including the Rails, Crakes and Coot जलकुक्कुट
  - Waterhens proper पारिप्लव, जलकुक्कुट
    - Small in size अम्बु कुक्कुटिका, कुलवारी, चित्रांगक
    - of medium size
      - White-breasted waterhen शुक्लकण्ठ दात्यूह, मेघराव, हुडुक्क दात्यूह.
      - Moorhen कृष्णा-जलकुक्कुटी
    - of large size
      - Purple coot or Moorhen मंजुल दात्यूह, जलरंकु दात्यूह राजीव, कमल.
      - Water-cock यष्टिक जल कुक्कुट, जलकुक्कुभ.
  - Coot कृष्णकारण्डव, जालपाद ,, सुमुख ,, प्लव.

Note—The meaning of पारिप्लव (v.l. परि०) as जलकुक्कुट has been missed in M.W. and other lexicons except वैजयन्ती. The commentators of the रामायण and रघुबंश also have overlooked it. See para 9 of the article.

1. All these birds are comprised within the general term जलकुक्कुट and possibly also पारिप्लव in Sanskrit (para 9 below). The Rails and Crakes which resemble slim chickens are the smallest of the group and are much alike in their habits. They spend the day among reeds and rushes and come out to feed early mornings and late evenings. They are the अम्बु-कुक्कुटिका (tiny water birds resembling a chicken) of सुश्रुत and अम्बुकुक्कुटी of चरक. The Blue-breasted Banded Rail and the Banded Crake are the कुलवारी (कुल+वारि, frequenting water near the bank ?) or चित्राङ्गद (having painted bands on the body) of कल्पद्रुकोश :—

"कुलवारी लघुः कृष्णः चित्राङ्गदः (चित्राङ्गकः ?)"

2. The larger birds like the Moorhen, the Purple Moorhen, etc. are जलकुक्कुट properly so called and each of them has one or more specific names as well. The Moorhen looks like a full-sized black chicken and is found

in the vicinity of thick cover near water, cultivated fields or gardens. It is the कृष्णा जलकुक्कुटी ("अथान्या जलकुक्कुटी कृष्णवर्णा") of कल्पद्रुकोश.

3. The White-breasted Waterhen, most remarkable for its "atrocious" and "roaring" calls, and named for this reason मेघराव in चरक and सुश्रुत, is one of the commonest water-birds of India, found wherever water is surrounded by a certain amount of thick cover. It is a dark coloured bird with white forehead, foreneck, breast and abdomen.

4. The Purple Moorhen is a large blue and purple-coloured bird with a red bill and shield and red legs and feet, found in reedy marshes and lotus-lakes, walking about over the partially submerged weeds and floating lotus leaves and "on the whole the bird is comparatively seldom seen unless beaten out of cover." From its striking colour and size it is "one of the greatest ornaments of our marshes" and, it may be added, of our tanks with lotuses and reedy margins. Not quite so noisy as the White-breasted Waterhen, it has a variety of loud calls. It feeds on tender shoots of the lotus, other water-plants and on the rice crop. Sanskrit nomenclature for these two birds is closely allied with certain names for the Pea-cock, the Black-Ibis and the Hawk-Cuckoo and they are considered in the following paragraphs.

5. अत्यूह, नत्यूह, दात्यूह, and मुगूह, as bird-names of obscure etymology would seem to be inter-related in some way, the first three from root ऊह् and the last from root गुह्, and an attempt is made here to distinguish and allocate the terms to their respective owners with the help of lexical synonymies not a few of which have sacrificed perspicuity for the sake of brevity. It may even be doubted whether the authors themselves had a clear idea of what they meant to define, and there is reason to believe that some of them at least have merely tried to summarize and compress what they found in the older but more detailed lexicons. Or it may be that they proceeded on the assumption that the names were too common and well-known to call for any elucidation.

(i) अत्यूह—the Peacock and Hawk-Cuckoo :

(a) अत्यूह, a प्रतुद bird in चरक corresponding to दात्यूह, in सुश्रुत is the Hawk-Cuckoo (Art. 37).

(b) "अत्यूहस्तु मयूरे स्यादत्यूहानीलिकौषधौ"—हेम, विश्व.

(c) "अत्यूहा नीलिकायां स्त्री कालकण्ठखगे पुमान्"—मेदिनी.

(d) अत्यूहः दात्यूहे, कालकण्ठके—शब्दार्थचिन्तामणि.

(e) अत्यूह—Peacock; gallinule—M. Williams.

कालकण्ठ in (c) and (d) is the Peacock and अत्यूह in (d) the Hawk-Cuckoo and Peacock. Both have a traditional relationship with the dark rain-cloud. If the one welcomes it with his loud calls, the other begs of it, equally vociferously, a few drops of water. It is interesting to note that दात्यूह also means a rain-cloud. M. W.'s rendering of अत्यूह as a Gallinule can only refer to the Purple Moorhen as अत्यूहा which means the indigo which yields the blue colour.

(ii) नत्यूह—"Probably = Dātyūha in the Rāmāyaṇa" (M.W.). Although this word occurs more than once in the Rāmāyaṇa it is surprising that the older lexicons and even Apte do not give it. From the context, however, it appears to be the White-breasted Waterhen. The term occurs as an alternative reading for दात्यूह in some editions but as the latter means both the Hawk-Cuckoo and the above Waterhen one has to deduce the meaning from the context. See examples given later.

(iii) दात्यूह—the Hawk-Cuckoo, the Black Ibis the White-breasted Waterhen, and the Purple Moorhen, each with a specific epithet.:

(a) दात्यूहः कालकण्ठकः—अमर. क्षीरस्वामी gives कालकण्टक as v.l. and explains कालकण्ठक as 'black-necked' and कालकण्टक as 'having black feathers. रामाश्रमी टीका, on the other hand, explains the former as "काले वर्षाकाले कण्ठो रवोऽस्य"—one that calls during the rainy season.

(b) दात्यूहे कालकण्टकः—अभि. चिन्तामणि which gives कालकण्ठक as v.l. and explains both like क्षीरस्वामी, and दात्यूह as "ददाति आनन्दं दात्यूहः" दात्यूह in this last sense is the Hawk-cuckoo but कालकण्ठ दात्यूह or कालकण्टक दात्यूह is the Black Ibis for which see Art. 80. According to the explanation in रामाश्रमी टीका, कालकण्ठ दात्यूह, as a homonym, should also be the Hawk-cuckoo and the White-breasted Waterhen both of which are very vocal during the rains.

(c) मादक-दात्यूहे—शब्दकल्पद्रुम; with "माद्यति वर्षागमे हृष्यति" the name can signify the Hawk-cuckoo if this etymology is parallel to "ददाति आनन्दं दात्यूहः"*

(d) "दात्यूहः कालकण्ठे स्याद् दात्यूहश्चातकेऽपि च"—विश्व.
"दात्यूहः कालकण्टके चातकेऽपि" —हेमचन्द्र, मेदिनी.

These two equations make it quite clear that दात्यूह as चातक,, the Hawk-Cuckoo, is quite different from the कालकण्ठ or कालकण्टक दात्यूह which is the Black Ibis. This makes the रामाश्रमी gloss on कालकण्ठ as "काले वर्षाकाले" untenable.

(e) "कालकण्ठस्तु दात्यूहे कलविङ्के च खञ्जने
सितापाङ्गे हरे पीते सारके नीलकण्ठवत् ॥"

"विश्व and हेमचन्द्र.

This synonymy is final on the question of interpretation of कालकण्ठ or नीलकण्ठ both of which, as applied to the different birds, simply mean 'black necked'. The Black Ibis, the Magpie Robin, the Large Pied-Wagtail and the Peacock are the birds meant here and everyone of them has an entirely black or blue neck.

(f) "जलकाकस्तु दात्यूहः स च स्यातकालकण्टकः"—धन्वन्तरि and राजनिघण्टु.
This places the identity of कालकण्टक दात्यूह beyond doubt, as जलकाक in the present context is no other than the Black Ibis.

---

*The Koel also calls persistently like the Hawk-Cu ckoo, and expressions like "माद्यत्कल-कण्ठ पञ्चमरुत"—रुक्मिणीपरिणय 4.3 for the former make it highly probable that मादक दात्यूह is the latter bird.

(g) "शितिकण्ठस्तु दात्यूहः"; "दात्यूहश्चातकेऽपि च"—त्रिकाण्ड.
With शिति for 'black' the first equation stands for the Black Ibis, and शिति for 'white' it is for the White-breasted Water-hen; see शुक्लकण्ठ below. The second equation calls for no remarks.

(h) "शुक्लकण्ठ दात्यूहे"—शब्दकल्पद्रुम and M.W.

(i) "......... दात्यूहः कालकण्ठकः
अत्यूहोऽपि च दात्यौहो मासज्ञोऽपि च स स्मृतः"— कल्पद्रुकोश.
This refers to (1) the Black Ibis, (2) the Hawk Cuckoo and (3) the White-breasted Waterhen (दात्यौह and मासज्ञ are explained later in this article).

(j) "बहुकःदात्यूहे"; "हुडुक्कः मत्तदात्यूहे"—हेम, मेदिनी etc.
"हुडुकस्तुमदोन्मत्ते वाद्यभिज्जलपक्षिणोः"—महीप.
The first as "बहुना कायति" is applied both to the Hawk-Cuckoo and the above Waterhen, while the second seems to refer to the Waterhen alone as it is actually known as डाहुक पाखी in Bengali and 'डाहुक' is clearly from हुडुक्क. This name or epithet has been explained by महेन्द्र in his notes on the अनेकार्थसंग्रह of हेमचन्द्रः— "हुडुक्कः वाद्यविशेषः । मुक्तहिक्काः हुडुक्काः" The second part of this is fully descriptive of the call-notes of the white-breasted Waterhen during the breeding season, actually described as "roars, hiccups and cackles" by EHA. The call of the Hawk-Cuckoo on the other hand does not at all resemble a "hiccup" or हिक्का. This helps us to fix हुडुक्क दात्यूह for the Waterhen, and मादकदात्यूह for the Hawk-Cuckoo.

(iv) (a) मुगूह is equated with दात्यूह in शब्दार्थचिन्तामणि and M.W., and with (1) पपीहा or the Hawk-Cuckoo and (2) a kind of deer in हिन्दी शब्द सागर. In view of the fact that deer-names like रङ्कु, कमल and राजीव are associated with the Purple Coot or Purple Moorhen as a kind of दात्यूह it would appear that मुगूह (गुह्-गोपने to conceal or hide) also refers to that bird and its identity with पपीहा in हिन्दी शब्द सागर is incorrect.

(b) "मञ्जुलं तु जलाञ्चले, रम्ये, कुञ्जे, मञ्जुलस्तु दात्यूहे"—हेमचन्द्र
"जलरङ्कुस्तु वञ्जुलः (मञ्जुलः ?) दात्यूहश्च"—वैजयन्ती
"मञ्जुलजलरङ्कू पतत्रिणि"—मेदिनी, शाश्वत
"दात्यूहो जलरङ्कुःस्यात्" —हलायुध
"मञ्जुलजलरङ्कके (जलरङ्कौ ?) —हारावली
"जलरङ्कौ तु मञ्जुलः"—विश्व
"गोरङ्कु = जलकुक्कुट in निघण्टरत्नाकर
जलरञ्ज = जलरङ्कु—M.W.

All the above equations apply to the Purple Moorhen as a kind of दात्यूह. It is "one of the most beautiful birds found on our Indian jheels", keeps to rushes, reeds and dense lotuses, is averse to flying and walks upon lotus leaves and other water vegetation and runs to cover when disturbed; rarely swims though it can swim, and has a variety of hooting, cackling and hoarse calls. It is particularly noisy during the breeding season. In short it has beauty and behaves like a skulking little deer on water and fully deserves the names मञ्जुल-दात्यूह, मृगूह-दात्यूह and जलरङ्कु-दात्यूह[1]. The only other birds that can claim these names are the Jacanas but they are small birds, have *no skulking habits, nor loud and powerful call-notes*.

It will be seen that the so-called substantives of the lexicons are really in the nature of descriptive epithets and the name दात्यूह principally means 'a noisy bird' and it is only the qualifying adjectives which make it specific for particular birds.

6. दात्यौह (v.l. दात्यूह) is named in "दात्यौहो मासानाम्" वाज. संहिता (24.25) for the deity presiding over the Months, and in all probability it is the White-breasted Waterhen which is dark or black above and a clear white below, and mystically represents the dark and the light halves of the month. Support for this view comes from the तैत्ति. संहिता (5.5.17) where a tortoise is dedicated to the same deity— "मासां कश्यपः", and here too the back of the animal is dark-coloured and the belly a pale white so that दात्यौह is the same as the शुक्लकण्ठ दात्यूह. It is from this dedication that the bird has earned the name मासज्ञ[2] (knowing the month) as in the synonymy (iii), (i) above.

7. In "क्वयिः कुटरुः दात्यौहस्ते वाजिनाम्"—वाज.संहिता, 24.29, again, it is the noisy White-breasted Waterhen with क्वयि the Screech Owl or the Common Owlet (Art. 48) and कुटरु, the Green Barbet (Art. 35), the last two being equally noisy birds. The alternative explanation of दात्यौह by Sāyaṇa on तैत्ति.संहिता as 'पुष्करिणी बसतिः' ('living on lotus-ponds') is perfectly true of this Waterhen. This selection is quite apt as the noise made by these birds is typical of the din and uproar attending horse races. The White-breasted Waterhen breeds during the rains when the males "become exceedingly obstreperous" and their calls begin with "loud raucous grunts, croaks and chuckles suggestive of a bear in agony and settle down to a monotonous and metallic ku-wak...ku-wak or kook...kook...kook...On cloudy days this is often kept up for 15 minutes at a stretch, and calling continues more or less throughout the night"—Salim Ali. EHA also remarks that "the clamour which this little bird can raise is something astounding". मेघराव of चरक is clearly this bird but डल्हण has incorrectly rendered it as the चातक which however, is not a water-bird at all.

---

1. Probably also जलरञ्ज-दात्यूह, one that gives colour or charm to a tank. In the synonymy— "दात्यूहे कालकण्टकः जलरङ्कुः : जलरञ्जः"—अभि. चिन्ता., दात्यूह has to be treated as a homonym referring to the Black Ibis (कालकण्टक), the Purple Moonhen (जलरङ्कु), and the Hawk-cuckoo (जलरञ्ज). क्षीरस्वामी or अमर, 2.5.17 gives जलरञ्ज for चातक, and on 2.5.22 for दात्यूह. Evidently जलरञ्ज is also a homonym or merely a descriptive epithet for more than one bird. As applied to the चातक 'जल' of जलरञ्ज means 'rain-water'.

2. Cf. पक्षाभ्यां शुक्लकृष्णाभ्यां मासस्तु परिकल्पितः—

पद्मपुराण, क्रियाखण्ड, 22.56.

The above syllabification of the calls of the bird helps to identify the दात्यूह of the following verse :

"प्रावृट्काले सुखी भूत्वा को वा कुत्र न गच्छति ।
इति वदति दात्यूहः को वा को वा क्व वा क्व वा ॥" —शब्दकल्पद्रुम

It roosts and often places its nest on low trees in the vicinity of water and is also "often found some distance from water". The दात्यूह of भवभूति spending hot hours of day in the hollow of a tree appears to be this bird :—

"दात्यूहैस्तिनिशस्य कोटरवति स्कन्धे निलीय स्थितम्" —मालतीमाधव, 9.7.

This verse, perhaps, helps to solve the following synonymy in वैजयन्ती:—

"अथ शकटाविले प्लवपरिप्लवौ
अन्वर्थनामधेयौ द्वौ जालपादाम्बुकुक्कुटौ ।"

that is, the name शकटाविल applies to two different birds viz. प्लव and परिप्लव (=पारिप्लव) called respectively जालपाद (the Coot) and अम्बुकुक्कुट (Rails and Waterhen). Now शकट is the तिनिश tree (Ougeinia dalbergioides, usually a small tree yielding valuable wood used for various purposes including carts and hence its name शकट or स्यन्दनतरु) and according to भवभूति, the White-breasted Waterhen occasionally does conceal itself (आविलति) in the hole (विल) of a शकट tree. One of the शकटाविल birds, therefore, is this दात्यूह and the other, in a homonymous sense of the term (शकटाविल = आविल confused, शकटव्यूह—mass formation or array, i.e., a bird moving in a confused mass) is the Coot, the "प्लवाः संघातचारिणः" of चरक.

8. नत्यूह in the following examples is जलकुक्कुट or दात्यूह according to the commentator and therefore, the present Waterhen :—

"रथाह्वहंसा नत्यूहाः प्लवाः कारण्डवाः परे ।
तथा पुंस्कोकिलाः क्रौञ्चा विसंज्ञा भेजिरे दिशः ॥" रामायण[1], 2.103.43.

"बद्धपद्मोत्पलवनाश्चक्रवाकोपशोभिताः ।
नत्यूहरुतसंघुष्टा हंससारसनादिता ॥" रामायण, 15.14.25

The humble Waterhen and its smaller cousins have not been overlooked in the Epics :

"सलिलकुक्कुटकारण्डवकलहंसादिभिर्विचित्रमुपकूजितामलजलाशय . . . ."
भागवत, 5.4.2.

"कारण्डैः सारसैर्हंसैर्वञ्जुलैर्जलकुक्कुटैः ।
चक्रवाकैस्तथा चान्यैः शकुनैः प्रतिनादितान् ॥" रामायण, 4.13.8.
"कादम्बैश्चक्रवाकैश्च कुररैर्जलकुक्कुटैः ।" महाभारत, 3.158.56

1. Mahābhārata III.146.44 is a similar verse probably taken over from the Rāmāyaṇa. Here the प्लवाः are the Cormorants and कारण्डवाः the Coots.

9. परिप्लव (v. l. पारिप्लव, agitated, confused), as just seen, denotes जलकुक्कुट and the term probably includes almost all the members of the Rallidae family, excepting the Coot which is a bird of open waters, skulking about nervously amongst the reeds and vegetation lining the banks of rivers and tanks. In the following examples, the term appears to have been used in this comprehensive sense. They are said to be within the cane and reed-beds flanking a river. तिनिश also figures as one of the river-side trees :

"वानीरैस्तिनिशैश्च व बकुलैः केतकैरपि ।"
"पारिप्लवशतैर्जुष्टाः बर्हिक्रौञ्चविनादिता ।
रमणीया नदी सौम्या मुनिसङ्घनिशेविता ॥" रामायण, 4.27.23.
"उपान्तवानीरवनोपगूढान्यालक्ष्य पारिप्लवसारसानि ।
दूरावतीर्णा पिबतीव खेदादमूनि पम्पासलिलानि दृष्टिः ॥"

रघुवंश, 13.30

It will be particularly noted that Kālidāsa has very correctly described the पारिप्लव birds as concealed within the reeds lining the पम्पा lake. The Saras Crane too looks for prey in such beds. पालकाप्य also mentions पारिप्लव birds with other water-birds in specifying the type of country in which royal elephants should spend the winter months.[1]

10. The Purple Moorhen, as seen above, is जलरङ्कु or मञ्जुल-दात्यूह. It goes under the name of कलीम in Hindi which is from Prakrit कलिमं for नीलोत्पलम् (देशीनाममाला) the blue lotus. Sanskrit राजीव too is the blue lotus. Now both राजीव and कमल also mean 'a kind of deer'. राजीव again, is one of the birds of diurnal habits (दिवाचर) and सारस one of the उभयचारी group, i.e., those which are active both by day and night, in the अग्निपुराण :—

खञ्जरीटकदात्यूहशुकराजीवकुक्कुटाः
भारद्वाजश्च सारङ्ग इति ज्ञेया दिवाचरा : ॥
श्वाविद्वृषभगोमायुवृककोकिलसारसाः
तुरंगकौपीननरा (?)[2] गोधा ह्युभयचारिणः ॥ 213, 16-19.

The list of birds in the मत्स्यपुराण (118, 52) includes कमल for a particular bird along with गोनर्द for the सारस ((गोचर्म is evidently a mistake for गोनर्द). Thus Hindi कलीम and Sanskrit कमल and राजीव are names for the Purple Moorhen from its blue colour and association with lotus plants amongst which it lives and moves like a pretty little deer.

11. "The Coot is a slaty black bird resembling a typical Waterhen on land but rather duck-like on water in the distance, with a white pointed bill and white horny shield covering the forehead. Gregarious by habit, it is always found in flocks on open sheets of water including slowly moving rivers. Large numbers visit India in winter when the birds collect in

---

1. See हस्त्यायुर्वेद p. 200.
2. The corrupt reading of the last line can be amended with the help of बृ॰ संहिता, 87.3.

'immense herds', and on the larger jheels of North India great patches of water are often literally black with their multitudes" (Salim All). Hume also speaks in the same strain... "Common Coots cover on the Manchar (Lake) a square mile of water which is perfectly black with them." (*Stray feathers*, 1.249). Their call, often heard, at night, is a clear and loud trumpet-like cry. It is one of the commonest birds and has naturally won several names for itself—some from its white bill and blaze on the forehead standing out against the dark body-colour, and others from its gregarious habits. It is the सङ्घातचारी प्लव ("प्लवाः सङ्घातचारिणः") of चरक and सहचारी सुमुख ("सुमुखाः सहचारिणः", सुमुख, from the white face against a black body) of सुश्रुत. The following lexical synonymies are based on the characters just mentioned :—

(i) "कारण्डवः काकवक्त्रो दीर्घाङ्घ्रिः कृष्णवर्णकः"—कल्पद्रुकोश

(ii) "......अथ शकटाविले प्लवपरिप्लवौ
अन्वर्थनामधेयौ द्वौ जालपादाम्बुकुक्कुटौ" —वैजयन्ती

(iii) "जालपात्पुरुदंशकः" —त्रिकाण्डशेष

(iv) "कारण्डवो महापक्षो" —वैजयन्ती
"सहस्रपाद कारण्डे" —हेमचन्द्र, विश्वप्रकाश
"कारण्डवस्तु मरुलः" —अभिधानचिन्तामणि

Before proceeding to a consideration of the above it is perhaps advisable to state that the terms प्लव, जालपाद and कारण्डव (v.1. कारण्ड) refer to more than one bird. प्लव means (1) a water-bird in general, (2) a Cormorant, which often takes a jump clean out of water before diving, (3) a Duck in general and the Pelican in particular as both swim or float like a boat and (4) the Coot which not only swims and dives but also patters along on the surface of the water with its feet like a frog ((प्लव) before rising into the air. जालपाद is (1) any web-footed water-bird and particularly a Goose or Duck, and (2) the Coot which moves in a mass (जाल, 'a multitude' with पद्, to go). कारण्डव means (1) the Coot from its gregarious habit—कारण्डव in Pali, 'chaff, sweeping'; cf यवकारण्डव, 'barley Chaff'; करण्ड 'a bee-hive'; 'a box or wicker-basket which may contain many things'—पेटक— 'a multitude';" "करण्डस्येव तदाकारं वा कारण्डवः" and, therefore, a bird that lives in large numbers like bees in a hive and that looks in the mass like so much chaff floating on water, or again that has the shape of a wicker basket, in reference, probably, to the duck-shaped baskets of old; and (2) a Duck e.g. पीततुण्ड कारण्डव, the Mallard and others.

12. The first quotation defines the Coot or कारण्डव as काकवक्त्र i.e. having a काक or sectarian mark, तिलक, on the face. The bird's facial white shield resembles such a mark. The bill of the Coot is white and far too small and thin(1.4″) to be comparable with that of a Crow. Its Hindi name दसरनी (fr. Telugu दसरी, a तिलक worn by the Hindus of South India, or from Sanskrit दर्शनीय corresponding to सुमुख of चरक) and टिकरी (fr. Sanskrit तिलक, Prakrit

टिक्क—Hindi टीका; टिकली in Hindi is such a mark or a spangle worn by women on the forehead) fully support the interpretation of काकवक्त्र. Emperor Jehangir mentions the Coot by the Persian name of "Qushq-ul dagh" (Qashq being the sectarian mark of white sandal worn by the Hindus, and 'a spot')[1]. It is immaterial whether the bird is actually known in Persia by the name given in the *Memoirs* but what is certain is that that was how the bird's Indian name was explained to, or rendered, for him, and it undoubtedly helps to get at the true significance of the epithet काकवक्त्र. The other two adjectives in the definition indicate the large feet and the dark colour of the Coot.

13. The quotation from the वैजयन्ती has already been considered earlier and it only remains to point out that शकटाविल as जालपाद is no other than the Coot and both these terms refer to its gregarious habit. It may also be pointed out here that जालपाद occurring with हंस in स्मृति or धर्मशास्त्र literature, where the birds that may or may not be eaten are discussed, means the Coot, but almost all the commentators have missed the true meaning, and I need not refer to some of their absurd explanations like, अजालपादाऽपि हंसाः सन्तीति हंसानां पुनर्वचनम्."[2] सायण माधवाचार्य, however, in his notes on पराशरधर्मसंहिता[3] has frankly stated that he does not know the birds named जालपाद and शरभ.

14. The equation "जालपात्पुरुदंशकः" stands for the Coot and not the Goose or Duck. पुरुदंशक[4] means 'crowded or standing closely together' and not 'many-teethed' as assumed by M. Williams. I have not come across any reference to the teeth of a Goose in Sanskrit though the action of their bill and tongue in sifting out food (क्षीर in the sense of पीयूष) from water is often mentioned. Both the terms of the equation thus mean the same thing—'moving or living in dense flocks'.

15. महापक्ष in "कारण्डवो महापक्षो" again, refers to the great or large (महा) parties (पक्ष) in which the birds are always found.[5] So too सहस्रपाद (moving in their thousands) as a descriptive epithet of कारण्डव is on a par with जालपाद as explained above. Lastly मरुल may mean a bird that cannot live without water as explained in the शब्दकल्पद्रुम or it may be a humorous reference to the birds in the mass as 'the devil's host'. This series of adjectives describing the gregarious habits of the Coot may be compared with the title of the Buddhist work- अवलोकितेश्वर गुण कारण्ड व्यूह, describing the thousands of the virtues of the बोधिसत्व अवलोकितेश्वरः "कारण्ड व्यूह" clearly refers to the packed mass of Coots containing hundreds of thousands of individual birds covering the surface of large waters by the square mile. The idea

1. *Memoirs* (Translation by A. Rogers, I.C.S.) p. 342.

2. मिताक्षरा on याज्ञवल्क्यस्मृति I.174.

3. Ch. 6.1; Bombay Sanskrit Series No.59, Vol.II. Pt. i, 1898.

4. For the use of दंश-दंशित in this sense see M.Bh. 3.7.18; 5.195.11; 6.56.8 (said of an army arranged in गरुडव्यूह).

5. Compare "महापक्षं मित्रम्" for 'a friend having a large number of supporters' in कामन्दक नीतिसार 7.66 (translated by M. Williams).

is that the good qualities of Lord अवलोकितेश्वर are as innumerable as the Coot birds in a व्यूह called कारण्डव्यूह. The name शकटाबिल for the Coot, where शकट stands for शकटव्यूह, is fully parallel to कारण्डव्यूह.

16. It will be seen that the majority of the epithets for Coot are clever synonyms for the simple terms, सहचारी and सङ्घातचारी of सुश्रुत and चरक, and only one, viz., जालपाद has been actually used in the स्मृति literature to avoid confusion with other bird-names. In the Purāṇic literature the term कारण्डव has been used probably in its homonymous sense i.e. meaning both Coots and Ducks particularly in the stock phrase "हंसकारण्डवाकीर्णा". In the alternative कारण्डव would include both Ducks and Coots by उपलक्षणा. Coots being a permanent feature of all waters including slow-running rivers flanked with rushes, canes and reeds there is no mistaking them as कारण्डव in the following :—

"हंसकारण्डवोद्‌गीता सारसाभिरुतास्तथा" (महाभारत)[1]

"कारण्डवाननविघट्टितवीचिमालाः
कादम्बसारसकुलाकुलतीरदेशाः ।" (ऋतुसंहार)[2]

"फुल्लपङ्कजषण्डानि प्रसन्नसलिलानि च ।
कारण्डवविकीर्णानि तटाकानि सरांसि च ॥" (रामायण)[3]

"जीवञ्जीवलसज्जीवं क्वणत्कारण्डवोत्कटम् ।" (स्कन्दपुराण, काशीखण्ड)[4]

"सदा कूजितलक्षेण तत्र कारण्डवद्विजाः " (ब्रह्माण्डपुराण, उत्तर.)[5]

17. Because of the Duck-like appearance of Coot when on water, the name कारण्डव has been applied to certain Ducks with suitable adjectives (Art. 84-c).

18. The Water-Cock equals the Purple Moorhen in size but is of a slate-grey colour. The bill, the shield on the forehead and the legs are red but the shield of the breeding male grows into a long horn. The note of the male consists of loud booming calls, chiefly heard in the breeding season. It is a skulking nocturnal bird frequenting reedy tanks and is known as कोरा, कोंगरा, or कोंड़ा in the vernaculars. It is a very pugnacious bird and is often kept by people in Bengal for fighting, and it is from its fighting habit that it has been named Water-cock in English (Whistler).

19. यष्टिक for जलकुक्कुट in शब्दकल्पद्रुम and शब्दार्थचिन्तामणि can only be this bird which carries, as it were, a stick-like horn on its head; cf. याष्टीक—"यष्टिधारियोद्धा"—शब्दकल्प० i.e., 'one armed with a stick' or fighter. It is also कोयष्टि (के शिरसि यष्टिरिव यस्य) in the same sense. Yet another very expressive name for the water-cock is जलकुक्कुभ after its booming call notes.

1. 3,38.20.
2. शरद्वर्णन
3. 3.8.14.
4. 32.101.
5. 35.10.

This name contrasts with the ground bird (स्थलज कुक्कुभ), the Crow pheasant or Coucal with a similar powerful voice (Art. 37-B). The lexical definition for the latter "कुक्कुभ: कुहकस्वन:"—अभि०चिन्ता० is applicable to both the birds. नलचम्पू, p. 159 mentions जलकुक्कुभ as calling from its nest in the reedbed bordering a river but यशस्तिलक चम्पू refers to it simply as कुक्कुभ in a list of water birds (पय: पतङ्गः) at p. 529.

20. Sanskrit कोणालक (Prakrit कोणालग) from कोण a stick, and अलक 'a curl on the forehead', may well be the present bird, and if so the name offers a better relationship with the vernacular कोंडा or कोंगरा than the name कोयष्टि..[1] कोणालक in the verse below should be the booming Water-Cock or the Black-crested Kalij which too lives in the neighbourhood of water (Art. 55) :—

"नित्यमत्तविहङ्गानि भ्रमरैः सेवितानि च ।
कोणालकविघुष्टानि सारसाभिरुतानि च ॥" रामायण All. Ed. 6, 39.11.

कुणाल or कुनाल is the Painted Snipe and these latter would seem to have got mixed up with कोणालक as a homonym for two other birds the water-cock and the above named Pheasant (कोण Prakrit for black and अलक a crest).

1. Lapwings and certain members of the Heron group also share the name कोयष्टि Arts. 71 and 82.

59

MASKED FINFOOT

This bird occurs in the most inaccessible places in the extreme east of India, and from its Rail-like characters it would pass for a variety of जलकुक्कुट.

60

JACANAS

1. The two species of Jacana found in India are about the size of a Pigeon and entirely aquatic by habit. The Bronze-winged Jacana is of a blackish colour with bronzed back and wings and a stumpy chestunt tail. It is a noisy bird specially when a number of them are together and tripping about lightly on their extraordinarily long toes on lotus leaves and floating vegetation in a tank and they give an impression of having an irritable temper. A flight of them as they move from one part of a tank to another reminds one of a flock of Blue Rock-Pigeons despite a pronounced difference in their mode of flying. It is the जल-कपोत, जल-पारावत or कोपी of the lexicons :

जलपारावतः कोपी प्रोक्तो जलकपोतकः——धन्वन्तरि, राजनिघंटु.

Sanskrit कोपी (अवश्यं कुप्यति—शब्दकल्प०) is the same as कोपङ्का of डल्हणाचार्य incorrectly equated by him with कोयष्टि[1] of सुश्रुत (Jeevanand's Cal. edn.; N. Sagar edn. reads कोयङ्का and कोयङ्ग which are incorrect). These names are after the bird's supposed bad temper and correspond to its Prakrit names[2] like कोभंगक, कोहंगक, or कोभक. पारेवत or पारेपत as a water-bird in वेस्संतर-जातक, verse 2107, is the same as जल-पारावत in Sanskrit. I have not met with this bird in literature. Its Bengali name जल-पीपी may be a corruption from जल-कोपी.

2. The Pheasant-tailed Jacana, on the other hand, is a decidedly beautiful bird with a striking plumage of white, gold and brown with a distinctive, long, pointed sickleshaped tail which is often held well above the water in a beautiful curve. The nesting and other habits of this are similar to those of its cousin but in all its actions it is more elegant and has earned the poetical name of "The Little white water-Princess" in English (S. Baker). It has a piping note which is rather pleasant and musical though it has also a mewing call (hence its names पीहो and मीवा in Hindi). It is the जल-शिखण्डिन (शिखण्ड a tail) the long-tailed water-bird or Water-Peacock; cf. the Peacock-Snipe for the Painted Snipe (Art. 61) in Telugu after the ring of white feathers round its eyes, a character shared with the Peacock—शुक्लापाङ्ग, (Art. 55) of याज्ञवल्क्यस्मृति, प्रायश्चित्ताध्याय, 272, where both the ground and the water-Peacocks are prohibited as food :

1. Articles 71 & 82.
2. ओववाइय सुत्तं, 4; अभिधानराजेन्द्र; कोहङ्गक = क्रोधाङ्गक (अर्धमागधी कोश)

हंसश्येनकपिक्रव्याज्जलस्थलशिखण्डिनः ।

Commentator विज्ञानेश्वर offers a rather curious explanation of the compound जलस्थलशिखण्डिनः which runs as under :

"जलशब्देन जलचरा बकादयो गृह्यन्ते । स्थलशब्देन स्थलचरा बलाकादयः (v.l. बकादयः) । शिखण्डी मयूरः ।"

He thus renders the word जल as 'water-birds like Storks and Herons', and स्थल as 'land-birds like Egrets', and separates शिखण्डिनः, Peacocks, from both. In the first place Storks, Herons and Egrets are all water-birds in an equal degree and cannot be separated as proposed, and secondly there is no warrant to interpret the simple terms like जल and स्थल to mean water and ground birds. It is submitted that the correct way is to split the compound as जल-शिखण्डिन् and स्थल-शिखण्डिन् as noted above. The Pheasant-tailed Jacana goes by the name of जल-मंजोर (? जल-मंजुर) in Hindi whose मंजुर should mean the Peacock (vide *F.B.I.*). The forms मजुर or मुजुर for मयूर occur in Nepal according to Turner's Nepali Dictionay. जलमंजुर is thus the same as जलमयूर or जल-शिखण्डिन्.

3. The Pheasants as a group are comprised within the expression जीवज्जीवक जाति (Art. 55) and most of them are characterised by long tails; and corresponding to the name 'Water-Peacock' we have the name 'Water-Pheasant' as well, viz. जीवज्जीवक[1] 'a water-bird' in सुश्रुत and at p. 198 in पालकाप्य. Again, जीवज्जीवक in the following examples, descriptions of lake-scenary, can only be the Pheasant-tailed Jacana :—

जीवज्जीवलसज्जीवं क्वणत्कारंडवोत्कटम् । —स्कन्दपुराण, काशीखंड, 32.101.
एक एव प्रियाहीनो रामोऽस्मि कुसुमागमे ।
इतीव जीवज्जीवोऽयं विरौति दयितासखः ॥ —रामायण मञ्जरी, 3.1149.
उत्फुल्लविविधविकसिताम्बुजजातिजीवितजीवज्जीवकम् ।
—नलचम्पू, 5, above verse 57.

अभिधानचिन्तामणि, on the other hand, has mixed up this जीवज्जीव with the चकोर in the following equation :

जीवञ्जीवस्तु गुन्द्रालो विषदर्शनमृत्युकः ।

Here the first part describes जीवज्जीव as गुन्द्राल i.e. as a bird that constructs a nest with the गुन्द्रा veriety of watergrass whereas the चकोर, which lays it eggs in a hollow in the bare ground, only sometimes lines it with dry leaves and grass but never with the गुन्द्रा grass. Both the Jacanas on the contrary make a nest of rushes and water-grass and place it on floating vegetation. गुन्द्राल जीवज्जीव is therefore the same as जलशिखण्डिन् and not the चकोर which is supposed to die at the sight of poison (विषदर्शनमृत्युकः; Art. 55-c).

---

1. जीवज्जीवः appears to be a homonym; (i) जीवान् शावकान् जीवयति जीवज्जीवः, the Peacock Pheasant; and (ii) जीवनं जलं जीवो जीविका यस्य जीवज्जीवः, the Pheasant-tailed Jacana.

4. The देशीनाममाला of Hemacandra has कामिजुल for a particular water-bird with कायंधुअ and कायंचुल as synonyms. These are difficult to solve or resolve but if कायंधुअ can be analyzed as कायं देहं धुअ धुन्वइ धुनोति i.e. an unsteady or agitated bird, the name may refer to the Bronze-winged Jacana. Similarly कायंचुल may be explained as कायं देहं चुलु चुलुइ (चुलु-चुलु--स्पन्दने--पा.स.म.). कामिजुल on the other hand may be closer to जलमंजुर and would then refer to the other Jacana. In this sense the letter का would stand for Sanskrit कं-जलं like the का in Prakrit काहारो, 'a water carrier'. If so the synonyms also would belong to the Pheasant-tailed Jacana with perhaps a different analysis. It is also worth noting that the second line in the following illustrative verse in देशीनाममाला, 2. 29 is comparable with the verse from रामायणमञ्जरी quoted above :

> कालिंजणि सामल घणत्थेवे रुअन्ति विरहिजणा ।
> रे कायंधुअ कायंचुलीयइ सहिओ सि कूजसु तुमंता ॥

Trans.: People separated from their beloved do cry out of sorrow when a cloud dark like the Tamāla tree begins to rain, but how strange O कायंधुअ ! that thou shouldst cry even when thy mate is with thee.

It is quite possible, however, that कायंधुअ of the verse is the noisy Browny winged Jacana with a predominantly black body and therefore supposed to be in sympathy with a dark rain cloud.

1
2
3
4
5
6
7
8
9
10
JPIrani
0 10 20 30 40 50 cm

PLATE VIII

1. Demoiselle Crane
2. The Black-necked Crane
3. The Hooded Crane
4. The Great White or Siberian Crane
5. The Eastern Common Crane
6. Macqueen's Bustard (or Houbara)
7. The Little Bustard
8. The Lesser Florican
9. The Great Indian Bustard
10. The Bengal Florican

PLATE IX

1. Rosy Pelican
2. White Stork
3. Black Stork
4. Flamingo
5. Lesser Flamingo
6. Bearded Vulture
7. Himalayan Griffon
8. Scavenger Vulture
9. Common Peafowl

PLATE X

1. Red-tailed Tropic Bird
2. Great White-Bellied Heron
3. Indian Reef Heron
4. Bittern
5. Giant Heron
6. Black Ibis
7. Glossy Ibis
8. Spoonbill
9. Yellow Bittern
10. Little Bittern

1 ♂
2 ♂ ♀
3 ♂
♀
4 ♂ ♀
5 ♂ ♀
6
7 ♂ ♀
8 ♂
♀
9 ♂ ♀
10 ♂
0 10 20 cm
0 4 8 in
John H. Dick

1
2
3
4
5
6
7
8
9
10
John H. Dick
0 10 20 30
cm

61

THE PAINTED SNIPE

The Painted Snipe is not a Snipe at all but an aberrant type of Sandpiper and as it cannot be fitted in with any well defined group of birds it has been separated as a family by itself. It is one of those few forms in which the female is the larger, brighter coloured of the sexes and the dominating partner in sexual matters. The females fight for the males and challenge one another with a loud note. After a male has been secured and eggs have been laid the female entrusts the duties of brooding the clutch and rearing the young to her partner and so soon as she is ready to lay again she seeks another partner in the usual manner, and so on. From her larger size, handsome colouration and the ways just referred to she is often mistaken for the male of the species. These birds inhabit rushy, reedy swamps or margins of tanks and lakes up to about 5,000 ft. in the Himalayas and at suitable places in the plains. Being birds of crepuscular habits they possess, like the Snipe, very large eyes which, unlike the Snipe, however, are placed in a forward position.

The female is olive-brown and bright olive-green, closely barred with black above: rich chestnut on the upper breast which is separated from the white belly by a blackish-brown pectoral band. A white ring surrounds the large eye and is prolonged into a streak behind it. The male has a duller plumage, a drab or brown breast and a white belly. The ring round the eye is buff. The wind-pipe of the female is longer than that of the male, and curves into a full loop, and it thus provides her with a powerful voice apparatus, for it is she who does all the calling with a deep mellow note. Frank Finn's remarks about the eyes of the bird, quoted by S. Baker in *Game Birds of India, Burma and Ceylon*, Vol. II, 132, are very interesting : "Like Owls, also, this bird has a singularly expressive countenance. ... On the rare occasions, however when one sees the bird walking about at ease, the feathers over the eyes are raised so as to be higher than the crown, which gives quite a wide awake expression. In moving about thus, the head is carried high, and the bird looks tall and graceful." No wonder it is called the 'Peacock Snipe' in South India because of the beautiful plumage of the female and particularly the white ring round her eyes and its extension (cf. शुक्लापाङ्ग; a Peacock).

कोनालक as a water-side bird included in the list of प्लवा: in सुश्रुत is explained by डल्हणाचार्य as "श्यामपृष्ठ श्वेतोदरः—पानीयवर्तिका इति लोके", and the कल्पद्रुकोश also defines the कोनील (?कोनाल) as a kind of 'water-quail' or Snipe :

"श्वेतोदरः श्यामपृष्ठः कोनीलो जलवर्तिका"

i.e. the water-quail known as कोनील is dark above and white on the abdomen. This agrees fully with the description of डल्हणाचार्य and there is reason to hold that the original कोनाल has been deliberately or mistakenly changed into कोनील by the scribe to make the name correspond in sense with the descriptive epithet श्यामपृष्ठ. M. Williams gives the forms कुनाल, कुणाल, कोनालि, कोनील, and कोनालक as names of waterbirds. Evidently names of more than one bird and some wrong spelling are involved here.

The Painted Snipe is known as ओहरीचाहा (चाहा a Snipe) in Nepal, from Sans. अवरोहण, Prak. ओहरण 'to descend' in reference to the bird's descent from higher to lower levels in winter (in Nepal), or from Prak. ओहीरिअं उद्गीतम् after its mellow call-notes. It is कोनेबट्टा (कोनाल-कुनाल-वर्तक) in the Singbhoom district and पानलवा (जलवर्तिका) in South India. Taking these with the definition in कल्पद्रु it appears that कोनील (कुनाल) is the Painted Snipe, कोणालक is the Water-Cock (Art. 58) and possibly also the Black crested Kalij pheasant (Art 55 B).

कुनाल as an auspicious bird of ललितविस्तर[1] and कुणाल of the कुणालजातक (536) are most probably this bird. The beautiful story of the birth of Aśoka's son कुणाल is given in दिव्यावदान[2] where the new-born child is named कुणाल because his eyes were as bright and beautiful as the कुणाल bird's. That it is a water-bird is clear from the following verse :—

"हिमेन्द्रराजे गिरिशैलशृंगे प्रवालपुष्पप्रसवे जलाढ्ये ।
कुनाल नाम्नेति निवासपक्षी नेत्राणि तेनास्य समान्यमूनि ।।"
Page 406

The कुणालजातक mentions also a lake कुणालदह, in the Himalayas, apparently so named, as its shores abounded in these birds. In the ललितविस्तर[3] the sweet voice of the Lord Buddha is compared with that of the कुनाल bird whose deep mellow note fully justifies the comparison.

The name कुनाल appears to be analogous to सुनाल for the Red Munia, both being derived from the bad or coarser and good or finer reeds or grasses (कु-bad, नाल-reed or grass, and सु–नाल) in which they live and breed. It is also possible, on the other hand, to derive the word from कुण् शब्दे, referring to the soft "kone-kone-kone" notes of the Painted Snipe (Tickell).

---

1. Chapter 5,44; 13,186 and 21,377.
2. Pp. 405 et seq.
3. Ch. 19.357.

62

CRANES

1. The Cranes are among the largest wading birds with long bills, necks, and legs, large broad wings and short tails. They fly with the neck and legs straight out like the Storks and since they bear a superficial resemblance to them members of both the groups are often confounded one with the other. They may, however, be readily distinguished from the Storks by their graceful form, thin and smaller bills and the fact that the hind toe is rudimentary and does not touch the ground. Unlike the Storks, therefore, they are unable to perch on the trees. Another radical difference between a Crane and a Stork consists in their breeding habits and the nature of the young. Indian Storks always nest on trees and the Indian Crane, the Sarus, whose habits have been well known in India, nests on ground or in shallow water. The young of a Stork are helpless and must remain in the nest until they are well able to fly, whereas the young of the Crane are active from the start like young chickens, and follow their parents. A majority of cranes have fine trumpeting calls while the Storks, having no voice clatter their bills during courtship or when excited. The former are mostly vegetarian while the latter feed on fish, frogs, reptiles and insects. No Stork or Heron ((बक) is mentioned as a pet-bird in literature but the Common Crane and Sarus have ever been favoured as pets. It is necessary to stress these differences as the term क्रौञ्च for a Crane has often been rendered as बक-विशेष (a kind of Stork or Heron) in commentaries and lexicons.[1]

2. Of the seven species of Crane described in the *Fauna of British India* by Stuart Baker only three are regular winter visitors to India and one, the Sarus, is a permanent resident over the greater part of the country.

---

1. कुङ्‍ क्रौञ्चः—कोंच बक इति भाषा,—शब्दकल्पद्रुम.
क्रुञ्चः—बकविशेषः, Ibid. बकभेदः—वाचस्पत्यम्.
क्रौञ्चा—कोंच बकी इति भाषा.—शब्दकल्पद्रुम.
क्रौञ्च—कोंच बक;– कुररपक्षी,—शब्दकल्पद्रुम.

None of the older lexicons connects the क्रौञ्च with the बक and it is only from a very superficial likeness between a crane and a stork that commentators and compilers of present-day lexicons have fallen into the error. Explanations like the above should therefore be understood to mean 'a bird resembling a stork or heron'.

Amongst the visitors the commonest and the most numerous are the Common and the Demoiselle Cranes. They are powerful fliers and form into huge flocks before moving from their breeding grounds in Central Europe and Central and Northern Asia and again on their return journey from India. They arrive in India in September-October and leave by March-April. "The observer who is favourably situated will hear one morning a loud clanging call (of the common crane) and looking towards the sound will see in the distant sky a vast tangled skein of birds. As it approaches it resolves itself into an immense concourse of Cranes flying at a tremendous height. The stream of birds travels across the sky like an army. ... As they go a single bird trumpets, answered by others" (Whistler). The flight is generally in the form of open V-formation which was the model for the क्रौञ्चव्यूह of ancient Indian military science.[1] They walk in a stately manner and "are lively and cheerful to a degree, devoted to their mates, and addicted to social amusements and athletic exercises, in the way of dancing and running and playing with sticks when on the ground. ... They display much affection for the young. and are easily tamed, often becoming very affectionate" (F. Finn). The great white or Siberian crane arrives in much smaller numbers and is fairly common in N. W. India and is found as far east as Bihar. The Hooded crane from Japan and Eastern Siberia is a rare visitor to Assam. The Black necked crane is canfined to the Himalayas (Ladakh, Tibet etc.) while the Burmese Sarus is found in Eastern Assam.

3. The following information (A) and lexical synonymies (B) bearing upon their Sanskrit nomenclature may be considered before setting out a brief description of the different species and allocating the appropriate name or names to each :

A. क्रौञ्च, पुष्कराह्व, and सारस for three different species of Crane, and मृणालकण्ठ for the flamingo, are included in the list of प्लवाः or water birds in चरकसंहिता.

क्रौञ्च, पुष्कर, कुरर and सारस, as above, in पराशरस्मृति quoted by भट्टोत्पल in his commentary on बृहत्संहिता, 85.28.

क्रौञ्च, महाक्रौञ्च, कुरर and सारस as above, listed with other water-birds by पालकाप्य in ch. 13, p. 198 where मृणालग्रीवक refers to the flamingo.

B (i) "क्रुङ् क्रौञ्चः"—अमर, वैजयन्ती, अभि. चिन्तामणि

(ii) (a) "कुररः खरशब्दः क्रुङ् क्रौञ्चः पंक्तिचरः खरः । —राजनिघण्टु

---

1. क्रौञ्चानां खेगतिर्यादृक् पंक्तितः सम्प्रजायते ।
तादृक् सञ्चारयेत् क्रौञ्चव्यूहं देशबलं यथा ॥

शुक्रनीतिसार, 4.7.279.

Eagles never fly in formation and श्येनव्यूह is the arrangement of an army in the shape of an Eagle on the wing.

(b) "अथाऽपस्वरः क्रौञ्चः क्रुङ स्यात्पंक्तिचरः पुनः ।
शरत्पक्षी वक्रचञ्चू रक्तको रात्रिजागरः ।
शेवलादः पुण्डरीकनयनः ।" —कल्पद्रुकोश

(c) "क्रौञ्चः शरद्विहङ्गे कुररपक्षिणि"—शब्दार्थचिन्तामणि

(iii) (a) "कर्करेटुः करेटुः स्यात्"—अमर.

(b) "कर्करेटुः करेटुः स्यात् करटुः कर्कराटुकः"—अभि. चिन्तामणि

(iv) (a) "पुष्कराह्वस्तु सारसः"—अमर.

(b) "सारसस्तु लक्ष्मणः स्यात् पुष्काराख्यः कुरङ्कुरः ।
सारसे दीर्घजानुकः गोनर्दो मैथुनी कामी श्येनाख्यो रक्तमस्तकः ।"
—अभि. चिन्तामणि

(c) "सारसस्तु कलाङ्कुरः[1] गोनर्दः" —त्रिकाण्डशेष

(d) "कुरङ्कुरः पुष्कराह्वः" —हारावली

(e) "अथ लक्ष्मणसारसौ लक्ष्मणो रसिकः कामी
काकुवाक् कामिवल्लभः । नीलकण्ठः पुष्कराह्वो ।"—कल्पद्रुम

(f) "सारसो रसिकः कामी नीलाङ्गो भणितारवः" (मणितारकः[2]—M.W.)
"नीलकण्ठो रक्तनेत्रः काकुवाक् कामिवल्लभः ॥" —राजनिघण्टु

(g) "सारसः सुस्वरश्चैव नीलाङ्गश्चित्रकन्धरः ।
रक्ततुण्डो रक्तनेत्रो रक्तपादोऽस्रवल्लभः ॥"[3] —धन्वन्तरि

4. The information brought together in section A of the last paragraph shows that at least four different varieties of Crane have been recognized in literature, viz., क्रौञ्च, पुष्कराह्व, (v.l. पुष्कर, पुष्कराख्य), सारस, and कुरर. These are actually the best known members of the family since the others are of rare occurrence and have not been known to visit India during recent times. The attention of classical poets and dramatists has been chiefly confined to two of the commonest, the Common Crane and

---

1. कलानां कामकलानां अङ्कुरो उद्भवो यत्र—कलाङ्कुरः, as the Sarus Couple is known to indulge in love-dance and sport as a preliminary to consummation. This is at the bottom of other poetic epithets like कामी, कामिवल्लभ, काकुवाक् and रसिक for the सारस alone as the breeding crane of India.

2. Compare मणिबीज for the pomegranate fruit with red seeds. मणितारक (having red-eyes, रक्तनेत्र) for the Sarus is out of place in Verse 120 at p. 331 of कल्पद्रुकोश where the text has suffered mutilation as at other places.

3. In this synonymy the epithets सुस्वर, चित्रकन्धर (having a painted or beautiful neck), रक्तनेत्र and रक्तपाद hold true of the Sarus Crane while रक्ततुण्ड, रक्तपाद and अस्रवल्लभ (blood i.e. flesh-loving) would seem to refer to the beautiful white stork which looks like a Small White Crane and feeds on frogs, mice, lizards, etc. It has evidently been regarded as a kind of Sarus and included here. No Crane has a red bill. The legs of the Sarus and the Great White Crane are merely of a pink colour and it is doubtful how far they can be described as रक्तपाद whereas the white stork has a blood-red bill and red legs and feet, the eyes brown. For Storks see Art. 81.

the Sarus while the harsh-voiced Demoiselle is mentioned only occasionally either as कुरर or simply as सारस.* During the later Vedic period when the Brāhmaṇas and the Saṃhitās like the तैत्तिरीय, वाजसनेयी, etc. were compiled the Flamingo (Art. 83) and the Common Crane, both very common in the North-West and further East, were the first to be named क्रुङ or क्रुञ्च and क्रौञ्च respectively. It is quite probable that the resident Indian Crane, with a trumpeting call similar to that of the Common Crane, was also included within the term क्रौञ्च. Later on it came to be distinguished from the Common Crane principally because of its red head and larger size and name लक्ष्मण-सारस. The lexicographers, as seen from the synonymies collected in section B, have since maintained the distinction between the Common Crane as क्रौञ्च and the Indian Crane as सारस or लक्ष्मण and treated the other species of Crane simply as varieties of the Sarus. The next step was probably to separate the Demoiselle as कुरर, नीलाङ्ग सारस, and ककेंरुटु, the Great White Crane as पुष्कर–, or श्येन-सारस, and the Black-necked species as नीलकण्ठ-सारस as we shall presently see. That is how we find क्रुङ and क्रौञ्च put together and all the rest either defined as सारस or put under that name in mixed synonymies like those in B (f), (g), and (h). At the same time a vague consciousness that they were all allied forms, i.e. were merely varieties of क्रौञ्च was also present and we have a name like खर-क्रौञ्च for the Demoiselle with a harsh note quite unlike that of the trumpeting Cranes, and the Sarus proper described under the name of क्रौञ्च in the second introductory chapter of the रामायण. The Buddhist work दिव्यावदान (circa 300 A.C.) has a verbal form क्रोञ्चति from root क्रोञ्च् for 'trumpeting of an elephant (M.W., Appendix) which makes it highly probable that the term क्रौञ्च was applied principally to such Cranes as have a trumpeting call note.

5. The first equation with क्रुङ and क्रौञ्च** as synonymous terms, though slightly incorrect, may be taken to imply that they refer to two birds possessing some features in common. The name क्रुङ-क्रुञ्च (क्रुञ्च-कौटिल्याल्पीभावयोः, to be crooked or to shorten) stands for a bird capable of curving or contracting some important part of its body, e.g. a long and flexible neck, and क्रौञ्च (क्रुञ्चेव आकृतिरस्य) for one resembling the क्रुञ्च. Allied to root क्रुङ-क्रुञ्च् is the root कुच् which means 'to curve or bend' and also 'to sound'. Root क्रुश्, again may have contaminated the root क्रुञ्च् and the idea of 'making a sound' is perhaps involved in or associated with the word क्रौञ्च. During the later संहिता and ब्राह्मण period क्रुङ and क्रुञ्च meant Flamingo, and कौञ्च the

* Illustrative passages from literature are quoted later on.

**The rendering of क्रुञ्च and क्रौञ्च as "the curlaw on snipe" in the *Vedic Index of Names and Subjects* is pure guesswork and wholly incorrect. For Curlaw and Snipe see Art. 72.

Similarly the entry—'an osprey' against क्रौञ्च on the authority of some lexicon in M.W. is incorrect and is due to a misunderstanding of the name कुरर which means both a crane (the अपस्वर क्रौञ्च) as well as the fishing Eagles including the Osprey (Arts. 50 and 52).

Common Crane, the former having a very long and flexible neck and the latter a long neck and a powerful voice:

(i) अद्भ्यः क्षीरं व्यपिबत् क्रुङङाङ्गिरसो धिया। वा. सं. 19.73

(ii) इन्द्राग्निभ्यां क्रुञ्चान्। Ibid. 24.22; मैत्रा. सं. 3.14.3

(iii) क्रुञ्चौ श्रोणिभ्याम्। Ibid. 25.6

(iv) क्रौञ्चं बृहस्पते : (सामन्)। छान्दोग्योपनिषद्. 2.22

(v) वाग्वै क्रौञ्चम्। ताण्ड्यब्राह्मण, 11.10.19

(vi) उच्चैः क्रौञ्चमिव वषट् कुर्यात्स्वर्गकामस्य। हिरण्यकेशी श्रौतसूत्र,21.2.44

In the first three of the above passages क्रुङ and क्रुञ्च refer to the Flamingo as a long necked bird having the power of separating क्षीर from अपस् (Art. 83). The others refer to the Common Crane with a loud and sonorous trumpeting call which is the relevant element in each case. According to the commentary on Aphorism, 11 of the आपस्तम्बगृह्यसूत्र the सामिधेनी hymns have to be recited in a tone lying between the उपांशु (low) and the क्रुष्ट (high) defined as तार or क्रौञ्च which would seem to connect the bird and its name क्रौञ्च with the क्रुष्ट (क्रुश् to cry) or high note.

6. The synonymies in B (ii) describe the क्रौञ्च birds as 'birds of the autumn' (शरद्विहङ्ग) and 'flying in formation' (पंक्तिचर), while कुरर is a क्रौञ्च with a 'harsh voice' (खरशब्द, अपस्वर).). The epithets वक्रचञ्चु (curved or bent bill), रक्तक (having red in the plumage), शेवलाद (living on minute water plants) and पुण्डरीकनयन (lotus-eyed) belong to the Flamingo, regarded as a kind of क्रौञ्च. The equations in B (iii) exclusively refer to the खर क्रौञ्च,* the Demoiselle Crane, as कर्करेटु corresponding to its Hindi name, करकटिया, both after its call, 'kurr-kurr-kurr' (कर्कं कर्कशब्दं रेटते भाषते—शब्दकल्प.). The series in B (iv) contains a mixed list of names and adnouns apparently for the Sarus alone but including the Great White Crane (पुष्कराह्वव, श्येनाख्य), the Black-necked (नीलकण्ठ) and even the White Stork (रक्ततुण्ड) regarded as a सारस allied to the Great White Crane (Art. 81). All these will be dealt with more fully when we take up the individual species for consideration. Returning to the term क्रौञ्च which is also specific for the Common Crane it is to be noted that in later literature it has been utilized as a base for coining the names of some Storks, Herons and also the Flamingo, all sharing the common feature of a long and flexible neck with a क्रौञ्च or Crane; and which have happily been described as क्रौञ्चनिभा (resembling the क्रौञ्च in general outline) by वसन्तराज at 4.48 of his book. We thus have नील क्रौञ्च for the Purple Heron; नक्त क्रौञ्च for the Bitterns and Night-Herons (Art.82); दर्वि कौञ्च for the Spoon-bill (Art.79); कालिक क्रौञ्च for the Black Stork; and अरुण क्रौञ्च for the Flamingo (Art.83), and finally the Open-bill Stork has been mentioned simply as a क्रौञ्च in the following:—

*Marathi करकोंचा is directly from Sansk. खरक्रौंच for this Crane.

"क्रौञ्चश्चञ्चुपुटेन कुञ्चितवपुः शम्बूकमन्वेषते ।"
सुभाषित, Page 14

The phrase कुञ्चितवपु describing the attitude of the bird in action is worth noting, for it strengthens the derivation of कुञ्चand क्रौञ्च from क्रुञ्च to 'curve or bend'. Similarly the term सारस means (i) a water-bird in general, e.g., in "अम्बुसारस"—कथासरित्सागर, 70.59 and क्षुद्रसारसाः of कल्पद्रुकोश, p. 331 and राजनिघण्टु, p. 471; (ii) any Crane and specifically the Indian Sarus according to the rule "सामान्योऽपि विशेषे वर्तते";* (iii) a Goose in बृहत्कथामञ्जरी, 9.1,145; 359 and in शिशुपालवध, 12.44 (cf. also 'चक्राङ्गसारसौ हंसे, from the शब्दार्णव quoted by वल्लभदेव in his commentary on the latter). That the Indian Crane, though popularly named as सारस, was known to be a kind of क्रौञ्च is clear from the story of sage वाल्मीकि, cursing, out of righteous indignation, the fowler who killed the male of a pair of क्रौञ्च birds engaged in love on the sands of the तमसा :

तस्याभ्याशे तु मिथुनं चरन्तमनपायिनम् ।
ददर्श भगवांस्तत्र क्रौञ्चयोश्चारुनिस्वनम् ॥
तं शोणितपरीताङ्गं चेष्टमानं महीतले ।
भार्या तु निहतं दृष्ट्वा रुराव करुणां गिरम् ।
वियुक्ता पतिना तेन द्विजेन सहचारिणा ।
ताम्रशीर्षेण** मत्तेन पत्रिणा सहितेन वै ॥
रामायण, 1.2.9-12

The poet's description of the birds possessing a beautiful voice and a red head leaves no doubt as to their identity with the Indian Sarus which, it may be pointed out, is the only resident and breeding क्रौञ्च of India. Despite the extended use of the terms क्रौञ्च and सारस, and the mixed synonymies noticed above, it is, however, possible to determine the names and epithets appropriate to the different species of Crane found in India with a very fair degree of approximation and an attempt is made in this direction in the following paragraphs.

7. The Eastern Common Crane (45″) is a medium sized Crane of a light to rather dark grey colour with long neck and legs. The bald crown is black in front and red behind, the bill dull green and the legs black. The eyes are red, brown or even yellow (F. Finn). The tertiary plumes of the wing are particularly well developed, long and loose textured which this Crane, more than others, has the power of raising and showing off though all Cranes do so to a more or less degree. Elegant in form and

---

*This rule applies equally to the specific name of क्रौञ्च for the Common Crane as against the general meaning of the term—'any Crane'.

**राम, the author of the तिलकव्याख्या on रामायण (Bombay edition) had apparently no clear idea of the क्रौञ्च for he explains it as a bird having a red crest like the Common Cock—कुक्कुटादिवत्ताम्रवर्णशीर्षगतचूडायुक्तेन which is incorrect. No Indian Crane has a crest.

carriage, it is "the Crane par excellence', occurring in flocks, often of large size, throughout North India and south to Deccan in the cold weather. It is very destructive to the crops. Like the Sarus it has a very fine trumpeting call, uttered both on the ground and in flight. It is known as कुरुंच (fr. क्रौञ्च) and कुलंग* in Hindi and being the commonest Crane of North India is the क्रौञ्च proper of Sanskrit literature. In the following examples the wailing cries of hundreds of women have been compared with the trumpeting calls coming from large flocks of the Common Crane, but due to the nature of the simile and poetic necessity the birds have been mentioned in the feminine gender (क्रौञ्ची) :

> जज्ञेऽथ तासां संनादः क्रौञ्चीनामिव स्वनः । रामायण, 2.39.40
> क्रौञ्चीनामिव नारीणां निनादस्तत्र शुश्रुवे ।
> आर्तानां करुणं काले क्रोशंतीनां सहस्रशः ॥ Ibid. 2.76.21

According to मनुस्मृति, 12.64 a person stealing cotton-fabrics is condemned to be reborn as a क्रौञ्च (कार्पासतान्तवं क्रौञ्चो), the reason for which would seem to lie in the long disintegrated tertiary plumes drooping gracefully over the short tail of the bird. The grey colour of hand-spun and hand-woven cotton fabrics is an additional reason for selecting the Common Crane with a grey plumage. In the alternative कार्पासतान्तव may mean a long warp prepared with yarn ready to be placed on the loom for weaving. This would seem to agree with "रज्जु-क्रौञ्चम्" of ताण्ड्य ब्रा० 13.9.17 based upon the flight of Cranes in long skeins. The Demoiselle and the Common Cranes both appear to travel together (Whistler) and this is borne out by the following passage relating to their return journey from India:—

> जलाप्लुतानीक्ष्य महानदीनां
> सुगात्रि ! हंसाः पुलिनानि हृष्टाः ।
> गताः श्रमं मानसवासलुब्धाः
> स सारसाः क्रौञ्चगुणानुविद्धाः ॥—हरिवंश, 2.95.13

The 'सारसाः' are the नीलाङ्गसारसाः, the Demoiselles flying in mixed formations with the Common Cranes. The phrase क्रौञ्चगुण is worth noting in connection with both "रज्जुः क्रौञ्चम्" and कार्पासतान्तवम्.

8. The Sarus or Indian Crane (58") is a huge french-grey bird with the bare head and upper neck of a red colour, becoming bright scarlet

*The story of the कुलिङ्गमिथुन related in भागवत, 7.2.50-56 is clearly based upon that of the क्रौञ्चमिथुन in the रामायण. There it is the female (कुलिङ्गी) which is trapped by a fowler and the male cries and bewails his own and his young ones' lot. In the mean time he too is killed with an arrow by the fowler. The Common Crane is known as "Kulanga" (Kulangi in *F.B.I.*) or perhaps as 'Kulinga' in Telugu and the author would seem to have used the Telugu name for purposes of the story though the word क्रौञ्च is also used in the भागवत. The use of the Telugu name of the Common Crane probably goes to show that the author was a South-Indian. The great Sanskritist, C. V. Vaidya, also held a similar opinion which is recorded by Winternitz in his History of Indian Literature, Vol.1, p. 556, f.n. 3, Calcutta, 1927.

during the breeding season. The legs are pink, the eyes red, and the bill of a greenish colour. The Sarus is "always to be found in pairs usually accompanied by the last hatched young" and hence the Sanskrit name or adnoun मिथुनिन् or मैथुनी for it. "They are most affectionate birds, pairing for life, and if one is killed the grief of the other is quite distressing" (S. Baker). Salim Ali, an authority on Indian bird-life and a keen observer, remarks that the devotion of a pair of Sarus to each other has earned them a degree of popular sentiment amounting to sanctity, and if one of a pair is killed the survivor haunts the scene of outrage for weeks calling distractedly, and has been known to pine away to death. Emperor Jehangir also relates in his Memoirs a most pathetic and touching example of a Sarus sitting continuously and without food upon the bones of its mate so much so that when the dying bird was lifted up its breast was found to have been eaten into by worms and maggots. It was such knowledge o the Sarus that made वाल्मीकि lose his temper with the fowler who killed one of a pair of them. The reason why the exemplary conjugal devotion of the Sarus has not received poetical recognition in Sanskrit literature, excepting the Rāmāyaṇa, is to be found in the fact that the similarly devoted चक्रवाक couples (the Ruddy Sheldrake or Brahminy Duck, Art. 84 C) would seem to have gripped the imagination of the Indo-Aryans from the Vedic times as both the Ṛgveda and the Atharva-Veda mention them in couples. It is therefore more than probable that the Indo-Aryans were already familiar with them before they got to know the Sarus whose habitat does not extend beyond the Indus.*

9. The Sarus Cranes are essentially birds of well watered open plains and avoid hills, forest country and desert lands. Their flight is powerful but they rise slowly and seldom fly at any great height from the ground (Salim Ali). Like all Cranes they indulge in dancing. more so in the breeding season than at other times, which is much less graceful than their dignified quiet walk (S. Baker). The call is a fine trumpet uttered mornings and evenings, and if the pair happen to feed apart during the night they keep in touch by constantly calling to each other as the चक्रवाक couples also do. They are much less gregarious than other Cranes and move from their favourite grounds in small flocks only if forced by drought or other cause and at such times they adopt the usual V-shaped flight.

10. Lexical adnouns for the Sarus are लक्ष्मण**, रक्तमस्तक, मिथुनिन्, मणितारक, etc. These are self-explanatory but the name गोनर्द for the male and गोनन्दी for the female Sarus call for a few remarks. गोनर्द as a bird-name is a homonym and belongs to (i) the Great Bustard who bellows like a bull (गोइव नर्दति-

*The Burmese Sarus is very similar to the Indian but is of a darker colour. Being more of a forest-bird it flics much higher and is far moe shy than our Sarus. It occurs in Eastern Assam. The call, like that of his Indian cousin, is a beautiful trumpet—"a fine sound when it rings out in the early dawn of a clear Indian winter morning" (S. Baker). Its Assamese name is कुरसंग (कुरचंग—क्रौञ्च).

**लक्ष्मणं, one possessing a distinctive mark (लक्ष्म), e.g. a red or white head contrasting with the body colour; also 'handsome or beautiful'—लक्ष्मण: श्री: शोभायुते as in अभि. चिन्तामणि.

Art. 63), and (ii) the Bittern with a booming call in reed beds by the water-side (गवि जले नर्दति-Art. 82). In the latter sense the name may well be applied to the Sarus as well but as the lexicons have no feminine form of गोनर्द and give गोनन्दी* instead for the female there is good reason to believe that the proper name or adnoun for the Sarus is गोनन्द and not गोनर्द. Fortunately however the विष्णुधर्मोत्तर mentions this name:

"पुत्रप्रियांल्लोहपृष्ठान् गोनन्दगिरिवर्तकान्" —1.151.44

The confusion between गोनन्द and गोनर्द is probably on a par with पिचुमन्द and पिचुमर्द for the निम्ब tree (M. W.) and is due to a graphical error of copying from MSS in an older script. The correct names for the male and female Sarus should thus be गोनन्द and गोनन्दी in the sense that a couple perform their marital rites on the ground: गवि भूमौ जलाभ्याशे वा सुरतानन्दो यस्य.**

11. A few of the Sūtras of Āpastamba dealing with the question of particular birds permitted or not permitted as food are as below:

"कुक्कुटो विकिराणाम्"— 1.5.17.32
"प्लवः प्रतुदाम्" — ,, ,, ,, 33
"क्रव्यादः "— ,, ,, ,, 34
"हंसभासचक्रवाकसुपर्णाश्च"— ,, ,, ,, 35
"क्रुञ्चक्रौञ्चवाध्र्राणसलक्ष्मणवर्जम्" ,, ,, ,, 36

The last aphorism quoted above permits three categories of birds as food, viz., (a) the Flamingo, (b) the Common Crane, and (c) the Hornbill, but makes an exception in favour of लक्ष्मण, i.e. the Sarus Crane. Both Haradatta in his उज्वला-टीका and Dr. Bühler in his translation (S. B. E. Vol. 2, 64-65) have missed something in explaining this particular aphorism. वाध्र णिस being an unknown thing to both, they have treated it simply as an adjective of लक्ष्मण and translated the compoud literally as the "leather-nosed Lakshmana" thus creating a non-existent curiosity, 'a leather-nosed Sarus'. For वाध्र णिस as the Hornbill see Art. 42 and for क्रुञ्च, the Flamingo, Art. 83. As regards the correct interpretation of the सूत्र itself it will be noted that Sūtras Nos. 32 and 33 permit the whole of the विष्किर and प्रतुद classes of birds as food *subject to only one exception in each case*. Sūtras 34 and 35 are entirely prohibitory while No. 36, as suggested by Bühler and Hara-

* Lexicons do not give the masculine form of गोनन्दी.

**Substituted for 'गवि जले नन्दतीति' of शब्दकल्पद्रुम. It will be noticed that my explanation of the term is based on the quotation from the Rāmāyaṇa given in para. 5.

datta, each in his own way, permits some and prohibits one or more of the birds named in the list.* Reading Sūtra 36 with No. 34 Bühler is of opinion that the mainly vegetarian, and therefore not क्रव्याद, क्रुञ्च and क्रौञ्च are permitted and the वाघ्रिणस-लक्ष्मण (singular) is disallowed. On the other hand Haradatta holds that the latter alone is permitted and both क्रुञ्च and क्रौञ्च are disallowed. Now that we know that वाघ्रिणस too is a particular bird and that one was sacrificed to god विष्णु as a most favourite dish of his (Art 42), Bühler's interpretation is obviously the correct one and we have only to add the Hornbill to the Flamingo and the Common Crane to complete the list of three great birds permitted, leaving out the लक्ष्मण (सारस) as an exception. This finds support from a somewhat similarly worded Sūtra in another Smṛti which permits वाघ्रीणस with विष्किर birds like तित्तिर, मयूर, etc.:—

पक्षिणस्तित्तिरिकपोतकपिञ्जलवाध्रीणस-
मयूरवारणावारणवर्जाः पञ्च विष्किराः। बौधायनस्मृति, 1.5.154

Here, it will be noted, the first five out of the six विष्किर birds including the वाघ्रीणस (same as वाघ्रिणस) are permitted while the last, viz., the वारण (the Great Bustard, Art. 63) is not allowed. All Cranes are good eating and the reason for the exception in favour of लक्ष्मण, the Sarus, is to be found in the extraordinary devotion observed between the Sarus couple which has endeared them to the Indians from very ancient times.** It is also worth noting that poet वाल्मीकि includes क्रौञ्च and कुरर but not the Sarus in the list of water-birds recommended as food by कबन्ध to Rāma when the latter made a long halt at the Pampā lake (para. 15 below).

12. The Hooded Crane (35″) is of a dark grey colour with the neck and the whole head except the bald red crown, pure white in contrast with the rest of the body colour. The bill is yellowish horny, the eyes orange-brown, and the legs horny-black (Finn) though the colours of these parts are slightly different according to the *F.B.I.* Breeding in Eastern Siberia and Japan it migrates south to China and in smaller numbers to Eastern Assam within Indian limits. It is possible that in the

---

*The विष्णुसंहिता, chapter 51, disallows all five-toed animals and all birds except these expressly named — "शशकशल्लकगोधाखड्गकूर्मवर्ज्जं पञ्चनखमांसाशने सप्तरात्रमुपवसेत्। तित्तिरिकपिञ्जललावकवर्तिकामयूरवर्ज्जं पक्षि-मांसाशने चाहोरात्रम्।"

** The voice and sight of a Sarus couple are amongst the best of auguries :

इष्टार्थसिद्धिः सकलासु दिक्षु ससारसद्वंद्वविलोकनेन।
श्रुत्वास्य पृष्ठे निनदं न गच्छेत् सिध्यत्यभीष्टं गृह एव यस्मात्॥
वामेन योषिद्धनलाभकारी शब्दस्तथाग्रे नृपतोऽर्थलब्ध्यै।
पार्श्वद्वये सारसयुग्ममेकं कृतारवं जल्पति कन्यकाप्तिम्॥

वसंतराज, 8.9-10, p. 234.

The first and fourth quarters of the second verse furnish an additional clue to the significance of the adnoun कामिवल्लभ (beloved of the pleasure-seeker) for the Sarus. See f. n. 1, p. 311.

long past it travelled further west and was known to the ancient Indians, may be even as an aviary bird in Royal establishments. The लक्ष्मण सारस according to Haradatta on the आपस्तम्ब धर्मसूत्र, 1.5.17.36 quoted and discussed in para. 9 above, is of two kinds, one with a white head and the other with a red head:

"श्वेतो लोहितो वा येषां मूर्धा ते लक्ष्मणाः ।"

The श्वेतमूर्धन्, or श्वेतमस्तक–लक्ष्मण should therefere be the Hooded Crane and the लोहितमूर्धन्-or रक्तमस्तक–लक्ष्मण the Sarus i.e. the Indian Crane. The Hooded variety being a bird of rare occurrence the लक्ष्मण of the Sūtra in question, as already pointed out in para. 9, must be taken to be the well known Sarus.

13. The Black-necked Crane (about 46") is slightly larger than the Common Crane and is known to breed in Tibet and Kokonor, not very far from India, and Frank Finn says that it may be expected to visit India in winter (*How to Know the Indian Waders*, p. 67). The body plumage is greyish white and the whole of the head, neck and tail black. The bill is horny-grey or-green, iris yellow and the legs black. The bare skin of the crown is dull red. Like the Common Crane it has a trumpeting call. The breeding grounds of the Bar-head Goose also are the lakes of Ladakh and Tibet and if the ancients knew, as they certainly did, the home and habits of the Goose they must have known this Crane as well, and the नीलकण्ठ सारस of the mixed synonymy, B (iv) (f) quoted above from कल्पद्रु and धन्वन्तरि, should be this Black-necked Crane. It is mantioned with the Ruddy Sheldrake, the Bar-head Goose, the Pin-tail Duck, and other healthy and happy-looking water-birds ('प्रमत्तसारसैः') *as giving character to a Himalayan scene in the शिवपुराण under the name of नीलस्कन्ध क्रौञ्च **:

शोभितं चक्रवाकाद्यैः कादम्बैर्हंसशङ्कुभिः
प्रमत्तसारसैः क्रौञ्चैर्नीलस्कन्धैश्च शब्दितैः ॥

The second रुद्रसंहिता, सतीखण्ड, 22.59

This Crane is therefore the नीलकण्ठ सारस or नीलस्कन्ध क्रौञ्च.

14. The Great White Crane (54") comes next after the Sarus in size and is mentioned as the महाक्रौञ्च with the क्रौञ्च and सारस by पालकाप्य (Para. 3 A). It is pure white throughout except for the wing-quills which are black. The naked skin of the head is reddish, eye pale yellow, bill brown, and legs pink. Breeding in Siberia it visits North India in winter in small flocks. A large number of them was caught and taken to the Calcutta

---

*The Indians Saras is not a hill-bird and the compound प्रमत्तसारस must be translated as above.

**स्कन्ध also means 'the neck', "गलः स्कन्धे"—विश्वलोचनकोश. Compare . तुरङ्ग-स्कन्धकेशाः, सिंहस्कन्धकेशाः for the neck-mane.

market about the year 1916-17 (Finn). They feed more exclusively on water-plants than do other Cranes and do not attack crops. Closely associated as it is with weedy tanks and Jheels it has been regarded as a kind of सारस and its specific names, पुष्कर, पुष्कराख्य, श्येनाख्य ("श्येन: शुक्ले"—हेमचंद्र, hence 'श्येन-सारस'—'the White-Sarus'), and पुष्कराह्व (पुष्करे जले आकाशे वा ह्वयति*—'one heard calling near about water or in the sky') have been assimilated with those for the सारस in the lexicons. Its call is not a trumpet but a soft one which is syllabified in its Hindi name 'Kare-khar' repeated rapidly but rather softly (S. Baker). It will be seen that the Hindi कारेखर**corresponds closely to Sansk. कुरङ्कर which is synonyous with or an adnoun for the पुष्कराह्व in हारावली. Not having a क्रुष्ट or क्रौञ्चस्वर (a trumpeting call) it is not one of the क्रौञ्च birds whose loud notes are discussed in para. 17 below. It is rarely found on dry land and the name पुष्कराह्व as explained above is fully justified. चरक and सुश्रुत mention it by this name.

15. The Demoiselle Crane (33") is the smallest क्रौञ्च of India but very elegant both in form and demeanour. Unlike others it has a fully feathered head and wears a pair of pure white aigrettes springing from the region of the ear and projecting beyond the head in a beautiful downward curve. The crown is grey but the rest of the head and neck including the very long and lanceolate ornamental plumes overhanging the breast are black while the wings and the greater wing-coverts are blackish. The rest of the body plumage is grey. The bill is dull green, eyes bright red and the legs black. It arrives in India crossing the Himalayas about October and returns in March-April in huge flocks, flying across the skies in broad bands often a mile or more long. It does not stay for any length of time in North Indian plains except as a passage migrant but makes straight for the peninsula where it attacks the rice and other crops. The call is a harsh 'kurr-kurr-kurr' distinctly heard below as a flock passes very high overhead. Epithets like अपस्वर and खर refer to its harsh voice contrasting with सुस्वर for the trumpeting Sarus, and it is the अपस्वर–or खर-क्रौञ्च, कुरर, and ककंरेटु of the lexicons corresponding to करकोंचा (खरक्रौञ्च) in Marathi, कुर्रा, करकर्रा and करकटिया in Hindi for it. The हिन्दीशब्दसागर also renders ककंरेटु as 'a kind of सारस'. It is also the नीलाङ्ग सारस of the lexicons because it is the darkest coloured crane of India. Like the Common Crane the Demoiselle too is a luxury for the table and is much sought after by sportsmen who call it by the name of कूंज (Prakrit कोञ्ज, accepted as Sanskrit in अभि. चिन्ता. as v. l. for क्रौञ्च). Its flesh was appreciated in ancient India as well and we find कबन्ध advising Rāma to kill and eat the rich and fat Geese and Ducks, Coots

*Compare "कह्व—के जले ह्वयति"—रामाश्रमी टीका on अमर. See also चक्र for the Ruddy Goose in M.W. and compare चक्रवाक and चक्राह्व—uttering a call like that of a cart-wheel (Art. 84).

**It is distinguished in Hindi as चीनी कुलंग, the Chinese Crane from कुलंग the Common Crane.

(प्लवा :, Art. 58), the Common and the Demoiselle Cranes frequenting the Pampā Lake:

"तत्र हंसाः प्लवाः क्रौञ्चाः कुरराश्चैव राघव ।
× × ×
घृतपिण्डोपमान् स्थूलांस्तान्द्विजान् भक्षयिष्यथ ॥"
Rāmāyaṇa, 3.73.12-14.

Some thoughtless commentators have unfortunately rendered प्लवाः as 'frogs', as for example, in तिलकटीका, Nirnayasagar edition, Bombay, 1930.

16. The identifications made in the preceding paragraphs are summarized below:

1. The Eastern Common Crane—क्रौञ्च,
2. The Hooded Crane—श्वेतमूर्धन्—or श्वेतमस्तक लक्ष्मण,
3. The Black-necked Crane—नीलकण्ठ सारस or नीलस्कन्ध क्रौञ्च,
4. The Great White Crane—श्येनाख्य—कुरङ्कुर—सारस; पुष्कराह्व,
5. The Sarus or Indian Crane—रक्तमस्तक लक्ष्मण, (सुस्वर) सारस
6. The Demoiselle Crane— कुरर, कर्करेटु, खर-क्रौञ्च, नीलाङ्ग-सारस

17. As there is reason to believe that Sanskrit scholars have very hazy and often mistaken ideas about the क्रौञ्च and his cousins, barring of course the well known Sarus, and particulary as Dr. S.C. Law, F. Z. S., misled by the rendering of क्रौञ्च as कोंचबक in Bengali in शब्दकल्पद्रुम, has identified the क्रौञ्च of Poet Kālidāsa with the Pond-Heron or Paddy-Bird (Ardeola grayii) in his well known book, '*Kalidaser Pakhi*' (in Bengali), page 93, it is neceasary to add a few more words about the voice of the क्रौञ्च described by Kālidāsa as a far carrying resonant sound (क्रौञ्च निनाद). The Pond-Heron known in Bengal as 'koncha-Baka' "is a silent bird but invariably utters a low, hoarse croak as it rises, whilst at night, when the colonies settle down to roost, there is a considerable amount of querulous croaking and fluttering" (S. Baker in *F. B. I.*). Neither the occasional low croak nor the querulous croakings on the trees can come anywhere near the sonorous trumpeting calls coming from a flock of Common Cranes feeding in the rice fields or flying in formation high up in the air. The powerful and far-reaching call of the क्रौञ्च has indeed been stressed in the following description of a particular way of reciting a मंत्र:—

"यत्क्रौञ्चमन्वाहासुरम्"—तैत्ति. संहिता, 2.5.11.

where the adjective आसुर refers to its high note. सायणाचार्य commenting on "वाचे क्रौञ्चः"—ibid. 5.5.12 describes क्रौञ्च as दारुणस्वनः पक्षिविशेषः, i.e. a particular bird with a very loud call. At a sacrifice to secure heaven to the host (यजमान) the होतृ priest must pronounce the exclamation वषट् in a very loud tone:—"उच्चैः क्रौञ्चमिव वषट् कुर्यात् स्वर्गकामस्य"—हिरण्यकेशी श्रौतसूत्र, Pt. 8, 21.2.44. Again, कोंचस्सर (क्रौञ्चस्वर) has been explained as follows in अभिधानराजेन्द्रः—

"क्रौञ्चस्येव मधुरः स्वरो यस्य स तथा । क्रौञ्चस्येव मधुरारावके । क्रौञ्चस्येव अप्रयासेन विनिर्गतोऽपि दीर्घदेशव्यापी स्वरो येषां ते क्रौञ्चस्वराः । क्रौञ्चसदृशेषु निर्ह्रादिस्वरेषु ।"

Sub Voice कोंचस्सर.

"महया महया सद्देणं कोंचारवं करेमाणा ।"—"महता महता शब्देन दीर्घतर निनादिनः क्रौञ्चस्येव बहुव्यापित्वाद् बहुअनुनादित्वात्"।

Ibid. Vol. 5. pp. 1445-46.

The क्रौञ्च mountain in the Himalayas is described as resounding with the loud calls of the क्रौञ्च birds:

"क्रौञ्चं महामन्यु*: क्रौञ्चनादनिनादिनम् ।" MBh. 9.46.84.

The trumpeting of elephants in pain or when wounded with a shower of sharp arrows:

"अभीक्ष्णं क्रौञ्चवन्नदति"—पालकाप्य, 3.5 (p. 385);
"क्रौञ्चवद् विनदन्तोऽन्ये नाराचाभिहता गजाः ।" MBh. 7.20.52.

The sharp neighing of a spirited war-horse:

"क्रौञ्चवद् रिपुवधाय ह्रेषितम्" । बृहत्संहिता, 97.7.

18. A selection from literature, illustrative of the associations and habits of these birds as also in support of the earlier remarks that the term सारस (स with आरस, having a loud call) has been used not only for the Sarus but also for other Cranes, is given below:

"अद्यापि छिद्रं तत्पार्थ क्रौञ्चस्य परिवर्तते ।
येन हंसाश्च क्रौञ्चाश्च मानसाय प्रयान्ति च ।।**

स्कन्दपुराण, कौमारिका खण्ड, 33.182

The arrival of the Cranes in autumn and their flight in formation:

क्रौञ्चहंससमाकीर्णा शरत् प्रमुदिताऽभवत् । MBh. 3.183.10

सततमतिमनोज्ञः क्रौञ्चमालापरीतः
प्रदिशतु हिमयुक्तः काल एषः सुखं वः । ऋतुसंहार, 4.18

श्रेणीकृता व्यरोचन्त राजन् क्रौञ्चा इवाम्बरे । MBh. 7.139.33.

दृष्ट्वा च विमलं व्योम गतविद्युद्बलाहकम् ।
सारसारवसंघुष्टं विललापार्तया गिरा ।। रामायण, 4.30.5.

---

*महामन्युः कार्त्तिकेयः क्रौञ्चनादनिनादितं क्रौञ्चं शक्त्या बिभेद——is the principal sentence.

**This statement is based upon facts observed by the ancients that the migratory Geese, Swans, and Cranes avoiding the higher Himalayas pass through the valleys one of which is known as the क्रौञ्चरन्ध्र.

पंक्त्यः शरदि मत्तानां सारासानामिवाम्बरे। हविवंश, 3.55.19.

श्रेणीभूता प्रकाशन्ते यान्तः श्येना इवाम्बरे। Ibid. 3.55.95

श्येन in the last line clearly stands for the श्येनाख्य (the Crane known by the name of श्येन, 'the white') or the Great White Crane, for no Hawk or Eagle is known to fly in numbers or in formation (श्रेणीभूत) 'सारस' as a bird of the autumn, शरत्पक्षी, in the above passages is synonymous with क्रौञ्च, for the Sarus proper is not a winter visitor (शरदिमन्त) with us nor does it fly very high or in large formations. The Demoiselles may also be intended by the term सारस.

19. Small numbers of Sarus, flying low in V-form have been compared to a decorative festoon hanging in a curve over an arch-way in one of the most beautiful similes of Kālidāsa:

श्रेणीबद्धाद् वितन्वद्भिरस्तम्भां तोरणस्रजम्।
सारसैः कलनिर्ह्रादैः क्वचिदुन्नमिताननैः॥ रघुवंश, 1.41

But the poet would seem to be indebted for the beautiful picture to the following from the Rāmāyaṇa:

विपक्वशालिप्रसवानि भुक्त्वा प्रहर्षिता सारसचारुपंक्तिः।
नभः समाक्रामति शीघ्रवेगा वातावधूता ग्रथितेव माला॥ 4.30.48.

A very large flight of Cranes, probably the Demoiselles, called सारसपंक्ति in the text, is beautifully described in the following verse:

ऋज्वायतां च विरलां च नतोन्नतां च
सप्तर्षिवंशकुटिलां च निवर्तनेषु।
निर्मुच्यमानभुजगोदरनिर्मलस्य
सीमामिवाम्बरतलस्य विभज्यमानाम्॥ स्वप्नवासवदत्तम्, 4.2.

The charming association of the Common and the Demoiselle Cranes with the larger rivers, the Common and the Sarus Cranes announcing their presence in the wheat and barley crops covered by the heavy morning mist, their undisturbed happiness in the rice-fields combined with a cloudless autumn, crystal waters and smiling flowers—all these have been recalled with affection. The ancients loved their birds and did not grudge them a share in the rich bounties of mother earth:—

हंससारसचक्राह्वैः कुररैश्च समन्ततः।
पुलिनान्यवकीर्णानि नदीनां पश्य लक्ष्मण॥ रामायण, 4.30.63
प्रोद्घुष्टां क्रौञ्चकुररैश्चक्रवाकोपकूजिताम् (नदीम्)। MBh. 3.64.113.

बाष्पच्छन्नान्यरण्यानि यवगोधूमवन्ति च ।
शोभन्तेऽभ्युदिते सूर्ये नदद्भिः क्रौञ्चसारसैः* ॥ रामायण, 3.16.16.

मत्तक्रौञ्चावघुष्टेषु कलमापक्वपाण्डुषु ।
निर्विष्ट रमणीयेषु वप्रेषु रमते मनः ॥ हरिवंश, 2.16.21.

जलप्रसन्नं कुसुमप्रहासं क्रौञ्चस्वनं शालिवनं विपक्वम् । रामायण, 4.30.53.

The Common Crane and the Sarus were among the pet birds of Royalty, e.g., the palaces of Queen Kaikeyī and Crown-Prince Rāma had them:

शुकबर्हिसमायुक्तं क्रौञ्चहंसरुतायुतम् । रामायण, 2.10.12.
सारसैश्च मयूरैश्च विनदद्भिर्विराजितम् । Ibid. 2.15.34.

The well-known hetaera, वसन्तसेना, of मृच्छकटिक maintained a large aviary induding the सारस as a domestic pet:

"एतेऽपरे वृद्धमहल्लका इव इतस्ततः संचरन्ति गृहसारसाः** ।"
Act 4, after verse 28.

*Compare the appreciative remarks of S. Baker quoted in the footnote to para. 8.

**This would seem to contain an ironical hit at the institution of eunuchs in Royal harems.

63

BUSTARDS

1. This family of birds is a link between the Cranes on one side and the Plovers on the other, the Stone Plovers being intermediate between them and the Plovers proper. Bustards are endowed with large wings and stand rather high on the leg; have small heads but rather long necks. They are ground birds affecting dry open country or grass lands. With broad and flat backs, their carriage, with neck and legs perpendicular to the body, is peculiarly their own The larger birds of the group fly heavily like herons but with necks and legs stretched out like the Storks, and "in general superficial appearance they are perhaps, most like the gallinaceous birds, especially in regard to their heads and wings" (Stuart Baker). When disturbed they run at great speed. Their young, like the common fowl's, are hatched covered with down, and can run about almost immediately after leaving the egg. Six species of Bustard occur in India, three of them as winter migrants and three as permanent residents.

2. The following Sanskrit names refer to these birds some of which, being crested, have been regarded as a kind of Peacock :-

गोनर्द and वारट (वार- a field or open plain, therefore, a bird that frequents these) as विष्किर birds in चरक and वाग्भट. These two names belong to the Great Bustard and the Florican respectively as we shall see presently.

गोक्ष्वेडक and सारङ्ग (pied, or a horse) as प्रतुद and विष्किर respectively in सुश्रुत. These are the Great and the Little Bustard respectively. It is interesting to note that Persian 'kodan' like सारङ्ग also means both 'a Bustard' and 'a pack pony'.

गुरुकण्ठ, in M. Williams is an adnoun for the Great Bustard;

कृशकण्ठ, adnoun for सारङ्ग the Little Bustard, in कल्पद्रु. where गुरुकण्ठ and तिलशिखी are listed with synonyms for मयूर.

बहुलग्रीव, in the Synonymous list for a Peacock in अभि. चिन्तामणि the same as गुरुकण्ठ.

तिलमयूर, a kind of Peacock in M. W. is the Houbara.

कुरण्टक, v.l. गुरण्डक, incorrectly for तिलमयूर in त्रिकाण्डशेष. This and the next three names refer to the Great Bustard again; cf गुरण्टक for a kind of Peacock in M. Williams, the same as कुरण्टक.

मरुबक, (Desert-Stork) a kind of Crane in M. W.

वारण, a विष्किर bird in बौधायन स्मृति, 1. 15.154.

विदीगय, a kind of Cock (कुक्कुट विशेष per Sāyaṇa on तै. संहिता, 5.6.22) and श्वेतबक,* also per Sāyaṇa on तै. ब्राह्मण 3.9.10.

खिलखिल, a kind of bird in वैजयन्ती. This and the next three names belong to the crested Bengal Florican.

खिलखिल्ल, in the list of Peacock-names in अभि. चिन्तामणि.

तृणबर्हिन्, in श्यैनिकशास्त्र, 7.12;

शाड्वलि, in मिताक्षराटीका on याज्ञवल्क्यस्मृति, 1.175.

अञ्जलिकर्ण, in सुश्रुत, 1. 7. 10. This is the lesser florican.

3. The Eastern Great Bustard is a winter visitor to the extreme North-West of the country. The fully grown male attains a length of three and a half feet and weighs up to 30 pounds. The Great Indian Bustard is larger and heavier with a wing-span of eight feet and weighs up to 40 pounds. He is in fact the largest and the heaviest land-bird of India corresponding to the elephant as the heaviest land-animal. The plumage is deep buff above finely vermiculated with black, the general effect being a rufous brown which is well described as "खदिर वर्ण" in कल्पद्रुकोश while the neck and under parts are white with a black band across the lower breast. The head carries a recumbent black crest. This magnificent bird occurs in pairs or parties in semi-desert land and about cultivation in the Punjab, Sind, Rajasthan, Kathiawar, etc., and the stately Cock can be spotted from a distance from its long white neck as he proudly struts about. He has an inflatable gular-pouch connected with a small opening beneath the tongue. The call "usually uttered before daylight, is a booming cry, not unlike a distant shout" but when alarmed the note is a bark. When feeding, however, the members of a party keep up a sort of cackle. During courtship the Cock greatly inflates his neck and throat** and struts before the hens w th the tail raised into a

*Because of superficial similarity of a Crane (क्रौञ्च) with a Stork (बक) the term क्रौञ्च has often been rendered as बक-विशेष in the lexicons and commentaries. Similarly a certain amount of resemblance between the Great Indian Bustard with his long white neck and white lower parts and the Crane or Stork is responsible for names like मरुबक and श्वेतबक for the former.

**After a few preliminary attempts at inflation "out goes the whole throat down to the breast, and that part of it next the latter swells more and more........and the lower throat bag gets bigger and bigger, and larger and larger, till it looks to be within six inches of the ground....and looked at in front, he seems to have a huge bag covered with feathers hanging down between his legs, which wobbles about as he struts here and there." (Hume quoted by S. Baker). The old name, वारण, is thus seen to be after the Cock's dangling pouch suggestive of the trunk of an elephant. The elephant is a वारण because his great strength enables him to offer resistance and this Bustard is also a वारण a he wards off or resists (वारयति) with his horrible smell—See paras. 4 and 10 below.

fan, drooping wings and the feathers of the body turned the wrong way about. At the same time he makes a deep moaning call, heard at a great distance. The food consists of principally large grass-hoppers and other insects but lizards, mice. young birds, etc.; grain and green shoots are equally welcome. In addition this Bustard has a "curious taste for snakes and the natives give it credit for being a constant slayer and devourer of these reptiles". (S. Baker).

4. The Great Bustard has a peculiar and very disagreeable smell when alive, and its flesh is not now held in much esteem. Dr. E. T. Aitchinson informs us that when he was on the Afghan Delimitation Commission, a flock of these Bustards was met with, and Lieut. Rawlinson succeeded in shooting one, but the stench of the bird was so great he almost thought of leaving it; it was so dark that he scarcely knew what it was that he had got, and the scent was almost enough to put off any one from even a new acquisition.[1] This writer also refers to the comments of F. Finn 'on this curious smell of the Bustard'.

5. As the habits of both the Great Bustards (Eastern and Indian) are similar they share common names in Sanskrit. In the above list it will be seen that गोनर्द and गोक्ष्वेडक (bellowing like a bull) are after the bird's bellowing call corresponding to its name गुनाद (गोनाद-गोनर्द) in Hindi. The names गुरुकण्ठ and बहुलग्रीव (thick-necked) are again for these birds with reference to their habit of puffing out their necks during courtship, while names like कुरुण्टक and गुरण्डक are merely Prakrit forms of गुरुकण्ठ unless गुरण्डक is from गुर्वण्डक (laying a large egg). The Peacock is दार्वण्ड (woody-egg) and the eggs of the Great Indian Bustard are larger than those of the former. मरुबक would however appear to refer to the Indian form which has a white neck and under-parts and lives in semi-desert areas. This name corresponds to Marathi मरटोंक (मरु and टङ्क fr. ध्वांक्ष, meaning बक); cf. also the Turkish name for the allied Little Bustard which means 'Sand-fowl'.[2] कल्पद्रु कोश defines the female as हंसका but the author is incorrect in attributing a booming call to her. "गुरुड्का' is however, the same as गुरण्डका.

6. Is it possible that the name कुरुण्टक (flower of the yellow amaranth) is independent of गुरुकण्ठ and really refers to the European Cock Bustard (found in the extreme North-West of India), for it fluffs out all his plumage and looks "like a surprising animated giant white Chrysanthemum"[3]?

7. The बोधायन स्मृति mentions वारण (वारयतीति one that wards off or forbids) as a विष्किर bird that must not be eaten :- "पक्षिणस्तित्तिरिकपोतकपिञ्जवाध्रीणसमयूरवारणा वारणवर्जाः पञ्च विष्किराः।" 1.5.154.

---

1. Stuart Baker, *Game Birds of India*, pp.150-151.
2. *Stray Feathers*, IV.184.
3. H. G. Wells, *Science of Life*, p. 1144.

वारण also means an elephant. The great Bustard, with its large size, weight and the forbidding stench, answers to the name in both the senses. The Chinese also consider its flesh as inferior.

8. It is also suggested that विदीगय of the following is very probably this bird :—

"छगल: कल्माष: किकिदीवि: विदीगयस्ते त्वाष्ट्रा: ।

तै. सं. 5.6.22; तै. ब्रा. 3.9.10.

Sâyaṇâcârya in his commentary on the संहिता renders विदीगय as कुक्कुटविशेष which agrees well with the Bustard's resemblance to a gallinaceous bird and justifies its inclusion under the name of गोनर्द in the विष्किर list by चरक; but in the ब्राह्मण he equates it with श्वेतबक which also agrees with मरुबक for this bird with a long white neck and white under-parts and looking like a Stork in the distance. त्वष्टृ being the expert artizan of the gods beautiful victims alone would seem to be appropriate for him, and that is what we find in the beautifully marked goat and the chestnut and blue Kingfisher, so that the Great Bustard with his "magnificent plumage" could very naturally be the third item in the list. The etymology of विदीगय is however beyond me and I can only offer a guess that the word is Prakrit—'वि' 'a bird' and दीर्घक—दिग्घक—दीगय, large; or fr. 'वि' and दिग्गज—दीगय,, 'elephant'. वारण* as a bird occurs in कुणाल जातक (536) and वेस्संतर जातक, verse 2105.

9. The Little Bustard is quite a miniature of the great bird just described. It is only about eighteen inches long and weighs less than two pounds. It is however a very pretty bird, sandy buff above pencilled with black. The wings are black and white and the under-parts white. The neck and breast of the cock in breeding plumage are black with a white necklace and a white breast-band below it. It is a winter migrant chiefly to the North-West including Kashmir and straggles as far east as Saharanpur in the Uttar Pradesh. It frequents mustard fields, flies high, fluttering and skylarking about in the air, whence its other name, the Butterfly Houbara (Finn). It does not inflate its neck, has a very graceful gait and runs very fast on the ground. It has therefore been most appropriately named सारङ्ग (= शबल, black and white, & 'a pied horse') and described as चटकाकार from its small size and habit of 'skylarking', and कृशकण्ठ (thin-

---

*In both the Jātaka stories वारण has been rendered as the हत्थिलिंग सकुन. In the वेस्सतरजातक the expression वारणाभिरुदा रम्मा can only refer to the booming call of the Great Bustard, but in the commentary on verse 2249 the हत्थिलिंग is also said to be capable of carrying away small children. Apparently this last name was applied to two different birds, the Great Bustard and the Adjutant Stork. See note on the भारण्ड bird, Art. 81. It may also be noted here that the Turkey-cock goes by the name of 'feel-murg'—elephant-bird, in Persia. If the word दीगय for दिग्गज is not found in the lexicons it only shows that it has not been used in literature.

necked) as against गुरुकण्ठ for the great Bustard. सारङ्ग as a विष्किर bird of सुश्रुत is certainly this bird. सारङ्ग also means 'a black and white horse' and it is more than probable that the name implies an underlying similarity of the breeding male with a smart pony decked out with silver trappings. The erect gait of the bird and its speed on the ground also are quite suggestive. That similarity with the horse did strike the ancients is apparent from the vernacular names like घोड़ाकङ्क (horse-heron) given by चक्रदत्त for गोनर्द of चरक, and Hindi घोरर (घोटक, घोड़ा) for the Great Bustard. An alternative note of डल्हणाचार्य on सारङ्ग runs : ""अन्यो कृष्णकर्बुरवर्ण चटकाकारो विष्किर:" which is clearly reflected in "सारङ्गश्चररादार: कृशकण्ठ:" of कल्पद्रुकोश. It is interesting to note that one of the riddles posed in वाज. संहिता 23.11 is, "किं स्विदासीद् बृहदद्वय: ?" Which is the great bird ? The answer in the next मन्त्र, is "अश्व आसीद् बृहद्वय:" । "The great bird is the अश्व, the horse". Is विदीगय the same as बृहद्वय ? The riddle would thus consist of a double meaning of अश्व as an animal and as a bird : cf सारङ्ग and the vernacular names noted above.

10. Macqueen's Bustard or Houbara resembles in build the Great Indian Bustard but is much smaller, being only about twenty nine inches in length. It is sandy brown above, beautifully marked with minute pencilling of black on buff. Both sexes have a black crest. It is known as तिलूर in North-India which is from Sansk. तिलमयूर from the fine pencilling of black (तिलाङ्कित) in the upper plumage of the bird and the long crest. The equation from त्रिकाण्डशेष given above should be interpreted—'the तिलमयूर is a kind of कुरण्टक or Bustard', otherwise it would be incorrect as the two are altogether different birds. The Houbara, when attacked by a trained Falcon and probably also in nature, protects itself by ejecting foul-smelling liquid excreta on the body of the attacking bird which gives up the chase in disgust. Would the name वारण apply to this bird as well? Perhaps not. But it is evidently the हिंगुराज mentioned with वारण in वेस्संतरजातक, 2105, so named from the habit just described (fr. हिङ्ग, the evil smelling asafoetida). It is also possible that "वारणा-हिंगुराजा" is a compound name (हिङ्ग-राज-वारण) for the evil smelling Great Bustard: cf. मदवारण an elephant in rut exuding scented ichor from the temples. The flesh of all Bustrads except the adult Great Indian Bustard is excellent.

11. The Bengal Florican is practically a black bird in the breeding plumage with wings mostly white, and back pencilled with buff markings. It has a long black crest and long black hackles on the lower neck and a tuft of still longer feathers hanging down from the lower breast. The male is twenty six inches long. Out of the breeding season both the cock and hen wear a plumage of mottled buff and black. They love cover and live in the grassy plains between the Himalayas and the Ganges though they have been found as far west as the Jumna. The male is known as चरट in Hindi (fr. चर, a spy and अट् to move ? because of the bird's habitat and movements in grass cover) and उलुमोर (उलुप or उलूक, 'kind of grass' and मयूर, a peacock) in Assam, and तनमोर (तृणमयूर) in Marathi. It has been a favou-

rite for hawking and is mentioned by the name of तृणबर्हिन् in the श्यैनिक शास्त्र :—

"नैकधा वाजिना सोऽयं तृणबर्हिर्यया हतः ।"—7.12.

It is also probably the वारट of चरक and शाड्वलि mentioned in the मिताक्षरा टीका on याज्ञवल्क्यस्मृति 1.175. Both these names evidently refer to the habit of the bird frequenting grass covered plains

12. The Lesser Florican or Likh is the smallest Bustard known, and is in form and general colour a fairly accurate miniature of the larger Florican. The cock in breeding plumage has neither crest nor hackles on the neck or breast but from each side of his head, behind the ears, spring a number of long feathers and three of these on each side are the longest "sometimes reaching as much as five inches in length, and generally exceeding three and a half inches. As a rule, the three longest feathers are graduated, and though in some cases they are subequal, three is nearly always a great difference in length between these three feathers and the others, which may vary between one and two inches. These feathers, more specially the longer ones, are spatulate in shape".* Evidently, therefore, the total number of such feathers is not less than five on each side. The illustration in *The Indian Waders* by Finn shows five, two small and three long.

13. One of the different kinds of forceps mentioned in सुश्रुत, 1.10 was designed after the shape of the bill of the bird अञ्जलिकर्ण which seems to be no other than the Lesser Florican with the separated feathers of the ear tufts jutting out well behind the head. Now if one raised one's palm to cover one's ears with the fingers spread out, the latter would represent the spatulate feathers in position about the bird's head, and the picturesque aptness of the name अञ्जलिकर्ण would be apparent. The Prakrit expression "दसंगुलि अंजलि" for a palm or hand with the fingers branching out offers a very good comparison. It is explained as follows :—

"अन्योऽन्यान्तरिता दश अङ्गुलयो यत्र सा दशाङ्गुलिः तामञ्जलिम् ।"

आवश्यक सूत्र, p. 188.

14. Another Hindi name for it is लिख which is merely a truncated form of खिलिखिल or खिलखिल्ल (playing, delighting in uncultivated or grass land). Both forms of Florican, particularly the breeding males, are in the habit of constantly springing or jumping up high above the grass, as a part of their love-play to attract the hens and the name clearly refers to

*Stuart Baker, *Game Birds of India, Burma and Ceylon*, p. 200.

this habit. As however the crested bird is तृणबर्हिन् and this bird is लिख in Hindi it would follow that the name though applicable to both was probably reserved for the Lesser Florican. The original name may well have been खिलखेलि (खेलि, 'a bird', i.e. a bird of the grass-land) or simply खेलि— 'the playful bird'; cf. खञ्जखेल for the sportive Wagtail.

64

STONE PLOVERS

1. In this article we are concerned with only two birds of the group, viz. the Indian Stone-Plover and the Great Stone-Plover. They form a very natural link with the Bustards and lead on to the Plovers proper, and are found throughout Old World. They are ground birds of a brown plumage, with a large head and large eyes, the latter necessitated by their nocturnal habits. During the day they rest on the ground in the shade of bushes or a grove of trees. The call of the Indian Stone-Plover is mostly heard during the night (after dusk), more particularly on moonlit nights —a series of sharp and clear whistling notes...pick...pick...pick followed by quickly repeated double notes, pick-wick...pick-wick...pick-wick..., and very often duets are indulged in (Salim Ali). The voice of the Great Stone-Plover which frequents river-beds and sand-banks is a harsh croak though "it is also heard occasionally piping at night" (Smythies). The piping call of the smaller bird is quite musical in effect, resembling that of sharp taps on a well-strung small drum and has indeed been described as "wild and musical".

2. The Stone Plover goes by the name of करवानक or करौनक in Hindi. चरकसंहिता has पानविक (v.l. पाणविक) in the list of प्रतुद birds. The name, from पणव, means a 'drummer' and कलपाणविक would be a 'pleasant drummer'. Now the Hindi name करवानक is directly from Sansk. कलपानविक with ल and प of the latter changed to र and व and the omission of वि so that both the names कलपाणविक and पाणविक belong to the Stone-Plover. The मानसोल्लास mentions it as करवाण —vol, 2,276. 39.

3. दीर्घशिर (large-headed), is a kind of bird in M. Williams and exactly corresponds to Hindi बड़सिरी (v.l. बरसिरी), another name for the Stone Plover. There is thus दीर्घशिर for both the Great and the Indian Stone-Plovers.

65

COURSERS & PRATINCOLES

Three species of Genus Cursorius are found in India. They frequent dry plains and are of the size of a Lapwing. They are fast runners, so much so that like the spokes of a swiftly turned wheel their legs become invisible[1], and the best known among them, the Indian Courser, found throughout the country, except East Bengal and Assam, is characterised by ivory or even china-white feet. It is evidently the श्वेतचरण of सुश्रुत placed in the प्लव group. Most editions of सुश्रुतसंहिता give श्वेतवारल instead which however has been rightly omitted by M. Williams as it does not make good sense. The Nirnaya Sagar edition mentions श्वेतचरण in the foot-note as an alternative reading, and this is given by M. Williams. Another name for the bird is क्षिप्रचला which is included in the quotation from पाराशर given by भट्टोत्पल in his commentary on बृहत्संहिता, 95.28. Its name in Telugu (Durawayi) also means 'a fast runner' and is the same as क्षिप्रचला of पाराशर and 'Swift-foot' of Jerdon.

The Pratincoles (Sand-Swallows or Swallow-Plovers) have short legs and Tern-like action and flight. They have Swallow-like bills with a large gape which helps them in catching insects on the wing. They hunt in flocks both on the ground and in the air. "They keep to the open ground ...running at great speed in short dashes hither and thither as they feed on various insects and small grasshoppers. They fly very strongly and at great speed, constantly whirling and wheeling about as they go" (Stuart Baker). Two of the species frequent dry land while the third is associated with wide stretches of sand and shingle beds of the larger rivers. Many birds are known to perform "the broken-wing trick" when their nests containing young chicks are approached by man but the behaviour of the Pratincoles in this respect is particularly noteworthy—less so of the Ring-Plovers. Douglas Dewar describes his experience in the following words : "Swallow-Plovers were surrounding me. They were nearly all on the ground and striking strange attitudes. Some were lying on the sands as though they had been wounded and fallen on the ground; others were

1. Cassell's *Book of Birds.*

floundering in the sand as if in pain; some were fluttering along with one wing stretched out limply, looking as though it were broken; while others appeared to have both wings broken."[1] Hume also records a similar experienee in *Nests and Eggs of Indian Birds.*[2] Dewar comments that "the little pratincole appears to be a bird having a singularly unbalanced mind while it is breeding", and again, "it would seem that the pratincole when in breeding condition, is sometimes so excitable that if one of a flock takes fright, the alarm is communicated to its fellows, and they then often behave as if attacked by an epileptic fit."[3]

The त्रिकाण्डशेष and हारावली of पुरुषोत्तम देव give names of some water-birds as below :

i "अथ सर्षपी
हापुत्रिका खञ्जनिका । तुलिकास्फोटिके समे"—त्रिकाण्डशेष.
ii "गोभण्डीरः पङ्ककीरः । कोयष्टिर्जलकुक्कुमः ।" Ibid.
iii "गोभण्डीरः पङ्ककीरो । हापुत्री राजभट्टिका ।" हारावली, अर्धश्लोकावधि
iv "गङ्गाचिल्ली तु देवट्टी । विश्वका जलकुक्कुटी ।"
v "शरारिराटिराडिश्च । हापुत्री राजपुत्रिका" ।
जटाधर in शब्दकल्पद्रुम under राजपुत्रिका[4]

The extract (iii) from हारावली is from its अर्धश्लोकावधि section which implies that the names in every half-verse are synonymous, but a comparison with the extracts (i) and (v) from त्रिकाण्डशेष and जटाधर shows that the equation "गोभण्डीरःपङ्ककीरः" is complete by itself and independent of the equation "हापुत्री राजभट्टिका" which latter therefore corresponds to "सर्षपी हापुत्रिका खञ्जनिका" of त्रिकाण्डकोष and "हापुत्री राजपुत्रिका" of जटाधर. The second part of त्रिकाण्डशेष, viz.," तुलिका स्फोटिके समे" refers to a different bird (Pipit, Art. 26-B). It is submitted that both the lines from हारावली belong properly to the पादावधि part of it and have been wrongly placed in the अर्धश्लोकावधि section.

No. (iv) would then be divisible into two equations: (a) गङ्गाचिल्ली तु देवट्टी, and (b) विश्वका जलकुक्कुटी each referring to a particular type of bird. Now as the name हापुत्रिका is placed with सर्षपी and खञ्जनिका in त्रिकाण्डकोष and with राजभट्टिका in हारावली, and also as the last three names mean the Little Ringed Plover (Art. 71) it would seem that the author intends हापुत्रिका also for the same bird. It has already been stated that the Little Ringed Plover's behaviour at the nest is similar to that of the Pratincole, though not so markedly, so that it is just possible that the name हापुत्रिका was applicable to both. Considering, however, the particularly exaggerated reactions of the pratincole the name seems to have been originally meant for it and

1. *Glimpses of Indian Birds*, p. 206.
2. Vol.III,p. 231.
3. *Birds at the Nest*, p. 183.
4. Each of the above half verses consists of two equations each containing synonyms for a single bird and forms allied to it with, however, the exception of the first half of No. (v) which mixes up two members of the Ibis group—See Art. 80.

came later to be mistaken for the Plover as well. This would explain the mixing up of the names of the two birds, and once हापुत्रिका was equated with the Ringed Plover the author was under a necessity to give a separate synonymy for the Pratincole which he did with "विश्वका जलकुक्कुटी". Now जलकुक्कुटी clearly signifies a very small water-side bird (cf. जलकुक्कुटी and अम्बुकुक्कुटिका for the Rails and Crakes, Art. 58) and if गङ्गाचिल्ली is a Gull, which is as big as a Crow if not larger (M. Williams, and Art.68), जलकुक्कुटी would be a most improper synonym for it. The name, therefore, belongs to a small bird otherwise known as विश्वका. This last implies a bird that moves and flies in all directions (विश्व) and the Pratincoles, as we have seen, fully answer to this meaning, and their small size suits the name of जलकुक्कुटी. विशुवि (विषुवि from विषु+वि a bird that flies in all dircetions) is one of the birds prohibited as food in वसिष्ठसंहिता (Chap. 12) and is probably the same as विश्वका हापुत्री as a bird name is included in the list quoted by भट्टोत्पल्ल from पराशर in बृहत्संहिता (85.28). We thus have विषुवि, विश्वका, and हापुत्रिका for the pratincoles. The very apt name of हापुत्री is based on human behaviour, e.g. शिलाद, a Brahman, on being told by an astrologer that his little boy of seven would not live beyond a year, falls to the ground, calling bitterly, "My son, oh My son."

"हा पुत्र पुत्र पुत्रेति पपात च ।"—लिङ्गपुराण, Pt. I, Ch. 43-11

Compare also :

"राजा ह्यशोकः पतितो धरण्यां हा पुत्र ! शोकेन हि दह्यमानः ।"—दिव्यावदान, p. 415

Commenting on अनर्घराघव (V.8) रुचिपति उपाध्याय has rendered कुररी (Tern, Art.69) incorrectly as हापूती इति प्रसिद्धा चटकविशेषस्त्री, but the statement that हापूती (हापुत्री) is a चटक विशेष i.e. of the size of a Sparrow is correct, for the small Indian pratincole of the larger rivers in North India is not over 6.5 inches in length. This supports the interpretation of जलकुक्कुटी given above.

66

CRAB PLOVER

This "very extraordinary bird" with a peculiar nesting habit has been placed in a family by itself. It is a Plover-like white bird (16 inches) with a black back. It nests "in colonies, often of great size, scooping burrows anything from one to four feet long in the sand or, occasionally among the loose boulders and rocks, in which it lays its one pure white egg" (S. Baker). It feeds mostly on crabs and hence the name Its breeding grounds are on the islands at the Adam's Bridge, Ceylon, and some islands in the Persian Gulf Ancient indian Law-givers were undoubtedly men of religion and some of them must have come to know this bird and its curious habits during their pilgrimage to Rameshvaram situated on an island next to Adam's Bridge. Law-giver वसिष्ठ was probably one such and he has included a bird called वैलातक in the 14th chapter of his Saṃhitā in the list of birds prohibited as food for the twice-born Hindus of the time. This वैलातक is perhaps the same as विलाता, 'a kind of bird' in M. Williams. Both are from विल 'a hole' or 'to conceal' and imply a bird that lives or nests in a hole. वैलातक, however, may also be from वेला sea-coast, and would seem to imply a coastal bird (cf. वेलाचर – M. W.). Most probably, therefore, both the names refer to the Crab-plover which nests in a hole and along the sea-coast. No other Saṃhitā or स्मृति mentions these names so far as I know, nor do the commoner lexicons give them. Had the name applied to any of the North Indian birds nesting in holes* some at least of the lexicons would surely have given it. In the circumstances it may be presumed that sage वसिष्ठ having known the bird during his visit to Rameshvaram made it a point to include it in his list not only as a curiosity but also to prohibit the Hindus of the neighbourhood from killing it for food, particularly as it is so easy to catch it in its nest-hole. All this is pure conjecture, and there may be nothing in it, and if so, the Crab-Plover of the extreme South must go like so many other birds even in North India, without an old Sanskrit name. In fact one has no right to expect Sanskrit names for uncommon birds even of North India, much less of birds beyond its limits, except perhaps as curiosities in royal aviaries.

---

*For example, Bee-eaters, Kingfishers, Bank-Mynas, and many others.

67

SKUAS

The Skuas are large Gull-like birds seen along the Sind coast. They live on fish which they rob from Gulls and Terns, pursuing them in the air until they drop the desired morsel, which they then seize (S. Baker). Their call is a piercing scream or gull-like "gack, gack". There is no Sanskrit name for them, but from their general appearance and habits they would be included in the general name of समुद्रकाक for the large sea-birds like the Sea-Gulls and others.

68

GULLS

1. Alfred Newton, the great British Zoologist and author of *The Dictionary of Birds* seriously questioned the wisdom of separating the Skuas, Gulls, Terns and Skimmers, all placed in the genus Larus by Linnaeus, into separate families (see *Ency. Brit.*, 11th ed., Vol. 12, 714), and the last three were indeed so placed by Blanford and Oats in the first edition of *The Fauna of British India* (*Birds*), but, following the classification of Lowe, Stuart Baker has separated them into distinct families in the second edition and yet he admits the correctness of the earlier grouping of all three in a single family. Since I have followed throughout the plan of the second edition I must stick to it in the case of these birds as well.

2. Gulls, the "most beautiful dwellers of the coasts and marshes" are medium to fairly large sized birds with long, moderately broad wings, almost square cut tails and webbed feet. The bill is stout and wedge-shaped with the upper mandible hooked at the tip, and when hunting for food they usually fly with their bills nearly on a line with their body. The predominating colour of the adult birds is white with a grey mantle, varying in shade from the most delicate pearl-grey to dark blackish-slate, and the head is often more or less marked with black in summer. The seasonal change is not great and affects chiefly the colour of the head. The young are a mottled brown and take three or four years to assume the adult plumage. They are grand fliers and show perfect mastery of the air and wind, remarkably quick and clever in their manoeuvres. They have voracious appetites and live mostly on dead fish, floating garbage, offal of all sorts, insects, grasshoppers, etc. They are in fact perfect scavengers of the waters and coastal areas just as the Vultures are on the land. They pick up their food from the surface of the water and never dive for it like the Terns, but they are experts in catching with their feet any tit bits thrown up to them in the air. They often swim and rest on the water floating highly like the Ducks. The Terns, on the other hand, are of a small to medium size with long, tapering wings, deeply forked tails, narrow and straight bills, short legs and small webbed feet. Expert on the wing, their flight is exceedingly graceful and when out for their fish food they carry their bills pointed downward, scanning the waters below with their searching eyes for an

individual fish or shoals of small fish at which they dive from a height of 10 to 20 feet. Unlike the Gulls they never touch any dead or putrid stuff. The colour scheme of their body plumage is, in the majority of cases, similar to that of the Gulls—black on the head, grey on the upper and white on the lower parts. Writing of these birds in his interesting little book, *Birds of the Sea* R. M. Lockley observes that the Gulls and Terns are closely related. "They seem to fly like embodied spirits clad in grey and white, though some have black hoods and some have black on their wings. The long-winged and long-tailed Terns are altogether more volatile and dainty and less aggressive than the larger and heavier built Gull-tribe." Both are sociable, breed in large dense colonies, and are very noisy when feeding in company and at their nesting grounds.*

3. Of the nearly fifty known species of Gulls in the world seven are represented in India, four along the coasts and four of these occur also on large inland rivers, lakes, and marshes. All except the Sooty Gull and the Slender-billed Gull, which breed on islands off the Mekran coast and on the Mekran coast respectively and may be called resident birds, are winter visitors with us. The Brown-headed Gull breeds on the lakes and marshes of Ladakh in Kashmir and further east in Tibet. The Indo-Aryans may well have been familiar with the Gull and its breeding habits before they moved into India but at any rate they must have got to know about those breeding nearer home.

4. Four of the species that spend the winter in North India are briefly described below:

(1) The Great Black-headed Gull (length 26", wing-expanse 68") has black head and neck, the upper parts pale grey and the lower parts white. The bill is yellow and the legs and feet yellow to orange yellow. In winter the head and neck become white streaked with black but the summer garb is assumed as the bird leaves India for its breeding home in Central Asia by about March-April. Its great size and magnificent flight render it conspicuous wherever it occurs. In India it is found on all the great rivers. In addition to the usual food of the tribe this Gull has a bad reputation for stealing the young and eggs of other birds. Its call is a very loud raucous cry, much like that of the Greater Black-backed Gull, which is described as a low ha-ha-ha-ha, a braying ha-ha-ha, a deep keow-keow, a short barking note and a long drawn moan (*Birds of America*, 1936).

(2) The Black-headed or Laughing Gull (length 16") is about the size of a Crow but with a much longer wing-expanse. In summer the head

*The male Gull invites the female for copulation but amongst the Terns either may invite either, and, unlike most other birds, copulation may be continued by the Black-headed Gulls and common Terns even after the eggs have hatched (J. Fisher in *Watching Birds*, p. 173—Pelican Books). During courtship the Greater Black-backed, the Lesser Black-backed and the Herring Gulls indulge in communal aerial dances (J. Fisher in *Bird Recognition*, pp. 140 ff. Pelican Books).

and neck are chocolate brown, the upper parts pearl grey and the underparts white. The bill and legs are deep bright red. In winter the head and neck become white with a few dark spots here and there. It lives largely on worms and insects, following the plough for this purpose. They also eat all sorts of grain, shoots of crops, sand eels, small fish, snails, slugs, etc. and at times young and eggs of other birds. In addition to a harsh "gek, gek" and a loud wailing "ka-yek, ka-yek" cry it also utters "long derisive though far from unpleasant ha-ha-ha-ha-ha-ha-ha, from which it derives its name, 'the Laughing Gull', for seemingly it laughs and no great imagination is needed to assume that its loud cries are those of real mirth." "Some observers call the sound demoniac or lunatic laughter, but to the writer's ears it is the joyous, buoyant, free laugh of the open sea" (*Birds of America*). Numbers are found together flying and wheeling backwards and forwards over lakes, jheels and the larger rivers and when not feeding they rest either on the water or sands and banks.

(3) The Brown-headed Gull (17″) resembles the Black-headed but the colour of the head in summer is ashy-brown instead of chocolate-brown. The bill and legs are deep red. In winter the head turns white. It visits the plains of Eastern India during the winter and its habits and voice are those of the Black-headed variety, following the plough for insects and worms brought up by the ploughshare.

(4) The Yellow-legged Herring Gull (23″ to 25″, wing-expanse 58″ to 60″) is, like the Great Black-headed Gull, a large bird with white head, neck, tail and underparts, and a dark slaty-grey mantle. The bill and legs are bright yellow.* Its call notes are similar to those of the common Herring Gull, described as a loud and raucous series of "cack-cack-cac-cac-cac-cac; or sometimes a querulous scream, kuh-r-e-e-e-e, kuh-r-r-e-e-e-e-e-ah, mingled with cluckings and subdued hen-like gobblings" (*Illus. Ency. of American Birds*). Like others they are omnivorous scavengers and in

---

*Sanskrit lexicons mention (i) the white (गौर or सित), (ii) the red (रक्त), and the black (कृष्ण) varieties of Rape-seed or Mustard (सर्षप) corresponding to Brassica Alba, B. Juncea and B. Nigra or Napus respectively but not the yellow (पीत) variety. A fourth variety is however mentioned by the name of देव सर्षप defined as कुरराङ्घ्रि (of the colour of the feet of the कुरर bird) with ऐन्द्र (coming up naturally with the rains i.e. self-sown and therefore wild) and निर्जर (not dying out, hence the same as the preceding). Now the variety Brassica Campestris, the yellow Rape-seed, though cultivated, grows wild in North India and is known in Hindi as पीला सरसों. It is, therefore, submitted that देवसर्षप (cf. देवखात) is this yellow Rape-seed and कुरर in its descriptive synonym, कुरराङ्घ्रि, is no other than the Yellow-legged Herring Gull or the Great Black-headed Gull having yellow feet.

No other bird sharing the name कुरर has really yellow feet. "कुररकामिनी" (poetic for कुररी) has been rendered as 'उत्क्रोश भार्या' in the commentary on यशस्तिलकचम्पू, page 248. The synonym कङ्कणहारिका given there is however incorrect.

addition are experts in breaking hard and soft clams. These they pick up from the shore in their feet and drop them on hard ground or rock from a height of 50 to 60 feet for the contents. They are coastal birds of Western and North-West India but straggle far inland to the larger rivers and lakes as far North as Kashmir and East as Cachar in Assam.

5. The ancient Indians had evidently noticed the similarity of physical features, close association with the water, and the noisy habits of both the Gulls and Terns and regarded them as closely allied forms, so much so, that they named the former कुरर (from roots कु, कुङ or कुर्—to make a sound: कौति, कवते, कुरति—कुररः) and the latter कुररी as if the former, with their heavier build and greater dash, were the males and the latter, with a graceful form and finer discrimination as to food, were the females of closely allied species. It is also probable that with Gulls named as कुरर the smaller Terns were distinguished as कुररी on the principle, "स्त्री स्यात् काचिन्मृणाल्यादिर्विवक्षापचये यदि" – अमरकोश, 3.5.7; e.g. we have वर्तक for the larger Common Grey Quail and वर्तिका for smaller Rain Quail (Art. 55). Some of the Sanskrit lexicons mention only three birds sharing the name कुरर, viz., the Osprey, the Demoiselle Crane (क्रौञ्च) and 'a kind of Eagle' (see शब्दकल्पद्रुम and M. W.).* Both चरक and सुश्रुत place कुरर in their lists of 'Birds of Prey' (प्रसहाः) for the Fishing Eagles including the Osprey, while both have उत्क्रोश (very noisy) in the lists of 'Water Birds' (प्लवाः) for the noisy Gulls. But as both the Fishing Eagles and the Gulls are very noisy the terms कुरर and उत्क्रोश have been treated as synonymous both in literature, particularly Pali literature, and the lexicons. M. Williams' rendering of 'उत्क्रोश as 'a sea-eagle' is certainly correct but it is not so on the authority of चरक as we have just seen. The earliest homonymous equation for these noisy birds, barring of course the D. Crane which is a कुरर but not उत्क्रोश, but including the noisy Terns and the Curlew is "उत्क्रोशकुररौ समौ" of अमरकोश. The अभि. चिन्ता. expressly includes the Fishing Eagles and Osprey in the extended synonymy: "अथोत्क्रोशो मत्स्यनाशनः कुररः", while the कल्पद्रुकोश includes the Terns and Curlew also within it:–

(a) अथोत्क्रोशः स्त्रियां पुमान् कुररः खरशब्दः ।
(b) उत्क्रोशो मत्स्यनाशनः ।
(c) कुररो (? कुररी) जलकुक्कुटी ।

The first equation includes उत्क्रोश—उत्क्रोशी and कुरर–कुररी (cf. कुङ शब्दे, कवतीति कुररः स्त्रियां तु कुररी—कातंत्रीय उणादि) as homonyms applicable to several different birds possessing a harsh voice (खरशब्द); the second to उत्क्रोश (= कुरर) as noisy fish-killing birds; and the third to कुरर or कुररी as a noisy bird resembling a

---

*पा. स. म. renders कुरर as उत्क्रोश and कुरल; and कुररी as the female of कुरर, but कुलल (the same as कुरल, कुरर) is equated with (i) पक्षिविशेष, (ii) गृध्रपक्षी (pointing to the fishing Eagle), (iii) कुररपक्षी, and (iv) a Cat.

श्रुतसागर सूरि, commentator of यशस्तिलक चम्पू, renders कुरर as जलकाक at page 144 and the bird meant is no doubt a Gull.

water-hen, viz., the Curlew. Now since commentators like मल्लिनाथ have interpreted कुररी as उत्क्रोशी (रघुवंश, 14.68; see also commentary on चम्पूरामायण, काण्ड 6, verse 90) it follows that the feminines उत्क्रोशी and कुररी for the Terns and Curlew are included in the general and comprehensive equation, "उत्क्रोशकुररौ समौ" of अमर.

The several different birds sharing the names कुरर and कुररी may be distinguished as below:

(i) the पंक्तिचर-कुरर is the Demoiselle Crane (Art. 62);
(ii) the मत्स्यनाशन-कुरर ,, ,, Osprey* (Art. 50);
(iii) the उत्क्रोश-कुरर ,, ,, (मत्स्यनाशन) Fishing Eagles (Art. 52);
(iv) the खरशब्द or उत्क्रोश-कुरर ,, ,, Gull;
(v) the उत्क्रोशी-कुररी ,, ,, Tern (Art. 69);
(vi) the ,, ,, Curlew, rarely कुरर as perhaps in the रामा-
or कुक्कुटी-कुररी यण (Art. 72).

It follows, therefore, that the particular bird or birds intended in a given passage must be determined from the context, e. g. in the lists of प्रसहा: and प्लवा: in चरक and सुश्रुत as explained earlier in this article; कुरर in association with water-birds like the सारस or क्रौञ्च would refer either to the Gulls and Terns or the Demoiselle Crane; and कुरर in धर्मशास्त्र literature should be taken to include the Gulls, Terns and Curlew, for the Demoiselle Crane would be included in term क्रौञ्च for all Cranes, and the Osprey and Fishing Eagles would fall within the general terms like श्येन and गृध्र or क्रव्यादपक्षी. The feminine कुररी on the other hand always signifies either the Tern or the Curlew as the context may demand. It must also be noted here that according to a well established convention birds of prey are held to be rather inauspicious (cf. अनिष्टविहग in बृहत्संहिता, 47. 4-7 and commentary of भट्टोत्पल) and are not mentioned in passages descriptive of beautiful natural scenery while they are inseparable concomitants of battle fields, burial or cremation grounds, etc. where the sentiments of disgust (बीभत्स) and fear (रौद्र) are involved. Turning to the call notes of कुररी, so common in similes, the reference is always to the sorrowful wail of women when in personal danger or when in fear of the loss of their near and dear ones. Such a reference to a large number of women crying over a threatened loss during the day time is to the Terns as birds of diurnal habits who gather in large flocks, crying plaintively, whenever their eggs and young are in danger. On the other hand, references to a single woman or a number of women crying piteously at night or before dawn are always to the Curlew or Curlews as these are chiefly heard at night and when on

---

*The Osprey is a winter visitor to India and as it is noisy mostly during the breeding season it is seldom heard in this country though its call notes are a loud Kai-Kai-Kai (Salim Ali in *The Book of Indian Birds*). The epithet or adnoun उत्क्रोश, therefore, is not applicable to it though it is included in a general way within the term उत्क्रोश for any Fishing Eagle.

the wing (Arts. 69 & 72)[1]. Bearing these considerations in mind it is not difficult to see that the numerous कुरर birds in the following passages relating to day-time scenes can only be the Gulls and Terns:

कादम्बैश्चक्रवाकैश्च कुररैर्जलकुक्कुटैः ।
कारण्डवैः प्लवैर्हंसैर्बकैर्मद्गुभिरेव च ॥—महाभारत, 3.158.56
—भागवत, 3.21.43

ददृशुः सहिता रम्यं तडागं योजनायतम् ।
शरारिहंसकुररैराकीर्णं जलचारिभिः ॥—रामायण, 3.15.6 (Cal. edn.)
अस्माद्धंसा जलक्लिन्नाः पक्षैः सलिलविस्रवैः ।
कुरराः सारसाश्चैव निष्पतन्ति पतत्रिणः ॥—रामायण 4.52.12 (Bom. edn.)

The sportive duels of Gulls or a Gull trying to snatch fish from a Tern in the air over the Tapti river is referred to as चटुलकुररद्वन्द्वम् in नलचम्पू, उच्छ्वास 6, verse 25. An important point worth noting in the above passages is the fact that the poets have taken care to mention birds that are on the water, at the water's edge, on the bank and those that fly in the air above, for it is all these taken together that give character to a lake or river scene.

Coming to the later names for a Gull we have गङ्गाचिल्ली for the Black-headed Gull (M. W.) or, for the matter of that, for any Gull and which is perhaps from the following synonymy:

गङ्गाचिल्ली तु देवट्टी, विश्वका जलकुक्कुटी[2]—त्रिकाण्डशेष

The name गङ्गाचिल्ली (Ganges-Kite) refers to the Kite-like scavenging habit of the Gulls picking up offal from the surface of the water or tit bits thrown up to them in the air which they greedily catch with their feet. Referring to the coastal Gulls Salim Ali remarks: "Gulls are to seaports and docks what kites are to inland towns and bazaars – efficient scavengers." The name देवट्टी (दिवि आकाशे अटति, देवाय क्रीडार्थं वा अटति) refers either to their magnificent flight or (देवलोकात् अटति आगच्छति) to their seasonal visit to the country from beyond the Himalayas (cf. देवलोकोद्भवा कोकिलाः for the Himalayan Cuckoos, Art. 37). Gulls being essentially sea-birds who "swim excellently and can be seen even on the roughest day, bobbing up and down on the waves as happy as can be" fully deserve the picturesque names of वीचीकाक (Wave-bird or Crow) and समुद्रकाक (Sea Crow). The latter term is wide enough to include, in a general way, all other sea-birds as well.

Hindi ढामरा (Dhomra in *F.B.I.* is probably a Bengali transliteration like 'Jol' for जल) for a Gull should be from Sansk. डमर onomatopoetic for 'uproar or tumult' of festivity or strife (cf. आडम्बर, डामर, डमरू) and emphasizes their screaming and scrambling habits. The equation, "ढामरा हंस्याम्" in वाचस्पत्यम् and शब्दकल्पद्रुम would seem to be based upon the story of an old हंस eating the eggs of other water-birds related in the Mahābhārata,

1. Illustrative examples from literature have been given in these articles.
2. For the second half of this synonymy see Art. 65.

2. 42. 32ff. No bird of the Goose family is known to eat eggs in a state of nature and it is probable that some egg-eating Gull like the Great Black-headed Gull has been called a हंस in a mystic (कूट) or etymological sense of हिनस्तीति हंसः, and some old commentator perhaps rendered this हंस of the story correctly by the local vernacular term of डामरा, a Gull. The lexicographer would then seem to have picked up the term डामरा as a Sanskrit feminine form and rendered it back as हंसी.

The Gulls as a class, we have seen, are of great help in maintaining the cleanliness of the waters and the surrounding areas by making a clean sweep of all dead and putrid animal matter and it has also been pointed out that some particular species are of particular service to humanity by destroying large quantities of harmful worms and insects which if allowed to multiply unchecked would produce famine in the country, and history records how at one time the people of the State of Utah in North America would have suffered grievously but for the timely help rendered to them by the California Gulls and how they expressed their gratitude to these wonderful birds: "That at least one community has not been unmindful of the substantial debt it owes the Gull is attested in Salt Lake City, where stands a monument surmounted by bronze figures of two Gulls, erected by the people of that city 'in grateful remembrance' of the signal service rendered by these birds at a critical time in the history of the community. For three consecutive years—1848 to 1850—black crickets by millions threatened to ruin the crops upon which depended the very lives of the settlers. Large flocks of California Gulls came to the rescue and devoured vast numbers of the destructive insects, until the fields were entirely freed from them. It is no wonder that the sentiment of the people of Utah, as reflected through their laws, affords Gulls the fullest protection" (*Birds of America*, 1. 38). In India, also we have the Black-headed and the Brown-headed Gulls who follow the cultivator's plough, gobble up all the pernicious vermin exposed in the furrows and thus render a great service to us, and one would not be surprised if the Vedic Aryans too were fully conscious of their services and left a still more lasting memorial of their gratefulness to them.

69

TERNS

1. A tern in general outline is an altogether more graceful, more beautiful but a smaller edition of a Gull.[1] Unlike the latter it has a straight but thinner and more pointed bill, long pointed wings, and in many species a deeply forked tail. In size they range from ten to twenty inches in length. They have a beautiful plumage, black on the head and neck, pearl to ashy-grey on the upper and white on the lower parts. Bill, legs and feet are often red. They are as noisy as the Gulls but unlike them again they exclude offal and garbage from their dietary and live mainly on small fish, sand-eels, crustacea and insects. They are very active and seem to have a ceaseless flight which is buoyant, fast, easy and exceedingly graceful.[2] They are "among the most beautiful of God's creatures. The beauty of their form is perfect. Their shape is a dream of comeliness and their movements are the poetry of motion. Wherever there is a river or lake in India, there you will see Terns. You cannot mistake a Tern; the slim white body, the long racing wings, the easy flight and the frequent descent to the water are a combination of characteristics peculiar to these feathered exquisites" (Douglas Dewar).

2. They nest, as a rule, in large or small colonies on sand-banks along the larger rivers and the sea-coast, the nests being mere hollows scraped in the sand. We can form some idea of the reasons behind this communal breeding if we recall the well known fact that people are particularly stimulated when working in cooperation in various fields like sports, community dances, social activities, war, etc. and in times of danger group consciousness helps to create confidence and a sense of security, and ensures ultimate success of an undertaking. Applying this analogy to social birds like the Flamingos, Terns and others it would seem that the presence of large numbers on their breeding grounds has the effect of

---

1. The reader is requested to read the first two paras of the preceding article.

2. Compare the name आति (अत्—सातत्यगमने: one that is constantly on the move) for the allied form, the Skimmer. It is more than probable that आति of the Ṛgveda meant a Tern as well as the closely allied Skimmer. The name is discussed in the next article.

stimulating their sexual impulses which leads to simultaneous mating and breeding among them. In other words the Terns would seem to have realised in the course of evolution that their safety and survival in the struggle for existence lies in keeping together and breeding in packed colonies.[1] As a preliminary to mating they indulge in lock-displays and social flights resembling the communal aerial dances of some of the Gulls, e.g. the Herring Gull. The courtship display of mated pairs includes (i) what has been aptly described as a 'fish-flight' where a bird with or without a fish is sportingly pursued and overtaken by another; (ii) swift glides from a height; (iii) slow-motion flights; and (iv) parading, bowing, scraping, stretching and 'scissor-billing' when on the ground. Both sexes brood the eggs and young and take part in feeding the latter, and some, like the Sandwitch Tern, are known to 'pool the young' of a colony after they are a few weeks old.[2] They are extremely demonstrative in their affection for young and eggs, for "a human being has only to set foot on a sand-bank for a scene of great excitement to ensue. Sitting birds rise from the nests, others arrive from the river,...and the air is filled with Terns flashing backwards and forwards and wheeling round and round overhead, their shrill plaintive cries indicating only too surely the presence of the eggs and offspring they seek to protect" (Whistler). They also appear to be very sympathetic towards their fellows that may get into difficulties. If one is killed the others in the neighbourhood will at once come and fly anxiously about uttering their plaintive cries all the time.[3] Salim Ali's explanation of such behaviour when one has been actually shot down into the river, is that "the unwounded birds think their companion has discovered some food and are anxious to share the spoils" and in the particular circumstances stated it would appear to be correct. Mated Terns, again, are very attentive to each other, and "one of the most charming sights of a visit to a colony is to see one of these little, gentle creatures feed his mate as she sits brooding her eggs".

3. About fifty species of Tern occur throughout the world and India claims no fewer than thirtytwo of them either as winter visitors to her coasts and inland waters or as resident birds. Brief notes on some of the more important Terns found in India are given below :

(i) The Indian Whiskered Tern (10") has a velvety black head and neck, ash-grey body and black abdomen. It is a resident bird of lakes and marshes. It breeds in colonies and makes a nest of reeds and rushes which is placed on lotus leaves or other water plants in lakes or swamps. When

---

1. R. M. Lockey in *Birds of the Sea* (1945), p. 17.

2. J. Fisher in *Bird Recognition* Vol. 1 (1947), pp. 124-150. According to S. Baker in *F.B.I.* (*Birds*), 1929, however, the Sandwitch Tern is very careless of its eggs. 'Pooling the young' refers to the feeding of the young in a colony by the adult birds irrespective of whether the young are their own, i.e., they are all fed in common.

3. T. Gilbert Pearson on the Least Terns (Ternlets) in *Birds of America* (1936).

fishing a whole flock generally works in unison, commencing at the end of a lake and working their way to the other end, when once more they return to their original starting point. In this they resemble the Skimmer who, however flies over the water very low, just a few inches above the surface. The flight is most light and elegant, and the sight of a flock feeding is a really beautiful one.

(ii) The Caspian Tern (20") is easily recognised by its great size, large red bill, black legs and feet, black head and grey and white body as it flies singly or in pairs over the larger rivers of India. It breeds on the lakes of Central and Western Asia, and the Mekran Coast within Indian limits. It is often mistaken for a Gull because of its large size and is known as केकरा (a dialectical variant of कुररी ?) in Sind after its loud harsh cry. Describing its ways in *The Birds of America,* W.L. Finley remarks that its greatest anxiety seems to be to keep them (the young) crouching low in the nest, so that they do not run away and get lost in the crowd (of other young from the neighbouring nests). If a young bird did start to run out of the nest, he was immediately pounced upon by his own parents and pecked and beaten until he dropped flat on the ground or hid in the leaves. A similar trait was observed by the ancient Indians as we shall see.

(iii) The Gull-billed Tern (15") is rather stoutly built and in point of body-shape stands intermediate between a Gull and a typical Tern. It is pearl-grey above and pure white below but its stout Gull-like black bill and legs of the same colour help to distinguish it from other Terns of the same size. Its scientific name of 'Gelochelidon nilotica' (lit. 'Laughing Swallow of the Nile') is after its call-notes described by Dr. Ridgway as 'a chattering laugh' (*Birds of America*). It shows great courage in defending its young. It breeds in Kashmir and other places in India and frequents the larger rivers and lakes often singly or in twos and threes. It feeds on small fish and insects and like so many Terns and Gulls, is especially fond of grasshoppers.

(iv) The Large Crested Tern (20"), which occurs in several races in India, is practically equal in size to the Caspian Tern but is readily distinguishable from it by the yellow bill and a well-developed, long, black and slightly curved crest.* They are coastal birds and one sub-species breeds off the Mekran Coast and another off the Sunderbans in lower Bengal.

(v) The Indian River Tern (15"-18") and the allied forms, the Black-bellied Tern (13"-14"), and the Tibetan Tern (15"-18") are the commonest Terns of North Indian rivers and lakes, the first two breeding in large colonies on sand-banks of our rivers, and the third on rivers and lakes of Ladakh and Tibet and winters in India. Other members of the group

*Smythies *in Birds of Burma* (1940).

like the White-cheeked and the Common Terns[1] are coastal birds. All these have black heads and crests, grey upper parts and white or white suffused with vinous-grey lower parts. All have deeply forked tails. The bill, legs and feet are yellow or red. The Black-bellied Tern frequents also small ditches and village ponds for food. The River Ternlet (10″) is practically a smaller edition of its larger cousin, the River Tern, which it resembles in breeding and other habits.

The common Sanskrit name for a Tern is कुररी as already noted in the preceding article, and for a small Tern or Ternlet, कुररिका as we shall see presently. The Indian River Tern, a permanent resident and the most numerous with us is known as कुररी in Hindi as well.[2] कुररी for a female Osprey or Fishing Eagle (Art. 50) is merely a grammatical feminine of कुरर[3] and the term is never used in literature in this sense because the names of all birds of prey like गृध्र, श्येन, कुरर, भास, etc. are always used in the masculine irrespective of sex except in mythology where गृध्री, भासी, and श्येनी are said to be the 'original mothers' of certain groups of birds in the Epics and Purāṇas[4] and गृध्री is occasionally used for the Common Kite e.g. in प्रबोधचन्द्रोदय, 4.3 (see Art. 52). Moreover the Osprey breeds very rarely in India and its callnotes are seldom heard in the country as pointed out by Salim Ali in his *Book of Indian Birds*. The कुररी, of literatures is therefore either the Tern or the Curlew according to context. It must also be noted that the cries of birds of prey have always been regarded as inauspicious and are never used as a simile for the plaintive wail of women of noble birth like सीता, or dramatic heroines like मालती of 'मालतीमाधव'. To render कुररी, in such contexts as the female Osprey or the Lapwing ((टिट्टिभ) is wholly indefensible.

The Curlew[5] breeds outside India and is only a winter visitor with us. The कुररी of अश्वघोष, crying plaintively at the loss of her young, is therefore the River or Black-bellied Tern, both breeding on the North-Indian rivers :

विषादपरिप्लवलोचना ततः प्रनष्टपोता कुररीव दुःखिता ।
विहाय धैर्यं विरुराव गौतमी तताम चैवाश्रुमुखी जगाद च ।।

बुद्धचरित, 8.51.

---

1. Writing about the Common Tern, which is a winter visitors to India along the Mekran coast and is closely allied to our River Tern, E. H. Forbush says that these birds are useful to the fisherman as they serve to mark the schools of edible fish. These fish drive the small fry to the surface, the telescopic eyes of the Terns mark the disturbance from afar and when the fishermen see the gahering, plunging flocks, they put off in their boats, well knowing that their work lies there. (*Birds of America*.)

2. Suresh Sinha in हमारी चिड़ियां (Allahabad, 1941).

3. See Art. 68 for the different meanings of कुरर.

4. रामायण, 3.14.19; म.भा. 1.66.58; मत्स्यपुराण, 6.31-32; हरिवंश, 1.3.107; ब्रह्म पु. 3.93-94; and other Purāṇas.

5. See Art. 72 for कुररी the curlew.

Terns rarely settle on the water, and "it is a pretty sight to watch a flock of Terns following a shoal of little fishes with clamorous glee, dropping one after another with a splash and rising again and chasing one another ceaselessly" (EHA). Such a scene is recalled in the following :

> प्रसन्नसलिलाः सौम्य कुररीभिर्विनादिताः ।
> चक्रवाकगणाकीर्णा विभान्ति सलिलाशयाः ॥ —रामायण, 4.30,59.

> क्रीडाकृतार्थकुररकामिनीव्याहार (कुररकामिनी, कुररी)
> —यशस्तिलकचम्पू, p. 248

and the wailing of hundreds of women of Rāvaṇa's household on the occasion of his death at the hands of Rāma is reminiscent of the clamorous scene witnessed on a sand-bank when a large colony of nesting and brooding Terns is alarmed;

> विलेपुरेवं दीनास्ता राक्षसाधिपयोषितः ।
> कुर्यं इव दुःखार्ता वाष्पपर्याकुलेक्षणाः ॥ —रामायण, 6.110.26

Similar scenes are noticed elsewhere as well :

> स गङ्गामनुवृन्दानि स्त्रीणां भरतसत्तम ।
> कुररीणामिवार्तानां क्रोशन्तीनां ददर्श ह ॥ —म. भा. 11.12.5.

> तासां नादो रुदतीनां तदाऽऽसीद्
> राजन् दुःखात्कुररीणामिवोच्चैः । — Ibid. 15.15.11

> श्येनपक्षाभिमृष्टानां कुररीणामिवध्वनिः ।—प्रतिज्ञायौगन्धरायण, 4.24.

The above passages, it may be noted, relate to events occurring in day time. श्येन, a falcon, it may be noted, is a bird of diurnal habits.

The Whiskered Tern unlike others, as we have seen, constructs a nest of rushes and water weeds wound round a lotus leaf in a marsh or tank and has therefore been very aptly named पुष्करशायिका (पद्मशायिन्या in कल्पद्रुकोश) explained as पद्मपत्रशायिका by डल्हणाचार्य on सुश्रुत and this is the same as पोक्खरसातक[1] (v.l. पोक्खरसाति, i.e. पुष्करसाद—पुष्करसादी) for a water-bird in वेस्संतर जातक, verse 2104. The Vedic पुष्करसाद[2] or पुष्करसद is therefore this Tern :

> कलविङ्कः लोहिताहिः पुष्करसादस्ते त्वाष्ट्रा —वाज. संहिता, 24.31

---

1. This is a compound name for a single bird but has been incorrectly split up into पोक्खर and सातक, and rendered as two different birds in the *Pali Dictionary* (P.T.S. edition).

2. पुष्करसाद is rendered simply as 'lotus-sitter' by Keith on तैत्ति. संहिता, 5.5.14; 'पुष्करसर्प : भ्रमर इत्येके' by सायण on ibid., and पुष्करभक्षी पक्षिविशेषः by उव्वट on वाज. संहिता. It is hardly necessary to state that no Tern feeds on any part of the lotus plant.

त्वष्ट्रा being the expert artisan of the gods three beautiful creatures have been named as his sacrificial victims at the अश्वमेध—(i) कलविङ्क i.e. the पीतमुण्ड कलविङ्क, the Weaver Bird which builds a beautiful rain-proof nest (Art. 22); (ii) लोहिताहि, the prettily marked Coral Snake; and (iii) पुष्करसाद (one nesting on a lotus leaf), the Whiskered Tern. This Tern is no bigger than a Ternlet and has been correctly called कुररिका and its nesting habit as also its love for the young have been accurately described by कुलशेखर वर्मा (see para. 3 (ii) above):

अर्द्धाभ्युद्‌गतपत्रकं परिलुठत् पत्रेषु पङ्केरुहाम् ।
प्रायः पोतकजातकं कुररिकाः पक्षैः समूहन्त्यमूः ॥ —तपतीसंवरण, 3.2.

कुररिका means a small Tern or Ternlet but the poet would seem to have used the term with a feeling of compassion also (अनुकम्पायां कन्) as is clearly implied by the earlier pitiful remarks of the boy-hermit in the drama :

अहो पतत्रिणामप्यतिकृपणः संसारधर्मः ।

In the above context the expression संसारधर्मः has been correctly rendered as पुत्रवात्सल्यम् by the commentator.

70

SKIMMER OR SCISSORBILL

The Skimmer is a white Tern-like bird with a black cap, a white collar and very long black wings. It is purely a water bird found on the larger, broader rivers where their course is placid, flowing smoothly between sand-banks. Occasionally it visits jheels and tanks, but only where there is a clear expanse of water free from weeds. It is the most curious and highly specialized bird and its method of feeding is correlated to its peculiarly formed bill. Both mandibles are deep and greatly compressed, much as if two knife-blades had been set edge to edge; the upper mandible is considerably shorter than the lower which projects beyond it by nearly an inch. When feeding the bird skims along the surface of the water with the beak wide open, the lower mandible inserted into the water and the upper quite clear of it. As soon as a small fish strikes the razor edge and runs up the incline the jaws close swiftly upon it. A party of Skimmers flying steadily backwards and forwards along the surface of the water appear "literally to plough the main" with the lower mandible of their bills.[1] Though the flight is slow and leisuerly when feeding, they can go at immense speed when frightened. Their note is a shrill chattering scream (S. Baker). Only one species of Skimmer is found in India. Other species, known in America, have names like 'Cut-Water'. 'Razor-bill' and 'Scissorbill'. It is known as पनचिरा ('water-cleaver' or 'cut-water') in Hindi. It is a faithful rendering of Sanskrit शरारी (fr. शरम् 'water', and आर्, 'to insert, to place in, Cf. आरा, a cobbler's awl or a probe, and "शरारिका रन्ध्रकारिणी"—कल्पद्रुकोश).

Existing lexical synonymies notwithstanding, शरारी and आटी (v.l. आटि, आडि, आडी) are two different birds possessing two different types of bills after which two surgical instruments named शरारीमुख and आटीमुख were designed by सुश्रुत as mentioned in the सुश्रुतसंहिता.[2] The शरारीमुख instrument is recommended as a blood-letting lancet[3] and as a pair of scissors[4]. It is, therefore, a dual purpose instrument and commentator डल्हणाचार्य accepts

1. Whistler & *Ency. Brit.* 11th and 14 editions.
2. 1.8.3.
3. Paragraph 4, ibid.
4. Para. 7, Ibid,

this and calls it by the alternative name of कर्तरी or scissors. Conscious of the fact that शरारी and आटी were different, he was, however, misled by the incorrect synonymies of अमर and हलायुध, and equated आटी with जलवर्धनी and postulated two varieties of शरारी characterised with long bills, one having a white shoulder and the other a red head, the first of which he called the शरारी proper :—

> शरारीमुखमिति, शरारिर्दीर्घचञ्चुः पक्षिविशेषः स द्विविधः — धवलस्कन्धो रक्तशीर्षश्च, धवलस्कन्धस्य शरारीति संज्ञा तन्मुखवन्मुखमस्य तच्छरारीमुखं, तस्य शस्त्रस्य लोके कर्तरीति संज्ञा ।

As already stated, there is only one variety of the Skimmer in India and the red-headed bird mentioned by him is no other than the आटी or the Black Ibis with a red papillated head (Ast. 80). His equation "आटी जलवर्धनीनाम पक्षिविशेषः" also confuses between the Ibis and the Skimmer, for the name जलवर्धनी (वर्ध् to cut', and वर्धनी 'a broom') means (i) 'water-cutter' and (ii) 'water-sweeper' or 'water-broom', i.e. a bird that cuts the water or sweeps over it. Both these senses are perfectly applicable to the Skimmer but none of them to the Ibis. The epithet धवलस्कन्ध may be said to be true of the Skimmer with reference to the broad white collar it has, but if it refers to the white shoulder patch of the Black Ibis, it would be difficult to maintain a distinction between the two birds intended by the commentator as both the epithets धवलस्कन्ध and रक्तशीर्ष would then signify the Black Ibis alone.

The editors of the Nirnayasagara Press editions of सुश्रुत have failed to understand the dual nature of the शरारीमुख instrument as explained by डल्हणाचार्य and also by the statement "दशाङ्गुला शरारीमुखी या सा कर्तरीति कथ्यते ।"[1] in the text itself and, falling back upon वाग्भट, they argue that शरारीमुख, as a lancet and pair of scissors, must be two different instruments, for one and the same instrument cannot perform both the operations :

> (सुश्रुत) वाक्येन शरारीमुखस्य विस्रावणमेव कर्मोक्तं, कर्तर्यास्तु कर्म छेदनमेव, तस्मादेतच्छस्त्रद्वयं पृथगेव भवितुमर्हति ।[2]

Hārānchandra's identification of शरारि with सरल (i.e. शरालि or Whistling Teal—Art 84c) is also quoted in this footnote and as the Duck's bill is flat and broad a rider is added that सुश्रुत refers only to the length of the Duck's bill and not to its breadth ! Nothing could be more absurd, particularly when it is remembered that डल्हणाचार्य prescribes a length of 12 fingers or approximately 7 inches and the Duck's bill is less than even 2.5. inches. The fact is that the identity of the two birds, आटी and शरारी and the exact

1. I.8.7. The Persian name for the bird is also derived from a word (maqass) meaning scissors.

2. Foot-note to सुश्रुत I.8.8 (1938 ed).

nature of their bills have been completely missed and for this not the commentators but the later lexicographers, who were each more of a grammarian than a field-naturalist, are responsible. The confusion dates back at least to the time of अमरसिंह, and his false synonymy on the identity of the names of several birds has been copied in the later lexicons including M. Williams. We have thus the following lexical equations :—

(i) शराटिराटिराडिश्च—अमर.

(ii) आटिः शरारिराटिः स्यात्—हलायुध and हेमचन्द्र (अभि. चि.)

(iii) आतिस्त्वाटिः शराटिका —वैजयन्ती

(iv) शरारिरारिराटिश्च शरार्यार्यातिरित्यपि
शरालिश्च शराली च —कल्पद्रुकोश

(v) आतिः —शरातिपक्षी —उणादिसूत्रवृत्ति of उज्वलदत्त.

(vi) आतिः —जलोपरिसंचारिणि खगे—

(vii) आटिः शरारिराडिश्च विचित्रा जलचारिणी—मदनपालनिघण्टु

It would be seen that while अमर, हलायुध and हेमचन्द्र have confused शरारि or आति with आटि or आडि, वैजयन्ती goes further and includes शराटिका in the same equation. कल्पद्रुकोश goes still further and brings in शरालि as well. It may perhaps help if, before proceeding with the identification of शरारी the above names are allocated to their respective owners :

(i) शरारि, आरि, आति, शराति —the Skimmer

(ii) आटि, आटी, आडि, आडी —the Black Ibis (Art. 80)

(iii) शराटिका (v.l. शराटी) —the White Ibis (Art. 80)

(iv) शरालि, शराली —the Whistling Teal (Art. 84 C)

The other synonymies for शरारि found in शब्दार्थचिन्तामणि and शब्दकल्पद्रुम have proved of considerable help in identifying it as one of the names of the Skimmer. They are ध्रुव and हिल्ल. Wilson's Dictionary also equates हिल्ल with शरारि. Now ध्रुव means 'fixed', 'constant' and in music 'the introductory verse of a song recurring as a kind of burthen'. ध्रुवका (ध्रुवतीति ध्रुवका, आवपनविशेषः —गणरत्नमहोदधि*) is a particular mode of ploughing the land where a plough or a team of ploughs proceeds straight in a direction to the end of the field and works back to the starting base-line, and so on. हिल्ल is fr. हिल्-हावकृतौ, भावकरणे and means 'to sport' and हिल्लोल, cognate with हिन्दोल, refers to a 'to and fro motion' (हिल्लोलयति, दोलयति). If these senses of the words ध्रुव and हिल्ल are checked up with the habits of the Skimmer as described by Whistler, no doubt is left as to the identity of ध्रुव, हिल्ल, and शरारी. The bird is constantly on the move going back and forth over a fixed beat, and

*I.62.

the names आति (अत् सातत्यगमने) and शराति (शरे जलोपरि अतति) also refer to this trait of the bird; cf. विचित्रा जलचारिणी in synonymy (vii) above. The statement "नद्यां आति: नद्याति:" in पतञ्जलि महाभाष्य[1] also brings out the close association of the आति with a river. It flies very low over the surface of the water—hardly a couple of inches above it—for it must cut the surface with the lower mandible all the time—and, therefore, appears to cut or sweep the surface of the water as it were and this has given it the name of जलवर्धनी (वर्धनी, 'a cutter' or 'broom'). The name आरि in कल्पद्रु is merely short for शरारि and supports the derivation of the latter suggested above. The open position of the two blades of the bill and their closing upon a tiny fish clearly resembles the action of a pair of scissors and this, evidently suggested the शरारी मुखयन्त्र as a dual purpose surgical instrument. The lower mandible of the Skimmer projects considerably beyond the upper and resembles a knife-blade with a vertically flat and rounded point so that if a pair of scissors resembling this bird's bill is made it will act as a scissors up to the tip of the upper blade while the projecting flat tip of the lower blade, if sharpened, will serve as a blood-letting lancet. One can only admire the power of acute observation and originality of the Sage सुश्रुत in designing his instruments. आटी and शराटि for the Ibises, and शरालि for the Whistling Teal Duck will be found discussed in the articles noted against them above, but a word or two in explanation of how the different names came to be confused, one with the other, would not be out of place here. It appears that the earliest lexicons, now lost, gave the names separately for 'a kind of bird' but later when the identity of the birds themselves was forgotten, lexicographers who, working within the four walls of their study were concerned more with considerations of Grammar and brevity than anything else, treated the names as examples of substitution (according to "रलयोरैक्यम्", "डलयोरभेद:", etc., and the changes of त—ट—ड— e.g. in words like प्रतिमा — पटिमा, पतङ्ग—पटंग, घट—घड, चटक—चडग etc.) and therefore held them to be identical, that, in short, all of them were variae lectiones (पाठभेदा:) of one or two original names. At the same time it is difficult not to blame them for overlooking the distinction between शरारी and आटी so evident in सुश्रुत.

In Vedic literature the Skimmer occurs under the name of आति in RV[2]. and in the वाज.संहिता.[3] In the former उर्वशी and her companion-maids are discovered sporting at a lake by पुरूरवस् who goes in search of her. She asks him to return home, adding, that fast like the wind as she is, it would be

---

1. 6.1.127.

2. 10.95.9.

3. 24.34.

difficult for him to capture her.[1] The शतपथ ब्राह्मण[2] also mentions the story and describes the birds as frisking, skipping or flying over the water :—

ता अप्सरस आतयो भूत्वा परिपुप्लुविरे ।

We have already seen how parties of the Skimmers fly up and down their beat over a given stretch of water (river or lake) and how when alarmed they are capable of immense speed. The behaviour of उर्वशी and her friends in the form of आति birds is therefore perfectly in keeping with the ways of the Skimmer. The dedication of आति with वाहस (a particular type of Python, a snake being वायुभक्ष in Sanskrit), and दर्विदा (the Spoonbill, Art.79) to the Wind-god is quite in keeping with what उर्वशी as an आति says of herself—

दुरापना वात इवाहमस्मि ।

and no further comment is called for. It is submitted that to render आति as हंस is incorrect.

In secular literature also the Skimmer has been mentioned, once in the Rāmāyaṇa :[3]

ददृशुः सहिता रम्यं तडागं योजनायतम् ।
शरारिहंसकुररैराकीर्णं जलचारिभिः ॥

and again in the ऋतुसंहार 4. 6 :

प्रफुल्लनीलोत्पलशोभितानि शरारि(शरालि)कादम्बविभूषितानि ।
प्रसन्नतोयानि सुशीतलानि (सशैवलानि), सरांसि चेतांसि हरन्ति पुंसाम् ॥

Here if it is remembered that the Skimmer is associated with perfectly clean sheets of water and the Whistling Teal prefers weedy waters, the alternative reading of शरालि necessitates the reading 'सशैवलानि' while शरारि goes well with प्रसन्न and शीतल (clear and cool) waters.

Like the Vultures, the most unlikely entry of a Skimmer (वर्धनी) into a residential house is considered an ill omen :

क्रौञ्चश्च वर्धनी चैव निपतन्ति गृहे यदि—भविष्यपुराण, 2.20.17.

An appreciative reference to the charm that the आति bird adds to a lake should be a fitting close to this article : The Ducks are at home in the lotus-bed at one end; White Ibises (बक) fishing along the edges; a pair of

---

1 "दुरापना वात इवाहमस्मि" 95.2.

2. 11.5.1.

3. III.15.6 (Cal.Edn.), quoted under जलचारी in शब्दकल्पद्रुम.

the Ruddy Goose resting on the water elsewhere; beautiful young ladies singing in the shade on the bank, and the Skimmer sporting over the clear waters complete the picture :—

हंसैर्लब्धप्रशंसैस्तरलितकमलस्रस्तरङ्गैस्तरङ्गैः ।
नीरैरन्तर्गभीरैश्चपलबककुलत्रासलीनैश्च मीनैः ॥
पालीरूढद्रुमालीतलसुखशयितस्त्रीप्रणीतैश्च गीतैः ।
भाति प्रक्रीडदातिस्तवसलिलचलच्चक्रवाकस्तडागः ॥

सुभाषित, p. 220,19

71

PLOVERS

1. Plovers are round-headed and short-billed birds of open meadows and sandy ground, not resorting to cover. They range in size from a small Quail to a Dove, have rather long legs and walk and run freely on the ground. They have no hind toe or only a rudimentary one and are, therefore, unable to perch on trees. A majority of them undergo seasonal changes of colour-pattern and, being winter-visitors to the country, their identification from a distance is a matter of some difficulty, and yet quite a number of them have Sanskrit names based on some physical characteristics and the nature of their call-notes.

2. The Little Ringed Plover (6.5″), the smallest member of the group, is सर्षपी (fr. सर्षप mustard, indicative of its small size and rolling or tripping movement on the ground) and खञ्जनिका (खञ्जन इव आचरति—शब्दार्थचिन्तामणि, or 'a little Wagtail') from the black band* below the white collar and the habit of running nimbly in short spurts along sand-banks and edge of the water. Its smart, neat and trim appearance has won for it other pretty names like राजभट्टिका and राजपुत्रिका 'the Little Princess'. Its larger allies, e.g. the long-billed Ringed Plover of Nepal must naturally share the above names with it. The synonyms in त्रिकाण्डशेष and हारावली for these birds and the Pratincoles have been considered in Art. 65.

3. The Red-wattled Lapwing (13″) with its well-known call of 'ti-tee-tee-it' or 'did he do it' is the most familiar of resident Indian Plovers while the allied form, the Yellow-wattled Lapwing (10.5″) is less common. The Spur-winged Plover, (12″) also has a 'did-he-do-it' call. These are undoubtedly the टिट्टिभ of अमरकोश and other lexicons. कोयष्टि however is a different bird according to चरक, मनु, etc., but it has been equated with टिट्टिभ and other birds by others. An attempt must, therefore, be made to clear the confusion if possible.

---

*Because of this black band the Ringed Plover indirectly shares the epithet of कालकण्ठ with the खञ्जन, a White Wagtail, and as it is smaller than a Wgtail it has been called खञ्जना or खञ्जनिका—खञ्जनः खञ्जरीटे, स्त्री सर्षप्यां, खञ्जनं गतौ—मेदिनी. The grammatical feminine often indicates the small size of an object—स्त्री स्यात् काचिन्मृणाल्यादिविवक्षापचये यदि— अमर. 3.5.7.

4. Some of the relevant dictionary meanings, lexical synonymies and a couple of other references given below would perhaps be found useful:—

(1) यष्टिक—'A kind of water-fowl' and the Lapwing in M. W., and 'जलकुक्कुट' in शब्दकल्पद्रुम and शब्दार्थचिन्तामणि.

(2) कोयष्टि—'having legs like sticks', the Lapwing (or a small white Crane, commonly called Paddy-bird) in M. W.

(3) शिखरी Parra jacana or goensis—M. W. (=the Red-wattled Lapwing)

(4) टिट्टिभ and टिट्टिभक – Parra jacana—M. W.

(5) कोशिकी—कोयष्टि

(6) कोयष्टि : शिखरी समौ—हेमचन्द्र, वैजयन्ती

(7) कोयष्टिः शिखरी जलकुक्कुभः—अभिधानचिन्तामणि

(8) कोयष्टिः जलकुक्कुभः—त्रिकाण्डशेष

(9) कोयष्टिः टिट्टिभः—धन्वन्तरि

(10) कोयष्टिष्टिटिभष्टिट्टिः—कल्पद्रु.

(11) कोयष्टि or कोयष्टिक and टिट्टिभ are different birds in (i) मनुस्मृति, 5.11 & 13; (ii) मत्स्यपुराण 118.50-51; (iii) अमरकोश; and (iv) याज्ञवल्क्य, 1.173, where कोयष्टि has been loosely rendered as क्रौञ्च, i.e., Egret or Heron in the मिताक्षरा टीका (cf. the expression क्रौञ्चनिभा for 'birds resembling a Crane' in वसन्तराज, 4.48).

5. A consideration of the above material shows that originally the terms कोयष्टिक and टिट्टिभ, corresponding to कोयष्टि and कुयष्टिका of चरक,[1] applied to different birds and it was through the already existing कुयष्टिका as a synonym for टिट्टिभ that the name कोयष्टि also came very early to be identified with the red and yellow-wattled Lapwings. The terms यष्टिक, कुयष्टिका (diminutive from masc. कुयष्टिक), कोयष्टि and कोयष्टिक seem to form a sort of homonymous series based upon two different senses of यष्टि for (i) a stick or support, with reference to the longish legs or horn-like crest of a bird, and (ii) hair or anything thin or slender, referring to the thin and longish crest-feathers possessed by others. Similarly the prefixes and suffixes कु, को and क would seem to have been understood in several senses, e.g., (i) कुत्सितार्थे, अल्पार्थे, (ii) a variant of कं—जलम्; (iii) कं—शिरः; (iv) कं—केशः and (v) कन्—प्रकारार्थे. Thus यष्टिक as a homonym should be (i) the Water-cock (शिखरी or जलकुक्कुभ) with a horn or stick like appendage on the head and (ii) the Black-winged Stilt, a bird of the Lap-wing family, characterised by very long legs and called लामगोड़ी (the long-legged) in the vernacular. कुयष्टिका would then be (i) the Lapwings with shorter legs in comparison to the Stilt and (ii) the Green Plover or the Peewit with its long, thin, pointed and recurved crest. कोयष्टि of चरक, मनु, etc. and कोयष्टिक (प्रकारार्थे कन्) of अमर, सुश्रुत, and भवभूति are the smaller crested Herons and Bitterns which

1. M. Williams gives ककुयष्टिका by separating "चिरिटीककुयष्टिका" of चरक in correctly.

keep standing in shallow water for hours waiting for prey to come to them. This trait of theirs and the possession of thin crests may be explained with reference to the derivation of the name given in the रामाश्रमी टीका on अमर and elsewhere, "कं जलं यष्टिरिवास्य" to which I would add another "के मूर्ध्नि यष्टिरिवास्य". If the word यष्टि in the latter derivatlon is taken for 'a stick' it would be true of the Water-cock as well. See Art. 58 for Water-cock and Art. 82 for Herons.

6. The equation "कोयष्टिः शिखरी समौ" is, therefore, equally true of the Green Plover and the Water-Cock. This is evident from the fact that it has been extended to include जलकुक्कुभ in Nos. (7) & (8) above. The name शिखरी means 'pointed', 'crested' and 'erection of the hair on the body'. कोयष्टि or कोयष्टिक again, as a bird with powerful call-notes is either a टिट्टिभ, the Red or Yellow-Wattled Lapwing, or the Water-Cock according as the bird is placed in a drier or wet zone or with water birds. On the other hand कोयष्टि, or more correctly कोयष्टिक, as a water-side or tree-perching bird is any (one or more) variety of the *smaller crested* Herons or Bitterns.[1] Unlike the piercing and persistent notes of the Lapwings the voice of these birds is a mere croak, uttered at intervals.

7. Names like कोयष्टिभ[2] and कोयष्टिभक[3] are clearly formed on the analogy of टिट्टिभ and टिट्टिभक and point to the adaptation and appropriation of the term कोयष्टि (small crested Heron) for the commoner Lapwings and they too, like कुयष्टिका, mark another stage in the assimilation of the name कोयष्टि, with टिट्टिभ for the Lapwings. It must, however, be noted that the poets have used all the variants of कोयष्टि indiscriminately for the Lapwings or small Herons according to the needs of the metre in hand. Thus even the form कोयष्टिभक has been used for the smaller Bitterns in रामायण (Art. 82). In the following examples the birds meant by कोयष्टि, कोयष्टिभक, and कोयष्टिक are the Lapwings:—

कोयष्टिभिश्चार्जुनकैः शतपत्रैश्च कीचकैः ।
एतैश्चान्यैश्च बहुभिर्नादितं तद्वनं महत् ॥

रामायण 3.75.12

प्रहृष्टकोयष्टिभकोकिलस्वनै-
र्विनोदयन्तं च सुखं परं शिवम् ॥

Ibid., 2.54.43

उद्दामद्युमणिद्युतिव्यतिकरप्रक्रीडदर्कोपल-
ज्वालाजालजटालजाङ्गलतटीनिष्कूजकोयष्टयः ॥

अनर्घराघव 2.30

---

1. कोयष्टि has been rendered as क्रौञ्च, i.e., a Heron like bird or alternatively as बक in the same sense in याज्ञवल्क्यस्मृति, 1.173.

2. Rāmāyaṇa 2.54.43.

3. Ibid. 5.1.44, and Allahabad Ed., 6.38.9.

दात्यूहकोयष्टिकाद्यः क्वचिच्चातिमनोहरैः ।
पुंस्कोकिलकलालापैः श्रुतिहारिभिरन्वितम् ॥

मार्कण्डेय पुराण, 58.24.

हंसकारण्डवाकीर्णं चक्राह्वैः सारसैरपि ।
जलकुक्कुटकोयष्टिदात्यूहकुलकूजितम् ॥

भागवत, 8.2.15.

8. The Red-wattled Lapwing being one of the commonest birds of India has earned for itself several other names and finds a place in literature under the name of टिट्टिभ. It is a very demonstrative bird, is greatly agitated and becomes noisy whenever a human being appears anywhere near its nest. Its anxiety for its eggs or young accounts for names like अण्डीरक (अण्ड+ईर् कम्पने ?) of the बृहत्संहिता and अण्डुक (कै शब्दे ?) of वैजयन्ती. The epithet उत्पादशयन indicates its habit of resting or sleeping while standing on one or both legs, but the story-teller forgetting the original sense of the expression has founded a wonderful conceit upon it. The bird is said to sleep on its back with legs stretched straight up with the deliberate idea of protecting itself should the heavens fall down upon it !

उत्क्षिप्य टिट्टिभः पादावास्ते भङ्गभयाद्दिवः ।*

पञ्चतन्त्र, समुद्रटिट्टिभकथा

A king is advised simply to ignore the unworthy pressing his request repeatedly like the Lapwing :–

टिट्टिभं तमनुपेक्षेत वाशमानमिवातुरम् महाभारत, 12.114.4.

Both this and the Yellow-wattled Lapwing, as also the Spur-winged Plover are कटुक्वाण from their harsh cries and the first two are पीतपाद from their yellow legs and सदालूता (लूता चर्मव्रणे—a scar—धन्वन्तरिनिघण्टु) from their permanent scar-like wattles:

टिट्टिभी पीतपादश्च सदालूता नृजागरः

राजनिघण्टु

9. The कटुक of मत्स्यपुराण, 'कटुकान्टिट्टिभान्भटान्' would also seem to refer to a particular Lapwing as the name is analogous to कटुक्वाण. The Sociable

*Similarly, the poets, commentators and lexicographers have misunderstood the name अष्टापद, a Giraffe, and interpreted it as a fabulous monster with eight legs, the normal four and a second set growing upwards from the back. See जैन आदिपुराण of जिनसेन 27, 70 and 31, 25 where the अष्टापद taking a somersault into the air is described as landing safely on his second set of legs. The body of the Giraffe is marked with a chequered pattern resembling a chess-board (अष्टापद), and hence the name. Lexical epithets like उत्पादक (standing high on legs), महास्कन्ध (high-shouldered), उष्ट्राकृति, and ऊर्ध्वनयन (looking high up) also belong to him. It is incorrect to describe अष्टापद as a fabulous animal though as described in the above work it is certainly unreal.

Lapwing has a mewing wail of a single loud and harsh note and occurs as a 'not uncommon' winter visitor in North India. The name कटुक, therefore, most probably refers to it.

10. The शयाण्डक* bird (?), has been dedicated to the sun in his friendly aspect along with two others, शार्ग the Bee-eater and सृजय the Paradise Flycatcher (Arts. 40 & 11):

शार्गः सृजयः शयाण्डकस्ते मैत्राः ।

वाज. संहिता, 24.33

As the first two are insect-eating birds it is probable that शयाण्डक too has similar habits. The name perhaps bears some analogy to अण्डरिक and अण्डुक for the Red-Wattled Lapwing, and may possibly be derived, शय+अण्ड+क, i.e., a bird that lays its eggs on the ground and cries (कै शब्दे) anxiously for them when in danger. If so, it should be the same as टिट्टिभ. All the three birds are beneficial to the crops in the field, orchard or grove. Moreover their striking colour-patterns are best set off during flight in the sun. The mild sun of the winter-months is indeed a friend to man as are these birds:

विवस्वान् श्रावणे मासि प्रौष्ठपद्यां भगः स्मृतः ।

*   *   *

मार्गशीर्षे भवेन्मित्रः पौषे विष्णुः सनातनः ।

कूर्मपुराण, 43.21-22.

11. The most prominent feature of the Avocet is its long, flexible and upcurved bill with which it probes into the mud for worms and insects. The upturned bill reminds one of a digging tool or a ploughshare. Its Hindi name कुसिया चाहा (a Snipe with a bill like a ploughshare; fr. कुशिक, a ploughshare) is the same as कशिकानी, a water-bird in चरक, and कशीका, काशीका, and कषिका ("कषिका पक्षिजातिः"–उणादि 4.16; "खनित्रे कशी"–गणरत्नमहोदधि 51; कषीका [illegible]. and कश a thong which is of course flexible). कुषीतक, again, (from कुष् to draw out or extract) occurring in तैत्ति.संहिता, 5. 5. 13 appears to be the same as कषिका. Prakrit हलीमुख also is the Avocet. यष्टिक as a probable name for the Black-winged stilt has already been mentioned. Another vernacular name for it is लालगोड़ी (red-legged) which helps to identify प्रवालपाद (red-legged), a water-bird in पालकाप्य, as this bird.

---

*More probably, it is the same as शयण्डक, the Spiny-tailed Lizard known as सांडा in Hindi. It is found in open sandy places. Like the garden lizard, प्रतिसूर्यक, it loves the sun. In fact, like other reptiles, the lizards dislike cold and are active in bright sunny weather.

12. The beautiful, though curious-looking, Ibis-bill has been rather doubtfully placed with the Plovers in *The Fauna* (*Birds*) *of India*. It has a long, curved and red bill, red legs and feet, and wears a double band of white and black as a gorget or necklace separating the blue neck from the white under-parts. It is a bird of the banks and beds of the Himalayan streams, ranging in summer between 8,000 and 15,000 feet and in winter between the edge of the plains and 10,000 feet.

13. The पारस्कर गृह्यसूत्र recommends the flesh of the कृकषा bird (कृक+ष श्रेष्ठे, having a beautiful or ornamented neck) at the अन्नप्राशन ceremony of a male child if his father wishes that he should be long-lived. The commentator gives कङ्कणहारिका as a synonym for कृकषा. Now कङ्कण means प्रतिसरः, माल्यः, a garland in शब्दकल्पद्रुम and "मण्डलं यागाद्यर्थं नानावर्णो रेखासन्निवेशः" in मङ्खकोषटीकासार. The bi-coloured gorget of the Ibis-bill is certainly a कङ्कण both in the sense of a garland and a multi-coloured set of lines, and it is therefore more than probable that the above synonymous names belong to the Ibis-bill. It is known as पग्गा (fr. प्रग्राह a halter or neck-rope) in Nepal. It will also be seen that the bill of this pretty bird resembles that of the आटी (Black Ibis) the flesh of which is said to ensure holy lustre to the growing boy, and like the latter the auspicious red colour is very prominent in the Ibis-bill. The bird's habitat would seem to protect it against persecution by man and so to ensure it a full normal life. Considerations like these would account for the selection of the bird in the above context.

14. Finally the भूलिङ्गशकुनि* of the महाभारत (2.41.19-21) cannot be omitted even though it is not one of the present-day Indian birds and therefore not included in *The Fauna* (*Birds*) *of India*. The relevent verses describing the curious behaviour of the bird are reproduced here:—

भूलिङ्गशकुनिर्नाम पार्श्वे हिमवतः परे ।
भीष्म ! तस्याः सदा वाचः श्रूयन्तेऽर्थविगर्हिताः ॥
मा साहसमितीदं सा सततं वाशते किल ।
साहसं चाऽत्मनाऽतीव चरन्ती नाऽवबुध्यते ॥
सा हि मांसार्गलं भीष्म ! मुखात् सिंहस्य खादतः ।
दन्तान्तरविलग्नं यत्तदादत्तेऽल्पचेतना ॥

The word सिंह in the above passage stands for पुष्करव्याघ्र, a Crocodile (Cf. synonymous expressions like पुरुषसिंह and पुरुषव्याघ्र), and भूलिङ्गशकुनि is the African Plover, Pluvianus aegyptius, commonly known as the Crocodile Bird, so called from its frequent association with the Nile Crocodile from

---

*भुवि लिङ्गतीति भूलिङ्गो बिलशायी पक्षिविशेषः— नीलकण्ठ on the above verse. The bird is named मासाहस शकुनि by हेमचन्द्र in परिशिष्ट पर्वन्, 3.141. The author, however, did not know that the bird was a kind of plover, for in the story related by him he makes the bird perch upon a tree which the Plovers never do. He has also modified the version in the M.Bh.

the body of which it picks up parasites and as the monster is sunning himself on the bank with the mouth agape, the bird boldly enters it to draw out the leeches sticking to his jaws. It renders another service as well to him, in that being a very wary bird, it flies off with warning cries at the approach of danger and the crocodile taking the warning slips into the water. Another Plover popularly known as the Zick-zack (Hoplopterus spinosus) is also said to have similar habits. It will be readily seen that the leeches are the मांस and the warning cry of the birds is the मासाहस cry of the story. It is probable that in former times one of these birds frequented the Sind coast or the estuary of the Sind river where Crocodiles occur, or else the ancient Indians heard of the bird's habits from the seafaring merchants of ancient India. The Plover lays its eggs in a hole in the sand and hence the name भूलिङ्गशकुनि. The habitat mentioned as "पार्श्वे हिमवत: परे" would seem to refer to the country beyond the south-western out-spurs of the Himalayas, viz., the Suleiman Range, considered as a wing or extension of the Himalayas. Evidently the territories to the North-west of the Indian Ocean are meant.

72

CURLEW, GODWIT, SANDPIPER, RUFF & REEVE, WOOD-COCK, & SNIPE

1. This family comprises the longer-billed waders some of which are as large as a common fowl, others as big as a dove and yet others no bigger than a sparrow, the majority, however possessing long legs.

2. The Curlew is a sandy-brown bird as big as a common fowl, or to quote from the *Britannica*: "In bulk the Curlew is not less than a crow, but it looks larger still from its long legs, wings and neck" (11th Edn.).

3. It is a winter visitor to India, arriving in September and leaving by the middle of May. In winter it is found inland in small numbers—singly, pairs or small parties—about jheels, marshland, and rivers, but it is rather more plentiful along our seacoasts (Salim Ali). It is active during both day and night but its call is mostly heard at night. "The commonest notes are a loud musical quoi quoi and crooee, crooee, crooee,... with the second syllable higher-pitched and more emphatic than the first and often uttered in long sequences. The song begins with a succession of low long drawn-out liquid notes, the first three or four delivered in a rather slow measured manner, Oorrr-oorrr-oorrr..., then gaining speed and passing into a louder and higher-pitched bubbling trill impossible to render in words, finally sinking again and often ending with some low notes like the opening ones" (Smythies). S. Baker describes the notes of the Curlew as a haunting cry of 'curlew cur-lew' heard far overhead at night and a loud screaming note when frightened or disturbed. It is quite possible that the Curlew in India does not give us its full repertoir but a shorter version of it. The relevance of the above detailed description of the bird's "plaintive voice" fully manifests itself when we come to references to कुररी (masc. कुरर, the Curlew) in Sanskrit literature. The name कुररी (कुररो is probably a copying error) in the single-names-list of कल्पद्रुकोश is perhaps different from the feminine of कुरर of the equation "कुररोत्क्रोशः" in the same lexicon and most probably refers to this bird. In other lexicons, however, the synonymy is comprehensive enough. The following simile based on the plaintive notes of the Curlew gives us a very vivid picture of the sorrowful wail of a young lady in distress:

तां क्रन्दमानामत्यर्थं कुररीमिव वाशतीम् ।
करुणं बहुशोचन्तीं विलपन्तीं मुहुर्मुहुः ॥

महाभारत, 3.63.20

माधव, the hero of the drama मालतीमाधव by भवभूति compares the soft and high-pitched piteous cries of his beloved मालती as she is on the point of being sacrificed to the goddess कालका with the 'most mournful wail' of the कुररी bird:

नादस्तावद्विकलकुररीकूजितस्निग्धतारः ।
चित्ताकर्षी परिचित इव श्रोत्रसंवादमेति ॥ Act V. 20

One of a group of love-lorn maidens (गोपी) of Gokul, when they find it impossible to go to sleep at night for thinking of their beloved Kṛṣṇa, questions a solitary Curlew calling in the air in the following words:

कुररि ! विलपसि त्वं वीतनिद्रा न शेषे,
स्वपिति जगति रात्र्यामीश्वरो गुप्तबोधः ।
वयमिव सखि ! कच्चिद्गाढनिर्भिन्नचेता,
नलिननयनहासोदारलीलेक्षितेन ॥
भागवत, 10.90.15.

It will be noticed that both the above examples relate to occurrences late in the evening or at night when the Curlew is often heard high up.

4. When Rāma returns to his hermitage after killing Mārīca he expresses his fears to his brother that Sītā has probably been carried away by blood-thirsty Rākṣasas and how she must have wailed like a कुररी: "नूनं विनादं कुररीव दीना, सा मुक्तवत्यायतकांतनेत्रा"—रामायण, 3.63,11. Similarly the wail of Sītā, when she was abandoned by Lakṣmaṇa at the bidding of Rāma near the hermitage of sage Vālmīki, has been compared by Kālidāsa to the plaintive cries of the कुररी :

सा मुक्तकण्ठं व्यसनातिभारात् चक्रन्द विग्ना कुररीव भूयः ।
Raghu, 14.68.

The following verses refer to the great sorrow of the ladies and maids at the palace of prince अनिरुद्ध who had been suddenly abducted away at night, and the poet wishing to present an impressive picture of the pathetic scene has campared their wail to the plaintive cries of hundreds of Curlews:—

ततोऽनिरुद्धस्य गृहे रुरुदुः सर्वयोषितः ।
प्रियं नाथमपश्यन्तः कुर्यः इव सङ्घशः ॥ हरिवंश, 2.121,1.

तासां हर्म्यतलस्थानां पूर्ण आसीन्महास्वनः ।
कुररीणामिवाकाशे रुदतीनां सहस्रशः ॥ Ib., 2.121,12.

5. The Whimbrel is a smaller edition of the Curlew but it has quite a different voice—"titti-titti-titti-titti-titti-tit in very even time and with even emphasis throughout" (Smythies). This bird is also known as 'titterel' from its voice in England, and it would seem that Sanskrit टिष्टि is for it though the name has been confused and treated as synonymous with टिट्टिभ. The name, however, occurs with single names of several other birds in the कल्पद्रुकोश- "कोयष्टिः टिट्टिभः टिष्टिः कुररो (?कुररी) जलकुक्कुटी". Everyone of these names stands for a different bird just as single names of thirteen different birds are given in अमरकोश—"तेषां विशेषा हारीतो मद्गुः...". हलायुध also gives a similar list. It is the proximity of कोयष्टि and टिट्टिभ in passages like these that has led to their being wrongly treated as fully synonymous and some commentators have incorrectly explained both कुररी and कोयष्टि as टिट्टिभ.

6. The Black-tailed Godwit (16 inches) is a migratory bird, visiting Northern India in flocks of ten to over a hundred from October to March. It has a particularly long and straight awl-like bill, 3" to 5" long with which it probes into the mud for worms, insects etc. It is evidently the very expressive आरा or आरामुखी (आरा चर्मप्रभेदनी—having an awl-like beak) of the कल्पद्रुकोश, corresponding to its Hindi name in Nepal, मलगूझा from मल, 'Mud' and गुज्झा, 'a bamboo-pin'. It is also known as बड़ा चाहा (large Snipe) in Hindi (per Jerdon) and गुदेरा also in Hindi from Sansk. क्षुद्, खुड्, खुण्ड् to break or pierce—H. खोदना to dig and गोदना to prick or pierce, whence गुदेरा one that pierces (the ground).

7. Snipes are चाहा (चह् विस्मापने ?) in Hindi from their habit of springing suddenly out of cover in marsh-land and their confusing zig-zag flight. In Bengal they are known as कादा खोंचा (कर्दम, mud and कुच, विलेखने, to scratch), the same as Sanskrit पङ्ककीर (पङ्क, mud and कॄ, to scatter or disturb). The resemblance of the colour of their plumage to that of the Quails accounts for their name पानलावा (Water-Quail) in Marathi and जलवर्तिका in Sanskrit. The Eastern Fantail Snipe breeds in Kashmir and the Himalayas, and the behaviour of this bird during the breeding season was certainly observed by the ancients who named it गोभण्डीर (गवि आकाशे भण्डते or गवि आकाशे भण्डीर इव, भण्डीर, the शिरीष tree, Accacia sirissa, so called because its numerous dry seed-pods vibrate and produce a rattling sound when shaken by the breeze). The Fantail, when flushed from its nest, soon mounts aloft and executes a series of aerial evolutions of an astounding kind after wildly circling about, and reaching a height at which it appears a mere speck it abruptly shoots downwards and as abruptly regains its former elevation. This process is repeated many times. A few seconds after each of these headlong descents a mysterious drumming sound is heard—evidently produced by the rush of air through its tail feathers as the bird shoots downwards (adapted from *Ency. Brit.* 11th Edn.; see also Whistler and other authorities). The bird is silent on the ground and when alarmed rises with just a 'pench' call which cannot justify the alternative derivation—"गवि जले भण्डीरः अति वाचालः"—शब्दकल्पद्रुम. The term भण्डीर implies a continuous sound (अतिवाचालत्व) and it is in

recognition of such a sound that the शिरीष has been named भण्डीर or शङ्खिनी-फल. The above description of the bird's flight and the consequent 'drumming' therefore fully bears out the beautiful name, गोभण्डीर, given to it and the त्रिकाण्डशेष equation—"गोभण्डीरः पङ्ककीरः" should be interpreted to mean that गोभण्डीर is a kind of पङ्ककीर or Snipe, for every पङ्ककीर is not exactly a गोभण्डीर. Thus we have पङ्ककीर and जलवर्तिका as common names for all Snipe, and गोभण्डीर for the Fantail, indicative of its peculiar drumming habit.

8. The Woodcock is a medium-sized and long-billed Himalayan bird (14 inches) whose russet-coloured plumage somewhat resembles that of the Common Grey Partridge. It is also about the same size. It moves down from its breeding haunts in the Himalayas from 8000 to 12,000 feet to the plains in winter. It is known in Nepal as सिमकुकरा or सिमतीतर, names which directly derive from सिम-or हिम-कुक्कुट; or सिम-or हिम-तित्तिर in Sanskrit ("तुषारः शिशिरः स्फीतःसेम्यः सीमो हिमोऽपि च"—for 'snow'—वैजयन्ती) and it must have been so named though these terms are not to be found in the present day lexicons. भण्डुतित्तिर (Pseudo- or imitation-Partridge) is mentioned in वेस्संतर जातक (547) with कपिंजर and तित्तिर for the Grey and the Black Partridges in verses 2098-2099. As a Himalayan bird, therefore, भण्डुतित्तिर is most probably the same as Hindi सिमतीतर, and the name may well be from Sanks. भण्ड-तित्तिर (a mimic or false Partridge). भण्ड also means 'a jester' and the name most probably refers to:

(i) the male Woodcock's habit of flying playfully backwards and forwards in an arc with alternate croaks and squeaks during the breeding season ;

(ii) its curious and twisting flight in and out of trees at a pace that is very deceiving; and

(iii) its 'acting' to entice one away from the nest and young by shamming injury and then flying clean out of sight after a while (S. Baker).

If so, the name भण्डु-or भण्ड-तित्तिर for it is really a very picturesque one.

9. The Watercock bores holes in soft ground for worms, grubs, etc., and its presence is often inferred from the holes made by its three inch bill. It is, therefore, possible that it also shares the name of आरामुखी with the Godwit, particularly as both are sub-equal in size and fowlers often pass a Godwit for a Woodcock at the Calcutta market because the latter is considered a greater delicacy for the table than the former (*F.B.I.*, first edition).

10. Sandpipers and Stints are comparatively speaking long-billed (less than one to two inches) waders of medium to small size which are rarely found away from water. They are more or less alike, the majority being grey-brown above and white below and with a good deal of white in or above the tail. Their constant connection with sandy ground near water and their piping call notes account for their common name of

Sandpipers. From a distance they look like Snipe and are therefore known as 'Snippets' which gives the unsportsman-like Anglo-Indian an excuse to shoot them for the pot. Unlike Snipe, however, they are birds of the open, do not take to cover and have not the tricky and fast flight of the Snipe. They are thus easy to kill and are not regarded as 'sporting birds'. Excepting a few like the Common Sandpiper and the Redshank most of the members of this group are winter visitors only, and of these the Wood Sandpiper and the Little, Temminck's and the Curlew Stints are the commonest. The Redshanks are known as बटान or सूरमा, the Greenshank as टिमटिमा (after its piping call), and the Little Stint as पनलोहा (lit., 'water-greedy') in Hindi.

The name बटान would seem to be related to भट for a kind of bird in the मत्स्यपुराण, 118--"कटुकान् टिट्टिभान् भटान्" where the association of the name with those for the Lapwings, birds of the same family, is significant. The alternative name सूरमा (शूरमान्य 'a self-proclaimed warrior') also points to भट, 'a fighter'. That is because the birds often parry against one another on the ground or indulge in aerial mock-fight out of the breeding season but more seriously during that season. The हारीतसंहिता, now extant, mentions पिङ्ग and पिक in its list of waterbirds (chapter, 11) and the first name पिङ्ग (पिञ्ज् शब्दे) most probably refers to the larger Sandpipers because of their piping notes. We thus have two names for these birds, भट and पिङ्ग.

The call of the Little and Curlew or Pigmy Stints is a 'wick-wick-wick' or the same as 'pick-pick-pick' which makes it highly probable that पिक is an onomatopoetic name for them. The Little Stint is पनलोहा (पनलोभा) in Hindi corresponding to जललोभिन्—जलरङ्क (जलार्थे रङ्कः दीनः) in Sanskrit. This last name has been thoughtlessly confused and equated with जलरङ्कु in the lexicons and commentaries. The latter, as we have seen, is the Purple Moorhen (Art. 58). The Stints as a group are therefore जलरङ्क and पिक.

Birds like the Marsh Sandpiper and the Greenshank are known as गोत्रा in Bengali and if the name is from गोत्रः—गो जलमेव त्राणमस्य, it would appear to be but a rendering of जलरङ्क. If this is correct जलरङ्क may well be a common name for the Sandpipers and Stints together as birds whose mainstay is water.

11. The Ruff and Reeve arrive in India towards the end of August and leave, "the males often in nearly full dress", in April. As the birds breed in northern Europe and Asia, the fights of the males for the possession of the females probably do not take place in this country and they have been named in Hindi and Sanskrit after the extraordinary ruff grown by the male as an ornament during the breeding season. The ruff extends from the nape downwards and covers the entire breast. It is known in Hindi as गरवाल (गर-गल neck, and वाल hair or feathers); Gehwala noted against the bird in the *F.B.I.* is an obvious misprint just as Panloha (पनलोहा) for the Little Stint has become 'Pauloha'. There are also

several other errors of this type in the work. Hindi गरवाल corresponds to Sansk. कण्ठवाल or कण्ठपाल as प and व often change places in Prakrit, and these latter are known as epithets for the Great Crested Grebe because it wears a ruff of long feathers round its neck. This feature is possessed by the male Ruff as well, and in an exaggerated form, and it, therefore, shares the names कण्ठवाल and कण्ठपाल with the Grebe.

73

PELICANS

Pelicans are huge, squat-looking birds of rivers and lakes living mainly on fish which they systematically hunt in parties in a semi-circular formation, driving the fish into the shallows and then gobbling them up. Their most characteristic external feature is the enormous elastic skin-bag which hangs below the large flattened bill, and this is large enough to contain a man's head. Besides fish they pick up and swallow young birds and even half-grown Ducks coming within their reach. The species that are found in India range from 5 to 6.5 feet in length and up to over 10 feet in wing-expanse. No wonder such a bird is called जलसिंह in Hindi and also in Sanskrit. "Jalasind" in the *F.B.I.* is a printing error. The water-bird called केसरी in चरक, and पुण्डरीक in सुश्रुत (lion and tiger respectively) is no other than the pelican; Cf. पक्षिसिंह for गरुड or the Golden Eagle. शार्दूल of the lexicons and शरभ of पराशरस्मृति, 6.2, are additional names for it. Lastly it is also प्लव in a special sense as defined in कल्पद्रुकोश :—

प्लवो महाप्रमाणः स्यात् प्रसेवकगज(गल ?)श्च सः ।

But it would be more correct to call it महाप्लव as against प्लव for the cormorant and the coct. डल्हणाचार्य also defines पुण्डरीक in a similar way, and the धन्वन्तरिनिघण्टु referring to its size, calls it a महापक्षी. As the different species of Pelican are difficult to distinguish in the field they are not differentiated in Sanskrit nomenclature.

Prakrit कासिह (=जलसिंह) and हय-पोंडरीय[1] of प्रश्नव्याकरण and पोंडरीग (पुण्डरीक) of अभिधानराजेन्द्र, all refer to this bird. The following corrupt synonymy in धन्वन्तरि probably includes जलसिंह for it:

जलपक्षी महापक्षी जलसाघ(संह)तिवासकः ।

If the second half of the above is read "जलसिंहोऽतिवासकः" the expression अतिवासक may refer to the belief that fish are attracted to Pelicans by their oily secretion (Jerdon). The first half of the verse (not reproduced) is also corrupt but includes yet another Prakrit name for it, viz. पाशगड (पाशगल), the same as प्रसेवकगल of कल्पद्रुकोश.

1. हय पोंडरीय equated with ह्रद पुण्डरीक—Lake-tiger in पा. स. म. is the same as कासिह of the same lexicon.

74

CORMORANTS & DARTER

1. Three species of Cormorants are found in India, viz., the Large Cormorant which measures about 32 inches in length, the Indian Shag (25 inches) and the Little Cormorant (20 inches), all of them of a generally black colour with a green gloss. They live entirely on fish which is caught by diving under water with the thin but hooked bill. When not feeding they perch on rocks, stakes in the water or on trees with wings spread out in the sun for drying. They frequent both fresh and salt water, the latter near the sea-coast.

The Darter or Snake-bird is about three feet long including its long snaky neck. It is of a black colour but with white on the neck. It has a long, thin and sharp pointed bill with which it impales fish under water. It is a much better diver than the Cormorants.

2. The well-known naturalist "E H A" speaking of Cormorants and the Darter says, "The Cormorant is a thoroughly shabby bird, with large, ragged tail, and coloured all over a sordid black,...the Snake-bird so called from its serpentine head and neck...sitting on a low tree, with its wings held out to dry, looks like a big Cormorant[1] with the neck of a Heron fitted on its shoulders; but at close quarters it is a very handsome bird. Its plumage is peculiar, the feathers on the shoulders especially being long and narrow, like the hackles of a Cock. Each feather is black or dark brown, with silvery border, or spotted with a silvery white, and the effect is very beautiful."[2] Because of its plumage it is also known as the silver-laced Snake Bird.

3. The Hindi names for the Cormorants are बड़ा- or छोटा-जलकौआ (Skt. जलकाक) corresponding to the Large and the Little Cormorant, but there is no separate name for the Shag which being larger than the Little Cormorant would pass as बड़ा पनकौआ. In Sanskrit they are प्लव or जलकाक though the name पानीयकाकिका would seem to imply the Little Cormorant.

---

1. This is the reason why both प्लव, the cormorant, and मद्गु, the Darter, have been described as a kind of water-crow जलकाक, in equations Nos. 1 and 3 reproduced in Para. 3 below.

2. *The Common Birds of Bombay*, 2nd Ed., pp. 186-187.

Some of the lexical synonymies bearing on these birds and the Darter are noted below:—

(i) प्लवः कारण्डवे जलकाके (जलवायसे)—विश्वप्रकाश; हेमचन्द्र

(ii) प्लवस्तु गात्रसम्प्लवः—अभिधानचिन्तामणि

(iii) मद्गुस्तु जलकाकः (जलवायसः)—वैजयन्ती; हलायुध; अभि. चिन्तामणि

(iv) मत्स्यवेधन (v.l. मत्स्यवेधनी) मद्गुपक्षिणि—वाचस्पत्यम्; M. Williams

(v) काकमद्गुः पानीयकाकिका—चक्रपाणिदत्त on चरक; रभसकोश quoted in नामचन्द्रिका (टीका on अमर)

(vi) शितिकण्ठस्तु दात्यूहः काकमद्गुः कचाटुरः—त्रिकाण्डशेष

(vii) काकमद्गुः जलरङ्कः— हारावली

The first shows that प्लव means both 'the Coot' (कारण्डव, Art. 58) and the Cormorant (जलकाक, 'the Water-Crow'). The second speaks of प्लव in its two meanings and states that both go down completely under water, i.e., are divers. M. Williams has rendered गात्रसम्प्लव as 'the Pelican', but this is not usually a diving bird and the error has, perhaps, arisen from the fact that प्लव also means a Pelican. Nos.(iii)and(iv)taken together show that मद्गु is a bird that spears fish and is a kind of जलकाक or Cormorant, i.e., the two have nearly similar habits, and they are indeed members of the same family. अमर mentions मद्गु, कारण्डव and प्लव as different birds and since कारण्डव is the coot (Art. 58) and none of the Commentaries on अमर seen by me renders प्लव as the Pelican, we are left with प्लव for the Cormorant and मद्गु for the Snake-bird. मद्गु is also a water-snake and the fact that the name is shared by bird and reptile is significant. The Cormorant swims and also "dives with a jump into air" and has been very appropriately named प्लव (प्लवन swimining, leaping). No. (iv) makes मत्स्यवेधन ('Fish-impaler') and मद्गु synonymous which appears to be perfectly correct as the principal difference between the fishing habits of a Cormorant and a Darter is that while the former always just catches a fish under water with its hooked bill, the latter, as a rule, transfixes it with a sudden rapier-like thrust of its thin and sharp pointed bill (aptly described as "spear of a beak"). This action is greatly helped by a peculiar arrangement of some of the vertebrae in its long neck, which act like a powerful spring and suddenly straighten out for each thrust at a fish (Whistler).

4. The aptness of the name मद्गु for the Darter is reinforced by the remarkable likeness borne by the long and flexible neck and small head of the bird, as it swims very low in the water, to a snake coming up to breathe. This has been well brought out by E H A and other observers. If follows, therefore, that मद्गु is the particular type of जलकाक which is by habit a मत्स्यवेधन. काकमद्गु (काक इव मद्गुः) occurs in चरक 1.25.38 and चक्रदत्त renders it as पानीयकाकिका (No. (v) above) which clearly refers to the Little Cormorant which is just as big as the Common Crow and is also by far

the commonest of the Cormorants. The feminine gender of the name also implies the smallness of the bird, cf. "स्त्रीत्वेन वर्तकाद् वर्तिकाया लाघवं स्यात्"[1] Equation No. (vi) refers to शितिकण्ठ (the black-necked)[2] as two kinds of Ibis, viz., दात्यूह, the Black Ibis and कचाटुर, the White Ibis but काकमद्गु is certainly misplaced with them for none of them is a diver. The error is due to the fact that all the three share the descriptive epithet of जलकाक (cf. "जलकाकस्तु दात्यूहः"—धन्वन्तरि). The last synonymy from हारावली is wholly incorrect as जलरङ्कु belongs as a group-name to the Stint and Sandpiper type of birds which again do not dive for food or sport.

5. The names मद्गु and उपमद्गु borne by two of the sons of अक्रूर in हरिवंश[3] (see alternative readings) are worth noting, for मद्गु as the Snake-bird and काकमद्गु as the Cormorant, preferably the Large one, which is about six inches shorter than the Snake-bird, are evidently the physical basis for them. Finally प्लवक or प्लवग are merely variae lectiones for प्लव.

6. "जलं हृत्वाऽभिप्लवः"—विष्णुस्मृति, 44.16 condemns a water-thief (probably a farmer misappropriating water from a canal belonging to another[4]) to be reborn as the aquatic bird अभिप्लव. प्लव being the Cormorant अभिप्लव should mean a superior (अभि) bird of the same type and the Large Cormorant is certainly intended. During the breeding season the male of this species is readily distinguished from other members of the family by the white cheeks and a broad white patch on the flanks and it is this feature combined with its large size which has given him the name of अभिप्लव. This inference is fully borne out by the fact that a particular Vedic rite derives its name from this bird. The अभिप्लव षडह is defined as "उभयतो ज्योतिषोऽभिप्लवा भवन्ति, अन्यतो ज्योतिःपृष्ठ्यः"—शत. ब्राह्मण, 12.2.2.1, and Eggling explains in a footnote at p.149 of Vol. 44, S.B.E., that the अभिप्लव षडह has light (ज्योतिस्) on both sides of it because the ज्योतिष्टोम सामन् is sung both at the beginning and at the close of the ceremony, i.e. on the first and the last days. This ज्योतिस् is clearly, in reference to the snow-white patches on both sides of the face and body (or in front and rear of the body) of the अभिप्लव bird, the Large Cormorant of India.

7. A few examples from sacred and secular literature should prove interesting:

मित्राय मद्गून्—वाज. संहिता, 24.22.
प्लवो मद्गुर्मत्स्यस्ते नदीपतये— Ibid., 24.34.

Here the comparatively beautiful Darter is named for the Sun-god because the bird seems to love the sun, as it were as it often perches with expanded wings in the sun for long periods. Similarly the Cormorant,

1. Per चक्रदत्त on चरक, 1.27.47.

2. The equation शितिकण्ठः दात्यूहे also refers to the white-breasted Waterhen, the शुक्लकण्ठ दात्यूह with शिति taken in the sense of 'white'.

3. 1.34.12.; and 38. 52.

4. cf. परकीयं जलं हृत्वा केदारार्थं द्विजो यदि। ... । स एव नरकं गत्वा मण्डूको जायते भुवि। हेमाद्रि, चतुर्वर्गचिन्तामणि, Vol. 4.277.

Darter and fish are quite appropriate for the Lord of the Rivers as all three are permanently associated with the water.

8. The interpretation of शुन्ध्यु as the clean मद्गु bird by यास्क[1] may not be correct but the view that a bird who spends much of his time in or upon the water shares the purity of that element seems to have been in favour with the ancients, for we find two spiritual preceptors named हंस and मद्गु and 'flying down' (उपनिपत्य) to impart spiritual knowledge to young.[2] The supposed association between cleanliness and spirituality is obvious in this picture and the position of honour given to the lowly Silverlaced Snake-bird is perhaps unique. The graceful Swan has of course been honoured in every country and particularly in India where the Sun and the Moon ("हंस: शुचिषत्)" and the liberated human soul have frequently been pictured as the Swan par excellence.

9. मनु[3] prohibits प्लव, the Cormorant, as food and[4] decrees that a water-thief would be reborn as that bird and thus condemned to an aquatic life. In the same way a person stealing animal-fat is destined to be a Darter (मद्गु). काकमद्गु in

> घृतं हृत्वा तु दुर्बुद्धिः काकमद्गुः प्रजायते । —महाभारत and ब्रह्मपुराण,[5]

is again the Little Cormorant with the glistening oily plumage not affected by constant immersion in water. मनु[6] punishes theft of drinking water, the punishment this time consisting of a denial of all but a few drops of rain-water, for the thief must be reborn as a Hawk-Cuckoo (स्तोकक). Do these point to the Indo-Aryans having lived in areas stricken with drought or of the nature of a desert before they settled down in the happy land of the Five-rivers? Or did they suffer from a long period of water-scarcity in the Punjab itself?

10. The reference to these birds in the रामायण and जानकीहरण are more interesting. रावण offers his love to सीता in captivity and she insults him with a number of disparaging similes two of which are based upon a comparison between the mean-looking Darter on the one hand and the princely Peacock and the graceful Goose on the other:—

> यदन्तरं वायसवैनतेययोः यदन्तरं मद्गुमयूरयोरपि ।
> यदन्तरं सारसगृध्रयोर्वने तदन्तरं दाशरथेस्तवैव च ॥
>
> —रामायण[7]

---

1. On RV 1.124.4.
2. जाबाल सत्यकाम—छान्दोग्य उपनिषद्, 4.7.1 and 4.8.1-2.
3. 5.12.
4. 12.62.
5. 13.111.122 and 217.107 respectively.
6. 12.7.
7. 3.47.47.

क्रीडन्ती राजहंसेन पद्मखण्डेषु नित्यशः ।
हंसी सा तृणमध्यस्थं कथं द्रक्ष्येत मद्गुकम् ॥ —Ibid.[1]

It need hardly be added that the Darter is most awkward on the land as compared with the beautiful and dignified gait of the Peacock on land and of the Goose both on land and on water.

11. The characteristic pose of the Darter as it perches on a stake in the water with wings spread out to dry finds poetical expreession in :

इयत्प्रमाणोऽपि सरःप्रदेशः, तव प्रसादेन ममास्तु भोग्यः।
इत्येष सन्दर्शयतीव मद्गुः, हंसाय शोषाय विसारितांसः ॥
—जानकीहरण[2]

Here the wooden stake would seem to demarcate the clear waters of a lake from the area covered with lotuses and lilies, and the bird extending his arms as it were, addresses the Goose sporting in the lotus-bed, "I may be permitted, Sir, to have the water on this side for my own use." The Darter fishes only in clear and weed-free waters.

1. 3.56.20.
2. 3.30.

75

GANNET OR BOOBY

Gannets are large long-winged sea-birds with stout conical pointed bills, serrated along the commissure. They are expert fishers, fly round over a shoal of fish at a height of 60 to 100 feet above the surface and periodically dive headlong into the water with the half-closed wings; this dive comes next to the stoop of the Peregrine as the most impressive sight afforded by a bird on the wing (Smythies). They have been frequently seen along the coasts of India but I have not come across any name for the bird in any Indian language including Sanskrit. Its method of fishing however, reminds one of the following verse (already quoted with reference to the Osprey which sometimes fishes in the tidal waters) :—

मत्स्यरङ्कक निरातङ्कक लवणाम्भसि मज्जसि ।
इयं हि जाठरी ज्वाला व्याकुलीकुरुते न कम् ?॥ —उद्भट

It may well share the name मत्स्यरङ्क with the Osprey or the King-fisher associated with inland lakes and rivers.

76

TROPIC BIRD

Tropic-birds are about the size of the small Gulls and resemble them in habits and appearance. They are rare along the Indian coasts and no Indian name is recorded for them. Generally speaking a Tropic Bird would pass for a समुद्रकाक.

77

ERIGATEBIRD

These are large black tropical sea-birds given to piracy. Their food principally consists of fish snatched from other fishing birds like Pelicans, Gannets, Cormorants, or Terns. They are the most aerial of birds except the Swifts. No Indian name is recorded for them but their habits remind one of the Hindi name लुटेरवा (robber) for a "kind of bird" and Sanskrit लुष्टाक as one of the names for a Crow. Like other sea-birds without specific names this too would go by the general name of समुद्रकाक or समुद्र-लुष्टाक.

78

PETRELS

Petrels are, with some exceptions, the smallest of sea-birds about the size of the Common Myna and despite their fragile appearance they have wonderful powers of flight and are perfectly at home at sea in the wildest storm. They have slender but long legs and webbed feet, and, when feeding, pat the water with their feet, springing along the surface in a series of hops with wings outspread. I know of no Indian name for them but Sanskrit वीचीकाक would be as good for them as for the Gulls.

79

SPOONBILL

A tall white wading bird recognized by its black spoon-shaped bill, yellow at the tip. It is seen in flocks on the margins of the larger jheels, sand-banks of large rivers, etc. When feeding it wades in shallow water with its neck stretched out and moves the half-immersed bill from side to side with a regular action. "It rises spirally to float aloft" (*Cambridge Natural History*), and is often seen "flying in single file in long white gleaming lines at a considerable height above the ground—moving—in a very regular and stately manner (Smythies).

It is undoubtedly the दर्विदा (v.l. दार्विदा) of the वाज. संहिता[1] —"आतिर्वाहसो दर्विदा ते वायवे", and the name is after the दर्वि shape (a spoon) of its bill. The definition and synonymy given in वैजयन्ती कोश is definite :

बकजातिः दर्वितुण्डो दर्विक्रौञ्चश्च दर्विदा ।

This makes it clear that the दर्वितुण्ड (lit. Spoon-bill) belongs to the tribe of Herons or Storks ("बकजाति", corresponding almost exactly to ORDER "Herodiones" as accepted in the *Fauna of Birtish India, Birds*). The selection of the bird for the Wind-god is based on the bird's flight as already set forth above. A flock rising spirally aloft typyfies a tornado or wind-storm marked by an inward spiral motion of the air with an upward current in the centre carrying up with it leaves, sprays of grass, etc., while the straight flight in a line represents a regular breeze. Yet another name for the bird is खजाक or खजाका (fr. खज 'a churning stick' and 'a ladle, spoon'):

खजाकः पक्षिणि ख्यातः खजाका दर्विरुच्यते—औणादिकपर्व टीका

खजाकः स्यात्पुंसि दध्नो विकारे विहगान्तरे—पेरुसूरि औणादिक पदार्णव[2]

This name is justified in both senses of the word as the bird moves its bill both right and left like a churn and the bill also resembles a spoon. "दब्बिमुख सकुन" of the commentary on वेस्संतर जातक[3] is no other than this bird although it has been mistaken there for आटा, the Black Ibis.

1. 24.34.
2. 4.68.
3. verse 2106.

80

IBISES

1. Three different species of Ibis belonging to बकजाति (Art. 79) are found in India. A long, slender and curved bill is common to all three but there are differences in body-feathering and colour of the plumage. They also differ in their habits.

2. i) The White Ibis is wholly white except for the skin of the head and neck which is bare and of a bluish-black colour. The young bird, however, has a feathered head and neck which becomes bald as it reaches the adult state. It is a bird of inland waters, like swamps, tanks and rivers and feeds principally on small fish, frogs, insects etc. Ordinarily it is a silent bird but during the breeding season it has a remarkably loud booming call. The flesh of this bird is described as being "execrable" to eat.

ii) The Black Ibis is a dark brown and black bird except for a conspicuous white shoulder-patch and a bare black head ornamented with a triangular patch of brilliant red papillae with the apex at the crown and cut off square at the nape. Here again the head of the young is feathered. This Ibis is found more often in open country or dry cultivation as fish does not form any part of its diet which consists chiefly of insects and most kinds of fallen grain, and it is only on occasion that it resorts to water for frogs. Unlike its white cousin and the Storks it is less inclined to rest and meditate, and is always on the move in search of food. Its call is a scream consisting of two or three notes. The important difference as regards habits between the White and the Black Ibises is that the former is always associated with water and finds its food along the water's edge and by wading in the shallows while the latter has to wander about a good deal on dry land and fields in search of its insect and grain food. This is the main reason why it cannot afford to "rest and meditate" like the other. Their names शराटि (शरे जले अटतीति) and आटि (यत्र तत्र अटतीति i.e. 'a wandering bird') respectively are based on their way of life just described.

iii) The Glossy Ibis is distinguished by a permanently feathered head and the plumage is dark-brown and chestnut. It moves about locally in an extraordinary manner changing places as a breeding and non-breeding bird, but it is essentially a bird of the marshes and large masses of water and does not frequent cultivated fields and open meadows. This bird is the पत्राटी of the कल्पद्रुकोश and the oldest names of the three forms, Black, White and Glossy are आटि, शराटि, and पत्राटि, respectively. कवार (के मूर्ध्नि वाला: केशा: सन्ति अस्य) is another name for the Glossy Ibis and fully corresponds to पत्राटी. 'Tantalus falcinellus' given for it in M. Williams has now been changed to 'Plegadis falcinellus'.

3. The white and the black varieties are known in Hindi as कचाटोर (also मुण्डा, 'the bald' and सफेद बुज्झा 'white striker'?—fr. श्वेतविद्धक ?), and करांकल, respectively and the Glossy Ibis as कोवर or कोवारी. In Western India (Cutch) the Gujarati names of the Black and White Ibises are रण नो कागड़ो and रण नो धोलो कागड़ो i.e. 'the crow and the white crow of the Runn' respectively.

4. Sanskrit synonyms relating to these birds are :—

(i) शरारिराटिराडिश्च—अमर.

(ii) आतिस्त्वाटि: शराटिका—वैजयन्ती.

(iii) आटी भेदे तु पत्राटी स्यान्नान्दीमुख इत्यपि—कल्पद्रु.

(Cf. कवार, Tantalus falcinellus, the Glossy Ibis, per Wilson in M. Williams).

(iv) दात्यूह: कालकण्ठक:—अमर.

(v) कालकण्ठनीलकण्ठौ...दात्यूहे ...शिखावले—हेमचन्द्र.

(vi) शितिकण्ठस्तु दात्यूह: काकमद्‌गु: कचाटुर:—त्रिकाण्डशेष.

(vii) दात्यूहे कालकण्टक:—अभि. चिन्तामणि; मेदिनी.

(viii) जलकाकस्तु दात्यूह: स च स्यात्कालकण्टक: । —राजनिघण्टु.

(ix) बक: कह्व:—अमर.

(x) काकमत्स्यात्खगौ ध्वाङ्क्षौ—अमर.

(xi) ध्वाङ्क्ष: काके बके—हेमचन्द्र.

धूङ्‌क्ष्णा तु श्वेतकाक: स्यात्—वैजयन्ती.

(xii) बके कह्वो बकोटवत्—अभि. चिन्तामणि.

(xiii) बक: कङ्को बकोटश्च तीर्थसेवी च तापस:—धन्वन्तरि.

(xiv) बकोट: शुक्लवायस:—त्रिकाण्डशेष.

बकस्तु शुक्लवायस:—कल्पद्रु.

(xv) पिचुल: जलवायसे—मेदिनी.

5. The first two synonymies mix up several birds including the आटि (v.l. आडि, आट, आटा, etc.) and शराटि as discussed in Art. 70, while the third regards पत्राटी (the fully feathered), Glossy Ibis, as a variety of आटी but incorrectly includes the नान्दीमुख (v.l. नन्दीमुखी), the Nukhta Duck, Art. 84-c. Nos. (iv) to (viii) relate to the Black Ibis as a black-necked bird like the Peacock, and call it दात्यूह and जलकाक. The epithet कालकण्टक most probably does not refer to its plumage as assumed in अभि. चिन्तामणि but to the red papillae on its head—कालं सिन्दूरमिव रक्तवर्णा: कण्टका: अङ्कुरा: शिरसि यस्य; कालं 'red lead',

cf. कठाहक below and रक्तशीर्ष आटी of डल्हणाचार्य in Art. 70. काकमद्गु,—the Cormorant, is placed in No. (vi) (see Art.74) where कचाटुर (v.l. कचाटुः fr. कच hair or a scar and अट् to move, or कचेन शुष्कव्रणेन सह अटति in reference to the bald head and neck which also look as if burnt or scarred) is the White Ibis known as कचाटोर in Hindi. The name जलकाक for the Ibises is preserved in Cutch, where the black form is known as the Crow of the Runn and the white as the White Crow of the Runn. More correctly, however, जलकाक should be the White and भूकाक the Black Ibis. The name जलकाक connects equations Nos. (x) to (xiv) with the White Ibis, which is, therefore, ध्वाङ्क्ष (ध्वाङ्क्ष्—घोर वाशिते from the bird's booming call), कह्व (calling near water), बक, बकोट and शुक्लवायस as well. The constant association of this Ibis and the Common Grey Heron (कङ्क) with water and their habit of resting in meditation are stressed by the epithets तीर्थसेवी and तापस in No. (xiii).

6. Reverting to equation Nos. (iv)-(viii), it seems advisable to consider the name दात्यूह a little more closely. In its application to these birds it is possible to derive the word in two ways: First from दात्रं or दाति—for a curved knife or sickle used in villages, in reference to the sickle-like bill of the birds-दात्रेण दात्या वा भक्ष्यमूहति प्राप्नोति; स्त्रियां दातिः न द्वयोः दात्रं लवित्रं—कल्पद्रु; ऊहः पूर्वप्राप्तस्य उत्क्षेपणम्—शब्दकल्पद्रुम. Cf. "Father Sickle", the name for the White Ibis in Egypt. Secondly, per क्षीरस्वामी on अमर—"द्वितीयं तृतीयं वा रूपं वहति दित्यवाट्, तस्यापत्यं दात्यूहः" and this may well refer to a change from the feathered head or head and neck of the young to the baldness of these parts in the adult birds, as also to the third form, viz., the fully and permanently feathered Glossy Ibis; or again, the statement may refer to the three different forms (रूपाणि) of the Ibis found in the country.

7. आटी as 'Turdus ginginianus', now 'Acridotheres ginginianus', i.e. the Starling known as the Bank Myna; आटी मेद (w.r.of आटीभेद) as "a name of a bird"; and वाटी for "a species of bird in Charaka" in M. Williams are all incorrect. आटीभेद is merely a descriptive expression, meaning 'a kind of आटी' used to define पत्राटी in No. (iii) above, and वाटी is the result of a faulty separation of the compound कारण्डवाटी into कारण्ड and वाटी instead of कारण्डव and आटी. It occurs as "कारण्डवाटीजलवायसानां" (Coot, Black Ibis and White Ibis) in वसन्तराज, 8.14. Some editions of चरक also incorrectly give वाटी for आटी.

8. Other names for the Black Ibis are (i) भूकाक[1] (भूमौ काक इव) as a kind of क्रौञ्च in शब्दकल्पद्रुम, (ii) कठाहक same as दात्यूह or a 'kind of fowl' (M.W.). This is from कटाह the shell of a turtle (कटाहः कूर्मकर्परः, तादृशं कं शिरो यस्य; the

---

1. भूकाकः—स्वल्पकङ्कः, क्रौञ्चः, नीलकपोतः. These are (a) the Pond Heron, (b) the Black Ibis as against जलकाक for the White Ibis, and (c) the Blue Rock Pigeon respectively. It may be noted that जल-, or वारि-वायस (—काक) also means the Cormorant. In the former काक stands for 'a bird' in general so that भूकाक is 'a ground-bird', and in the sense of a Cormonant the expression जलकाक means a 'water-crow' though it is not always possible to maintain this distinction, e.g., in Cutch the Gujarati names for the Black and White Ibises are रण नो कागड़ो and रण नो धोलो कागड़ो respectively.

papillated head of the bird resembling the rough and grannular shell of a turtle; cf. कालकण्टक), and (iii) पक्ष-बिन्दु (–बक) from the white patch on the wing. The first two names are evidently in opposition to जलकाक (i.e. शराटि) and कचाटुर (implying a bald and smooth head) for the White Ibis.

9. The Pali for आटि is आट or आटा mentioned in वेस्संतर जातक, 2106 where the White Ibis with a booming call is distinguished as "आटा परिवदंतिका". The Commentator's rendering of आटा as दब्बिमुख सकुन is, however, incorrect, for दब्बिमुख is the same as दर्विक्रौञ्च, the Spoonbill (Art.79). आडि is really a Prakrit form of आटि and is given by Hemachandra in his देशीनाममाला, 8.24 along with साराडि for शराटि. The निघण्टुरत्नाकर translates आटी as a kind of Heron (बगली).

10. पिचुल for 'a kind of water Crow' should really signify the White Ibis as पिचुल means 'Cotton' and the name implies the white cotton-like plumage of the bird. आडा सेतीय of प्रश्नव्याकरण and आडा सेतीक of पाइयसद्दमहण्णवो are from Sanskrit श्वेत+आटा i.e. the White Ibis. आटि or आडी is thus both a general name for any Ibis and specific for the Black Ibis as will appear presently.

11. The struggle between the Brāhmaṇas and Kṣatriyas for social and political supremacy in ancient India has been beautifully allegorised as a duel between their leaders, sage वसिष्ठ and sage विश्वामित्र, transformed by mutual शाप or curse into the आडी and बक birds in मार्कण्डेय पुराण, styled as "आडी-बक-युद्ध". The combatants, आडी and बक, are described as brothers, being sons of अन्धक (probably formed form अन्धकाक[1] for a 'Heron' or दात्यूह) in मत्स्य पुराण—"बकभ्राता रणोत्कटः आडिर्नामा"—156.12 and also in स्कन्दपुराण, कौमारिका खण्ड, ch. 28.

This relationship indicates similarity of form and family affiliation, and the inconclusive fight shows practical equality in size and strength as well; Cf.—

तुल्ये बले तु बलवान्परिकोपमेति—पंचतंत्र

पराक्रमन्ते युद्धेषु सममेवोभये भटाः—सभारञ्जन शतक

The birds, therefore, are the Black and the White Ibis. The importance of the fact that वसिष्ठ, the Brāhmaṇa sage, possessed of ब्रह्मवर्चस्, i.e. spiritual power or lustre, assumes the form of आडी would be clear from what follows.

12. The flesh of the Black Ibis (आटि)[2], must be given to a baby-boy at the अन्नप्राशन ceremony according to पारस्कर गृह्यसूत्र, 1.19; if the father wants the child to acquire ब्रह्मवर्चस् (holy lustre) when he grows to manhood. Why should the Black Ibis typify ब्रह्मवर्चस्? First, because it has a white wing-

---

1. दात्यूह = अन्धकाक in अष्टाङ्गहृदयकोश.

2. The White Ibis is "execrable to eat" while the flesh of the Black Ibis is "very good" (Jerdon). The हारीत संहिता, मांस वर्ग, Ch. 11 also recommends the flesh of आडी—"आडी वातविकारकासहृननी बल्या तथा दीपनी."

patch on a dark body signifying the sun against a deep blue sky.[1] Second, because the bird has a bald head indicative of spiritual wisdom, and third, it wears an auspicious triangular patch of red papillae on the back of the head representing the sacrificial fire. The last two characteristics and the metallic gloss on the plumage are acquired by the bird in adult life only and these strange features, unique in the bird world, would seem to invest it with special spiritual significance The above points are, perhaps, borne out by the following few extracts from sacred literature :—

(i) मयि अग्निस्तेजो दधातु...मयि सूर्यो भ्राजो दधातु ।
—आश्वलायन गृह्यसूत्र, 1.21.4

(ii) अथ यत्रैतदङ्गाराश्चाऽऽकश्यन्त इव । तर्हि हैष भवति ब्रह्म स यः
कामयेत ब्रह्मवर्चसी स्यामिति तर्हि ह स जुहुयात्...।
—शतपथ ब्राह्मण, 2.3.2.13

(iii) पसिस्रजी होता भवति. . .एतद्वै ब्रह्मवर्चसस्य रूपम् ।
—कृष्णयजुर्वेदीय तैत्तिरीय ब्राह्मण, 2.7.1

Sāyaṇa comments : 'परिस्रजी खलतिः, शिरसि स्रगाकारेण परित एव केशा न तु मध्ये । यदेतद् द्विजवेशस्य लक्षणं खलत्यादि तद् ब्रह्मवर्चसस्वरूपम् । अतः तदनुकूलेन रूपेण ब्रह्मवर्चसं प्राप्नोति ।

(iv) स्वस्तिकस्तु त्रिकोणकः—वैजयन्ती, i.e. स्वस्तिक is an auspicious triangular mark, a triangular crest-jewel (M.W.).

It is interesting to note that the Glossy and the White Ibises were held sacred in Egypt.

13. The Black Ibis, found in the open and away from water, was a favourite quarry for purposes of hawking with the Peregrine or Shaheen and is mentioned by the name of दात्यूह (=कालकण्ठदात्यूह) in a book on Falconry :

अतिदूरगतानान्तु कङ्कदात्यूहपक्षिणाम् ।
लक्ष्ये मोको बहर्या हि जनयत्यद्भुतं रसम् ॥ —श्यैनिक शास्त्र, 6.37.

The quarry tries to out-wit the Falcon by mounting higher and higher but the latter rises still higher and finally makes her stoop and brings the bird down. The Ibis often escapes by rising very high into the sky. It is this flight of the bird which has probably given it the name of खेगमन (flying high into the sky). This is, however, subject to M.W.'s rendering as 'a gallinule' being correct.[2] It has also inspired a beautiful simile where

---

1. Cf. Dr. A. B. Keith's observation in his introduction to the translation of the तैत्ति. संहिता, "white of course is the Vedic symbol of the Sun as in the round white skin which represents the Sun at the महाव्रत..." p. cxxxvi.

2. In the alternative खेगमन (=कालकण्ठ) would be a White Wagtail which is supposed to disappear into the sky and descend again to the earth from there. Cf. आकाशभद्र or अम्बरभद्र in Art. 26; Cf. also खेचरता the magical power of flying into the sky.

the pearl necklace of king महाबल with a deep blue sapphire in the centre has been compared to a V-flight of Bar-headed Geese with a Black Ibis as the leading bird :—

तद्वक्षसि पृथाविन्द्रनीलमध्यमणिर्बभौ ।
कण्ठिका हंसमालेव व्योम्नि दात्यूहमध्यगा ।।
—जैन आदिपुराण (गुणभद्र), 5.6.

आडी and काक (i.e. जलकाक White Ibis) dwell at a lake on the Vindhya mountain :

आडीकाकबलाकाभिः सेवितं कोकिलादिभिः
—स्कन्दपुराण, रेवाखण्ड, 2.22.

Verse 8 of the Subhāṣita, p.219 mentions आटि, the Black Ibis, as moving along the edge of a lake :

चरतु स्वच्छन्दमाटिस्तटे ।

It will now be seen that the आटीमुखयन्त्र of सुश्रुत is a pair of long curved tongs and the illustrations of it in published books including *The Surgical Instruments of the Hindus* by Dr. G. N. Mukhopadhyaya are incorrect. पालकाप्य (3.12.74) calls the instrument as दात्यूहं (दात्यूहमुखं), दात्यूह being the Black Ibis or आटी.

14. The strikingly white plumage of the White Ibis and its constant association with water has appealed to Sanskrit poets more than the other Ibises, but it is always mentioned by the name of बक. This name, it must be remembered, includes in a wider sense also the Herons, Storks and even the Flamingo and it is, therefore, very necesary that the identity of the particular bird meant in a given context is carefully determined. A few examples of बक, बकोट, श्वेतबक, श्वेतकाक, and ध्वाङ्क्ष or धुङ्क्षा as the White Ibis are given below :— मनुस्मृति prohibits this Ibis (बक) as food as also its wanton killing, while it decrees that a person guilty of stealing fire would be reborn as a बक[1]. The origin of this last punishment is to be found in the dedication of the White Ibis to the Fire-god at the Horse-Sacrifice—धुङ्क्षाग्नेयी —वाज. संहिता, 24.31; and "अग्नये धूङ्क्ष्णा"–तैत्ति. संहिता, 5.5.19 where धुङ्क्षा and धूङ्क्ष्णा mean the White Ibis (from ध्वाङ्क्ष्-घोरवाशिते, to utter a loud cry; both the Crow and the White Ibis are noisy and share the name ध्वाङ्क्ष between them). The reason for naming the bird to the Fire-god is to be found in the bluish-black colour of the bare skin of the white bird's neck resembling skin that has been scorched or burned by fire.[2] A parallel idea occurs in the शतपथ where a yoke-bullock is said to partake of the nature of fire because that part of his neck which bears the yoke loses the hair and appears to have been scorched by fire :

...दक्षिणा अनड्वान् वा, स हि वहेनाऽग्नेयोऽग्निदग्धमिव ह्यस्य वहं भवति । —शतपथ ब्राह्मण, 4.5.1.15

1. 5.14; 11.135; and 12.66.

2. It is also very significant to note, in this connection, that the God of Fire himself has been called असितग्रीव black-necked, in V. S. 23.13, and animals having black necks in particular are sacrificed to him, e.g. कृष्णग्रीवा आग्नेयां-VS 24.6, 9, 14, i.e., यः पाप्मना गृहीतः स्यात् स आग्नेयं कृष्णग्रीवमालभेत—TS 2.1.4.6.

The White Ibis occurs in parties which have been called बकप्रकराः by लोलिम्बराज who, however, makes them stop eating fish in their immediate neighbourhood because they have been charmed into inaction by the sweet tunes of Lord Kṛṣṇa's flute :—

निकटेऽपि गतान्गतकेलिकरान् मकरान्नसरःसुबकप्रकराः ।

हरिविलास, 2.10.

These Ibises flock to the shallow edges of tanks and rivers.

दुष्टबकोटसंकटतटोद्देशास्तडागादयः ।

सुभाषित, 222.33.

The deceitful tactics of the apparently gentle and polished ministers of state dressed in spotless white have been beautifully compared with the fishing methods of the White Ibis :—

'बहिरविकृतवेषैर्मन्दमन्दप्रचारैः
निभृतनयनपातैः साधुताकारसारैः ।
निकृतिनयविनीतैश्चान्तरेतैरमात्यैः
तिमय इव बकोटैर्वञ्चिता के न लोकाः ॥

यशस्तिलकचम्पू, 3.191.

Verse 13 under स्थानमाहात्म्यम् in सुभाषित, 86, institutes a parallel between the moon and the White Ibis (बक) and declares the superiority of the latter because it has entirely white wings (पक्षौ) as against the two fortnights (पक्षौ) of the former both of which are partly light and partly dark. Numbers of these birds moving quietly through the reeds or resting amongst them until the next urge of hunger, have been held up as a model of prudent and cautious behaviour for persons finding themselves in a difficult situation in enemy country. The श्वेतबक, श्वेतकाक, and ध्वाङ्क्ष in the examples below is the White Ibis in groups :—

मर्कवच्छ्वेतबाकीयैरुपायैः स्थयितां सुराः ।

—स्कन्दपुराण[1]

भजस्व श्वेतकाकीयैर्मित्रधर्ममनर्थकैः ।

—महाभारत[2]

ईदृशैः श्वेतकाकीयैः राज्ञःशासनदूषकैः ।

—मृच्छकटिक[3]

यस्य दस्युगणा राष्ट्रे ध्वाङ्क्षा मत्स्यान् जलादिव ।

—महाभारत[4]

This bird is never found away from water except when roosting for the night, and the sight of one on a hill-top is, therefore, considered unlucky :

1. Kaumārikā Khaṇḍa, 21.236.

2. XII.105.15; also I.47.12. To separate the compound श्वेतकाक as श्वा+एत+काक as suggested by some is absurd. See R. B. Raddi's edition of मृच्छकटिक, Bombay, 1909.

3. IX.41, Raddi's edition.

4. XI.142.29.

"शिखरे शुक्लवायसः (अशुभः)—नारदीय महापुराण.[1] शुक्लवायस does not mean the albino form of the common Crow, for it would be inauspicious anywhere and not only on the top of a hill.

15. Poets have often instituted a comparison between a White Ibis (बक) and the Swan (both all-white with black bills and feet) stressing the difference between their feeding habits, gait, etc. The Swan is praised for his supposed power of separating milk from water which the poor Ibis can not do. Such poetry is, of course, of अन्योक्ति type containing a satire on persons devoid of merit but aspiring to high rank. A single example should be enough :

> हंसः श्वेतो बकः श्वेतः को भेदो बकहंसयोः ।
> नीरक्षीरविवेके तु हंसो हंसो बको बकः ॥ सुभाषित[2]

The White Ibis shares the habit of 'resting and meditation' with the Storks and Herons—all going under the common name of बक, and it is a familiar theme with the poets to describe the seemingly innocent but really fraudulent conduct of men in different walks of life as बकवृत्ति, and such men as बकसाधु or ध्वाङ्क्षव्रती.

> स्तब्धग्रीवो मौनी पिहितार्धलोचनः शश्वत् ।
> सजलो जनो य आस्ते स किल ध्वाङ्क्षव्रती प्रोक्तः ॥[3]

The first line describes correctly the attitude of the White Ibis when fishing in the shallows. For other examples see Art. 82.

---

1. Ch. 56.750.
2. 221.6.
3. महेन्द्रटीका on हेमचन्द्र, 2.550.

81

STORKS

Eight species of Storks are found in India. They are tall and stately birds with long legs, long, stout and powerful bills, and a plumage of striking colours—characters which make them conspicuous wherever they are found. They often soar very high, like and in company of Vultures. They are almost omnivorous and feed on all sorts of animals, such as frogs, fish, crabs, snakes, locusts, small birds and mice. Some, like the Adjutant Stork, feed also on carrion. A few serve as food for another type of omnivorous creature —Man. With one exception (the Adjutant) they are voiceless and give expression to their emotions by clattering their long bills and indulging in a sort of dance during the breeding season. As a class or group they are बृहद्बकाः and fall under the larger category of बकाः* which corresponds to the Order Herodiones. Their voicelessness has been recognised in a verse on the virtue of silence :—

> आत्मनो गुणदोषेण बध्यन्ते शुकसारिकाः ।
> बकास्तत्र न बध्यन्ते मौनं सर्वार्थसाधनम् ॥—सुभाषित, 86.1.

Four of the larger Storks are named after their physical features in स्मृति and पुराण literature, e.g., the White and Black Storks with red bills and feet are called (जलजा) रक्तपादतुण्डाः in गौतमस्मृति, ch. 17; the महाभारत calls the White-necked and Black-necked Storks as शितिकण्ठाः (शिति black and white), while, शंखस्मृति, 17.26 and गरुडपुराण, 1.97.70 name all the above four as रक्तपादाः. The specific individual names for the different members of the group may now be considered.

1. The White Stork (42 inches) is only a winter visitor to North India and remains with us from September to about the end of March. It is all white except for the wing-quills and some wing-coverts which are black. With his red bill and legs and a predominantly white plumage set off by black wings it is a beautiful object when seen on green grass near

---

*Prakrit derivatives like ढिंक and ढेंक from Sansk. ध्वाङ्क्ष for the White Ibis or बक have been applied not only to the Ibis but also the Storks and the Flamingo, and it is from the Storks (ढेंक) that ढेङ्की and ढेङ्किका for a particular dance resembling that of the storks, and measure of time in music, have passed into Sansk.—See M. W. under ढेङ्कु.

water, and he is the बकराज or राजबक described as :

मृष्टाभरणसम्पन्नो भूषणैरर्कसन्निभैः ।

महाभारत, 12.170.21.

Here the ornaments of the colour of fire or the rising sun (अर्क) are the red bill and legs of the bird and, as this is the most beautiful of the Storks, he has been well named बकराज.* He is also the बक of the बककुलीरककथा, पञ्चतंत्र Pt. 1, 7th tale, where his Egret-like thin and white neck is described as "मृणालनाल-धवला मृदुग्रीवा", and he is also the Stork par excellence of Aesop's Fables. He has been incorrectly listed with the Sarus in धन्वन्तरिनिघण्टु where the adnouns like रक्ततुण्ड, रक्तपाद and अस्रवल्लभ suit him better than the Sarus (Art. 62).

2. The Black Stork (40 inches) is principally of a black colour glossed with purple, bronze and green, and has red bill and legs. It is a bird of open marshes and wet ground away from villages. He is the कालिक or कालीक ("क्रौञ्चे, बके"—वाचस्पत्यम्, शब्दकल्पद्रुम, etc.) corresponding to Hindi सुरमाई (of the colour of सुरमा, collyrium, and hence black; cf. कालिक-कृष्णचन्दन). The name नीलाङ्ग (black-bodied) as a synonym for सारस in धन्वन्तरि and राजनिघण्टु is probably due to a confusion between a Stork and Crane or to misunderstanding of an older equation like "नीलाङ्ग सारसे" where सारस meant 'a water bird' only, for the Sarus is neither blue nor black. नीलाङ्गः should, therefore, be an adnoun for this Stork just as it is for the Purple Heron and कालबक is yet another name comparable with the last but it has incorrectly been given as synonym for अतिजागर in शब्दकल्पद्रुम for the नीलक्रौञ्च. This latter is the most wary and suspicious Purple Heron as defined in the कल्पद्रुकोश:—

नीलक्रौञ्चोऽतिजागरः । दीर्घग्रीवश्च नीलाङ्गो

3. The White-necked Stork (36 inches) is a glistening black and white bird with a conspicuously white neck, black bill and red legs. As a soaring bird this and the Black-necked Stork have been mentioned as शितिकण्ठाः in महाभारत where Arjuna speaks of the great speed of his chariot drawn by white steeds :—

मृगाः शृगालाः शितिकण्ठाश्च काका, गृध्रा बकाश्चैव तरक्षवश्च ।

5.48.104.

बकाः in the verse are the Adjutant Storks mentioned elsewhere in the company of Vultures as carrion eaters. शितिकण्ठ is a homonym for the Black-necked and White-necked Storks as already stated. The solemn looking White-necked Stork occurs single, in pairs or in small parties about rivers, jheels, tanks, etc., and is often seen "standing motionless on one

*The great Tulasidas, author of रामचरितमानस, compares this बक with the राजहंस (cygnus davidu):—

चरनचोंच लोचनरंगौ चलौ मराली चाल ।
छीर नीर बिबरनं समय बक उघरत तेंहि काल ।।—दोहावली, 333.

leg as if absorbed in meditation" (Salim Ali), thus recalling the following verse of क्षेमेन्द्र which is true not only of Storks but also of the Common or Grey Heron, also called a बक :—

मत्स्यार्थी चरति तपः सुचिरं निस्पन्द एकपादेन ।
तीर्थेषु बकतपस्वी, तेन विहङ्गान् गतो दम्भः ॥

कलाविलास, 1.93 (का.मा. Pt. 1)

He is known in Hindi as मानिकजोड़ (मणिचूड ?) from his green-glossed black crown though our Muslim friends explain the name with reference to a story which need not detain us. He also shares the name सारङ्ग बक with the next species.

4. The Black-necked Stork (52 inches) is also a black and white bird with red legs and black bill. He is लोह सारङ्ग in Hindi because of the black parts being glossed with metallic hues (लोह) and the pied plumage (सारङ्ग), and सारङ्गबक in Sanskrit. सारङ्ग is 'a large kind of Crane'—Ardea sarunga—according to Carey quoted in M. Williams and the term evidently refers to both the birds*. Another name for him is कृष्णग्रीव by which he is mentioned as an inauspicious bird in महाभारत :

कृष्णग्रीवाश्च शकुना रक्तपादा भयानकाः—5.143.25.

Again, the Griffon Vultures (पाण्डुराः) and Storks in the रामायण:

पाण्डुरा रक्तपादाश्च विहगाः कालचोदिताः—6.35.31.

The name कृष्णग्रीव makes it just possible that the name शितिकण्ठ may not after all be a homonym covering both the White-necked and the Black-necked Storks as suggested above and may be specific for the former alone.

The dancing propensity common to Storks as a class is more highly developed in the Black-necked variety than in others. This dance and music of their clattering bills has been fully described by Hume in his *Nests and Eggs*, vol. 3 and by other observers as well. "Two birds (male and female gravely stalk up to each other and when a yard or so apart stand face to face, extend their long wings, and flutter them rapidly, with the points of one bird's wings flapping against those of the other; they then advance their heads till they nearly meet and both simultaneously clatter their bills. This display lasts for nearly a minute after which one walks a little apart, to be followed after a moment by the other, when they repeat the performance; and so on for perhaps a dozen times" (Smythies). It will now be seen that the equation "जायानुजीवी बके"—(विश्वप्रकाश and हेमचन्द्र) can only refer to this Stork who is a नट i.e., a dancer, actor and even musician, all in one. जायानुजीवी बक is thus this particular Stork. In the

---

*The Painted Stork is also a kind of सारङ्ग बक known as कठ सारंग in Hindi (Sansk. काष्ठ सारङ्ग as a back-formation).

alternative, it may also be a common name for the Storks as a group. The करालफाल बक (stork, having terribly large mandibles looking like plough-shares) in the following should be the Black-necked stork with a twelve inch bill. He is a "more regular fisher than most Storks" and has, next to the Adjutant, the largest bill of all. The Adjutant is excluded as the verse is descriptive of the शरद् season :—

अस्यां तरङ्गितनुतोयपलायमान—
मीनानुसारिबकदत्तकरालफालाः ॥

काव्यमीमांसा, Ch. 18

5. The Gigantic or the Adjutant Stork is not only the largest but also the ugliest and most formidable member of the present series. The male is five feet long and stands four and a half feet high, distinguished by a bare red head and neck, and a long pouch of skin hanging from the neck and resting against the chest. The enormous, thick, four-sided bill is wedge-shaped and measures no less than thirteen inches. The wing-expanse exceeds twelve feet. He is indeed a monster among birds. The English name Adjutant is derived from his "deliberate, high-stepping military gait as it paces up and down" (Salim Ali), and fully corresponds to Sanskrit दीर्घपाद (दीर्घः पादन्यासः अस्य, long-paced) as against दीर्घजङ्घ (long-legged) for other Storks and the larger Herons. Names like बृहत्-or महा-चञ्चुबक are after his bill. He is essentially a scavenger and performed his duties as such in India till not very many years ago and was one of the most familiar birds of towns and villages, and naturally won for himself quite a number of epithets with कङ्क and बक as the basic names. They are listed below :—

उरगारि—, उरगाशन—, दीर्घपाद—, कालपृष्ठ—, कोलपुच्छ—, गलेगण्ड—, गलेशुण्ड—, गृहबलिप्रिय—, द्वारबलिभुक्—, दारबलिभुक्; ;, स्त्रीदत्तबलिभुक्—, मर्कट (पर्कट ?)—,मर्कक (v.l. मरकक)—, स्कन्ध-मल्लक—, कर्कटस्कन्ध—, शुक्लाक्ष—, पुण्डरीकाक्ष—, बृहच्चञ्चु—, महाचञ्चू—, सिंहनाद—, etc.

अभि. चिन्तामणि and वैजयन्ती have mixed up some of the above names with those for the Brahminy Kite and Pallas's Fishing Eagle, but त्रिकाण्डशेष and हारावली have kept the Kite and Stork apart (Art. 52-C &E). Coming to the propriety of the names in the above list, उरगारि and उरगाशन (both in Wilson and the latter in M. Williams) means the Garuḍa and a kind of 'crane' and this 'crane' clearly refers to both forms of Adjutant who eat snakes, apparently from analogy with the snake-eating habit attributed to the mythological Garuḍa. These names are the origin for Hindi हरगिला (fr. हरि frog or snake and गिल् to swallow, later, corrupted to हड़गीला bone-swallower) and probably also the element 'argala', in the older scientific name of 'Ardea argala'. Unfortunately, however, the name हड़गीला led some-one to identify it with Sansk. अस्थिभक्ष (a dog) and to apply the latter to this bird, and that is how it finds place in शब्दकल्पद्रुम. M. Williams also, no doubt similarly influenced, gives अस्थिसंहारक as a name for this Stork. This

*The वाचाटित (noisy) बकोट in the next verse is the White Ibis (Art. 80).

last really means the medicinal plant or creeper अस्थिसंहारी of भावप्रकाश, गुडूच्यादि वर्ग (Vitis quadrangularis), Hindi हाड़जोड़ी, supposed to help join up broken bones. Both the Adjutants are known as गरुड़ in Hindi because they eat snakes which supports the derivation of हरगिला given above.

Adnoun कालपृष्ठ is from the Stork's black back and this is shared by Pallas's Fishing Eagle and the Black Buck antelope, while कोलपुच्छ (कोल is Prakrit for क्रोड chest, and the name means 'a bird with a tail in front of the chest') and गलेगण्ड (also गलेशुण्ड—निघण्टुरत्नाकर) refer to the long pouch. The series द्वारबलिभुक्, दारबलिभुक्, and स्त्रीदत्तबलिभुक् is after the scavenging habits of the Adjutant. A Hindu woman does not make any daily ceremonial बलि and what is humorously described as 'बलि' in these names is the house-rubbish, offal, scraps of animal and other food which were formerly, and in the villages are even now, thrown out of doors (द्वार) by the women, and these the Adjutant turned up for offal, scraps, etc. It is in this sense that this (द्वारबलिभुक्) कङ्क is placed in the list of विष्किर birds in चरकसंहिता (Lahore edn.). It is also possible that the original name was only द्वारबलिभुक् and due to an error in copying द्वार became दार which in turn led to "स्त्रीदत्त" as a clear substitute for दार. No other Heron or Stork found in India turns up at these rubbish heaps, though the White Stork takes its place in Europe.

No Indian male Stork or Heron is known to receive food from the female during courtship or when sitting on the eggs, and the following verse from the आर्यासप्तशती would seem to be based upon a misunderstanding of the name स्त्रीदत्तबलिभुक् for a बक which is on a par with the absurd statements about the अष्टापद and उत्पादशयन (Art. 71):—

स्वयमुपनीतैरशनैः पुष्णन्ती नीडनिर्वृतं दयितम् ।
सहजप्रेमरसज्ञा सुभगा गर्वं बकी वहतु ॥—599

मर्कट (a monkey) is yet another humorous name for this quaint looking bird, and मर्कक, if from मर्क् to cleanse, as assumed by सायण on RV 10.27.20 where he interprets मर्कः as मार्जयिता or शोधयिता, would mean a 'scavenger' which the bird certainly is. Or again, the name may mean 'a small devil' after the mythological demon मर्क. The name, however, may well be from root मृ-मर, in which case the correct form would be मरकक, and this would make the bird an attendant on 'death' with Vultures, e.g., upon cholera epidemic or the battlefield, as a carrion-eater.

The first of the following two synonymies has mixed up the adnouns or epithets for three different कङ्क birds, viz. the Brahminy Kite (लोहपृष्ठ or कमनच्छद—), Pallas's Fishing Eagle (प्रियापत्य–), and the Adjutant, while the second has confused those for the first and the third bird :—

कङ्कस्तु कर्कटस्कन्धः (कर्कर-?) पर्कटः (मर्कटः ?) कमलच्छदः (कमन-?)
दीर्घपादो प्रियापत्यो लोहपृष्ठश्च मल्लकः—वैजयन्ती

कङ्कस्तुकमनच्छदः ।
लोहपृष्ठो दीर्घपादः कर्कटः स्कन्धमल्लकः ॥ —अभिधानचिन्तामणि*

The correct names कर्कटस्कन्ध (कर्कर—?) and स्कन्धमल्लक for the Adjutant have suffered mutilation in both, i.e., one of them in each synonymy. Both the names refer to the bird as if he is holding a pot or vessel about his neck or shoulder, and correspond to क्रोडमल्लक for a beggar who carries his bowl hanging from the neck and in front of his chest (क्रोड). स्कन्ध by itself cannot mean a Heron as in M. Williams. The epithet कमनच्छद belongs to the above named Kite with a white and bright chestnut plumage and not to the repulsive looking Adjutant "with the coarsest and most tumbled of plumage." Both the Adjutants, funny-looking bald-heads, have been jocularly named in Hindi चन्दियारी (चन्द्रिलारि—enemy of the barber; Cf. Prakrit चंदला—bald) as they never need a hair-cut !

The उणादि of श्वेतवनवासिन्, 3.66 equates गृत्स with कङ्क. Now if गृत्स is from गृध् as suggested by M. Williams कङ्क would be the Brahminy Kite which greedily snatches away tit bits from other birds like the Kite. If on the other hand we accept Sāyaṇa's derivation "निगरणाद् गृत्सः"—ऐतरेय आरण्यक, 2.2.1, com., कङ्क would be either the Common Grey Heron or the Adjutant from their habit of swallowing their food. The latter, however, is known to gulp down or swallow at one stroke an entire dead cat or half a leg of mutton and the probability is thus in his favour. If so he would be the गृत्स कङ्क.

गृत्समद (proud of his powers of eating or swallowing) is the name of a Vedic sage and is camparable with जाष्कमद of the अथर्ववेद for Pallas's fishing Eagle—Art. 52-C. On this analogy, however, गृत्स would seem to refer to the Brahminy Kite which shares the names of जलाटन and कङ्क with the fishing Eagle, and it is possible that this particular Kite was also known as गृत्समद कङ्क— Art. 52, E.

Finally, three more synonyms for the Stork, one each from चरक, सुश्रुत and बृहत्संहिता, must be mentioned. पुण्डरीकाक्ष of चरक corresponding to शुक्लाक्ष of सुश्रुत refers to the Adjutants, both of whom have white irides. The Adjutant bellows like a buffalo or a cow separated from her calf (Hume in *Stray Feathers*, vol. 7, pp. 32 & 51) and was also believed to "roar like a tiger" (Charles Knight in *Pictorial Museum of Animated Nature*, vol.2, 1871), and would therefore seem to be the सिंहनाद of बृहत्संहिता, as a bird of augury. It is doubtful, however, how far this last is a bird-name and does not refer to the roar of a lion as lions were quite common in North India till a few centuries ago.

The Adjutant is the only बक that eats carrion and numbers of these have been known to consort with the Vultures both when soaring high and at a feast on dead animals (*Stray Feathers*, vol. 4, 21 and Cassell's *Book of Birds*) and the बक mentioned in the following in company with

---

*For other syonymies see Art. 52, Section E.

Pallas's fishing Eagle (कङ्क), Tawny Eagle (श्येन), Imperial Eagle (सुपर्ण), and Vultures as feeding on dead human bodies and animals killed in battle is the Adjutant Stork :—

अतीव हृष्टाः श्वशृगालवायसाः
बकाः सुपर्णाश्च वृकास्तरक्षवः—महाभारत, 7.50.9;
see also 6.2.17

गृध्राः कङ्का बकाः श्येना वायसा जम्बुकास्तथा—
Ibid. 7.97.13; see also 5. 143.19

शृगालगृध्रवायसाः परं प्रमोदमादधुः
क्वचित्स्थितोऽतिभीषणः श्वचञ्चु (शवं तु ?) चर्वितो बकः
मत्स्यपुराण, 153. 137.

Similarly the बक of the बकजातक, 300 ready to attack a lamb or kid, if near enough, is the Adjutant. The कङ्क, again, in the following is the snake-eating Adjutant who in an atmosphere of spirituality prevailing at hermitage permits snakes to play about freely in his body plumage :—

फणिनः कङ्कबर्हेषु निर्विशङ्कं विशन्ति च ।
पद्मपुराण, 6 उत्तरखंड, 184. 28

This ugly and fierce looking Stork is also the physical basis of the बकासुर of Indian mythology e.g., in the भागवत, 10.11 where he is called महाबक.

6. The Smaller Adjutant resembles the Adjutant but has no pouch, and not being a scavenger does not "haunt civilization". He naturally shares such of the names for the larger bird as do not refer to the pouch. Prakrit कंडूर for a बक refers to these Storks as if they have lost the hair on their heads from itches, cf. "मुंडा कंडू विणट्ठंगा—कण्डू कृतं क्षतैर्विनष्टशरीरे— अभि. राजेन्द्र under कंडूविणट्ठंगा.

7. The Painted Stork in a little smaller than the White Stork, with a white plumage closely barred and marked with shining greenish-black above and with a black band across the breast. The eyes of the young are brown and of the adult, straw-yellow. If the Adjutant is शुक्लाक्ष this should be the काचाक्ष* of सुश्रुत.. This name has been rendered as a बृहद्बक in the Chowkhamba Sanskrit Series edition of सुश्रुत (Benares). The शब्दार्थचिन्तामणि also has काचाक्ष for बृहद्बक, while डल्हणाचार्य takes it for the Indian Pied Kingfisher with hazel irides and the epithet may well belong to both the birds—this Stork as काचाक्षबक and the Pied Kingfisher as काचाक्ष मत्स्यरङ्ग. The Hindi for this Stork is कठसारंग (काष्ठ सारङ्गबक), i.e., a smaller variety of सारङ्गबक, and it was probably known as काष्ठसारङ्ग as the name is in line with काष्ठशुक and काष्ठकदली. पिंगलक्खग (पिङ्गलाक्ष having yellowish eyes) of the Jain औपपातिक सूत्र and प्रश्नव्याकरण should be the same as काचाक्ष or this Stork.

8. The Open-bill Stork is easily distinguished from its curious bill which has a clearly visible gap between the two mandibles. It feeds

*काच, wax, hence, having yellowish eyes.

chiefly on fresh-water molluscs or shells which it breaks open before swallowing. In many Indian dialiects it is known as 'the shell-breaker' and घोंघल (Sansk. घोङ्गक a shell- विश्व) in Hindi and शामूक भंग (शम्बूक with भञ्जन breaker) in Bengali. Sansk. घोङ्क (more correctly perhaps घोङ्ग) for a kind of bird in विश्वप्रकाश may be for this bird. सुश्रुत mentions अवभञ्जन (अव may be a mistake for वट or पुट for a shell ?) as a particular bird in connection with surgical instruments one of which was designed after the shape of its bill. Now a bill with a curious gap like the present bird's is not likely to have escaped the keen eyes of सुश्रुत and he must have modelled an instrument upon it resembling a pair of black-smith's tongs. No particular instrument is however mentioned by the name of अवभञ्जन मुख but one called अन्तर्मुख (having space between the jaws ?) is described as मध्यमुख regarded as synonymous with the former :—

अन्तर्मुखमि मध्यमुखम् तल्लक्षणमाहः—अष्टाङ्गुलप्रमाणेन
जिह्मधारेण चाप्लुतम् । शस्त्रमन्तर्मुखं नाम चन्द्रार्धमिव चोद्गतम्
—डल्हणाचार्य

The expressions मध्यमुख, जिह्मधार and अर्धचन्द्र clearly point to the inter-space between the jaws, their curved edges and crescent shape respectively, characters that fit in admirably with the inner and outer contours of the bird's bill, and it is suggested that this अन्तमुंख is the instrument made after the bill of अवभञ्जन or the Open-bill Stork. शम्बूकभञ्जन too may well have been its name.

The list of water-birds given at p. 198 of हस्त्यायुर्वेद of पालकाप्य contains several incorrect readings, e.g., वर्चका for वर्तका, परिप्लुत for परिप्लव; and कुक्कुर for कुक्कुभ and I would amend the expression कुटभेदक to पुटभेदक which would make sense with पुट-पुटक meaning 'a shell', and may be rendered as the 'shell-breaker' or the Open-bill; Cf. Pali पुटभेद, 'breaking open a bean'. Is Pali पटिकुट्टक of वेस्संतरजातक, verse 2098 a wrong reading of पुटकुट्टक ?

It has already been stated that the larger terms क्रौञ्च and बक comprehend the Storks and Herons, and the Open-bill has naturally been referred to by these names in अन्योक्ति type of poetry :—

क्रौञ्चश्चञ्चुपुटेन कुञ्चितवपुः शम्बूकमन्वेषते
सुभाषित, 41.70

शम्बूका अपि सन्ति नेति च बकैराकर्ण्य ही ही कृतम्
Ibid. 221, 30.

Pali सिथिलहनु (having the lower mandible loose or relaxed) is mentioned as one of the birds the quills of which could be used to feather an arrow :

यस्य पत्तेए वाजितं, यदि वा गिज्झस्स . . .
यदि वा सिथिलहनुनो'ति—मज्झिमनिकाय, सुत्त 63

I need hardly add that शिथिलहनु is a most fitting name and a correct redering of the English name Open-bill for the bird.

As there is reason to believe that the physical basis of the semi-fabulous भारण्ड (भार+अण्ड, looking like a huge egg, or laying a large or heavy egg), भारुण्ड, भेरुण्ड, etc. of the Purāṇas, Pañcatantra, etc. may be the Adjutant Stork or some other bird, I conclude this article with just a suggestive note on it and it must be clearly understood that what follows is pure conjecture. Some of the references to these mythical birds and lexical information bearing upon them are noted below :—

(1) एकोदरा पृथगग्रीवा भारण्डा इव पक्षिणः—पञ्चतन्त्र

(2) भारुण्ड सामगीताभिः अथर्वशिरसोद्गतैः—महाभारत, 1.70.39

(3)a भारुण्डा नाम शकुनाः तीक्ष्णतुण्डा भयानकाः
ते निर्हरन्ति मृतान् दरीषु प्रक्षिपन्ति च— Ibid. 6.8.11

b भारण्ड उत्तरकुरुदेशजशकुनपक्षिणि—शब्दार्थचिन्तामणि

(4) मनुष्यवदनाश्चान्ये भारुण्डा इति विश्रुताः— Ibid. 12.169.9.

(5) भेरुण्डा वायसा गृध्रा हंसाद्या पक्षिजातयः—नारदपुराण, 77.88

(6) चिञ्चिकः (चर्चिकः) पक्षिराट् तत्र भेरुण्डो योऽभिधीयते (द्विमुखः) ब्रह्मपुराण, Ch. 164.

(7) भेरुण्डचाषभासाश्च परावतकपिञ्जलौ—पाराशरस्मृति, 6.7

(8) गिद्धूलुय भारयडो=गृध्रोलूक भारण्डः—रिष्टसमुच्चय, 176

(9) द्विमूर्द्धाशकुनिः— Progeny of दनु in मत्स्यपुराण, 6.17.

(10) भेरुण्ड son of जटायु in Ibid. 6.36.

(11) वेलाधरः भारण्डः—परिशिष्टपर्वन्, 2.408.

(12) भारण्डः—उत्तरकुरुदेशजशकुनपक्षी । इति पुराणम्—शब्दकल्पद्रुम

(13) भेरुण्डौ भीषण खगौ; वारुण्डः खगउद्रिणि—हेमचन्द्र
भेरुण्डोभीमदर्शन पक्षिणो भिदि—विश्व.

(14) हत्थिलिङ्ग शकुन— a vulture with a bill like the trunk of an elephant—Pali Dictionary (P.T.S.)

(15) गलेशुण्ड—पक्षिविशेष in निघण्टुरत्नाकर

(15)a भेरुंडो चित्रयः—दे.ना.

(16) रुण्ड— mutilated body

Examination of the above extracts shows that भारण्ड and its variants refer to (i) a so called two-faced bird, (ii) a human-faced (moustached and bearded ?) bird, and (iii) bird with a powerful vioce and carrion-eating habits of a Vulture—all of great size and formidable or fearful appearance.

First, the two-faced bird: The giant, flightless and now extinct Pigeon, the Dodo, of Mauritius was known to European navigators by names like 'Dodaarsen', 'Dodaars' and 'Duodo'. The etymology of these names has not been satisfactorily solved even though all the facts about the bird and these names do not go beyond the sixteenth century. The Indian voyagers too must have known or at least heard about the bird which had a huge body—larger than the Turkey-Cock and standing near about two feet six inches high—rudimentary stumps in place of wings, head with a large massive bill in front and a short curly tail at the rear. It is probable, therefore, that, looked at from a distance, the bird appeared as a large egg-shaped object (भार+अण्ड) or having two heads, as it were, one at either end of its body, and from this last feature the Indian sea-men probably called it द्विदर्शन (cf. द्विमुख in No.6 and द्विमूर्धा शकुनि in No.10 above). This द्विदर्शन was probably taken up by the Dutch and others as 'Dodaarsen' which later got corrupted to Dodaars, Dodaers, and finally to Duodo (See 'Dodo' in *Enc. Brit.* 11th ed.). That one of the भारण्ड birds had its origin across the seas is amply proved by the story of the adventures भीम related in Book X of the Jain work शत्रुञ्जय माहात्म्य of धनेश्वर, a poet at the court of शिलादित्य, king of सुराष्ट्र (the Kathiawar peninsula on the west coast of India) who ruled over the country about 1100 A.C. भीम sailing overseas in a merchant vessel runs aground in mid-ocean on a coral reef. The name भारण्ड may thus refer either to the large egg-shaped body of the bird or the large egg laid by it. This would furnish a basis for the mythical भारण्ड of पञ्चतंत्र, द्विमुख of ब्रह्मपुराण and भारण्ड as वेलाधर (a coastal bird), also वारुण्ड as a water-bird (खग उद्रिणि) of Hemchandra, No.8 above.

Second, the so-called human-faced भारुण्डा: said to carry dead bodies to a deep valley would seem to refer to an old practice of exposing the dead. After the flesh had been picked out by other Vultures the Bearded Vultures would then work upon the bones, pick up and drop them from a great height on the rocks below to break them into bits for their own food. This would explain भेरुण्ड as the son of जटायु who is no other than th Bearded Vulture (Art. 51), and also भारण्ड as a bird of omen with Vultures and Owls—Nos. 3,4,9&11 above. The mention of the synonyoms शकुन and गृध्र in these is very significant. The thick black rictal bristles overhanging the bill and the tuft of bristly hair hanging down from the chin against the white face of this Vulture combined with his large and intelligent looking eyes are comparable with the moustache and beard on the human face—No.4 above. It may also be recalled how जटायु of the Rāmāyaṇa has been very nearly anthropomorphised; Cf. also 'यत् श्मश्रुण: तत् पुरुषाणां रूपम्' said of a bearded goat in तैत्तिरीय संहिता, 2.1.1.9.

Third, as a fearful bird with a powerful voice भारण्ड or भेरुण्ड may well be the awful looking Adjutant Stork with a bellowing or roaring call attributed to him. The भारुण्ड साम गीत (No.2) should therefore be a charm sung so loudly as to strike terror in the heart of the enemy. This Stork would also seem to be the हत्थिलिंग (No.13) bird of Buddhist literature, the twelve to fifteen inch pendent pouch of the bird being supposed to resemble the trunk-characteristic mark (लिङ्ग) of an elephant. In the वेस्संतर जातक the commentator explaining the expression सकुनानं च ओपातो in verse 2249 refers to हत्थिलिंगसकुण as a bird capable of taking away small children. It is well known that this Stork readily swallows a leg of mutton or a dead cat entire, and he would also strike at any living thing he can swallow at a gulp; cf. the story in बक जातक, 300 where this Stork is said to be ready to attack a lamb or kid, and if he can have a chance he would certainly not fail to make a meal of a small human baby as well. The reference in वेस्संतर जातक may also be to the Bearded Vuture formerly reputed to carry off little children. The name गलेशुण्ड (No.14), however, significantly points to the Adjutant as the हत्यिलिङ्ग bird.

That भेरुण्ड, prohibited as food in No.7, was a real bird hardly admits of a doubt as the passage expressly mentions both kinds of भासा:, the Bearded and the Neophron Vultures, and the probability of भेरुण्ड as a fearful (भीषण) bird is definitely in favour of the Adjutant Stork (Nos. 5,7&8). It is also to be noted that Hemachandra's equation, "भेरुण्डो भीषणखगौ" —note the duals— clearly refers to two different birds of that name and it is suggested that the two birds are the Bearded Vulture and the Adjutant Stork.

We, therefore, have three different kinds of भारण्ड or भेरुण्ड birds—(i) the वेलाघर or द्विमुख भारण्ड, the Dodo; (ii) the मनुष्यवदन भारण्ड,, the Bearded Vulture; and (iii) the हस्तिलिङ्ग or गलेशुण्ड भारण्ड, the Adjutant Stork.

82

HERONS, EGRETS AND BITTERNS

1. Birds comprised within the Heron group are easily distinguished from the storks by their thin, dagger-shaped and pointed bills. The epithet or adnoun कृशचञ्चु for a Heron is really descriptive of the whole group as कृशचञ्चुबकाः as against बृहच्चञ्चुबकाः for the Storks (बृहच्चञ्चु—पक्षिविशेषे, दीर्घपादे, i.e. a Stork— शब्दार्थचिन्तामणि; दीर्घपाद, a long-legged heron—M. W.) Barring a couple of exceptionally large Herons, like Great White-bellied Heron of Bhutan, the majority of the birds in this group are of medium and small size which also helps to separate them from the much heavier and long legged Storks.

2. The typical Herons, with the exception of the Pond-Heron, are fairly large birds, over a yard long, and their plumage is a mixture of grey, white and black or these with some rufous-buff and chestnut. The commonest are the Grey Heron and the so-called Purple Heron which has no purple in its plumage.

3. The Grey Heron (39"), who e prototype in Europe is known as the Blue Heron, is a tall grey bird marked with black and white, often seen brooding "almost motionless by the side of water." It has a long drooping black crest and white long feathers falling over the breast. It is a solitary bird and sometimes "wades in shallow water with slow deliberate paces, the neck outstreched" (Whistler), watching for fish or frog to come within striking distance. It is one of the five different birds bearing the common basic name of कङ्क mentioned in the lexicons and is the कृशचञ्चु कङ्क [1] (having a thin pointed bill), and simple कङ्क or वारिकङ्क. for short. कल्पद्रुकोश has बलाहक in the list of names for Herons, Egrets, etc., and as the term also means a cloud (cf. श्वेतनील for 'a cloud' in M.W., and note that the black and white colour-pattern of the Grey Heron is also श्वेतनील) it should be another name for this bird. The complexion of lord Kṛṣṇa has been compared with the colour of a dark cloud and the plumage of the बलाहक bird :

बलाहकाञ्जननिभं बलाहकतनूरुहम्—हरिवंश, I.24.

---

1. कङ्कमुख forceps of सुश्रुत and कङ्कमुखबाण of रामायण (Cal. Edn.) 6.79.69 quoted in शब्दकल्पद्रुम, refer to the shape of the thin, pointed bill of this Heron or the next,

It is rather significant to note that the bird is known in Hindi as अञ्जन (collyrium) which is also the colour of the cloud in the above verse. This Heron was a great favourite with falconers both in Europe and India and has been mentioned by the name of कङ्क in श्यैनिकशास्त्र :—

अतिदूरगतानान्तु कङ्कदात्यूहपक्षिणाम् ।
लक्ष्ये मोको बहर्व्या हि जनयत्यद्भुतं रसम् ॥—6.37.

4. The Grey Heron is not a skulker like its cousin, the Purple Heron, and has been the subject of popular observation so that its ways have been well described as a बक in poetry :—

स्थित्वा धैर्यादुपाम्भः समजठरशिराश्चक्रमूर्त्तिर्मुहूर्तं म् ।
धूर्त्तः संत्यक्ततीरः कतिचिदपि पदान्युच्चकैः कुञ्चिताङ्घ्रिः ।
पश्चाद्ग्रीवां प्रसार्य त्वरितगतिरपां मध्यमाविश्य चञ्च्वा
चञ्चन्तीमूर्ध्वंकण्ठः कथमपि शफरीं स्फारिताक्षो बकोऽत्ति ॥
—सुभाषित, 208.24.

Again,

न भ्रूणां स्फुरणं न चञ्चुचलनं नो चूलिकाकम्पनं
न ग्रीवाचलनं मनागपि न यत्पक्षद्वयोत्क्षेपणम् ।
नासाग्रे क्षणमेकपाददमनं कष्टैकनिष्ठं परं
यावत्तिष्ठति मीनहीनवदनस्तावद् बकस्तापसः ॥
—Ibid. 229.232.

Reference to the birds' habits and the crest in these examples helps to identify the बक as the Grey Heron.

5. कङ्क as a sporting bird is also mentioned in the पद्मपुराण :-

चकोरांश्च मयूरांश्च कङ्कतित्तिरिमूषकान् (कुक्कुटान् ?)
—उत्तरखण्ड, 51.25.

कौटिल्य distinguishes the cautious and slow-stepping Grey Heron as वारिकङ्क from the long-paced Adjutant, दीर्घपादकङ्क, in describing the different styles of the movements of a horse trained for purposes of war. Slow and cautious steps are वारिकाङ्कगति and high-stepping long-paced motion the काङ्कगति (अर्थशास्त्र, अधिकरण 2, ch. 30). The renderings of the different gaits or foot-movements of a horse have gone wrong at least in some cases in the translation by R. Samasastry. जलसूचि is not a crow as in M. Williams but the कङ्क (Grey Heron) with its thin and sharp-pointed bill with which it spears fish in water. हेमचन्द्र and विश्वप्रकाश both equate it with कङ्क and not काक.

6. The Eastern Purple Heron (38") is a bird of about the same size as the Grey Heron whose prevailing colour is grey on the wings and back, black on the belly and chestnut in the remaining parts. It is a great skulker and spends most of its time amongst reeds in marshes, tanks, etc. It is intensely curious and its long neck may often be seen stretched up above the reeds

to watch passers-by. In other respects it does not differ from the Grey Heron. The definition of नील क्रौञ्च given in कल्पद्रुकोश would seem to refer to this bird :

नीलक्रौञ्च ऽतिजागरः दीर्घग्रीवश्च नीलाङ्गः,

where अतिजागर refers to the wariness of the bird and नीलाङ्ग to the dark grey colour of the wings and back. The epithet बिसनासिक for a Heron is most appropriate for it as it is descriptive of its long neck, small head and pointed yellow bill held perpendicularly amongst reeds like a new lotus shoot. It is also the कङ्केर as defined in 'कङ्केरः निश्चलाङ्गः स्यात्' —कल्पद्रु., where the adjective निश्चलाङ्ग describes its attitude when "frozen". The Grey Heron being कङ्क, its cousin, the Purple Heron, is appropriately named कङ्केर[1] and the त्रिकाण्डशेष would seem to be in error when it equates कङ्केर with द्वारबलिभुक्, the Adjutant (cf. बकेरु below). The mistake is due to the fact that the Adjutant is also a कङ्क. In the same way, कङ्केर is wrongly equated with a Crow because the Crow is गृहबलिभुक् and the latter has been mistaken by some for a बक (see शब्दकल्प. and M.W.). Here the error arises from a confusion between द्वारबलिभुक् and गृहबलिभुक् (the House Crow and the House Sparrow). The Little Egret (Ardea nivea in M.W.) or any other Egret or Heron in nature is never a गृह- or द्वारबलिभुक्.

7. No individual Sanskrit name is available for the rare but the largest of Indian Herons, the Great White-bellied Heron (55") of the Bhutan Terai, but who can say if it was not known as महाकङ्क on the analogy of names like महाक्रौञ्च, महाहंस, महासुपर्ण, etc.? The fact that one of the smallest Herons, the Pond Heron, goes by the name of स्वल्पकङ्क lends considerable support to the above suggestion.

8. Three kinds of the True or White Egrets are common in India. They are pure white at all times and of a slenderer build than the Herons. The Large Egret occurs in two sizes: the Western form is a little larger than the Eastern but both are similar in all other respects. They are all बलाका in Sanskrit but each kind has also been separately named, principally according to size and certain other characters.

(a) The Lage Egret (35"-36") is the ज्येष्ठ बलाका[2] of चक्रदत्त on चरक; बकेरु of the lexicons and महाश्वेता of the Mahābhārata. We have seen that the related terms कङ्क and कङ्केर refer to the allied birds, the Grey and the Purple Heron respectively. Similarly, when बक is the all-white White Ibis, बकेरु (resembling the बक) should be the Large Egret, all white and of a comparable size with it. महाश्वेता in the following verse has perhaps been doubtfully rendered as a बलाका or Egret, for it appears to be merely a

1. The equation लोहपृष्ठस्तु कङ्कः स्यात्—अमर, may well be homonymous and includes this Heron which has a chestunt back like the Brahminy Kite. This is supported by its Hindi name, लाल अंजन, the Grey Heron being simply अंजन.

2. Incorrectly equated with श्वेतवारल, a wrong reading for श्वेतचरण, one of the water-birds in चरक. M, W. gives only the latter (Art. 65).

descriptive epithet of a full-grown white heifer, nevertheless it is clear that the term, independently of the context, has that meaning, and as the simile relates to a full-sized cow the particular Egret meant by the commentator, Nīlakaṇṭha, must be the Large Egret :—

महाश्वेतेव माहेयी वने जाता त्रिहायणी ।
उपातिष्ठत पाञ्चाली वासितेव वरर्षभम् ॥— M.Bh. 4.17.11.

This Egret grows three sets of long plumes from the region of the shoulder and they extend some inches beyond the tail during the breeding season. This particular feature accounts for the Pali name चेलावक (चेलबक)[1] for it in the कुणालजातक, 536; cf. Pali चेलकेदु for the Paradise Flycatcher which too carries two white ribbons in its tail (Art. 11). The बलाका of VS 24.22-33 should be the Large Egret.

(b) & (c) The Smaller ($28''$) and the Little ($20''$) Egrets are बलाका and बलाकिका respectively. बकेरुका, again a diminutive of बकेरू for the Large Egret, is a synonym for बलाकिका ("बकेरुका बलाकिका" and "बकेरुका बलाकाभिद्" —हेमचन्द्र and विश्वप्रकाश).

The equation, "बलाका बिसकण्ठिका"[2]—अमर and अभिधान चिन्तामणि applies to both these Egrets of small size after their thin white necks, and the following examples refer to one or the other:

स्थलकमलमुग्धवपुषा सातङ्काङ्कस्थितैकचरणेन ।
आश्वासयति बिसिन्या: कूले बिसकण्ठिका शफरम् ॥
—आर्यासप्तशती, 607.

पश्य निश्चलनि:स्पन्दा बिसिनीपत्रे राजते बलाका ।
— Sansk. of गाथासप्तशती, 1.4.

The story of a बलाका perched upon a tree and 'dropping' into the face of a Brahman who was sleeping under it, and who reduced the bird to ashes with the fire emanating from his angry eyes, told in the Mahābhārata, relates to one of these very common small Egrets:

उपरिष्टाच्च वृक्षस्थबलाका सन्यलीयत ।
तथा पुरीषमुत्सृष्टं ब्राह्मणस्य तदोपरि ॥—3.206.3.

The story is retold in the पद्मपुराण, 5—सृष्टिखंड, 47, with बक (White Ibis) substituted for the बलाका.

The Little Egret wears "a crest composed of two very long attenuated but not decomposed feathers" as part of the breeding plumage and is the बलाका सिखिनी (शिखिनी बलाका) of the लोलजातक, 274, while the homonymous

1. बक that wears, as it were, a चेल or skirt about its waist.

2. बिस and मृणाल are different in सुश्रुत 6.46.17 and mean thin and thick lotus roots or stalks; cf. मृणालकण्ठ for the Flamingo (Art. 83). The names बलाकिका and बिसकण्ठिका have been inadvertently used for the flamingo (बलाक, मृणालकण्ठ) in नेमिनिर्वाणकाव्य, 4.43,46. This illustrates the danger of mixed synonymies in our lexicons.

equation "शिखी चन्द्रविहङ्गमः"—त्रिकाण्डशेष, refers to it as शिखी (crested) and चन्द्र विहङ्गम (shining like the moon and hence, white).

Prakrit सेडी for a kind of bird in अभि. राजेन्द्र is the same as श्वेता for बलाका; cf. सेडिया-श्वेतिका, खटिका (Ibid), i.e. chalk. For बलाका as the female of the Flamingo see Art. 83.

(d) The Cattle Egret (20″) is also a बलाकिका but as it undergoes a change of colour from white into a beautiful golden-buff on the head, neck and back during the breeding season it has been named पिङ्गला or पिङ्गलिका and करायिका in Sanskrit though the last name appears to be a Prakrit form. This Egret is a constant companion of cattle as it feeds on their insect parasites and chiefly on grass-hoppers and other insects disturbed by them while grazing, and this habit accounts for yet another name, गोबक for it corresponding to गाय बगला or ढोरिया बगला (ढोर—cattle) in Hindi.

9. The Pond Heron or Paddy-bird (18″) is the commonest of the family and seen sitting hunched up on the mud, standing knee-deep in the water along the edges of tanks, streams, etc., or on water plants among the lilies and lotuses. "Its dull colours assimilate with the mud and the herbage, and the bird is tame and confiding, with the result that it is seldom noticed until it rises close to the passer-by, springing into life with a sudden flash of the white wings. To this invisibility is due the name of 'blind-heron' that it bears in several dialects (Whistler). It is known in Hindi as अन्धाबगला (Sanskrit अन्धबक or अन्धकाक). The lexicons do not give the Sanskrit terms placed within brackets, but there seems to be little doubt that the bird had them for its names. The commentator of अष्टाङ्गहृदय, however, gives अन्धकाक in the sense of जलकाक, as a synonym for दात्यूह. अन्ध means both 'ditch water'[1] and 'a blind person'. अन्ध is also a particular type of परिव्राजक or wandering mendicant:—

तिष्ठतो व्रजतो वाऽपि यस्य चक्षुर्न दूरगम् ।
चतुष्पदां भुवं मुक्त्वा परिव्राडन्ध उच्यते ॥
—Apte's Practical Sansk. Eng. Dict., 1890

The point about this definition is that the mendicant is not supposed to look beyond a space of four paces or feet about him. Next, there is the special meaning of अन्ध in the निरुक्त :—

अन्धो भग इत्याहुरनुत्सृप्तो न दृश्यते—12.14.1.

Here the sun, not visible until it rises above the horizon, is called अन्ध भग and the special meaning of अन्ध is explained as under:—

नास्मिन् द्रष्टृणां ध्यानं दर्शनमस्तीति अन्धः

which means that an object which escapes observation is known as अन्ध (blind). The idea of absence of movement or movement upwards (उत्सृप्त-उत्सरण) is also involved. The invisibility of the Pond Heron as it sits

1. अन्धं तु कलुषं तोयं—हेमचन्द्र (शेषनाममाला) and hence 'puddle on pond' : the name अन्धकाक thus corresponds to 'Pond-Heron'.

hunched up, camouflaged in its surroundings and intently watching a few feet of mud or water about it for prey, and the sudden white flash with which it rises are thus fully comprehended in the name अन्धबक and also probably in अन्धकाक. अन्धाबगला, the popular Hindi name for it, is just a rendering of these names and in the sense discussed above. Names like तापस and मृषाध्यायी for Herons and Storks (बक) humorously refer to their habit of standing on one leg and apparently innocuous contemplation until an unwary frog or fish appears on the scene. The term स्वल्प कङ्क for a very small Heron should belong to this, the most common member of the group.

The Pond Heron, like the Little Egret, grows a long white occipital crest in the breeding season and for this reason shares the name of कोयष्टि with the Egret, the Night Heron and the Little Green Heron (See Art.71 for the different meanings of कोयष्टि). In the verse below कोयष्टि affecting a Pond (during the day) is this Heron or the Little Egret :—

बककोयष्टिभिर्जुष्टे पल्वले मानसं कुतः ।

—सुभाषित, 221.7.

10. Bitterns and Night Herons, with the exception of the Bittern, are birds of a shorter and stouter build. They also differ from Herons and Egrets in that they are all night-birds and generally solitary at all times (Finn). They are designated as नक्तक्रौञ्च (Night-Herons) by पालकाप्य in हस्त्यायुर्वेद, 2.20, निशैत or निशैड in the mixed synonymy of त्रिकाण्डशेष, and रजनीबक in विष्णुधर्मोत्तर, 1.151. 48 where रजनीयकान् is a wrong reading of रजनीबकान्.

(a) The Night Heron (23″) is truly nocturnal in its habits. Not until after the sun has set for half an hour or so do the birds leave the trees where they remain all day in the deepest shade they can get. During flight they utter every few minutes a loud, though not unmusical, squak. It has several names in Hindi after its voice, वाक, क्वाक and कुकराई (क्वाकराविन् ?) corresponding to Sanskrit वाक ("वाकश्चन्द्रविहङ्गमः"—कल्पद्रु, चन्द्रविहङ्गम is thus the same as नक्तक्रौञ्च). This equation corresponds to "शिखीचन्द्रविहङ्गमः" both for the Little Egret which is crested and white and for वाक, the Night-Heron which is also crested, and the expression चन्द्रविहङ्गम as a homonym means (i) a white bird, as well as (ii) a night-bird or one that feeds during moon-light. Like the Little Egret the Night Heron also wears a crest of long, thin, black and white feathers and shares the name of कोयष्टि or कोयष्टिक with it and also with the crested Little Green Heron, another night-bird. क्षीरस्वामी on अमर explains the name कोयष्टि as "ओको यजति कोयष्टिः" which fits in admirably with the habit of these night-birds resting all day in heavily foliaged trees. This fact has been beautifully brought out in the following verses :—

स मत्तकोयष्टिभकान् पादपान् पुष्पशालिनः ।
उद्वहन्नुरुवेगेन जगाम विमलेऽम्बरे— ॥ —Rāmāyaṇa, 5.1.44.

काश्मर्याः कृतमालमुद्गतदलं कोयष्टिकष्टीकते

—मालतीमाधव, 9.7.

and it is incorrect to render कोयष्टिभक or कोयष्टिक in the above contexts as a Lapwing (टिट्टिभ), for the latter, not having an effective hind toe, never perches on a tree. The terms कुयष्टिका and कोयष्टि for different birds have been considered in Art. 71 and the latter as the Water Cock in Art. 58.

(b) The Little Green Heron is a greenish grey bird (18") with a long black pendant crest glossed with green. It is a forest bird found singly along forest streams. During the heat of the day it sits hunched up on the lower branches of some thick water-side bush, refusing to move until the bush is almost hit, when, with a squak (वाक), it flaps lazily away to another dark and shady bush (S. Baker). वाक being the Night Heron, वाकरुका (making the 'wak' sound, or having a call similar to that of the वाक, the Night Heron) should be this bird. Resembling the Night Heron in habits and possessing an erectile crest it can also claim the name कोयष्टिक with it. The following excellent verse mentions the booming White Ibises (बकाः in the first line), the Cormorants (काकमद्गु, loosely or for brevity called मद्गु) taking a jump into the air before diving, the Storks frequenting a tank during the day and the Night Herons and Bitterns resorting to it at night (both called बकाः in the third line), and finally, the Swan, the 'high-brow' amongst aquatic birds, who very properly quits the Lotus-tank which shelters such a mean assortment:—

यामालिङ्ग्य बका रटन्ति कटुकं दीर्घोच्छ्वसत्कन्धरा
यस्यामंसतटावघट्टितजलं वल्गन्त्यमी मद्गवः ।
या शश्वन्मलिनात्मकैरपि बकैर्नक्तं दिनं सेव्यते
सा हंसेन मनस्विना कमलिनी युक्त यदि त्यज्यते ॥

—सुभाषितावलि, 714.

(c) The Chestnut Bittern (15") of noctural habits belongs of course to the नक्तक्रौञ्च or चन्द्रविहङ्गम group of Herons and one of the Hindi for it is जुनबगला which is from Sanskrit ज्योत्स्नाबक. ज्योत्स्ना 'moon-light' is जुन्हाई in Hindi, and this last has been shortened to जुन्ह—जुन in the compound name जनबगला which thus fully corresponds to चन्द्रविहङ्गम (cf. ज्योत्स्नाप्रिय for the चकोर). This Heron spends the day in dense reeds or feeds in deep shade along streams. It has no crest and is not, therefore, a कोयष्टि.

(d) The Bittern (30") is of a golden brown colour mottled with black. It is a winter visitor only and has been found breeding at Quetta within (pre-partition) Indian limits. Its ordinary note is a hoarse low croak but it booms loudly in the breeding season. It has the habit, when danger threatens of standing with the head and neck extended sky-wards—the whole attitude and colouration being protective amongst the varied lights and shade of a reed-bed (Smythies). This behaviour of the Bittern is quite similar to that of the Purple Heron so that the equation "कङ्केरुः निश्चलाङ्गः स्यात्"—कल्पद्रु. applies to it as much as to the other. The Hindi name for it is नीरगाँग (नीर-water, and गङ्ग्‌य-to shout) corresponding exactly to गोनर्द

(गो—water, and नर्द्—to call aloud) which has been wrongly equated with the Sarus due to confusion between गोनन्द and गोनर्द (cf. पिचुमन्द and पिचुमर्द). गोनन्दी is the female Sarus and गोनन्द should, therefore, be her mate. गोनर्द as a homonym is (i) a game bird, the Great Bustard, which has a bellowing call (from गो—a cow) and (ii) the Bittern (fr. गो—water) (see Arts. 62 and 63). Similarly the equation "बकः कह्वः" of अमर (के जले ह्वयते = गवि जले नर्दति) should apply to (i) the White Ibis and (ii) the Bittern both of which have a booming call and belong to the बक group in the wider sense.

83

FLAMINGOS

1. Flamingos, with very long necks and legs and thick bills, 'broken' or bent in the middle, are quite unlike other birds and appear to stand in a class by themselves, but from anatomical and other features they would seem to occupy a position intermediate between the Storks (बक) on one side and the Geese and Ducks (हंस) on the other. They combine the look of a Stork and the ways and voice of a Goose. They have indeed been placed by scientists sometimes with the Ciconiiformes (Stork-like birds) and at others with Chenomorphae (Swans, Geese, and Ducks), and although Stuart Baker has "for the present" separated them under Order Phoenicopteri (Phoenicopterus, 'red-winged'—a Flamingo—the 'flame-coloured') he is strongly inclined to the opinion that they will have to be finally classed with the Swans and Geese under one common Order. It is interesting to note in this connection that, except for its original Vedic name of क्रुङ or क्रुञ्च, so named after its extraordinarily long and very flexible neck, the later Sanskrit names for the Flamingo, viz., वरहंस, बलाक, and even बक, seem to recognise its affinity to the Swan or Goose on the one hand and to the Storks on the other. Again, names like मृणालकण्ठ or मृणालग्रीव (having a thin, long neck like a lotus stalk) are merely a paraphrase of the original क्रुङ or क्रुञ्च.

2. India claims two out of the five known species of Flamingo, viz., the Common Flamingo (50") and its smaller cousin, the Lesser Flamingo (33"). The former has one of its breeding sites in the Rann of Kutch[1]

---

1. बककच्छ (बकविशिष्ट: बकप्रधानो वा कच्छ: जलप्रान्त:) as an ancient place-name probably belonged to what is today the Rann of Kutch in Western India where Flamingos are known to breed in their thousands. According to the St. Petersberg and M. Williams' Dictionaries the name is mentioned in कथासरित्सागर, 6. 76 & 166 but the निर्णयसागर edition of the work reads भरुकच्छ instead and it is placed on the Narmada. भरुकच्छ is Prakrit for भृगुकच्छ which has been correctly identified with the present Broach or भड़ोच. Evidently बककच्छ is a different place and is probably the Rann of Kutch or the island of Kutch to the south of it. The name is analogous to other place-names like खट्वाङ्गवन, क्रौञ्चवन, गृध्रकूट, etc., named after the particular birds that abounded at each of these places. My friend, Dr. Raghu Vira, brought to my notice the name of another country viz. बलाया लोय (बलाकालोक) mentioned as a country of the Mlechhas or Non-Aryans in the ancient Jaina

within Indian limits, while the nearest breeding grounds of the latter are on the shores of the Red Sea, but so far as the mainland of India is concerned both the species are winter visitors, arriving about September and leaving for their breeding homes in May-June and some time as late as July. Both move in parties or large flocks though the Lesser Flamingo s an erratic visitor, occurring plentifully in the North-West up to the Sambhur Lake in Rajasthan in certain years and scarce or altogether absent in others.[1]

3. The Common Flamingo (50″) is a tall, white bird with rosy upper parts, black flight-quills, a flame-red patch on the wing and scarlet axillaries and underwing coverts. The eyes are yellow, the orbital skin pink to bright red, bill flesh-coloured and legs pinkish-red. With very long legs and neck it stands about four feet high but its body is no bigger than that of a common Goose. The heavy 'goosy' bill with an obtuse bend in the middle, the upper mandible freely moveable as if on a hinge (unlike the Goose whose lower mandible is moveable) and adapted for feeding in an inverted position is characteristic. Its webbed feet, anserine voice and the fact that young chicks are active as soon as hatched link it up more closely with the Swans and Geese than its long legs with the Storks. Nevertheless this apparently dual character of the Flamingo is reflected both in its Sanskrit and vernacular names:

Sanskrit—कुञ्ज, कुञ्च (fr. कुञ्च् 'to curve or become small' after the long, flexible neck which when coiled round the body and with head tucked into the back makes the bird look very much smaller than at other times)

बलाक, बक after its superficial resemblance to a Stork (बक);

बर हंस (वरं, कुङ्कुमे, श्रेष्ठे; cf. वरा turmeric; and hence either 'a superior type of Goose' or 'the Red-Goose' as it is actually called in Persian.

4. The effect that the Flamingo, seen singly or in the mass, whether on its feeding grounds or high up in the air, produces upon a cultured mind cannot be described better than in the words of Stuart Baker—"Although so ungainly in shape when viewd individually, the Flamingo when seen in the vast herds in which they so often collect is one of the most beautiful of Avian sights. In the distance they look like a field of

---

work, जम्बूद्वीप प्रज्ञप्ति, 3.52. We will see in later paragraphs that बक, बलाक, and the feminine बलाका, are names of the Flamingo in Sanskrit, so that if बककच्छ within Aryan limits is the Rann of Kutch, बलाकालोक may well refer to the territory near the Red Sea where the Lesser Flamingos breed. It is, therefore, highly probable that the ancient Indians knew the two nearest breeding grounds of both kinds of Flamingo.

1. The Lesser Flamingo is more richly coloured than the Common Flamingo and there is some crimson on the tail feathers as well. The eyes, bill and legs are different shades of red. In its habits it closely resembles the common Flamingo.

snow with a rosy sunset glow upon it, then as one approaches, the snow suddenly melts into a flaming scarlet as the birds unfold their wings and sail away. When just moving from one feeding ground to another they adopt no particular formation but when in full flight form into either a wide V or a long waving ribbon."[1] Their food consists chiefly of minute vegetable matter and to some extent of tiny animal organisms, crustacea, mullusca, etc. found in the mud of fresh and salt water lakes and lagoons. When feeding, the bird wades in a regular line with others of its kind, and bending down its long neck and head between the legs, uses its inverted bill like a shovel in which to catch and collect its food. This it obtains by moving the head backwards and forwards or from side to side and gently stirring up the mud which is sifted through the seive-like bill. Then it erects its long neck to swallow the selected food.

5. To the bird's peculiar method of feeding the Prakrit and Hindi languages owe the picturesque terms ढेंका and ढेंकी for the country-gardener's shadoof or simple water-lever commonly seen working at a water-hole or crude well. It consists of two posts supporting a cross beam at the top with a bucket suspended from the longer end and a counterpoise at the other. Not much of imagination is required to see that the contrivance works exactly like a Flamingo as it feeds. Prakrit ढेंकी means बलाका, a female Flamingo (fem. of बलाक) and ढेंका a 'water-lift' defined as कूपतुला in देशीनाममाला of हेमचन्द्र. Now this कूपतुला ('a pair of scales at a well') is none other than the water-lever described above.[2] Prakrit ढेंक; ढंक, are the same as Sanskrit ध्वाङ्क्ष equated with बक, viz., the White Ibis and a Stork (Arts. 80, 81). बलाक, as we shall see, is the Flamingo defined loosely as 'a sort of बक or Stork'. The feminine of बक is बकी and of बलाक, बलाका.[3] Closely associated with the picture described here and lending considerable support to it is the Hindi name लमढेंक (लमढींग in the Pujnab, fr. Sansk. लम्ब pendent, but 'long लम्बा' in Hindi with ढेंक—ध्वाङ्क्ष, 'the tall or long Stork-like bird') for the Flamingo.

---

1. Writing earlier S. Baker made the following remarks about these remarkable birds: "Flying or wading they are a lovely sight, and, often as they have been described, no one has yet been able to do justice to their beauty." Again, "Typically their flight is distinctly anserine, not perhaps exactly V-shape, but more in the form of a curved ribbon, the ends fluttering backwards and forwards as the birds, more especially those at the two extremes, alter their position." On shorter flights the birds rise in one indiscriminate mass and continue as they have risen. (*Indian Ducks and Their Allies*, 1908).

"To witness the simultaneous unfolding of a thousand lovely crimson and black pinions under brilliant sunlight is a sight the recollection of which will not readily be effaced from our memories" (Eagle Clarke, quoted, ibid. page 5).

These extracts fully bear out the appreciative references to Flamingos (flying *en masse* or in formation) in Sanskrit literature of a thousand to two thousand years ago.

2. Compare 'crane' as a machine, so named after the bird with the long neck.

3. The term बलाका for the Egrets is a जातिवाचक संज्ञा and is always in the feminine gender, but बलाका for the female flamingo is the feminine of बलाक for the male.

6. In the following lexical synonymies, which are mostly of a mixed character, the terms क्रुञ्च, बलाक, बक and मृणालकण्ठ refer to the male Flamingo, and बलाका, मेघानन्दा and दीर्घकन्धरा to the female. बलाका in a special sense means also 'a flight of Flamingos in formation', described also as बलाकमाला or बकपंक्ति :

(i) क्रुङ क्रौञ्चः—अमर, अभिधानचिन्तामणि

(ii) अथाऽपस्वरः क्रौञ्चः क्रुङ स्यात् पंक्तिचरः पुनः ।
शरत्पक्षी वक्रचञ्चू रक्तको रात्रिजागरः ॥
शेवलादः पुण्डरीकनयनः—कल्पद्रुकोश,
—p. 329, verses 107-108

(iii) मृणालकण्ड (?कण्ठ) काकस्तु बलाकः स्यात्—Ibid.

(iv) बलाका विषकण्ठी स्याच्छुष्काङ्गी दीर्घकन्धरा ।
घर्मान्तिकामुकी श्वेता मेघानन्दा जलाश्रया ॥—राजनिघण्टु

(v) बलाका बकपङ्क्तिः स्यात् बलाका बिसकण्ठिका ।
बलाका कामुकी प्रोक्ता बलाकश्च बको मतः ॥[1] —विश्वशाश्वतौ

Reserving the terms क्रुङ and क्रुञ्च for discussion a little later let us take up the other names and adnouns for the Flamingo. Except for अपस्वर क्रौञ्च the remaining terms in (ii) above refer to our bird as a bird of the autumn (शरत्पक्षी), flying in formation (पंक्तिचर), having red in the plumage and a bent bill (रक्तक, वक्रचञ्चू), living on minute water-plants (शेवलाद) and wary or wakeful at night (रात्रिजागर). This last trait of the bird has been brought out by Salim Ali in his Article on the Flamingo in *J.B.N.H.S.*, XLV, page 589, and S. Baker also describes it as "extremely wary and cute". बिस and मृणाल are different parts of the lotus plant both in चरक and सुश्रुत (चरक, 6.21.78 & 82; सुश्रुत, 1.21.23 and 6.46.17), the former is the white root, the same as Hindi भिस्स or भिस and the latter the पद्मनाल or the long stalk of the lotus flower. The मृणालकण्ठ काक (काक i.e. जलकाक, water-bird) in (iii) equated with बलाक is the long-necked Flamingo, while 'बलाका' of the equation "बलाका बिसकण्ठिका" of कल्पद्रु., अमर and other lexicons is the pure white Egret which too has a comparatively long and white neck.[2] अष्टाङ्गसंग्रह like चरक

1. Quoted in the commentary on उणादि सूत्र "बलाकादयश्च", 462, at page 524 of सिद्धान्तकौमुदी with तत्त्वबोधिनी व्याख्या, Nirnayasagar edition, 1908, and attributed to विश्वशाश्वतौ though the editions of these two lexicons issued by the Chowkhamba Office, Banaras and the Oriental Book Agency, Poona, respectively do not have this verse. The औणादिक पदार्णव of पेरुसूरि, Madras, 1939, however, gives the following : बलाकाबकपंक्तौ च बिसकण्ठ्यां च वर्तते । कामुक्यामप्यथ पुमान् बलाको बकपक्षिणि ॥ 4.69-70.

2. If बिस and मृणाल are identical it is possible to take बिसकण्ठ and मृणालकण्ठ for the taller bird, the Flamingo with an extremely long neck and बिसकण्ठी and बिसकण्ठिका for the smaller bird, the Egret, according to the rule "स्त्री स्यात्काचिन्मृणाल्यादिर्विवक्षापचये यदि"—अमर., 3.5.7.

It is also highly probable that with बलाक for the Flamingo the equally white but smaller Egret with comparatively long necks have been named as बलाका irrespective of sex, under this rule.

has the correct reading of मृणालकण्ठ and मृणालकण्ड in कल्पद्रुकोश is an obvious error. पालकाप्य has मृणालग्रीव instead (p. 198). In synonymy (iv) बलाका is probably a homonym and stands for both the Egret and the female of the Flamingo as they share the majority of the epithets in common. Both are शुष्काङ्गी (i.e. waders and not swimmers, though they can swim), घर्मान्तकामुकी (having their breeding season in North India at the end of summer or beginning of the rains), and जलाश्रया (associated with water, the Flamingos more than the Egrets). Adnoun विष– or बिसकण्ठी is specific for the Egret while दीर्घकन्धरा being the feminine of दीर्घकन्धर equated with बक in शब्दकल्पद्रुम is clearly more appropriate for the female of the long-necked Flamingo. श्वेता (the white), again, is common to both. That leaves मेघानन्दा[1] which, if treated as a homonym, would apply (i) in the sense of घर्मान्तकामुकी to both, and (ii) with मेघेन सह सुरतानन्दो शिशुप्रसवानन्दो वा यस्याः, to the female Flamingo in particular (See para. 13 where this topic is discussed in greater detail). The last synonymy also is mainly homonymous, for बलाका means (i) a flight of Flamingos in formation, (ii) an Egret, and (iii) कामुकी i.e. a passionate woman metaphorically called बलाका on the analogy of the female Flamingo supposed to fly up eagerly to meet the rain-cloud for fertility, and finally बलाक, the Flamingo, is defined as a sort of बक or Stork. M. Williams' rendering of कामुकी as a kind of Crane is incorrect.

7. The Kalmuks and the Russians call the Flamingo as 'the Red Goose' (per Jerdon in *Birds of India*) from the red colour in the wings, also the Persians (Qaz-i-surkh). Hindi हंसावर for it corresponds to Sansk. वरहंस which may well mean 'the superior' or 'the red Goose' (वरः श्रेष्ठे, वरं कुङ्कुमे—हेमचन्द्र; cf. वरा, वराङ्गी turmeric, and वरकाष्ठका the plant Clerodendron siphonanthus, the blue drupe of which rests upon an enlarged and spreading red calyx—Brandis, p. 508). वरहंस in the following verse should therefore be the Flamingo or the Red Goose:

गायत्री नाम या सन्ध्या रक्ताङ्गी रक्तवाससा।
वरहंससमारूढा श्रीमत्पुष्करसंस्थिता ॥—गरुडपुराण, 1.217.5.

This verse refers to the personification of the early morning prayer (गायत्री) when the sun rises with a red glow while in the next two verses the mid-day prayer is conceived of as clad in white and described as "श्वेतपद्मासना" and "श्वेतपुष्पोपशोभिता" because then the sun is at its brightest. The evening गायत्री is "पीतवस्त्रा" and "अतसीकुसुमप्रख्या" representing the orange-yellow of the setting sun and the advancing darkness, the अतसीपुष्प, linseed-flower, being of a sky-blue colour. Taking all the three representations of गायत्री and her colour associations it is highly probable that वरहंस in the above quotation is the white Flamingo with a rosy tinge on the upper parts and red on the wings. The Hindi हंसावर lends special support to this view. It is also

1. Cf. मेघाभिकामा said of a flight of Flamingos in the verse from the Rāmāyaṇa quoted in para. 13 below; also गोनन्दी for the female Sarus who consummates her love on the ground, Art. 62 para. 10.

particularly significant that भट्टोत्पल in his commentary on the verse from the बृहत्संहिता quoted at the end of this article renders बलाक as a kind of हंस "हंसविशेष:".

8. The red colour in the plumage of the Flamingo has been recognized in the name अरुणक्रौञ्च by which it has been mentioned in the Mahābhārata. A particular array of an army has been named (metri causa) "व्यूहः क्रौञ्चारुणः"[1] which in plain prose should be read as अरुणक्रौञ्चव्यूह. This arrangement is evidently different from the क्रौञ्चव्यूह and was set up like a श्येनव्यूह (see f. n. to para. 1, Art. 62) but with a difference, viz., that the front or head part of the array was like a दण्डव्यूह representing the outstretched long neck of the Flamingo on the wing and a similar arrangement at the back of the main body corresponding to the long out-stretched legs behind, the body and the flanks of the formation being after the body and broad wings of the bird. This अरुणक्रौञ्चव्यूह is fully described in the Epic beginning with the verse:

व्यूहः क्रौञ्चारुणो नाम सर्वशत्रुनिबर्हणः ।
यं बृहस्पतिरिन्द्राय तदा देवासुरेऽब्रवीत् ॥ —6.50.40ff.

On shorter flights, i. e. when moving from one feeding ground to another the Flamingos rise indiscriminately in a huge mass and fly very much lower than during migration. In such a position the red in the plumage is distinctly visible from below and this particular type of flight *en masse* has been utilised with considerable effect for a beautiful simile which, based as it is on actual observation, combines wonderful poetic imagery with typical Indian exaggeration. A great mass of arrows feathered with the chestnut-red wing and tail-feathers of the Brahminy Kites (कङ्क) discharged by warriors at the enemy has been compared with a ceiling (पृष्ठ) of Flamingos (अरुणक्रौञ्च) rendering the sun and the sky invisible to people in the field:

अन्वधावत्किरन्बाणैः कङ्कपत्रैरजिह्मगैः ।
राजानमभिधावन्त शरैरानृत्य रोषरी ॥
क्रुद्धः प्रच्छादयामास शरजालेन मारुतिः ।
* * *
क्रौञ्चपृष्ठारुणं रौद्रं बाणजालं व्यदृश्यत ।
नैव सूर्यप्रभा राजन् न दिशः प्रदिशस्तथा ॥ —MBh. 8.51.60-66

9. We have just seen in the preceding paragraph that the अरुण क्रौञ्चव्यूह was the invention of sage बृहस्पति. Another invention of his, based upon a natural formation of Flamingos in the sky against a back-ground of dark rain clouds, has been called the great बार्हस्पत्य व्यूह:

1. क्रौञ्चारुण by itself therefore does not mean a व्यूह as assumed by M. W.

बार्हस्पत्यः सुविहितो नायकेन विपश्चिता ।
नृत्यतीव महाव्यूहः परेषां भयमादधत् ॥
तस्य पक्षप्रपक्षेभ्यो निष्पतन्ति युयुत्सवः ।
हस्त्यश्वरथमातङ्गाः प्रावृषीव बलाहकाः ॥ MBh. 8.46.27-28

In this connection I would invite the reader's attention to Stuart Baker's description of the flight quoted in the foot-note to para 4 above. It is "in the form of a curved ribbon, the ends fluttering backwards and forwards as the birds, more specially those at the two extremes, alter their position." A comparison of this with the passage from the Mahābhārata clearly shows that (i) नृत्यतीव refers to the fluttering movement; (ii) निष्पतन्ति युयुत्सवः to the change of places by the birds at the ends of the formation (पक्षप्रपक्ष); and (iii) the heavier elements of the army consisting of हस्त्यश्वरथमातङ्गाः at the rear and flanks look like the dark rain-clouds (प्रावृषीव बलाहकाः)".[1] We thus have two kinds of अरुणक्रौञ्चव्यूह just as we have two types of क्रौञ्चव्यूह formed after the flying formation and the body of the क्रौञ्च, the Common Crane (Art. 62 para. 2, f. n.). Both forms of अरुणक्रौञ्चव्यूह are bigger than the क्रौञ्चव्यूह as the Flamingo (50″) is larger than the Common Crane (45″) and also occurs in larger masses.

10. We have seen in paragraph 6 that in later Sanskrit the Flamingo was known as बलाक and regarded as a kind of बक ("बलाकश्च बको मतः") and the following half verse from the पद्मपुराण recognizes its power of sifting out पय (i. e. क्षीर which by लक्षणा means 'food' in the context) or minute semi-liquid food from water exactly as the हंस is supposed to do:

क्षीरार्णवः पयो दत्ते हंसाय न बकाय किम् ?[2]
—उत्तरखण्ड, Ch. 247. 160

The same Purāṇa refers again to the Flamingo as living upon small water-organisms and rejecting other living things like frogs, fish, etc.:

बको जलचरान् भुङ्क्ते मण्डूकादींश्च वर्जयन् । —Ibid. 129.151

This naturally leads to a consideration of the bird क्रुङ or क्रुञ्च of the वाजसनेयी संहिता where it is said to separate milk from water, and as explained in Art. 62, it is a bird with a long and flexible neck and the Flamingo as we have seen has the best claim to these names. If the faculty of separating the whole of its minute food from water is literally true of any bird it is true of the Flamingo alone. The Swans, Geese and Ducks also do so

1. A similar picture is depicted in Mbh. 7.20.35, quoted in para. 14 below where white flags fluttering in the air and the chariots, elephants, horses, etc. carrying them have been compared with Flamingos and clouds. This close parallelism between the two passages helps to identitify the बार्हस्पत्य व्यूह also as modelled on a formation of Flamingos.

2. 'Does not a Lake give milk to the Flamingo as it does to a Swan? (i.e. it certainly does give milk to the Flamingo as well,

to some extent but the greater portion of their food consists of coarse stuff like green grass, water-weeds, crops, the larger mollusca, fish, etc. The क्रुञ्च and हंस (i.e. the sun pictured as the heavenly Swan) have been regarded as different birds in the following passages with reference to their power of separating क्षीर (liquid food) and सोम (pure water) respectively from the impure natural waters:

अद्भ्यः क्षीरं व्यपिबत् क्रुङाङ्गिरसो धिया[1]— VS 19.73.

सोममद्भ्यो व्यपिबच्छन्दसा हंसः शुचिषत्— VS 19.74.

In the first verse क्रुञ्च is described as आङ्गिरस which may possibly mean two things: (i) अङ्गिरस् being an epithet of अग्नि the reference may be to the red or flame colour in the plumage of the bird क्रुञ्च, the Flamingo; and (ii) resembling अङ्गिरस् and possessed of magical power (cf. धी 'art, science, intelligence', in the text) enabling the क्रुञ्च to separate क्षीर from अप्. Perhaps both the ideas are involved. Similarly the term छन्दसा (छन्द desire, will) in the second verse should refer to the wonderful power of the sun (the pure white Swan of the clear blue sky) who by his own free will or innate power sucks up सोम (pure water) out of impure waters of the earth. A special capacity to extract some essential element out of the impure waters of the earth is thus common to both, viz., the earthly क्रुञ्च and the heavenly हंस, one taking out क्षीर and the other सोम. Now if we examine some of the numerous Vedic equations or statements reflecting the diverse mental processes of the highly imaginative Indo-Aryans we will find that the term क्षीर stands for what to the क्रुञ्च is the essential part of the impure waters, viz., its food. The following equations are particularly interesting from the above viewpoint:

(1) सोमः पयः— शतपथ ब्राह्मण, 12.7.3.13.
(2) रसो वै पयः— Ibid. 4.4.4.8.
(3) अन्तर्हितमिव वा एतद् यत्पयः— ताण्ड्य ब्राह्मण, 9.9.3.
(4) आपो वै क्षीररसा आसन्— Ibid. 13.4.8.
(5) आपो वै सूदो अन्नं दोहः— शत. ब्रा. 8.7.3.21
(6) सोमो वै वाजपेयः—तैत्तिरीय संहिता, 1.3.2.3.
(7) अन्नं वै सोमः—शत. ब्रा. 3.9.1.8.
(8) सर्वमेतदन्नं यद्दधिमधुघृतम्— Ibid. 9.2.1.11.

The first three of the above statements place milk and Soma juice on a par as the two are drawn from the cow or the plant; regard them as the

1. Cf. "विद्वा पजहाति पापकं कोंचो खीरपको व निम्नगम् ।"—उदान viii, 7. The कोंच of this Pali passage is evidently the क्रुञ्च—'The wise man leaves the evil as the milk-drinking Flamingo the water'. C.R. Lanman's rendering of कोच as 'Curlew' is incorrect. See his article, "The milk-drinking Haṁsas of Sanskrit Poetry" in *J.A.O.S.* Vol 19., page 151,

'essence' and as hidden (अन्तर्हितम्) i.e. within the body of the cow or the plant. The क्षीर and सोम for the कुञ्चः and हंस (the sun) are equally essences hidden in the muddy waters and are drawn, as it were, by both for their respective purposes. Nos. (4) & (5) connect the waters with milk (क्षीर) and food (अन्न) while Nos. (6) & (7) regard Soma and milk with which it is always mixed as a drink or food for strength. क्षीर, again, in the sense of 'milk', occurs in the Ṛgveda and Atharvaveda as an item of food both for gods and men.[1] It is also used metaphorically for all kinds of wealth which in Vedic times consisted principally of cattle and food stuffs (RV, 1. 104. 3). It is therefore submitted that क्षीर in VS 19. 73 quoted above stands metaphorically for the almost liquid food (वाजपेय) extracted by the Flamingo from the water with its bill which works like a seive and separates the unwanted water and retains what is क्षीर or food for itself. The same is true of the sun, pictured as a Swan, for it takes up with its rays a different essence, viz., the Soma or clean water out of the impure waters. This pure water, though named as सोम, is also क्षीर but in a different sense, for it is sent back in the form of rain-water, which, dropping from above in thin streams like milk from the cow's udder, is truly a kind of क्षीर (क्षीरम् क्षरतेः—यास्क, 2. 5. 4).

11. The above passages from VS 19. 73-74 and their parallels in KS 38.1; MS 3.11.6; and TB 2. 6. 2 contain to my knowledge the oldest version of the क्षीरनीरविवेक attributed to the हंस or Swan in later literature and which has served as a beautiful argument in the Vedānta and Nyāya Philosophies or as a motif in story. Bloomfield in his Foreword to Vol. VII of Penzer's edition of *The Ocean of Story*, 1926, pp. xviii-xix, has opined that attempts to explain the drinking apart of milk from water "as a feature of the natural history of the haṁsa are, in my opinion, fatuous" and he cites the example of क्रुञ्च mentioned in the texts cited above. He however makes the mistake, in common with the authors of the '*Vedic Index of Names and Subjects*', of rendering क्रुञ्च as the Curlew. The Curlew feeds on "insects, reptiles, coleoptera, slugs, worms, and at times, berries, seeds and seaweed" (S. Baker) and the Snipe, suggested as an alternative in the Vedic Index, also feeds on worms, grubs, tiny snails, etc. for much of which it bores into soft ground with its sensitive bill. It is thus impossible to consider these birds as separating their food from the water. The Flamingo alone as we have seen does it to perfection and is the कुञ्च of the above texts which also clearly indicate the next step

---

1. क्षीर is described as food (अन्न) in the following passage : "तस्मै हान्वागताय सर्पिःक्षीरम् आमिक्षां दधीत्येतद् उपनिदधुः, तस्य ह सुहित आस, तं होचुः सुपर्णेष एव ते बलिर्भविष्यत्येतद् अन्नम्"—"Contributions from the Jaiminīya Brāhmaṇa to the History of Brāhmaṇa literature" by Prof. H. Gertel, *JAOS*, vol 19, pp. 97 ff. For an explanation of the story see Art. 52. अन्न and क्षीर are closely associated in AV 10.10.8 where वशा, गो stands for earth and cow both.

which led the people to substitute the more beautiful Swan for the Flamingo in later literature. Colebrook certainly understood the phrase, अद्भ्यः क्षीरं व्यपिबत्, in the correct sense when he said—"Because the bird seems, as the Hindus apprehend, to extract his food by suction from solution in water" (quoted by Bloomfield in a foot-note to his Foreword, referred to above, at p. xviii).[1] I would only modify his statement to this extent, viz., that the bird is not the हंस but the क्रुङ, that it did not merely seem to extract food 'by suction from solution in water' but actually did so in the manner explained in para. 4 above, and that the ancient Indians had a correct knowledge of it based upon observation. The following verse not only clinches the issue but also shows a clear consciousness on the part of the author that क्षीर in the context means simply food and nothing else and that it is definitely incorrect to assume that क्षीर-अप् or क्षीर-नीर is intended to mean literally a mixture of milk and water. No doubt the idea is very beautiful and tempting and has been used with great effect in didactic and other poetry but the true basis of it must be understood:

मत्स्यादयोऽपि जानन्ति नीरक्षीरविवेचनम् ।
परं प्रसिद्धिर्हंसस्य यशः पुण्यैरवाप्यते ॥—सुभाषित, p. 155, verse 116.

This statement is perfectly correct of the Carp family of fishes which feed exclusively on micro-organisms like the zoo-planktons and phyto-planktons, and in this respect they resemble the Flamingos. The Vedic Indians killed and ate the Flamingo and had ample opportunities to examine the contents of its stomach as well. This is clear from the following aphorism which permits the eating of Flamingo, the Common Crane and the Hornbill:

क्रुञ्चक्रोञ्चवार्ध्रणसलक्ष्मणवर्जम्

—आपस्तम्बधर्मसूत्र, 1.5.17.36.

For a discussion of this aphorism see Art. 62, para. 10.

12. क्रुञ्च in the following passages is the Flamingo:

(i) इन्द्राग्निभ्यां क्रुञ्चान्— VS 24.22; MS 3.14.3.
(ii) क्रुञ्चौ श्रोणिभ्याम्[2]— VS 25.6.

The reason for selecting the Flamingo for the dual deity in (i) would seem to be the white and red colour of the bird, the flame colour being particularly representative of the god of fire, अग्नि; and the bird's association, during its homeward flight, with the rain clouds high up in the sky goes well with the rain-god Indra. In the second passage a pair of Flamingos are the deities to whom cuts from the श्रोणी or the waist-region of the sacrificial horse are offered. The propriety of this assignment does not seem to have

1. Dr. Elliott Cones of Washington quoted by Prof. Lanman in the aritcle refered to on the f.n. to para 6. is also of the same opinion as Bloomfield.

2. "श्रोणिभ्यां दक्षवामाभ्यां कटिप्रदेशाभ्यां क्रुञ्चौ देवौ प्रीणामि ।"—महीधर भाष्य,

been understood so far (see the *Vedic Index* sub voce कुञ्च), but, as it seems to me, श्रोणी refers to the 'fold of the flank' situated in the region of the waist of the horse. The cutaneous muscle, 'Musculus cutaneus trunci', of the horse covered by skin constitutes 'the fold of the flank' which ends on the fascia above the stifle. It has been illustrated in Fig. 276 at page 289 of *The Anatomy of the Domestic Animals* by Septimus Sisson (W. B. Saunders Company). This 'fold of the flank' keeps constantly expanding and contracting as the horse runs, gallops, or even walks in the ordinary way and this action of the muscle is typical of the long and flexible neck of the Flamingo in its various activities. This would, therefore, seem to offer a very probable explanation of the passage.

13. कुञ्च in the following appears to be a mistake for क्रौञ्च which is the reading in the parallel passages in TS 5.5.12; MS 3.14. 12; and KS 5.7.2 :—

वाचे कुञ्चः—VS 24.31.

क्रौञ्च is the loudly trumpeting Common Crane (Art. 62) and suits the context best, for the anserine voice of the Flamingo would be a poor substitute;[1] cf. also वाग्वै क्रौञ्चम्— 11.10.1. That कुञ्च and क्रौञ्च are two different birds has already been made clear by the passage quoted from the आप. धर्मसूत्र in para. 11 above.

14. The descriptive epithet, मेघानन्दा, for the female Flamingo has already been mentioned at the end of para. 6. Its importance lies in the especial relationship established by tradition and poetic convention between the Rain god पर्जन्य and clouds on the one hand and the Flamingos or a flight of them on the other. Knowledge of the fact that these birds leave the country, flying in large formations, just as the rains are approaching undoubtedly helped in establishing the connection. Thus in the षड्विंशब्राह्मण 1-2 "पुरोबलाक" (moving with a vanguard of Flamingos) is an epithet of god पर्जन्य. It is however not clear why in spite of numerous references to the constant association of बलाक and मेघ (Flamingo and cloud) in literature beginning with the Rāmāyaṇa and Mahābhārata सायणाचार्य interprets पुरोबलाक as "सर्वेषां पुरोगामी मेघो भूत्वा..." and a few illustrative examples are therefore given below to elucidate the point:

पुरोबलाकैरसितैर्मेघैर्ज्योत्स्नामिवावृताम् ।
—रामायण, 5.20.27.

मेघपृष्ठे बलाकानां रराज विमला ततिः ।[2]
—विष्णुपुराण, 5.6.41.

आवृतं गगनं मेघैर्बलाकापंक्तिहासिभिः ।—म. भा. 1.138.23.

---

1. It is not however impossible that the author of the संहिता deliberately chose the low voiced कुञ्च for the goddess of speech.

2. This indicates the great height at which Flamingos travel when migrating from one country to another. The bright red underwing coverts became invisible, and the black wing-quills merging with the clouds the birds simply look white at a great height.

तत्प्रकीर्णपताकानां रथवारणवाजिनाम् ।
बलाकाशबलाभ्राभं ददृशे रूपमाहवे ।। —Ib. 7.20.35
बलाकिनी नीलपयोदराजी दूरं पुरःक्षिप्तशतह्रदेव ।
—कुमारसंभव, 7.39.
ताडका चलकपालकुण्डला कालिकेव निबिडा बलाकिनी ।
—रघुवंश, 11.15.
एतैरेव यदा गजेन्द्रमलिनैराध्मातलम्बोदरै—
र्गर्जद्भिः सतडिद्बलाकशबलैर्मेघैः सशल्यं मनः ।।
—मृच्छकटिक, 5, verse 18.
घनप्रदेशेषु बलाकपंक्तयः—हरिवंश, 2.95.4.

Clouds are said to be responsible for making the females of the Flamingo fertile:

बलाकागर्भदाश्चैव बलाकागर्भधारिणः (मेघाः) ।
—वायुपुराण, 51.53; ब्रह्माण्ड पु., 1.22.36.
हृष्टा बलाका घनमभ्युपैति कान्ता सकामा प्रियमभ्युपैति
—रामायण, 4.20.25.

The exiled यक्ष reminds the Cloud of flights of Flamingos :

गर्भाधानक्षणपरिचयान्नूनमाबद्धमालाः ।
सेविष्यन्ते नयनसुभगं खे भवन्तं बलाकाः ।। —मेघदूत, 10.

The expression "गर्भाधानक्षणपरिचय"[1] used by the poet definitely points to his knowledge of the birds' annual migration to repeat their 'happy experience of love and parental instinct.' The courtship of Flamingos was naturally a most rare thing in North India, for they go to breed elsewhere, and popular or poetic fiction attributed a sort of parthenogenesis to them under the influence of rain-clouds. This is reflected in the passages given above and also in a quotation from कर्णोदय given by मल्लिनाथ in his commentary on the मेघदूत :

गर्भं बलाका दधतेऽभ्रयोगान्नाके निबद्धावलयः ।

According to the Buddhist tradition also the female Flamingo becomes gravid on hearing the thunder of rain-clouds :

बलाका च नाम मेघसद्देन गब्भं गण्हंति ।—लोलजातक, 274.

We can now see that just as the female Sarus, who consummates her nuptials on the ground, is called गोनन्दी (Art. 62) the female Flamingo, the बलाका, is मेघानन्दा i.e. happy in the fulfilment of her life's mission only by association with the cloud (cf. मेघाभिकामा in the verse from the Rāmāyaṇa in the next para).

---

1. Literally—'The past experience of the pleasure of fecundation or consummation (in association with the fertilising rain-clouds).

Artistic use of this association between bird and clouds was made in summer-houses of royal palaces where a row of Flamingos sculptured in marble, set against a ceiling painted with dark clouds, showered water from their rose-fitted beaks :

क्वचित्स्फटिकबलाकावलीवान्तवारिधारा लिखितेन्द्रायुधाः
सञ्चार्यमाणा मायामेघमालाः[1]—कादम्बरी, p. 323.

15. The Flamingo is undoubtedly one of the "भद्रपक्षिणः" or auspicious birds of India and has naturally won for itself a place of honour with the Rain-god, पर्जन्य, as we have seen, just like the Golden Eagle (सुपर्ण) of Lord विष्णु, the Peacock of कार्त्तिकेय, and the Swan of ब्रह्मा and सरस्वती. We have also noticed the Flamingo as the वरहंस of the morning गायत्री and as the wise क्रुञ्च of इन्द्राग्नी. It now remains to cite a few examples from literature just to show how well the ancients had observed the bird and its ways in nature. Hume, struck with the beauty of these birds massed near the water or flying above it exclaims: "How shall I describe the countless myriads of Flamingos that are seen either massed upon the water, huge rosy islands, or floating above it like a sun-set cloud, in all the larger lakes of Sind ?"[2] But the great poet वाल्मीकि anticipated this description, though in a different setting, a couple of thousand years ago :

स तया शुशुभे श्रीमान् लतया कण्ठसक्तया ।
मालयेव बलाकानां ससन्ध्य इव तोयदः ॥
—रामायण, 4.12.41.

Here a garland of white गजपुष्पी[3] flowers set against the dark reddish body of सुग्रीव is compared with a flight of Flamingos seen against a dark cloud in the glow of sun-set.

Their aerial westward migration to their breeding grounds during June-July when the rain clouds are advancing from the East is more often described than their return in autumn :

मेघाभिकामा परिसंपतन्ती संमोदिता भाति बलाकपङ्क्तिः ।
वातावधूता वरपौण्डरीकी, लम्बेव माला रुचिराम्बरस्य ॥
—रामायण, 4.28.23.

विद्युत्पताकाः सबलाकमालाः. . .गर्जन्ति मेघाः
—Ibid. 4.28.20.

विद्युन्मण्डलसंनद्धाः सबलाका इवाम्बुदाः— Ibid. 4.42.36.

---

1. The expression सञ्चार्यमाणा मायामेघमाला shows that some sort of moveable screen painted with clouds in different shades was fitted to the ceiling above the sculptured row of Flamingos.

2. *Stray Feathers*, Vol. 1.257.

3. गजपुष्पी according to हिन्दीशब्दसागर is the नागदौन plant, Staphylea Emodi which bears white flowers in panicles. See Brandis, p. 181, and Forest Flora by B. L. Gupta (1928), p. 138,

This striking association between these white birds and the dark rain-clouds became so very fixed that a convention grew up among the poets not to refer to the return flights, quite impressive enough though they must have been, in their descriptions of the शरत् or autumn season. Even Kālidāsa could not resist this tradition and is forced to sing :

धुन्वन्ति पक्षपवनैर्नं नभो बलाकाः ।
पश्यन्ति नोन्नतमुखाः गगनं मयूरा : ॥

—ऋतुसंहार, 3.12.

The हरिवंश has the following :—

विजला विमला व्योम्नि विबलाका विविद्युतः ।—2.16.13-15.

Not that the poet's eye is blind to the Flamingos' return in autumn but it is naturally more sympathetic to the newer and more varied arrivals, the Cranes, Geese and Ducks that are quite conspicuous both in the air and at all waters throughout North India :

क्रौञ्चहंससमाकीर्णा शरत्प्रमुदिताभवत्—महाभारत, 3.923.90.

Nevertheless, the Flamingos are not forgotten altogether, for the unconventional author of the ब्रह्मवैवर्तपुराण has actually defied the poetic tradition :

मालतीमालया श्यामकण्ठवक्षःस्थलोज्ज्वलम् ।
बकपङ्क्त्या यथाऽऽकाशं शारदीयं सुनिर्मलम् ॥"—4.21.41.

Needless to say that to translate expressions like बलाकमाला, बकपंक्ति or बलाका as 'a flight of Cranes' or of Egrets is entirely incorrect. Cranes, with the exception of the resident Sarus which flies low and in small numbers, are not to be seen in India during the rains while the Egrets are always with us and though they too often fly in V-form like the Sarus they do so at a very low level. It is only the Flamingos, Cranes and the Geese that fly very high, almost at the level of the clouds. In the following verse वराहमिहिर, describing the beauty of the skies (आकाशम्) at the beginning of the rainy season pictures the dark clouds as huge elephants with Flamingos in V-form for their white tusks :

तडिद्धेमकक्ष्यैर्बलाकाग्रदन्तैः स्रवद्वारिवानैश्चलत्प्रान्तहस्तैः ।
[illegible] ॥

—बृहत्संहिता, 24.17.

84

SWANS, GEESE, DUCKS AND MERGANSERS

Sanskrit nomenclature corresponding to the common names in the title of this Article is हंस or महाहंस, कलहंस or कादम्ब-हंस, क्षुद्रहंस or हंसक, and कारण्डव respectively, and the epitomised expression हंसकारण्डवा:[1] approximates in meaning to the scientific name of the family, viz., Anatidae. Indian mythology recognizes the unity pervading the family when it regards the Swans, Grey Geese and Ducks as the progeny of the first Swan-Mother धृतराष्ट्री :—

धृतराष्ट्री तु हंसांश्च कलहंसांश्च सर्वशः ।
चक्रवाकांश्च भद्रं ते विजज्ञे साऽपि भामिनी ।।
—रामायण 3.14.19.; म. भा. 1.66.60.

In this verse कलहंस (the Grey Lag noted for its mellow call note) stands for all grey Geese and चक्रवाक (the beautiful Brahminy Duck) for all Indian Ducks. In the same way हंस (note the plural in each case) denotes the all-white Swans as is clear from references to them in the Ṛg Veda, literature and the Lexicons. Amarasiṃha and others name the Grey Geese like the Grey Lag and the Bar-headed Goose as कलहंस and कादम्ब, and define हंस as an entirely white bird with white wings (श्वेतगरुत्) and distinguish three different varieties of it as we shall see presently. All the northern breeding grounds of the Swans and Geese are conventionally placed at or near the मानस lake in the Himalayas. These birds do not breed within Indian limits, nevertheless poetical convention treats them as being under the influence of love during the cold season. The reson is that they are in a good condition and keep calling to one another, and hence expressions like मत्तहंस or मत्तकलहंस, for according to पाराशर quoted by भट्टोत्पल in बृहत्संहिता, 85, 28, the मदकाल for हंस, कादंब, etc. is the शरद् ऋतु.

A. SWANS

1. The Swans with which this section is concerned are Goose-like birds, pure white when adult but with heavier bodies and longer necks.

1. The expression, however, includes also the 'सुमुखकारण्डव' or the 'कृष्णकारण्डव' or the Common or Black Coot—Art. 58.

Rather awkward on land, they are very graceful on water. The Whooper and the Mute Swan are known to visit the extreme North-West of the subcontinent including Sind in small 'herds' during the non-breeding season i.e., from about December-January to June-July. When the winter is very severe in Northern and Central Asia the numbers visiting this country are larger than usual. The present position according to Hume is that Swans do not occur anywhere within Indian limits outside the Himalayas except in the extreme North-West.[1] It is, however, more than probable that in the hoary past when the so-called sportsman of the present day with his rifle and gun was not known, they travelled further east and, were, therefore, met with at least, on the upper reaches of the Jumna and the Ganges. Being large and conspicuous birds and visiting the country in small numbers they now rarely escape slaughter and have no chance to renew their acquaintance with the country. That the ancient Indians were quite familiar with them admits of no doubt. Not only did they know the two species named above but also the smaller but rarer and more striking Chinese Swan, Cygnus davidii, pure white like the others but with red bill, legs and feet. The possibility of Cygnus davidii visiting India has been admitted by noted ornithologists like Hume and Le Messurier.[2] In any case these three varieties of Swan could at times be seen on the Himalayan rivers and lakes, and the ancient Indian princes must have had them, at least occasionally as ornamental birds on their private lakes like the Mute Swan in Europe during recent times. The pair of Swans on a Lotus tank in the pleasure grounds of a temple of Śiva in Banaras mentioned in the स्कन्दपुराण[3] could only be tame birds :—

मरालीगलनालीस्थबिसासक्तसितच्छदम्

Frequent references to pet Cranes, Geese and Ducks also occur in literature.

2. According to a story related in the रामायण, 7.18 god वरुण avoided रावण by transforming himself into a हंस and later granted a boon to the bird for his help and made him permanently white ;—

वर्णो मनोरमः सौम्यश्चन्द्रमण्डलसन्निभः ।
भविष्यति तवोदग्रः शुद्धफेनसमप्रभः ॥—7.18.29.

हंसानां हि पुरा राम न वर्णः सर्वपाण्डुरः ।
पक्षा नीलाग्रसंवीताः क्रोडाः शष्पाग्रनिर्मलाः ॥—7.18.31.

क्षेमेन्द्र also describes this favourite bird (हंस) of वरुण as wholly white :—

1. *Stray Feathres*, IV.33.

2. *Game, Shore and Water-birds of India*, 4th Edn., p. 252.

3. काशीखण्ड, पूर्वार्घ 32.99. The verse means that out of affection the male Swan is keen on sharing the soft lotus stalk which is being eaten by the female.

हंसोऽपि हिमकर्पूरशीतांशुरजतद्युतिः ।
वरुणस्य वराज्जातस्तोयेशप्रीतिमान्सदा ॥—रामायणमंजरी, 7.339.[1]

The हंस of the story is clearly a Swan and the change of colour from Juvenile to adult plumage has been explained mythically. The mount of ब्रह्मा (हंसवाहन) is also a Swan so that the epithet सुरप्रिय for a हंस denotes a Swan—see para. 11 of this and para. 6 of section B.

(1) The young Whooper is pale grey-brown throughout but the adult is pure white; the bill black with a yellow base, legs and feet black. The male bird is nearly five feet long, has a wing span of about eight feet and weighs up to 19 lbs. General Osbourne, who shot one out of four Whoopers on the Beas (विपाशा) in the Hoshiarpur district of the Punjab in 1900, says about the wounded bird, "as long as its companions remained in sight it continued to utter its long, loud, musical trumpet call" (Stuart Baker). According to Hume and Marshall also this Swan has a loud and musical call which much resembles 'hoop' 'hoop' but when uttered by a large flock of different sexes and ages and mellowed by the winds and waves has "a really fine effect".[2] Flocks fly in V-formation and smaller numbers in a line (Edmund Sandars).

It breeds on the northern shores of the Caspian, Asiatic tundras and probably as far as South Seistan so that "breeding so near India as this we may hope to have many more records of its visiting our borders" (S. Baker). This Swan has frequently occurred in the Punjab and Sind, and has been observed in Nepal and even in Rajasthan.[3]

The breeding and the other habits of all Swans are alike. When nests placed in shallow water or on the borders of a marsh or swamp are threatened by flood they raise the level of the nests by introducing new materials under the eggs to protect them from danger. "They are very good parents and look after their young with the greatest care, the duck-bird often carrying her young ones about on her back whenever they want a rest."[4] No wonder the Swan is a wise bird in Epic and story-literature.

Bewick's Swan is very similar and subequal in size to the Whooper. It has occurred in the Punjab and Sind aud must have passed for a Whooper in the past.

(2) The Mute Swan is also wholly white when adult with the base of the bill, the knob and the nail black, and the remainder of the

---

1. तोयेश the मानसरोवर lake, the mythical home of all Swans and Geese; hence also the name सरप्रिय for Swans as v.l. for सुरप्रिय.

2. *Game Birds of India, Burma and Ceylon* 1881.

3. Poet माघ, it will be seen, rightly places a flight of Swans in the autumnal sky at रैवतक in the Kathiawar peninsula, not far from the Sind coast:—

"स्मितसरोरुहनेत्रसरोजलाम् अतिसिताङ्ग विहङ्ग हसद्दिवम् ।
अकलयन् मुदितामिव सर्वतः स शरदं शरदन्तुरदिङ्मुखाम् ॥

The स्कन्द पुराण pt. 4, अर्बुदखण्ड, Ch. 30.56 places the धार्तराष्ट्र or Whooper Swan in the neighbourhood of the Aravali Hills in Rajasthan, and this is correct.

4. *F.B.I.* & S. Baker.

bill reddish horny. The legs and feet are dull black. The colour-pattern of the young is different from the young of the Whooper. The head is brown with white tips of the feathers; sides of the head and neck are mixed grey and white; upper parts pale grey-brown and underparts white suffused with grey-brown.

Its nearest breeding place is in Western Turkestan and Siberia and it is a regular winter visitor to the Northwest straggling up to Rawalpindi and Sind. They often keep in pairs and when one of a pair is wounded the other keeps company and often pays dearly for his fidelity. Parties of eight to ten birds have been observed in the Punjab. They are as large as the Whooper but have a very weak voice and for this reason are known as the Mute Swans. Both parents vigorously defend their nest and young. The female when disturbed hisses angrily and the male utters a defiant grunt. The Whooper and the Mute sometimes hybridise with each other.

(3) Cygnus davidii is a much smaller species. It is entirely white like other two but has the bill vermilion-red with the nail black, and legs and feet orange. It is apparently a very rare bird but an instance of its occurrence in Dera Ghazi Khan (Punjab) in the year 1892 is given by Le Messurier in his book.

3. The Ṛg Veda contains references to हंस as (i) a solitary bird (ii) going in pairs, and (iii) flying and calling together in a line. There is also mention of the नीलपृष्ठ हंस, the Bar-head Goose (Section B, para 5). The following references are evidently to the Swan :

The सोम plant when crushed exudes the juice with a hissing sound due to air bubbles coming out and bursting. This is compared to the hissing of a Swan when disturbed on the water :—

"श्वसित्यप्सु हंसो न सीदन्— RV 1.65.5.

We have seen that the female of the Mute Swan hisses angrily when disturbed. Writing about the voice of Swans, B. Vesey Fitzgerald also says : "The Mute Swan very rarely does more than hiss severely at unwelcome visitors."[1] It is, therefore, incorrect to translate श्वसिति as "pants" as Griffith does, for there is no reason for the bird of powerful flight to 'pant' and the comparison is between the effects produced on the सोम and हंस when they are teased (crushed being the proper word for सोम corresponding to 'teased' or 'annoyed' for the हंस).

The Sun is called "हंस : शुचिषद्" in RV 4.40.5, and the reference can only be to a solitary Swan floating upon a wide expanse of deep blue water, Cf:

प्रजगाम नभश्चन्द्रो हंसो नीलमिवोदकम् ।—रामायण, 5.17.1.

The Aśvins invited to the Soma sacrifice like a pair of Swans hastening to the water:—

हंसाविव पततमा सुतां उप— RV 5.78.1-3.

---

1. *Birds, Trees and Flowers*, p. 57.

हंसाविव पतथो अध्वगाविव— RV 8.35.8.

The Swan is monogamous and a pair, being greatly attached to each other, keep together. This is particularly the case with the Mute Swans (see above). The last two references are, therefore, to these birds. None of the Geese can be intended as they live and move in flocks of some size when away from their breeding grounds.

White horses (दिव्यासः 'shining' and therefore 'white') running, in a race or otherwise, in a line are compared to Swans flying in a line :

दिव्यासो अत्याः हंसा इव श्रेणिशो यतन्ते — RV 1.163.10·

Freshly cut to size and barked (and therefore white) wooden sacrificial posts carried on their shoulders by men walking in a single file along a forest foot-path look like long-necked Swans flying in a line

हंसा इव श्रेणिशो यतानाः शुक्रावसानाः—RV 3.8.9

The Whoopers, when in small parties, fly in a line. The Geese, on the other hand, always occur in large flocks and fly in "bunches" on shorter and in wedge-formation or very long lines on longer flights.

A party of Whoopers answering the sonorous call of their leader :

हंसा इव कृणुथ श्लोकम्— RV 3.53.10.
आदीं हंसो यथा गणं विश्वस्यावीवशन्मतिम्— RV 9.32.3.

The हिरण्यपर्ण हंस with a beautiful voice (मधुमन्त) in the verse below is the same as the सुवण्ण हंस of the जातक, and the हिरण्य हंस of कुमारसंभव (see paragraphs 7 & 8 below) and, therefore, a young Whooper with a greyish brown plumage :—

हंसासो ये वां मधुमन्तो अस्रिधो हिरण्यपर्णा उहुव उषर्बुधः
—RV 4.45.4[1]

The हंसाः dedicated to the Moon-god (VS 24.22) and the Wind-god (Ib.24.35) are clearly Swans. The Sun and Moon have often been pictured as a Swan, and its powerful flight and migratory instinct are fully in keeping with the spirit of the Wind.

4. It would appear that in the post-Vedic period when the commonest Geese of India, the Bar-head and the Grey Lag were named कादम्ब हंस and कलहंस respectively, the Swans, known simply as हंस came occasionally to be distinguished as राजहंस. An echo of this last fact is preserved in the following equation, probably taken over from some old lexicon :—

---

1. Cp. "वदन्तो मधुरं" in paragraph 10 below.

"मल्लिको मल्लिका चैव (मल्लिकाख्यैव ?) राजहंसान्तरे द्वयम् ।"
—विश्वलोचनकोश

i.e. मल्लिक and मल्लिकाख्य[1] are two names for a kind of राजहंस. In other words, the Whooper and the Mute Swan, the धार्तराष्ट्र and मल्लिक of later times, were regarded as varieties of राजहंस. This finds support from धन्वन्तरिनिघण्टु whose skeleton at least is very much older than अमरकोश. It does not refer to the Swan with red bill and feet but only to the Whooper (धार्तराष्ट्र) and the more graceful Mute Swan (मनोरम राजहंस) and the Grey Lag Goose (कलहंस) which probably shows that धन्वन्तरि lived in the North-West of India :

हंसः श्वेतो धार्तराष्ट्रो, राजहंसो मनोरमः
कलहंसोऽपरः प्रोक्तो...

Later on both the Swans came to be known as राजहंस as indicated above. The Whooper (धार्तराष्ट्र or मराल) which is the vehicle of ब्रह्मा has also been called रथ-राजहंस (See para 11 below). Similarly राजहंस in रामायण and महाभारत, where कादम्ब and कलहंस are also mentioned, is a Swan :—

क्रीडन्ती राजहंसेन पद्मषण्डेषु नित्यशः ।
हंसी सा तृणमध्यस्थं कथं द्रक्ष्येत मद्गुकम् ॥—रामायण, 3.56.20.
कल्याणवाचः शकुना राजहंसाः—महाभारत, 6.3.68.[2]

क्षेमेन्द्र relates in बृहत्कथा-मञ्जरी 9. 140-142, how one धर्मसेन and his wife intently watched a pair of Swans flying high in the sky before their death and were re-born as a pair of राजहंस and verse 143, ibid. describes the Swan with its long and curved neck as कुटिल कन्धर.

The later names, viz., धार्तराष्ट्र and मल्लिकाख्य as also पाकहंस do not occur in very early works like the Rāmāyaṇa and the Mahābhārata and seem to have been borrowed from Pali literature of the Buddhists. They had travelled widely in Central Asia, China, Tibet, etc. and having observed the differences in Cygnus Davidii, the Whooper and the Mute Swan, named them afresh; and in doing so they appropriated the name राजहंस to the beautiful Chinese Swan (Cygnus davidii) with red bill and feet and renamed the Whooper, the next best, as धार्तराष्ट्र[3] and the Mute

1. 'मल्लिकाख्य' is the reading in the नामचन्द्रिका edition (Bombay); क्षीरस्वामी टीका, Index III (Special words), Oriental Book Agency, Poona, 1941; रामाश्रमी टीका, Bombay 1944; Devadatta Tiwaree's edition, Bareilly College, 1875 and as v. 1. in महेश्वर टीका, Bombay 1907;—all editions of अमरकोश.

2. These कल्याणवाचः राजहंसाः are the Whoopers with their beautiful trumpeting calls. The राजहंस समूह in Mahābhārata 12.327.6 on the other hand should be the Bar-head Geese as the passage appears to be a later addition by an inexpert hand who has placed the कृष्ण परभृत (the Koel) with the Golden Eagle in the Central Himalayas—an impossible thing, for the Indian Koel is "not found in the Himalayas and is scarce in the foot-hills at their base" (Whistler). It is however possible that the scribe has changed श्वेत into कृष्ण not knowing that there is such a thing as a श्वेत कोकिल as well. If so राजहंस समूह could well be a party of Swans, and not necessarily the Bar-head Geese.

3. Coined from धृतराष्ट्री, the first Swan-mother, or धृतराष्ट्र as explained in the next para.

Swan as मल्लिकाख्य or पाकहंस. This राजहंस being a very rare bird even in the Himalayas has naturally been left severely alone and does not figure in the Jātaka stories. The title of the महाहंस जातक, which deals principally with the two varieties of Swan, the घतरट्ठ and the पाकहंस, and their young, shows that these Swans went by the common name of महाहंस. पालकाप्य, ch. 26, however, mentions धार्तराष्ट्र and महाहंस[1] in juxtaposition, and if one reads the two words as a single name it would mean 'the धार्तराष्ट्र type of Swan' but as two different names they would refer to the Whooper and the Mute Swan respectively. That they are not the Geese is clear from the fact that the latter are named in the same passage as कादम्ब (Bar-head) and कलहंस (Grey Lag). The presence of महाहंस on the गङ्गाह्लद lake in the Himalayas is mentioned in the पद्मपुराण :—

सर्वतो भद्रतां प्राप्तो महाहंसैः प्रशोभते ।—भूमिखण्ड, 101.27.[2]

It must be noted that महाहंस does not include the much smaller Cygnus davidii which is the राजहंस of अमरकोश whose author was a Buddhist.

5. Apart from the Geese, कलहंस and कादम्ब, the lexicons give हंस (in the original sense of an all-white Swan), श्वेतगरुत् (white-winged, a Swan alone has white wing quills), सितच्छद (white plumaged), etc. as common names for a Swan and mention three different kinds of it, viz., राजहंस, धार्तराष्ट्र and मल्लिकाख्य :—

हंसास्तु श्वेतगरुतश्चक्राङ्गा मानसौकसः,
राजहंसास्तु ते चञ्चुचरणैर्लोहितैः सिताः,
मलिनैर्मल्लिकाख्यास्ते, धार्तराष्ट्रा सितेतरैः—अमर.; अभि. चिन्ता.
हंसो श्वेतः धार्तराष्ट्रो, राजहंसो मनोरमः—धन्वन्तरि.
हंसो मरालो नीलाक्षः चक्रपक्षः सितच्छदः
मानसौकाः परिप्लावी वक्राङ्गो जालपादकः—वैजयन्ती.
हंसेषु तु मरालाः स्युः—अभि. चिन्ता.
मरालो धूसरच्छदः. . . अभव्यः स च हंसः स्यात्—कल्पद्रुकोश
कालेषु तेषु (i.e. चञ्चुचरणेषु) धवलः किल धार्तराष्ट्रः
सोऽप्येष धूसरतनुस्तु भवेदभव्यः—राजनिघण्टु.
चक्राङ्गः सारसो हंसे—शब्दार्णव cited by मल्लिनाथ on शि. वध, 12.44.
हरिः, हरिणः हंसः—शब्दकल्पद्रुम

मल्लिकाक्ष in some editions of अमर and in अभि. चिन्ता. is a mistake for मल्लिकाख्य, for मल्लिक is हंसभेद both according to हेमचन्द्र and विश्वप्रकाश. मल्लिकाक्ष proper is the Duck known as the White-eyed Pochard and this explains the error. Brief notes on some names and epithets in the above quotations are added below :

1. Cf. महाहंस as विष्णु (M.W.), the Sun, can only be a Swan.
2. The कलशब्द महाहंस of मार्कण्डेय पुराण 1.11 is the Whooper Swan.

चक्राङ्ग and चक्रपक्ष (M. Williams)—refer to the circular or spiral flight of the birds as they survey their landing ground or water, and also to the vigorous rotary motion of their wings preparatory to settling down.

मानसौकस्—All the Swans and Geese come across the Himalayas and as the Bar-headed Geese were known to have their breeding grounds at the Himalayan lakes including the मानसरोवर the Swans also have been placed there and the name merely signifies their northern home across the Himalayas; cf. देवलोकोद्भव[1] and सुरप्रिय as epithets for a Swan.

मराल—is a Swan according to वैजयन्ती and अभि. चिन्ता. but with a grey-brown plumage as defined in कल्पद्रुकोश.

As for the अभव्य हंस (one that is not beautiful, i.e., is not white) राजनिघण्टु makes it clear that the धार्तराष्ट्र (the Whooper) when in the brown phase is known by that name. It follows, therefore, that मराल and अभव्य हंस denote young Swans that have not yet assumed the white plumage of the adult. कल्पद्रुकोश supports this when it says, "अभव्यः स च हंसः स्यात्".

नीलाक्ष—'having black or dark-brown eyes' should be the Mute Swan which has the darkest eyes of all.

क्षीराश—'whose food is milk' after the supposed power of a Swan to separate milk from water. क्षीर also means 'clean or pure water' and the name may well have been transferred back to it after the Sun had been pictured as a Swan in the blue sky. The Sun sucks up pure water out of the impure waters of the earth and this power of the heavenly Swan came later to be attributed to the earthly Swan. It is more probable, however, that the power of the क्रुञ्च bird (the Flamingo, and not the Curlew) of separating milk (very fine food) from the water came later to be transferred to the हंस— see Art. 83, and Prof. C.R. Lanman's article, "The Milk-drinking Hansas of Sanskrit Poetry" in the *Journal of the American Oriental Society*, vol. 19, p. 151ff. (1898).

वक्राङ्ग (Pali वक्कंगो) and सङ्कुचित (वैजयन्ती) are after the long flexible neck of a Swan.

परिप्लावी—refers to the permanent association of a Swan with the water and its swimming habit as against a Goose which is more of land than a water-bird.

ज्येष्ठ, प्रास्थिक and धोरण (in वैजयन्ती)—'the largest', 'the migratory' and 'flying in formation' respectively. 'ज्येष्ठहंस' corresponds to 'महाहंस'.

राजहंस—has red bill and feet according to अमर but the colour is bright red (अतिलोहित) according to अभि. चिन्ता. It is particularly to be noted that धन्वन्तरि, older than अमरकोश, makes no mention of red bill and feet.

मलिन— 'soiled, tarnished, or of a dark colour.'

---

1. देवलोक is evidently the देवक्षेत्र or उत्तरकुरु the vaguely known or conjectured areas including central Asia, Tibet, i.e. lying beyond and to the North of the Himalayas (ऐतरेय आरण्यक, 8.23). The description of Swans as coming from देवलोक is thus fairly correct though later they came to be placed with the Geese at, and in the neighbourhood of, the मानस Lake in the Himalayas.

मल्लिक, मल्लिकाख्य—white like the Jasmine flower.

धार्तराष्ट्र—patronymic from (i) धृतराष्ट्री, the mythological Swan-Mother of all Swans, Geese, etc., and (ii) धृतराष्ट्र, 'a king'. धार्तराष्ट्र— son of a king and therefore next to him in status. The real significance of the name, despite its last place in the above verses, must be determined, as shown by क्षीरस्वामी on अमर, with reference to राजहंस as 'the king or best of Swans':— "धृतराष्ट्रे अमात्ये भवा धार्तराष्ट्राः, राजहंसेभ्यो न्यूनत्वात्" cf. also :—

परस्मिन्न्यूनतामेति यथाऽमात्यः स्थिते नृपे

quoted by पतञ्जलि, 5.3.57. धार्तराष्ट्र is thus the next best Swan after the राजहंस[1]. धन्वन्तरि defines राजहंस as beautiful and धार्तराष्ट्र as a white हंस.

सारस—सारं असति, i.e., one that takes out the essence from the water—after the नीरक्षीरविवेक conventionally attributed to a Swan. It is in this etymological sense that क्षेमेन्द्र uses the phrase "विलासरससारसः" for a Swan in a metaphor in बृहत्कथामञ्जरी, 9. 359 and सारसी for राजहंसी at 9.145. सारस is again a Swan in रामायण 3. 19.8; cf. the following :—

यत्सारभूतं तदुपासितव्यं हंसो यथा क्षीरमिवाम्बुमध्यात्

—सुभाषित, 173. 878.

माघ has used the term rather loosely for the Geese in शिशुपालवध, 12.44 where it may well refer to water-side birds in general. See also किरातार्जुनीय, 8.9 & 31, and Art. 62.

हरि and हरिण, adnouns for a हंस or Goose must refer to (i) a juvenile Swan or (ii) the Grey Lag Goose as the terms denote a tawny or brown colour (M. W.). If हरिण also means white (शुक्लवर्ण—शब्दकल्पद्रुम), हरिण हंस would also be an adult Swan.

6. Now looking back to the physical characters and habits of the three different Swans set out above, it should not be difficult to fix their identity in Sanskrit. The rare Chinese Swan, Cygnus davidii, is the राजहंस proper of the later lexicons, a mere memory of the past which readily led to the transference of the name to the familiar Bar-head. राजहंस, as Cygnus davidii, is not mentioned in the Rāmāyaṇa or Mahābhārata but the much later Harivaṃśa certainly mentions it at 3.41, 61-62 (quoted in para. 5 of Section B). The Whooper with its black (partly yellow) bill and feet is the धार्तराष्ट्र हंस, celebrated alike in the Jātaka, the Indian Epics, and European literature from the time of Homer. It is the wise and talking Swan described as 'सुरप्रिय' or 'beloved of the gods', for did not ब्रह्मा, the Creator, assume its beautiful and spotlessly white form as related in the Epics ? Its far northern home is देवलोक. The Mute Swan's bill is mainly reddish-horny and the feet dull-black so that the description of मलिनचञ्चुचरण is fully applicable to it and the name मल्लिकाख्य हंस is descriptive of its spotless white plumage. It has a weak voice and is generally silent and this is the reason why it does not figure as a talking Swan in Purāṇic stories. Nevertheless it finds its proper

1. The simplest way to interpret the name is to equate धृतराष्ट्र with 'King' and धार्तराष्ट्र as the king's son, and hence next in status to the King, i.e. राजहंस.

place in the चुल्ल हंस (533) and the महाहंस जातक (534) under the names of सुमुख and पाकहंस respectively. As सुमुख हंस it is the Army-chief of the धतरट्ठ हंसराजा,, the king of the Swans, and the name refers to the black knob or 'berry' worn like an ornament at the base of its bill; compare the name नन्दीमुख for the Comb Duck after a similar but larger knob on the bill, and सुमुख for (i) the Black Vulture with red face and ear-lappets, and (ii) the Common Coot with a white bill and shield against a dark body.

7. Juvenile Whoopers are clothed in a uniform grey-brown and take from eighteen months to two years to assume the white plumage of the adult. They are the सुवण्ण वण्ण हंस or सुवण्णहंस (सुवर्ण हंस cf. जातरूप हंस below) of जातक, 534 where the queen dreams of one discoursing upon religion to the king and feels an irresistible longing to see it. The धतरट्ठ and पाकहंस type of Swans, both with their kings, come into the story at a later stage, and while both types are said to have the same body-colour (white) the young daughter of the king of the पाकहंसा: is also said to be of a golden colour—"पाकहंसरण्णो पन धीता सुवण्णवण्णा अहोसि", and she is married to the धतरट्ठ king.[1]

The पाकहंस, therefore, is evidently the Mute Swan, the name being true of it in a double sense : (i) पाक as indicating a change of colour from brown of the young to white of the adult through lapse of time or advancing age (पाक, 'ripening'— "जरसा केशस्य शौक्ल्यम्" मेदिनी; cf. पाकशुक्ला for chalk, i.e. lime in reference to the change undergone by dark coloured lime-stone on baking), and (ii) पाक, 'a child or ignorant person' in view of the bird not having the full voice of the धतरट्ठ, the Whooper.[2] In the चुल्लहंस जातक (533) the King of the धतरट्ठ Swans and his Army-chief, the सुमुख हंस, are trapped and taken to the king. The धतरट्ठ king holds a learned discourse on religion with the king but when the latter requests सुमुख for his views as well, he excuses himself by saying that he is not so cultured or educated and is, therefore, unable to discourse seriously in the presence of the great :—

अहं खलु महाराज नागराजारिव' श्रंतरं
पतिवत्तुं न सक्कोमि न मे सो विनयो सिया— verse 75.

Evidently सुमुख is the Mute Swan with a weak voice. Thus सुमुख and पाकहंस are one and the same.

8. Parties of golden-plumaged Swans on a Himalayan lake mentioned as हिरण्यहंसावलि and हिरण्यहंसव्रज in कुमारसम्भव, 13. 27 and 39 are the same as सुवण्ण हंस of the महाहंस जातक. This accords well with the statement of S. Baker that the great majority of Swans visiting India are young birds in brown plumage.

1. Does this statement not show that the ancients knew that the two species occasionally interbreed, a fact now acknowledged by orinthologists ?.

2. In the first sense both the Whooper and the Mute Swan would be पाकहंस. It is in this sense that चरक (1.23.37) uses the name पाकहंस for an adult Swan and चक्रदत्त renders it correctly as श्वेतहंस.

9. The Whooper and the White Ibis have an entirely white plumage and black bill and legs, and these form the slender basis of comparison between the two in several सुभाषित verses where the Ibis is always taunted for not being able to match the Swan either in its graceful movement or the power of separating out milk from water. In verse 229 at page 229 of the सुभाषित (1935 Edn.) a pure white body, a pleasant voice (the booming call of this Ibis is well known) and even a slow-stepping gait (during fishing) are conceded to the Ibis, while in verse 230 it is despised for its animal diet and for not enjoying the honour of serving as a mount for god ब्रह्मा. It may be added that the comparison is hardly fair to the Swan but it is allowable in अन्योक्ति which chiefly involves a satire upon a person of false perfections.

10. The large size and strength of पाकहंस are clearly stated in the Jātaka story, 534— "पाकहंसा. . .महब्बला", the वेस्संतर जातक (547)— "पाकहंसा अतिबला" verse, 2106, and also in जातकमाला, 22.40—"सज्जपत्ररथी बली" and we can now see that the हंसा: described as बलवीर्योपपन्न, बली हंस or simply as बलिन् in the following verses are no other than Swans :—

बलवीर्योपपन्नानां रूपयौवनशालिनाम् ।
षष्ठस्तु पन्था हंसानां, वैनतेयगतिः परा ॥–रामायण, 4.58. 28.
कथं नु हंसं बलिनं चक्राङ्गं दूरपातिनम्—महाभारत, 8.41.23.
सामिषं कुररं जघ्नुः बलिनो ये निरामिषाः—भागवत, 11.9.2.

11. The golden-coloured हंस caught by love-distracted Nala was no other than a young Whooper :

स ददर्श ततो हंसाञ्जातरूपपरिष्कृतान्—महाभारत, 3.54.19.[1]

The bird promised to plead Nala's cause with Damayantī and was thereupon released. He flew with his party to her place and allowed himself to be caught by her and then performed his mission.[2] The circular flight of the bird before it settled down is described in the verse below :—

भ्रमणरयविकीर्णस्वर्णभासा खगेन
क्वचन पतनयोग्यं देशमन्विष्यताधः ।
मुखविधुमदसीयं सेवितुं लम्बमानः
शशिपरिधिरिवोर्ध्वं मण्डलस्तेन तेने—नैषधचरित, 2.108.

The talking धार्तराष्ट्र birds with a beautiful voice engaged upon a mission similar to the above are again the Whooper Swans :—

1. It is to be noted that a majority of Swans visiting India are young birds who have not yet attained the adult white plumage.

2. Damayanti found the bird to be अद्भुतरूप i.e., quite unlike the Geese she had been accustomed to see. It will be seen that जातरूप हंस is the same as सुवण्ण हंस of the जातक.

ततो हंसान् धार्तराष्ट्रान् देवलोकनिवासिनः—हरिवंश, 2.91,36.
ते वै नदन्तो मधुरं संस्कृतापूर्वभाषिणः—Ib. 2.92.3.
आलपन्तं सुमधुरं धार्तराष्ट्रा जनेश्वर—Ib 2.92.5.
सकान्तैर्धार्तराष्ट्रैश्च राजहंसैः[1] सुरप्रियैः—Ib.2.41.61.

It may be added that the Swans have also been described as देवपक्षिणः (Ibid. 2.91 37) ; हंससत्तमाः, 'best of their kind' (Ibid.2.91.39).

The occurrence of adult Swans in Kashmir is mentioned in the पद्मपुराण where मृणालधवला देवहंसाः and मृणालवर्चसो हंसाः are referred to—VI. उत्तर खंड, 176.70, and the Whoopers are placed on the Himalayan waters :

हंसान्सुमधुरांश्चापि तत्र शुश्राव पार्थिवः ।
—महाभारत, 13.54.14.

The normal change from the juvenile grey-brown to the all-white plumage of the adult धार्तराष्ट्र has been utilized, though not quite artistically, to glorify the purifying effects of a certain holy place on the Narmadā in the Padma Purāṇa, II. भूमिखंड, ch. 92 and the adult birds are described a little earlier as entirely white but with the bill and feet black :

सितेतरैश्चञ्चुपादैरन्यतः शुक्लविग्रहाः— Ib. 90.43.

भट्टनारायण has used धार्तराष्ट्राः with a double meaning in the following, as (i) the कौरवाः, the sons of धृतराष्ट्र and (ii) the Whooper Swans :—

सत्पक्षा मधुरगिरः प्रसाधिताशा मदोद्धतारम्भाः ।
निपतन्ति धार्तराष्ट्राः कालवशान्मेदिनीपृष्ठे[2] ॥
—वेणीसंहार, 1.6.

Again the visiting (अभ्यागत) सुरप्रिय and चारुविशालपक्ष are Swans and हंसाः the Geese in the following :

अभ्यागतैश्चारुविशालपक्षैः सरः (सुर ?) प्रियैः पद्मरजोवकीर्णैः ।
महानदीनां पुलिनोपयातैः क्रीडन्ति हंसाः सह चक्रवाकैः ॥
—रामायण, 4.30.31.

Nothing brings out the true significance of the name विशालपक्ष better than a comparison of the size and wing-expanse of a Swan with that of a Goose. The former is sixty inches long and has an expanse of ninety to nintyfive inches as against only thirtytwo and sixty inches respectively of the latter. सुरप्रिय are the Swans, हंसाः the Geese, and चक्रवाक the Ruddy Sheldrakes, and the verse gives a picture of a great river with these birds, sporting on the sands (and presumably some on the waters as is their habit). The Swan of god वरुण is described in रामायण, 7.18.28 as "गङ्गातोयविचारिन्" and this supports the above identification of विशालपक्ष.[3]

1. राजहंस here refers to the Mute Swan.

2. The expression कालवश refers to (i) the severity of winter which forces the Swans to move from the higher latitudes to the lower and warmer one in India, and (ii) the adverse fate awaiting the कौरवाः.

3. विशालपक्ष qualifying सुरप्रिय may also mean 'a large party' of Swans.

In the following pen-picture the full moon in a clear blue and starry sky is compared with a single हंस or राजहंस on a large lake studded with lilies. Both are obviously Swans :—

तमांस्युत्सार्य भगवांश्चन्द्रो जृम्भति सो ऽम्बरे ।
कुमुदालङ्कृते हंसो यथा सरसि विस्तृते ।। मत्स्यपुराण, 139.16.

स्फुटकुमुदचितानां राजहंसस्थितानां
मरकतमणिभासा वारिणा पूरितानाम् ।
श्रियमतिशयरूपां व्योमतोयाशयानां
वहति विगतमेघं चन्द्रतारावकीर्णम् ।। ऋतुसंहार, 3.21.[1]

The sun and the spiritually elevated man are compared with the wise Swan in the following :—

हंसस्य चोर्ध्वगमने गतिर्भवति निश्चला ।
तत्त्वातत्त्वविवेकोऽस्ति जलदुग्धविभागवत्[2] ।।
—शिवपुराण, रुद्र सं. 2, Ch. 15, 10.

The Mute Swans (मल्लिकाख्य हंस) are known often to go about in pairs and they are greatly devoted to each other. These, therefore, should be the हंसमिथुन in the examples below.
Swans in pairs add to the charm of a river :—

हंसमिथुनैर्नद्यः (भान्ति) —सुभाषित, 188·1042

Swans resting on the sand-bank of a river were a favourite theme for the painter's brush :—

कार्या सैकतलीनहंसमिथुना स्रोतोवहा मालिनी ।
—शाकुन्तल, 6.17.

अश्वघोष was certainly aware of the affection between a pair of Swans and the following appeal to Prince Siddhārtha to return to his wife based upon the behaviour of these birds is particularly forceful :

हंसेन हंसीमिव विप्रयुक्तां त्यक्तां गजेनेव वने करेणुम् ।
आर्तां सनाथामपि नाथहीनां त्रातुं वधूमर्हसि दर्शनेन ।।
—बुद्धचरित, 9.27.

---

1. Even with the reading "राजहंसाश्रितानां" in the first line it is incorrect to separate the compound with the plural राजहंसाः as the comparison with the Moon postulates only one Swan.

2. The change of attitude in the rising and setting sun is readily noticeable but its movement or change of position near the zenith is not easily perceptible. It is then that the sun is at its brightest and hottest and its power of sucking up pure from impure ground water is at its best. The critical faculty of a person who has attained perfect wisdom and balance of mind does not falter and he instinctively, as it were, and with certainty discriminates between good and evil.

The last three items in the synonymies quoted in paragraph 5 above relate to मराल or अभव्य हंस as a grey-brown bird and as belonging to the हंस group which includes the three pure white Swans. Evidently, therefore, मराल signifies a juvenile Swan. मराल is often associated with god ब्रह्मा whose mount is said to be a हंस, the adult Whooper. In पद्मपुराण, 6, उत्तरखंड, 180,41ff. ब्रह्मा assumes the form of a talking Swan (मराल) who was once pure white (पक्वकर्पूरपाण्डुर) but underwent a sudden change of colour and is contemptuously called a कलहंस because of its resemblance with the grey-brown of the Grey Lag (कलहंस):

देवेश धूर्जटे विद्धि मां मरालं स्वयंभुवः ।
* * *
कलहंस गतोऽसि त्वं मां विलङ्घ्य विहायसा ।

The Swan story, based on छान्दोग्य उपनिषद्, 4, related in स्कन्दपुराण, ब्रह्मखंड, सेतु-माहात्म्य, ch.29.48ff. would seem to confirm the above interpretation of मराल. Here certain sages have assumed the form of talking Swans which can only be Whoopers, and one of them jocularly addresses the leading bird as an inexperienced young Swan (मरालक) having a poor eye-sight :—

एको हंसस्तु संबोध्य हंसमग्रेसरं तदा
सोपहासमिदं प्राह............ ।
भो भो भल्लाक्ष भल्लाक्ष पुरोगच्छन् मरालक
............न पश्यसि किमन्धवत् ॥[1]

The statement "हंसेषु तु मरालाः स्युः" seems to show that there are more than one kind of मराल and they are all Swans, and as the मराल of today is the pure white Swan of tomorrow the name came to be used for the adult bird as well, and it is in this sense that मराल is the mount of ब्रह्मा and called रथ-राजहंस (राजहंस as a रथ or vehicle) in ibid. 16.31. (Compare also ibid. 9, 37-38 "वर्णेनैव परं मरालधवलः—सुभाषित, 222, 31.) The name मराल, having lost its identity, has been used indiscriminately by the poets for a हंस (Swan) in general or even for a कलहंस.

B. GEESE

1. The Geese stand midway between the larger and heavier Swans at one end and the smaller Ducks at the other. If the Swans are almost entirely aquatic and the Ducks chiefly so, the Geese may be said to be almost terrestrial in their habits. The legs being placed forward they walk easily and well and have none of the waddling gait of the domestic Goose. They feed on grass and green crops, causing considerable damage to winter

1. भल्लाक्ष means 'bear-eyed', i.e. having weak eyes. It may also mean 'having excellent eyes' used in an ironical sense.

rice and wheat in India. Occasionally, however, they also feed in shallow water. Except on shorter flights when they "bunch", they normally fly in V-formation or in long lines. Out of the breeding season, i.e., when they visit India in the cold weather, they are thoroughly gregarious and are always seen in small parties or flocks of several hundred birds at a time. Ordinarily they feed in the morning and in the evening and return for rest and sleep to sand-banks or sandy churs (islands) of large rivers, jheels or lakes with some bird on the watch and some always on the water. They differ from the Ducks in that the sexes are alike and the male assists the female in the duties of rearing the young.

2. They are commonly divided into two groups, the Grey and the Black Geese. Of these latter only the Red-breasted Goose is occasionally found in India at the present day, though it may have been more common a thousand years ago. It is black above, including the head and neck, and chestnut and black below. It is probably the कालहंस of बुद्धघोष[1] in संयुत्त निकाय, 277. The Grey Geese, on the other hand, are much more common in India and of these the most important and numerous are the Grey Lag and the Bar-headed Goose. As regards numbers, however, five Bar-heads visit India to every Grey Lag and "taking upper India as a whole this (the Bar-head) enormously outnumbers all the other species of Geese put together," and "as for all the rest of the Geese, they are apparently so rare that when one comes to consider numbers they are not worth speaking about" (Hume & Marshall in *The Game Birds of India, Burma and Ceylon*). According to the same authorities the loud trumpet calls of a flight of Grey Lags high up in the air are very sonorous and musical while the notes of the Bar-heads are distinct from those of the other and are sharper, harder, less sonorous and more strident. The voices of the two are thus easy to differentiate. Moreover the two species never mingle companies, and always keep at some distance—flying, feeding, resting or swimming, always a little apart. The Bar-head is a lighter built, more graceful and more active bird than the other. It is also of a much lighter colour and has more white in its body plumage. The ancient Indians could certainly not have been unaware of these striking differences and must have named the two species differently. It is necessary to stress this point because according to a majority of the lexicons कलहंस and कादम्ब mean one and the same thing although the two species are differentiated in Sanskrit literature and also in Hindi nomenclature.

3. Hindi names for the Grey Lag (much browner than the Bar-head) are करहंस (Skt. कलहंस), मोगल (मधुगल), सोनाहंस (cf. Pali सुवण्ण हंस for a young Swan in brown plumage), राजहंस and धितराज (Skt. धृतराष्ट्र). The first name is after the bird's sonorous call-note and the second its brown colour. The last is

1. बुद्धघोष enumerats six varieties of Ducks, Geese and Swans : हरित, तंब, खीर, काल, पाक and सुवण्ण after the colour of the plumage. The first two are for Ducks, the next two for Geese and the last two for Swans.

an adaptation from धार्तराष्ट्र for the Whooper Swan. Both हेमचन्द्र and विश्वप्रकाश give धृतराष्ट्र for 'a kind of bird' in close proximity with धार्तराष्ट्र :—

धार्तराष्ट्रः कौरवेऽह्नौ कृष्णास्याङ्घ्रि सितच्छदे—हेमचन्द्र

धृतराष्ट्रः सुराज्ञि स्यात् पक्षिक्षत्रियभेदयोः—विश्व.

Evidently, therefore, धृतराष्ट्र stands for a bird other than the Swan, and when we find the Grey Lag actually going under the name of धितराज its identity with धृतराष्ट्र of the lexicons becomes fairly certain. In other words the Grey Lag would seem to have been regarded as a smaller edition of the young Whooper after the former's brown plumage and sonorous call. It is also called राजहंस from its size. The Bar-head, on the other hand, is known in Hindi as करेइ हंस (fr. केरव हंसे under कैरव in शब्दकल्पद्रुम and शब्दार्थचिन्तामणि), बिरुआ हंस (fr. विराविन् after its harsher call?), and राजहंस. This last name is again by way of substitution for the original राजहंस, viz., the Chinese Swan with deep red bill and orange legs as the Bar-head is of a much lighter colour and a more graceful build than the Grey Lag and has yellow or orange bill and legs. The name सारङ्ग for a हंस in शारदीयनाममाला and equated with राजहंस in शब्दकल्पद्रुम and M. Williams can only refer to the Bar-head Goose with a conspicuously सार i.e. शबल body.

4. The adult Grey Lag (32″), heavier than the Bar-head, is, generally speaking, a grey-brown bird with fleshy-pink bill and feet. Its breeding grounds are in Europe, Persia and Eastern and Northern Afghanistan. It is, therefore, very common in the North-West of India but working East it occurs in smaller numbers. A majority of those visiting India are, however, the young of the year and these are far less marked underneath and are nearly white on the lower parts as compared with the adults. This fact is well worth noting as it not only explains the description of कलहंस, during flight high up in the air, as white, e.g. in :—

यासां व्रजद्भिः शितिकण्ठ ! मण्डितं ।
नभो विमानैः कलहंसपाण्डुभिः ।। भागवत, 4.3.12.

but to a certain extent also the confusion of कलहंस with कादम्ब in the lexicons. The other Grey Geese like the Bean Goose, the Pink-footed and the White-fronted Goose that occur in very small numbers resemble the Grey Lag so very closely that they are very hard to tell apart in the field. The name and description of कलहंस would, therefore, apply to them all :

पक्षैराधूसरैर्हंसाः कलहंसा इति स्मृताः—हलायुध.

The adjective आधूसर (आ समन्तात् धूसरवर्णः) means 'mainly brown all over' which is perfectly true of the Grey Geese except the Bar-head which is generally of a pale grey colour and has more of white in its plumage than the others. The name कलहंस for the Grey Lag is particularly appropriate as, of all the Grey Geese, its call-note is the most sonorous "कलेन मधुरास्फुटध्वनिना विशिष्टो हंसः" —शब्दकल्पद्रुम,. It is therefore the कलकण्ठ हंस of M.W. and

कलहंस proper of Sanskrit literature. In accordance with the old belief that all Swans & Geese coming from the North had their breeding grounds about the मानस lake the latter is expressly said to be the birth-place of the कलहंस:

उत्पत्तिसदनं कलहंसयसां... मानसं नाम दिव्यं सरः

—बालरामायण, 10.34.

If कलहंस is understood in the wider sense of 'Grey Geese' as in the Mahābhārata genealogy, the above statement would include the कादम्ब or Bar-head Geese as well.

5. The Bar-headed Goose (30″) is pale grey above with two black bars on a white head, brown on the neck with a white streak on each side, brown on the flanks and pale grey and white below. The bill and feet are yellow or orange. "It is a far more graceful bird both on land and water, than the Gray, our only other common Goose, walking more easily and sitting higher in the water" (F.Finn). It breeds nearer India, on the lakes of Leh, Ladakh and Tibet, which accounts for its occurrence throughout North India in flocks of various sizes and these, when on a sand bank or during flight, have a pretty grey-white effect. From its occurrence and movement in flocks it is the कादम्ब हंस of the Epics and the Purāṇas ("कदम्बे समूहे भवः, सङ्घचारित्वात्"—अभि. चिन्तामणि) and राजहंस of classical literature. The term हंस in its original sense means a Swan but the Geese also because of their size, are ordinarily designated by that name, and, it is only when there is reason to specify a particular variety, e.g., from the point of voice, colour or numbers, that the distinctive names, कलहंस and कादम्ब are used. Thus the नीलपृष्ठ हंस of the Ṛgveda is probably the Bar-head with its grey-brown upper parts which would certainly appear fairly dark as compared with the bright white of an adult Swan :

सस्वश्चिद्धि तन्वः शुम्भमाना आ हंसासो नीलपृष्ठा अपप्तन् ।

—RV 7.59.7.

Here the expression नीलपृष्ठ should have the same sense as in RV 3.7.3 where it is descriptive of the mantle of smoke of a grey-brown colour through which the fire is shooting forth. In the above verse the wind-gods, मरुतः, are supposed to have bedecked themselves in secret and seated round the soma offering like a flock of Bar-head Geese (ornamented with orange-yellow bills and feet, black bars on their white heads, white stripes on their grey neck, etc.) on the sands, and like finely dressed young men sitting round a vedic sacrifice. It is perhaps after this Vedic name of नीलपृष्ठ हंस for the later कादम्ब हंस that मल्लिनाथ on रघुवंश, 13.55, and शङ्कर on हर्षचरित, p.12, have explained कादम्ब as नीलहंस and कृष्णहंस respectively. The author of नैषधचरित also has pictured कादम्ब as a dark bird, an embodiment of कलि, in the garden of नल which, from a profusion of white flowers, competed in beauty with the full moon. The कादम्ब is a dark spot in the garden comparable with the लाञ्छन in the moon—rather hard on the beautiful Goose which most certainly adds to the charm of the inevitable lotus pool in a garden (See नैषध चरित, 17.220).

6. In the following examples the occurrence of the Bar-heads in flocks is clearly indicated :—

हंसकादम्बैः सङ्कुलं (तटाकम्)— रामायण, 3.11.6.
कादम्बसारसकुलाकुलतीरदेशाः— ऋतुसंहार, 3.8.
कादम्बकदम्बकैर्युतम्— bank of a river in स्कन्दपुराण, 2.8. ch. 9.
कादम्बकदम्बकैरासेवितं (पम्पासरः)
—कादम्बरी (पूर्वभाग), p. 44.
कादम्बकदम्बकास्तडागाः— हरिविलास 3. 11
राजहंसकुलाकुला (गङ्गा)— स्कन्दपुराण, काशीखण्ड, 29.70
राजहंससमूह— on the Himalayas, महाभारत, 12.327.6.

7. The original distinction between the Grey Lag Goose and the Bar-headed Goose as कलहंस and कादम्ब respectively is fully borne out by the following evidence: हलायुध for instance names both of them separately :—

पक्षैराधूसरैर्हंसाः कलहंसा इति स्मृताः
* * *
कारण्डवकादम्बक्रकराद्याः पक्षिजातयो ज्ञेयाः

पालकाप्य mentions महाहंस (Swan), कलहंस and कादम्ब as different in हस्त्यायुर्वेद, ch. 13, while the following from भागवत and लोलिम्बराज distinguish between राजहंस (Bar-head) and कलहंस :—

मोदमदमुदितराजहंसकलहंसजलकुक्कुटकारण्डव चक्रवाकादिभिः. . उपकूजितेषु
—भागवत, 5.17.13.

श्रमनुत्सु सरःसु राजहंसाः कलहंसाश्च मनोरमा रमन्ते
—हरिविलास, 3.9.

In his discription of शरद् ऋतु (autumn) राजशेखर refers to कादम्ब, कलहंस and other birds arriving in the country in large numbers :

कादम्बकारण्डवचक्रवाकससारसक्रौञ्चकुलानुयाता ।
उपानयन्ती कलहंसयूथमगस्त्यदृष्ट्या पुनती पयांसि ॥
काव्यमीमांसा, Ch. 18 (Baroda Edn. p. 101)

Simlarly कलहंस and कादम्ब are mentioned separately in a single passage at pages 45, 144 and 145, of Kale's edition of कादम्बरी (पूर्वभाग). The passage below from the हरिवंश, again, makes the position very clear. It names धार्तराष्ट्र (the Whooper), राजहंस (the Mute Swan), कादम्ब, कलहंस and other birds occurring on the Himalayan lakes :—

सकान्तैर्धार्तराष्ट्रैश्च राजहंसैः सुरप्रियैः ।
कादम्बैश्चक्रवाकैश्च सारसैः कुररैरपि ॥
* * * *
कलहंसोपगीतानि सारिकाभिरुतानि च— 3.41.61-62.

The मदनविनोदनिघण्टु, on the other hand, defines कादम्ब as a kind of कलहंस with yellow legs and bill :—

कलहंसस्तु पीतैः (पदाननैः) कादम्ब उच्यते

This statement goes to show that, applying probably a too literal and narrow interpretation to the genealogy of the Grey Geese from धृतराष्ट्री, quoted in the opening paragraph in Section A of this Article, both the Geese have been regarded as कलहंस. Nevertheless it is clear that the Grey-Lag with fleshy-pink bill and feet is just a कलहंस but not a कादम्ब in which these parts are yellow. The राजहंस of a whitish colour and with yellow bill and legs in the following verse is no other than the कादम्ब as defined in मदनविनोदनिघण्टु :—

सर्वाङ्गपाण्डुरैः पिच्छैश्चञ्च्वा च कनकत्विषा ।
हरिद्रापिञ्जरैः पादैः राजहंसो विराजते ।। मानसोल्लास, 2.175.

There is thus hardly any doubt that कादम्ब is the Bar-head and कलहंस the Grey Lag Goose and, it may be noted, that these names are so used in the रामायण, महाभारत, हरिवंश, etc. But as the centre of Sanskrit culture moved eastwards people and poets rarely saw a Swan, and since the Bar-head with its grey and white plumage, orange-yellow bill and legs and slimmer and smarter body-lines stood out prominently amongst the Grey Geese including the Grey Lag they readily transferred the name राजहंस to it. It also became the conventional White Goose, the सितच्छद or धवलपक्ष-हंस of the classical poets in comparison with the darker and heavier Grey Lag exactly as the light-grey Ring Dove is the धवल कपोत amongst the Doves. None of the two is pure white but each is the lightest coloured member within its own group; cf:—

पूर्वेण स्पर्द्धमानोऽयं उत्तरो लभते सितः—पतञ्जलि महाभाष्य, 5.3.57.
काकस्य कार्ष्ण्यात् धवलः प्रासादः— Proverb

i.e., 'even a grey building looks white as compared with the Crow perched upon it'. And once the Bar-head came to be known as राजहंस, the name कादम्ब lost its specific character with some of the poets and became synonymous with कलहंस for the Grey Lag Goose. This change must naturally have come about before अमरकोश was written. At the same time the increasing artificiality of classical poetry aided by a freer exercise of poetic license and the stress of metre led to a further confusion resulting in the obliteration of the originally sharp distinctions. This is reflected in the not always true equations like the following and its permutations elsewhere:—

राजहंसस्तु कादम्बे कलहंसे नृपोत्तमे—हेमचन्द्र[1]

हेमचन्द्र follows अमर in his definitions of राजहंस and कलहंस in अभि. चिन्तामणि but falls into line with विश्वप्रकाश in the अनेकार्थसंग्रह, and मेदिनी follows suit. In the same way the names मराल and मरालक for a young Swan came to be applied

1. राजहंसो नृपश्रेष्ठे कादम्बकलहंसयोः—विश्वप्रकाश implies a difference between the two. Nevertheless other synonymies for कादम्ब and कलहंस in the same lexicon obliterate the difference. The हंस type of King, नृपश्रेष्ठ is described in बृ० सं०. 68.24-26.

to the Grey Lag Goose and this is recognized by the राजनिघण्टु in the following :—

कलहंसस्तु कादम्बः कलनादो मरालकः ।

and शब्दकल्पद्रुम rendering मरालक as कलहंस gives the following derivation :

मराल इव प्रतिकृतिरिति, मराल+कन्

i.e., the Grey Lag is a मरालक because it resembles a मराल (in the colour of its body-plumage). This agrees with the statement, "हंसेषु तु मरालाः स्युः in the अभि. चिन्तामणि which shows that more than one bird went by the name of मराल.

We have already seen in Section A that a young Swan in grey-brown plumage is the मराल proper and now we see that the name has been applied to the Grey Lag as well.

7. It is perhaps clear by now that if one wants to know with a fair degree of certainty the particular kind of Swan or Goose meant in a given context one cannot always go by the dictionary meanings of the names used or the published commentaries and translations but must try to examine the overall context in each case roughly with reference to the period of the composition (Vedic, epic or classical), the geographical setting, the picture an author wants to present and the object he has in view. This is however easier said than done, for many an instance in the Purāṇas and classics would be found to be extremely vague and it is perhaps true to say that poets, with of course some exceptions, have striven in their compostions more after general effect and word symphony than faithfulness to Nature. At the same time it cannot be denied that there is a considerable volume of high class poetry which is quite as close to Nature as poetry can be, and the above considerations should help if the alternative meanings illustrated below are borne in mind :—

(i) हंस and राजहंस, both used for Swans in the older sense, the latter for the more graceful Mute Swan for preference :

सुप्तैकहंसं कुमुदैरुपेतं महाह्रदस्थं सलिलं विभाति ।
घनैर्विमुक्तं निशिपूर्णचन्द्रं तारागणाकीर्णमिवान्तरिक्षम्"।।—रामा. 4.30,48.
गाङ्गमम्बु सितमम्बुयामुनं कज्जलाभमुभयत्र मज्जतः ।
राजहंस तव सैव शुभ्रता चीयते न च न चापचीयते" ।।—काव्यप्रकाश, 10.174.

राजहंसमिथुन described later as हंसमिथुन in कुन्दमाला, Act.4 are a pair of tame (wing-clipped?) Mute Swans on an artificial lake in the palace grounds.

(ii) हंस for (a) any of the common Geese in the Epics, and (b) all members of the Goose family (Anatidae) in स्मृति and धर्मशास्त्र literature :

(a) महानदीनां पुलिनोपयातैः क्रीडन्ति हंसाः सहचक्रवाकैः ।
—रामायण, 4.30.31.

क्रौञ्चहंससमाकीर्णा शरत्प्रमुदिताऽभवत्—म. भा. 3.183.10.

मङ्गल्यार्थप्रदैः शब्दैरन्ववर्तन्त सर्वशः।
सारसाः शतपत्राश्च हंसाश्च मधुसूदनम् ।। म. भा. 5.83.25.

(b) See मनुस्मृति, 5.12, याज्ञवल्क्य स्मृति, 1.172, etc. where हंस in the singular or plural signifies all Swans, Geese and Ducks prohibited as food. For the separate mention of चक्रवाक everywhere see Section C, para. 7 & 8

(iii) राजहंस for (a) the Chinese Swan very occasionally, and (b) mostly the Bar-head Goose which is more graceful on land and water than the Grey Lag Goose :

(a) See passage from हरिवंश, 3.41.61-62 quoted in para 7 above.

(b) पदगतिं शिक्षमाणानीव कामिनीनां पश्चात्परिभ्रमन्ति
राजहंसमिथुनानि—मृच्छकटिक, 4.28.
वामाङ्गनासुगतिनिर्जितराजहंसी—बिल्हण काव्य, 40.
सा राजहंसैरिव संनताङ्गी गतेषु लीलाञ्चितविक्रमेषु—कुमारसंभव, 1.34.
येऽपि त्वद्गमनानुकारिगतयस्ते राजहंसा गताः
—सुवृत्ततिलक, 2.39 (काव्यमाला, pt. 2).

(iv) मराल for (a) a young Swan; (b) an adult Swan; and (c) the Grey Lag Goose, as a Swan, with legs placed farther back, is very awkward on the land:

(a) See Section A. para. 11.

(b) यस्याच्छमानसपथे विजिहीर्षयेव
याता विमानपदवीं कति नो मरालाः—श्रीकण्ठचरित, 16.30.

Note—these मराल birds are called रथ-राजहंस in the next verse, and Swans serving as vehicles of the gods are described as embracing the sky with the wide expanse of their wings in किरातार्जुनीय, 18.19.

(c) निजतीरशेखरमरालकुलगतितस्करीः (त्रिदिवसुन्दर्यः)
—श्रीकण्ठचरित, 9.37.

The "केलिमराल यूथ" in Ibid. 11.37 are a party of tame Grey Lag Geese, while the wording of the following line clearly shows that the poet is referring to the same Geese (viz., कलहंसाः) as मराल on the Ganges:

संमिलद्भिर्मरालैः सा कलं कूजद्भिरुन्मदैः—कुमारसंभव, 10.33.

(v) कादम्ब is the Bar-head Goose in the Epics and Purāṇas but the name has been very sparingly used in classical literature as it was replaced by राजहंस and to a certain extent by the euphonious कलहंस. For examples see para. 6 and (viii) below.

(vi) कलहंस for (a) the Grey Lag, and (b) the Bar-head:

(a) विमलस्फाटिकाभानि पाण्डुरच्छदनैर्द्विजैः ।
कलहंसैरुपेतानि सारसाभिरुतानि च[1] ॥—म.भा. 3.158,72.
कलहंसगणैर्जुष्टामृषिकिन्नरसेविताम् (महागङ्गाम्)—Ibid. 3.159,99
ततः स कूजत्कलहंसमेखलां सपाकसस्याहितपाण्डुतागुणाम् ।
—किरातार्जुनीय, 4.1.

See also para. 6.

(b) The pale grey Bar-heads, having a white head and a good bit of white in the neck, and not the brown grey Lags, assimilate with white lotuses where their existence is known only from their conversational notes :

सितारविन्देषु चर्यषु लीनाः संसक्तफेनेषु च सैकतेषु ।
कुन्दावदाताः कलहंसमालाः प्रतीयिरे श्रोत्रसुखैर्निनादैः ॥
—भट्टिकाव्य, 2.18.

भवनकलहंसमालाभिर्धवलिताङ्गण—कादम्बरी, 145.

The Moon moving through dark clouds looks like a Bar-head floating in the midest of the Dark waves of the Jamna:

सितकरः कलहंस इवाभितस्तरति संवलितो यमुनोर्मिभिः ।
—क्षेमेन्द्र in सुवृत्ततिलक, 1.27.

(vii) सितखग, धवलविहग, etc., literally a Swan, have often been used for the Bar-head Geese. "कूलसितविहग" and "कूलधवलविहग" (श्रीकण्ठ चरित, 9.16 & 38) on the banks of the Mansarovara Lake can only be the Bar-heads which breed in the neighbouring territory and are plentiful there. Poet माघ, who knew full well that सितविहंग had come to mean the Bar-head, has deliberately used the descriptive "अतिसिताङ्गविहङ्ग (the extremely white bird) for a Swan :

स्मितसरोरुहनेत्रसरोजलाम् अतिसिताङ्गविहङ्गलसद्विम् ।
अकलयन्मुदितामिव सर्वतः स शरदं शरदन्तुरदिङ्मुखाम् ॥—6.54.

(viii) The compound "हंसकारण्डव" or हंस and कारण्डव named separately in the same verse refer to a mixed assemblage of Geese, Ducks and Coots. The phrase हंसकारण्डवाकीर्ण is the commonest epithet for rivers, lakes and tanks where some of these birds are often present, and the picture is sometimes made richer by naming other common water-side birds along with हंस and कारण्डव :

कादम्बैश्चक्रवाकैश्च कुररैर्जलकुक्कुटैः ।
कारण्डवैः प्लावैर्हंसैर्बकैर्मद्गुभिरेव च ॥—म.भा. 3.158.56.
कारण्डैः सारसैर्हंसैर्वञ्जुलैर्जलकुक्कुटैः ।
चक्रवाकैस्तथा चान्यैः शकुनैरुपनादितान् ॥—रामायण, 4.13.8.

---

1. The first line refers to white birds like white Ibises, Egrets, etc. and not to Swans as it would amount to circumlocution and poetic pedantry which is quite foreign to Epic poetry. The कादम्ब Geese are mentioned a little earlier in the same chapter, verse 56.

कादम्बकारण्डवहंसजुष्टाः पद्माकुलाः पुष्करिणीरपश्यन् ।

—म.भा. 3.164.5.

मानसं हंसकारण्डवाकुलम्—पद्मपुराण, सृष्टिखंड, 43.178.

(ix) In अन्योक्ति poetry हंस, राजहंस, हंसकुलावतंस, मराल, राजमराल and मरालकुलनायक are all used for a Swan as representing the highest standard of personal grace, dignity and ethical behaviour for an honourable person.

8. A pilgrimage to the मानस Lake, south or south-east of the कैलास range in the inner Himalayas, has been dear to the religious-minded and enterprising Indians from very ancient times and they thus became familiar not only with the breeding grounds of myriads of Bar-headed Geese and Cranes but also the valley or valleys by which they crossed the Himalayas to and back from India. This association of the क्रौञ्च or राजहंस with the great Lake and the क्रौञ्चरन्ध्र valley recurs quite often in Sanskrit literature. Incidentally, it also helps to solve the equation, "सरःकाकस्तु हंसः स्यात्"—त्रिकाण्ड-शेष, where "सर" stands for "मानसर" and "काक" either for a bird in general or a Crow. The reference is thus to the Bar-head as the bird of the मानस Lake or to its being as common a bird there as the Crow is elsewhere. A few relevant references to राजहंस for the Bar-head are given below:

(i) हंसद्वारं भृगुपतियशोवर्त्म यत् क्रौञ्चरन्ध्रम् ।

—मेघदूत, 59.

(ii) अद्यापि छिद्रं तत्पार्थ क्रौञ्चस्य परिवर्तते ।
येन हंसाश्च क्रौञ्चाश्च मानसाय प्रयान्ति च ॥

—स्कन्दपुराण, कौमारिकाखण्ड, 33.181.

(iii) सम्पत्स्यन्ते नभसि भवतो राजहंसाः सहायाः ।

—मेघदूत, 11.

(iv) मेघश्यामा दिशो दृष्ट्वा मानसोत्सुकचेतसाम् ।
कूजितं राजहंसानां नेदं नूपुरशिञ्जितम् ॥

—विक्रमोर्वशीय, 4.14.

(v) यस्य सानुमतां पृष्ठे सरः काञ्चनपङ्कजम् ।
कारण्डवसमाकीर्णं राजहंसोपशोभितम् ॥

—वामन पुराण, 85.16.

(vi) आहारो बिसपल्लवाः पुलिनभूर्लीलाविहारास्पदं
रेवावारिणि राजहंसशिशवस्तिष्ठन्ति धन्याः सुखम् ॥

—नलचम्पू, 5.71.

The first four examples refer to the last homeward flights of the Bar-heads late in spring or in early summer when a few spring-showers are common.

This has been poetically associated with the beginning of the rainy season, unless the Geese stayed on much longer or the rains set in much earlier some two thousand years ago than they do now. The convention has been followed by all poets as कविसम्प्रदाय or poetic fiction.

9. The ancients also knew from their visits to the northern Himalayas that the Geese, like almost all members of the family, lose their wing-quills after the breeding season and are helpless for some time. This is clear from the following verse where the female (who is now busy attending to her young) is said to be happy in the thought that her mate must be feeding amongst the lilies somewhere, little knowing that the poor fellow deprived of his power of flight, is almost starving in the muddy reeds :

हंसी वेत्ति परागपिञ्जरतनुः कुत्रापि पद्माकरे
प्रेयान्मे बिसकन्दलीकिसलयं भुङ्क्ते ह्ययं निर्वृतः ।
नो जानाति तपस्विनी यदनिशं जम्बालमालोडयन्
शैवालाङ्कुरमप्यसौ न लभते हंसो विशीर्णच्छदः ॥

—सुभाषित, 222.34.

10. Some additional appreciative references to the Geese and a couple of examples of striking poetic imagery showing in what high regard they have been held in India may now be given:

(i) The sonorous 'honking' calls of the Grey Lag high up in the sky, or their conversational notes when feeding in the fields have been greatly admired:

कर्षन् नितान्तमधुरान् कलहंसनादान्—कुन्दमाला, 2.4.
या पुरा कलहंसानां कलेन कलभाषिणी—रामायण, 4.30,9.
श्रोत्रं हंसस्वनोऽयं सुखयति दयिता नूपुरह्लादकारी—प्रियदर्शिका, 1.15.

(ii) The distant 'gaggle' of long lines of the Bar-head Geese, flying high in different directions and each flock answering the call of another, in the cloud-free autumnal sky has inspired a truly picturesque image. 'The goddesses presiding over the Cardinal Points are, as it were, carrying on a lively conversation accross the skies':

सितच्छदानामपदिश्य धावतां रुतैरमीषां ग्रथिताः पतत्रिणाम् ।
प्रकुर्वते वारिदरोधनिर्गताः परस्परालापमिवामला दिशः ॥

—किरातार्जुनीयं, 4.30.

(iii) Flights of Geese in lines or V-formation have served as excellent similes. Thus arrows feathered with the brown wing-quills of Eagles resemble Grey Lags on the wing:

रुक्मपुङ्खा व्यराजन्त हंसाः श्रेणीकृता इव—म.भा. 6.137.7.

Warriors (dressed in light grey) marching in single file to battle likened to a flight of the Bar-heads :

शरदभ्रप्रतीकाशा हंसावलिरिवाम्बरे—रामायण, 6.69.36.

A necklace of large white pearls with a deep blue sapphire in the centre, lying on the breast in a V-shape:

कण्ठिका हंसमालेव व्योम्नि दात्यूह[1]मध्यगा—जैन आदिपुराण, 5.6.

Comparing Geese, returning in autumn to a hazardous life in their old haunts, with ascetics, half-way through their spiritual evolution and, therefore, beset with difficulties, the following verse strikes a sympathetic but melancholy note as the dear birds would now often have to face heartless bow-men or the secretly laid trap-nets of prowling fowlers:

पूर्वं त्यक्तैः सरोम्भोभिः हंसा योगं पुनर्ययुः ।
क्लेशैः कुयोगिनोऽशेषैरन्तरायहता इव ॥—विष्णु पुराण, 5.10.9.

All arts and sciences, acquired in her previous births, return to Pārvatī like Geese descending in quick succession on the old familiar sands of the Ganges:

तां हंसमालाः शरदीव गङ्गां महौषधिं नक्तमिवात्मभासः ।
स्थिरोपदेशामुपदेशकाले प्रपेदिरे प्राक्तनजन्मविद्याः ॥—कु.सं. 1.30.

(iv) Kālidāsa compares the clear (supposed to be of a dark colour according to poetic convention) and the slightly turbid (poetically white) waters of the Jamna and the Ganges at their confluence with lines of the Bar-head (कादम्ब) and Swans swimming as it were side by side:

क्वचित्खगानां प्रियमानसानां कादम्बसंसर्गवतीव पंक्तिः ।
—रघुवंश, 13.55.

Again, neck-laces of large वैडूर्य[2] gems (the cat's eye variety of beryl) resting on the breasts of the tipsy ladies of the harem of Rāvaṇa have been compared with a row of कादम्ब Geese:

अपरासां च वैडूर्याः कादम्बा इव पक्षिणः—रामायण, 5.9.49.

It is suggested that the original basis of comparison for the dignified gait of a shapely young lady of noble birth was the gentle gliding movement of the beautiful Mute Swan, the मनोरम राजहंस of धन्वन्तरि carrying its long neck in a graceful curve on the water, but with the shifting of the centre of Indo-Aryan culture from the Punjab to the मध्यदेश the Geese replaced the Swan in this as in other respects. The quotation from the रघुवंश given below would seem to support the idea. The Grey Lag, being a larger and heavier bird than the slimmer and more beautiful Bar-head,

---

1. दात्यूह, Black Ibis.

2. वैडूर्य is बिडालेक्षण in शिशुपालवध 3.45. It is defined as a gem resembling the eye of a cat or civat and having a moveable white line in it.

has naturally a less graceful gait on land than the latter, and the expressions कलहंसगामिनी and मरालगमना should properly describe the rather heavy though dignified step of the "श्रोणीभारभरालसा" or "श्रोणीभारादलसगमना" type of beauty cast in an ampler mould:

घनजघनस्तनभारभरे दरमन्थरचरणविहारम् ।
मुखरितमणिमञ्जीरमुपैहि विधेहि मरालविकारम् ।। —गीतगोविंद, 11.20.2

अलसपदमनोरमं प्रकृत्या जितकलहंसवधूगतिप्रयातम् ।
स्थितमुरुजघनस्थलातिभाराद् उदितपरिश्रमजिह्मितेक्षणं वा ।।
—किरातार्जुनीय, 10.60.

गतैः सहावैः कलहंसविक्रमं कलत्रभारैः पुलिनं नितम्बिभिः ।
—Ibid. 8.29.

Comparisons with the राजहंस (Bar-head on the ground or Swan on the water) on the other hand suggest a slim and elegant figure of the 'सकलतनुसुवेशा'—तन्वी type of womanhood. In the first quotation below Kālidāsa compares the graceful movement of the young इन्दुमती at the स्वयंवर, from one royal suitor to another, with a Swan's on the water and in the second her heavier gait, when she had grown into a stately looking queen with that of a Grey Lag :

समीरणोत्थेव तरङ्गलेखा पद्मान्तरं मानसराजहंसीम् । रघु. 6.26.
कलमन्यभृतासु भाषितं कलहंसीषु मदालसं गतम् । Ibid. 8.29.

Finally, Swans and Geese had an important place in the arts of ancient India, for we find the Goose motif in the printing industry, wood-carving, and metal work. Their soft feathers were used to stuff quilts and cushions for the rich, and their quills for making royal umbrellas or canopies for thrones.

C. DUCKS

Ducks, as a rule, are smaller and much more aquatic than the Geese, and with legs placed less forward they cannot walk as well. Altogether about thirty different species of Duck including four members of the Subfamily, Merginae (characterised by a tapering, narrow and sub-cylindrical bill quite unlike the broad, flat bill of the Ducks proper)

---

1. Cf. वधूदुकूलं कलहंसलक्षणम्—कु० सं० 5.67.
शालकाष्ठेन घटितो हंसमालोपशोभितः ।
* * * *
चरणाग्रे हंसरूपं पुत्रिकास्त्वेकविंशतिः ।
* * * *
हंससिंहासनं नाम सर्वानिष्टविनाशनम् ।। युक्तिकल्पतरु, p. 52.
हंसतूलमयी शय्या—स्कन्द पु० अरुणाचल मा०, उ. खं. 19.9.
छत्रं राज्ञः प्रशस्यते । हंसपक्षैर्विरचितं—अग्नि पु०, 245, 1-2.
Swan-shaped receptacle of gold in नैषधचरित, 6.72.

occur in India but of these only eight are permanent residents and the others are with us for a period of about six months—Sept.-Oct. to April. Of these latter again some seven or eight species are rare and a few are only casual visitors or are found in the extreme Eastern part of Assam. Some species confine themselves exclusively to tanks and lakes while others prefer rivers and lakes. A rough list of these two groups is appended at the end of this section which would help in forming some idea of the sort of birds that are referred to when the stock phrase हंसकारण्डवाकीर्ण is used to describe Lake or River scenery. Some Ducks possess a multi-coloured bright wing-patch, called a 'speculum' which may be rendered as पक्ष-ज्योति in Sanskrit. Ducks as a group go by क्षुद्रहंस or हंसक (Pali चुल्ल हंस) but quite a number of them have also specific names in Sanskrit and these are considered below.

(1) The Comb-Duck, Nukhta, or 'the Black-backed Goose' of Jerdon, is 30 inches long and as large as the Bar-head Goose. It is black above and white below with a white head and neck spotted with black but the most characteristic feature of this Duck is a black, fleshy knob on the base of the bill of the male which becomes greatly swollen during the breeding season and "shrinks up almost to nothing" in winter. This Duck is met within family parties of four to ten birds but flocks of 25 or 30 are also seen. They are strong and rapid fliers, walk and dive well and freely perch on the thicker branches of trees. Their voice is like that of the Goose and when an intruder approaches the nest they utter loud trumpet calls. It occurs in the Punjab but is at present of rare occurrence west of the Sutlej and is found throughout the rest of India except the North and West Sind.

The Hindi name for it is नकटा, i.e. 'having the nose cut off' in reference to the great reduction in size of the comb or knob during the non-breeding season, and the name is just a translation of नासाच्छिन्ना, the first name in the synonymy—"नासाच्छिन्ना तु पूर्णिका"—त्रिकाण्डशेष, Here the second name, पूर्णिका, clearly implies the fuller phase of the comb during the breeding season (cf. अजातककुत् and पूर्णककुत् for a young and full-grown bull respectively). The breeding period lasts from June to September and it is therefore perfectly correct of poet भवभूति to mention the bird by the name of पूर्णिका in his description of a mid-day scene at the height of the summer season:

तीराश्मन्तकशिम्बिचुम्बनमुखा धावन्त्यपःपूर्णिकाः

—मालतीमाधव, 9.7.

चरक calls it नन्दीमुखी and भावप्रकाश leaves no doubt whatever about the name and its owner:

स्थूला कठोरा वृत्ता च यस्याश्चञ्चूपरिस्थिता ।
गुटिका जम्बुसदृशी ज्ञेया नन्दीमुखीति सा ॥

अभि. राजेन्द्र, explaining the Prakrit णंदिमुह, gives a cryptic and apparently nonsensical definition:—

नन्दिमुख—द्व्यङ्गुलप्रमाणशरीरके पक्षिविशेषे

i.e., a particular bird with a body measuring only two fingures. The अर्धमागधी कोश also repeats the above. Evidently an earlier and fuller statement regarding the nature of the bird's bill has been inexpertly condensed by a person who did not know the bird, and the mutilated version has been thoughtlessly repeated by later lexicographers. Now if we bend our middle finger and place its tip on the back of the fore-finger we have quite an accurate shape of the bill of this Duck—the curved middle-finger representing the swollen knob. This is the idea behind the absurd descrption "द्व्यङ्गुलप्रमाणशरीरके".

सुश्रुत has a pair of surgical forceps, named नन्दीमुख यन्त्र, shaped after the bird's bill and consisting of an upper jaw the fore-end of which rests flat upon the straight lower jaw, forming the gripping part of the instrument, while the remaining part of the upper jaw turns up and comes down in a loop (like the shape of the bent middlefinger) near the pin holding the two together. Such a pair of forceps was very useful in extracting or pulling out arrowheads and other missiles from the body of a warrior which were flat or thin at the lower but thicker at the upper and exposed end. The loop of the forceps would accommodate the thicker part and the tip would grip fast the thinner part and help pulling it out.

2. The White-winged Wood Duck (32") has a spotted white head and neck, a white wing-patch and a bluish-grey speculum. It is known as देवहंस (fr. दिव् shining), a purely Sanskrit name, in Assam. The eyes of old birds are blood-red and the name रक्ताक्षहंस[1] corresponding to रत्तच्छो for a kind of हंस in देशीनाममाला should belong to it. The Geese have brown or dark brown eyes and no Ducks have such blood-red eyes except the Goosander which, however, is not looked upon as a हंस as it does not possess the typical flat bill of one and is entirely carnivorous. It therefore goes by the name of मणितुण्ड कारण्डव (see Nos. 24-25 below) The White winged Wood Duck, comparable in size to a Goose, is therefore रक्ताक्षहंस or देवहंस.

3. The Pink-headed Duck (23") is resident throughout North India and is known as लालसिर in Hindi corresponding to रक्तशीर्षक mentioned by चरक in the list of water-birds. It shares this name with some of the Pochards as varieties of क्षुद्र हंस while the Indian Sarus also claims the term as a descriptive epithet to distinguish it from other Cranes (सारस).

---

1. If the name is in contra-distinction to मल्लिकाक्ष for the White-eyed Pochard, it may well be for the Pochard or Red-crested Pochard both having reddish-brown or reddish-yellow eyes and belonging to the same genus. The Cotton Teal also has crimson-red eyes but it is too small a bird in comparison with others.

4. The Cotton Teal (13″) is the smallest Indian Duck which nests in hollows or holes in trees near water. It is गंगरैल or गुरगुर्रा in Hindi, the same as Sansk. घर्घरक for a kind of Duck in M. Williams. These names are clearly after the bird's voice. M. Williams gives also काणूक for a kind of Goose (i.e., हंस in the wider sense) and the name, derived from कण 'a little bit', clearly implies a little or tiny Duck (cf. काण कपोत for the Red Turtle Dove, the smallest of all Doves—Art. 53). The brown upper parts in the male are glossed with metallic green or purple and the names तृणहंस of the महाहंस जातक (534) and हरित हंस of बुद्धघोष on संयुत्त निकाय, 277 would again seem to point to it. तृण means 'green grass' and is also indicative of the minute size of a thing, and हरित is the 'green colour', and both the names are fully descriptive of this tiny 'goslet'. The Cotton Teal, the commonest of Indian Ducks, frequenting even ponds and ditches, is thus the घर्घरक-, काणूक-, तृण-, or हरित-हंस.

5 & 6. The Whistling Teal occurs in two forms, the Lesser (17″) and the Large (20″). The former is resident throughout India and the latter chiefly in Bengal and sparsely in North India. Both frequent swamps, lakes and tanks, and being good walkers, graze on the land as well. They are very tame and confiding birds and can be easily domesticated. The Common Whistling Teal, plentiful all over, is known as सिलही in Hindi and as सरल, शरैल, सरालि, and हरालि in Bengal and Assam. All these names are local variants from Sansk. शरालि or शराली but most Sanskrit lexicons have confused the last two names (शरालि, शराली) with शरारि or शरारी which are specific for the Skimmer, on the strength of the rule, "रलयोरैक्यम्" though the two are quite different. The following verse from ऋतुसंहार with alternative readings of शरारि and शरालि in the second line has been considered in Art. 70:

प्रफुल्लनीलोत्पलशोभितानि शरालिकादम्बविघट्टितानि —4.9.

and as the tank in question is said to be covered with lotuses and the water-weed शैवाल, the probability is in favour of शरालि as the correct reading, for the Whistling Teal would readily take to such a tank but not the Skimmer. The Large whistling Teal bears a good deal of resemblance to the Lesser and naturally shares the name शरालि with it. Brown above and chestnut below, they are the तंबहंसा (ताम्र red) of बुद्धघोष (ibid.), मनोसिला हंसा (मनःशिल mineral red-arsenic) of महाहंस जातक, अलुने (अरुण reddish) of the Fifth Pillar Edict of Aśoka, and रविहंसा (रविसंज्ञक ताम्रम् and therefore the same as तंबहंसा) of वेस्संतर जातक, verse 2107.

7 & 8. The Sheldrake (24″) and the Ruddy Sheldrake or the Brahminy Duck (26") are closely related and though they have been separated under two different genera by S. Baker in *F.B.I.*, other authorities keep them together as sub-species of a common genus. The Indians too have regarded them as closely allied birds. The two are respectively known as 'Safed Surkhab' and 'Surkhab' in Persian or Hindustani, and उपचक्र and चक्र or चक्रवाक in Sanskrit. The names चक्र, चक्राह्व, and चक्रवाक are after the bird's

'a-oung' call resembling the sound of a badly greased wheel mounted on a wooden axle (चक्र इव वाक् शब्दोऽस्य; cf. रथाङ्गतुल्याह्वयन 'calling like a wheel' used for the bird in हरिवंश, 2. 95. 14; see also चक्र in M. Williams). The Ruddy Sheldrake[1] has much of rich orange-brown in its plumage while the Sheldrake has a black head and neck and much white on the lower parts with a chestnut band accross the breast. Resembling as it does the former it has very appropriately been termed उपचक्र (चक्रेण चक्रवाकेन तुल्यः). उपचक्र is also the See-see Partridge resembling the चकोर (Art. 55-C).

The noblest of associations surround the चक्रवाक and practically date back to the beginnings of Indian civilization. The attachment of a pair to each other, their constant company during the day, conversational contact maintained by both at night as they graze or feed apart on land or water, and their re-union at sun-rise have invested them in popular imagination with the halo of the highest conjugal virtues. No wonder, they are sacred birds not only with the Hindus of India but also the Mongolians and the Kalmucks. They are equally sacred to the Chinese through Mongolian or Indian influences. All through Indian history they have afforded a rich theme to the poets, and a high compliment is paid to them in the Ṛgveda where they are regarded like the inseparable Aśvins:

चक्रवाकेव प्रतिवस्तोरुस्रा—2.39.3.

and in the Sūkta dealing with the marriage of सूर्या and चन्द्र the Atharva-veda holds them up as the ideal of conjugal love and fidelity:

इहेमाविन्द्र संनुद चक्रवाकेव दम्पती[2]—14.2.64.

The habit of a pair of these birds of calling to each other at night has been recognised in वाज. संहिता where one is named for the deity presiding over the Echoes:

प्रतिश्रुत्कायै चक्रवाकः—24.32.

The fidelity of a pair to each other, the rich orange-brown of their plumage, and their habit of keeping together during the day fully justify their selection for god वरुण who is the chief upholder of the moral law, wears a golden mantle, and is the lord of the celestial light of day :—

वरुणाय चक्रवाकान्—VS, 24.22.

Sanskrit literature is, of course, full of warm and tender references to them and just a few examples should suffice:

---

1. The simile of चक्रवाक birds for full, round breasts is appropriate only where the latter are closely draped in saffron or orange, and, if exposed, have received a fragrant wash of saffron or the like; cf. कुङ्कुमारुणपयोधरगौर—किरात. 9.23; तन्वंशुकैः कुंकुमरागगौरैः अलङ्क्रियन्ते स्तनमण्डलानि—ऋतुसंहार, 6.4.

2. The 'red Geese' a pair of which is given to a newly married couple in China may well be these birds though the Snow Goose of the Arctic region is commonly known as the Red Goose—See *Ency. of Religion and Ethics*, 1.518.

Herself undergoing severe penance in ice-cold water to secure union with her beloved Śiva, Pārvatī pities quite naturally the चक्रवाक couple separated for the night:

परस्पराक्रन्दिनि चक्रवाकयोः पुरोवियुक्ते मिथुने कृपावती ।

—कुमारसंभव, 5.26

The poetic conventions regarding the painful separation of the चक्रवाक couples and the closing of the lotus flowers at night have been utilized with considerable effect in the following verse:

विश्लेषाकुलचक्रवाकमिथुनैरुत्पीडमाक्रन्दिते
कारुण्यादिव मीलितासु नलिनीष्वस्तं च मित्रे गते ।
शोकेनेव दिगङ्गनाभिरभितः श्यामायमानैर्मुखै-
र्निःश्वासानलधूमवर्तय इवोद्गीर्णास्तमोराजयः ॥

—नलचम्पू, 5.75

See also नेमिनिर्वाण काव्य, 9.11

People living in the रमणक country, somewhere in or beyond the Himalayas, are truly happy since they are free from marital jealousy:

एकैकमनुरक्ताश्च चक्रवाकमिव ध्रुवम् ।
अनामया ह्यशोकाश्च नित्यं मुदितमानसाः ॥

—मत्स्यपुराण, 113.76

The desolate condition of Sītā in the garden of Rāvaṇa:

सहचररहितेव चक्रवाकी जनकसुता कृपणां दशां प्रपन्ना ।

—रामायण, 5.16.30

All Swans, Geese and Ducks pair for life but as the Geese are seen moving in flocks as against the चक्रवाक, always seen in pairs, the मार्कण्डेयपुराण indirectly attributes promiscuity to the Grey Lags in a conversation between a कलहंसी and a चक्रवाकी. The former, seeing a number of pretty women sporting amorously with a prince on a hill overlooking a lake, praises the good luck of the women and the latter criticising their behaviour as unworthy of good women makes the following reply:

कलहंसि ! पतिर्धन्यो मम धन्याहमेव च ।
यस्यैकस्यां चिरं चित्तं यस्याश्चैकत्र संस्थितम् ॥ —62.18

The चक्रवाक, it will be seen, occupies a status of its own in Hindu culture and this explains why it is particularly named in scenic descriptions of river and lake or in the protective clauses of all works on धर्मशास्त्र. It is quite useless as a table bird, nevertheless sportsmen abuse and defame it for its alertness and the timely warning of approaching danger it gives to its cousins. There is not a single eye-witness or other authentic evidence, e.g., examination of stomach contents, in support of the vile charge made against it that it feeds on dead human bodies. If there were any truth in the allegation the observant Indians would not have missed the fact. On the contrary there is evidence that it is mainly a vegetable feeder and does not eat fruit or flesh. The चक्रवाक of the जातक named after it, No. 434, makes the following reply to a Crow who envied the former's golden plumage:

न अण्णवे संति फलानि ढंक ! मंसं कुतो खादितुं चक्कवाके ।
सेवालभकख' म्ह अवाकभोजना, न घासहेतुं पकरोम पापं ॥

What, however, seems probable is that, the bird being held sacred in India, some shrewed Brahman assistant of a sporting Sahib of the old John Company told his boss a deliberate lie to protect the bird and the lie is still persisting.

9. The Mallard or Wild Duck (24″) breeds in the Himalayas as elsewhere in Europe and Asia, is resident in Kashmir, and descends to the plains of North India from the Punjab to Assam and South to Rajasthan and through Madhya Pradesh to Bombay. It prefers large open sheets of water but does not disdain small rivulets, ponds and even ditches. The drake is greyish-white with the head and upper neck glossy emerald-green separated by a white collar from the chestnut breast. It possesses a beautiful violet-purple speculum bordered both above and below with black and white bands. The four central tail feathers are black glossed blue-green and curled up backwards. It is a most handsome Duck and "one of the greatest dandies of the bird-world". It is known in Hindi as नीलसिर नीरुगी and लिलगही (fr. नीलशीर्ष or नीलग्रीवक) after the drake's bright green head and neck. पालकाप्य mentions नीलग्रीवक as a water-bird in हस्त्यायुर्वेद, ch. 13, p. 198 and the name clearly refers to the Mallard.

The name कारण्डव, in a wider sense, serves as a common base with appropriate epithets to denote quite a number of water-birds including the Mallard (Art. 58). The Mallard with a yellow bill is the पीततुण्ड कारण्डव; see पीततुण्ड in Apte and शब्दकल्पद्रुम[1]. As the most beautiful Duck it is the बन्धुर (Goose-like or beautiful) कारण्डव and मञ्जुप्लव (charming Duck or water-bird) of धन्वन्तरि:

अथ बन्धुरः कारण्डवः प्लवो मञ्जुः

कारण्डव in the following example is the Mallard as an ornamental bird on a garden-tank:

---

1. The synonymy—"चञ्चुसूचिस्तु सुगृहः पीततुण्डः" with an alternative reading of पीतमुण्ड for पीततुण्ड in त्रिकाण्डशेष has been misunderstood by the commentators in the सारार्थचन्द्रिका and नामचन्द्रिका editions (Bombay) and as पीततुण्ड is a kind of Duck or कारण्डव the first two names, which really belong to the Weaver Bird, have been incorrectly appropriated to the कारण्डव. M. Williams also renders all the three incorrectly but as 'Sylvia sutoria', the Tailor Bird, though his rendering of पीतमुण्ड as the Weaver Bird (Loxia philippensis) is correct. The entire synonymy with the correct reading of पीतमुण्ड refers exclusively to the Weaver Bird—Art. 22.

तप्तं वारि विहाय तीरनलिनीं कारण्डवः सेवते ।

—विक्रमोर्वशीय, 2.23.

The period of courtship in the Mallard is a prolonged one and it pairs very early in the year. During courtship a female may be frequently seen at a considerable height pursued by one or more drakes and performing many coy evolutions, flying in circles with extreme rapidity and keeping up the chase for a considerable time (see Birds of Great Britain and Ireland, Naturalists' Library, Ornithology, Vol. XIV, Part IV, Natatores, under 'Common Wild Duck, the Mallard'). The ancients had certainly observed the behaviour of the bird at its breeding haunts on the lakes in Kashmir and the Himalayas and they very appropriately named it कामिक कारण्डव ('the amorous Duck'—शब्दकल्पद्रुम and M. Will.; cf. also कामी as an epithet for the Ruddy Sheldrake, the Indian Sarus and the House Sparrow). The drakes of a few other species also have characteristic ways of courting the female but they do not breed within Indian limits. The playful circling flight and gaggling high up in the air of the Geese, Mallards, Ruddy Sheldrakes, etc., is called नादावर्त्त :—

हंसकारण्डवचक्रवाकादीनां व्योम्नि क्रीडतामावर्त्तो नादावर्त्त ।

—अभि. राजेन्द्र under 'आवट्ट'

10. The Spot-bill or Grey Duck (24″) may be readily distinguished by the orange-yellow of the terminal third of its bill and two red spots, one on each side of the forehead, at the base of the bill. It is गुगरल in Hindi, बरमुघी हंस (prob. a phonetic error for वरमुखी हंस fr. वर-कुङ्कुम, saffron, and मुख face, in reference to the partly orange-yellow bill and the red spots) in Assam, and हुंघुर (fr. हिङ्गुल vermillion?) in Sind. The Hindi name points to Sansk. घर्घरक for a Duck so that both the Cotton Teal and this Duck share it, while the name वरमुखी हंस (cf. नन्दीमुखी) though lost to the lexicons has been preserved by the people of Assam. It is one of the resident and common Duck of India.

11. The Gadwall (20″) is a brown Duck of medium size. "In India the Gadwall is perhaps the most numerous of our non-diving Ducks, occurring in immense flocks from Sind to Assam...." (S. Baker). It is known in Hindi as मैल which is the same as (Prakrit मइल for dirty) Sansk. मलिन for a kind of हंस in हिन्दी शब्दसागर. The निघण्टुरत्नाकर also has मलिन for a कलहंस which, however, is a little incorrect as no other lexicon supports it. The Gadwall, being of a dark colour (मलिनवर्ण), is the मलिनहंस proper.

12. The Wigeon (19″) is a Duck of shallow swamps and marshes and "loves feeding in a few inches of water or in water where the weeds come close to the top" and they also graze on young crops, and instead of resting during the day like other Ducks it continues to feed "in jheels throughout the day near the edges where they remain among reeds and vegetation" (S. Baker). This Duck is known as पियासन in Hindi, fr. Sansk.

प्रियाशन[1] (fond of eating) which however is not found in any Sanskrit lexicon as a bird-name, but there is reason to believe that प्रियाशन हंस must have been its Sanskrit name, for it is so very apt.

13. The Common Teal (15″) is easily identified from the male's painted face and chestnut-red head and upper neck. A broad shining green band runs through the eye and is bordered both above and below by a white edging. It is this colour pattern on the face contrasting with the surrounding chestnut which accounts for its Sanskrit name of रोहिणी defined as लोहिता तु या रोहिणी स्यात्—कल्पद्रु.; cf. लोहित, रोहित for a form of incomplete rainbow; रोहिणिका, a woman with face red coloured with pigments. Its name लोहिया केर्रा in Hindi corresponds to लोहिता of the lexicon, while रोहिणीक as a water-bird in पालकाप्य, ch.13, is this beautiful Duck.

Hindi पतारी for Ducks like this and the Blue-winged Teal with a conspicuous white eye-brow against a pink-brown head is probably derived from Sansk. पत्राली for 'face-decoration with various scented pigments'.

14. The principal feature of the graceful Pintail Duck (22″) are its long, pointed pin-like central tail feathers which project at an angle well beyond the tail. It is known as सींकपर (शङ्कुपत्र) in Hindi; शलांच (शल्यहंस, same as शङ्कु हंस below) in Bengali; and द्रिगुच्छ (दीर्घपुच्छ) in Cutch. Its proper Sanskrit name is शङ्कु हंस which occurs with स्यूति (a needle?) in वैजयन्ती in a mixed list of names for हंस. The occurrence of this Duck on the Himalayan lakes is mentioned in the शिवपुराण :—

शोभितं चक्रवाकाद्यैः कादम्बैर्हंसशङ्कुभिः—2.22.59.

"For the table they (Pintails) are among the best of all the Duck" and they were certainly eaten in India. The medical treatise, भावप्रकाश, prohibits the शङ्कु हंस to a patient suffering from piles in the chapter, अर्शोऽधिकार.

15. The Garganey or Blue-winged Teal is a brown and black Duck streaked white in parts, with blue and grey on the wings and a broad white supercilium. It is common all over India from September onwards and visits large swamps, village tanks and even ponds. Being a nightfeeder it rests by day and causes a good deal of damage to winter rice and wheat crops. One of the peculiarities of its flight noticed by Stuart Baker is that like the White-eyed Pochard, the Scaup and the Goosander it rises obliquely from the water.

The वैजयन्ती describes हंस साचि as a क्षुद्र हंस or Duck, and the descriptive epithet साचि in the name ("तिर्यगर्थे साचिः"—अमर, going or moving side-ways) would seem to refer to its oblique flight. The word has perhaps some such significance in the following passage :

.....साचीव वै वयः पक्षौ कृत्वा पतीय; पतति

—पञ्चविंशब्राह्मण, 5.1.12.

---

1. This name is on a par with मुहुर्भुज (constantly eating) for a horse who, not being a ruminant, need not stop like cattle to chew the cud.

Sāyaṇa explains the above as follows :

> वयः पक्षी साचीव वै तिर्यगिव पक्षौ कृत्वा पतीयः पतति, अतिशयेन पतनं करोति........

In a साचि or oblique flight the bird's wings must assume a different attitude from that in a straight and forward flight. Now the question is which of the above four birds is the साचि हंस. The Scaup is a very rare visitor to India and must be left out of account. The Goosander, being entirely carnivorous and having a thin, toothed and pointed bill designed for catching fish, is not regarded as a हंस but a special kind of कारण्डव (See Nos.24-25 below). मनु, 5.13 almost certainly includes it with birds like the Cormorant and Darter in the comprehensive expression— "निमज्जतश्च मत्स्यादान्"—'all birds that catch fish by diving'. That leaves us with the White-eyed Pochard and the Garganey. The former is the मल्लिकाक्ष हंस, which is a very old name since it occurs as an alternative reading, though incorrect, for मल्लिकाख्य in अमर, वैजयन्ती, itself, and other lexicons. What is more, वैजयन्ती does not identify हंससाचिः with it. Further, the Pochard "gets off (the water) badly, fluttering about and rising very obliquely" but the Garganey "rises quicker off the water, getting up obliquely" and is really a fast flier. This last, therefore, seems to answer best the description of a fast साचि flight given by Sāyaṇa. The only mention of the हंससाचिः is to be found in the तैत्तिरीय संहिता :

> आदित्ये हंससाचिः—5.5.20.

where अदिति is the Sky-goddess and the Garganey or the Blue winged Teal having a fast flight and some blue on the wings would seem to have commended itself to the author of the Saṃhitā as a bird having some esoteric connection with the sky.

16. The Shoveller (20″) is a beautiful Duck, the male having a shining dark-green head and neck. It occurs singly or in small parties on dirty ditches, village ponds and weedy jheels. The peculiarly spatulate or shovel-like bill, very much broader towards the tip than at the base, is specific. It is known as खंतियाहंस in Hindi and खातहंस in Sanskrit from its habit of frequenting ditches and pools (खात):—

> दिदृक्षुरन्तः सरसीमलङ्ध्यं यत्खातहंसः समुदीक्ष्य वप्रम् ।
> सस्मार नूनं दृढकौञ्चकुञ्ज–भागच्छिदो भार्गवमार्गणस्य ॥
>
> —जानकीहरण, 1.5.

The reference to क्रौञ्चरन्ध्र has misled the annotator to translate खातहंस as a Swan but the poet certainly knew better than to place the nobler Swan or Goose in a ditch or moat. He knew not only the habits of the Shoveller but also the fact that, being one of our winter visitors, it came accross the Himalayas and therefore through the traditional हंसद्वार and would return home the same way. It is this memory of the familiar passage which the poet has attributed to the bird and made it think of the arrow of Parashuram to cut a hole through the high city-wall.

Newton describes in his *Dictionary of Birds* the peculiar habit of the Shoveller, a surface-feeder, "as swinging round in circles with its bill in the water above the spot where Pochards are diving and feeding beneath, and sifting out the substances that float up when disturbed by the operation of the diving Ducks." This peculiar habit and the shape of its bill would justify the Sanskrit name of खजाक (खज् मन्थे, churning) for 'a kind of bird' as specific for it:

खजाकः स्यात्पुंसि दध्नो विकारे विहगान्तरे

—पेरुसूरि, उणादि, 4. 68 & शब्दकल्पद्रुम

खजाक also means 'a ladle or spoon' so that the Duck answers to the name in both senses, the 'churning rod' typifies its feeding habit and the 'spoon' its bill broad at the tip. Even at other times it feeds by moving its bill in the water from side to side like the Spoon-bill Stork to which also the name would apply, and the two would be खजाक हंस and खजाक बक respectively (see Art. 81). The Bengali name खंतामुखी (खंता a spade; पंतामुखी in *F.B.I* seems to be an error) for the Duck is the same as खजाक.

17. The Marbled Teal (18.5″) is a resident Duck wherever found but is most common in Sind and less so in the Punjab, Gujarat, and Uttar Pradesh. It seldom shows itself in open water and keeps to and feeds in reeds, swampy vegetation, lily-beds, etc. It is known in Sind as छह and is obviously the क्षयि हंस defined by वैजयन्ती as a bird of the lily-beds: "क्षयिस्तु कुवलायिकः". उणादि भोजीयानि, Pt. 2 gives this name but M. Williams has perhaps omitted it as a corrupt reading. The name is from क्षि–2, to live in an undisturbed or secret place (M.W.).

18 & 19. The Nyrocinae subfamily of Ducks, which includes the Pochards, consists of diving Ducks many of which feed on deep-water plants, roots, etc. and are often known as बुडार (divers) in Hindi. Sansk. मज्जिका (fr. मज्-मस्ज् to dive or sink under water), perhaps rendered incorrectly as the 'female Sarus' (which never dives) by M. Williams, should be a common name for these diving Ducks just as मद्गु, from the same root, denotes the Darter; cf. also the phrase "निमज्जतश्च मत्स्याद" in मनु, 5.13 referring to birds like the Cormorants, Darter, Goosanders, etc. all of which dive for their fish-food. These Ducks as a class are also the पद्मकन्दाद हंस (lily-root eaters) of कल्पद्रुकोश.

The Red-crested Pochard with a red bill (21″) is लालचोंच (रक्तचञ्चु) and लालसिर or रंगपुड़िया (रक्तशीर्ष, रक्तमूर्द्धन्) while the Pochard or Dun-bird with a blackish bill (18″) is simply लालसिर in Hindi and both would therefore share the name of रक्तशीर्षक with the Pink-headed Duck in Sanskrit with probably रक्तचञ्चु as an additional epithet for the former, the Red-crested Pochard. The Dun-bird may also be रक्तमूर्द्धन्.

20 & 21. The White-eyed Pochard (16″) and the Eastern White Eye (18″) are closely allied forms and are the मल्लिकाक्ष हंस (white-eyed) of literature:

एतस्मिन्मदकलमल्लिकाक्षपक्षव्याधूतस्फुरदुरुदण्डपुण्डरीका:
—मालतीमाधव, 9.14; उत्तररामचरित, 1·31.

It is one of the water-birds in सुश्रुत. The call-note of this Pochard is a "koor-ker-ker", uttered both when feeding in a lake and when rising from the water. This agrees very well with the description of the bird as मदकल. The alternative reading of मल्लिकाख्य (the Mute Swan) is incorrect as the epithet is inapplicable to it, for it is a silent bird and utters its soft low call chiefly when pairing (Sanders). Moreover the Swan on the Pampa lake placed in the extreme south of India in उत्तररामचरित is an impossibility. मल्लिकाक्ष is, therefore, the correct reading and it means the White-eyed Pochard. The last paragraph of the third काण्ड of चम्पूरामायण also places the मल्लिकाक्ष on the Pampa lake.

22. The Tufted Pochard (17″) has a black head and wears a long pendant occipital crest glossed with purple. It goes by the name of मालक in Nepal and बम्हनियां हंस (fr. ब्राह्मण) in Assam. मालिक (v.l. मालक, one wearing a wreath) is a kind of bird in मेदिनी and evidently refers to this Duck.[1]

The Assamese name clearly refers to the bird's long crest resembling a Brahman's शिखा or top-knot which is often allowed to hang behind the head. पालकाप्य has ब्रह्मपुत्र as a water-bird in हस्त्यायुर्वेद. The शिखा of a Brahman is also known as ब्रह्मपुत्री ("ब्रह्मपुत्री शिखायाम्"—शब्दार्थचिन्तामणि) and sage Nārada, famous for his शिखा is also ब्रह्मपुत्र. The ब्रह्मपुत्र of पालकाप्य is therefore no other than the Tufted Pochard which is found from Sind to Assam.

23. The Smew and the Goosanders are members of the subfamily Merginae consisting of fish-eating Ducks of great diving powers. Their legs are placed far back on the body which makes it very difficult for them to walk. The bill is armed with hard tooth-like serrations which enable the birds to catch and hold fish under water. The male Smew (17″) is a beautiful black and white bird with a black patch on either side of the white head and face and the underparts pure white. It often goes under the name of the White Nun in England. It is very common in Sind and fairly so in North India. In Sind it is called जाली (a basket) and निहन्नी (Skt. निधानी a receptacle) in the Uttar Pradesh. Both the names are analogous to Skt. करण्ड for 'a basket' and point to

1. मालिका for a kind of bird in M. Williams would seem to be a mistake as the term means an open semi-circular loop with a horizontal bar at the base serving as a perch for a pet bird tied to it with a ring (on the bird's leg) and chain—"पक्षिमल्ले च मालिका"—विश्व and हेमचन्द्र. पक्षिमल्ल means 'a thing i.e. a cage that holds a bird'.

कारण्डव being the bird's Sanskrit name. Its thin and dark slaty-coloured bill accounts for the name काक-तुण्डक (crow-billed) in चरक where the name has been correctly rendered as श्वेतकारण्डव by चक्रदत्त, कृष्णकारण्डव being the Coot. The Smew is thus the श्वेत- or काकतुण्डक-कारण्डव. It may be noted that the members of this group are not regarded as varieties of हंसक or Duck, probably because they are fish eaters.

24 & 25. The Goosander and the Eastern Goosander (25″ & 22″ respectively) are allied birds. The first is a winter visitor from Northern Europe and Asia, to Sind and the second breeds in the Himalayas and visits North India in winter. Both are black above and white below, the white underparts being suffused with a beautiful rosy-salmon colour. The bill and legs are red in both, and from the colour of the bill they are the मणितुण्डक (कारण्डव) of चरक ; cf. मणितारक for the Sarus with red eyes. Both are voracious fish-eaters: "The gorging ended, the birds sit on some sand-bank so full that when disturbed they have to disgorge before moving" (S. Baker), and they probably owe their name कारण्ड or कारण्डव to this habit of gorging themselves to the neck and thus resembling, so to say, a मत्स्य करण्ड or fish-basket.

The word भसत् means कारण्डव or a sort of Duck, and the sun according to शब्दकल्पद्रुम and M. Williams. Evidently it is meant as a descriptive epithet or adnoun for कारण्डव as a particular bird, viz., the Goosander. This is supported by a striking simile in the Rāmāyaṇa where the clear blue sky is pictured as a large placid lake looking beautiful with lilies and birds dotted here and there. The moon (presumably less than full and therefore above the horizon at sun-rise or sun-set, and not very bright either) is a white lily, the sun, a Goosander, the constellations of Aquila and Cancer, the Bar-head Geese, the star Arcturus, a Swan, the Gemini constellation, a whale; the Mars, an alligator; the mythological Airāvata elephant, a large island; and stray clouds, the Śaivāla weed in the heavenly lake:—

सचन्द्रकुमुदं रम्यं सार्ककारण्डवं शुभम् ।
तिष्यश्रवणकादम्बमभ्रशैवालशाद्वलम् ॥ —5.57.2-4.

The कारण्डव of this picture can only be the Goosander with white underparts suffused with pink, red bill and red legs, described elsewhere as the 'golden' कारण्डव. No other member of the कारण्डव group would be appropriate. We thus have two names for the Goosanders, मणितुण्डक- and भसत्-कारण्डव.[1]

Similarly epithet तरत् for a कारण्डव in विश्वप्रकाश refers to these birds after their quick movements on water when fishing or sporting as described

---

1. The Goosanders can be भसत् कारण्डव in a different sense as well if the term भसत् is derived from root भस् to chew with the jaws or teeth as the bills of these birds are particularly well armed with toothed serrations to enable them to catch fish. The name would then mean the 'gorging or glutton Duck' but the quotation from the Rāmāyaṇa seems to negative this suggestion.

by S. Baker: "They seem to be equally at home in the deep slowly-moving pools or in the wildest torrents and it is a most beautiful sight to see a party of these birds playing in either kind of water." They fish forming a wide semi-ring and although "the birds dash hither and thither, both on and under water, with almost incredible speed, the formation is never broken...". Exactly such a scene is described as 'a beautiful dance' of a party of 'golden कारण्डव birds' upon a certain river:

काञ्चनमयाङ्गविलसत्कारण्डवषण्डताण्डवमनोज्ञाम्

—श्रीललितास्तवरत्नम्, 84; काव्यमाला, Pt. 10.

काञ्चनमयाङ्ग refers to their vermilion bill and feet.

Finally, the following two lists of Ducks showing their preference for (i) tanks and lakes, or (ii) rivers and lakes should help a student of Sanskrit literature in forming a rough idea of the sort of birds a poet has in mind when using the phrase, हंसकारण्डवाकीर्ण, to describe a lake, tank or river. It must, however, be remembered that हंस in this phrase includes the Geese and Ducks, and कारण्डव, the Mallard, the Smew, the Goosander and the Coot.

85

GREBES

Grebes constitute a group of water-birds easily distinguished from others by their being practically tailless and the peculiar structure of their feet, which are placed far behind and have toes furnished with broad lobes and flat blunt nails.

1. The Little Grebe or Dab-chick is common on tanks and reedy margins of slower rivers. It is a small bird about 9 inches long, and feeds on insects, vegetable matter and small fish for which last it is an expert diver. It is mentioned in वसन्तराज as वञ्जुल (पाणंतरा in Rajasthan corresponding to Hindi पनतिरी or पनडुब्बी) as a bird of omen in ch. 4, 21. It has a curious tittering note, a shrill rippling whinny audible for some distance, and its alarm note is a sharp 'tui, tui'. As the bird is common on all way-side tanks and even ponds of some size its inclusion in the list of birds of augury is easily understood. It is mentioned twice in the Rāmāyaṇa both as a river and tank bird:

सरितं वापि सम्प्राप्ता मीनवञ्जुलसेविताम् ।[1]
कारण्डैः सारसैर्हंसैर्वञ्जुलैर्जलकुक्कुटैः ।[2]

Poet भवभूति's appreciation of the soft notes is to be seen in the following verse:

आमञ्जुवञ्जुलरुतानि च तान्यमूनि ।
नीरन्ध्रनीलनिचुलानि सरित्तटानि ।।—उत्तररामचरित.[3]

Scribes who knew वञ्जुल merely as a kind of reed or cane and could not therefore make sense of the words "वञ्जुलरुतानि" introduced their own emendations like "वञ्जुललतानि" or "मञ्जुललतानि" for them, forgetting for the moment that the poet would not refer twice to vegetation on the river bank in the same verse. On the other hand the dense reedy growth is indeed the place for the वञ्जुल birds who actually derive their name from the वञ्जुल reeds they live in.

---

1. III.61.16.
2. IV.13.8.
3. 2.23.

2. The Black-necked Grebe is a larger bird, about 12 inches long, found in India as a winter visitor. The place nearest to India where it breeds is Baluchistan. In the breeding plumage the birds have a line of long, silky, hair like feathers of a golden colour commencing behind the eye and running down the neck, and the synonyms "वञ्जुलकः कर्णवालखगे" in शब्दार्थचिन्तामणि would seem to belong to it. The name or epithet कर्णवाल is clearly indicative of the tufts of hair-like feathers growing from behind the eye which is the region of the ear in a bird. The Black-necked Grebe is also known as the Eared Grebe and is कर्णवाल वञ्जुल in Sanskrit. Its call note is a soft 'pee-ep' and alarm note is a sharp 'whit, whit'.

The largest bird of the group occurring in India is the Great Crested Grebe (18″ to 22″). It is distinguished by a short bifid black crest and a ruff of long black feathers round the neck and falling over the breast. It breeds in the Himalayas, occasionally in Kashmir and locally in North India. It is the कण्ठपाल वञ्जुल of the equation in वैजयन्ती "कण्ठपालस्तु वञ्जुलः" the epithet कण्ठपाल referring to the protective sort of ruff round the neck.

The call note of this Grebe is a harsh 'krek, krek' as against the softer notes of the Little Grebe and it is more probably the वञ्जुल of augury in बृहत्संहिता[1] and वसंतराज.[2] It is defined in the former as खदिरचञ्चु (having a brown-bill) which agrees with the dark brown bill of this bird as againt the black bill of the other Grebes. It has been regarded as a bird of good omen under the name of वञ्चुलक (v.l. वञ्जुलक) in the Rāmāyaṇa:[3]

> एष वञ्चुलको नाम पक्षी परमदारुणः ।
> आवयोर्विजयं युद्धे शंसन्निव विनर्दति ।।

The तिलक व्याख्या (NS. Press Edn.) renders वञ्चुलक as कण्ठवाल bird, clearly the same as कण्ठपाल. For वञ्जुलक as a possible name for the diver see the next Article.

The Great Crested Grebe "carries the long neck upright and from a distance looks somewhat like a cygnet" (Dewar). This fact coupled with its black crest is responsible for the name शिवहंस by which it is known in Assam.

1. 87.5.
2. 4.21.
3. 3.69.23.

86

DIVERS

The Divers seem to stand midway between the Auks, Puffins, etc., on the one hand and the Grebes on the other. Like the Grebes their legs are placed far back on the body, and like them again they are unable to walk more than a few paces on the ground. They have great powers of submergence and dive and swim under water in pursuit of their fish-food just as the Grebes do. They have been separated from the latter on certain anatomical grounds including their fully webbed feet like the ducks.

The Black-throated Diver, the only one of the family, was once found in the Ambala district in the year 1922. It is much bigger than the largest Grebe and its call is a loud prolonged wail, audible at an immense distance.

The Divers are essentially sea-birds but they resort to fresh water for breeding purposes. Even otherwise they "are not unfrequently found far from the sea, being either driven inland by stress of weather, or exhausted in their migrations."[1] It is, therefore, quite likely that, though the bird is a very rare winter visitor to India at the present time, in the different conditions obtaining in the country nearly two thousand years ago, the bird visited India with some regularity and in larger numbers. If so, it would certainly be regarded as a larger variety of the Grebe which it so closely resembles in habits, and the name वञ्चुलक may well refer to it. The description of वञ्चुलक with reference to its loud call, as परमदारुण would seem to support this suggestion. The voice of the Great Crested Grebe, identified with वञ्चुलक in the preceding article (q.v.) is no doubt a harsh 'krek, krek' but it is doubtful how far the bird may be characterised as परमदारुण. Moreover, the different spelling also may imply a distinction between the Grebe (वञ्जुलक) and Diver (वञ्चुलक).

1. *Ency. Brit.*, 11th edition.

Index

D

K

L

Q

R

S

Y

Sanskrit-Pali-Prakrit Index with Scientific Names, English and French Equivalents

by André Couture and Elfrun Linke

The following Index was compiled using two earlier reference lists, those of Mrs. E. Linke (1997) and Prof. Dr. André Couture (1998). The present revision includes the Pāli [P] and Prākrit [Pkt] names as well as those Sanskrit [Skt] terms mentioned by K. N. Dave. In addition to the English names used by Dave, which are usually the same as those found in the well-known guides of Salim Ali (other colloquial names are placed in parentheses), we thought it useful to include those changes in nomenclature which appear in the authoritative guide to the birds of India and related countries, recently published by R. Grimmett, C. Inskipp, and T. Inskipp. The differences in the Scientific and English names occuring in this book are the result of the revision of the taxonomy of the birds of the world published by Sibley and Monroe (1990). To facilitate the consultation of this guide, we chose to place the new names in brackets. The French names, that follow the English names [Fr., if unclear], are drawn from the authoritative reference published by the *Commission internationale des noms français des oiseaux* in 1993. Words preceded by an asterisk (*) were not found in any dictionary. This Index is intended to facilitate the use of Dave's book. It does not indicate, except in a few cases, the status of these identifications which range from being practically certain to being no more than hypothetical.

Ali, S. *The Book of Indian Birds*. Bombay, [1]1941; Twelfth Revised and Enlarged Centenary Edition, Oxford University Press, 1996.

Commission internationale des noms français des oiseaux, *Noms français des oiseaux du monde avec les équivalents latins et anglais*, Sainte-Foy (Québec), Éditions MultiMondes; Bayonne (France), Éditions Chabaud, 1993.

Couture, A. "*Birds in Sanskrit Literature* de K. N. Dave : un index sanskrit-latin-anglais-français", *Bulletin d'études indiennes*, n° 16 (1998), p. 179-229.

Grimmett, R., Inskipp, C., and Inskipp, T. *A Guide to the Birds of India, Pakistan, Nepal, Bangladesh, Bhutan, Sri Lanka and the Maldives*, Princeton (N.J.), Princeton University Press, 1999.

Inskipp, T., Lindsey, N., Duckworth, W., *An Annotated Checklist of the Birds of the Oriental Region*, Oriental Bird Club, Sandy, 1996.

Kapadia, H.R., "The Jaina Records about Birds", *Annals of the Bhandarkar Oriental Research Institute* 43 (1962), p. 59-107; 45 (1964), p. 105-141.

Linke, E. "Birds in Sanskrit Literature : Sanskrit-English Index", *Annals of the Bhandarkar Oriental Research Institute*, Vol. LXXVIII (1997), p. 121-141.

Sibley, C. G., Monroe, B. L. Jr, *Distribution and Taxonomy of Birds of the World*, 1990.

a

agni-kaṇṭha, Mirafra javanica [M. cantillans], Singing Bushlark, Alouette de Java, 110

aṅga-hetuka (P), Phaenicophaeus tristis, [Large] Green-billed Malkoha, Malkoha triste; "the two Sirkeer Cuckoos, the Punjab Sirkeer and the Bengal Sirkeer Cuckoo" (ref. unclear, the only known Sirkeer is : Phaenicophaeus leschenaultii,

kurarī (feminine form of *kurara*, used for birds smaller than Gulls), any Laridae of the Sternini tribe (Tern / Sterne), 341-342, 347-348; also Numenius arquata, [Eurasian] Curlew, Courlis cendré, 185, 341-342, 348, 364-366

ku-ravaka, Dendrocitta vagabunda, Indian Treepie [Rufous T.], Témia vagabonde; Dendrocitta formosae, Himal-ayan Treepie [Grey T.], Témia de Swinhoe, 12, 13

**kurukuñcitā*, idem, 12

kuru-bāhu, Pomatorhinus ruficollis, Rufous-necked Scimitar Babbler [Streak-breasted S. B.], Pomatorhin à col roux; Pomatorhinus horsfieldii, Slaty-headed Scimitar Babbler [Indian S. B.], Pomatorhin de Horsfield, 28

kuru-bāhuka, esp. Garrulax ruficollis, Rufous-necked Laughingthrush, Garrulaxe à col roux, 28; Turdoides caudatus, Common Babbler, Cratérope indien; Tordoides striatus, Jungle Babbler, Cratérope de brousse, 28, 29

**kula-vārī*, small Rails or Crakes (Fr. Râles), esp. Gallirallus striatus, Blue-breasted Banded Rail [Slaty-breasted R.], Râle strié; Rallina eurizonoides, Banded Crake [Slaty-legged C.], Râle de forêt, 292

kulāla, large hooting Strigidae (Owl / Hibou, Chouette), 138; certain Wood Owls, esp. Strix leptogrammica, Brown Wood Owl, Chouette leptogramme, 180

kulāla-kukkuṭa, Centropus sinensis, [Greater] Coucal, Grand Coucal, 137, 138, 150; Gallus gallus, Red Junglefowl (Common or Wild Cock), Coq bankiva, 138

kulāla-kukkubha, Centropus sinensis, [Greater] Coucal, Grand Coucal, 138

kulālī śakunikā, Merops orientalis, (Small) Green (or Common Indian) Bee-eater, Guêpier d'Orient, 150

ku-liṅga, Dicrurus adsimilis (macrocercus), (Common) Black Drongo (or Kingcrow), Drongo brillant, 63; various small birds moving about on the ground in search of food (Sparrow, Finch, Bunting / Moineau, Roselin, Bruant), 92, 95; Grus grus, Common Crane, Grue cendrée, 315

ku-liṅgaka, Turdus boulboul, Grey-winged Blackbird, Merle à ailes grises; Copsychus saularis, [Oriental] Magpie Robin, Shama dayal, 50, 93; Passer domesticus, House Sparrow, Moineau domestique, and related species, 167; certain Accipitridae of the genus Accipiter, including Accipiter badius, Shikra, Épervier shikra, 235-236

ku-liṅgakā, Accipiter nisus, [Eurasian] Sparrowhawk, Épervier d'Europe, 199

kulīkā, Saroglossa spiloptera, Spotted-winged Stare [Starling], Étourneau à ailes tachetées, 83

kuvaya, Tyto alba, Barn (White, Screech) Owl, Effraie des clochers, 173

kuvi, idem, 173

kuṣītaka, Recurvirostra avosetta, [Pied] Avocet, Avocette élégante, 361

**kūnja* (read : *kunca* or *konca*; Pkt), Grus virgo, Demoiselle Crane, Grue demoiselle, 320

kūṭa-pakṣī, any of the Corvidae, tribe Corvini, genera Cissa, Urocissa and Pica (Magpie / Pie, Pirolle), 12

kūṇi, female of the Turnicidae (Bustard Quail [Buttonquail] / Turnix), 291

kṛkarāṭa, any of the Alaudidae, genus Mirafra (Bushlark / Alouette), as distinct from Mirafra javanica [M. cantillans], Singing Bushlark, Alouette de Java, 110, cf. *krakarāṭa*

kṛkala, cf. *krakara*; refers to Syrrhaptes tibetanus, Tibetan Sandgrouse, Syrrhapte du Tibet , 266, 267

kṛkalāsaka, Circus pygargus, Montagu's Harrier, Busard cendré, 247

kṛkavāku, Gallus gallus, Red Junglefowl, Coq bankiva, 273

kṛkālikā, Athene brama, Spotted Owlet, Chevêche brame, 177

kṛśa, any of the Apodidae (Swift / Martinet), 99, 165

kṛśa-kaṇṭha (*sāraṅga*), Tetrax tetrax, Little Bustard, Outarde canepetière, 325, 328

kṛśa-kūṭa, any of the Corvidae, tribe Corvini, genus Dendrocitta (Treepie / Témia), 12, 13, 20

kṛṣi-dviṣṭa, 96, cf. *anna-dūṣaka*

kṛṣṇa-kāka, Corvus macrorhynchos, Jungle Crow [Large-billed C.], Corneille à gros bec, 1, 3, 7; Corvus corone, Carrion Crow, Corneille noire and/or Corvus macrorhynchos, Jungle Crow [Large-billed C.], Corneille à gros bec, 1, 6, 7, 20

kṛṣṇa-grīva, Copsychus saularis, [Oriental] Magpie Robin, Shama dayal; Copsychus malabaricus, [White-rumped] Shama, Shama à croupion blanc, 94; Ephippiorhynchus asiaticus, Black-necked Stork, Jabiru d'Asie, 391

kṛṣṇa-cūḍa, Pycnonotus cafer, Red-vented Bulbul, Bulbul à ventre rouge, 35

kvayi, Athene brama, Spotted Owlet, Chevêche brame, 124; Tyto alba, Barn (Screech) Owl, Effraie des clochers, 124, 173

kṣatraka, Ceryle rudis, Pied Kingfisher, Martin-pêcheur pie [or Megaceryle lugubris, Greater Pied Kingfisher [Crested K.], Martin-pêcheur tacheté, which is the related species above 800 m in the Himalayas, 155

kṣayi-haṃsa, Marmaronetta angustirostris, Marbled Teal, Marmaronette marbrée, 457

kṣipra-śyena, Falco peregrinus, Peregrine Falcon, Faucon pèlerin, 210, 222, 225

kṣudra-gīdhrī, Milvus migrans, Common Pariah Kite [Black K.], Milan noir, 189, 245

kṣudra-valguli, cf. *khuddaka-valguli*

kṣudra-haṃsa, small and medium-sized Anatidae (Duck / Canard), 422

kṣudrolūka, the smaller Strigidae (Owlet / Chevêche, Chevêchette), 176

kṣemaṅkarī, Haliastur indus, Brahmany Kite, Milan sacré, 244

kṣviṅka, Sarcogyps calvus, Black (or King) Vulture [Red-headed V.], Vautour royal, 190, 196

kh

kha-kāminī, Haliastur indus, Brahmany Kite, Milan sacré, 243, 244

khajāka, Anas clypeata, Shoveller [Northern Shoveler], Canard souchet, 457

khañja-kheṭa, any of the Passeridae, subfamily Motacillinae, genus Motacilla (Wagtail / Bergeronnette), 102

khañja-khela, Motacilla alba, Pied Wagtail [White W.], Bergeronnette grise, 106

khañjana, any of the Passeridae, subfamily Motacillinae, genus Motacilla (Wagtail / Bergeronnette), 102; white Wagtails, esp. Motacilla alba, Pied Wagtail [White W.], Bergeronnette grise (and subspecies), 49, 52, 102ff.

khañjanaka, white Wagtails, esp. Motacilla alba, Pied Wagtail [White W.], Bergeronnette grise (and subspecies), 102

khañjanikā, Charadrius dubius, Little Ringed Plover, Pluvier petit-gravelot, 334, 357

khañjarī, Phoenicurus ochruros, Black Redstart, Rougequeue noir, 49

khañjarīṭa, *khañjarīṭaka*, yellow Wagtails : Motacilla flava, Yellow Wagtail, Bergeronnette printanière (and subspecies); Motacilla citreola, Yellow-headed Wagtail [Citrine W.], Bergeronnette citrine, 103ff.; but may also designate white Wagtails, 105

khañjarīṭī, female of the yellow Wagtails, cf. *khañjarīṭa*, 105

khaṭvāṅga(ka), Buceros bicornis, Great Hornbill, Calao bicorne, 160

khara-krauñca, Grus virgo, Demoiselle Crane, Grue demoiselle, 312, 320, 321

khara-śabda-kurara, any noisy Laridae, Larini tribe (Gull / Goéland, Mouette), 342

khargalā, Athene brama, Spotted Owlet, Chevêche brame, 177

khāta-haṃsa, Anas clypeata, Shoveller [Northern Shoveler], Canard souchet, 456

khīra-haṃsa (P; Paramattha-jotikā II 277,12), a kind of Goose, 436 n., cf. 429

khuddaka-valguli (P; Dhp-a III 223,6), Tit, a small bird, esp. Parus major, Grey Tit [Great T.], Mésange charbonnière; or Parus xanthogenys, Yellow-cheeked Tit [Black-lored T.], Mésange à joues jaunes, 21

khe-gamana, Pseudibis papillosa, Black Ibis, Ibis noir, 385; Motacilla alba, Pied Wagtail [White W.], Bergeronnette grise, 385

g

gaṅgā-cillī ("Ganges's Kite", cf. *cilla*), Larus ridibundus, Black-headed Gull, Mouette rieuse, 343; or any Laridae of the Larini tribe (Gull / Goéland, Mouette), 343

gandharva, may refer to Cuculidae with melodious voice : Cuculus canorus, European or Grey [Eurasian] Cuckoo, Coucou gris; Cuculus saturatus, Himalayan or Asiatic [Oriental] Cuckoo, Coucou oriental, 128

garuḍa, a mythical bird, 199ff.; may refer to : Aquila chrysaetos, (Himalayan) Golden Eagle, Aigle royal, 199; Haliaeetus leucogaster, White-bellied Sea Eagle, Pygargue blagre, 200, 207, 212; or even Aquila rapax, Tawny Eagle, Aigle ravisseur, 200

garutmat, Aquila chrysaetos, (Himalayan) Golden Eagle, Aigle royal, 202-204, cf. *garuḍa*

garud-yodhī, Quails (Fr. Cailles) or Bustard Quails [Buttonquails] (Fr. Turnix) which fight with their wings, 285

**galegaṇḍa* (Pkt), Leptoptilos dubius, [Greater] Adjutant (Stork), Marabout argala, 392f.

gh

ghanatola, a synonyme for *caṭaka*, 137, cf. *caṭaka*

ghargharaka, Tyto alba, Barn (White, Screech) Owl, Effraie des clochers, 173; Nettapus coromandalianus, Cotton Teal [Cotton Pygmy-goose], Anserelle de Coromandel, 450; Anas poecilorhyncha, Spot-billed Duck (Grey Duck), Canard à bec tacheté, 454

ghūka, refers to large hooting Strigidae (Owl / Hibou, Chouette), 176, 177, 179

ghūghū-kṛt, Streptopelia tranquebarica, Red Turtle Dove [Red Collared D.], Tourterelle à tête grise, 259

ghoṅka, Anastomus oscitans, Openbill Stork [Asian Openbill], Bec-ouvert indien, 396

ghoṅga, ghoṅgaka, idem, 396

ghoṣṭa-kukkuṭa, Neophron percnopterus, (White) Scavenger Vulture [Egyptian V.] (or Neophron Vulture), Vautour percnoptère, 23, 192

c

cakora, Alectoris chukar, Chukar (Partridge), Perdrix choukar, 282

cakra, Tadorna ferruginea, Ruddy Sheldrake [Common Shelduck], Tadorne casarca, 450

cakra-koka, Treron apicauda, Pin-tailed Green Pigeon, Colombar à longue queue; Treron sphenura, Wedge-tailed Green Pigeon, Colombar chanteur, 254

cakravāka, Tadorna ferruginea, Ruddy Sheldrake [Common Shelduck], Tadorne casarca, 450, 451

cakrāṅga-vāja, Accipiter gentilis, [Northern] Goshawk, Autour des palombes (juvenile), 219, 237

cakrāhva, Tadorna ferruginea, Ruddy Sheldrake [Common Shelduck], Tadorne casarca, 450

cañcu-sūcī, any Passeridae of the Ploceinae subfamily (Weaver / Tisserin), 88

caṭaka, birds in general, 92; small birds, esp. House Sparrow (Fr. Moineau domestique), Finches (Fr. Roselins), Buntings (Fr. Bruants), etc., 61, 92, 93; Hirundinidae (Swallow, Martin / Hirondelle) and Apodidae (Swift / Martinet), 92, 99, 101, 165, 167

caṭakikā, diminutive of *caṭaka*, small birds, esp. Flycatchers (Fr. Gobemouches), Warbler / Fauvette, Ground Warbler / Tésie, Bush Warbler / Bouscarle, Wren Warbler / Prinia, Tailorbird / Couturière, Flycatcher Warbler / Pouillot, 53, 56, 68, 92; also Regulus regulus, Goldcrest, Roitelet huppé, 70; Munia / Munia, 90, 92; or Zosterops palpebrosa, [Oriental] White-eye, Zostérops oriental, 92, 112

caṭikā, a diminutive of *caṭaka*, small birds, esp. Flycatcher / Gobemouche, Warbler / Fauvette, Ground Warbler / Tésie, Bush Warbler / Bouscarle, Wren Warbler / Prinia, Tailorbird / Couturière, Flycatcher Warbler / Pouillot, 53, 56, 68, 89, 92; also Regulus regulus, Goldcrest, Roitelet huppé, 70; Munia / Munia, 89, 92; Flowerpecker / Dicée, 116

caṭī, various Hirundinidae (Swallow, Martin / Hirondelle), 98-99, 167

candraka, Tyto alba, Barn (White, Screech) Owl, Effraie des clochers, 173

candra-kānta, Halcyon smyrnensis, White-breasted Kingfisher [White-throated K.], Martin-chasseur de Smyrne, 156

candrakolūka, Tyto alba, Barn (White, Screech) Owl, Effraie des clochers, 173

candra-vihaṅgama, small Ardeidae (Bittern / Blongios, esp. Ixobrychus cinnamomeus, Chestnut Bittern [Cinnamon B.], Blongios canelle, 406

caraka, Falco jugger, Laggar Falcon, Falcon laggar; Falco cherrug, Saker Falcon, Falcon sacre, 221, 228

carillī, cf. *cirillī*, 167, 168

carcarī, any of the Passeridae, subfamily Motacillinae, genus Anthus (Pipit / Pipit), 107

carcikā, Haliastur indus, Brahmany Kite, Milan sacré, 244

carmacūḍa, refers to two species of Junglefowl / Coq : Gallus gallus, Red Junglefowl (Common or Wild Cock), Coq bankiva; Gallus sonneratii, Grey Junglefowl, Coq de Sonnerat, 271

cala-picchaka, Phoenicurus ochruros, Black Redstart, Rougequeue noir; or any of the Passeridae, subfamily Motacillinae, genus Anthus (Pipit / Pipit), 49

cala-puccha, Coracias benghalensis, Indian Roller, Rollier indien, 18

cātaka, may refer to : Cuculus varius, Common Hawk Cuckoo (Brainfever Bird), Coucou shikra; Clamator jacobinus, Pied (Crested) Cuckoo, Coucou jacobin, 133-137; also Cuculus [Hierococcyx] sparverioides, Large Hawk Cuckoo, Coucou épervier; Cacomantis passerinus, Plaintive Cuckoo [Grey-bellied C.],

ch

j

jala-kapota, Metopidius indicus, Bronzed-winged Jacana, Jacana bronzé, 304

jala-kāka, Pseudibis papillosa, Black ibis, Ibis noir, 294, 382, 383-384; Phalacrocoracidae (Cormorant / Cormorant), 371, 372; Threskiornis aethiopica [melanocephalus], White Ibis [Black-headed I.], Ibis sacré, 383

jala-kukkuṭa, Gallicrex cinerea, Watercock, Râle à crête, 301, 358

jala-kukkubha, idem, 138, 301, 358

jala-cara, any of the Cinclidae, esp. Cinclus pallasii, Brown Dipper, Cincle de Pallas, 43

jala-pārāvata, Metopidius indicus, Bronze-winged Jacana, Jacana bronzé, 304

jala-madgu, any of the Alcedinidae (small Kingfishers), Halcyonidae (large Kingfishers), Cerylidae (Pied Kingfishers (Fr. Martin-pêcheur), 155

jala-raṅka, Calidris minuta, Little Stint, Bécasseau minute, 368; or generic term for certain Scolopacidae, subfamily Tringinae (esp. Sandpiper / Bécasseau), 368

jala-raṅku, Porphyrio porphyrio, Purple Moorhen [P. Swamphen], Talève sultane, 298, 368

jala-lobhin, Calidris minuta, Little Stint, Bécasseau minute, 368

jala-śikhaṇḍin, Hydrophasianus chirurgu, Pheasant-tailed Jacana, Jacana à longue queue, 305

**jala-siṃha*, any of the Pelecanidae (Pelican / Pélican), 370

**jalpaka-kāla-caṭaka*, Dicrurus adsimilis [macrocercus], (Common) Black Drongo (or Kingcrow), Drongo brillant, 63

javala-kaṇṭika, Accipiter trivirgatus, Crested Goshawk, Autour huppé, 220

jāṅgala, Francolinus pondicerianus, Grey Partridge [G. Francolin], Francolin gris, 283

**jāṇṭa-sārika*, Acridotheres fuscus, Jungle Myna, Martin forestier, 86

jāyānujīvī baka, Ephippiorhynchus asiaticus, Black-necked Stork, Jabiru d'Asie, 391; or generic term for any of the Ciconiidae family (Stork / Cigogne, Jabiru, etc.), 392

jāla-pāda, any web-footed waterbird, esp. Rails and Crakes (Fr. Râle), Coots (Fr. Foulque), 299

jāvala, Falco pelegrinoides (Shaheen Falcon), said to be conspecific with Falco peregrinus, Peregrine Falcon, Faucon pèlerin, 220

jāṣkamada, Haliaeetus leucoryphus, Pallas's Sea Eagle, Pygargue de Pallas, 214

jihmākṣa, fish-eating Strigidae (Owl / Hibou) : Fish Owl / Kétoupa, 175

jīrvi, any of the Apodidae (Swift / Martinet), 167, 168

jīvañjīvaka, Polyplectron bicalcaratum, [Grey] Peacock Pheasant, Éperonnier chinquis, 270, 273, 274, 281

jīvahara, *jīvāntaka*, Aquila pomarina, Lesser Spotted Eagle, Aigle pomarin, 209

jūrā, male of the Accipiter gentilis, [Northern] Goshawk, Autour des palombes, 221

jṛmbha, Oriolus oriolus, [Eurasian] Golden Oriole, Loriot d'Europe, 78-79, cf. *pipīlaka*

jyeṣṭha-balākā, Casmerodius albus, Large Egret [Great E.], Grande Aigrette, 403

jyotsnā-baka, Ixobrychus cinnamomeus, Chestnut Bittern [Cinnamon B.], Blongios canelle, 406

jh

jhampāśī, Alcedinidae (small Kingfishers), Halcyonidae (large Kingfishers), Cerylidae (Pied Kingfishers (Fr. Martin-pêcheur), 155

ṭ

ṭikaṭikī, Acrocephalus dumetorum, Blyth's Reed Warbler, Rousserolle des buissons, 69

ṭiṭṭibha, Vanellus indicus, Red-wattled Lapwing, Vanneau indien, 357, 360; Vanellus malabaricus, Yellow-wattled Lapwing, Vanneau du Malabar, 357; Vanellus spinosus [V. duvaucelii], Spur-winged Plover [River Lapwing], Vanneau à éperons, 357

ṭiṣṭi, Numenius phaeopus, Whimbrel, Courlis corlieu, 366

ṭuṇṭuka, Orthotomus sutorius, [Common] Tailorbird, Couturière à longue queue; other noisy warblers such as : Prinia socialis, Ashy Wren Warbler [Ashy Prinia], Prinia cendré; Cisticola juncidis, Streaked Fantail Warbler [Zitting Cisticola], Cisticole des joncs, 68-69

ṭunā, *ṭonā*, male of the Accipiter badius, Shikra, Épervier shikra, 237, 242

ḍ

ḍh

ṇ

t

d

dh

n

naṣṭa-kāka, Corvus frugilegus, Rook, Corbeau freux, 6n., 20; Corvus monedula, [Eurasian] Jackdaw, Corbeau calédonien, 6

**nahikuti* (*nahiḥ kutiḥ*), Riparia riparia, Sand Martin, Hirondelle de rivage; Hirundo rupestris, [Eurasian] Crag martin, Hirondelle de rochers, 99

nāgāśī, cf. *garuḍa*; Haliaeetus leucogaster, White-bellied Sea Eagle, Pygargue blagre, 201, 207; Circaetus gallicus, Short-toed [Snake] Eagle, Circaète Jean-le-Blanc, 201; Spilornis cheela, Crested Serpent Eagle, Serpentaire bacha, 211

nāsā-cchinnā (cf. MW *nāsā-chinnī*), Sarkidiornis melanotos, Comb Duck, Canard à bosse, 448

niśā-kara, Ichthyophaga ichthyaetus, Grey-headed Fishing Eagle [G. Fish Eagle], Pygargue à tête grise, 215

niśāntaka, cf. *nakta-krauñca*, 232

niṣaṇṇa-śyāmā, Hirundo rustica, Common Swallow [Barn S.], Hirondelle rustique; Hirundo smithii, Wire-tailed Swallow, Hirondelle à longs brins; Delichon urbica, House Martin, Hirondelle de fenêtre [now subdivided into : Delichon urbica, Northern House Martin, Hirondelle de fenêtre; Delichon dasypus, Asian House Martin, Hirondelle de Bonaparte; Delichon nepalensis, Nepal House Martin, Hirondelle du Népal], 100

nīla-kaṇṭha, Coracias benghalensis, Indian Roller, Rollier indien, 17, 18; Copsychus saularis, [Oriental] Magpie Robin, Shama dayal, 18, 103; Pavo cristatus, Peacock [Indian Peafowl], Paon bleu, 18, 49; Passer domesticus, House Sparrow, Moineau domestique, 93; various black-throated Wagtails (Fr. Bergeronnettes), 18, 103

nīla-kaṇṭha-sārasa, Ephippiorhynchus asiaticus, Black-necked Stork, Jabiru d'Asie, 319, 321

nīla-krauñca, Ardea purpurea, Purple Heron, Héron pourpré, 402, cf. 390

nīla-khaga, Corvus corax, [Common] Raven, Grand Corbeau, 7

nīla-grīva, Coracias benghalensis, Indian Roller, Rollier indien, 17

nīla-grīvaka, Anas platyrhynchos, Mallard, Canard colvert, 453

nīla-caṭaka, Niltava grandis, Large Niltava (or Niltava Flycatcher), Grand Gobemouche, 53; Irena puella, [Asian] Fairy Bluebird, Irène vierge, 71

nīla-cchada-śyena, Falco peregrinus, Peregrine Falcon (or Blue Hawk), Faucon pèlerin, 222

nīla-cchavi, Irena puella, [Asian] Fairy Bluebird, Irène vierge, 71, 138

nīla-laṭvā, Niltava grandis, Large Niltava (or Niltava Flycatcher), Grand Gobemouche, 53

nīla-skandha-krauñca, Grus nigricollis, Black-necked Crane, Grue à cou noir, 319, 321

nīlāṅga, Coracias benghalensis, Indian Roller, Rollier indien, 17, 18; Ardea cinerea, Grey Heron (or Blue Heron), Héron cendré, 18; any of the Gruidae (Crane / Grue), 18; Pavo cristatus, Peacock [Indian Peafowl], Paon bleu, 18

nīlāṅga-cāpa, Coracias garrulus, European (Kashmir) Roller, Rollier d'Europe, 16, 20

nīlāṅga-sārasa, Grus virgo, Demoiselle Crane, Grue demoiselle, 312, 320, 321

nīlāsya-kāka, Corvus corone orientalis, Eastern Hooded Crow [Carrion Crow, subspecies], Corneille mantelée (?), 2, 4, 20

P

pakṣa-kalikā, Falco subbuteo, [Eurasian] Hobby, Faucon hobereau, 221, 231, 232

pakṣa-gupta, Chloropsis hardwickei, Orange-bellied Chloropsis [O. Leafbird], Verdin de Harwicke, 33

pakṣi-pravara, Gypaetus barbatus, Lammergeyer (or Bearded Vulture), Gypaète barbu, 197

paṅka-kīra, any of the Scolopacidae, subfamily Scolapacinae, genus Gallinago (Snipe / Bécassine), 366

paṅkti-cara-kurara, Grus virgo, Demoiselle Crane, Grue demoiselle, 186, 342

pañcama-kāka, Corvus monedula, [Eurasian] Jackdaw, Corbeau calédonien, 2, 20

paṭa-kapota, Dukula aenea, Green Imperial Pigeon, Carpophage pauline, 251, 253, 255

paṭikutt(h)aka (so! Ja VI 538,10), Anastomus oscitans, Openbill Stork [Asian Open-bill], Bec-ouvert indien, 396

paṭṭi-valguli, Parus xanthogenys, Yellow-cheeked Tit [Black-lored T.], Mésange à joues jaunes, 22

paṇḍu-haṃsa (P; not PED, but Ja V 356,24), cf. *seta-haṃsa*

pataṅgikā, various small birds, esp. the Sylviidae (Warbler / Fauvette), 68

piñjolā, Oriolus oriolus, [Eurasian] Golden Oriole, Loriot d'Europe; may refer to : Oriolus xanthornus, Black-headed Oriole [Black-hooded O.], Loriot à capuchon noir, 80

piṇḍīka, any of the Apodidae (Swift / Martinet), 168

pipīlaka, Oriolus oriolus, [Eurasian] Golden Oriole, Loriot d'Europe, 77ff.

**pipīliya*) (Pkt; *pīpīliya* in Paṇhavāgaraṇāiṃ 1,3 [8a, 3]), idem, 77 (read : *pippiliya*, °*yā*), 79

pippala, Megalaima virens, Great (Hill Himalayan) Barbet, Barbu géant, 123, 124

pippika, Merops orientalis, (Small) Green (or Common Indian) Bee-eater, Guêpier d'Orient; or another Bee-eater, 149ff.

piriḍī (Hemacandra, Deśin. 6,47) (Pkt; *pirilī* "musical instrument" [PSM]), Lonchura malabarica, White-throated Munia [Indian Silverbill], Capucin bec-de-plomb; Lonchura striata, White-backed Munia [White-rumped M.], Capucin domino, 45 (read : *piriḍi*), 90

pirili, *pirilī*, Lonchura malabarica, White-throated Munia [Indian Silverbill], Capucin bec-de-plomb; and Lonchura striata, White-backed Munia [White-rumped M.], Capucin domino, 89f.

pilaka, *pilaga* (Ardhamāgadhī), cf. *pipīlaka*, 77, 79

pīta-tuṇḍa-kāraṇḍava, Anas platyrhynchos, Mallard (or Wild Duck), Canard colvert, 453

pīta-netrā, cf. *citra-netrā*

pīta-pāda, *pīta-pādā*, Acridotheres tristis, Common Myna, Martin triste; Gracula religiosa, Hill Myna (or Grackle), Mainate religieux, 85; also Vanellus indicus, Red-wattled Lapwing, Vanneau indien; Vanellus malabaricus, Yellow-wattled Lapwing, Vanneau du Malabar, 85, cf. 360

pīta-bhadra-śuka, Psittacula alexandri, Red-breasted Parakeet, Perruche à moustaches, 76, 140, 144

pīta-muṇḍa-kalaviṅka, yellow-headed birds : Ploceus philippinus, Baya Weaver, Tisserin baya; Ploceus manyar, Streaked Weaver, Tisserin manyar, 50, 88, 94

pīta-muṇḍa-caṭaka, idem, 94

puṭinī, Orthotomus sutorius, [Common] Tailorbird, Couturière à longue queue, 68

puṇḍarīka, any of the Pelecanidae (Pelican / Pélican), 222, 231, 370

puṇḍarīkākṣa, Butastur teesa, White-eyed Buzzard (Eagle), Busautour aux yeux blancs, 212

puttaka (P), Saxicoloides fulicata, Indian Robin, Pseudotraquet indien, 90

puttikā, a tiny bird, 90 cf. *putrikā*

putra-gupta, 33, 144, cf. *pakṣa-gupta*

putra-priya, Upupa epox, [Common] Hoopoe, Huppe fasciée, 162

putra-śuka, Loriculus vernalis, Indian Loriquet [Vernal Hanging Parrot], Coryllis vernal, 144

putrikā, small birds, esp. the Warblers (Warbler / Fauvette; Ground Warbler / Tésie; Bush Warbler / Bouscarle; Wren Warbler / Prinia; Tailorbird / Couturière; Flycatcher Warbler / Pouillot; etc.), 68; the Munias, 89, 90; Zosterops palpebrosa, [Oriental] White-eye, Zostérops oriental, 112; also the Hirundinidae (Swallow, Martin / Hirondelle) and the Apodidae (Swift / Martinet), 100

puṇya-darśana, Coracias benghalensis, Indian Roller, Rollier indien, 17

purallikā, *purillaka*, Prinia socialis, Ashy Wren Warbler [Ashy Prinia], Prinia cendré, 69

puruṣa-vāk-śāri, Gracula religiosa, Hill Myna (or Grackle), Mainate religieux, 82, 87

pulīkā, Saroglossa spiloptera, Spotted-winged Stare [Spot-winged Starling], Étourneau à ailes tachetées, 82, 83

puṣkara-śāyikā, Chlidonias hybridus, Whiskered Tern, Guifette moustac, 349

puṣkara-sad, *puṣkara-sād*, idem, 94, 349

puṣkara-sārasa, Grus leucogeranus, (Great White) Siberian Crane, Grue de Sibérie, 312

puṣkarākhya, idem, 311, 320

puṣkarāhva, 311, 320, 321

puṣpa-kokila, Cuculus saturatus, Himalayan (Asiatic) Cuckoo [Oriental C.], Coucou oriental, 129

puṣpaṃ-dhaya, Nectarinia asiatica, Purple Sunbird, Souimanga asiatique, 115

puṣpa-bhūṣī, Lonchura punctulata, Spotted Munia [Scaly-breasted M.], Capucin damier, 89

puṣpa-śakuna, any of the Phasianidae, genus Tragopan; may refer to : Tragopan satyra, Crimson Tragopan (or Horned Pheasant) [Satyr T.], Tragopan satyre, 281

puṣpāvataṃsaka, various whiskered Pycnonotidae, esp. Pycnonotus jocosus,

ph

b

bh

m

madhu-kara, Nectarinia asiatica, Purple Sunbird, Souimanga asiatique, 114, 115
madhu-ghoṣa, sweet-voiced Cuculidae : Cuculus canorus, [Eurasian] (or Grey) Cuckoo, Coucou gris; Cuculus saturatus, Himalayan Cuckoo [Oriental C.], Coucou oriental, 128
madhupa(-khaga), 115, cf. *madhu-kara*
madhu-sārikā, Sturnus roseus, Rosy Pastor [Rosy Starling], Étourneau roselin, 86
madhu-hā, Pernis ptilorhyncus, (Indian Crested) Honey Buzzard [Oriental H. B.], Bondrée orientale, 248
manaḥśila-caṭaka, Tarsiger chrysaeus, Golden Bush Robin, Rossignol doré, 52
manuṣya-vadana-bhāraṇḍa, Gypaetus barbatus, Lammergeyer (or Bearded Vulture), Gypaète barbu, 399
manosila-haṃsa (P; not PED, but Ja V 356,24), Dendrocygna bicolor, Large Whistling Teal [Fulvous Whistling-duck], Dendrocygne fauve, 450
mayaṇā (Pkt) (*madanā* is likely incorrect), Gracula religiosa, Hill Myna (or Grackle), Mainate religieux, 29 n. 2
mayūra, Pavo cristatus, Peacock [Indian Peafowl], Paon bleu, 55, 270
mayūraka, Lophophorus impejanus, Impeyan Pheasant [Himalayan Monal], Lophophore resplendissant, 271, 277
mayūra-kukkuṭa, idem, 257, 277ff.
mayūra-ghnī, Hieraaetus fasciatus, Bonelli's Eagle, Aigle de Bonelli, 211
maru-baka, any of the Otididae (Bustard / Outarde), 326
marula, Fulica atra, [Common] Coot, Foulque macroule, 300
malina, Anas strepera, Gadwall, Canard chipeau, 454
mallika, Cygnus olor, Mute Swan, Cygne tyberculé, 427
mallikākṣa(-haṃsa), Aythya nyroca, White-eyed Pochard or Ferruginous Duck [Ferruginous Pochard], Fuligule nyroca, 428, 458
**maharī* (Pkt), Copsychus saularis, [Oriental] Magpie Robin, Shama dayal, 47
mahā ukkusa (P), 214, cf. following entry
mahā utkrośa, Haliaeetus leucoryphus, Pallas's Sea-Eagle [Pallas's Fish Eagle], Pygargue de Pallas, 214
mahā-kaṅka, may refer to : Ardea insignis, (Great) White-bellied Heron, Héron impérial, 402
mahā-kauśika, Bubo nipalensis, Forest Eagle Owl [Spot-bellied E. O.], Grand-duc du Népal, 176, 181, 182
mahā-krauñca, Grus leucogeranus, Great White (Siberian) Crane, Grue de Sibérie, 319
mahā-cañcu-baka, Leptoptilos dubius, Adjutant Stork [Greater Adjutant], Marabout argala, 392
mahā-pakṣī, Bubo nipalensis, Forest Eagle Owl [Spot-bellied E. O.], Grand-duc du Népal, 176, 182; any of the Pelecanidae (Pelican / Pélican), 370
mahā-prāṇa, any black Corvidae, tribe Corvini, genus Corvus, except the Common Raven (Fr. Grand Corbeau), 3
mahā-plava, any of the Pelecanidae (Pelican / Pélican), 370
mahā-muktaka, Aquila chrysaetos, (Himalayan) Golden Eagle, Aigle royal, 206
mahā-yogī, Coracias benghalensis, Indian Roller, Rollier indien, 17, 18; domestic Cock, 18
mahā-rāvaṇa-vāja, "Icelander", a form of the Falco rusticolus, Gyrfalcon, Faucon gerfaut, 219 [N. B. A term used to refer to a form (Falco rusticolus candicans Gmelin) which is no longer classified in this way.]
mahā-vīra, Aquila chrysaetos, (Himalayan) Golden Eagle, Aigle royal, 206
mahā-śveta, Casmerodius albus, Large Egret [Great E.], Grande aigrette, 402
mahā-suparṇa, Aquila chrysaetos, (Himalayan) Golden Eagle, Aigle royal, 206
mahā-haṃsa, any of the Anatidae, genus Cygnus (Swan / Cygne), 422, 428
mājala, Coracias benghalensis, Indian Roller, Rollier indien, 17, 18
mātṛ-nindaka, any of the Bucerotidae (Hornbill / Calao), 159
mālāya, Spilornis cheela, Crested Serpent Eagle, Serpentaire bacha, 212
mālika, Aythya fuligula, Tufted Duck (or Pochard), Fuligule morillon, 458
māsa-vartikā, Calandrella rufescens, Lesser (Rufous) Short-toed Lark, Alouette pispolette, 110
mithunin, Motacilla alba, White Wagtail, Bergeronnette grise, 106
mīna-raṅka, any of the Alcedinidae (Kingfisher / Martin-pêcheur), 155,
mīnāmrīṇa, Motacilla alba, White Wagtail, Bergeronnette grise, 106

y

r

raktāṅga, Sarcogyps calvus, Black (or King) Vulture, Vautour royal, 188

raghaṭa, Falco jugger, Lagger Falcon, Faucon laggar, 227

raṅgaṇa(-śyena), Falco tinnunculus, [Common] Kestrel, Faucon crécerelle, 155, 220, 233

rajanī-baka, any nocturnal Ardeidae (Night Herons and various Bitterns / Fr. Bihoreaux and Blongios), except the Botaurus stellaris, [Great] Bittern, Butor étoilé, 405

rajju-dala, *rajju-dālaka*, Terpsiphone paradisi, Paradise Flycatcher, Tchitrec de paradis, 14, 54

rajju-vāla, idem, 54ff.

raṇa-pakṣī, Aquila rapax, Tawny Eagle, Aigle ravisseur, 208

raṇa-matta, idem, 208

raṇālaṅkaraṇa-kaṅka, Haliastur indus, Brahmany Kite, Milan sacré, 243

rata-nidhi, Motacilla alba, White Wagtail, Bergeronnette grise, 106

ralā, certain noisy ground insects, incorrectly identified as Bulbuls (family Pycnonotidae), 35, 38, 39, cf. *kaṃiyaka*

ravi-haṃsa (P; Ja VI 539,15), Dendrocygna bicolor, Large Whistling Teal [Fulvous Whistling-duck, Dendrocygne fauve, 450

rāga-pakṣi, Aquila rapax, Tawny Eagle, Aigle ravisseur, 208

rāja-putrikā, Charadrius dubius, Little Ringed Plover, Pluvier petit-gravelot, 357; Charadrius placidus, Long-billed (Ringed) Plover, Pluvier à long bec, 357

rāja-baka, Ciconia ciconia, White Stork, Cigogne blanche, 390

rāja-bhaṭṭikā, 357, cf. *rāja-putrikā*

rāja-vihaṅgama, Coracias benghalensis, Indian Roller, Rollier indien, 17

rāja-śuka, Psittacula eupatria, Large Indian Parakeet [Alexandrine P.], Perruche alexandre, 143

rāja-sārasa, Pavo cristatus, Peacock [Indian Peafowl], Paon bleu, 270

rāja-haṃsa, any of the Anatidae, genus Cygnus (Cygnus cygnus, Whooper Swan, Cygne chanteur; Cygnus olor, Mute Swan, Cygne tuberculé), 426ff.; Anser anser, Greylag Goose, Oie cendrée, 436, 437, 440

rāja-haṃsa (P), Cygnus cygnus, Whooper Swan, Cygne chanteur; Anser indicus, Bar-headed Goose, Oie à tête barrée, 427f.; Cygnus columbianus davidi, "Chinese Swan" [Tundra Swan], Cygne siffleur, 430 [N.B. According to Sibley and Monroe, "Cygnus columbianus davidi Swinhoe 1870, Swinhoe's Swan, known from the unique type from Tientsin, in Hopey, China, is probably a young C (columbianus) bewickii"]; Cygnus olor, Mute Swan, Cygne tuberculé, 433 n.

rāji-śuka, Psarisomus dalhousiae, Long-tailed Broadbill, Eurylaime psittacin, 118

rukkha-koṭṭaka (P), any of the Picidae (Woodpecker / Pic), 54n 2, 119

rucaka-pārāvata, Columba pulchricollis, Ashy Wood Pigeon, Pigeon cendré; Columba palumbus, [Common] Wood Pigeon, Pigeon ramier, 256

rociṣṇu, Leiothrix lutea, Red-billed Liothrix, Léiothrix jaune, 32

ropaṇākā, Gracula religiosa, Hill Myna (or Grackle), Mainate religieux, 81

rohiṇī, *rohiṇikā*, Anas crecca, Common Teal, Sarcelle d'hiver, 455

l

lakṣmaṇa, Grus antigone, Sarus (Indian) Crane, Grue antigone, 312

lagna, female of the Falco jugger, Lagger Falcon, Faucon laggar, 220, 221, 227

laghu-jaṅgala, 286, cf. *alpa-kapiñjala*

laṅgaṇa, male of the Falco jugger, Lagger Falcon, Faucon laggar, 227; cf. *raṅgaṇa(-śyena)*

laṭukikā, Amandava amandava, Red Munia [Red Avadavat], Bengali rouge, 91

laṭūṣaka, various Laniidae (Shrike / Pie-grièche), 57

laṭvā, any of the Pycnonotidae (Bulbul / Bulbul), 34ff.; Pycnonotus leucogenys, White-cheeked Bulbul [Himalayan B.], Bulbul à joues blanches, 34, 37, 54, 57; also Pycnonotus leucotis, White-eared Bulbul, Bulbul à oreillons blancs; Pycnonotus melanicterus, Black-headed Yellow Bulbul [Black-crested B.], Bulbul à tête noire, 37; Calandrella rufescens, Lesser (Rufous) Short-toed Lark, Alouette pispolette, 35; Rhipidura aureola, White-browed Fantail (Flycatcher), Rhipidure à grands sourcils; and Rhipidura albicollis, White-throated Fantail (Flycatcher), Rhipidure à gorge blanche, 35, 53, 54, 90

laṭvākā, Amandava amandava, Red Munia [Red Avadavat], Bengali rouge, 53, 54, 91

lāpa(ka-sakuna) (P), may refer to : Turnix suscitator, Common Bustard-Quail [Barred Buttonquail], Turnix combattant, 289

Short-toed Lark, Alouette pispolette, 109; cf. *vartaka*

vardhamāna-kapota, Dukula aenea, Green Imperial Pigeon, Carpophage pauline, 251, 253, 255

varṣa-priya, Cacomantis passerinus, Plaintive Cuckoo [Grey-bellied C.], Coucou à tête grise, 131

valgulā, Burhinus oedicnemus, Stone Plover (Curlew) [Eurasian Thick-knee], Oedicnème criard, 39

vāka, Nycticorax nycticorax, [Black-crowned] Night Heron, Bihoreau gris, 405

vāk-kāra, noisy birds including Laughingthrushes (Garrulaxes) and Babblers (Cratéropes), 28

vāja, Accipiter gentilis, [Northern] Goshawk, Autour des palombes, 220, 221, 235ff., 241

vāja-rāja, Spizaetus cirrhatus, Crested Hawk Eagle [Changeable H. E.], Aigle huppé, 211

vāji, *vājika*, Accipiter gentilis, [Northern] Goshawk, Autour des palombes, 220, 236

vājī, Accipiter gentilis, [Northern] Goshawk, Autour des palombes, 220, 235, 236, 241

vātāśin, Apus affinis, (Common) House Swift, Martinet des maisons, 166

vāyasa, any of the Corvidae, tribe Corvini, genus Corvus (Crow / Corbeau, Corneille), 1ff.; esp. Corvus splendens, House Crow, Corbeau familier, 2

vāyasāntaka ulūka, Bubo coromandus, Dusky Horned Owl [Dusky Eagle O.], Grand-duc de Coromandel, 181

vārața, Eupodotis bengalensis [Houbaropsis b.], Bengal Florican, Outarde du Bengale, 325, 330

vāraṇa, Otis tarda, Great Bustard, Grande Outarde, 327, 328

vāri-kaṅka, Ardea cinerea, Grey Heron, Héron cendré, 400, 401

vārtīka, not to be confused with : Calandrella rufescens, Lesser (Rufous) Short-toed Lark, Alouette pispolette, 109; cf. *vartaka*

vārdhrīṇasa, any of the Bucerotidae (Hornbill / Calao), 159, 161, including the Aceros nipalensis, Rufous-necked Hornbill, Calao à cou roux, 159, 160

vāsā, Accipiter nisus, Indian Sparrowhawk [Eurasian S.], Épervier d'Europe; Accipiter gularis, Asiatic Sparrowhawk]Japanese S.], Épervier du Japon, 220ff., 236; general term for small Hawks, 237

vikakara, Pterocles indicus, Painted Sandgrouse, Ganga indien, 265

viṭ-sārikā, Sturnus contra, [Asian] Pied Myna, Étourneau pie, 85, 87

vidīgaya, Otis tarda, Great Bustard, Grande Outarde, 328

viśālākṣa, cf. *garuḍa*, a mythical bird; esp. Aquila chrysaetos, (Himalayan) Golden Eagle, Aigle royal, 207

viśoka, Coracias benghalensis, Indian Roller, Rollier indien, 17, 18; domestic Cock, 18

viśvakā, any of the Glareolidae, subfamily Glareolinae, genus Glareola (Pratincole / Glaréole), 335

**viṣuvi*, idem, 335

viṣkirāḥ, "scratchers" (Fr. "gratteurs"), a group of birds identified in Āyurvedic texts, XV, 28, 92, 137, 170, 268, *passim*

viṣṇu-dharmā, 207, cf. *viśālākṣa*

viṣṇu-liṅgaka, Pericrocotus flammeus, Scarlet Minivet, Grand Minivet; Pericrocotus brevirostris, Short-billed Minivet, Minivet à bec court, 58, 59

vihāra, Rhipidura aureola, White-browed Fantail (Flycatcher), Rhipidure à grands sourcils, 54

vīcī-kāka, any of the Laridae, genus Larus (Gull / Goéland, Mouette), 343

vījana, a kind of Phaesant (Fr. Faisan), 273

vṛkṣa-kukkuṭa(-śakuna), a generic term for Picidae (Woodpecker / Pic), 26, 119

vṛtti-tittiri, Francolinus gularis, Swamp Partridge (S. Francolin), Francolin multiraie, 284

vṛddha-kāka, Corvus corax, [Common] Raven, Grand Corbeau, 4, 5, 20

vṛṣāyaṇa, Passer domesticus, House Sparrow, Moineau domestique, 92

vṛṣārāva, Cuculus varius, Common Hawk Cuckoo (or Brainfever Bird), Coucou shikra, 168, 169

velādhara, Dromas ardeola, Crab-plover, Drome ardéole, 336; Raphus cuculiatus, Dodo, Dronte de Maurice, 398f.

vesara, male of the Accipiter virgatus, Besra (Sparrow-hawk), Épervier besra, 220, 221; Accipiter nisus, [Eurasian] Sparrowhawk, Épervier d'Europe, 220, 236

vesarā, small Hawks, 237

vainateya, cf. *garuḍa*; esp. Aquila chrysaetos, (Himalayan) Golden Eagle, Aigle royal, 192, 199

vailātaka, Dromas ardeola, Crab-plover, Drome ardéole, 336

vyaghīnasa (P; **vyāgghīnasa* is likely incorrect; not in PED, but Ja VI vs 2099 v. *loha'[ā]piṭṭhā*), any of the Bucerotidae (Hornbill / Calao), including the Aceros

śikharī, Vanellus indicus, Red-wattled Lapwing, Vanneau indien, 358

śiti-kakṣa-gṛdhra, śiti-kakṣin, Gyps bengalensis, (Indian) White-backed Vulture [White-rumped V.], Vautour Chaugoun, 188, 190

śiti-kaṇṭha, Pavo cristatus, Peacock [Indian Peafowl], Paon bleu, 229; Ciconia episcopus, White-necked Stork [Woolly-necked S.], Cigogne épiscopale; Ephippiorhynchus asiaticus, Black-necked Stork, Jabiru d'Asie, 389, 390

śiti-pakṣa, Hirundo smithii, Wire-tailed Swallow, Hirondelle à longs brins, 101

śiti-pṛṣṭa, idem, 101

śitodarī, idem, 101

śilā-nīḍa, Aquila chrysaetos, (Himalayan) Golden Eagle, Aigle royal, 207

śilindhrī, any of the Sittidae (Nuthatch / Sittelle), 24ff.

śiva-haṃsa, Podiceps cristatus, Great Crested Grebe, Grèbe huppé, 462

śiñjirikā, any of the Nectarinidae (Sunbird / Souimanga), 114

śuka, any of the Psittacidae (Parakeet / Perruche), except the Loriculus vernalis [Vernal Hanging Parrot], Indian Loriquet, Coryllis vernal, 23, 142, 143

śuka-cchavi(-kapota), Chalcophaps indica, Emerald Dove, Colombine turvert, 257, 261, 262

śuka-tuṇḍa, any of the Sylviidae, subfamily Sylviinae, tribe Timaliini, called Parrotbills or Suthoras (Fr. Paraxodornis), 23

śuka-nāsa, idem, 23

śuka-pucchaka, idem, 118

śukānanā, idem, 23

śukikā, Aegithina tiphia, Common Iora, Petit Iora, 31

śukla-kāka, Corvus splendens, House Crow, Corbeau familier (albino), 8

śuddha-vesara, Accipiter virgatus, Besra (Sparrow-hawk), Épervier besra, 241

śusulūka, Bubo nipalensis, Forest Eagle Owl [Spot-bellied E. O.], Grand-duc du Népal; or may refer to one of the small Strigidae (Owlet / Chevêchette, Chevêche), 183

śṛgāla, Aquila rapax, Tawny Eagle, Aigle ravisseur, 208, 230, 231

śaiśira(-caṭaka), describes all Buntings (Fringillidae, subfamily Emberizinae) as winter visitors, 96

śyāma-kaṇṭha, Luscinia svecica, (Red-spotted) Bluethroat, Gorgebleue à miroir, 49

śyāma(-kalaviṅka), Saxicoloides fulicata, Indian Robin, Pseudotraquet indien, 45ff.; Copsychus malabaricus, [White-rumped] Shama, Shama à croupion blanc, 46, 50, 93; may refer to : Parus major, Grey Tit, Mésange charbonnière, 22

śyāma-gala-kāka, any black Corvidae, tribe Corvini, genus Corvus, except the Common Raven (Fr. Grand Corbeau, 6

śyāma-caṭaka, Emberiza melanocephala, Black-headed Bunting, Bruant mélanocéphale; and Emberiza bruniceps, Red-headed Bunting, Bruant à tête rousse, 95-96

śyāva-gṛdhra, Aegypius monachus, Cinereous Vulture, Vautour moine, 188, 190

śyeta-śuka, Psittacula alexandri, (Indian) Red-breasted Parakeet (or Paroquet), Perruche à moustaches, 144

śyena, a generic term which includes the Falconidae (Falcon / Faucon), and certain species of the Accipitridae family, esp. Eagles, Hawk Eagles, Buzzards, 199, 236; may refer specifically to the true Eagles, 199, 200, 204, 205, 208, 210; and to different forms of the Peregrine Falcon (Fr. Faucon pèlerin), 210

śyena-sārasa, Grus leucogeranus, Great White (Siberian) Crane, Grue de Sibérie, 312

śyenākhya, idem, 320, 321, 323

śyenolūka, Bubo nipalensis, Forest Eagle Owl [Spot-bellied E. O.], Grand-duc du Népal, 182, 183

śrīka, Myiophoneus caeruleus, (Himalayan) [Blue] Whistling Thrush, Arrenga siffleur; Motacilla alba, White Wagtail, Bergeronnette grise, 102

śrī-karṇa, any of the Pycnonotidae (Bulbuls) with a white, or white and red, patch in the ear-region, 39

śrī-vada, one of the various species of Sibia (Sylviidae, subfamily Sylviinae, tribe Timaliini, genus Heterophasia), 50; Myiophoneus caeruleus, (Himalayan) [Blue] Whistling Thrush, Arrenga siffleur, 50, 52

śrī-vada-pakṣī, Copsychus saularis, [Oriental] Magpie Robin, Shama dayal, 47

śveta-kāka, Corvus splendens, House Crow, Corbeau familier (albino), 8; Threskiornis aethiopicus [T. melanocephalus], White Ibis [Black-headed I.], Ibis sacré, 9, 386, 387